ORLANDO
& Walt Disney World

© Disney

2016

Simon & Susan Veness

foulsham
LONDON • NEW YORK • TORONTO • SYDNEY

W. Foulsham & Co. Ltd
for Foulsham Publishing Ltd
The Old Barrel Store, Drayman's Lane, Marlow, Bucks SL7 2FF

Foulsham books can be found in all good bookshops or direct
from www.foulsham.com

While every effort has been made to ensure the accuracy of all the information contained
within this book, neither the author nor the publisher can be liable for any errors. In
particular, since prices, times and any holiday or hotel details change on a regular basis, it is
vital that each individual checks relevant information for themselves.

ISBN: 978-0-572-04547-0

Text copyright © 2015 Veness Enterprises Inc

Series, format, logo and layout design copyright © 2015 Foulsham Publishing Ltd

A CIP record for this book is available from the British Library

Look out for the latest editions of Foulsham travel books:
Brit Guide to Las Vegas, Jane Anderson and the *Brit Guide* team
Brit Guide to Disneyland Resort Paris, Simon and Susan Veness
Brit Guide to New York, Amanda Statham

Dedication: To our special home-grown research team – Ben, Anthony and Mark – who help
make our work fun!

SPECIAL THANKS
Special thanks for this edition go to: Visit Orlando, Experience Kissimmee, Visit Florida, The
Walt Disney Company, Universal Orlando & SeaWorld Parks & Entertainment.

Our sincere thanks also go to Wendy Hobson and all the hard-working people at Foulsham
who help to bring our work to life every year.

Typeset in Great Britain by Chris Brewer Origination
Printed in Malta by Melita Press

CONTENTS

Foreword

Simon says… so you want to go to Orlando? Great idea, whether you're planning your first trip, or your twenty-first. There's just one thing you need to know in advance – exactly what you're getting into. There is nowhere on earth like this great Central Florida wonderland and, for all the fact it can dazzle and excite in equal measure, it can also confuse and exhaust those who are not prepared. We've been doing this for more than 20 years and have chapter and verse on everything in store: how to prepare and plan for it, how to enjoy it to the full – and how not to go into major debt as a result! It is an enchanting and mind-boggling place, both for its sheer scale and the amazing detail you'll encounter, and it has more options and variations than you can shake a magician's wand at (and there are plenty of magicians since Universal Orlando opened up their second Wizarding World of Harry Potter in 2014). The most important thing is to have a 'good companion' – that means us – to steer you through the complexity, choice and fun in store, taking you through the full Orlando experience stage by stage. You'll miss none of it with us, and you'll ensure your hard-earned holiday money gets full value for the long journey. Just be ready to Have A Nice Day…!

Susan says… Planning an Orlando holiday is a time of excitement and anticipation. It can also be a time of frustration and confusion. Disney dining reservations must be made months in advance; scheduling attractions is crucial with Disney's new FastPass+ system and, again, these decisions must be made well ahead of your arrival. What's a person to do? Relax. We've got you covered. From making the most of Universal's 'front of the queue perk' and early entry into the Wizarding Worlds of Harry Potter for onsite guests, to navigating Disney's My Magic Plus system, the following pages will walk you through it step by step so that you arrive in the Vacation Capital of the World feeling like a pro.

And if you want to make sure you get the very best out of your holiday without wasting time or money, let us help with our unique Touring Plans (p41).

So if you're ready, let's get on with the planning…!

Simon and Susan Veness
(visit us at www.venesstravelmedia.com, or email britsguide@yahoo.com, and follow Veness Travel Media on Twitter and Facebook).

1

Introduction

or Welcome to the Holiday of a Lifetime

Fun. Excitement. Thrills. Fantasy. Food (lots of food!). They are all waiting for you in this vast area of Central Florida we call Orlando. It is an amazing array of choice, temptation and all-out holiday appeal that has no equal anywhere else on earth. It is a fully-fledged assault on the senses in every respect, and it draws families, couples and singles, young and old alike. It runs the gamut from astounding theme parks to world-class shopping, superb nature and fabulous nightlife.

Most of all, though, this is a BIG venture in every sense and it's vital you have an idea of the extensive and complex nature of what awaits you. Walt Disney World is the leading attraction and is the size of a small city, and there is a strong supporting cast, led by Universal Orlando and SeaWorld. There's something for all tastes and ages, but it exacts a high toll. You'll walk a lot, queue a lot and probably eat a lot. You WILL have a fabulous time, but you'll probably end up exhausted, too. But stick with us, and you'll have the best possible preparation for what's in store.

Eight theme parks

In simple terms, there are eight major theme parks, and several need two days to enjoy fully. Add a day at a water park, a trip to one of the wildlife or nature attractions and the lure of the Kennedy Space Center, and you already have two full weeks of pure adventure mania. Then mix in the night-time fun of Disney Springs, Universal's CityWalk and a host of dinner shows, plus superb shopping, and you start to understand the awesome scope of the place. Even with two weeks, something has to give – just make sure it isn't your patience, wallet – or sanity.

So, how do you get full value from this truly magical holiday? The answer is Good Planning – read, reflect and prepare. On pages 345–46 is a handy outline guide for a typical two-week stay. Be aware of the time demands of the parks and make sure you build in a quiet day or two by the pool or at one of the smaller attractions. With SO much on offer, it just isn't possible to 'do it all', so try to ensure you get full value from your choices. Also, don't underestimate the vast scale involved – this is a huge area and it takes time even to get from park to park. But do stop to admire the imagination and detail of what's on offer as it is all world class.

There's all kinds of fun waiting to greet you!

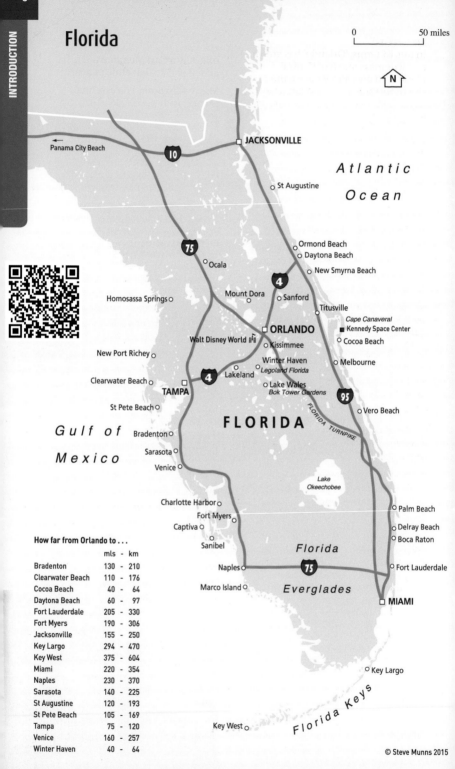

Florida

0   50 miles

N

← Panama City Beach

JACKSONVILLE

10

Atlantic

Ocean

○ St Augustine

75

○ Ocala

Homosassa Springs ○

○ Ormond Beach
○ Daytona Beach

○ New Smyrna Beach

Mount Dora ○   ○ Sanford

4

Titusville ○

Cape Canaveral
■ Kennedy Space Center

□ **ORLANDO**

Walt Disney World   ○ Kissimmee

○ Cocoa Beach

New Port Richey ○

Winter Haven
Legoland Florida

○ Melbourne

Clearwater Beach ○

4   Lakeland ○

St Pete Beach ○

□
TAMPA

○ Lake Wales
Bok Tower Gardens

FLORIDA

95

○ Vero Beach

Gulf of

Bradenton ○

FLORIDA TURNPIKE

Mexico

Sarasota ○

Venice ○

*Lake
Okeechobee*

Charlotte Harbor ○

Fort Myers ○

Captiva ○

○
Sanibel

○ Palm Beach

○ Delray Beach

○ Boca Raton

Florida

75

○ Fort Lauderdale

Naples ○

Everglades

Marco Island ○

□ **MIAMI**

○ Key Largo

Florida Keys

Key West ○

© Steve Munns 2015

How far from Orlando to . . .

	mls	-	km
Bradenton	130	-	210
Clearwater Beach	110	-	176
Cocoa Beach	40	-	64
Daytona Beach	60	-	97
Fort Lauderdale	205	-	330
Fort Myers	190	-	306
Jacksonville	155	-	250
Key Largo	294	-	470
Key West	375	-	604
Miami	220	-	354
Naples	230	-	370
Sarasota	140	-	225
St Augustine	120	-	193
St Pete Beach	105	-	169
Tampa	75	-	120
Venice	160	-	257
Winter Haven	40	-	64

Orlando

In tourist terms, 'Orlando' has grown to encompass much of Central Florida, an area almost twice the size of Yorkshire. Yes, that big. The city itself is north of the main tourist areas and many people won't even see it as they charge from park to park, which is a shame as it is a bright and happening place. When Walt Disney's dream of a vast resort opened in 1971 with the Magic Kingdom (sadly, he never saw it realised as he died in 1966), it led to a huge tourist expansion. New attractions pop up all the time and both coasts also vie for attention.

There are seven counties in Central Florida. **Orange County**, home to the city of Orlando, with Walt Disney World in the south-west corner, part of which is also in **Osceola County**, with Kissimmee its main town; **Seminole County**, home of Orlando Sanford International Airport, north-east of Orange; **Lake County** to the north-west, with Mount Dora its principal town; **Polk** to the south-west, home to many vacation villas and Legoland Florida; and **Brevard** and **Volusia Counties** to east, home to the Kennedy Space Center and Daytona Beach.

Each year, some 60 million people holiday in Orlando and the area boasts 116,000 hotel rooms, 26,000 vacation homes, more than 4,000 places to eat and 30 malls. Here's a taste of the main attractions.

Walt Disney World

This is where the magic really starts. This vast resort consists of four separate theme parks, 20 themed hotel resorts, a camping ground, two water parks, a sports complex, five golf courses, mini-golf and a huge shopping and entertainment district (Disney Springs). It covers $47ml^2/122km^2$ and Alton Towers and Thorpe Park would comfortably fit into its car parks! At peak periods, it holds 200,000-plus visitors. Disney does things with the most style and there are always new projects on the drawing board. It maintains a high

level of customer service, where everyone who works for them is officially a Cast Member, not just staff, and they take that ethic to heart.

Magic Kingdom: The essential Disney, with the magic of its wonderful films, the adventures of the Wild West and Africa, the excitement of thrill rides like Space Mountain (an indoor roller-coaster), the eye-catching new Fantasyland and splendid parades and fireworks.

Epcot: Disney's two-part park, with the technology-inspired Future World, plus a potted journey around the globe in World Showcase. More educational than adventurous, it has some memorable rides, including the superb Soarin', plus excellent dining.

Disney's Hollywood Studios: Ride the movies in style, meet Star Wars™, the Muppets and Indiana Jones; drop into the fearsome Tower of Terror; learn the tricks of the trade at the epic Lights, Motors, Action!™ Extreme Stunt Show; and try the Toy Story Mania ride.

Disney's Animal Kingdom: Another contrasting option, with realistic animal habitats, including a 100acre/40.5ha safari savannah, captivating shows and terrific rides, like the grand Expedition Everest.

Disney's Typhoon Lagoon Water Park: Splash down waterslides and learn to surf in the world's biggest man-made lagoon.

Disney's Blizzard Beach Water Park: The big brother of all the water parks, with a massive spread of rides in a 'snowy' environment.

Tranquility at Discovery Cove

Disney Springs: Almost a mile of themed restaurants, bars, shops, a cinema multiplex, the DisneyQuest arcade of interactive games, House of Blues music venue and world-famous Cirque du Soleil® company.

Wedding Pavilion: A fairytale venue overlooking Seven Seas Lagoon for picture-perfect marriage ceremonies.

ESPN Wide World of Sports: A huge sporting venue to both play and watch top events.

The other parks

If you think Orlando is only about Disney, prepare to be amazed.

Universal Orlando: The other main resort has two theme parks, an entertainment district and four themed hotels (five later in 2016). At Universal Studios you encounter The Simpsons, the Rip Ride Rockit roller-coaster, Woody Woodpecker's KidZone, TRANSFORMERS: The Ride – 3D and the new Wizarding World of Harry Potter – Diagon Alley. Islands of Adventure (IoA) features the original Wizarding World area, with a superb blend of thrill rides, family attractions, shows, great design and high-tech features such as the Amazing Adventures of Spider-Man. A full onsite water park is also under construction.

Wet 'n Wild: On International Drive, this Universal water park offers plenty of fun rides and slides.

SeaWorld: THE place for creatures of the deep, with killer whales, dolphins and penguins, a refreshing atmosphere, the Blue Horizons and One Ocean shows, fabulous new

Iceploration at Busch Gardens

© SeaWorld Parks

Antarctica attraction, thrill rides like Manta and Kraken, plus an area of rides and activities just for kids.

Discovery Cove: Its exclusive neighbour offers the chance to swim with dolphins, among other things.

Aquatica: A fab water park providing even more fun and animal encounters in a colourful South Seas setting.

BRITTIP

Be realistic about the tickets you need. You simply won't get full use out of, say, a 14-day Disney ticket and the Orlando FlexTicket Plus in a two-week holiday.

Busch Gardens: In nearby Tampa, the sister park to SeaWorld offers creatures of the land, with a good mix of rides and shows. Highlights are the Cheetah Hunt and SheiKra coasters, the new Falcon's Fury drop-tower ride, the Edge of Africa 'safari' experience and the ice-skating show, Iceplorations. A family treat, and a must for coaster fans.

Other key attractions

These include: the dramatically upgraded **Kennedy Space Center**, with the new Atlantis Exhibit; the surprisingly fun and humorous **Gatorland**; LEGOLAND Florida, great for the 2–12 age group; **I-Drive 360**, featuring the 400ft/120m Orlando Eye; **Forever Florida**, a mix of local nature and high-energy zipline adventures; and **Boggy Creek Airboats** and **Wild Florida**, for a close-up with Kissimmee nature. Plus there is great mini-golf almost everywhere and other attractions along International Drive.

BRITTIP

Buy your theme park tickets in advance, NOT at the park gates. You will save time AND money, as most outlets offer an advance purchase discount.

Disney tickets

This is where things get complicated and it's important to work out what tickets you need. Most people buy one of three multi-day passes specifically for the UK market that allow visits to more than one park a day. They are great value for a two or three-week visit and provide maximum flexibility. But they aren't cheap and, if you want to visit only two or three of the Disney parks, you have to buy a Magic Your Way ticket in Orlando. Be aware you can't walk between the parks (they can be miles apart) and trying to do more than one a day is hard work, especially in summer.

Disney's ticket system is called Magic Your Way and is horribly complicated (although there is a simplified choice for UK visitors; see below). Multi-day tickets offer savings against one-day tickets but unused days expire after 14 days of first use.

Magic Your Way: If you just turn up at the ticket booths (or buy in advance from a US broker), you must choose:

- The number of days you want (up to 10).
- Whether you want Park Hopping (the ability to move between parks on the same day) for $64/ticket.
- If you want the Water Park Fun & More Option (2–10 visits to the water parks, DisneyQuest and ESPN Wide World of Sports™) for $64/ticket. Disney also offers one free round at nine-hole Oak Trail golf course (book in advance on 407 939 4653; club hire NOT included) and two free rounds at its mini-golf courses.
- Or if you want both Park Hopping *and* Water Park Fun & More for $90/ticket. NB: The non-expiration option for multi-day tickets has been discontinued.

Per-day ticket savings increase with the more days you buy: 1 day = $97–105 plus tax; 10 days = $365 plus tax, or $36.50/day.

BRITTIP
Use the Guest Services at Downtown Disney to save time and queuing if you need to buy Disney tickets in Orlando or exchange vouchers for tickets.

UK tickets: In the UK, there are three tickets on offer: the 7, 14 and 21-day Ultimate Ticket (see chart p11). NB: in 2015, a new 2-day ticket, with mini-golf, was being offered on a trial basis.

Other tickets
The choice is equally complicated for Universal Orlando, Wet 'n Wild, SeaWorld, Busch Gardens and Aquatica. Do check periodic special offers (see Orlando Ticket Deals, p11).

- **Orlando FlexTicket:** 14 consecutive days to both Universal parks, Wet 'n Wild, SeaWorld and Aquatica. Add Busch Gardens with the **FlexTicket Plus**.

- **1, 2, 3 or 4-day Tickets:** For Universal alone, **one park per day** or **both parks each day**.

- **2 and 3-Park Bonus Ticket:** 14 days at Universal Studios and IoA or those two plus Wet 'n Wild; buy in the UK.

- **2 and 3-Park Tickets:** 14 days for SeaWorld and Busch Gardens or SeaWorld and Aquatica, or all three.

- **Discovery Cove:** A day ticket includes a 14-Day Pass for SeaWorld and Aquatica. The Ultimate Package adds Busch Gardens for 14 days for an extra $25.

- **Party Pass:** For Universal's CityWalk ($11.99 plus tax) or a Party Pass with Movie ($15 plus tax) at the 20-screen cinema.

- **14-Day Combo Pass:** Offered by many UK brokers, for Disney & Universal, or various combinations of Disney, Universal, SeaWorld, LEGOLAND and the water parks,

The Splash Zone at
Curious George Goes to Town

plus a Freedom Ticket, or similar, for all eight parks plus the water parks. This is NOT a single ticket but a bundle of two or three tickets.

- **Go Orlando Card:** Two, three, five or seven days of visits within 14 days to 33 attractions and activities, including Kennedy Space Center, LEGOLAND Florida, Gatorland, WonderWorks, Fun Spot, airboat rides, mini-golf and more ($120–320 adults, $110–250 3–12s). There is also a **Family Fun Pass** (just LEGOLAND, WonderWorks and Gatorland for $99/89) and a **Top Attractions Pass** (five attractions for $75/59). It represents 32–55% in savings and comes with a handy attractions guidebook. See **www.goorlandocard.com**.

- **I-Drive Four Pass:** New in 2015 was this combo ticket for four International Drive attractions, Ripley's Believe It Or Not, CSI: The Experience, WonderWorks and Titanic: The Artifact Exhibition. It costs $74.99 (adults) and $54.99 (under 13s), and saves more than $12 off visiting them all individually. See **www.idrivefourpass.com**.

- **Eat and Play Card:** A discount card for groups of up to four, valid for 90 days from first use. Save 10–20% off 50-plus restaurants, from McDonald's, Denny's, Pizza Hut and TGI Friday's to upmarket choices like Big Fin Seafood, Café Tu-Tu Tango and Bongos Cuban Cafe, all in the main tourist areas and including alcohol in some cases; 10–30% on attractions like golf, mini-golf, Gatorland, Ripley's Believe It Or Not and more; and

10–20% off shops like Macy's and Reebok Outlet Stores, plus the Outta Control Magic Dinner Show and Golfsmith shops. It costs a bargain $25 and covers the entire bill for up to 4 people each time, so there are significant savings possible. Available from **www.eatandplaycard. com** (or call 001 613 680 7109) or select ticket brokers and tour operators.

With annual price hikes, try to buy your tickets as soon as you can, but be aware that some discounted tickets must be used for the first time in the year of purchase (e.g. 'first use by 31 Dec 2015'). Shop around, as many outlets have sales and special offers, but use a reputable agent and use your credit card for added security. The following companies all come well recommended.

Attraction Tickets Direct: Britain's top direct-sell Florida ticket broker, with a sharp bookings team, no credit card fees, free delivery in seven days and a promise to match any UK brochure price, plus a huge range of dinner shows, excursions, sports, theme park backstage tours and special offers, and a keen online Florida Forum and info centre to which we contribute (0800 787 0182, **www.attraction-tickets-direct.co.uk**).

FloridaTix: Independent ticket specialist featuring all the theme parks, plus the likes of Kennedy Space Center, Blue Man Group, dinner shows, many tours and excursions, no credit card fees and a £10 deposit ticket offer (0800 980 5552, **www.floridatix.co.uk**).

Ocean Florida: Independent Florida specialist also offers a well-priced ticket service, featuring all the theme parks, plus Kennedy Space Center and Miami Seaquarium (020 7939 7775, **www.ocean-florida.co.uk**).

Orlando Attractions: A UK-owned ticket service based in Orlando, it will post tickets to the UK and offers all the parks and the likes of airboat rides, fishing and other activities, plus some good combo tickets. Fully ABTA-bonded. Free shipping, price

The Amazing Adventures of Spider-man

© Universal Orlando Resort

Choosing a ticket

Ticket type	Park	Allowance
1-Day Ticket	Any Disney park, Universal Orlando parks, SeaWorld or Busch Gardens	Access to one park ONLY for one day; not available in advance
7, 14 and 21-Day Ultimate Ticket	All Disney parks	Unlimited access to all Disney attractions, including water parks, *DisneyQuest*, *ESPN Wide World of Sports*™ and nine-hole Oak Trail golf course (clubs not included) for 14 days after first use; NO non-expiration option; available only in advance in the UK
Annual Pass	*Magic Kingdom Park, Epcot, Disney's Hollywood Studios, Disney's Animal Kingdom;* plus discounts for shops, dining and tours	Unlimited admission and *free parking* for 365 days after purchase date. If ordered online, you get a voucher that must be activated at a park; the 365 days start on the first day you activate the pass
Premium Annual Pass	All Disney parks; plus numerous discounts for shops, dining and tours	Unlimited admission and *free parking* for 365 days after purchase date; plus discounts on sports and recreation
2, 3 or 4-Day 1-Park Ticket	Universal Studios, Islands of Adventure	Access to one of the Universal parks each day for 2–4 days, plus CityWalk; valid for 14 days
2, 3 or 4-Day 2-Park Ticket	Universal Studios, Islands of Adventure	Access to both Universal parks each day for 2–4 days, plus CityWalk; valid for 14 days
2-Park Bonus Ticket	Universal Studios, Islands of Adventure and CityWalk	14 consecutive days' access to both Universal parks, plus CityWalk clubs; sold in UK only
3-Park Bonus Ticket	Universal Studios, Islands of Adventure, Wet 'n Wild and CityWalk	14 consecutive days' access to all three parks, plus CityWalk clubs; sold in UK only
Orlando FlexTicket	Universal Studios, Islands of Adventure, SeaWorld, Wet 'n Wild, Aquatica	Access to all five parks, with multiple parks on same day, for 14 days from first use, plus CityWalk clubs
Orlando FlexTicket Plus	Universal Studios, Islands of Adventure, SeaWorld, Wet 'n Wild, Aquatica, Busch Gardens	Access to all six parks, with multiple parks on same day, for 14 days from first use, plus CityWalk clubs
2-Park Ticket	SeaWorld and Busch Gardens	14 consecutive days' access to both parks
2-Park Ticket	SeaWorld and Aquatica	14 consecutive days' access to both parks
3-Park Ticket	SeaWorld, Busch Gardens and Aquatica	14 consecutive days' access to all three parks

includes tax and no credit card fees (0800 294 9458, **www.orlandoattractions. com/tickets**).

Orlando Ticket Deals: A keenly priced and helpful broker that also issues real tickets (not vouchers), has a next-day delivery service and offers a significant Price Promise for all its attractions, including all the parks, dinner shows and many excursions (0800 542 1280, **www.orlando-ticket-deals.co.uk**).

There are others, including the main tour operators (p20), while you can also visit the Official Visitor Center on International Drive (**www.visitorlando. com**), but beware offers for 'free' tickets as these are purely timeshare lures. And NEVER buy resale tickets from a booth in Orlando – they are often unusable. Stick with the main brokers, who offer good products, service and local knowledge. And don't forget to plan with our sample Busy Day Guide (p346). You'll be exhausted if you try to do all the parks in one go!

BRITTIP
For all your theme park tickets, be sure to check out *Brit Guide* partner Orlando Ticket Deals first, as it features an exclusive money-saving offer for our readers (see inside back cover).

The climate
This catches out a lot of first-timers. Florida's weather varies from bright but cool with the odd drizzly spell in winter (Dec–Feb), to furiously hot and humid, punctuated by tropical downpours in summer (May–Sept). The most pleasant option is therefore spring or autumn. In Sept and Oct, you will also avoid the worst of the crowds. However, as most families are governed by school holidays, Easter and July–Aug remain the most popular for British visitors, so we have plenty of advice on how to stay ahead of the high-season crush. If you do need to go in summer, opt for late Aug when the crowds drop off somewhat.

BRITTIP
The draining humidity levels – up to 100% – and daily rainstorms in summer take many visitors by surprise, so carry a lightweight rainproof jacket or buy a cheap plastic poncho locally.

The mood
Orlando is big, brash and fun, but above all it's American and that means everything is well organised, but with some cultural differences such as tipping (see right). It's clean, well maintained and eager to please: Floridians generally are an affable bunch, but they take affability to new heights in the theme parks, where staff are almost painfully keen to make sure you 'have a nice day'.

Tipping
With the exception of fast-food restaurant servers, just about everyone who serves in hotels, bars, restaurants, buses, taxis, airports and public amenities will expect a tip, not least because all service industry workers are taxed on the basis of receiving 15% in tips, whether they're given or not.

- Bars, restaurants and taxis: 15%.
- Porters: $1/bag.
- Chambermaids: $1/day per adult.

BRITTIP
Tipping guide

Bill	Suggested tip
$15	$2.25
$20	$3.00
$25	$3.75
$30	$4.50
$40	$6.00
$50	$7.50

ESTA and immigration
Anyone flying to the USA on the Visa Waiver Programme MUST register online via the Electronic System for Travel Authorization (ESTA) no later than three days before departure. For all flights to the US, this has now replaced the old green Visa Waiver form (I-94W).

ESTA: ESTA is a pre-authorisation process prior to arriving at US immigration. The fee is $10 per person (plus admin and credit card fees, taking the final cost to around $15) and is valid for any visits in a two-year span (so you do NOT pay the $10 fee again in that time).

Apply at **https://esta.cbp.dhs.gov** and fill in your basic immigration info – passport, address in the USA, flight details, email address and a few security questions. Have your holiday address details available both for the ESTA and your Advance Passenger Information for your flight online. Ask your tour operator if you don't have a specific address (e.g. for a villa allocated on arrival) as it will have a formula for this. Your application should generate an immediate

Springfield at Universal Studios

response of 'Authorization Approved' or 'Pending'. If the response 'Travel Not Authorized' is generated, the applicant is unable to travel under the Visa Waiver Programme and must apply for a visa in advance. Remember to record or print your Application Number during the process so you can amend it for future visits within two years.

BRITTIP

If you need to fill in the white I-94 immigration form for visa holders, do so carefully in block capitals. Mistakes are often sent to the back of the queue. Please be courteous to immigration officials – they do a difficult job in demanding circumstances, and jokes about terrorism are NOT appreciated.

The ESTA speeds up the immigration process and cuts out most form filling. An ESTA must be completed for each member of your group or family travelling under the Visa Waiver Programme. Those who have a US visa because they are not eligible to travel under the Visa Waiver Programme (i.e. because of a criminal record – see right) still need to fill in a white I-94 form en route (fill in the front only) but they do NOT pay the $10 entry fee. However, anyone with a US visa for work purposes and who is travelling to America for a holiday, WILL need to fill in an ESTA and pay the fee.

BRITTIP

Beware unofficial websites that offer to fill in the ESTA form for you – for a fee. Stick with the official US government website and just pay the $10/person fee (or 'Travel Promotion Act fee').

Customs: You still need to complete a white customs form en route (it'll be given to you on the plane or at check-in and it's best to complete it in advance). Fill in one customs form per family, with some of the same basic info but also the value of any goods that will stay in the USA (put $0 unless you are arriving with gifts for

friends). Hand the document(s) with your passports to the immigration official who checks you through and takes a fingerprint scan and photo. The customs form will be handed back to you to present to another official when you exit the baggage hall.

Visa requirements

Holiday visitors to America do not need a visa providing they hold a valid machine-readable British passport (MRP). Any passport issued from 26 October 2005 must include a digital photograph (not glued or laminated). All passports issued from 26 October 2006 must include the new biometric data. Each family member must have their own passport, valid for the FULL duration of the holiday. However, British subjects, those without an MRP or those who fail to meet the photo/biometric data criteria DO need a visa ($131), and should apply at least two months in advance to the US Embassy.

US immigration requires ALL visitors aged 14–79 to give fingerprint and photo ID on arrival. It is a simple process, though – first the four fingers and thumb of one hand, and then the same for the other hand, then stand still for the camera. Some US gateways require a full 10-finger scan.

Some travellers may NOT be eligible under the Visa Waiver Programme and will have to apply for a special restricted visa or they may be refused entry. This applies to those who have been arrested in the past (even if it did not result in a conviction), have a criminal record

Disaster: A Major Motion Picture Ride

© Universal Orlando Resort

Main Attractions & Routes

✈ **Sanford International Airport**

Sanford Airport via Interstate 4 has no tolls, but can be far busier, especially during rush-hour

Sanford Airport via 417 has a few tolls, but is much quieter

Daytona

Mount Dora

ALTAMONTE SPRINGS

━━━ Toll road (from 50c to $5)

Lake Apopka

WINTER PARK

OCOEE

WINTER GARDEN

WEST COLONIAL DRIVE

DOWNTOWN ORLANDO

EAST - WEST EXPRESSWAY

Orange County History Center

WINDERMERE

FLORIDA TURNPIKE

KIRKMAN RD

SEMORAN BOULEVARD

Universal Studios
CityWalk
Islands of Adventure

Cocoa Beach

Kennedy Space Center

Wet'n Wild

SAND LAKE RD

BEACHLINE

Ripley's Believe It or Not
I-Drive 360

north exit

INTERNATIONAL DRIVE

TURKEY LAKE RD

Orlando International Airport

Magic Kingdom

Aquatica

SeaWorld

ORANGE BLOSSOM TRAIL

south exit

BOGGY CREEK ROAD

PALM PARKWAY

Discovery Cove

JOHN YOUNG PARKWAY

Lake Buena Vista

EPCOT DRIVE

Disney Springs

Epcot

CENTRAL FLORIDA GREENEWAY

BUENA VISTA DRIVE

WESTERN BELTWAY

Disney's Hollywood Studios

Typhoon Lagoon

Animal Kingdom

Blizzard Beach

Gatorland

BOGGY CREEK ROAD

MainGate West

WORLD DRIVE

OSCEOLA PARKWAY

Toll road

FLORIDA TURNPIKE

OLD LAKE WILSON RD

Old Town
Celebration

KISSIMMEE

IRLO BRONSON MEMORIAL HIGHWAY

East Lake Tohopekaliga

Kissimmee Airport ✈

Champions Gate

✈ Busch Gardens, Bok Tower Gardens, Legoland Florida

ST CLOUD

Lake Tohopekaliga

Tampa, Clearwater, Gulf Coast

© Steve Munns 2015

0   5 miles

Miami

N

(the Rehabilitation of Offenders Act does not apply to US visa law), have a serious communicable illness (but no longer including AIDS/HIV), or have previously been refused admission into, been deported from, or have overstayed in the US on the Visa Waiver Programme. Minor traffic offences do not count. Visa appointments can be arranged online at **https://ais.usvisa-info.com/en-gb** or call 020 3608 6998.

Contacts:

- **England, Scotland and Wales:** Visa Office, US Embassy, 24 Grosvenor Square, London W1A 2LQ (020 7499 9000). NB: for mailing address use postcode W1K 6AH.

- **Northern Ireland:** US Consulate General, Danesfort House, 223 Stranmillis Road, Belfast BT9 5GR (028 9038 6100).

- **More detailed advice: http://london. usembassy.gov**

Travel information

Luggage is liable to random searches in the US and you are advised NOT to lock your suitcases at check-in for the flight home as TSA officials have the authority to break into them. Using zip-lock seals that can easily be snipped open is permissible and some airlines provide them free, while you can also buy TSA-approved reusable locks at some travel shops. It is best to leave any gifts you are taking home unwrapped, just in case screening requires them to be opened; and be sure to put scissors and other sharp items in checked bags, never in your hand luggage.

BRITTIP
Cabin baggage restrictions often change, so check with your airline in advance for up-to-date info.

What's new?

Walt Disney World will debut its fabulous new **Rivers of Light** evening special effects show at the Animal Kingdom in spring 2016, while the huge **Disney Springs** redevelopment (formerly Downtown Disney) should be complete by May. In the Epcot park, there will be added capacity on the popular **Soarin'** ride, while the same should be true for **Toy Story Mania** in Disney's Hollywood Studios. Also in Epcot, the dramatic **Frozen** makeover of the Norway pavilion will be unveiled, including the new Frozen Ever After ride and the Anna & Elsa meet-and-greet.

Over at Universal, their Islands of Adventure park will open **Skull Island: Reign of Kong** 3-D ride and the **NBC Sports Café** in CityWalk in summer 2016, while **SeaWorld** will add the eye-catching Mako, which will be Orlando's fastest and tallest coaster. **Busch Gardens** will also have a new ride for summer 2016 in the shape of unique spinning coaster Cobra's Curse.

Mardi Gras parade at Universal Studios

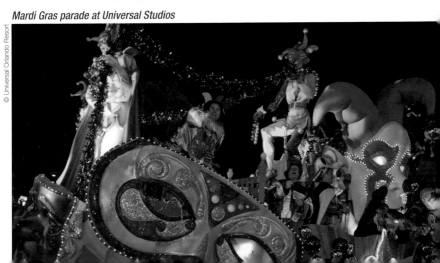

What's on?

Central Florida is home to some wonderful annual events that are well worth taking in:

February
Mardi Gras (to Apr), Universal Studios: **www.universalorlando.com**
Mount Dora Arts Festival, Mount Dora: **http://mountdoracenterforthearts.org/arts-festival**
Silver Spurs Rodeo, Kissimmee: **www.silverspursrodeo.com**

March
Flower & Garden Festival (to May), Epcot: **www.disneyworld.com**
Bands, Brew & BBQ, SeaWorld (to Apr): **http://seaworldparks.com/en/seaworld-orlando/events/bands-brew-and-bbq/**
Food & Wine Festival, Busch Gardens (to Apr): **http://seaworldparks.com/en/buschgardens-tampa/food-and-wine/**
Sidewalk Art Festival, Winter Park: **www.wpsaf.org**

April
Florida Film Festival, Orlando: **www.floridafilmfestival.com**

May
International Fringe Theatre Festival, Orlando: **http://orlandofringe.org/**

June
Sounds Like Summer concerts (to July), Epcot: **www.disneyworld.com**
Summer Nights (to July), SeaWorld and Busch Gardens: **www.seaworldparks.com**

September
Mickey's Not-So-Scary Halloween Party (to Oct), Magic Kingdom: **www.disneyworld.com**
Halloween Horror Nights (to Oct), Universal Studios: **www.universalorlando.com**
Howl-O-Scream, Busch Gardens (to Oct): **www.howloscream.com**
International Food & Wine Festival, Epcot (to Nov): **www.disneyworld.com**

October
Halloween Spooktacular, SeaWorld: **http://seaworldparks.com/en/seaworld-orlando/spooktacular/**
Silver Spurs Rodeo, Kissimmee: **www.silverspursrodeo.com**

November
World Food Championships, Celebration: **http://celebrationtowncenter.com/events/the-world-food-championships/**
Mickey's Very Merry Party (to Dec), Magic Kingdom: **www.disneyworld.com**
British Bonfire Night, Kissimmee: **http://guyfawkeskissimmee.com**
Snowing Nightly, Celebration (to Dec): **http://celebrationtowncenter.com/events/**

NBC Sports Grill is due to open in 2016

© Universal Orlando Resort

$ **BRITBONUS**
Don't forget to keep an eye out for the Brit Bonus, which features special offers and discounts with various hotels, attractions and restaurants. In addition, *Brit Guide* partners Florida Dolphin Tours now offer their exclusive 12.5% discount to our readers on a new live booking option on our website, **www.britguideorlando.net**.

Plan your visit

The next few chapters will tell you all you need to know to plan the ideal holiday. Make a rough itinerary and then fine tune it with this book. You can also take advantage of our unique Touring Plans Service (p41). Now read on and enjoy…

Planning and Practicalities

or **How to *Almost* Do It All and Live to Tell the Tale**

Advance planning has always been vital to a memorable Orlando holiday, and it is more important than ever since Disney brought in their My Magic+ system. You simply have to do some homework in advance, or risk being frustrated and/or exhausted!

This huge and demanding place can pull you in a dozen directions at once, with a dazzling array of options for practically everything. Nowhere else in the world can be so complex to navigate, so it's vital to plan your visit in advance. Start with WHEN you want to go; WHERE you'd like to stay; WHAT sort of holiday you want; WHO to book with; and finally HOW MUCH to try to do.

When to go

To avoid the worst of the crowds, the best times to go are Oct to Dec (but not Thanksgiving week in Nov or 20 Dec to New Year); early Jan to mid-Mar (avoiding President's Day in Feb); and the week after Easter to the end of May.

Busiest times: Orlando is seldom quiet but is busiest at:

- Christmas/New Year period (about 17 Dec–7 Jan).

- Mid-Mar to week after Easter.

- From Memorial Day (the last Mon in May, the official start of the summer season) to mid-Aug, notably around 4 July.

- Labor Day weekend in early Sept, the last holiday of summer.

Disney's Art of Animation Resort

Hurricane alert?

June–Nov is officially hurricane season, but it is not anything to worry about. Even the unprecedented extremes of 2004, when three major storms hit Central Florida, caused no significant damage to the parks and the biggest inconvenience was losing electricity for a few days. In the unlikely event of a major storm, switch your TV to the Weather Channel or local news station WESH 2 and follow its advice.

• Thanksgiving week (from the Wed–Sun).

The parks can close to new arrivals by mid-morning at these times – especially at Christmas.

BRITTIP

Thanksgiving is the 4th Thurs in Nov; George Washington's birthday, or President's Day, is the 3rd Mon in Feb, and both make for above-average long-weekend crowds.

Best times: The best combination of good weather and smaller crowds is in Apr (after Easter) and Oct. Rain isn't a big factor (although outdoor rides and the water parks will close if lightning threatens), but the crowds will noticeably thin out when it does rain and you can take advantage by bringing waterproofs or buying a cheap plastic poncho (all the parks sell them, but they are cheaper from local supermarkets). In the colder

months, take a few warm layers for early morning queues. Then, when it heats up, leave them in the park lockers. When it gets hot, take advantage of the air-conditioned attractions (and drink LOTS of water). The humidity alone will knock you sideways in summer and it's vital to rehydrate at regular intervals.

Where to stay

This is equally important and, again, there's a huge choice. As a rough guide, four main areas make up the great Orlando tourist conglomeration.

Walt Disney World: Some of the most sophisticated, convenient and fun places to stay are Disney's own hotels.

The same imagination that created the theme parks also worked on the likes of Disney's Polynesian Village and Animal Kingdom Lodge. They all feature free transport, MagicBand (your resort ID, room key, park entry, FastPass+ entry and charging privileges around the parks so you can have purchases delivered to the hotel), free parking and the BIG bonus of Extra Magic Hours. This allows Disney resort guests entry to one theme park each day, either one hour before official opening or for two hours after closing, so you can do many of the attractions with lower crowds (though evenings can still be busy). Many also have kids' clubs and babysitting services. However, with the exception of Disney's All-Star, Pop Century and Art of Animation

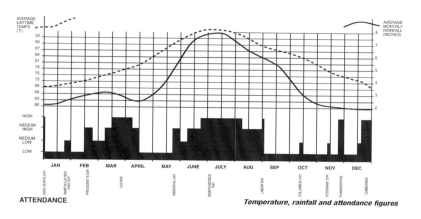

ATTENDANCE

Temperature, rainfall and attendance figures

Virgin's V-Room

All Virgin Holidays guests have the option of the V-Room lounge at Gatwick and Manchester, a private hideaway with a kids' play area, video games, big-screen TV, internet access, adults-only area, free breakfast, snacks, fruit, soft drinks, tea and coffee, and fast-track security channel. It costs £24.50/adult and £14/(2–11s) in advance (£25 and £15 on day of travel), free with Platinum bookings. NB: The Gatwick V-Room will close Feb–Dec 2016 and reopen in a new space in the North Terminal as part of the Gatwick revamp.

Resorts, its hotels are among the most expensive, especially to eat in, and are not close to other attractions you may wish to visit. They make a good one-week base, though.

BRITTIP

Beware holiday homes (and some hotels) that insist they are 'just minutes from Disney World' – which may actually mean 30mins or more from the parks. Try to get the exact address and check it.

Lake Buena Vista: On the eastern fringes of Walt Disney World and conveniently along Interstate 4 (I-4), this features a good mix of hotels. It is handy for Disney (and slightly cheaper), with most hotels offering free transport to the parks, plus there is excellent dining and shopping.

International Drive: The ribbon development known as I-Drive lies mid-way between Disney and downtown Orlando, running parallel to I-4, and is an excellent central location about 20mins' drive from Disney and close to Universal and SeaWorld. It is a well-developed tourist area in its own right, with great shops, restaurants and attractions like I-Drive 360, Wet 'n Wild, Ripley's Believe It Or Not, WonderWorks and iFLY Orlando, plus its own transport service, the I-Ride Trolley. The downside is it gets congested in peak times, but it is good value and one of the few areas with extensive

pavement, making it easy to explore on foot. A sub-district off I-Drive is the Universal area of Kirkman Road and Major Boulevard.

Kissimmee: Budget holiday-makers can be found in their greatest numbers along the tourist sprawl of Highway 192 (the Irlo Bronson Memorial Highway), an almost unbroken 20ml/32km strip of hotels, motels, restaurants and shops. It offers some of the best economy accommodation and is handy for Disney, though further from Universal and SeaWorld. A car is advisable here, although there is extensive pavement, landscaping, bus shelters and benches. **Highway 27** is often referred to as 'Kissimmee' but is actually either in Lake County (to the north) or Polk County (to the south). This is prime holiday home territory, with numerous developments along its 25ml/40km extent.

BRITTIP

I-Drive south of Sand Lake Road offers some of the best hotels and restaurants. To the north, it is more budget hotels, fast food and gift shops.

Split holidays

Florida has so much to offer, many opt to spend a week in Orlando and a week somewhere else. The Atlantic coast has great beaches an hour to the east; the Everglades are 3–4 hours to the south; and there are more wonderful beaches to the west. There's great shopping almost everywhere, stunning golf courses and opportunities to play or watch tennis, baseball and basketball, go fishing, boating or kayaking. The tour operators all offer a huge variety

Grand Bohemian Hotel in Downtown Orlando

Dining Plan options

Most tour operators offer the Disney Dining Plan as an optional extra with Disney hotel packages and it can be good value if you spend ALL your time in Walt Disney World, where there are few cheap dining outlets. But, because ALL members of the family must be included for the FULL length of your stay, even the Quick Service plan adds £1,120 for a family of four (with children 3–9) staying for two weeks; the main Dining Plan would be £1,512; and the Deluxe Plan a huge £2,632. It is a LOT of food to contend with, especially when it's hot, and you often need to book the full-service restaurants well in advance. You can eat cheaper elsewhere, so don't book unless you are sure. However, tour operators occasionally offer the Dining Plan as a FREE perk at quieter times of the year – a BIG bonus. See more on Disney Dining Plan on p58.

of packages, plus cruise-and-stay options. If you can afford it, the best option is to have two weeks in Orlando then a week relaxing on a beach. A two-week, half-and-half split is popular, but can make for a hectic time in Orlando. Some companies offer a 10/4 Orlando/coast split, which is a better idea for two weeks. Fly-drives offer great flexibility, but there is a lot to tempt you and you may find it better to book a two-centre stay that includes a car and accommodation so you can still travel but avoid too much packing and unpacking (see also Chapter 9).

Travel companies

There is serious competition for your hard-earned money – from the big boys, specialists and online agents – so choose one that best fits your needs on cost, flights, style and extras. Always ensure they are ABTA (for travel agents) or ATOL (for flights) bonded. During peak periods – notably the summer and Christmas holidays – it can be cheaper to book a package with charter flights rather than individual flights, hotels, etc, although it is also worth looking at flight-only prices.

Arriving at the Magic Kingdom parking kiosks

The Big Boys

British Airways Holidays: A well-established and varied choice, using direct BA flights from Gatwick to Orlando International Airport and Tampa year-round, with any range of stay (0844 493 0124, **www.britishairways.com/travel/holidays-in-florida**).

Cosmos Holidays: With a long history in Florida, Cosmos focuses on the key resort areas in Orlando and the Gulf Coast. Uses Thomson flights to Orlando Sanford International Airport from spring to late autumn (0483 227 1464, **www.cosmos.co.uk**).

Thomas Cook: A routine range of options from this former big mainstream operator, now offering just 7 and 14-day holidays with flights from Manchester and Glasgow from late Mar to early Nov, plus Stansted and Belfast in summer (01733 224 800, **www.thomascook.com**), although their travel agent arm can still sell packages from Gatwick (just with other airlines).

Thomson: Another one of the mainstream companies, with an especially extensive range of villa choice. Flights from Birmingham, Bristol, East Midlands, Gatwick, Glasgow, Manchester and Newcastle to Orlando Sanford International Airport with their own Thomson Airways, many using the latest Dreamliner aircraft from spring to late autumn (0871 231 4691, **www.thomson.co.uk**).

Travel City Direct: Popular budget-minded brand under Virgin umbrella

Complete Orlando

The highly rated Attraction Tickets Direct company has a full ATOL-bonded travel operator called Complete Orlando, which is well worth trying for packages, flights, hotels, car hire and travel insurance. It offers a wide range of accommodation (usually with some great deals, especially on Disney hotels), plus handy online videos, and no credit card fees or hidden extras. Call 0800 294 8844, **www.completeorlando.co.uk**.

and with mainly Virgin Atlantic flights (but also BA, Delta, United and Aer Lingus), with good range of Orlando-beach combos and great villa choice (0844 557 6969, **www.travelcitydirect.com**).

Virgin Holidays: Britain's leading tour operator to Florida, with by far the biggest choice and multi-centre option possibilities (including cruises, beach-hopper packages and even a Miami-Cancun combo), mainly using Virgin Atlantic's award-winning service but also Delta, Air France, United and US Airways. Some exclusive extra perks, like early entry to the Wizarding World of Harry Potter at Universal Orlando and to SeaWorld, plus return flight check-in at Disney Springs, wedding services, vow renewals and exclusive options on Singer Island, Marco Island and Key West (0844 557 4321, **www.virginholidays.co.uk**).

The specialists

Choose from the following smaller, specialist companies that all feature individual programmes to Florida:

- **Funway Holidays** (0844 557 0626, **www.funwayholidays.co.uk**).
- **James Villa Holidays** (0800 074 0122, **www.jamesvillas.co.uk**).
- **Jetsave** (0844 415 9880, **www.jetsave.com**).
- **Kuoni** (0800 092 4444, **www.kuoni.co.uk**).
- **Ocean Florida** (020 7939 7775, **www.ocean-florida.co.uk**).

- **Premier Holidays** (0844 4937 531, **www.premierholidays.co.uk**).
- **Trailfinders** (020 7368 1200, **www.trailfinders.com**).
- **Travelbag** (0871 703 4698, **www.travelbag.co.uk**).
- **USAirtours** (0800 0350 149, **www.usairtours.co.uk**).

Online agents

The recent growth of online travel agents has been huge, and you will find some great deals in this group, for packages, flights or accommodation:

- **eBookers** (020 3320 3320, **www.ebookers.com**).
- **Dial A Flight** (0844 811 4444, **www.dialaflight.com**).
- **Expedia** (020 3684 2911, **www.expedia.co.uk**).
- **LastMinute** (0800 083 4000, **www.lastminute.com**).
- **Opodo** (0871 277 0090, **www.opodo.co.uk**).
- **Travel Supermarket** (0845 345 5708, **www.travelsupermarket.com**).

For flights only, try:

- **Cheap Flights** (**www.cheapflights.co.uk**).
- **Flight Centre** (0800 587 0058, **www.flightcentre.co.uk**).
- **NetFlights** (01772 394 404, **www.netflights.com**).
- **Sky Scanner** (**www.skyscanner.net**).

Online search engines

The following selection search a number of travel agent sites at the same time:

- **kelkoo** (http://travel.kelkoo.co.uk).
- **kayak** (www.kayak.co.uk).
- **Travel Jungle** (**www.traveljungle.co.uk**).

Scheduled flights

Aer Lingus: The main Irish airline offers three flights a week from Dublin (0333 004 5000, www.aerlingus.com).

British Airways: The big national carrier flies direct from Gatwick to Orlando up to 14 times a week, as well as to Tampa and Miami (0844 493 0787, **www.britishairways.com**).

Virgin Atlantic: With up to 13 flights a week Gatwick–Orlando, up to 10 from Manchester, 2 from Glasgow, and 1 from Belfast (in summer peak), plus daily from Heathrow to Miami (0344 209 7777, **www.virgin-atlantic.co.uk**).

Norwegian: The low-cost carrier started a new direct Gatwick–Orlando route once a week in 2015, in addition to offering Gatwick to Fort Lauderdale in South Florida (a 3-hour drive from Orlando) at some tempting prices and all using the Boeing Dreamliner, as well as Orlando–Copenhagen (0330 828 0854, **www.norwegian.com/uk/**).

Icelandair: From Heathrow, Glasgow and Manchester; also offers a scheduled transatlantic route to Orlando Sanford Airport via Reykjavik, Iceland (0844 811 1190, **www.icelandair.co.uk**).

However, you can often save money on indirect flights with these carriers:

American Airlines: now incorporating US Airways, from Heathrow, Manchester, Glasgow or Dublin via Boston, Chicago, Charlotte, Dallas, New York, Philadelphia and Washington (0844 369 9899, **www.americanairlines.co.uk**).

Delta/KLM: Gatwick via Atlanta; Heathrow via Atlanta, Boston, Minneapolis, Detroit or New York; or Manchester via New York or Atlanta; (020 7660 0293, **www.klm.com**).

Cobra's Curse due to open at Busch Gardens

© SeaWorld Parks

United: (Heathrow via Washington, Houston, New York or Chicago, or Manchester, Birmingham, Belfast, Dublin, Glasgow or Edinburgh via New York; 0845 607 6760 **www.united.com**).

The obvious drawback is the extra journey time, and the connecting flight may land you in Orlando late in the evening. However, it does break the journey and places like Detroit and Dallas often process international passengers quicker than Orlando, meaning less hassle when you arrive in Florida.

What to see when

Once you arrive, the temptation is to head for the nearest theme park, then the next and so on. Except this is the best way to end up exhausted. Some days at the parks are busier than others, while you'll also need a few rest days. So here's what to do.

Using the Planner on p345 as an example (or with the Brit Guide Touring Plans service, p41), make a note of the attractions you want to see. The most sensible strategy is to plan around the 8 'must-see' parks. If you have only a week, drop Busch Gardens and focus on Disney, Universal and SeaWorld. The new-look Kennedy Space Center is also hard to overlook these days, though.

- **Magic Kingdom**: 2 days – the biggest hit with children.

- **Epcot:** 2 days – only the most fleet of foot can do it in a day, and then only with low crowds, but there are fewer rides to amuse children.

- **Animal Kingdom**: 1 day – a little short on appeal for the youngest.

- **Disney's Hollywood Studios:** 1 day – plus the evening Fantasmic! show.

- **SeaWorld:** 1–2 days.

- **Islands of Adventure:** 1–2 days.

- **Universal Studios:** 1–2 days.

- **Busch Gardens:** 1 day – extremely popular with British families, it is 75mins away in Tampa.

- **LEGOLAND Florida**, 45mins away

Our must-do experiences

- Soarin' and IllumiNations show (Epcot)
- Cirque du Soleil® (Disney Springs)
- Wizarding Worlds of Harry Potter at Universal Orlando
- Boggy Creek Airboats/Wild Florida (Kissimmee)
- Expedition Everest and Festival of The Lion King (Animal Kingdom)
- Wishes fireworks, Pirates of the Caribbean and Haunted Mansion rides (Magic Kingdom)
- Fantasmic! show and Star Tours ride (Disney's Hollywood Studios)
- The Orlando Eye at I-Drive 360
- Shopping!
- Antarctica: Empire of the Penguin and Blue Horizons show (SeaWorld)
- Cheetah Hunt and SheiKra coasters (Busch Gardens)
- Space Shuttle Atlantis (Kennedy Space Center)
- A Disney character meal
- A day at a water park

in Winter Haven, is also a full day's outing, while the attractions of **I-Drive 360** can be fitted around the main parks. Look at the detail in Chapters 5–8 before you plan.

Smaller attractions

Of the other, smaller scale attractions, **Forever Florida** is a full day out as it also involves an hour's drive to get there, but everything else can be fitted around your Big Eight itinerary. The **water parks** or the quieter **Bok Tower Gardens** make for a relaxing half-day, while **Gatorland** (at least half a day) is a unique look at some of Florida's oldest inhabitants and is a good combination with **Boggy Creek Airboats** or **Wild Florida**. Then there are the likes of **Ripley's Believe It Or Not** museum, the **WhirlyDome** and the **WonderWorks** house of fun, all offering several hours' entertainment, the thrills of **iFLY Orlando** (an indoor 'sky-diving' wind tunnel) and the lure of old-fashioned go-karts and other fairground-type rides at **Fun Spot**,

Magical Midway and **Old Town**. Many stay open after the theme parks close.

Disney also has **DisneyQuest**, an imaginative interactive arcade that guarantees several hours of fun (especially for older children) at **Disney Springs**, while each main area is also well served with creatively designed **mini-golf** courses.

Evenings

The evening entertainment features a similarly wide choice. By far the best, and worth at least one evening each, are **Disney Springs** and Universal's **CityWalk** – the latter will keep you busy until the early hours! Dinner shows provide a lot of fun: 2hr cabarets based on themes such as medieval knights, pirates, Al Capone and murder mysteries that all include a hearty meal.

Shopping

Shopping in Orlando is world class (see Chapter 12) and your battle plan should include at least a day to visit the spectacular malls and discount centres, like the two excellent Orlando Premium Outlets centres, Lake Buena Vista Factory Stores, Mall at Millenia and the Florida Mall. Busy at weekends, they're handy if it rains.

What to do when

There are several guidelines for avoiding the worst of the tourist hordes, even in high season.

Avoid busy days: Most Americans arrive at weekends and head for the main theme parks first, so Sun and Mon are often bad times to

Pat O'Brien's at Universal

© Universal Orlando Resort

visit the Magic Kingdom, while Tues is usually also busy at Epcot. New rides like Harry Potter (at Universal Studios) also create longer queues, notably at weekends. The Animal Kingdom is the hardest to navigate when crowded, while Epcot handles the crowds best. Disney's Blizzard Beach and Typhoon Lagoon water parks hit high tide at weekends, and Thurs and Fri in summer. If Walt Disney World is humming early in the week, that makes it a good time to visit SeaWorld, Busch Gardens or the Kennedy Space Center. Try to avoid Wet 'n Wild and Aquatica at weekends, too.

Disney's Extra Magic Hours: Allowing Disney guests early and late access (see p59) creates bigger crowds, too. So, if you are NOT staying at a Disney hotel, avoid these EMH mornings. For much of the year, they run as follows: Magic Kingdom, Thurs (morning EMH) and Saturday (evening EMH); Epcot, Tues (morning), Fri (evening); Disney's Hollywood Studios, Sat (morning), Mon (evening); Animal Kingdom, Wed and Sun (morning only). Be aware EMH days can change at short notice, and the Magic Kingdom can have multiple successive days at peak periods. See the Park Hours page at **https://disneyworld.disney.go.com/calendars/**

Universal Orlando: The picture is different here as only the two Wizarding Worlds of Harry Potter have daily early opening privileges (for guests at Universal hotels). This often means heavier crowds early in the week, while the parks also get busiest at weekends.

BRITTIP

If your hotel is not far away, take a mid-afternoon break from the park and return for a siesta or a swim. Your car park ticket is valid all day, and the evening is often the best time to be in the parks.

Arrive early: Getting the most out of your days at the parks is another art form, and there are several options. The opening times seldom vary from 9am (Magic Kingdom and

Medical marvels

The **Medical Concierge**® is a great choice for local medical care with doctors and paediatricians throughout the tourist areas, making house calls to hotels and villas 24/7. They also have several key clinic locations, notably close to Universal Orlando, and International Drive, Lake Buena Vista, Kissimmee and Haines City/Davenport, but you must call for an appointment. Their doctors have mobile pharmacies and even X-ray units and they specialise in providing healthcare to overseas visitors, hence their staff are familiar with dealing with Brits. They can often arrange same-day dental and other specialist appointments and take many UK travel insurance polices, meaning they deal directly with the insurance company. Their switchboard is manned around the clock with medically trained staff, ensuring you never deal with an answering machine. Call 1855 326 5252, and dial 1 to get straight through to medical care, or visit **www.themedicalconcierge.com**.

Animal Kingdom can be 8am at peak times), but arriving early is highly advisable. Apart from being near the head of the queues (and they are SERIOUS queues, or 'lines'), the parks occasionally open early if the crowds build up. So you can be a step ahead by arriving at least 30mins before opening time (or an hour early during peak periods). You will also be better placed to park in the huge car parks and catch the tram to the main gates.

Prioritise: Once you are in pole position, don't waste time on the shops, scenery and other frippery that will lure the unprepared first-timer. Instead, head straight for some of the main rides and get a few big-time thrills under your belt before the main hordes arrive. You will quickly work out where the most popular attractions are as the majority of early birds will flock to them. Use Chapters 5 and 6 to plan your park strategies.

Pace yourself: Disney's parks, notably the Magic Kingdom, stay open late for the main holidays, until midnight at times, and that can be a l-o-n-g day for kids. It's vital to pace yourself,

Footy frenzy

You don't need a specialist sports bar to find British football on TV these days. The Premier League is extensively covered by NBC (up to three games on Sat and Sun, plus the Mon night games) while the Champions League and FA Cup is on Fox Sports. You should check if your villa/hotel has NBC Sports for some games, though, as it is a cable channel that not everyone gets. And don't forget to check out our own team – Orlando City – at **www.orlandocitysc.com**.

especially if you arrive early. There are plenty of options to take time off for a drink or a sit-down somewhere air-conditioned, and these latter are vital in summer.

FastPass+: make *sure* you use this Disney system to your advantage in advance (see p101).

Meal breaks: Benefit from the American habit of dining en masse at lunchtime (noon–1.30pm) and dinner (5.30–7pm) by planning your own meals outside those times. It pays to take an early lunch (before noon), snack in mid-afternoon and then enjoy a relative drop-off in crowds in late afternoon. But try not to have all your meals in the parks; eating here can be expensive (at least $11/person for a basic meal). A good breakfast before you arrive and a light lunch will save you $$$s!

BRITTIP
The water IS safe to drink in the US, but it might not taste great as it's heavily fluoridated. If you buy bottled water, do so at supermarkets, not at the parks, where it is exorbitantly expensive.

Comfort and clothing

You may feel jetlagged for the first day or so after your arrival, but avoiding alcohol and coffee on the plane and keeping hydrated by drinking plenty of water can reduce this.

Shoes: The most important part of your holiday wardrobe is your footwear – you'll be on your feet a

LOT, even at off-peak periods. The smallest park is 'only' 100acres/40ha, but that is irrelevant to the time spent queuing. This is not the time to break in new sandals or trainers. Comfortable, well-worn shoes or trainers are essential (many rate Croc-type shoes as ideal park footwear).

BRITTIP
Look after your feet and avoid the onset of blisters by buying some moleskin footpads from a supermarket or 'drug-store' like Walgreens and CVS.

Casual clothes: You need dress only as the climate dictates. T-shirts and shorts are appropriate in all parks and nearly all restaurants will accept casual dress. However, swimwear is not acceptable away from pool areas. If you feel the need for a change of clothes or a sweater for the evening after a long day, use the handy lockers in all the parks (unlimited use all day for a small fee).

BRITTIP
Don't be tempted to pack a lot of smart or formal clothing – you really won't need it in hot, informal Florida.

Baby services: All the parks are well equipped with pushchairs, or 'strollers', for hire (although it pays to have your own), and baby services are located at regular intervals. You can even hire pushchairs for your full holiday period from Orlando Stroller Rentals from $100 for two weeks (1800 281 0884, **www.orlandostrollerrentals.com**).

Dragon Challenge

© Universal Orlando Resort

Attractions with warnings for expectant mothers

Animal Kingdom: Dinosaur!, Expedition Everest, Kali River Rapids, Kilimanjaro Safari, Primeval Whirl.

Busch Gardens: Cheetah Hunt, Congo River Rapids, Falcon's Fury, Kumba, Montu, Phoenix, Sand Serpent, Scorpion, SheiKra, Stanley Falls Log Flume, Tanganyika Tidal Wave, Ubanga-Banga Bumper Cars.

Epcot: Mission: SPACE, Soarin', Test Track.

Hollywood Studios: Rock 'n Roller Coaster, Star Tours, Twilight Zone Tower of Terror.

Islands of Adventure: Cat in the Hat, Dragon Challenge, Dudley Do-Right's Ripsaw Falls, Flight of the Hippogriff, Harry Potter and the Forbidden Journey, Incredible Hulk Coaster, Jurassic Park River Adventure, Popeye & Bluto's Bilge Rat Barges, Storm Force Accelatron, Dr Doom's Fearfall, The Amazing Adventures of Spider-Man.

Magic Kingdom: Big Thunder Mountain Railroad, The Barnstormer, Seven Dwarfs Mine Train, Space Mountain, Splash Mountain.

SeaWorld: Antarctica: Empire of the Penguin (Wild version of ride), Journey to Atlantis, Jazzie Jellies, Kraken, Manta, Rock Wall, Shamu Express, Swishy Fishies, Wild Arctic (ride portion).

Universal Studios: Disaster!, ET Adventure, Harry Potter and the Escape from Gringotts, Men in Black Alien Attack, Revenge of the Mummy, Shrek 4-D, Terminator 2: 3-D (stationary seats available), TRANSFORMERS: The Ride – 3D, Twister – Ride it Out!, Woody Woodpecker's Nuthouse Coaster.

Sunscreen: It is VITAL to use high-factor sun creams (30-plus) at all times, even during the winter when the sun may not feel strong but can still burn. Orlando has a subtropical climate and you need higher factor creams than in the Mediterranean, and waterproof if you are swimming. Use sun block on sensitive areas like nose and ears, and splash on the after-sun liberally at the end of the day. Skincare products are widely available and usually inexpensive (at Wal-Mart, Publix or Target). Wear a hat during the day, and avoid

Gringott's Bank

© Universal Orlando Resort

alcohol, coffee and fizzy drinks until the evening as they are dehydrating and make you liable to heatstroke. You must increase your fluid intake SIGNIFICANTLY in the summer, but stick to sports drinks and lots of water.

BRITTIP

One of the best ways to keep cool in the sun is to buy a simple mist spray fan (about $7.99) from a supermarket.

Medical help

Should you require medical treatment consult your tour operator's info about local hospitals and surgeries. In the event of a medical or other emergency, dial 911 as you would 999 in Britain. It cannot be over-stressed, however, you should take out comprehensive travel insurance (see p29) for any trip to America, as there is NO National Health Service and any form of medical treatment is expensive. Keep all the receipts and put in a claim on your return home.

BRITTIP

Look for local insect-repellent brands Cutter, Repel and Off! and use them away from the parks.

At-a-glance kids' height requirements

Height	Park	Rides
2ft 8in/82cm	Disney's Blizzard Beach	Chairlift
Must be with a child		
3ft–4ft 8in/91–142cm	Islands of Adventure	Pteranodon Flyers
3ft–4ft 8in/91–142cm	Wet 'n Wild	The Surge, Aqua Drag Racer, Flyer, Disco H2O
3ft/91cm	Disney's Magic Kingdom	The Barnstormer
	Universal Studios	Woody Woodpecker's Nuthouse Coaster
	Islands of Adventure	The Cat in the Hat
3ft 4in/101cm	Disney's Animal Kingdom	DINOSAUR!
	Disney's Hollywood Studios	Star Tours, The Twilight Zone Tower of Terror
	Disney's Magic Kingdom	Splash Mountain, Big Thunder Mountain Railroad, Seven Dwarfs Mine Train Ride
	Epcot	Test Track, Soarin'
	Islands of Adventure	The Amazing Adventures of Spider-Man
	Universal Studios	The Simpsons Ride, TRANSFORMERS: The Ride – 3D, Harry Potter and the Escape from Gringotts
3ft 6in/106cm	Aquatica	Walhalla Wave, HooRoo Run, Taumata Racer
	Busch Gardens	The Wild Surge (3ft 2in/96cm with adult), Congo River Rapids, Ubanga-Banga Bumper Cars, Scorpion, Sand Serpent (age 6 minimum)
	Disney's Animal Kingdom	Kali River Rapids
	Islands of Adventure	Jurassic Park River Adventure
	SeaWorld	Journey to Atlantis, Wild Arctic (Polar Express at Christmas)
	Universal Studios	Men in Black: Alien Attack
3ft 8 in/111cm	Disney's Animal Kingdom	Expedition: Everest
	Disney's Magic Kingdom	Space Mountain
	Epcot	Mission: SPACE
	Islands of Adventure	Dudley Do-Right's Ripsaw Falls
3ft 10in/116cm	Busch Gardens	Stanley Falls
Under 4ft/122cm only	Aquatica	Kata's Kookaburra Cove
	Disney's Blizzard Beach	Tike's Peak
	Disney's Typhoon Lagoon	Ketchakiddee Creek
Under 4ft/122cm only (with adult)	Wet 'n Wild	Kids Park
4ft/122cm	Aquatica	Dolphin Plunge, Ihu's Breakaway Falls, Omaka Rocka
	Busch Gardens	Tanganyika Tidal Wave, Jungle Flyers
	Disney's Animal Kingdom	Primeval Whirl
	Disney's Blizzard Beach	Summit Plummet, Slush Gusher, Downhill Double Dipper
	Disney's Hollywood Studios	Rock 'n' Roller Coaster Starring Aerosmith
	Disney's Typhoon Lagoon	Crush 'n' Gusher, Humunga Kowabunga
	Epcot	Sum of All Thrills (non-inversion)
	Islands of Adventure	Popeye And Bluto's Bilge-Rat Barges, Flight of the Hippogriff, Harry Potter and the Forbidden Journey
	Universal Studios	Revenge of the Mummy, Disaster! A Major Motion Picture Ride...Starring YOU (unless accompanied by adult), ET Adventure
	Wet 'n Wild	Bomb Bay, Der Stuka, Black Hole, The Storm, Brain Wash
4ft 3in/130cm	Universal Studios	Hollywood Rip Ride Rockit!
	Wet 'n Wild	Wild One
4ft 4in/132cm	Disney's Magic Kingdom	Tomorrowland Speedway (for child to drive alone)
	Epcot	Sum of All Thrills (with inversion)
	Islands of Adventure	Dr Doom's Fearfall
4ft 6in/137cm	Busch Gardens	SheiKra, Kumba, Montu, Cheetah Hunt, Falcon's Fury
	Islands of Adventure	The Incredible Hulk Coaster, Dragon Challenge
	SeaWorld	Kraken, Manta

Emergency outpatients: These can be found with Centra Care at Florida Hospital Medical Center in more than 20 Central Florida locations (407 200 2273; **www.centracare.org**), as well as full family and paediatric care. Open 8am–8pm (5pm at weekends), there are four locations open to midnight Mon–Fri, including at 12500 S Apopka-Vineland Road near the Crossroads shopping centre and Downtown Disney at Lake Buena Vista (8pm Sat and Sun; 407 934 2273). Other notable tourist area locations are: 8201 West Irlo Bronson Memorial Highway (192), by Orange Lake Resort (407 465 0846); on Sand Lake Road, between John Young Parkway and Orange Blossom Trail (9am–5pm Sat and Sun; 407 851 6478); and 4320 West Vine Street, near Medieval Times (407 390 1888).

BRITTIP

If you take regular prescription drugs, find out the different UK and US names from your doctor or pharmacist and carry the info with you (e.g. adrenaline is known as epinephrine, paracetamol is acetaminophen).

Two-way radio rentals

Many families buy 'walkie-talkies' to keep in touch around the parks in preference to mobile phones. You can pick them up locally for as little as $35 in stores like Wal-Mart, Best Buy, Radio Shack, Office Depot and Staples. However, they cannot be used in the UK as they use the same frequency as our emergency services.

The Dr P Phillips Hospital, 9400 Turkey Lake Road, also has an emergency outpatients open 24 hours (407 351 8500).

Better still, call The Medical Concierge® (407 648 5252 or freephone at 1888 648 5252, or **www.themedicalconcierge.com**; see panel on p24) who make hotel and villa 'house calls' 24 hours a day.

Chemists: The largest chemists ('drug stores' in the US) are Walgreens (**www.walgreens.com**) and CVS (**www.cvs.com**), and the Walgreens at 12100 S Apopka-Vineland Road (near Downtown Disney), 5935 W Irlo Bronson Memorial Highway (Highway 192 in Kissimmee), 6201,

Hollywood Rip Ride Rockit

© Universal Orlando Resort

Measurements

US clothes sizes are smaller than ours, hence a US size 12 dress is a UK 14, or an American jacket sized 42 is a 44. Shoes are the opposite: a US 10 should fit a British size 9 foot. The measuring system is imperial, not metric.

8959 and 12650 International Drive (among others, plus the new one at the corner of I-Drive and Sand Lake Rd), are open 24 hours.

Travel insurance

You shouldn't travel without insurance, but you shouldn't pay more than you need to and you don't need to buy your travel agent's policy. Your policy should cover all these options.

- Medical cover of at least £2m.

- Personal liability up to £2m (this won't cover driving abroad; you still need Supplementary Liability Insurance with your car hire firm).

- Cancellation or curtailment cover up to £5,000.

- Personal property cover up to £1,500 (but check on expensive items, as most policies limit single articles to £250).

- Cash and document cover, including your passport and tickets.

- 24hr emergency helpline.

- If you want to go horse-riding, check your policy includes dangerous sports cover.

Shop around at reputable dealers such as:

- **Allianz Assistance** (0871 200 0428, **http://www.allianz-assistance.co.uk/**).

- **American Express** (0800 587 4000, **www.americanexpress.com/uk**).

- **Aviva** (0800 051 3606, **www.aviva.co.uk**).

- **AXA** (0844 874 0360, **www.axa.co.uk/insurance/personal/travel/**).

- **Club Direct** (0845 888 8891, **www.clubdirect.com**).

- **Columbus** (0800 068 0080, **www.columbusdirect.com**).

- **Direct Travel** (0333 300 0029, **www.direct-travel.co.uk**).

- **Money Supermarket** also compares travel insurers at **www.moneysupermarket.com/travel-insurance** (0845 345 5708).

Florida with children

We are often asked what we think is the right age to take children to Orlando, and there is no set answer. Some toddlers take to it instantly, while some 6–7-year-olds are overwhelmed. Very often, the best attractions for young children are the hotel swimming pool or the tram ride to a park's front gates! Some love the Disney characters instantly, while others find them frightening. There is no predicting how they'll react but, at 4½, Simon's oldest boy loved just about every second of his first experience (apart from the fireworks!) and still talks about it. A 3-year-old may not remember much, but will have fun and provide you with great memories, photos and videos. Here are some top tips for travelling with youngsters.

The flight: Try to look calm (even if you don't feel it) and relaxed. Small children soon pick up on any anxieties and make them worse. Pack a bag with lots of little things for them (comics, sweets, colouring books, small surprise toys, etc.) and keep vital extras like Calpol (in sachets, if possible), a change of clothes, a small first-aid kit plasters, antiseptic cream, baby wipes), sunglasses, a hat and

Superhero Island at Islands of Adventure

© Universal Orlando Resort

sunscreen in your hand luggage.

Once you're there: Take things slowly and let your children dictate the pace to a large extent. In hot, humid summer, only the most placid children (and few under-5s, in our experience) will happily queue for an hour or more at a ride, so use Disney's FastPass+ system (p101) judiciously. The heat, in particular, can result in grizzly kids in no time, so take breaks for drinks and splash zones or head for attractions with air-conditioning. Remember to carry your small first-aid kit. Baby wipes always come in handy, and it's a good idea to take spare clothes, which you can leave in park lockers. Going back to the hotel for an afternoon snooze is a good idea – you will also dodge the worst of the heat and crowds.

BRITTIP

The **Kids-eat free** and **Eat & Play** cards (see p10) are great ways for families to save money in many tourist-area restaurants. They feature more than 50 options, from the standard McDonald's and Dunkin Donuts to upmarket Cedar's and Big Fin Seafood.

In the sun: Carry sun cream and sun block at all times and use it often, in queues, on buses, etc. Use a children's after-sun lotion and make sure they drink a lot of water or non-fizzy drinks; tiredness and irritability are often the signs of mild dehydration.

Dining out: Look for Kids-eat-free deals as they can apply to children up to 12, and take advantage of the

Enjoying a Butterbeer at Universal Orlando

© Universal Orlando Resort

many buffet options (see Chapter 11, Dining Out) to fill up the family or for picky eaters. Many restaurants do Meals To Go if you want a quiet meal in your own accommodation without the worry of the kids playing up. And try to let your children get used to the characters (especially the size of them) before you go to one of the many wonderful character meals.

Having fun: Let your children do some of the decision-making and be prepared to go with the flow if they find something unexpected – the many squirt fountains and splash zones in the parks are an example (bring swimsuits and/or a change of clothes!). The Orlando rule of 'You Can't Do It All' applies especially with kids. Be aware some youngsters find the evening fireworks too loud, but the hotels around the Magic Kingdom offer a view from a distance.

Baby centres: All the parks have facilities for nursing mothers and can provide baby food and nappies on request (locations are on the park map). The centres can even provide spare children's underpants for those little accidents. All Disney hotel gift shops stock baby food and nappies. Expectant mothers are strongly advised not to ride some of the more dynamic attractions and coasters, and there will be clear warnings on park maps and at the rides.

Pushchairs: 'Strollers' are essential, even if your children are a year or so out of them. The walking wears kids out quickly and a pushchair can save a lot of discomfort. You can take your own, hire them at the parks or buy one for as little as $25 at a local supermarket. Babysitting is available through many Disney resorts and some of the bigger hotels elsewhere.

BRITTIP

Avoid making phone calls from your hotel – they're hugely expensive. It's cheaper to buy a local phone card and use a normal payphone. British mobiles can also be costly to use in the US. To call the UK from the US, dial 011 44, then drop the first 0 from the UK area code.

Repeat visitors

Repeat visitors are a large part of the Orlando market and are usually on the lookout for something new. Chapters 8 and 9 (Off The Beaten Track and The Twin Centre Option) are largely designed with them in mind. Here are 10 things worth doing once you have Been There and Done That:

1   Behind the scenes tours at the Disney parks.

2   Dolphin watch cruise from Dolphin Landings at St Pete Beach.

3   Wildlife eco-tour with Island Boat Lines at Cocoa Beach.

4   The scenic boat ride and Morse Museum in Winter Park.

5   Bok Tower Gardens.

6   St John's River Cruise in Blue Spring State Park, Seminole County.

7   Boggy Creek Airboats or Wild Florida.

8   Eco-park at Florida EcoSafaris or Orlando Tree Trek.

9   Merritt Island National Wildlife Refuge at Titusville.

10 Kayaking at The Paddling Center in Kissimmee.

Travellers with disabilities

The parks pay close attention to the needs of visitors with disabilities and Florida is extremely disabled-friendly (although Americans use the word 'handicapped' as we use 'disabled').

Access: Wheelchair availability and access is usually good (though there are a few rides that cannot cater for them) and all hotels now have disabled-accessible rooms. For hearing-impaired guests, there are assistive listening devices and reflective captioning at attractions where a commentary is part of the show. Braille guidebooks are available, plus rest areas for guide dogs, and there are special tape cassettes for blind guests. Disney, Universal and SeaWorld offer Accessibility Guides for disabled guests in all their main parks (and online). Life-jackets are always on hand at water parks. For Disney disability assistance, call 407 824 4321 (TTY 407 827 5141); for Universal, call 407 224 4233.

Guest Assistance: If you need help with queuing or have children with special needs, visit any Disney theme park Guest Relations office, with the person in question, and request a Disability Access Service card (DAS), which has replaced the old Guest Assistance Card. It doesn't provide front-of-line access, but instead provides a return time based on the current queue at each attraction. As soon as the Guest finishes one attraction, they can receive a return time for another. This can be used in addition to Disney's FastPass+ service. Universal, SeaWorld and Busch Gardens provide similar assistance through their Guest Services offices.

The New York back-streets at Disney's Hollywood Studios

Parking permits: To use any of the plentiful designated disabled parking areas in all public areas (including the parks), UK drivers must obtain a **Temporary Disabled Parking Permit**, which costs $15. You can either go to a local tax collection office, with your UK blue badge and passport, when you arrive (most open 8.30am–4pm Mon–Fri only), OR apply by post, fax or email at least four weeks in advance (but no more than six). By mail, send a photocopy of your Blue Badge (both sides), a copy of your passport ID page, your home address and address while in Florida, arrival and departure date and a money order (in US dollars) for $15; do NOT send cash for safety reasons. The Osceola County tax office has a special service for UK visitors with a dedicated team to deal with all requests (8am–4.30pm Mon–Fri). By mail: Patsy Heffner Tax Collector, 1300 9th Street, Suite 101-B, St Cloud, Florida 34769, USA; by fax: 407 892 8076; and include an email address for return confirmation. By email: **TaxCollectorTPL@osceola.org** with a scanned copy of your details (as above, but NOT your credit card details) and they will email you back with a number to call to arrange payment (there is a 2.5% service charge for using a credit or debit card). If you cannot reach them for any reason or don't get a response within two working days, try **webinfo@osceola.org** or 407 742 4000.

For a list of tax offices in Orange County (for the Orlando area), call 407 836 4145 (**www.octaxcol.com**, and click Office Locations); in Osceola County (for Kissimmee), call 407 742 4000 (**www.osceolataxcollector.com**). The temporary permits are valid for 90 days from issue date so it's best to apply no sooner than 5–6 weeks before travelling to ensure it will be valid for your stay. However, you may renew a permit within 12 months for no fee.

- **Walker Mobility:** Specialises in electric scooters and wheelchair rentals, with free delivery and pick-up, even from holiday villas (407 518 6000, **www.walkermobility.com**).

- **Wheelchair Vans of America:** Has specially-equipped vans for hire for wheelchair users (1800 910 8267 or 407 977 3799, **www.wheelchairvansofamerica.com**).

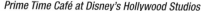
BRITTIP

'We used CARE Medical Equipment to hire a charger for our electric wheelchair as the 110v currency in the US does not work with a chair's 220v charging needs. They delivered to our villa within an hour and even stayed to make sure it worked. Some UK battery chargers will work but not all, so please check before you leave.' – Reader Lisa Smith, County Durham

- **CARE Medical Equipment:** Another company highly recommended

Prime Time Café at Disney's Hollywood Studios

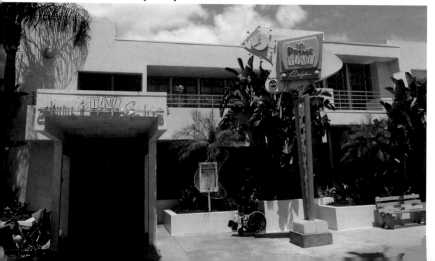

American-speak

Many words and phrases have a different meaning across the Atlantic. For instance, when Americans say the first floor, they mean the ground floor, the second floor is really the first, and so on. (NB: NEVER ask for a packet of fags; 'fag' is a crude, slang term for a homosexual.) Here are a few everyday words to help you:

American	English	American	English
ATM	Cash machine	Faucet	Tap
Appetizer	Starter	Fender	Car bumper
Band aid	Plaster	Freeway	Motorway
Bathroom	Private toilet	Fries	Chips
Biscuit	Savoury scone	Gas	Petrol
Broiled	Grilled	Graham cracker	Digestive biscuit
Cellphone	Mobile phone	Hood	Car bonnet
Check	Bill	Intersection	Junction
Chips	Crisps	Nickel	5 cents
Collect call	Reverse charge phone call	No standing	No parking OR stopping
		'Pound sign'	The # on a phone keypad
Cookie	Biscuit		
Cot/rollaway	Fold-up bed	Purse	Handbag
Crib	Cot	Quarter	25 cents
Diaper	Nappy	Ramp	Slip road
Dime	10 cents	Restroom	Public toilet
Divided highway	Dual carriageway	Seltzer	Soda water
Eggplant	Aubergine	Shrimp	King prawn
Eggs 'over easy'	Eggs fried on both sides but soft	Soda	Fizzy drink
		Stroller	Pushchair
Eggs 'sunny side up'	Eggs fried on just 1 side (soft)	Trunk	Car boot
		Turn-out	Lay-by
Entrée	Main course	Yield	Give way
Facecloth/washcloth	Flannel	Zucchini	Courgette

for sale, rent or repair of powered scooters and wheelchairs and other medical equipment (407 856 2273, **www.caremedicalequipment.com**).

The discussion forums on **www. wdwinfo.com** have a board geared to visitors with disabilities, while the excellent AllEars website has a big section on advice for a whole range of concerns, from children with ADD to vegetarian and vegan food. Visit **http://allears.net/pl/special.htm**.

Orlando for grown-ups

You don't need to have kids in tow to enjoy Orlando. There is so much clever detail and imagination, adults usually get the most out of the experience.

In fact, as many couples and singles visit the parks as do families with children. Certainly, when you look at the entertainment at Downtown Disney and CityWalk and the great range of bars and fine restaurants, it is easy to see the attraction for those

Antojitos at CityWalk

© Universal Orlando Resort

21 and over. As well as Florida being a key honeymoon destination, its friendly, sociable atmosphere is ideal for singles, while couples without children can also take advantage of late opening at the parks and clubs. Even better, the downtown area of the city of Orlando is coming back as a happening night-time venue, with a lot to recommend it for a lively evening out.

BRITTIP

If you have a fridge in your hotel, put drink cartons in the freezer overnight and they will be cool for much of the next day in your back-pack. Better still, buy a cheap coolbag, freeze it with some water bottles in, and leave it in the car – great after a day in the parks.

Orlando for seniors

Mature travellers can also benefit from a healthy dose of the Sunshine State, as they are likely to have just as much fun, just within slightly different parameters. Seniors can also take advantage of numerous discounts and special deals for their age group at the attractions, plus many restaurants and hotels. The official Visitor Center on I-Drive (p42) publishes a brochure of all the deals.

Hotels: For the older person, staying in a Disney hotel is highly recommended as it removes the stress of driving. The extra cost is offset by the convenience and relaxation factor.

Parks: There is still plenty to do here, even if the thrill rides are not a draw – just watching can be entertainment

Old Hickory Steakhouse at Gaylord Palms

Top 10 romantic restaurants

1   Tchoup Chop, Universal's Royal Pacific Resort
2   California Grill, Disney's Contemporary Resort
3   Todd English's bluezoo, Walt Disney World Dolphin Resort
4   Jiko, Disney's Animal Kingdom Lodge
5   Capa, Four Seasons Orlando
6   Old Hickory Steakhouse, Gaylord Palms Resort
7   Bice, Universal's Portofino Bay Hotel
8   Cala Bella, Shingle Creek Resort
9   Narcoossee's, Disney's Grand Floridian Resort
10   Park Plaza Gardens, Winter Park

We could actually list several dozen more, including Hillstone, Luma on Park and The Bistro on Park Avenue (Winter Park), Bull & Bear (Waldorf-Astoria), Norman's (Ritz-Carlton), The Venetian Room (Caribe Royale Resort), Seasons 52, Eddie V's and Roy's (Sand Lake Road), and Kres Chophouse, Ceviche and The Boheme (downtown Orlando).

enough! Both Epcot and Disney's Animal Kingdom have much to engage the older visitor, while the shows of Disney's Hollywood Studios make that a popular choice, too, and the Magic Kingdom, while a bit hectic, is still an essential experience.

Evenings: The Disney Springs area can feel a bit frenetic for the senior crowd, but the Boardwalk Resort is popular and the whole of the Epcot resort area offers much in the way of fine dining and relaxation. In fact, this is often a prime area for seniors, notably the quieter Disney's Yacht and Beach Club Resorts, and the superb Swan-Dolphin complex.

Attractions: We also highlight the following for the senior age group.

• **Animal Kingdom:** Kilimanjaro Safaris, the Maharajah Jungle Trek, Pangani Forest Trail, Finding Nemo show and Festival of the Lion King.

Top things to do for FREE!

Disney's Boardwalk Resort: Free nightly entertainment includes jugglers, comedians and live music. Time your visit to coincide with the 9pm IllumiNations fireworks extravaganza at nearby Epcot.

Downtown Concert Series: Four times a year, local radio station WMMO stages free open-air concerts in front of City Hall with the likes of Peter Frampton and Blues Traveler. Great day out, with festival atmosphere (**www.wmmo.com/s/dcs/**).

Downtown Orlando Historic Tour: From the Visitor Center on Orange Avenue, local historian Richard Forbes leads a free tour of downtown at 9.30am on the first Fri of every month from Oct–May. Must call in advance to check availability on 407 246 3789 (**http://downtownorlando.com**).

Lake Eola Park: Take a walk on the mild side in downtown Orlando. The kids can play or feed the swans and summer sees live music at the Walt Disney Amphitheater; **www.cityoforlando.net/parks/lake-eola-park/**

Lake Tibet-Butler Preserve: Just 5mins from Disney but a world away from the theme park bustle (on local highway 535, Winter Garden-Vineland Road) is this local nature preserve, with quiet trails, lake overlook and interpretive centre. Open 9am–dusk (not public holidays), it is on the Great Florida Birding Trail and is a minor gem of native wildlife); **www.sfwmd.gov**.

Lakeridge Winery and Vineyards: Join one of its fun, free wine-tasting tours and you'll know why Lakeridge (in nearby Clermont) has won more than 300 awards. Designate a driver as sample sizes are generous! 10am–5pm Mon–Sat, 11am–5pm Sun (**www.lakeridgewinery.com**).

Morse Museum of American Art: This superb little museum in tranquil Winter Park, dedicated to American paintings, ceramics and representative arts from the 19th and 20th centuries, is free 4–8pm every Fri, Nov–Apr (**www.morsemuseum.org**).

Old Town, Kissimmee: The biggest vintage car parade in the US every Sat, with cars on display from 1pm and the Classic Car Cruise at 8.30pm, plus a Muscle Car Cruise 8.30pm each Fri and Show 'N Shine each Sun with trucks, jeeps and SUVs, and live music 5–9pm (**www.myoldtownusa.com**).

Osceola County History Museum: Part of the new Welcome Center on Highway 192 in Kissimmee (by Marker 15), this offers a great insight into the region's back story and heritage (**www.osceolahistory.org**; see also p258; closed on public hols).

PLUS: Watching the participants at **iFLY Orlando** on I-Drive (p236); the **Cornell Fine Arts Museum** at Rollins College in Winter Park (p249); and the hiking trails of **Ocala National Forest**, north of Orlando (**www.stateparks.com/Ocala.html**).

- **Disney's Hollywood Studios:** Jim Henson's Muppet Vision 3-D, Great Movie Ride, Indiana Jones Stunt Show, Beauty and the Beast and Fantasmic!.

- **Epcot:** Spaceship Earth, Soarin', Universe of Energy, all of World Showcase and IllumiNations (plus the superb gardens and architecture).

- **Magic Kingdom:** The Haunted Mansion, Jungle Cruise, Pirates of the Caribbean, Mickey's PhilharMagic and the monorail ride.

- **Universal Studios and Islands of Adventure:** The amazing Wizarding Worlds of Harry Potter.

- **Others:** Watching the children at the many parades and character greetings; dinner at the California Grill in Disney's Contemporary Resort (and other fine dining locations); shopping at Orlando Premium Outlets.

- **More options:** SeaWorld remains hugely popular for seniors and even Busch Gardens, despite its many roller-coasters, has plenty to offer. The local Segway Tours (in Kissimmee, Mount Dora, St Petersburg, Port Canaveral and Clearwater Beach) are highly recommended, while Mount Dora and Winter Park (see also Chapter 8) are also perfect senior fare.

Weather: Mar and late Oct/Nov are ideal times to visit, but the summer months are hard going for older folks. Good coats (and gloves) may still be necessary at times in winter.

> **BRITTIP**
> Don't want to take your mobile with you for fear of high charges? Hire a phone for your holiday from Adam Phones and take advantage of its special local rates for the US (0800 123000, **www. adamphones.com**).

You've got mail

You won't find many post boxes and some post offices don't seem to know the fees for postage to the UK. All the parks have post boxes and you can get stamp books from most stamp machines and City Hall at the Magic Kingdom. A standard postcard or greetings card in an envelope to the UK both need a $1.15 stamp; standard postage within the US is 49c.

The main post offices are:

- **Disney area:** 10450 Turkey Lake Road (just north of the junction of Palm Parkway and Central Florida Parkway; 8am–7pm Mon–Fri, 9am–5pm Sat).

- **Kissimmee:** 1415 W Oak Street (8.30am–5pm Mon–Fri, 9am–2pm Sat).

There is also a small post office inside the **Mall at Millenia**, off the lower level of the Grand Court.

The Haunted Mansion at the Magic Kingdom

Wedding bells

Florida is a popular choice for couples wanting to tie the knot. Its almost guaranteed sunshine and lush, natural landscape make it a huge hit as a wedding backdrop. Orlando also has terrific services, co-ordinators and venues like Cypress Grove Estate House, Winter Park wedding chapel, Casa Feliz, Leu Gardens, Ceviche in downtown Orlando and hotels like Rosen Shingle Creek, Walt Disney World Swan and Dolphin and the Omni Orlando Champions Gate. Even scenic golf courses such as Celebration Golf Club and Grand Cypress can stage grand occasions extremely well. More unusual ones include the Hard Rock Café, a hot-air balloon or helicopter, Danville B&B (p262–3), on the beach or a luxury yacht, or even on the new Orlando Eye ride. All the tour operators feature wedding options and services, or you can pick a local specialist like Get Married In Florida (see right). Prices vary from around £300/couple (for a basic civil ceremony) to more than £4,000.

> **BRITTIP**
> Looking for essential travel accessories and useful knick-knacks, like TSA-approved locks, plug adapters and waterproof accessories? Try **www.essentials4travel.co.uk**. Asda supermarkets also sell a good travel range.

Walt Disney World's Wedding Pavilion: True fairytale romance, with the backdrop of Cinderella Castle, you can opt for traditional elegance in this Victorian setting with up to 260 guests or the full Disney experience, arriving in Cinderella's coach with Mickey and Minnie as guests. Disney's wedding planners can tailor-make the occasion for you (407 828 3400) but at a price – rates START at $5,000 for the basic ceremony and can top $60,000!

Licence: To obtain a marriage licence, visit a local courthouse: Osceola County Courthouse, Courthouse Square, Suite 2000, Kissimmee (just off Bryan Street in downtown Kissimmee) 8am–4pm Mon–Fri

(407 343 3500); Orange County Courthouse, 425 N Orange Avenue (downtown Orlando) 7.30am–4pm Mon–Fri (407 836 2067); or Clermont Courthouse at Minneola City Hall, 800 North Highway 27, Minneola, 8.30am–4.30pm (closed noon–1pm; 352 394 2018). All are closed on US bank holidays. Both parties must be present to apply for a licence, which costs $93.50 (in cash, travellers' cheques or by credit card) and is valid for 60 days, while a ceremony (equivalent to a British register office) can be performed at the same time by the clerk for an extra $20. You'll need passports, birth certificates and, if you have been married before, your decree absolute. After acquiring a licence, a couple can marry anywhere in Florida. It is also possible to obtain a licence BEFORE arriving in Florida (see **www.floridamarriagelicencebypost. com**). For flowers and floral design, be sure to look up Flourish on 407 601 4948 or **www.flourishproductions.com**.

Get Married in Florida: This local business has been dedicated to organising weddings for UK couples since 2002. Ideally placed to deliver great personal service, it offers the complete package for the perfect wedding (321 945 1563, **www.getmarriedinflorida.com**).

BRITTIP

Looking for a good pay-as-you-go mobile option for the USA? Check out Three and their £15 add-on option: **www.three.co.uk/Discover/Phones/ Feel_At_Home**.

Disney special occasions

Birthday badges: Get free badges from City Hall in the Magic Kingdom and Guest Services at Epcot, Disney's Hollywood Studios and Disney's Animal Kingdom. Cast Members make a fuss over children (and adults!) wearing a birthday badge.

Birthday cakes: Contact room service at your resort or Guest Services at one of the parks. All Disney restaurants can offer ready-made 15cm/6in cakes ($25 at each restaurant) or something larger ($35–120) if ordered 48 hours in advance on 407 827 2253. If someone in your group has a birthday, tell the Cast Member at check-in (or when you make your reservation), as well as hostesses and/or servers in restaurants. While not guaranteed, Disney staff often go out of their way to make the day special. If characters know it's a birthday when they sign a child's autograph book, they may add a special birthday wish.

The wedding venue at Celebration Golf

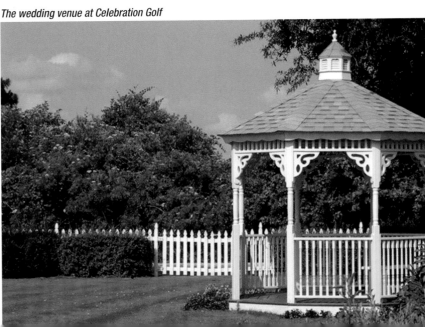

Birthday cruise: The IllumiNations Celebration Cruise (to Epcot) provides snacks, drinks, streamers and balloons for a 90min tour, for up to 10, from Disney's Yacht and Beach Club Resort marina for $371 (407 939 7529).

Disney's Pirate Adventure: This two-hour activity for kids 4–12 sails (on pontoon boats) from four of the resorts (Grand Floridian, Yacht/Beach Club, Port Orleans and Caribbean Beach at 9.30am) to find pirate 'booty' at different ports of call, with a final stop for lunch; $37 per child (407 939 7529, up to 180 days in advance).

Money matters

You'll need to carry ID for both cheques and some credit card purchases (take your UK driving licence card).

> **BRITTIP**
> American banknotes are all the same size and primarily green, with just the occasional splash of colour in the newer notes. The only real difference is the picture of the president and the denomination in each corner.

Cash: It is worth separating larger notes from smaller ones in your wallet to avoid flashing all your money in view. Losing £300 of travellers' cheques shouldn't ruin your holiday – but losing $600 in cash might. All the theme parks have ATMs (cash machines).

Credit cards: Having a credit card is almost essential (especially for car

Macy's Holiday Parade

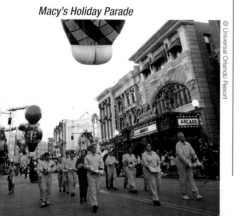

© Universal Orlando Resort

hire) as they are accepted everywhere and provide extra buying security. Visa, Mastercard and American Express are all widely accepted.

FairFX card: Perhaps the best option is this convenient card, which you preload to a chosen amount (**www.fairfx.com**). The exchange rate is fixed at loading and you can save 5–10% on High Street currency rates.

Travellers' cheques: Dollar travellers' cheques can be used as cash almost everywhere (though a few places, like Golden Corral restaurants, no longer accept them) and can be replaced if lost or stolen, so it is not necessary (or advisable) to carry lots of cash. Sterling travellers' cheques can be cashed only in major banks.

Safety and security

While crime is not a serious issue in Florida, this is still big-city America. Tourism is such a vital part of the economy, the authorities have a highly safety-conscious attitude. Just don't ignore the usual safety guidelines for travelling abroad.

> **BRITTIP**
> For your journey to the US, use a business rather than your home address on your luggage. It is less conspicuous and safer should any item be lost or stolen.

Commonsense tips: A bumbag (Americans say 'fanny pack'!) is better than a handbag or shoulder bag in the parks, and make sure bags are always firmly zipped up when not in use. Don't leave camera equipment on view in the car (especially as the heat could damage it anyway).

Christmas cheer

We're often asked our favourite time of year here and it has to be the festive season, from late Nov–1 Jan. Every park adds a fab Christmas overlay and there is more to enjoy everywhere, even at the smaller attractions and places like Disney Springs and the town of Celebration. It can get seriously crowded 20 Dec–4 Jan, but visit in early Dec and you get all the festivities with fewer crowds.

Walt Disney World: Every park has its own extensive decorations and magnificent Christmas tree, with a daily lighting ceremony at the **Magic Kingdom**, plus Mickey's Once Upon A Christmastime Parade, the Castle Dream Lights (a stunning effect on Cinderella Castle) and the chance to meet Santa, as well as the extra-ticket event of Mickey's Very Merry Christmas Party (p118). At **Epcot**, the standout feature is the Candlelight Processional, a choral retelling of the Christmas story with a guest narrator, as well as Holidays Around The World, with traditional storytellers at each World Showcase pavilion. Mrs and Mrs Claus visit at the American Adventure pavilion, where vocal group Voices of Liberty become carollers for the season. The daily IllumiNations show also has a special Yule finale. At **Disney's Hollywood Studios**, the dazzling Osborne Family Spectacle of Dancing Lights is a marvel – with 5 million twinkling, themed fairy lights that draw huge crowds – and the Frozen Christmas, with Anna and Elsa, is now a firm favourite. **Downtown Disney** features Festival Of The Seasons, with Santa's chalet, school choirs and more lavish decorations. Each resort also boasts plenty of Christmas cheer, with the best being **Disney's Grand Floridian**, offering a life-size Gingerbread House.

Universal Orlando: Miles more garland, lights and tinsel are on offer here, plus 2 daily features. At **Universal Studios**, Macy's Holiday Parade is the highlight, a fabulous cavalcade of floats, giant balloons, Father Christmas (and his Rockette-style dancers!) and a tree-lighting ceremony at dusk each day, as well as strolling carollers, hot cocoa kiosks and a Christmas Village of traditional fare and gifts. **Islands of Adventure** offers Christmas Dr Seuss style, with Grinchmas all around Seuss Landing, including the epic, family-friendly stage show of *The Grinch Who Stole Christmas*.

SeaWorld: Arguably the biggest Christmas celebration is here, with magnificent shows, special effects and extravagant theming. It starts with a Polar Express makeover for the Wild Arctic ride and continues with the Sea of Trees, an eye-catching sequence of well-lit 'trees' spread over the main lagoon. A Christmas Marketplace highlights one end of the park, while 2 unmissable seasonal shows are Winter Wonderland On Ice and O Wondrous Night, a nativity tale with a difference. Both the Shamu and Sea-Lion shows have their own festive additions, and nightly 'snowfalls,' dancers, musicians and the Christmas Celebration fireworks round out a glittering seasonal occasion.

Busch Gardens: The highlight here is Christmas Town, another after-dark spectacular throughout the park, with themed areas, shows and decorations (each Fri, Sat and Sun from late Nov/early Dec, and nightly from mid-Dec). Highlights include the Carol of the Bells, an Ice Show, the Three Kings Journey and a lavish array of seasonal dining and shopping, plus Santa's 'North Pole' home and some more superb lighting effects.

Gaylord Palms Resort: equally astounding is their annual ICE! exhibition, a mind-boggling presentation of 2 MILLION pounds of ice in marvellous tableaux, hand-carved by 40 Chinese artisans in the special 'Florida Freezer,' including 4 huge ice slides. There are festive presentations, shows, musicians, tree, kids' activities, character meet-and-greets from Dreamworks and the chance to meet Santa, making for an amazing Christmas offering. It MUST be booked in advance, though, at **www.marriott.com/hotels/travel/mcogp-gaylord-palms/**

Celebration: this pretty Disney-inspired town offers nightly 'snow-falls' 6–9pm on Market Street in Dec and also features ice-skating for kids, horse-drawn carriage rides, carollers and other festive touches.

And more: downtown Orlando is well worth a visit for its many festive touches, notably around **Lake Eola**, which has Christmas trees, ice-skating and the nightly Holiday Lights show. The child-sized fun of **LEGOLAND Florida** boasts a superb array of decorations and the daily Tree Lighting, while all the **dinner shows** add in suitably festive theming and extra Christmas elements. One final amazing event is staged at the huge First Baptist Church on John Young Parkway just off I-4, where **The Singing Christmas Trees** is a stunning choral show presentation of music, stage and lighting each Fri, Sat and Sun for the first 2 weeks in Dec. Find out more at **www.firstorlando.com/worship/singing_trees**.

The VERY strong police advice in the unlikely event of being confronted by an assailant is: DO NOT resist or 'have a go', because this can often make a bad situation worse. However, it is comforting to know Orlando does not have any no-go areas in the main tourist parts. The nearest is the portion of the Orange Blossom Trail south of downtown Orlando (a selection of strip clubs and 'adult bars' that can be downright seedy) and the Parramore area south-west of downtown.

TOPS: International Drive has its own dedicated police unit (the Tourist Oriented Policing Squad, a division of the Orlando City Police), with officers on patrol, arranging local crime-prevention seminars and ensuring I-Drive takes good care of its visitors. You'll often see these police out on mountain bikes, and they are a polite, helpful bunch.

Hotel security: While in your hotel, always use door peepholes and security chains when someone knocks at the door. DON'T open the door to strangers without asking for identification, and check with the hotel desk if you are still not sure. It is stating the obvious, but keep doors and windows locked and always use deadlocks and security chains. Take cash, credit cards, valuables and car keys when you go out (or put them in the room safe), and don't leave the door open, even if you just pop down the corridor to the ice machine. Most hotels now have electronic card-locks for extra security and can offer deposit boxes in addition to the standard in-room mini-safes. Don't

be afraid to ask reception staff for safety advice for surrounding areas or if you are travelling somewhere you are not sure about. Safety is a major issue for the Central Florida Hotel & Lodging Association (**www.cfhla.org**) and hotel staff are well briefed to be helpful.

BRITTIP

If your room has already been cleaned before you go out for the day, hang the 'Do Not Disturb' sign on the door. Always keep your valuables out of sight, whether in the hotel or the car.

Car safety: Make the basic safety checks of your hire car straight away and familiarise yourself with the car's controls BEFORE driving away. Try to memorise your route in advance, even if it's only a case of knowing the road numbers. Most hire firms now give good directions to all the hotels, so check them before you set off (or, better still, hire a GPS system). Make sure the fuel tank is well filled and never let it get near empty so you risk running out of 'gas' in an unfamiliar area. If you do stray off your pre-determined route, stick to well-lit areas and ask for directions only from official businesses like hotels and petrol stations, or the police. Try to park close to your destination where there are plenty of lights and DO NOT get out if there are suspicious characters around. Always keep windows closed (and air-con on), and don't hesitate to lock the doors from the inside if you feel threatened (larger cars have doors that lock automatically as you drive off). Don't forget to lock the car when you leave it – and note that not all rental cars have central locking.

BRITTIP

Remember, if you are calling Orlando (area code 407) from the UK, you must put the international dialling code for the USA, 001, first.

More info: For more info on safety, contact the Orange County Police (407 254 7000 or **www.ocso.com**) or the

Grinchmas Holiday Spectacular

© Universal Orlando Resort

Let us take the stress out of your holiday ...

...with our unique Touring Plans

The *Brit Guide* Touring Plans will ensure you get the most out of your time in central Florida. This is a service no one else can offer, as we provide you with daily touring plans for the parks, attractions and shopping in central Florida.

Your full Touring Plan (which usually runs to 40 pages for a 2-week holiday) will: walk you through your day so you make the most of your time and your tickets; highlight any rides that may be closed for refurbishment; include shopping guides if you plan to take advantage of all the savings to be had at the malls and outlets; provide key advice right from the source of the fun, as well as a host of Brit Tip Extras and Brit Picks (our special favourites) we can't fit into the book, plus a special Busy Day Guide for your visit. Just go to **www.britguideorlando.net** and click Touring Plans.

Fill out the online form with your travel dates, choose the type of Plan you need (be sure to see our FAQ to help you decide which Plan is right for you), and indicate which parks/shopping/etc you want to fit into your visit. Submit the form, with your payment, and you'll receive, by email, your unique Touring Plan, which will consist of:

1 An official *Brit Guide* welcome from Susan and Simon Veness.

2 A daily plan for each of the parks, water parks and shopping centres you will visit.

3 Touring strategies in each day's plan to help you avoid the longest queues and take advantage of the latest developments.

4 Alternative suggestions in case of bad weather.

5 A note of any rides/shows that are closed during your visit (please see our FAQ for further info).

6 A special selection of Brit Tip Extras and local advice.

7 Our Brit Picks – a guide to a range of personal favourites, from restaurants to shops.

8 The ultimate insider knowledge, as Susan and Simon are based in the heart of the Orlando magic and are fully up to date on all developments.

9 Our special bonus: an EXCLUSIVE Platinum VIP Passport for Orlando Premium Outlets (not available to the public), with extra savings at select stores at this great shopping venue.

10 Best of all, you will receive a Busy Day Guide especially for your holiday dates so that you can assemble the best possible day-by-day plan.

All in all, it adds up to the most comprehensive package of specialised holiday info anywhere, and it represents the secret to the most fun, in the most hassle-free way, in the most exciting place on earth. What more could you ask for? Just check out our website and we'll do the rest.

Please note: There is a minimum order period, so check online and apply in good time before your holiday (*at least* 10 days). Book owners receive a discount on the price of the Touring Plans, so have it with you when you register as you'll need a password from the book.

The password is random and expires on 31 Dec of the edition's year, NO EXCEPTIONS. We are not a travel agency or ticket service and you MUST know your park and shopping requirements in advance.

We urge you to read our FAQ before ordering, as it will assist you in choosing the right plan for your holiday, answer the most common questions we receive, and ensure you order with confidence.

International Drive police team office (407 351 9368). If you are the victim of theft in Orange County, call 407 836 4357.

Emergencies

Emergency services: For police, fire department or ambulance, dial 911 (9-911 from your hotel room). Make sure your children know this number.

General: For smaller-scale crises (e.g. mislaid tickets, lost passports or rescheduled flights), your holiday company should have an emergency contact number in the hotel reception.

Independent travellers: If you run into passport or other problems that need help from the British Consulate, its main office is now at 1001 Brickell Bay Drive, Miami, Florida 33131 on 305 300 6400, but there is still a small office in downtown Orlando offering consular services, such as lost documents and aid for those hospitalised or arrested and detained, on 407 254 3300 (**www.gov.uk/ government/world/usa**).

You'll find masses of info on all things Orlando on the discussion forums at

Cinderella Castle at the heart of the magic

www.attraction-tickets-direct.co.uk and, as we are both Moderators on the site, you can come and 'talk' to us and pass on your own ideas and experiences. It's a fun, friendly community and we're always happy to see new faces.

Know before you go

Here are the best sources for additional info before you go.

- **Kissimmee:** More useful online info and an e-guide to download on this link, **http://bit.ly/ExpKissMag**, plus the UK website **www. experiencekissimmee.com/uk/**.

- **Fan websites:** An ever-growing choice, try any of the **www.thedibb. co.uk** ('Disney with a British accent'), the fully comprehensive **www.allears. net** (notably for its Disney dining section) and **www.wdwinfo.com**.

- **Orlando Attractions mag:** (which we also write for) offers a superb website full of features and videos at **www.attractionsmagazine.com**, plus a weekly magazine-style programme called *The Show*.

- **Orlando Sentinel:** The online local paper (**www.orlandosentinel.com**) is packed with info (especially for shopping, dining and nightlife), while the free **Orlando Weekly** is also worth checking (**www.orlandoweekly.com**).

- **Orlando Visitor Center:** It's worth checking Orlando's ONLY official Visitor Center, 8.30am–6.30pm daily at 8723 International Drive (407 363 5872 or email **info@ visitorlando.com**) for discounted attraction tickets, and free brochures, accommodation advice, info pamphlets and maps.

- **Visit Florida:** Offers a free info pack, as well as many online e-brochures (01737 644 882, **www.visitflorida.com/ en-uk.html**).

- **Visit Orlando:** has a 24hr info line, plus a website where you order its free Holiday Planning kit (0800 018 6760, **www.visitorlando.com/en-gl/uk/**).

Now, on to the next step of the holiday, your transport…

3 Getting Around

or The Secret of Driving on the Wrong Side of the Road!

Arriving and driving in Orlando are among the biggest concerns for visitors, especially first-timers, but there's no need to worry. Although most people begin their holiday by leaving the airport in a newly acquired, automatic, left-hand-drive hire car on roads that can appear bewildering, driving here is a lot easier and more enjoyable than in the UK. Anyone familiar with the M25 should find Florida FAR less stressful.

Before you get to your hire car, though, you need to be aware of the arrival process at the two airports.

BRITTIP
Don't forget you must have filled in your ESTA form and immigration details online before you travel (see p12). For country of residence put UNITED KINGDOM; for Passport Issuing Country, put UK – BRITISH CITIZEN. You must give a valid US address for your accommodation.

Orlando International
This is one of the most modern and enjoyable airports in the world, but it can be confusing for newcomers. All flights arrive at one of four satellite terminals and you then take a shuttle tram (like a mini monorail) to the main terminal. Allow around an hour from landing to ground transportation.

International arrivals: If you arrive with British Airways, Virgin Atlantic or Thomas Cook, you disembark at the satellite for Gates 70–99. With Aer Lingus or Norwegian, it is 1–29. First, join one of the two main queues that feed into the individual immigration kiosks, and wait for the official to call you to the next open kiosk. Once through Immigration, collect your baggage from the carousel and go through the Customs check. The airport now has a series of self-service electronic processing kiosks, allowing you to input your flight info and passport details, fingerprints and photo before reaching the Immigration officer, which can save considerable time for whole flights at a time. Just follow the instructions and take your receipt, with your passports and customs form, to the officer. NB: Children under 14 cannot be processed by the electronic kiosks and will need to be checked by the Immigration officer. Then you have a choice.

BRITTIP
Visit www.orlandoairports.net for a photo preview of the arrival process at Orlando International Airport (click Airport Guide, then Arrivals Guide) and other info.

Option 1: Deposit your checked luggage on a second conveyor belt to take it to the main terminal while you go upstairs to the shuttle with your hand luggage only. Once in the main terminal you are on Level 3 and you follow signs down to Baggage Claim B on Level 2 (BA and Thomas Cook), Baggage Claim A on Level 2 (Aer Lingus and Norwegian) or Baggage Claim A Level 1 (Virgin).

Option 2: If you can manage your luggage without a trolley, take it on the escalator up to the shuttle and go straight to pick up your transport on Level 1 (or, if a specific driver is meeting you, Level 2).

Domestic arrivals: For anyone arriving on a US domestic flight (from another US gateway), you disembark at the satellite terminal and proceed straight to the main terminal on the shuttle to collect your baggage on Level 2 (either A or B side, depending on arrival gate). Once at the main baggage claim, porters can help you to Level 1 (for a $1/bag tip) for car hire, shuttles and buses. Trolleys need $3 in change (or a credit card) to operate.

BRITTIP

The biggest change in Orlando International Airport in recent years is with the automated arrivals process (p43) as well as the number of car hire companies now on site instead of needing a shuttle bus. There will be more changes in the next few years as construction is now underway on the new South Terminal.

Transfers: Kerbside pick-up is just outside the doors on Level 2. If a driver is meeting you, he or she will wait on Level 2, either at the bottom

Shamu Express at SeaWorld

© SeaWorld Parks

of the escalators or by your baggage reclaim. Several tour operators have help desks here, too, while Virgin has a reception desk on Level 1. The public bus system, Lynx (p46), operates ONLY from the A side of Level 1 (6am–10.30pm; 9.30pm on Sundays and public holidays), in spaces 38–41. Links 11 and 51 depart every 30mins (less often on Sundays and bank holidays) for Orlando city centre (about 45mins), while Link 42 serves International Drive (about a 1hr journey) and Link 111 goes to the SeaWorld area via the Florida Mall.

Car hire: All the main hire companies are on site (with 22 off-airport). The main 10 to choose from include *Brit Guide* partner Alamo (with new automated self-service kiosks), Dollar, National, Thrifty, Hertz and Avis, and all offer a full service. Complete your paperwork, then walk out of Level 1 across the road to the multi-storey car park to collect your car.

If you arrive late, consider staying overnight at the Hyatt Regency hotel at the airport rather than driving tired. You will be far more ready to drive next day (and the car hire queues will be shorter). Several tour operators also offer an arrival-day transfer, with car hire pick-up arranged the next day.

BRITTIP

If you are hiring a car from one of the on-airport companies, save time by sending the driver to complete the paperwork BEFORE collecting your luggage on Level 2.

Leaving the airport: When you drive out of the airport, DON'T follow signs to 'Orlando'. The main tourist areas are south and west of the city, so follow the signs for your accommodation.

The Martin Andersen Beachline Expressway (528) and Greeneway (417) are both toll roads, so make sure you have some US currency before leaving the airport. Toll booths hate to change notes above $20, while some auto-tolls take ONLY coins.

Welcome Sunrail!

Central Florida's first commuter rail system, Sunrail, arrived in 2014 and, while it is not extensive enough to be fully relevant to visiting tourists, it offers a few possibilities.

Sunrail currently operates over a 32ml/50km, 12-station stretch from east Sand Lake Rd (at the junction with S Orange Ave) to DeBary in the north. A northern extension is due in 2016/17 to DeLand and south to Poinciana (south of Kissimmee). From Sand Lake Rd station, it runs straight to downtown Orlando (three stations, including Church St. Station) and up to Winter Park, providing a handy way to visit these areas without driving. However, it ONLY operates Mon–Fri, every 30mins in peak periods and every two hours otherwise, 5.30am–10pm.

Fares are extremely modest ($3.75/adult for a round-trip from Sand Lake Rd to Winter Park while a weekly SunCard is $34 for unlimited 7-day use) and tickets can be purchased via the machines at each station using cash or credit card. Once you have your ticket, you 'tap on' by tapping it against one of the six validator machines on the platform before you board the train, then 'tap off' when you reach your destination. There are also Lynx bus connections at every Sunrail station, including Link 111 from SeaWorld and Link 42 from I-Drive to the Sand Lake Rd station, plus the free Lymo bus service in downtown Orlando. Look up more at **www.sunrail.com**.

- **For International Drive:** (or I-Drive), take the North Exit and the Beachline Expressway (Route 528) west until it crosses I-Drive just north of SeaWorld (you will need $2.25 in toll fees). Most hotels on I-Drive are to the north, so keep right at the exit.

- **For Kissimmee, Disney and villas in Clermont/Davenport:** Take the South Exit for 3ml/5km and pick up the Central Florida Greeneway (Highway 417) west.

- **For most Disney resorts:** Take exit 6 and follow the signs ($3 in tolls).

- **For Animal Kingdom resorts:** Use exit 3 and take Osceola Parkway west ($3.75).

BRITTIP

For traffic news and reports, tune to 96.5FM (WDBO) or **www.news965.com**. Call 511 on a mobile phone for motorway traffic info or **www.fl511.com**.

- **For eastern Kissimmee:** Come off Highway 417 at exit 11, the Orange Blossom Trail (Highway 17/92), and go south ($2.25 in tolls).

- **For west Kissimmee and Clermont/Davenport (Highway 27):** Take exit 2, turn right on Celebration Avenue and left (west) on Highway 192 all the way to Highway 27 (you will need $3.75 in toll fees).

Orlando Sanford International Airport

Arriving at Sanford (in Seminole County) couldn't be easier. The list of airlines visiting this easy-to-use airport currently includes Thomson Airways, Icelandair, Arke (to Amsterdam) and Jetfly (Brussels). It generally takes only 30–40mins from arrival to leaving the baggage hall, but there may be delays in peak season when several planes arrive at once, as its handling capacity is limited. It's a short walk from the plane to the immigration hall (where two queues feed through to the kiosks); you then collect your baggage, pass through Customs and walk straight out to car hire, shuttle or taxi pick-up.

Orlando Sanford Airport

> **BRITTIP**
> Don't want to drive? Consider a multi-centre stay within Orlando itself, staying first at, say, I-Drive or Universal Orlando and then a Disney resort, to get the best of the free or cheap transport options.

Car hire: As you exit the Customs Hall, the welcome desks for Thomson are across the road in front of you, next to the Car Rental centre, which also houses the Cosmos welcome desk. The one exception is for *Brit Guide* partner Alamo, which has its own centre via a covered walkway and boardwalk behind this building, and its British-dedicated operation is very smooth. Look up more on **www.orlandosanfordairport.com**.

Leaving the airport: It may be 35ml/56km to the north and involve more driving (and taxis and shuttles are much more expensive – a town car service would be around $140 one-way to Walt Disney World and a taxi $100, while Orlando Carriers charge $60/person round-trip on their shuttle; **www.orlandocarriers. com**), but you usually save time by your quicker exit. There is just one main road out, on to Lake Mary Boulevard, and you then take Seminole Expressway (Highway 417, which becomes Central Florida Greeneway in Orange County) south. The slip road to this toll motorway is just under the flyover on your LEFT, and you need $8 to reach Disney or Kissimmee or $6.50 for I-Drive (via the Beachline Expressway). You can avoid the tolls by staying on Lake Mary Blvd for 6ml/10km until you get to I-4, but you're likely to hit heavy traffic through the city centre. The Expressway/Greeneway is an excellent, easy-driving introduction to Orlando, even if it does cost a few dollars.

> **BRITTIP**
> If you suspect you may need more boot space in your car, upgrade when you book at home as it is usually more expensive to upgrade when you arrive.

ORLANDO WITHOUT A CAR

Although being mobile is advisable, it is certainly possible to survive without a car. However, few attractions are within walking distance of hotels, and taxis can be expensive. You also need to plan with greater precision to allow for extra travelling time (and with children, taking buses can be tiring). For non-drivers, your best base is either Walt Disney World itself (free transport throughout, but harder to get to the rest of Orlando) or International Drive for its location, 'walkability' and the great I-Ride Trolley. Many hotels have free shuttles to some of the parks or a cheap, regular mini-bus service. There are 4 main options: public transport; shuttle services; town cars and limousines; and taxis.

> **BRITTIP**
> Although Disney has free and extensive transport services, it can be slow. Bus rides from many hotels to the parks can take a good 30mins while getting from Disney Springs to Animal Kingdom Lodge – the longest journey from one side to the other – takes almost an hour.

Public transport

Lynx bus system: Reliable and cheap but slightly plodding, it covers much of metro Orlando. Its online system map shows all its routes (or 'links') and main attractions (407 841 5969, **www.golynx.com**).

- **Link 18:** From Kissimmee to downtown Orlando (from Osceola Square Mall, east on Highway 192 and north on Boggy Creek Road, Buenaventura Boulevard and Orange Avenue).

- **Link 38:** I-Drive to downtown Orlando (from the Convention Center via Wet 'n Wild, Kirkman Road and I-4).

- **Link 42:** From Orlando International Airport to I-Drive.

- **Link 50:** From Disney's TTC to downtown Orlando via SeaWorld and I-4.

Park Maps

For a detailed look at the layout of the parks, each of the park maps contains a QR code that you can scan with your smartphone or tablet to take you to a high-res online map. You'll need a QR reader, which you can get free from Apple at **https://itunes.apple.com/gb/app/ qr-reader-for-iphone/id368494609?mt=8** or for Android at **https://play.google.com/ store/apps/details?id=me.scan.android. client&hl=en**.

- **Link 55:** Kissimmee's Highway 192 from Osceola Square Mall west to Four Corners via the Summer Bay Resort.

- **Link 56:** From Kissimmee to Disney (from Osceola Square Mall, along Highway 192 via Old Town and Celebration to Disney's Transportation & Ticket Center (TTC) by the Magic Kingdom).

- **Link 300:** From Disney Springs via I-4 to downtown Orlando.

- **Link 304:** To Disney from the top of I-Drive (Oak Ridge Road to Disney Springs, via Sand Lake Drive).

BRITTIP

Lynx buses use the Disney Springs West Side Transfer Center as their Disney hub, with Links 301, 302 and 303 spreading out from there to the theme parks and resorts.

Lynx fares are $2 a ride (transfers are free) or $16 for a weekly pass (children 6 and under go free with a full-fare passenger). The service is every 30mins in the main areas, every 15mins 6–9am and 3.30–6.30pm, but you must have the right change. All buses are wheelchair accessible and stop at the pink paw-print Lynx stops. There can be long queues for buses at Disney at closing time, so you could take Disney transport to Disney Springs (via one of the resorts or the TTC), then get a taxi back to your hotel (about $30–35 to I-Drive).

I-Ride Trolley: Great-value service for the I-Drive area, it operates two routes along a 14ml/23km stretch of this tourist corridor.

- **The Main/Red Line:** With 77 stops, this runs from the Orlando Premium Outlets at the top of I-Drive to SeaWorld and Aquatica via Westwood Boulevard and Sea Harbor Drive, and on to Orlando Premium Outlets (Vineland Ave).

- **The Green Line:** With 33 stops, this goes from the Universal resort area (Windhover Drive and Major Boulevard) south to Orlando Premium Outlets via Universal Boulevard, the Convention Center and SeaWorld.

Running every day, 8am–10.30pm roughly every 20mins (30mins on the Green Line), it costs $2/trip ($1 kids 3–9, 25c for seniors) –have the right change – or you can buy Unlimited Ride Passes for 1, 3, 5, 7 or 14 days at $5, $7, $9, $12, $18. If you need to transfer between routes, ask for a transfer coupon when you board (not needed with Unlimited Ride Passes). All trolleys have hydraulic lifts for wheelchairs. Passes are sold at more than 100 locations in the I-Drive area, including the Official Visitor Center and most hotel desks, plus online, but NOT on the trolleys themselves (407 248 9590 or US freephone 1866 243 7483, **www.iridetrolley.com**). I-Ride has a high-tech vehicle location system that allows riders to check arrival times, maps and other info live on their mobile devices. It can be accessed on their mobile website **www.iDrive2Go.mobi** or if you text the code at each trolley stop.

The Knight Bus at Universal Orlando

© Universal Orlando Resort

Busch Shuttle Express: There are seven departure points in this regular daily service, 8.15–9.40am, from SeaWorld to Busch Gardens in Tampa. It costs $10/person but is FREE if you have Busch tickets in advance (included in the FlexTicket Plus or 3-Park Ticket with SeaWorld and Aquatica). For more info, call 1800 221 1339 in Orlando toll-free.

BRITTIP

The cheapest way to get from I-Drive to Disney is the $2 Lynx bus Link 50 from SeaWorld – 6600 Sea Harbor Drive – to the Transportation & Ticket Center next to the Magic Kingdom. All Disney transport then operates from there. Use the I-Ride Trolley to get to SeaWorld.

Shuttle services

Alternatives to public transport are the well-organised firms offering set-fee shuttles to the attractions that pick up at hotels. There are more than a dozen, with everything from stretch Hummer limos to buses.

Florida Fun Shuttle: An excellent range of attraction shuttle options (round-trip transportation only), with tours to the likes of St Augustine, Daytona and Cocoa Beach, plus winery excursions, a new Craft Beer tour, kayaking trips, sports events and other one-off trips. They can even do one-way visits to the beaches, with pick-ups a few days later, and Port Canaveral transfers (321 231 0005, **www.floridafunshuttle.com**).

Maingate Transportation: Another option from the Highway 192 area ($15 round-trip to Universal or Wet 'n Wild, $12 to SeaWorld and $11 to Disney parks; 407 870 5553, **www.maingatetaxi.com**).

Mears: The most comprehensive service, with a 1,000-vehicle fleet from limousines to town cars and coaches. Typical round-trip shuttle fares would be: airport to Walt Disney World, $36 adults, $27 under-12s, under-4s free ($22 and $17 one way); airport to I-Drive, $32 and $24 ($20 and $15 one way); airport to Highway 192 in Kissimmee $38 and $29 ($22 and $17 one way); Walt Disney World

to Universal Orlando, $20 round trip; I-Drive to Walt Disney World, $20; I-Drive or Walt Disney World to Kennedy Space Center, $36. You can book a shuttle on arrival at the Mears' desks in the luggage halls, but it can be a longish trip if it has a full van stopping at several hotels before yours (407 423 5566, **www.mearstransportation.com**).

Magic Shuttle: with services to and from both airports, all the main attractions, the dinner shows, restaurants and even shopping services (407 402 4283, **www.magicshuttle.net**).

Lake Buena Vista Factory Stores: offers a shuttle that collects guests free each day from 60 hotels in the Orlando and Kissimmee areas (407 363 1093, or **www.lbvfs.com**).

Excursions: There are also excursion services offered by the likes of *Brit Guide* partners Florida Dolphin Tours (407 352 5151, **www.floridadolphintours.com**) and Gray Line Tours (p266).

Town cars and limos

When it comes to limousine, town car and other transport services, there is again a huge choice (more than 150 at the last count). The following all earn a *Brit Guide* recommendation:

BRITTIP

With the abolition in 2015 of the old paper part of the UK driving licence, drivers are technically required to obtain an on-line code (from the DVLA website **www.gov.uk/view-driving-licence**) to show the rental company, if requested. It is highly unlikely any car hire company will ask for the code, or even the old paper part of the licence (*Brit Guide* partners Alamo say they will not require it for US rentals) but it is best to have it just in case.

FL Tours: This well-established and popular company specialises in both airport–Disney routes and Port Canaveral transfers. One-way trips start from $70 and round trips from $125 ($125 and $235 from Orlando Sanford International Airport), plus gratuity; it also offers a free 30min grocery stop, free kids' booster and car seats, 24-hour online reservation access, and no extra charge for late pick-ups (407 857 9606, **www.fltours.com**).

Quick Transportation: A good bet for airport transfers and tailor-made transport packages, its town cars comfortably cope with a family of 4, while luxury vans cater for larger parties and all offer a 30min grocery stop for an extra $20. Luxury van rates (for up to seven) one-way from Orlando International Airport range from $75 to the I-Drive area up to $120 for the farthest parts of Walt Disney World. Up to 11 can use a van for a small additional fee per person. Larger parties may need a luggage trailer for $25 extra each way. Town car rates are $125 from the airport to anywhere in Greater Orlando and $240 for a round trip, while stretch limos are $195 and $380. It serves all the parks and attractions and offers online quotes for all services, while it can also supply vehicles for the disabled (407 354 2456 or 1888 784 2522, **www.quicktransportation.com**).

Sky Limousine: This company has one of the largest selections of vehicles in town, from Lincolns and executive vans to the amazing Hummer limo. One-way airport transfers from $80 (plus a 20% driver gratuity), and vehicles can also be hired by the hour from $60/hour. Other options cover much of central Florida, offering cruise transfers, a night on the town, all-day services, beach trips, concerts and tailor-made excursions (407 352 4644, **www.skyorlando.com**).

Taxis

For groups of four or five, taxis can be more cost-effective than shuttles. Orlando International Airport to I-Drive would be around $45 (plus tip); $50–60 for the Kissimmee area; $65 to Magic Kingdom resorts and $60 for the Epcot resort area; $15–20 from I-Drive to Universal Orlando; and $20–30 from I-Drive to Downtown Disney. You'll find plenty of taxis in ranks at the parks, hotels and shopping centres, but they don't cruise around looking for fares, so it's often best to book in advance. Choose a reliable, fully insured company with its name and phone number clearly displayed on the cab, the driver's ID and insurance visible and the rates on the window or inside the car. Some drivers look for fares in the airport baggage hall, which is strictly illegal; all legitimate taxis should be in the rank on Level 1.

Mears: A group of Checker Cabs, Yellow Cabs and City Cabs (407 422 2222) – all of which are reliable. Mears is the main taxi company for Orlando Sanford International Airport, and you can pre-book cabs for around $105 to I-Drive, $125 to Lake Buena Vista and $130 to Disney hotels. Most taxis are metered but it is also acceptable to ask in advance what the fare will be.

Other reputable firms: Ace Metro Cab (407 855 1111), Star Taxis (407 857 9999) and Diamond Cab (407 523 3333). Several hotels have town cars at their ranks and these won't have meters, so you can either ask for the fare or call one of the companies listed above.

THE CAR

Ultimately, having a car is the key to being in charge of your holiday and, on a weekly basis, car hire tends to be quite reasonable: weekly rates can be as low as $135 for the smallest car. The scale of the car hire operation is huge, with as many as 1,000 visitors arriving at a time.

BRITTIP
Your first call for car hire should be to *Brit Guide* partner Alamo. See inside the front cover for our special offer.

The cars will be mainly American – Chevrolet, Dodge, Buick, Chrysler, Ford, Mercury and Lincoln, plus some other makes like Kia, Hyundai, Honda, Toyota and Nissan.

- **Economy or Subcompact:** The smallest cars are usually a Vauxhall Corsa-sized hatchback.
- **Compact:** Next up is a small family

saloon like a Nissan Versa.

- **Midsize or Intermediate:** A more spacious 4-door, 5-seater like a Toyota Corolla.
- **Fullsize:** This would be a larger-style executive car like a Ford Fusion.
- **Premium, Luxury, Convertible, SUV and Minivan:** All more upmarket options, while the Minivan is a Ford Galaxy or Renault Espace type.

Most holiday companies offer 'free car hire', but that doesn't mean it won't cost you anything. Only the rental cost is free and you must still pay the insurances and taxes (which makes the all-inclusive packages more attractive).

BRITTIP
Be firm with the car hire company check-in clerk. Some can push you into having extras, like car upgrades, you simply won't need.

Also beware low starting rates – there are essential insurances, taxes and surcharges that can take the weekly rate above $300. However, all the big rental companies now offer all-inclusive rates, which can work out cheaper if booked in advance in the UK, and you also benefit from easier processing in Orlando, making the whole business quicker.

BRITTIP
Be sure to pick the right car for your group size – and luggage. You simply won't get 7 people AND all their cases in a 7-seater van!

Car rental companies: Alamo is our *Brit Guide* partner and offers excellent rates and service (see inside front cover). You also benefit with Alamo from being able to choose your own car from the different ranges, where most other companies assign you a specific car. For alternatives, try Dollar (020 3468 7685), Avis (0844 581 0147), Budget (0844 544 3439) or Thrifty (01494 751 500), or try

Enter Mapman

By far the best and most up-to-date area map is a British production, created by Disney fan and cartographer Steve 'Mapman' Munns. It is superbly detailed for the I-4 corridor, Highway 192 and *Walt Disney World*, with special sections on I-Drive and villa locations. All the main attractions, hotels and even many restaurants are clearly indicated and there is accompanying text and photos, while the website adds updates and insider tips. We think it's the perfect companion to the *Brit Guide* and you won't go wrong with it at only £7.40 (plus £1.10 p&p). Go to **www.orlandomaps. co.uk** (online orders only). There should also be another revision in time for 2016, with all the latest developments and updates, once again printed on both sides in full colour. So be sure to check in advance of your visit. Even better, Steve is our resident 'mapman' for the *Brit Guide*.

the comparison website **www.carrentals.co.uk**.

Insurance: Having a credit card is essential, and there are 2 main kinds of insurance, the most important being the Loss or Collision Damage Waiver (LDW or CDW). This costs $25–27/day and covers you for any damage to your hire car. You can do without it, but the hire company will insist on a deposit around $1,500 on your credit card (and you are liable for ANY damage). You will also be offered Supplemental Liability Insurance (SLI) or Extended Protection at $12–15 a day, which is not essential but does cover you for most damage you might cause. Another option is Underinsured Motorists Protection (in case someone with minimal cover runs into you) at around $8 a day.

BRITTIP
Unless you have accepted the SunPass pre-pay auto-toll option from the car rental firm, you cannot drive through the toll booths marked 'Sunpass' or 'E-Pass' only. You must stop at the booths marked 'Change Given' (in green) or 'Exact Change Only' (in blue).

The satnav solution

The best way to navigate is by a GPS or satnav system. All car hire companies offer this as an extra (at around $90/week) or you can bring your own. If your system has only the base-level (i.e. UK) maps loaded, download the maps for south-east USA for around £35. If you are thinking of buying a GPS system, the likes of Wal-Mart offer new systems, fully loaded for the US, for around $150.

Specialist insurance: Those on a budget can cut costs by taking insurance through specialists like Insurance4CarHire (0844 892 1770, **www.insurance4carhire.com**), whose US and Canada cover offers up to 60 days' continuous rental, including CDW/LDW and SLI, for £109. You may still need to leave a credit card imprint with the hire firm, but it should accept these policies (check in advance).

Other costs: Drivers must be at least 21, and those under 25 have to pay an extra $25 a day. Other costs include local and state taxes, plus Airport Access and 'Facility' fees, which can add more than $40 a week. Many companies also offer a Roadside Plus (around $5/day), which covers flat tyres, running out of fuel or locking your keys in the car, but this is again totally optional.

Fuel: Then there is 'gas', though this is still cheaper than in the UK. You can either pre-pay for a full tank (so you bring it back empty; the charge is usually slightly under the local rate/gallon for this); fill it up yourself so you have a full tank on return; or pay a fuel surcharge at the end for the company to refill the tank (the most expensive option).

Pre-pay tolls: You can also opt for the SunPass auto-pay system for toll roads, so you just drive through without stopping; all your tolls are auto-recorded for payment when you return the car. Dollar and several other hire companies call it PlatePass and charge a flat-rate fee of $8–9/day. This is great for peace of mind but an expensive option unless you are using the toll roads a *lot*.

Getting used to your car

Most people soon find driving in America is a pleasure, mainly because nearly all hire cars are automatics and nearly new. And, because speed limits are lower (and rigidly enforced), you won't often be rushed into taking a wrong turn.

- All cars have air-conditioning, which is essential for most of the year. Turn on the fan as well as the A/C button or it won't work! A small pool of liquid will form under the car from condensation.

- Power steering is universal.

- Larger cars have cruise control, so you can set the desired speed and take your foot off the accelerator. There will be 2 buttons on the steering wheel, one to switch on cruise control, the other to set the speed. To cancel, either press the first button or touch the brake.

- Some cars have an extra pedal to the left of the brake, and you need to push this to engage the handbrake. To release it, you pull the tab just above it, if there is one, or give a second push on the pedal.

- Keep your foot on the brake when you are stationary as automatics tend to creep forward. Always put the gear lever in 'P' (Park) when switching off.

- The car probably won't start unless the gear lever is in 'P'. To put the car in 'D' for Drive, depress the brake pedal. D1 and D2 are extra gears for steep hills (none in Florida!).

Disney's car park tram

- Not all cars have central locking, so make sure you lock ALL the doors before leaving it. With an automatic, you won't be able to take the keys out of the ignition unless you put the gear lever in 'Park'.

Fuel: All local gas stations are self-service and you usually pay before filling up. However, the pumps should allow you to pay by credit card without having to visit the cashier (some stations ask for a local zip code with a credit card swipe, which means you DO need to go inside). To activate the petrol pump, you may need first to lift the lever underneath the pump nozzle. RaceTrac and Speedway petrol stations are often the cheapest. The 3 Speedway stations in Walt Disney World are, surprisingly, among the cheapest in the area, while the Wal-Mart on Vineland Road is also a cheaper option. Petrol stations just outside Disney and the airport are the MOST expensive.

Finding your way

Your car hire company should provide you with a basic map of Orlando, plus directions to your hotel – insist they do, as all the hire companies make a big point of this in their literature.

BRITTIP

Be organised – get your directions in advance off the internet at sites like **www.mapquest.com** or use Google Earth to source maps, directions and even check out the lie of the land in advance. Download it free from its website at **http://earth.google.com**.

Atlas V rocket launch at Kennedy Space Center

© Kennedy Space Center

Signposting: You'll easily find the main attractions, but retracing your steps can be tricky as the exit road may be different from the way in. Familiarise yourself with the main roads in advance and learn to navigate by road numbers (which are given on the signposts), exit numbers off the main roads, and directions around the attractions (i.e. if you want I-4 east or west or 192 as you exit Walt Disney World).

Lanes and exits: Exits off motorways can be on EITHER side of the carriageway, not just on the right, and you don't get much notice. You can overtake in ANY lane on multi-lane highways, so sit in the middle lane until you see your exit.

Road names: Around town, road names are displayed at every junction suspended ABOVE the road underneath the traffic lights. This road name is NOT the road you are on, but the one you are CROSSING. Again there is little advance notice of each junction and the road names can be hard to read as you approach, especially at night, so keep your speed down if you think you are close to your turn-off to allow time to get into the correct lane. If you do miss a turning, most roads are on a grid system, so it's easy to work back.

Occasionally you will meet a crossroads where no right of way is obvious. This is a Four-Way Stop, and the priority goes in order of arrival. So, when it's your turn, just indicate and pull out slowly (America doesn't have many roundabouts, so this may be the closest you get to one).

Local maps: The maps supplied by the car rental companies are pretty basic, as are the free maps in the tourist areas. AA members have their own map options (p54), but we recommend getting the Orlando Map by Steve Munns (p50).

Rules and regulations

As well as the obvious difference of driving on the opposite side of the road, there are several differences in procedure.

Tolls: For toll roads, have some change handy in amounts from 25c to $2. They all give change (in the GREEN lanes), but you will get through quicker if you have the correct money (in the BLUE lanes). On minor exits of Osceola Parkway and the Greeneway, there are auto-toll machines only, so keep some loose change to hand.

BRITTIP

On nearly all toll roads, for the manned toll booths you have to pull in to a slip road on the right to pay. It is SunPass/E-Pass only on the main carriageway. This can catch you out when you have just left the airport.

Traffic lights: The most frequent British errors occur at traffic lights (which are hung above the road). At a red light, you can still turn RIGHT providing there is no traffic coming from the left. Stop, check there are no pedestrians crossing and make your turn – unless there is a sign indicating 'No turn on red'. Turning left at the lights, you have the right of way with a green ARROW but must give way to traffic from the other direction on a SOLID green. The recent addition of a YELLOW flashing arrow means it is OK to turn left providing the way is clear.

Left turns: The majority of accidents involving overseas visitors take place on left turns, so take extra care. There is also no amber light from red to green, but there IS from green to red. A flashing amber light at a junction means proceed but watch for traffic joining the carriageway, while a flashing red light indicates it is okay to turn if the carriageway is clear.

BRITTIP

The Osceola Parkway toll road (522) that runs parallel to Highway 192 is a better route in to Walt Disney World from eastern Kissimmee and costs only $1.75. Use Sherberth Road for Disney access from west 192 or the new Western Beltway (Highway 429).

Speed limits: Speed limits are always well marked with black numbering on white signs and the police are pretty hot on speeding, with steep on-the-spot fines. There are varying limits of 55–70mph/88–113kph on the Interstates, where there is also a 40mph/64kph minimum speed limit. It can also be just 15–25mph/24–40kph in built-up areas.

Seat belts: These are compulsory for all passengers, while child seats must be used for under-4s and can be hired from the car companies at $10–15 a day (so bring your own or buy one locally for $70–80). From 4–5, they can use regular car seatbelts if they are at least 49in/124cm tall; otherwise use a booster seat.

Parking: It is illegal to park within 10ft/3m of a fire hydrant or a lowered kerb, and never park in front of a yellow-painted kerb – they are stopping points for emergency vehicles and you will be towed away. Never park ON a kerb, either. Park bonnet first – reverse parking is frowned upon because number plates are only on the rear of cars and police then can't see them. If you park parallel to the kerb, you must point in the direction of traffic.

Other traffic laws: Flashing orange lights over the road indicate a school zone and school buses must NOT be overtaken in either direction when they are unloading and have their hazard lights on. U-turns are forbidden in built-up areas and where there is a solid line down the middle of the road. You must pull to the side of the road to allow emergency vehicles to pass, in either direction,

About to take an airboat ride

when they have lights and/or sirens going. Also, on multi-lane highways in Florida, the Move Over law means you must pull into an adjacent lane if you see a police car on the hard shoulder, or slow down if you can't move over. And you must put on your lights in the rain.

Finally, DON'T drink and drive. Florida has strict laws, with penalties of up to 6 months in prison for first-time offenders. The blood-alcohol limit is lower than in Britain, so it is safer not to drink at all if you are driving. It is also illegal to carry open containers of alcohol in the car.

Bonus for AA members: Your membership is recognised by the equivalent AAA in the US and you benefit from various special offers. Take your AA card and produce it where you see the AAA 'Show & Save' signs in to enjoy the same discounts as the locals. Visit **www.aaasouth.com** and click AAA Discounts for the full range, which includes shopping and dining, like 10% off at Hard Rock Cafe and Dennys restaurants (use the zip code 32819 when prompted). You can also get maps and books from their office in Lake Mary in Seminole County (near Sanford).

There are no fixed speed cameras in Florida (although many traffic lights DO have cameras to catch red-light offences), but the police often go out with hand-held radar guns.

Accidents

In the unlikely event of an accident, no matter how minor, you must contact the police before the cars can be moved (except on the busy

Meet and greet at Cheetah Run, Busch Gardens

I-4). Car hire firms will insist on a full police report for the insurance. If you break down, there should be an emergency number for the hire company in its literature or, if you are on a main highway, raise the bonnet and wait for one of the frequent police patrol cars to stop (or dial *FHP on your mobile). *Always* carry your driving licence when driving, as well as your car hire forms in case you are stopped by the police.

Key routes

All main motorways are prefixed I, the even numbers going east–west and odd numbers north–south. Federal Highways are the next grade down, with black numerals on white shields, while state roads are prefixed SR (black numbers on white circular or rectangular signs).

All American motorways have their junctions numbered in mileage terms, which makes it easy to calculate journey distances. I-4 starts at exit 1 in Tampa and goes to exit 132 at Daytona, 132ml/211km away. In Orlando, the main junctions run from exit 55, at Highway 27, to exit 83 (downtown Orlando) and exit 101 for the Seminole Expressway (417) and Orlando Sanford International Airport.

Interstate 4: I-4 is the main route through Orlando, a 4, 6 or 8-lane motorway linking the coasts. Interstates are always indicated on blue shield-shaped signs. For most of its length, I-4 travels east–west but, around Orlando, it swings north–south, though directions are still given east (for north) or west (for south). All the attractions of Walt Disney World, plus SeaWorld and Universal Orlando are well signposted from I-4. LEGOLAND Florida in Winter Haven, Lake Wales and Bok Tower Gardens are a 45min drive from Orlando west on I-4 and then south on Highway 27, while Busch Gardens is 75–90mins down I-4 to Tampa. Be aware I-4 can be packed with traffic for long sections in the morning and evening rush hours. You can check for major roadworks on **www.cflroads.com**.

International Drive: I-Drive is the second key local roadway, linking a 14½ml/24km ribbon of hotels, shops, restaurants and attractions like Wet 'n Wild, Pointe Orlando and Orlando Premium Outlets (I-Drive South, from Highway 192 in Kissimmee north to Route 535 is NOT the main stretch and the two sections are linked via Route 535 and World Center Drive). From I-4, take exits 71, 72, 74A or 75A going east, or 75B, 74A or 72 going west. To the north, I-Drive runs into Oak Ridge Road and the South Orange Blossom Trail, which leads to downtown Orlando (junctions 82C–84 off I-4). I-Drive is also bisected by Sand Lake Road and runs into World Center Drive (536) to the south, also convenient for Disney.

> **BRITTIP**
> Be ready for MAJOR roadworks on I-4 north of Universal (at Kirkman Rd) all the way to north of downtown. It is a road widening project that will add toll lanes for the first time. Completion date 2021! See http://i4ultimate.com/.

I-Drive is a major tourist centre and makes an excellent base, especially around the Sand Lake Road junction, as it is fully pedestrian-friendly. It's a 20min drive to Disney and 10mins from Universal. However, at peak times, heavy traffic means it's best to avoid the stretch from the Convention Center north. Use Universal Boulevard instead.

Kissimmee: The other main tourist area, south of Orlando and south-east of Disney, its features are grouped along a 20ml/32km stretch of the Irlo Bronson Memorial Highway (192), which intersects I-4 at junction 64B, and is close to Walt Disney World (though a good 25mins from SeaWorld and Universal). Downtown Kissimmee is off Main Street, Broadway and Emmett Street, and is ideal for walking.

Highway 192: A handy visual along here is the Marker Series from Formosa Gardens (number 4) to just past Medieval Times (number 15). These highly visible signs are good locators for hotels, restaurants and attractions, and much of this stretch is also walkable (though few places are close together). Try to avoid the area of the 192 east of Marker 15, though; it is rather run-down and unappealing. For downtown Kissimmee (which we DO recommend) use the Osceola Parkway and S Orange Blossom Trail (441). The unique Disney-inspired town of Celebration is also here (just south of Walt Disney World).

Highway 27: This is at the west end of Highway 192, running north to Clermont and south to Davenport (and Haines City). A major area of holiday villa developments, these are generally quite convenient for Disney. Many home owners claim they are 'only 5 mins from Disney' but it is at least 10mins from Highway 27 to the edge of Disney property; often more. The area is also starting to add shops and restaurants, notably in the Cagan Crossings junction (just north of where 192 meets 27), where there is also a large Wal-Mart, and Berry Town Center (to the south).

Western Beltway: Highway 429 provides a western Orlando bypass, avoiding the often-crowded I-4 to link with the Florida Turnpike and Apopka to the north. It also offers a western gateway to Walt Disney World at Exit 8 (Western Way), which is handy for the Davenport/Clermont areas. This junction is also destined for future tourist development as an area called Flamingo Crossings at the junction of the 429 and Western Way, with the first two hotels now under construction.

Now, let's go on to the next vital step – your holiday accommodation…

Travel of a different kind on the Hogwart's Express

4 Accommodation

or Making Sense of American Hotels, Motels and Condos

Metro Orlando has the second highest concentration of hotels in the world (after Las Vegas) and more are being built all the time. There are currently 118,000 rooms, and counting, not to mention 26,000 villas for rent. Therefore, what follows is only a general guide to the various types, plus our recommendations and favourites.

The main choice is between a traditional hotel option and one of the many self-catering types of accommodation, which can be villas/vacation homes, town homes or condos.

HOTELS

Many American hotels, particularly in the tourist areas, tend towards the motel type, where everything is not necessarily located in one building. Your room may be in one of several blocks sited round the pool, restaurant or other amenities. Room size rarely alters, even from 2 to 4-star hotels; their amenities and services form the basis of their star ratings. A standard room usually has two double beds and will accommodate a family of four (couples without children should ask for a king room, with an extra-size bed), while most rooms are now non-smoking. Motel-type accommodation can also lack a restaurant as they operate on a room-only basis.

Disney's Animal Kingdom Lodge

Most hotels are big, clean, efficient and great value. You'll find plenty of soft-drink and ice machines (though it's cheaper to buy drinks from a supermarket), with ice buckets in all rooms. All accommodation will be air-conditioned, but you'll get used to the drone of the A/C unit. If you need a more spacious room, look for one of the many suite hotels, which provide sitting rooms and mini-kitchens, as well as 1–3 bedrooms.

BRITTIP

Don't make calls from your hotel – most add a 45–70% surcharge (Disney resorts even add a connection fee), while you can be charged for an unanswered call if it rings five or more times. Buy a phonecard instead (p30 and 36).

Deals and bookings: If you've just arrived and need a hotel, visit the official Visitor Center at 8723 I-Drive, just north of Pointe Orlando (on the corner of Austrian Court; 8.30am–6.30pm daily; closed 25 Dec; 407 363 5872), where they have brochures on all current deals. There are also many online hotel specialist agents like **www.priceline.com**, Expedia (0330 123 1235, **www.expedia.co.uk**), Hotels.com (**www.hotels.com**), Orbitz (1888 656 4546 in the US only, **www.orbitz.com**) and Hotwire (**www.hotwire.com**).

BRITTIP

Buy soft drinks at the supermarket, and (if your hotel room doesn't have a fridge) buy a polystyrene cooler for about $5 that you can fill from your hotel ice machine to keep drinks cold.

Prices: Hotel prices are always per room (not per person) and they will be cheaper out of the main holiday periods, with special deals at times. Always ask for rates if you book directly and check if special rates apply during your visit (don't be afraid to ask for their 'best rate' at off-peak times, which can be lower than published or 'rack' rates). There may be an additional charge ($5–15 per person) for more than two adults sharing a room ($5–15 per person), plus there is state tax and, sometimes, a sneaky resort fee that can add $10–15/day.

There is no widely accepted star rating, so (with the exception of Disney's resorts), we group hotels into 4 ranges: where the (rough) price groups/night will be:

- Budget   =   up to $50
- Value   = $51–99
- Moderate = $100–160
- Deluxe   = $161 plus

The main factor is the extra facilities. Thus, a Deluxe rating will include the highest level of facilities and service, while a Budget will be a basic motel-type. A key pricing factor is location (the closer to Disney and other parks, the higher the price), so you can save if you don't mind a longer journey.

Suite things

Suites hotels provide a combination of hotel and apartment, with extra value for large families or groups. Typically, a suites room gives you a living room and kitchenette, including microwave, coffee-maker, fridge, cutlery and crockery, while many offer a complimentary continental breakfast (or better). All have pools and grocery stores or snack bars and several have restaurants. They vary only in the number of bedrooms and can usually sleep 6–10.

Disney's monorail terminus

Disney Dining Plan

This is another perk of staying onsite with Disney. Hotel guests can pre-pay most meals at a set fee per day. However, it is an EXPENSIVE option if you are staying for a week or more. There are 3 different Plans to choose from (prices shown as of spring 2015):

Quick Service Dining Plan: Provides 2 counter-service meals and 1 snack a day, plus 1 refillable resort mug/person. Counter-service meals are defined as 1 entrée or combo meal, plus 1 dessert and 1 (non-alcoholic) drink for lunch or dinner, and 1 juice, 1 entrée or combo meal and 1 drink for breakfast. Snacks can be any item such as an ice-cream, popcorn, pastry, a piece of fruit, a bag of crisps, a bottled drink, a medium soda or tea/coffee. Cost: $41.99/day for adults, $16.03 for 3–9s (children must order off the Children's Menu).

Disney Dining Plan: Provides 1 table service meal, 1 counter-service and 1 snack per person per day. Table-service meals are 1 entrée, 1 dessert and 1 (non-alcoholic) drink, or 1 juice, 1 entrée and 1 drink OR a full buffet for breakfast. Cost: $60.64 and $19.23/day (slightly more in peak season).

Deluxe Dining Plan: Provides 3 meals (either table or counter-service) and 2 snacks per person per day, plus 1 refillable resort mug per person. Cost: $109.53 and $29.86/day (slightly more in peak season).

All meals do NOT have to be used per day and can be spread over the duration of your stay, so you can miss a table-service meal one day, then use 2 table-service credits another day for a signature restaurant or dinner show. Gratuities are NOT included. When you check in at a Disney hotel, your MagicBand is loaded with all your Dining Plan meals and that monitors your daily usage. The Dining Plans CAN be used for Character Meals, when 1 table-service meal is required per person (2 at ultra-popular Cinderella's Royal Table in Magic Kingdom), and for the 13 Signature Restaurants in Walt Disney World (notably Jiko at Animal Kingdom Lodge, California Grill at the Contemporary Resort and Citricos at the Grand Floridian Resort), which all require 2 table-service meals. They can even be used at Disney's Dinner Shows (p295), subject to availability, at 2 table-service meals per person.

However, ALL members of the group must book the Plan for the full duration of the stay and inclusive of park tickets. It is also advisable to pre-book (on 407 939 1947 or 0800 16 60 748 in the UK) full-service meals well in advance as the sit-down restaurants usually book up early. Not all restaurants are on the Plan but you still have 100 options. More info at **www.disneyworld.co.uk**, where you can book all table service restaurants online.

Disney hotels

Our review of Orlando's hotels starts with Walt Disney World. Situated conveniently for all its attractions – and linked by an excellent free transport system of monorail, buses and boats – Disney's hotels, suites and campsites are all magnificently appointed and maintained. It groups them into Value, Moderate and Deluxe Resorts, the Deluxe Villas (Disney's timeshare properties) and the Campground of Fort Wilderness (with a strong element of self-catering for the latter two). They range from the swanky Grand Floridian Resort & Spa to the more basic but fun style of the Pop Century Resort. And Disney's imagination and attention to detail here are as good as at the parks. There are more than 22,000 rooms, while Fort Wilderness has 1,195 campsites and cabins. All Disney hotels are non-smoking, with designated smoking areas outside.

Grand accommodation comes at a price, though. A regular room at the Grand Floridian can be over $900 a night in high season (suites can top $2,000) and even the Moderate Port Orleans Riverside can be $330 a night. Dining at resort hotels is not cheap, and you'll find few fast-food outlets on site. However, staying with the world-famous Mouse is one of the great thrills, for the style, service and extras. The 20 resorts offer superb facilities that children especially love. The benefits are:

Kidsuites = happy families

Orlando has pioneered a great family accommodation style, worth seeking out if you have kids who enjoy bunk beds. Basically, a kidsuite is a separate area within the hotel room that gives the kids their own 'bedroom' (with bunks), usually also with their own TV and games console.

- **MagicBand:** Every guest receives this wristband, which is the room key, theme park entry, FastPass+ reservations and PhotoPass collector, as well as a 'charge card' for almost all on-site purchases. Disney hotel guests can also book FastPass+ 60 days in advance instead of 30.

- **Package delivery:** Park purchases can be sent back to your hotel.

- **Free parking:** At all the parks.

- **Free Wi-fi:** At the parks.

- **Refillable mugs:** All Disney resorts sell collectable drinking mugs, which are well worth buying (from $8.99 for a one-day stay to $17.99 for four or more days) as you then get free refills at their self-service cafés.

- **Dining priority:** Many Disney restaurants hold tables for resort guests, and you can book 180 days in advance plus the length of your stay (i.e. 194 days if you're going for 2 weeks). Call 407 939 1947 or 0800 16 90 748 in the UK (non-Disney hotel guests can book only 180 days in advance).

- **Children's services:** All resorts have in-room or group babysitting (subject to availability) and eight of the nine Deluxe resorts have supervised activity centres and dinner clubs (around $15/child per hour), usually open till midnight.

- **Mickey on call:** An alarm call from the Mouse himself.

- **Extra Magic Hours:** The BIG bonus is getting into one of the parks each day either an hour early or for 2 hours after regular park closing to enjoy rides with reduced crowds.

- **Disney's Magical Express Service:** The free airport transfer service for guests at Disney hotels. Book at least 10 days before arrival through **www.disneyworld.co.uk** or a travel agent.

BRITTIP

All of Disney's deluxe resorts offer valet parking. If you would like to take advantage of it but aren't sure how to tip, the average tip is $3–5, handed to the valet when he or she returns with your car.

Value resorts

Disney's All-Star Resorts: Here you can stay in one of five Sports-themed blocks centred on a massive food court, 2 swimming pools, a games arcade and shops; the Music-themed version; or the Movies complex – possibly the most imaginative, with its Fantasia pool and kids' play areas, the most popular blocks being Toy Story and 101 Dalmatians.

Standard rooms are bright and compact (read 'tight' for families with older children), but well designed for those who want the Disney convenience but not the price. The All Star Music Resort (Jazz and Calypso buildings) also has 192 impressive two-room Family Suites (combining two standard rooms) that sleep up to six. Each suite has two bathrooms, a well-stocked kitchenette, a lounge and private master bedroom, making the space much more flexible.

All three centres, with 5,794 rooms, have pool bars, shops, laundry facilities, video games rooms and a pizza delivery service. Close to the entrance is a large McDonald's if the resort's food courts don't appeal. All resort transport is provided by an efficient bus service.

BRITTIP

To make a reservation at any Walt Disney World hotel call 407 939 1936, 0800 16 90 730 from the UK, or see **www.disneyworld.co.uk**.

Disney's Pop Century Resort: In a similar vein, themed round the decades of the 2nd half of the 20th century, here are 5 blocks with giant icons – such as yo-yos, Rubik's cubes and juke-boxes – and a riot of period sayings and visual gags. Opened in 2003, it features a pool like a 10-pin bowling lane (others shaped like a computer and a flower), a huge table football set-up and open-air Twister mats. Blocks are grouped around a main building housing the check-in area (with a large-screen TV showing Disney films), an imaginative food court, a lounge (with quick-breakfast bar), a Disney store and a games arcade. The 177acre/72ha complex also features a central lake and lots of bright landscaping. It also has a well-organised bus service to the parks. The drawbacks? Long queues to check in and a rather hectic feel, even late in the evening. You need to request a hairdryer from reception and rooms are, again, rather small.

Disney's Art of Animation Resort: This Budget suites-style resort builds on the popularity of the Family Suites at the All Star Music Resort. Originally intended to be part of the Pop Century Resort, it is a four-part, 1,984-room complex (1,120 suites, 864 standard rooms) based around classic animated films *The Lion King,* *The Little Mermaid, Finding Nemo* and *Cars,* and with an elaborate main pool and children's play areas themed with *Finding Nemo* characters, two 'quiet' pools, the animation-themed Landscape of Flavors food court with four sections (themed to the movies and one of Disney's best), enormous games arcade and the Ink and Paint gift shop. The four courtyards are heavily themed, with larger-than-life icons, interactive sculptures, fountains, extensive photo ops, and other play features, and theming in all the rooms (look for fun 'character reveals'), with the suites offering a master bedroom, two bathrooms and three separate sleeping areas in the living space, including the 'Inovabed' – a piece of furniture that converts from a table or work-desk into a bed, plus a small kitchenette with mini fridge, microwave and coffee maker. The pool area is vivid and colourful with plenty of kid-appeal as it even features an underwater sound system! Like Pop Century, all park transport is by bus.

Moderate resorts

Disney's Caribbean Beach Resort: This 2,112-room complex is spread over five Caribbean 'islands' (with an inter-island bus service). The resort's basic rooms are relatively plain, but comfortably sleep four, while the

Disney's Art of Animation Resort

Pirate Rooms (request at booking) take the swashbuckling theme to a fantastic level, with ship-shaped beds and other decor. The Market Street food court, main restaurant Shutters and outdoor activities (with a lakeside recreation area with themed waterfalls, slides, games arcade, bike and boat rentals) are a big hit with kids. The six Market Street outlets at the Old Port Royale resort hub can get busy in the morning, and the Trinidad South and Barbados 'islands' are a fair walk from the centre. Trinidad South rooms feature the pirate theming (for a supplement) and there are other imaginative touches, like Parrot Cay Island with its tropical birds and play area. Transport to all the parks is solely by bus.

Disney's Coronado Springs Resort: Possibly the best value of this trio, it has slightly more facilities for its 1,921 rooms spread over 125acres/50ha: four pools (including the massive Lost City of Cibola activity pool with waterslide), two games arcades, restaurant, food court and café/convenience store, lounge bar, gift shop, beauty salon, health club, business centre and two launderettes. There's also the chic and upscale Rix Lounge – a bar/nightclub serving unique cocktails and appetisers. Constructed on a scenic Mexican/Spanish theme in three 'villages' (Casitas, Ranchos and Cabanas), Coronado is an often-overlooked treasure. Check out the Maya Grill and its New Latino cuisine; sample the recently revamped food court dining style of the Pepper Market or a snack or drink from Café Rix to enjoy with the splendid lake views from the outdoor terrace. Coronado Springs is only 5mins from Disney's Animal Kingdom and is well served by the bus network.

BRITTIP

Disney resort restaurants can (and, we think, should) be visited even if you aren't staying there. Advance book at any of the parks, call 407 939 1947 or 0800 16 60 748 in the UK, or visit **www.disneyworld.co.uk**.

Disney's Port Orleans Resort: This is a two-part complex. The 2,048-room Riverside has a steamboat reception area, a great Riverside Mill food court, Boatwright's full-service restaurant, the River Roost lounge (with live entertainment on certain nights) and an old-fashioned General Store (gift shop). It also features the new Royal Guest Rooms, themed for Princes and Princesses right down to headboards that perform fibre-optic fireworks! Also here is the 1,008-room French Quarter, with the Sassagoula Floatworks and Food Factory court, two bars, a games room and shopping arcade.

The Riverside includes the magnificent Ol' Man Island, a 3½acre/1.5ha playground with swimming pool, kids' area and a fishing hole, while the French Quarter has Doubloon Lagoon, with Mardi Gras dragon slide, alligator fountains and a play area. The eye-catching landscaping and design vary from rustic Bayou backwoods to turn-of-the-century New Orleans. Transport for both is by bus to the parks and bus or boat to Downtown Disney.

Deluxe resorts

More than anything, Disney specialises in high-quality hotels with grand design features, amenities and restaurants. All nine offer a Concierge level, which adds an exclusive, personalised service, and a private lounge with meals and snacks.

Boma restaurant at Animal Kingdom Lodge

Disney's Animal Kingdom Lodge:
This stunning 'private game lodge' is set on a 33acre/13ha animal-filled savannah, which many rooms overlook. The pervasive African theme and the effect of opening your curtains to a vista of giraffes and zebras is immense. The lavishness and detail are superb, right down to the guides who can tell guests about the animals and their habitats, the African folklore around the outdoor fire pit and the chance for children to become junior safari researchers while Mum and Dad do some wine-tasting (there's a huge collection of South African wines).

All this creativity comes before you consider the amenities: two restaurants, café, bar, elaborately themed 'watering-hole' main pool (with waterslide) and kids' pool, massage and fitness centre, large gift shop, children's play area and an awesome four-storey atrium.

The main restaurant, Jiko, is spectacular, but there is also the superb buffet-style Boma, a 'marketplace' restaurant featuring African-tinged dishes from a wood-burning grill and rotisserie for breakfast and dinner.

> **BRITTIP**
> Wine aficionados take note: Jiko at Disney's Animal Kingdom Lodge offers a fabulous array of South African wines in a wonderfully romantic setting. A superb choice for date night.

Disney's Contemporary Resort

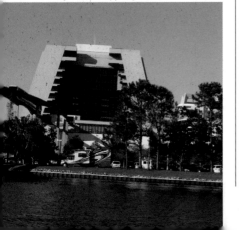

Rooms range from standard doubles to 1 and 2-bedroom suites, some of which have bunk beds. Part of the main building, Jambo House, has been converted into studios and 1 and 2-bed villas (the latter with full kitchens) for Disney Vacation Club guests, sleeping 4–12, but these are also available to regular guests when not in use by DVC. The newer Kidani Village wing adds still more (p68). Simba's Cubhouse is for 3–12s (4.30pm– midnight), and all transport is by bus (with the Animal Kingdom barely 5mins away).

Disney's Boardwalk Inn and Villas:
One of the Crescent Lake resorts next to Epcot is this 45acre/18ha extravagant Inn and entertainment 'district'. It features a 512-room hotel, 383 villas, four themed restaurants, a TV sports club and two nightclubs, plus shops, sports facilities and a huge, free-form pool with a waterslide, all on a semi-circular boardwalk around the lake. The effect is stunning, and the in-room attention to detail excellent, notably in the 'summer cottage' Villas (also part of the Disney Vacation Club).

For dining, the Big River Grille is a great bar/restaurant with its own micro-brewery while the Flying Fish is an upmarket seafood option with a hugely creative menu (if a bit pricey). Trattoria al Forno opened in 2014, replacing Kouzzina, with creative Italian 'comfort food', wood-oven pizza and risottos. You can also try the Boardwalk Bakery for a snack. It's a delightful place to visit for a meal, the nightlife (especially Jellyrolls piano bar and ESPN Club) or just to wander along the boardwalk. Transport is by boat to Epcot and Disney's Hollywood Studios and bus to the other parks.

Disney's Contemporary Resort:
On the monorail next to the Magic Kingdom, this 15-storey resort boasts 655 rooms, a cavernous foyer, 5 shops, 4 restaurants, 4 lounges, a real sandy beach, a marina, 2 pools (1 with waterslide), 2 tennis courts, a video games centre and health club – and fabulous views, especially from the superb, hotel-top California Grill

(one of the most romantic settings in Orlando; try to get a reservation to coincide with the park's fireworks), completely refurbished in 2013. Don't miss Chef Mickey's for a breakfast or dinner buffet with your favourite characters, while the monorail runs right through the hotel – great for kids. Rooms are some of Disney's largest, with elegant décor, dark-wood furniture and comfy duvets. Chic restaurant/lounge The Wave features a modern bar and dining area with a highly varied menu and is well worth trying for dinner or just a cocktail, while the Contempo Café adds a light meal option 6am–midnight. Within walking distance of the Magic Kingdom, transport to other parks is by bus.

Disney's Grand Floridian Resort & Spa: This true 5-star hotel is built like an elaborate Victorian mansion, with 867 rooms, an impressive domed foyer, and staff in period costume. Again on the monorail, one stop from the Magic Kingdom, the rooms and facilities are truly luxurious – hence the mega prices, though it's worth a look even if you're not staying. Its 6 restaurants include the top-of-the-range Victoria and Albert's (where the set 6-course dinner with wine costs $200, or you could sample the Chef's Table at $315 – with wine – per person), the chic seafood-based Narcoossee's (one of our favourites), with its excellent view over Seven Seas Lagoon, and Mediterranean-styled Citricos. There are also 4 bars and impressive sports and relaxation facilities, notably the fabulous Senses Spa. There's a wonderful second pool area with zero-depth entry and waterslide, while the main pool has been heavily remodelled. The Mouseketeer Club caters for 4–12s (4.30pm–midnight) and the 1900 Park Fare restaurant is hugely popular for character breakfasts and dinners, plus various children's activities (p102). The Garden View Lounge serves a variety of traditional Afternoon Teas 2–5pm daily, $30–48/person. Transport to the Magic Kingdom is by boat and monorail; by bus to the other parks.

BRITTIP

Watch out for the free nightly Electrical Water Pageant on Bay Lake and Seven Seas Lagoon, on view from all the Magic Kingdom resorts.

Disney's Polynesian Village Resort: This is a South Seas tropical fantasy – with modern sophistication and comfort. Beautiful beaches, lush vegetation and architecture are home to 853 rooms built in wooden long-house style, all with balconies and superb views. Also on the monorail opposite the Magic Kingdom, it boasts a lovely three-storey atrium, with landscaped seating areas and an iconic Tiki god. The large rooms have been extensively refurbished to revive the Pacific isles theme, with custom-made furniture, tapestries and warm colours. The dining is excellent: 'Ohana is a stylish dinner venue with lively character breakfasts, while the Kona Café is less formal but still with an extensive menu and Captain Cook's Snack Company has more basic counter-service fare. New in 2015 was interactive tropical lounge Trader Sam's Grog Grotto (4pm–midnight) with appetisers and exotic cocktails. Then there is a beautiful 'Volcano' pool area with waterslide, a games room, shops and children's playground. Lilo's Playhouse caters for 3–12s (4pm–midnight). Catch the monorail or boat to the Magic Kingdom and buses to the other parks. The Poly is also home to the

Disney's Grand Floridian Resort and Spa

Spirit of Aloha dinner show (p295), which is open to non-resort guests and makes a great evening among the torch-lit gardens. The Resort's beach is a great area from which to view the nightly Magic Kingdom fireworks. A major renovation in 2015 added 360 Disney Vacation Club deluxe studios with private balcony or porch, and room for 5. Then there are 20 gorgeous lakefront 2-bed, 2-bath bungalows (on stilts over Seven Seas Lagoon), large enough to sleep eight people, with full kitchens, living and dining rooms, deck with individual plunge pool, and a grandstand view of the Magic Kingdom fireworks. But beware the price – from $2,000 a night!

Disney's Wilderness Lodge: One of the most picturesque and romantic resorts, this is a re-creation of a National Park lodge, from the stream running through the massive wooden balcony-lined atrium into the gardens, past the swimming pool (with hot and cold spas) to a geyser that erupts each hour. Offering backwoods charm with luxury, the resort is connected to the Magic Kingdom by boat and bus (and buses to the other parks). Rooms are all spacious and well furnished, while the Courtyard View rooms are the best of the regular rooms (though at a slight premium). Deluxe rooms sleep up to six and the suites (at up to $1,000/night) are sumptuous. It also has 2 restaurants: the brilliant Artist's Point (lunch and dinner) and

The view from the Grand Floridian Resort

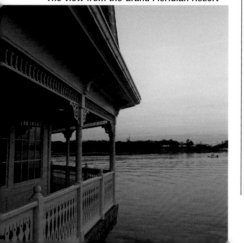

the Whispering Canyon Café (lively breakfast and huge all-you-can-eat family meals) – plus a snack bar and pool bar. The Cubs' Den is for 4–12s (4.30pm–midnight). The Villas at Wilderness Lodge is a Disney Vacation Club development of 136 studios and 1 and 2-bed villas. Facilities include living areas, kitchens, private balconies and whirlpool baths. There is a quiet pool area, a spa and health club.

Disney's Yacht and Beach Club Resorts: There is more refined quality with this duo, featuring 630 and 580 nautical-themed rooms respectively. Set around Crescent Lake next to the Epcot park, they help to form a massive resort area that is a delight to walk around at any time but especially at night. For dinner, the Yachtsman Steakhouse offers friendly, elegant dining at the Yacht Club, while the sister hotel features Cape May Café for lovely character breakfasts and a nightly New England-style clambake buffet. Beaches & Cream can also be found here, a classic 1950s-style diner for burgers, shakes and sundaes. Both resorts are set along a white-sand beach like a tropical island paradise and share water fun at Stormalong Bay, a superb 2½acre/1ha recreation area with waterslides and a sandy lagoon. You can go boating or catch a water-shuttle to Epcot or Disney's Hollywood Studios; other park transport is by bus. The Sand Castle Club here caters for youngsters aged 3–12 (4.30pm–midnight).

BRITTIP

Look out for the nightly Disney film shows on the big outdoor movie screen by the beach at the Yacht and Beach Club Resorts.

Walt Disney World Swan and Dolphin Resort: These unmistakable twin hotels are not owned by Disney but conform to the same high standards, with some of the most extensive facilities, a great location, fab restaurants and a night-time view second to none, while they

Walt Disney World and Lake Buena Vista Accommodation

Big Sand Lake

Hilton Garden Inn
Residence Inn
Embassy Suites
Hampton Inn
Quality Suites Lake Buena Vista
Floridays
Clarion Inn
Comfort Inn
Hilton Grand Vacation Suites

Extended Stay America

Hawthorn Suites

Crossgrounds Center
Radisson Lake Buena Vista
Marriott Village
Courtyard by Marriott, Fairfield Inn, Springhill Suites

Holiday Inn LBV Resort
Blue Heron Beach Resort
Bryan's Spanish Cove
Grand Beach Resort
Caribe Royale
Buena Vista Suites

APOPKA – VINELAND ROAD

Cypress Pointe Resort

Staybridge Suites

Fairfield Inn & Suites
Sheraton LBV Resort

Courtyard LBV

Hyatt Regency Grand Cypress

Doubletree Guest Suites
Best Western LBV
Wyndham LBV Resort
B Resort Lake Buena Vista
Holiday Inn
Hilton Orlando Resort

LBV

Vistana Resort

Marriott Vacation Club
Orlando World Center Marriott Resort
Nickelodeon Family Suites

Buena Vista Palace
Saratoga Springs Resort & Spa, & Treehouse Villas

DISNEY SPRINGS

Old Key West Resort
Typhoon Lagoon

Four Seasons Hotel and Disney's Golden Oak Villas

Port Orleans Riverside Resort
Port Orleans French Quarter Resort

Waldorf-Astoria, Hilton Orlando and Wyndham Grand Resort at Bonnet Creek

Caribbean Beach Resort
Pop Century Resort

Fort Wilderness Resort & Campground

Epcot
Beach Club
Yacht Club
Dolphin Boardwalk
Swan
Disney's Hollywood Studios
Disney's Art of Animation Resort

Walt Disney World

Contemporary Resort & Bay Lake Tower
Wilderness Lodge

Bay Lake

Transportation & Ticket Center

Magic Kingdom
Grand Floridian Resort & Spa
Polynesian Village Resort

BAY LAKE

Coronado Springs Resort
Blizzard Beach

All-Star Resorts

Animal Kingdom
Animal Kingdom Lodge Resort & Kidani Village

© Steve Munns 2015

N

are usually slightly cheaper than most Deluxe resorts. They're within walking distance of Epcot and Disney's Hollywood Studios, Disney's Boardwalk Resort and the Fantasia Gardens Miniature Golf Courses, but also have a boat service to both parks (and bus to the others). The unique architecture is extensive, with the Swan topped by a 45ft/14m statue, as well as 758 large rooms (including 55 suites), while the Dolphin (1,509 rooms, 112 suites) is crowned by two even bigger statues. Both are being extensively refurbished to include the Westin Heavenly Bed® and high-speed wi-fi, while adding a sumptuous Grand Deluxe room category with enhanced bathrooms, personalised in-room fridge, new furniture and contemporary décor. The $125m upgrade should be complete by early 2016. The Dolphin also boasts the Balinese-inspired Mandara Spa, with a relaxing tea garden and Meru Temple. This resort has 17 restaurants and lounges, 4 tennis courts, 5 pools (one an amazing grotto pool with hidden alcoves and waterslide), a kids' pool and white-sand beach, 2 health clubs, a great range of shops, a video arcade and the Camp Dolphin centre for 4–12s (5.30pm–12am, $10/hour per child). Even for non-guests, Shula's Steak House and celebrity chef Todd English's Bluezoo (both Dolphin) are worth seeking out, along with Il Mulino Trattoria,

New York's top Italian restaurant (in the Swan). Fresh, the Dolphin's Mediterranean-style market, serves breakfast and lunch, featuring all made-to-order menu items and both à la carte and tableside dining. The decor and atmosphere at the Swan's Garden Grove Café is inspired by the gardens of Central Park, and it serves à la carte or buffet breakfasts, with Disney characters each evening and breakfasts at the weekend. The intimate Kimonos, in the Swan, offers sushi and a karaoke bar. Picabu in the Dolphin is open 24 hours with all-American favourites, while The Fountain is a great choice for ice creams, sundaes, milkshakes and other speciality desserts, as well as classic diner fare. With its ideal location and amenities, this is possibly the perfect resort (407 934 1609, www.swandolphin.com).

Four Seasons Resort: (see Golden Oak, p69).

BRITTIP

Most Disney hotel rooms will accommodate only 4, with the exception of Port Orleans Riverside (which can take an extra child on a trundle bed). For larger groups, consider Old Key West, Saratoga Springs, the Boardwalk Villas, the villas at Animal Kingdom Lodge, Wilderness Lodge Villas, Fort Wilderness cabins or 2-room suites at the All Star Music Resort and Art of Animation Resort.

Port Orleans Riverside

Campground and cabins

Disney's Fort Wilderness Resort & Campground: This is possibly the best value of all the Disney properties. Situated on Bay Lake across from the Magic Kingdom, it offers impressive camping facilities and chalet-style cabins housing up to 6 in a 750acre/304ha spread of countryside. Two 'trading posts' supply fresh groceries and there are 2 bars and cafés plus a range of on-site activities, including 2 swimming pools, the thrice-nightly Hoop-Dee-Doo Musical Revue, Mickey's Backyard Barbecue (a seasonal character buffet dinner), campfire programme, open-air films, sports, games and a prime position to view the nightly Electrical Water Pageant. You can rent bikes or boats or take horse rides around the country trails, while the Tri-Circle D ranch has a small petting zoo. There is even a Segway Tour (the great 2-wheeled personal transports), the Wilderness Back Trail Adventure, providing a unique two-hour trundle around the many trails ($96/person, over-15s only; 8.30 and 11.30am Tue, Fri, Sat; call 407 939 8687 to book). The Trails End restaurant (sit-down and takeaway) offers a great value buffet breakfast, à la carte lunch and buffet dinner, while Crockett's Tavern serves pizza and appetisers (dinner only). Buses and boats link the resort with other areas (and the short boat ride to the Magic Kingdom is a great start to the day). If you need a break from the Magic Kingdom, hop on the boat here and try the family-friendly Trail's End for lunch or the dinner buffet ($27 for adults, $16 3–9s).

Disney Vacation Club resorts

Disney's Old Key West Resort: Disney's first Vacation Club resort, this is primarily a 5-star holiday ownership scheme (one of eight such timeshares), but the 1, 2 or 3-bed studios in a Key West setting can also be rented nightly when not in use by members. Facilities include 4 pools, tennis courts, a games room, shops and a fitness centre, plus the lovely Olivia's restaurant. Transport to all parks is by bus.

> **BRITTIP**
>
> Looking for a handy diversion from Downtown Disney Springs? Take the boat from the West Side (not Marketplace) to Old Key West and try a meal at Olivia's for a lovely, laid-back holiday vibe.

Disney's Saratoga Springs Resort & Spa: The most extensive DVC resort, this 65acre/26ha apartment complex is opposite Disney Springs, has some wonderful views over the lake and is next to scenic Lake Buena Vista Golf Course. It boasts 828 units, from standard 2-bed hotel-style studio rooms to massive 2-storey, 3-bed apartments sleeping 12. The theme is the 1880s' New York resort of the same name, with a gracious look and great facilities, from the free-form, zero-depth entry main pool (with waterslide and squirt-fountains), a smaller quiet pool, varied dining (the Artist's Palette for counter-service breakfast, lunch and dinner, the Paddock Grill for more quick-service fare and the upscale Turf Club Bar & Grill, with a cocktail lounge and pool table, plus food shop), a large video arcade, tennis courts and a wonderful full-service spa and gym. All but the hotel-style studios have a kitchen (with dishwasher and microwave), washer-dryer, whirlpool bath and DVD player, with TVs in each living room and bedroom. The resort includes room service, babysitting and childminding services plus a water taxi to the shops and entertainment at Disney Springs.

Disney's Fort Wilderness Resort

B Resort at Walt Disney World

Looking for something different, hotel-wise? Formerly the Royal Plaza Resort, the **B Resort at Walt Disney World** is its new-look replacement after a total refurbishment in 2014, offering 394 rooms in 5 categories, with suites accommodating up to 5 and family rooms with kids' bunks. It features fresh, contemporary decor and excellent personal amenities in the upscale-but-relaxed style of the new B brand. There is a high-quality signature restaurant called American Q (serving barbecue specialities at dinner), a Grab 'n Go deli-café, landscaped pool (with interactive water elements) and pool bar, 4 tennis courts, stylish Aveda Spa, fitness centre, coin-op laundry and kid-zone area with films and games. Standard rooms have a sitting area while the magnificent two-room suites boast a huge lounge and all feature clean, crisp design, Blissful beds, 47in/120cm flatscreen TVs, mini-fridge and superb bathrooms. Other signature elements include free technology amenities like high-speed Internet access throughout the resort, courtesy iPads, game consoles and Monscierge®, a digital touchscreen concierge and destination guide. The attention to detail and that 'something different' style is highly noticeable here but be aware there is a $20 resort fee and self-parking is $16/day (407 828 2828, **www.bresortlbv.com**)

Rates for the 3-bed villas top $1,900 a night, but the 1-bed units are more modestly priced and, although it is a Vacation Club property, rooms are usually available to the public.

Also here are 60 3-bed Treehouse Villas, beautiful chalets raised 10ft/3m off the ground and set among a heavily wooded area next to Sassagoula River. Sleeping up to 9, they feature some sumptuous furnishings, including granite counter-tops and flatscreen TVs, as well as two full bathrooms and outdoor barbecue grills. They also have their own leisure pool and whirlpool spa. Transport to all parks is by bus.

Bay Lake Tower at Disney's Contemporary Resort: This resort is linked to the Contemporary Resort by a 5th-floor bridge and features its own pool, waterslide and whirlpool spa, kids' water-play area, shuffleboard

B Resort at Walt Disney World

and bocce courts. The 14-storey, 295-room Tower, studio rooms and spacious 1, 2 and 3-bed villas have modern decor. The studios (sleeping up to four) all have small fridges, microwaves and coffee-makers, while the villas (sleeping up to 12) have full kitchens and laundry facilities. The Tower superbly complements its neighbour resort and affords wonderful views over the Magic Kingdom and nightly fireworks from its exclusive rooftop lounge and viewing deck (DVC members only). There is also a gourmet coffee bar and easy access to the restaurants of the Contemporary Resort. Transport by monorail or bus (or on foot to Magic Kingdom).

Disney's Animal Kingdom Lodge – Kidani Village: An addition to the Animal Kingdom Lodge, this is divided into hotel-room studios (sleeping up to four) and 1, 2 and 3-bed villas (sleeping five, nine or 12), all offering full kitchens and laundry facilities. The low-rise architecture and decor continue the African theme and the 3-bed villas are very spacious. There is a separate wildlife preserve in four animal savannah areas, a fabulous pool and kids' play area, and another restaurant, Sanaa, which continues the Lodge's reputation for fine dining. The stunning Samawati Springs – a huge zero-depth entry pool – is open to guests, while children will make a beeline for Uwanja Camp, a three-part interactive water playground (for ages 4 and under, 5–7s, and 8 and over). Other amenities include a video arcade, basketball court, fitness centre, gift shop and animal programmes, from flamingo-feeding to campfire story-telling. Transport to all the parks is by bus.

Grand Floridian Villas: These sumptuous additions to the DVC inventory provide 147 stylish 1 and 2-bed villas sleeping 5–9, plus 'grand villas' that sleep 12 and include a media room with home theatre system. The elegant building, with subtle Mary Poppins theming, has its own reception, children's water-play area and private beach.

Golden Oak: In an ultra-exclusive corner of Walt Disney World is this small-scale community of holiday homes for private sale. Like most villa developments, it has its own luxurious Clubhouse, but homes are NOT rented out and feature VIP perks such as concierge service, private transport to the parks and special events. The price is equally exclusive – they START at $1.8m!

Four Seasons Resort: Within the gates of Golden Oak but a separate entity (and also open to non-guests for its spectacular dining opportunities), the first Central Florida hotel of this fabulous 5-star brand opened in August 2014 and features 444 capacious rooms and even larger suites, all with marbled bathrooms, and in an oasis of tranquillity within the Disney confines. Built in Spanish Revival style and with luxury throughout, it has an amazing array of amenities, including 5 restaurants, 3 pools, a lazy river and water-play area, tennis courts, extensive spa, state-of-the-art gym and its own golf course. The huge kids club (for 4–12s, open 10am–6pm) is free to guests and offers a superb spread of games and activities and there is a good choice of inter-connecting family rooms, as well as adults-only rooms with luxurious king beds and great views to both sides. Rooms with views of the parks – and the Magic Kingdom fireworks – come at a premium while

the rooftop Spanish steakhouse restaurant Capa is one of Orlando's most spectacular. Authentic Italian restaurant Ravello, with its show kitchen, is another show-stopper and the golf clubhouse diner Plancha features Cuban-American cuisine in a lakeside setting. It offers a full Disney Planning Centre, grab-and-go café, teen hangout and the kind of deluxe 'extras' – including a shoe-shine service, twice-daily housekeeping, refrigerated private bar and unobtrusive service – that go with the brand. However, regular room rates start at $545/night and reach $12,000/night (!) for the nine-bedroom Royal Suite (1800 267 3046, **www.fourseasons.com/orlando/**).

BRITTIP
Book dinner at Capa at the Four Seasons to coincide with the nightly Wishes show at the Magic Kingdom and you will have a superb high-level view of the fireworks.

Disney Hotel Plaza

If Disney's hotel prices are out of your range, consider the seven 'guest' hotels that are on site but come with a less hefty price-tag, on Hotel Plaza Boulevard on the doorstep of Disney Springs. There's a free bus service to the parks, guaranteed admission (even on the busiest days), and you can make reservations for shows and restaurants before the general public. The convenience of being able to walk to Disney Springs and the Crossroads shopping plaza is also handy.

BRITTIP
Look out for a 'Free Breakfast' and special Advance Purchase offers at the Holiday Inn Walt Disney World. Book seven nights or more and qualify for free breakfast for two adults. Look them up on **www.hiorlando.com/specials.htm**.

Take your pick from the well-priced **Best Western Lake Buena Vista** (407 828 2424; Value); the new-look **B Resort** (407 828 2828; Moderate; see also p68); the outstanding **Buena Vista Palace Hotel & Spa** (407

827 2727; Moderate); the versatile **DoubleTree Suites by Hilton** with its array of two-room suites (407 934 1000; Moderate); the **Hilton Orlando Resort** (a smart choice but without Disney's Extra Magic Hours benefit as of Jan 2016; 407 827 4000; Moderate); the South Beach vibe and excellent dining of the **Holiday Inn** (407 828 8888; Moderate); and the recently renovated **Wyndham Lake Buena Resort** (407 828 4444; Moderate).

For more info on these, go to **www.downtowndisneyhotels.com**.

Beyond Disney

Once you move away from Walt Disney World, your hotel choice becomes more diverse. The Budget and Value types are most common, and the area you stay in also has an effect on price: the further you go from Disney on Kissimmee's Highway 192, the cheaper (and more basic) the hotel/motel, while parts of I-Drive are more expensive than others (north of Sand Lake Road is usually cheaper). Facilities vary little and what you see is usually what you get. All the chain hotels can be found here, with rates as low as $35/room off-peak (but remember the local sales tax). Some also have rooms with a kitchenette (an 'efficiency'). Be prepared to shop around, especially on Highway 192, where many hotels advertise their rates, and feel free to ask to see a room before you book. Here are the main options.

BRITTIP

Coffee-makers are standard in most hotel rooms, but tea-making facilities are rare. Bring your own teabags or look for PG Tips and Yorkshire Tea in the International aisles at Publix and Wal-Mart.

Econolodge Kissimmee

Budget hotels

Chain hotels can be found at their most numerous in this category and you'll find few frills. All have pools, but not many have restaurants, bars or lounges (though some provide a free continental breakfast and many offer fridges and microwaves).

- **America's Best Value Inn:** Basic motel type with some newer properties that are worth seeking out, with free wi-fi and continental breakfast (1888 315 2378, **www.americasbestvalueinn.com**).

- **Days Inn:** Chain that varies widely from tired older hotels to smart newer ones, and with free continental breakfast (1800 225 3297, **www.daysinn.com**).

- **Econo Lodge:** Also with free wi-fi and continental breakfast (1877 424 6423, **www.econolodge.com**).

- **Howard Johnson:** Mainly older properties, many with a Kids-eat-free option and free breakfast, but rooms are often more spacious (1800 221 5801, **www.hojo.com**).

- **Knights Inn:** Several smarter choices in the Orlando area (1800 477 0629, **www.knightsinn.com**).

- **Motel 6:** 'Bargain basement' choice (1800 899 9841, **www.motel6.com**).

- **Red Roof Inn:** Several renovated properties in Orlando, plus free wi-fi (1800 733 7663, **www.redroof.com**).

- **Rodeway Inn:** Chain that has slipped from Value to more Budget territory, but still offers a free breakfast (1877 424 6423, **www.rodewayinn.com**).

- **Super 8 Motel:** Chain varies a lot, but has several newer motels (notably on American Way, just off I-Drive) and all offer free breakfast; look for its 'Pride' hotels, which are above average (1800 454 3213, **www.super8.com**).

- **Travelodge:** With an excellent property on American Way, plus free breakfast and wi-fi (1800 525 4055, **www.travelodge.com**).

Our Budget recommendations

Hotels we rate as above average for this category include:

Champions World Resort: Converted Howard Johnson on west Highway 192, a sound budget choice with 3 pools, free theme park transport and wi-fi (1800 638 7829, **www.championsworldresort.com**).

Destiny Palms Hotel Maingate East: Well situated for Disney, this pleasant motel also offers free wi-fi and a continental breakfast (407 396 1600, **www.destinypalmshotel.com**).

EconoLodge Inn International Drive at Universal: Basic, clean and reliable, with free wi-fi, coffee and pastries, and a nice picnic area (407 313 1090, **www.econolodge.com**).

Golden Link Resort Motel: On Highway 192, this quaint little retro motel with free breakfast and wi-fi consistently gets rave reviews (407 396 0555, **www.goldenlinkresortmotel.com**).

Super 8 Kissimmee/Maingate: Well above average for this low-cost chain, with good customer feedback (407 396 8883, **www.super8maingate.com**).

Travelodge Suites East Gate Orange: Higher quality from a basic chain motel, with wi-fi, microwave and fridge in all rooms, a good pool and kiddie pool (407 396 7666, **www.travelodge.com**).

There are dozens of smaller, independent outfits that offer special rates periodically, especially a battery of cheap and cheerful motels along Highway 192 in Kissimmee (but try to stay west of Marker 14).

BRITTIP

Hotels designated Maingate East or Maingate West should be close to Disney's main entrance on Highway 192, though it is wise to check.

Value hotels

At first glance there may not seem much difference here between these Value options and the Budget category, especially as some are still motels, and the big chains dominate. They should have smarter facilities, but not all have their own restaurant.

- **Baymont Inn & Suites:** Highly worthwhile group, boasting several new properties, all with free breakfast and wi-fi (407 994 1900, **www.baymontinns.com**).

- **Choice Hotels:** Group comprising Comfort Inn, which is a bland chain, but offers a free breakfast; Comfort Suites, which has some smart, newer properties; Quality Inn, with a reputation for good value, some with an exercise room and free continental breakfast;

and the smarter Clarion Inn (and Suites), often including restaurants, though the age of the properties varies (1877 424 6423, **www.choicehotels.com**).

- **Extended Stay America:** No-frills, clean and consistent chain with more space than many in this group, a free grab-and-go breakfast and wi-fi, plus fully equipped kitchens (1800 804 3724, **www.extendedstayamerica.com**).

- **Fairfield Inn:** Budget version of the Marriott chain, usually with newer hotels, many with gyms and most with free breakfast (1800 1927 1927 in the UK, 407 581 5600 in the US, **www.marriott.com**).

- **Hampton Inn and Suites:** Usually above average in this category, with free wi-fi, hot breakfast and tea/coffee in the lobby 24 hrs (1800 426 7866, **www.hamptoninn.com**).

- **Ramada:** Good value at this level, many have free wi-fi and breakfast or a restaurant (1800 854 9517, **www.ramada.com**).

There are more options at the upper end of the category.

- **Best Western:** Good, family-style facilities with more amenities (0800 393 130 in UK, 1800 780 7234 in US, **www.bestwestern.com**).

Our Value recommendations

Notable properties in this range:

Avanti Resort: This former EconoLodge in the heart of I-Drive has been heavily refurbished to provide an individual touch, with a fabulous new resort pool area (including kids' water fun section), interactive games room, state-of-the-art fitness centre, coffee shop and poolside bar & grill. Rooms have been given a sleek new look and vary from standard queen doubles to a king Jacuzzi room, while double queen and king rooms can be connected to sleep a family of 6, all with free wi-fi and flatscreen TVs. There are free daily shuttles to Universal, SeaWorld and Epcot, as well as Wet 'n Wild and Aquatica (407 313 0100, **www.avantiresort.com**).

Drury Inn & Suites: New in 2013, this smart choice includes a lot for your money (like free wi-fi, parking, hot breakfast, phone calls, snacks and drinks at their daily 5.30pm Kickback sessions and popcorn and soft drinks in the lobby 3–10pm). Well situated for I-Drive, Universal and Sand Lake Road, room choice includes 2-room suites and there is an indoor/outdoor pool and fitness centre (407 354 1101, **www.druryhotels.com**).

Extended Stay America Orlando-Universal Studios: A high-quality choice in this chain, in a great location for Universal and I-Drive, with all rooms recently renovated (407 903 1500, **www.extendedstayhotels.com**).

Galleria Palms Hotel: In Kissimmee at Maingate West, just off Highway 192, has a smart, contemporary look, ultra-comfy rooms, a great location close to Disney, free shuttle to the parks, free breakfast and wi-fi, and a relaxing pool area (there is no restaurant but plenty nearby; 407 396 6300, **www.galleriakissimmeehotel.com**).

Holiday Inn Maingate East: In Kissimmee (between Markers 8 and 9), offering well-maintained rooms (including kidsuites) in 2 high-rise towers, plus an oversized pool, kids' pool, waterslides, gym, children's theatre, food court and lobby lounge, plus a Kids-eat-free programme (407 396 4222, **www.holidayinnmge.com**).

Ramada Plaza Resort & Suites: Top value-for-money choice in a good I-Drive location with a free continental breakfast, wi-fi and Disney transport, plus over-sized rooms all with fridge, microwave and coffee-maker (407 345 5340, **www.michotel.com**)

Palms Hotel & Villas: Just off Highway 192 in Kissimmee (close to I-4), resort with spacious 1 and 2-room suites with full kitchens, 2 large pools and kiddie pool, sports court, free shuttle to Disney parks and free breakfast (407 396 2229, **www.thepalmshotelandvillas.com**).

Wyndham Orlando Resort: Heavily remodelled in the heart of I-Drive and with great facilities, this boasts two pools, a delightful poolside bar and restaurant, ice-cream shop, fitness centre and sauna, all set in landscaped grounds but without the high price tag you might expect. There is also a free shuttle to Universal and SeaWorld. The $18/day resort fee includes parking and wi-fi (407 351 2420; **www.wyndham.com**).

- **Holiday Inn and Holiday Inn Express:** Recently rebranded to be more upmarket, there are still bargains in Value/Moderate territory as they offer Kids-eat-free (with parents) at all properties and many include sophisticated pools and extra facilities such as games rooms (0800 405060 from the UK, 1888 465 4329 in the US, **www.holidayinn.com**).

- **La Quinta Inn and Suites:** Some notably smart hotels in Orlando (1800 753 3757, **www.lq.com**).

- **Radisson:** Possibly the best overall value here, this group has some excellently priced hotels, all with above-average amenities and services, free wi-fi and well situated for the parks (0800 374 411 in UK, 1800 976 9033 in the US, **www.radisson.com**).

- **Wingate Inn:** Modern chain, with gyms, free breakfast and wi-fi (1800 337 0077, **www.wingatehotels.com**).

💲 BRITBONUS

Enjoy a special *Brit Guide* rate of $69/night, plus resort fee and tax, at the Palms Hotel & Villas on Parkway Boulevard in Kissimmee (just off Highway 192). This includes: full suite (sleeping 1–5) with kitchen and living space, free hot breakfast daily, free wi-fi, use of recreational facilities and parking. Use code BRIT2015 when calling (407 396 2229) or email palmshotelandvillas@gmail.com. Offer valid until 31 Dec 2016.

Moderate Hotels

This is a category with fewer of each brand, so we highlight a few worthy individuals as well as the chains. All properties provide a good pool (often with extras like a waterslide, kids' pool and/or playground), at least one restaurant, bar and café, and extra in-room comfort.

🇬🇧 BRITTIP

Not all hotels provide hairdryers, though they can often be ordered from the front desk. For your own, you will need a US plug adaptor (with 2 flat pins). The voltage is 110–120AC (ours is 220) so UK appliances will be sluggish.

Main chains:

- **Country Inn & Suites:** A smart choice, with spacious rooms and a pleasant country-house lobby, with an extensive free breakfast (0800 973 217, **www.countryinns.com**).

- **Hyatt Place:** A chic, contemporary choice with stylish, comfortable rooms, free continental breakfast (or hot breakfast upgrade), 24-hour café and evening bar service, plus free wi-fi (1888 591 1234, **www.hyatt.com/hyatt/place**).

- **Residence Inns:** Identikit but consistent, with free breakfast and exercise rooms, plus microwave, fridge and tea/coffee-making facilities (00800 1927 1927, **www.marriott.com/residence-inn/travel.mi**).

- **Springhill Suites:** Also part of the Marriott group, they offer reliable, comfortable value (00800 1927 1927, **www.marriott.com/springhill-suites/travel.mi**).

More upmarket

- **Crowne Plaza Hotels:** Some eye-catching properties featuring great pool areas, smart restaurants, fitness centres and ultra-comfy rooms (**www.ihg.com/crowneplaza/**). The Crowne Plaza Orlando-Universal is a fine example, with 398 rooms and suites in 2 stylish blocks and a spectacular atrium. Two restaurants, a cocktail lounge and fitness centre, plus a huge heated pool add up to quality and value in an ideal location on Universal Boulevard's junction with Sand Lake Road (407 355 0550, **www.cporlando.com**).

🇬🇧 BRITTIP

It is usual to tip hotel chambermaids by leaving $1/adult each day before your room is made up.

- **Doubletree by Hilton:** A contemporary, upscale choice with fewer frills but spacious, ultra-comfy rooms featuring their Sweet Dreams sleep experience and signature welcome cookies, plus a rare B&B option (1800 222 8733, **http://doubletree3.hilton.com/en/index.html**). A good example is the Doubletree by Hilton Orlando at SeaWorld, a recently remodelled hotel just off I-Drive set in 28acres/11ha. It offers 3 pools, 2 kids' pools, a playground, mini-

Country Inn & Suites

golf and extra-large suites. Limited dining, but tropical grounds give it a luxury feel (407 352 1100, **www.doubletreeorlandoidrive.com**).

- **Hilton Garden Inn:** The Hilton chain has really struck the right note with this modern, comfortable and family-friendly brand, with a number of attractive, modern hotels (1877 782 9444, **http://hiltongardeninn3.hilton.com/en/index.html**).

- **Marriott:** Another well-represented group, with some of the smartest hotels in this category, often providing extra facilities and more landscaped grounds, a choice of restaurants and some of the largest standard rooms. Features include its signature Revive beds for a guaranteed good night's sleep (00800 1927 1927, **www.marriott.com**).

- **Sheraton hotels:** These boast a smart, revamped look. Several are themed and feature extra facilities and good dining (1800 325 35353, **www.starwoodhotels.com/sheraton**). The Sheraton Lake Buena Vista Resort remains a popular choice with Brits, with spacious, well-

Cabana Bay Beach Resort

© Universal Orlando Resort

furnished rooms, a spectacular pool complex and fitness centre, and impressive restaurant and lounge. (1800 325 3535, **www.sheratonlakebuenavistaresort.com**).

Notable individuals

There are only a few non-chain properties in the Moderate category.

- **Cabana Bay Beach Resort:** New in March 2014, Universal's first fully Moderate hotel is split into 2 impressive parts either side of a central reception area with classic 1950s styling. There are 1,800 standard rooms and family suites with kitchenettes that sleep up to six, set either side of an efficient 600-seat Food Court, with food stations including burgers and milk shakes, salads, pizza and pasta, a bakery, sandwiches and a Grab & Go section. There are also 4 huge video screens showing period TV shows and vintage holiday home movies! Other options include a retro Starbucks coffee shop, lobby bar and 2 elaborate pool bars offering signature frozen drinks and smoothies. The Lazy River Courtyard also offers the Hideaway Bar & Grille for lunch and dinner. Guests can even have pizza delivered to rooms that feature all mod cons, with flatscreen TVs, mini fridge, free wi-fi and a clever bathroom arrangement that features two wash-basins as well as a bathtub/shower. Amenities include a 10-lane bowling alley, which has its own bar/restaurant, and 2 feature-packed resort pool areas, with zero-depth entry, sandy beaches, waterslide and Universal's first lazy river, while the period theming is extensive and all-pervading. Other notable extras include a large video games room and themed fitness centre with lockers and showers (very handy if your room isn't ready yet and you want to change for the parks). However, this is the one Universal resort that does not benefit from the free Universal Express pass perk, although there is still early entry to the parks. It also requires

Our Moderate recommendations

Embassy Suites International Drive South: A consistent 'old faithful' in the heart of I-Drive, with spacious rooms (either standard two-room suites sleeping 4 or double-doubles for six) providing 2 TVs, coffee-maker, fridge and microwave. There's a great outdoor pool deck, kids' splash pool and indoor pool, plus a sauna and gym and good dining options, with a free breakfast. It is rare in this area in offering a free shuttle service to Disney, Universal and SeaWorld (407 352 1400, **www.embassysuitesorlando.com**).

Four Points By Sheraton Orlando Studio City: A 21-storey I-Drive icon near Universal Orlando, this features a heated tropical pool and paddling pool, games room, mini-golf, fitness room and free shuttle to Disney and Universal. All 301 well-appointed rooms have coffee-makers, Nintendo games and free wi-fi, plus superb views (ask for a Universal view if possible). The Tropical Palms restaurant is a minor gem, with a fun ambience for breakfast, lunch or dinner, and an imaginative dinner menu, while you can also grab a drink at the Oasis Lounge or Tropical Breezes patio pool bar (407 351 2100, **www.fourpointsorlandostudiocity.com**).

Radisson Hotel Lake Buena Vista: A dramatically remodelled property, convenient for Disney and the Crossroads area, with sleek rooms and furnishings, the stylish Liquid Bar & Grill, a small gym and free wi-fi. Extra-spacious rooms feature a fridge, microwave, coffee-maker, large, flatscreen TV and the signature comfy Sleep Number bed (407 597 3400, 0800 374 411 from the UK, **www.radisson.com**).

Rosen Center Hotel: This spectacular 24-storey property, one of the area's largest, caters heavily to the Convention Center next door but also offers excellent facilities. It has a huge swimming grotto, tennis courts, an exercise centre, high-quality restaurants (the excellent steak-and-seafood Everglades and casual 24-hour deli, Café Gauguin), the chic Banshoo Sushi bar and 98Forty Tapas & Tequila bar. The style is luxurious, yet prices aren't (1800 204 7234, **www.rosencenter.com**).

Holiday Inn at Walt Disney World: Among the seven along Hotel Boulevard adjacent to Disney Springs, this is a fresh and quality-conscious offering in a great area. It features an excellent, family-friendly pool area, pool bar, lounge and surprisingly high-quality restaurant, and there is an overall South Beach vibe that would not be out of place in chic Miami (407 828 8888, **http://www.hiorlando.com/**).

its own shuttle bus to CityWalk (or a 15min walk). 1888 430 4999, **www.loewshotels.com/Cabana-Bay**.

BRITTIP
Need a Moderate hotel that is truly family friendly? Consider the CoCo Key Hotel and Water Resort, one of the most thoughtful and feature-packed hotels we've seen in ages.

- **CoCo Key Hotel & Water Resort Orlando:** This ultra-family-friendly option offers excellent amenities, notably the extensive water park. It has been transformed from an old Ramada, from the chic new lobby area to the 391 rooms (all with flatscreen TVs, smart bedding and furniture, coffee-maker and free wi-fi). There is a quiet adults' pool, with fountain and Jacuzzi, buffet

breakfast room (Tradewinds), food court (Callaloo Grill, featuring Pizza Hut), indoor sports bar and outdoor Tiki Bar overlooking the Key West-themed water park, with a canopy roof to protect from the sun (but also an uncovered play area and terrace). There is a fitness centre, extensive games arcade, gift shop and convenience store,

CoCo Key

Coming up Rosen

One notable local operator in Orlando is the Rosen Hotels & Resorts group, with a good variety of seven well-run, value-conscious properties. Four are budget-minded, the Brit-popular **Rosen Inn at Pointe Orlando**, **Rosen Inn International** and **Rosen Inn** on I-Drive, and the **Clarion Inn Lake Buena Vista**. All have been impressively refurbished and offer standard amenities but thoughtful touches, like family-style buffet restaurants, kids facilities, plenty of pool choice and free wi-fi. The other hotels are the flagship deluxe **Rosen Shingle Creek Hotel** (p80–1), and the Moderate pair of **Rosen Centre Hotel** and **Rosen Plaza Hotel**, a distinctive 800-room property with excellent facilities – including two restaurants, a pizza shop, deli, fitness centre and nightclub – and spacious, well decorated accommodation (1866 337 6736, **www.rosenhotels.com**).

private rooms for birthday parties and a kids' club. The water park is a marvel: Parrot's Perch, an interactive jungle-gym; Minnow Lagoon, for pre-school kids, with a zero-depth entry pool and water cannons with mini-slides and other small-scale fun (with life-jackets, and life-guards); Coral Reef Cove, the teen activity pool, with the Cyclone body-slide; and the outdoor Water-Park, with nine different slides, including the Over The Falls and Surfer Splash body-slides and Boomerango double-rider tube slide. There is a 'resort fee' for use of the water park, but at $24/room/day, it isn't unreasonable. Day guests are also allowed when the resort is not full, at $25–27/person (kids under 3ft are free) (407 351 2626, **www.cocokeywaterresort.com**).

Hard Rock Hotel guitar fountain

© Universal Orlando Resort

• **Monumental Hotel:** A converted Crowne Plaza hotel and still ultra-stylish, with a Key West theme, 94 spacious, well-equipped rooms, beautiful pool area and Pineapple Grill Restaurant for daily breakfast and dinner Fri and Sat (1877 239 1222, **www.monumentalhotelorlando.com**).

Deluxe hotels

When it comes to the best hotels, it is largely a question of individuals. The growing selection of genuinely deluxe properties in this area are all highly distinctive, with excellent facilities, outstanding service and, usually, at least one 5-star restaurant. They can be divided into five main areas: Universal Orlando, International Drive, Lake Buena Vista, Kissimmee and Further Afield.

Universal Orlando

Universal teamed up with the Loews group to create its hotels, and the four upscale offerings come with the Universal Express front-of-queue bonus to the main attractions with your key card. Universal resort guests also enjoy other benefits, like a resort ID card (for buying food, merchandise, etc. throughout the resort), priority seating at most restaurants (show your room key card), package delivery to your room, special golf privileges at four nearby courses, and early entry to the Wizarding World of Harry Potter in both parks. The deluxe all feature boat transport to the parks, plus kids' activity centres with a meal option

The Sky's the limit

For a good cross-section, from Value hotels to villas and community resorts, try **Sky Hotels & Resorts**, a specialist management company. Its one-stop shop includes the reliable **Enclave Suites** just off I-Drive, **Hawthorn Suites Lake Buena Vista**, the excellent **Lake Buena Vista Resort Village & Spa** (p90) and the highly rated **Coral Cay Resort** in Kissimmee, a well-designed gated development of 3 and 4-bed town-homes (terraced villas), plus the spectacular views of the 3-star **Hawaiian Inn** at Daytona Beach. An interesting prospect is their own branded **StaySky Suites** just off I-Drive on Canada Avenue. A converted Hawthorn Suites property, it features 1 and 2-bed suites, all with full kitchens and sleeping 4–8. There is free breakfast, shuttle transport to the parks and wi-fi, as well as a fitness centre, heated pool and hot tub, games room and free parking (1866 455 4062, **www.staysky.com**).

(for 4–14s; 5–11.30pm Sun–Thurs, to midnight Fri and Sat; $15/hour per child, plus $15 for meal). Anyone booking a Universal hotel package via their reservation system (**www.universalorlandovacations.com**) can also add a daily Dining Plan to the park experience (p20). For all Universal hotels, call 1888 273 1311 or visit **www.universalorlando.com**.

✠➤ BRITTIP

Hard Rock Hotel guests – and music fans – should make a note of the monthly Velvet Sessions at the hotel, live gigs by well-known bands ('rock 'n' roll cocktail parties' as they call them), on the last Thurs of each month. There's music, free drinks and finger foods. Book tickets at **www.velvetsessions.com**.

Hard Rock Hotel: Possibly the coolest hotel in Orlando, this icon of rock chic is themed as a former rock star's home, with 650 rooms and suites in California mission style. High ceilings, wooden beams, marble floors and eclectic artwork give an eye-catching style, with a rock-star theme to most public areas, music memorabilia, black-suited foyer staff and fairly constant music. The 14acre/6ha site includes 3 bars (including the ultra-cool Velvet Bar), 2 restaurants (the full-service The Kitchen and the 5-star, dinner-only Palm Restaurant), plus a takeaway café, fitness centre, gift shop and games room. The lido area features a huge, free-form pool and 240ft/73m waterslide, 2 Jacuzzis, a beach volleyball court, shuffleboard and life-size chess and draughts. The

pool even has an underwater sound system! The 650 rooms (including 12 kidsuites and 10 king suites) are big, beautifully furnished in the hotel's chic style and superbly comfortable.

Portofino Bay Hotel: The stunning jewel in Universal's crown is a splendid re-creation of the famous Italian port. The elaborate porticos, trompe l'oeil painting, harbourside piazza and faithful ornamentation of the waterfront make it one of Florida's most memorable settings. The 750 rooms were all completely refurbished in 2012–13 and are impeccably appointed, with lashings of Italian style. Standard rooms are sumptuous, with huge beds, spacious bathrooms, mini-bar and coffee facilities, ironing board and hairdryer, while the 94 Club Rooms feature concierge service with private lounge, extra room amenities and free entry to the Mandara Spa fitness centre. There are 18 superbly-themed *Despicable Me* kidsuites with separate bedrooms each (complete with missile beds!) with their own TV. The resort facilities are equally

Portofino Bay Hotel

breathtaking – a Roman aqueduct-style pool with waterslide (and poolside films on Sat evenings), an enclosed kids' play area and wading pool, a separate quiet pool, Jacuzzis, the beautiful Mandara Spa, business centre, an array of gift shops and a video games room. The Portofino also has an amazing 8 restaurants and lounges, including the 5-star (and very romantic) Bice Ristorante (p324), the boisterous Trattoria del Porto, Mama Della's, an authentic Italian family dining experience (watch out for Mama herself!), an aromatic deli, a pizzeria, gelateria and swanky Bar American. It is only a short way from the parks, but is light-years away in terms of its tranquil ambience.

Royal Pacific Resort: This 53acre/21ha, 1,000-room resort has an exotic 1930s South Seas style, and you feel as if you have stepped into another world as you cross the bamboo bridge into the elegant lobby, faced by the splendid Orchid Garden courtyard. Extensive use of rich, dark woods, cool stone floors and masses of greenery give the place an opulent, colonial feel. Standard rooms feature hand-carved Balinese furniture among many refined touches, and there is also a Club level, with separate lounge and extended facilities, and 51 superlative suites – including 8 Jurassic Park-themed kidsuites (dinosaurs not included!). The Islands Dining Room offers breakfast, lunch and dinner in an oriental setting (children have their own buffet area with TV screen,

Royal Pacific Resort

© Royal Pacific Resort

plus character dining on select nights), while fine dining is taken to a new dimension by a magnificent restaurant run by celebrity chef Emeril Lagasse called Tchoup Chop (possibly the best in Orlando; p326). There's a pool snack bar and luau garden area, with the Wantilan Luau Saturday nights, featuring an eye-catching Polynesian feast and dinner show ($66–73 adults, $35–40 under-13s; 407 503 3463 to book). The huge freeform pool is ideal for kids, with zero-depth entry at one end and a boat-shaped interactive play area of squirting fountains. Add a health club (with Jacuzzi, sauna and gym), kids' club (with computer games, TVs and organised activities), video arcade and 2 shops and you have excellent value, even at this end of the scale.

Sapphire Falls Resort: Due to open in summer 2016 is this Caribbean-themed tropical oasis, with 1,000 rooms (including 77 suites) and a glittering array of amenities. A resort-style pool will boast a water slide, children's play area, sand beach and fire pit, forming a central courtyard surrounded by guest rooms. A full-service restaurant with scenic views and outdoor dining, a quick-service marketplace, a lobby lounge and poolside bar also will be included, along with a fitness centre, sauna and Jacuzzi. Like the other three deluxe resorts, there will be water taxi and shuttle access to all parts of Universal. It should also be one of Universal's most picturesque hotels, with flowing water in the shape of rivers and waterfalls in addition to the main pool and elegant outdoor terraces for enjoying the view.

International Drive

There are four eye-catching hotels here that take advantage of I-Drive's great location.

Hilton Orlando: This impressive 1,400-room hotel on I-Drive next to the big Convention Center and set in 26acres/10.5ha boasts superb leisure facilities. It features upscale steakhouse, Spencer's, along with David's Club bar and grill, casual

The SeaWorld bonus

For anyone planning on a lot of SeaWorld and Aquatica visits, consider a **SeaWorld Official Partner Hotel** for a range of benefits and money-saving offers. All seven feature free Quick Queue at SeaWorld, a free behind-the-scenes Rescue Tour, free shuttle service to SeaWorld and Aquatica, early park entry on select days, free signature show seating, 10% off dining and 10% off merchandise purchases of $50 or more. These benefits are available at each of the Renaissance Orlando, Doubletree by Hilton, Hilton Garden Inn, Hilton Grand Vacations, SpringHill Suites, Fairfield Inn & Suites and Residence Inn, all at SeaWorld. Be sure to pick up a Benefits Card when you check in at any of these hotels. Alternatively, there are another nine hotels nearby that offer the early entry, show seating, and 10% discounts. See details at **http://seaworldparks.com/en/seaworld-orlando/vacations/hotels/benefits/**.

dining at The Bistro, a 24-hour Marketplace and an inviting pool bar and grill. A full-service spa, a large state-of-the-art fitness centre, 2 pools, lazy river (in a wonderful 'tropical island' setting), tennis, volleyball and basketball courts, and a neat 9-hole putting golf course complete the impressive amenities. The Resort pool boasts a waterslide and kids' fountain, while the Quiet pool has several Jacuzzis and both have cabanas, with fridges and TVs, for hire. Rooms feature Hilton 'Serenity' bedding, 37in HD TVs and high-quality toiletries, while an executive level includes a private lounge and extra services (407 313 4300, **www.thehiltonorlando.com**).

Hyatt Regency Orlando: Formerly the Peabody and, sadly, no longer with its trademark ducks, this remains an upmarket choice right in the heart of I-Drive, appealing largely to convention business but also well-stocked for holiday fun. The original 891-room tower has an Olympic-size pool, tennis courts and two superb restaurants in the gourmet Italian of Fiorenza and the amazing 24-hour B-Line Diner. Larger-than-average rooms and huge suites add to the quality, but conference business can make this side of the hotel a bit hectic.

⚓ BRITTIP

The impressive 2,178m²/22,000ft² The Spa at the Hyatt Regency features a blissful array of treatments and make-up services, plus a full-service nail and hair salon, and all-day spa packages with lunch, all open to non-hotel guests on a daily basis.

The 34-storey tower adds real cutting-edge sophistication and holiday appeal, with another 1,641 luxurious rooms; a lushly landscaped 3acre/1.2ha recreation area with 3 pools (and you'll feel a million miles from busy I-Drive), with tropical pool bar and cabanas; Urban Tide seafood and coastal cuisine; a chic cocktail bar, Rocks (perfect in the evening, with live music); a grab-and-go Café; lobby coffee bar; and a superbly stylish spa and fitness centre. Rooms feature the Hyatt Grand Bed, fridges, cordless phones and even mini LCD TVs in bathroom mirrors! (407 284 1234, **www.orlando.regency.hyatt.com**).

Renaissance Orlando Resort: This superb resort (788 rooms on Sea Harbor Drive, next to SeaWorld) features a wonderful two-part children's water-park, complete with water-jets, rain-tree and more. It gives the outdoor amenities a real boost

Renaissance Orlando Resort

Suite choice

These are our top-rated suites hotels.

Embassy Suites: With smart interior courtyards, good restaurants and relaxing pool areas (1800 362 2779, http://embassysuites3.hilton.com/en/index.html).

Homewood Suites: Provide extra room for larger families in 1 and 2-bed suites with full kitchens, free breakfast and an upmarket feel with mid-range pricing (1800 225 5466, **http://homewoodsuites3. hilton.com/en/index.html**).

Hawthorn Suites by Wyndham and Staybridge Suites: Both feature spacious 1 and 2-bed suites that sleep up to 6 and fully fitted kitchens, plus a hearty free breakfast, wi-fi and free local phone calls (1800 337 0202, **www.hawthorn.com** or 1877 238 8889, **www.ihg.com/staybridge/**). Sister properties the **Buena Vista Suites**, a well-appointed and more individual choice, and **Caribe Royale Resort** (1800 823 8300, **www.cariberoyale.com**) are on World Center Drive just off the lower end of I-Drive. The former is the more basic type, with spacious 2-room suites, a free full breakfast, heated pool, whirlpool, tennis courts, gift shop, mini-market and the Vista Bistro. The Caribe Royale is more luxurious, with a choice of 1-bed suites and 2-bed villas, a tropical pool with waterslide, tennis courts and 2 fitness rooms. Award-winning Venetian Room restaurant is a treat for lovers of fine continental cuisine, and there are 4 other cafés and lounges.

Nickelodeon Family Suites: Not so much a hotel as a theme park resort is this striking, kid-friendly choice on I-Drive South. With loads of character interaction, daily activities, shows and celebrations, this has huge kids appeal, especially as the facilities – including 2 huge water-play areas, video arcade, mini-golf and various shops – are all child-friendly. Rooms come in 1-bed kitchen suites and 2 and 3-bed kidsuites, with living room and bathroom, microwave and fridge (and full kitchen with some). Nicktoons Café offers buffet dining (plus à la carte in the evening), while the character breakfast with Spongebob and pals and Dora the Explorer costs $14/ages 4–13 and $25/adults (Teenage Mutant Ninja Turtles at dinner, $17 and $33). Plus there is a food court, pool bar and grill, and adult-friendly Lounge Bar (407 387 5437; **www.nickhotel.com**).

Sonesta ES Suites: Newly converted from Staybridge Suites on I-Drive (right opposite the I-Drive 360 complex), this refreshing, spacious and Brit-friendly choice features 146 1- and 2-bed suites sleeping 4–8 in 3 configurations, including full kitchens and a master bedroom with its own bathroom. The versatile Trio 2-bed suite features a master bedroom, two double beds in the second bedroom and a sleeper sofa in the lounge. A hot and cold breakfast buffet is included and the pool area and hot tub provide a great retreat at the end of the day. The inviting bar area extends to an outdoor patio that guarantees a good social gathering and there is also a fitness centre, snack shop, coin-op laundry and daily housekeeping. There is free wi-fi and a daily shuttle to the parks (407 352 2400, **www.sonesta.com/orlando**).

(parents may struggle to get their young 'uns out of here!) and creates more of an adults-only vibe to the main pool area and gardens. It has a massive 10-storey atrium lobby and some equally large rooms and suites, a lavish spa and fitness centre and a video arcade. All rooms feature extra bathroom amenities, flatscreen TVs and Marriott's Revive bedding. The dining line-up consists of Mist Sushi & Spirits (cocktails and full-service dining, plus an amazing 'aquarium' video wall), Boardwalk Sports Bar, the upscale but casual Tradewinds for breakfast, lunch and dinner, Palms Pool Bar & Grill, a smart Starbucks café and ice-cream parlour. The hotel offers great packages in conjunction with SeaWorld, which is a 2min walk across the car park, and its rates are often the best in Deluxe territory (1800 327 6677, **www.renaissanceseaworldorlando.com**).

Rosen Shingle Creek Hotel: This 230acre/93ha resort ranks among the grandest for its location, quality and style. In the middle of the award-

Condo hotels

A condo-hotel is a cross between a villa and a hotel. People buy 'rooms' in these big properties (which look like resort hotels), which they then own – unlike timeshare, where you just 'own' a time period for a resort. All rooms are identically furnished, unlike villas, and feature 1, 2 or 3 bedrooms, living/dining room and kitchen or kitchenette. A management company then rents them out on behalf of the owners. For guests, they are booked as you would for any hotel. Some are owned by hotel groups such as Starwood while others are just managed by hotel specialists to ensure they maintain the right standards. They are usually built in tower blocks around communal facilities like the Clubhouse check-in and swimming pool (often with elaborate water features), and can include restaurants, fitness centres and even spas.

winning Shingle Creek Golf Club on lower Universal Boulevard, it boasts 1,500 rooms and suites, all with sumptuous decor and comfort, as well as a full-service spa and fitness centre. Rooms vary from standard doubles to presidential suites, but all with fabulous flatscreen TVs, wi-fi, fridges and first-class toiletries. Amenities include 5 restaurants, 4 bars, a lounge, coffee house, deli and ice-creamery, plus 3 outdoor pools, tennis, basketball and volleyball courts and nature trails. There is also a shopping gallery and babysitting service. The resort is built in a 1900s Spanish revival style and offers flawless service (especially at concierge level). Don't miss A Land Remembered, one of the best steakhouses in the state, in the Golf Clubhouse, and Cala Bella, a fine-dining Italian restaurant, with heavenly desserts from its renowned pastry chef (407 996 6338, **www.rosenshinglecreek.com**).

Westin Imagine Orlando: Also on Universal Boulevard, this chic condo-hotel property features 315 king rooms and 1 and 2-bed suites, with either kitchenettes or full kitchens, and the trademark Westin Heavenly bed and bath, plus

distinctive decor and extras like flatscreen TVs and marble-topped desks. Signature Italian restaurant Fiorella's Cucina Toscana features delicious casual lunches and upmarket dinners surrounded by unique decorative glass designs, with the option of al fresco dining. The bar area is equally distinguished plus there is a huge South Beach-style pool with Tiki Bar and a modern fitness centre to complete a very fresh and modern offering (407 233 2200, **www.westinimagineorlando.com**).

> **BRITTIP**
>
> Most villas and resorts do not have electric kettles, but you can find them at stores such as Wal-Mart and Super Target. Small versions are reasonably priced.

Lake Buena Vista

Moving to the next major resort area, there is a growing range of Deluxe choice here, too.

Hilton at Bonnet Creek Resort: This rare and extensive development is in a unique position inside Walt Disney World but privately owned (the only piece of land Walt was unable to buy from the original landowners in 1966). It is part of a 482acre/194ha resort complex with the Waldorf-Astoria (below) and shares some of the same facilities. The Hilton features 1,000 rooms, 4 restaurants, a

Blue Horizons at Sea World

© SeaWorld Parks

lagoon pool complex with lazy river and waterslide, 18-hole golf course, tennis courts and the adjoining full-service European spa and fitness centre. The chic modern Italian-themed La Luce restaurant provides fine dining, while the Harvest Bistro offers the main alternative (with kids 12 and under eating free with a full-paying adult), along with the Muse grab-and-go deli (with coffee bar), Zeta bar/lounge and Beech Pool Bar and Grill. One of its prime draws, though, is that it is just minutes from the Disney parks, and benefits from the full Hilton package of stylish accommodation and excellent kids' activity programmes, as well as some blissfully comfy rooms (407 597 3600, **www.hiltonbonnetcreek.com**).

BRITTIP

The Hilton Bonnet Creek Resort's splendid La Luce restaurant is usually featured in Orlando's Magical Dining Month each September, when a selection of the best restaurants offer three-course prix fixe dinners for a bargain $33/head. See more at **www.visitorlando.com/magicaldining** (and p304).

Hyatt Regency Grand Cypress: The area's first genuine Deluxe hotel in 1984, this is still one of the best. A mature 1,500acre/608ha resort with a unique mix of facilities, it has a rare 9-hole pitch-and-putt golf course, 27 holes of regular golf (designed by Jack Nicklaus), a golf academy, boating

lake and superb pool complex with a kids' water park, rock-climbing wall and snack bar. Other extensive enhancements were made to every guest room, the fitness centre and the restaurants. The elegant lobby boasts Zen-inspired décor with some highly relaxing touches, while all 750 rooms have been given a bright, contemporary finish, with large, flatscreen TVs, large shower units and elaborate lighting. The dining choice is among the best of any Orlando resort, and the location remains ideal, almost on the doorstep of Disney yet blissfully reclusive (on Winter Garden-Vineland Road, around the corner from the Crossroads area). The huge freeform swimming pool boasts Jacuzzis, waterfalls and slide, while the white sand beach and magnificent restaurants make for a sumptuous stay, especially Hemingway's, its Key West-styled dinner spot, and Cascade American Bistro, the all-day option with its 2-storey atrium and beautiful lake views. There is also the On The Rocks pool bar and deli-style Palm Café; an inviting lobby lounge and sushi bar; and Marilyn Monroe Spa. Watersports, such as boating, kayaking or fishing on scenic Lake Windsong, tennis and bike rentals are covered by the one-off resort fee. And, once among its richly landscaped grounds, you could easily be light years from the theme-park bustle (407 239 1234, **http://grandcypress.hyatt.com**). New here in 2015 was the Marilyn Monroe Spa, a fun and varied option

Hyatt Regency Grand Cypress

International Drive Accommodation

© Steve Munns 2015

for a chillout break, whether you are staying at the hotel or not. It offers hairstyling, manicures, pedicures, a make-up bar, facials and massages, and it all comes with a suitably glamorous touch (321 558 7818 for appointments).

Orlando World Center Marriott: We love this impressive landmark on Disney's outskirts, set in landscaped 200acres/810ha and surrounded by a beautiful golf course. With 2,000 rooms and suites (most boasting fabulous views up to 28 storeys high), 6 restaurants and a series of pools, including a huge freeform tropical pool and three amazing water slides, it is a monumental prospect, set among landscaped foliage and with fabulous facilities, including a Bill Madonna Golf Academy, tennis courts, volleyball, basketball, spa and state-of-the-art gym. Highlights are the Mikado Japanese Steakhouse, Hawk's Landing Steakhouse, Siro Urban Italian Kitchen and High Velocity Sports Bar, while there are excellent children's amenities and programmes. It gets busy with convention business, but the picturesque pool complex offers true relaxation bliss and there were extensive renovations in 2013/14 (407 239 4200, **www.marriottworldcenter.com**).

Waldorf-Astoria: The second part of the huge Bonnet Creek development, this 497-room hotel was the first US Waldorf outside New York and added a new level of luxury to the Orlando scene when it opened in 2009. Stately and serene, the famous-name hotel

features 313 standard rooms with Italian marble bathrooms and HD flat-screen TVs, plus 185 truly grand suites with butler service. The zero-entry pool boasts cabanas and waiter service, while the dining choice is superb, from the poolside grille and classic Bull & Bear Steakhouse to the small-plate cuisine of Peacock Alley, gourmet style of signature Oscar's brasserie and private club atmosphere of Sir Harry's Lounge. The spa is unashamedly 5-star. Other amenities include basketball and tennis, jogging trails, bike rentals, a state-of-the-art fitness centre (with personal trainers), yoga and aerobics classes and boutique shops on a par with the Waldorf's luxury cachet. Even children aren't forgotten, with the WA Kids Club providing active, creative fun for 5–12s (10am–5pm, $15/hour per child) and the After Dark programme with dinner and games 6–10pm at $75/child (407 597 5500, **www.waldorfastoriaorlando.com**).

Kissimmee

The more budget-oriented area of Osceola County also has its share of upmarket properties.

Bohemian Hotel: In the Disney-inspired town of Celebration just off Highway 192, this unique hotel offers refreshing small-town America style that is a long way from the usual tourist hurly-burly. With just 115 rooms in its 1920s' wood-frame design, it has a classy ambience and a wealth of high-quality touches, notably in the ultra-comfy rooms: Standard or Lake View (with either a king or 2 queen-size beds), Studio or a 2-room suite, all beautifully furnished. Lovely artwork, courteous staff and a good array of facilities – pool, Jacuzzi and fitness centre, plus the highly-regarded Lakeside Bar & Grill (excellent for breakfast, it becomes a signature steakhouse at night) – mark out this hotel as a real gem. In addition, it is within a short stroll of the town's shops, restaurants and lakeside walks and makes a great romantic choice (407 566 6000, **www.celebrationhotel.com**).

Orlando World Center Marriott

© Orlando World Center

Kissimmee Accommodation

© Steve Munns 2015

Gaylord Palms Resort: One of the most dramatic hotels, with 1,406 rooms, is on the junction of I-Drive South and Osceola Parkway (ideal for Disney). A cross between a convention centre and a vast turn-of-the-century Florida mansion, it features 4½acres/2ha of indoor gardens, fountains and 'landscaped' waters under a glass dome, with live entertainment nightly. Three themed indoor areas bear witness to great creativity and the resort offers every creature comfort, with an array of restaurants and bars (including the spectacular 2-level Wreckers sports bar, with more than 50 HDTVs and a 20ft/6m high video screen), full-service spa and children's centre. The Cypress Springs Family Fun Water Park adds a huge zero-entry pool featuring 4 water slides, a massive multi-level water play structure, lagoon, toddler splash area, and 'dive in' family-friendly movies. Grown-ups will appreciate the relaxed ambience of the eye-catching South Beach Pool (with the option of private cabanas). Standard rooms are some of the smartest and most spacious, while the suites are enormous. The central Emerald Bay offers even more choice with a concierge level. One area is landscaped like the Everglades (with alligator feeding!); another copies St Augustine's old-world charm, with a replica Spanish fort; and the third is eclectic Key West, with a mock-up marina and sailboat. To walk into the resort's marbled lobby and cavernous interior at night is like entering a future world. Then there is the signature fine dining, with the choice of Old Hickory Steakhouse, MOOR (featuring fine seafood),

Gaylord Palms Resort

the Mediterranean buffet-style Villa de Flora and SORA Sushi Bar. The Relâche Spa is one of the area's largest, with 25 treatment rooms, fitness centre and beauty salon. Find unique shopping along the indoor 'retail street', plus the Cocoa Bean coffee shop and Honeybells Frozen Yoghurt. The hotel stages regular special events and is a great wedding venue (407 586 0000, **www.gaylordpalms.com**).

BRITTIP
The Gaylord Palms features the stunning Christmas celebration ICE!, a wonderland of ice sculptures, snow scenery and ice slides, plus other festive touches. Early Nov–3 Jan, tickets $30 adults, $29 over-55s and $17 4–12s, extra for snow tubing.

Meliã Orlando Hotel (formerly Mona Lisa Suites Hotel): One of the finest condo-hotels, on Highway 192 at the entrance to Celebration, this is a luxury 5-storey, 240-unit property set around a spectacular 'vanishing edge' swimming pool and boasting upmarket dining at the Gastrobar, with its small-plate dining and signature sangrias, and Fuego Restaurant with its Latin flavours. The 1 and 2-bed suites feature beautifully furnished living areas, full kitchens and ultra-comfy bedrooms, with designer toiletries. Balconies overlook the infinity pool or lush landscaping. There is a free shuttle to all the parks and privileged use of the Celebration Spa and Golf Club (407 964 7000; **www.meliaorlando.com**).

BRITTIP
If you're like many travellers who have trouble falling asleep with a whirring air conditioner in your room, drop by Wal-Mart, Walgreens, or CVS and pick up a packet of soft foam earplugs. Effective enough to filter out the drone without making you deaf to 'important' noises.

Further afield
Grande Lakes Orlando: You'll find extensive luxury at this 500acre/200ha combination of a 584-room, 5-star

Ritz-Carlton Hotel, a 1,000-room JW Marriott Hotel, grand spa, 18-hole Greg Norman-designed golf course, tennis centre and an upscale range of shops and restaurants, like the outstanding Norman's, featuring the 'new world' cuisine of celebrity chef Norman Van Aken. Located on the edge of a forestry preserve, it feels secluded and remote – quite a feat in this area. It is slightly off the beaten track – at the junction of John Young and Central Florida Parkway – yet is only 10ml/16km from Disney and Orlando International Airport.

JW Marriott: This flagship hotel of the Marriott group has Spanish-Moorish design and fabulous dining including the fresh organic produce of Whisper Creek Farm: The Kitchen (with its own craft brewery), classic Italian at Primo, a Starbucks lounge, Sushi Bar and a pool bar and grill. It has a great lazy river mini-water park, plus a kids' pool and splash fountain. Rooms are plush and ultra-comfortable; 70% with balconies, and there are 64 grand suites.

BRITTIP

Always wanted to visit the American south but can't give up your Orlando holiday? Highball and Harvest at the Ritz-Carlton gives you a taste of upscale Southern cuisine without the extra travel. Try the boiled peanuts. You'll thank us!

Ritz-Carlton: This offers a wonderful blend of scale and detail, with lush gardens, abundant lakes and streams, Venetian-inspired architecture and a wealth of genuine antiques. It has a large, sloped-entry pool, kids' pool, 3 floodlit tennis courts, a signature shop and 5 dining choices, plus a separate children's check-in and the excellent Ritz Kids Club (5–12s; also for JW Marriott guests), while all restaurants offer child menus. As well as the highly rated Norman's, the restaurants include Southern inspired Highball and Harvest (one of our faves), Fairways Pub and Bleu pool bar and grill. The rooms are beautifully furnished, with high-quality products in the

marbled bathrooms, plasma-screen TVs, radio/CD, mini-bar, slippers and robes, and all have balconies. There are 66 spacious suites and 92 Club rooms on the top 2 floors, with concierge and butler service, food and drink presentations in the Club Lounge and Bulgari amenities. Two kidsuites feature a separate bedroom and bathroom, with toys, games, TV and video games for 100% child appeal. The golf course is immaculate and offers a Caddie Concierge programme for the ultimate in service. The beautiful citrus-tinged spa boasts a huge fitness centre and aerobics studio, lap pool (all free to guests at both hotels), lovely spa-cuisine restaurant and a huge array of massages and therapies. The pricing is suitably upmarket, but it is a rare treat. Note the $30 daily resort fee. (407 206 2300/2400, **www.grandelakes. com**).

Omni Orlando Resort at Champions Gate: A real golfing paradise, this offers 720 rooms and suites overlooking a superb golf set-up with two Greg Norman-designed courses. An imposing hotel with impressive facilities, including the HQ of the renowned David Leadbetter golf academy, main swimming pool and activity pool (including a lazy river, fountains and waterslide), four restaurants (notably the superb Asian cuisine of Zen and the chic David's Club bar-restaurant), coffee bar, deli, three lounge bars, state-of-the-art health club and full-service spa. Just 15mins south of Disney off I-4, this is well situated yet off the beaten track for those (especially golfers) looking for something different. Set in 1,500 landscaped acres/607ha and with

Doubletree at Orlando Airport

a magnificent vista as you walk in, it suits both business travellers and leisure-seekers. It also has 59 superb 2 and 3-bed villas, affording a more private stay, with full kitchens and opulent furnishings (407 390 6664, **www.omnihotels.com/hotels/orlando-championsgate**).

Airport convenience

If you need to stay near the airport, either if you have a late arrival or if you'd prefer the convenience of collecting your hire car in the morning rather than straight after a long flight, consider this duo.

Hyatt Regency: It doesn't get more convenient than a hotel inside the airport, and this is a great choice as well for its excellent restaurants, pool deck, fitness room, lounge and business centre. Rooms are ultra-spacious, particularly the corner rooms, and many feature internal balconies overlooking the airport atrium. We especially enjoy dining or just drinks at McCoy's (breakfast, lunch and dinner) restaurant, with its appealing menu and sushi bar, while Hemisphere, on the 8th floor, boasts award-winning steaks and seafood (breakfast and dinner only) as well as great views. There is no noticeable aircraft noise and none of the bustle you expect at an airport hotel and staying here is a real boon if you're looking for a stress-free arrival (407 825 1234, **http://orlandoairport.hyatt.com**).

Doubletree by Hilton at Orlando Airport: This impressive hotel is just 5mins north of the airport and especially well equipped after a big renovation completed in early 2014. A great pool area provides a lot of relaxation potential while all the ultra-spacious rooms are fully refurbished, with the latest flatscreen TVs, wi-fi, coffee-makers and either a king bed or two doubles. The junior suites add a living area, larger TV, kitchenette and dining table. The lobby features welcome cookies (a Doubletree speciality) and a combination lounge-bar and restaurant that is especially inviting at night. There is a modern fitness centre and business centre with computers. Bistro 436 features the trademark Wake-up Doubletree breakfast buffet, plus lunch and dinner. Extremely disabled-friendly, it used to be the Crowne Plaza but benefits more from the Hilton brand name (407 856 0100, **www.OrlandoAirport.DoubleTree.com**).

SELF-CATERING

Once you venture beyond pure hotel territory, your choice varies through a range of 'Resorts' to timeshares, villa communities, studios and condos, all of which are essentially self-catering (although some still offer restaurants and other hotel-type amenities). They all tend to be further away from the parks, but they represent a flexible option, especially for larger groups.

Ritz Carlton

Self-catering definitions

To avoid confusion, here's the correct terminology for self-catering accommodation (but check with the operator for the exact type if it's not clear):

Villa: Detached vacation home, usually with its own screened-in pool, in self-contained residential communities.

Townhome: 2-storey terraced-style house, rarely with its own pool; found in many Resorts.

Condo: 1, 2 or 3-bed apartment-style unit, usually in a low-rise block but sometimes 10 or more storeys.

Studio: 1-room accommodation unit that includes kitchen facilities.

Resort: Collection of condos (or townhomes) built around central features like pools, recreation facilities and (sometimes) a restaurant/bar or 2.

Barefoot'n Resort: This boutique timeshare of 82 1- and 2-bed condos is nicely tucked away next to Old Town in Kissimmee. There's a main pool, kids' pool, whirlpool, children's play area, volleyball and barbecue stations. (407 856 7190, **www.barefootn.com**).

BRITTIP

If you prefer a tranquil Lake View room at the Blue Heron Beach Resort, you can still get a view of Disney's fireworks at night from the outdoor corridor/terrace on each floor.

Blue Heron Beach Resort: A superb complex of two high-rise towers (16 and 21 storeys) on Apopka-Vineland Rd (Highway 535) in Lake Buena Vista, this features 283 beautifully furnished 1 and 2-bed condos, all with 2 bathrooms, a balcony and fully equipped kitchen, including washer-dryer. There are bunk beds for kids in the spacious 1 and 2-bed units, which can comfortably sleep 6–8. All master bedrooms also include a whirlpool tub in the en-suite bathrooms. All have balconies overlooking scenic Lake Bryan while the 2-bed Deluxe

suites have a second balcony with a Disney firework view.

There is a superb lido deck, with a large freeform pool, kids' pool, hot tub and Tiki Bar, plus a boardwalk fronting the lake and watersports (jet-skis and water-skiing, for an extra charge), with the 36-hole Hawaiian Rumble mini-golf course outside (for a fee). There is a video games room and 2 fitness centres, but no restaurant (but plenty nearby, including a CiCi's Pizza, Starbucks, Dunkin' Donuts and Subway). As a self-catering resort, daily housekeeping is available only for a charge, but there is a free daily shuttle to Disney and SeaWorld and for $12/person to Universal (407 387 2200, **www.blueheronbeachresort.com**).

BRITBONUS

Get 7 nights for the price of 5 or 14 for the price of 10 at the Blue Heron Beach Resort. Book online or call 407 387 2914, and use booking code 'BRIT75'. Valid until 18 Dec 2016; not valid with any other discount or coupon. Based on availability and certain blackout dates.

Floridays Resort Orlando: One of the smartest of the area's condo-hotels, this is well situated in a quieter part of I-Drive, but close to Orlando Premium Outlets and with a free shuttle service to the parks. The full site consists of six condo blocks (each with 72 rooms), 2 pools (including the elaborate main zero-depth entry pool and great water-play area), a pool bar and grill, fitness centre, stylish Welcome Center, kids' activity centre and games room, a small grocery store, plus concierge services, business centre and meeting facilities. The 2 and 3-bed grand suites are beautifully furnished, sleep 6–10, and have either a balcony or patio. Living rooms include large plasma TVs, high-speed internet, games console and stereos, while each bedroom also has a TV. There's also a delivery service (8am–10pm) from the Café & Marketplace, which serves Starbucks coffee. All rooms are wheelchair-accessible and some are adapted for the disabled with roll-in showers (1866 994 6321, **www.floridaysresortorlando.com**).

Fountains Resort: This high-quality timeshare, available to the public when not fully booked, is on the quieter stretch of I-Drive (south of SeaWorld). It has superb 2-bed, 2-bath condos, with full kitchens, plus a huge pool area with waterslides and poolside bar, all in a beautiful tropical environment, complete with the large Clubhouse boasting a games room, kids' activity centre, bar, coffee lounge and spa services (1800 456 0009, **www.bluegreenrentals.com**).

Hapimag Orlando Resort: An unusual combination of vacation home and resort, this is the Swiss timeshare operator's only US property (but with NO timeshare solicitation), inside the mature Lake Berkley villa community in Kissimmee (almost behind Medieval Times). It encompasses a self-contained circle of 2 and 3-bed town-homes, grouped around a busy clubhouse with pool, volleyball court, small fitness centre and gift shop.

BRITBONUS
Stay 6 nights in a row at Hapimag Orlando Resort and the 7th is free. Special rates for 1, 2 and 3-bed units of $97, $108 & $129/night low season and $120, $130 & $151/night high season; and $140, $151 & $172 at Christmas (plus tax). All offers valid to end 2016; subject to availability; some blackout dates apply. Just quote code 'Brit Guide 2016' when booking on 407 390 9083 or email www.orlando@hapimag.com.

Floridays Resort Orlando

There are also a handful of fully furnished 4-bed villas elsewhere in the community, which has its own clubhouse and smart pool area with kids' pool, plus another gym, games room and internet room. There is then a scenic walkway around the lake, with two white-sand beaches (407 390 9083, **www.orlando-hapimag.com**).

Lake Buena Vista Resort Village & Spa: This stylish condo-hotel features five tower blocks of 2, 3 and 4-bed condos, next to Lake Buena Vista Factory Stores on Highway 535. The impressive facilities include a superb freeform swimming pool, with pirate play-ship, a second quiet pool, a state-of-the-art fitness centre, video games room and Kids' Club. There is a convenience store and gift shop, a Pizza Hut Express, specialist bar-restaurant Frankie Farrell's Irish Pub & Grille and Lani's Luau, the pool-side bar and grill, as well as a shuttle to the main theme parks (as part of the resort fee). The rooms (all with full kitchens, Jacuzzi tubs, digital TVs and internet) are comfortable and stylish, with the 4-bed condos very spacious. Housekeeping services are available either daily or weekly for a charge, while the resort fee covers a grocery delivery and dry-cleaning service, although all rooms come with their own washer and dryer. The blissful Reflections Spa & Salon offers some wonderfully relaxing treatments (407 597 0214, **www.lbvorlandoresort.com**).

BRITTIP
Visiting Lake Buena Vista Factory Stores? Relieve aching limbs by popping next door to the Resort Village for the Reflections Spa for a soothing pedicure, massage or other spa treatment (407 597 1695).

Liki Tiki Village: On the western fringe of Highway 192, this timeshare set-up often has good-value condos to rent on a weekly basis. It features spacious 1, 2 and 3-bed condos, all with well-equipped kitchens (including coffee and ice-makers), while the 64acre/26ha complex boasts 2 pools, a mini water park, tennis courts, paddle boats, mini-golf, pool-bar and grill, free wi-fi and kids activity programmes Mon–Fri (407 239 5000, **www.likitiki.com**).

Mystic Dunes Resort & Golf Club: This holiday ownership property is tucked away in a quiet corner of Kissimmee and offers hotel-type rentals, often at terrific rates. It features just about every facility, including 4 resort pools, water-slide and water-play area, plus an impressive array of 1, 2 and 3-bed condos that sleep up to 12, a championship-quality golf course and mini-golf (1877 747 4747, **www.mystic-dunes-resort.com**).

Orange Lake Resort: This vast resort on west Highway 192 offers a mixture of well-furnished 1, 2 and 3-bed condos (NB: Orange Lake refers to them as 'villas' but they are definitely apartment-type) and studios that sleep 4–12, plus golf, watersports and cinema. Then there are kids' activities, exercise classes, tennis, racquetball, mini-golf and a Marketplace of general store, pizzeria and golf shop. The amazing River Island water park has a lazy river, 2 zero-depth entry pools, mini-golf, whirlpool tubs, waterfalls and a clubhouse, arcade and fitness centre, while the Water's Edge Beach Club adds a restaurant, pool bar, cabañas, stage and gift shop, plus an Olympic-size pool with beach-style entry. There is also a Publix supermarket, and this resort gets consistently good feedback, if occasionally a bit strong on the timeshare sales (407 239 0000, **http://experienceorangelake.com/**).

BRITBONUS

Holiday Inn Club Vacations @ Orange Lake Resort are offering a Resort Credit package for use in the resort for things like pizza, lazy-river tube rentals, play passes or a family dinner. Enjoy villa-style accommodation and receive a $50 resort credit when you stay two nights, plus an extra $25 credit for each additional night. Call 1866 892 5890 and mention IKREC or book online at **www.hiclubvacations.com**.

Palisades Resort: A real find out at the rural western end of Highway 192 in Kissimmee, this smart condo-hotel features spacious 1, 2 and 3-bed condos that sleep 4–8, with fully equipped kitchens, including washer-dryers, and private balconies. Each unit offers generous living and dining areas, 2 bathrooms (master bed with oversized bath) and flatscreen TVs. The tropical lido deck has a large outdoor pool in lush surroundings, plus there is a sauna, fitness centre, small shop for sundries and free wi-fi. It is close enough to benefit from the shops and restaurants along Highway 192 (and be just 10mins from Disney), but still be tranquil. There is no bar or restaurant, but a Publix supermarket is only 5mins away (321 250 3030, **www.palisadesvacations.com**).

Regal Oaks at Old Town: This mix of stylish town-homes, from 3-bed, 2-bath units to grand 4-bed, 3-bath villas, follows the successful blueprint of accommodations set around an elaborate clubhouse, with fabulous water features (zero-entry pool, waterslide, whirlpool and lazy river), Tiki Bar and other facilities. Right next to all the fun and shopping of Old Town in Kissimmee, it offers terrific value (407 997 1000, **www.regaloaks.com**).

Regal Palms Resort & Spa: Next door to the serene Highlands Reserve villa community on Highway 27 is this mix of 3 and 4-bed townhomes and 4 and 5-bed villas set around a beautiful Clubhouse that includes a mini water park (with lazy river and waterslides), pools, Jacuzzis and extensive sun terraces, as well as free

Palisades Resort

wi-fi. The sister resort to Regal Oaks, it also features a pub that shows live UK sports, a business centre, gym and gift shop/grocery store, plus an indulgent Spa & Health Club (407 965 3887, **www.regalpalmsorlando.com**).

Reunion Resort & Club: One of the most extensive resorts, this will be of interest to golfers who appreciate the chance to stay where they play. On Highway 532 in Kissimmee (just off exit 58 of I-4 south of Disney), this 'community' boasts a vast line-up of condos, town-homes and luxury villas set around 3 superb golf courses (designed by Arnold Palmer, Tom Watson and Jack Nicklaus). The choice is deluxe, featuring 1, 2 and 3-bed condos (many with stunning golf course views); a range of private homes, from modest 3-beds to mansion-style 8-beds; a stylish golf clubhouse with excellent bar and restaurant; a full-service spa, with a superb array of treatments; the scenic Seven Eagles pool, complete with The Cove bar and grill, Jacuzzis, fitness room and kids' play centre; floodlit tennis courts; an amazing water park consisting of lazy river, slides, pools, waterfalls and interactive kids' area; and miles of biking and hiking trails. High-rise condo, the Reunion Grande, features 82 luxurious 1 and 2-bed suites, magnificent Italian cuisine restaurant Forte, a state-of-the-art fitness facility and ultra-chic rooftop pool and bar, Eleven, offering American fare, cocktails and panoramic views. It all comes with concierge service and even private in-room dining that marks this out as one of Florida's most upmarket

Reunion Resort and Club

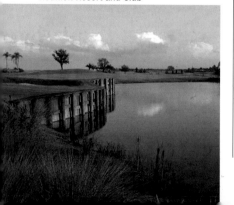

resorts. Only those staying here or members can play on the courses, but the scale of the resort is superb (407 662 1000, **www.reunionresort.com**). Reunion is also home to the state-of-the-art ANNIKA Academy, created under the direction of top golfer Annika Sorenstam.

> **BRITTIP**
>
> At both Sheraton Vistana properties, for a nominal fee, you can arrange to have your condo pre-stocked with food and laundry products.

Sheraton Vistana Resort: This sprawling family-friendly timeshare set-up in Lake Buena Vista, close to Walt Disney World, is a mature development of roomy 1 and 2-bed/2-bath condos (sleeping 4–8; again, they are called 'villas' but are definitely apartment-type) with fully equipped kitchens and magnificent resort facilities. Furnishings and facilities are all modern, with multiple TVs, DVD player and a screened-in private patio or balcony, plus large washer-dryers, which all serves to underline the great self-catering value of this type of accommodation. There are 7 giant pools, 13 floodlit tennis courts, smart Marketplace deli (with Starbucks coffee), casual café/restaurant and 3 pool bars, plus massage treatments. There is complimentary scheduled transport to select Disney parks and lots of family-orientated activities, including poolside parties, crafts and more (407 239 3100, **www.sheraton.com/vistanaresort**).

> **BRITBONUS**
>
> Reserve a 1 or 2-bed villa at the Sheraton Vistana Resort or Sheraton Vistana Villages and receive $50 in resort credit. You must reserve directly by calling toll free: 0203 564 6335 ask for Rate Code BGRC50 and stay a minimum of 5 consecutive nights. You must also show your *Brit Guide* upon check in to receive the credit; no cash value/no refund on unused portion. The credit is not available through third party reservations.

Rental Accommodation

© Steve Munns 2015

Sheraton Vistana Villages: The sister property, located on I-Drive south of SeaWorld, this upmarket family resort offers spacious 1 and 2-bed/ 2-bath condos with fully equipped kitchen or kitchenette, dining area, washer-dryer and more, all in 5 and 6-storey blocks and all set around scenic landscaping or pool areas. The beautiful lobby opens on to a stunning pool boasting waterfalls, Jacuzzis and children's play areas, while there's the smart Flagler Station Bar & Grill for breakfast, lunch and dinner and a mini-market/deli. Less than 6ml/10km from Disney, guests enjoy extensive amenities like complimentary scheduled transport to select Disney parks, daily activities, 3 pool areas (some with slides and water-play areas), a state-of-the-art fitness centres, games rooms, basketball and tennis courts and a grocery store, plus there is a big Publix supermarket and the Premium Outlets shops nearby (407 238 5000, **www.sheraton.com/vistanavillages**).

BRITTIP

As the Sheraton Vistana resorts are both timeshare properties, you may well be asked if you'd like to take their property tour, but there is no pressure to sign up or hard-sell if you do.

Summer Bay Resort: Out on west Highway 192 is a mix of hotel (The Crown Club Inn), and 1 and 2-bed condos sleeping 4–8. The 700 rooms spread over 400acres/162ha are all smart, while the facilities include outdoor heated pools and kiddie pools, pool bars, an elaborate children's water-play area, mini-golf,

Villas at Grand Cypress

clubhouse with volleyball, tennis, basketball, shuffleboard and fitness room, video arcade, gift shop and snack bar. The family Adventure Park activity centre features zip-lines, bungee jumping, wipe-out style Inflatable Zone, rock-climbing wall, bumper boats and picnic area. The lake provides jet-skis, paddleboats, waterskiing and more, plus daily kids' activities and organised sports. Even those in The Crown Club Inn (which has its own pool and breakfast area) benefit from the clubhouse facilities, while next door is a Denny's diner and Publix supermarket, plus another 12 restaurants within a few miles (1855 849 2205, **www.summerbayresort.com**).

Tuscana: This Mediterranean-inspired condo-resort bordering the Champions Gate golf courses offers 288 elegant, oversized 2 and 3-bed condos, each with 2 full baths, balcony, fully equipped kitchen, washer and dryer. The excellent clubhouse boasts the Tuscana Tavern bar and grill, poolside sports bar, kiddie pool, cabanas, fitness centre and spa treatments (407 787 4800, **www.tuscanaresort.com**).

Villas at Grand Cypress: Arguably Orlando's top golf resort, this is also a wonderfully upmarket option in a beautiful setting behind Walt Disney World, making it among the most convenient villa options in Orlando. It offers 146 single-room club suites and 1, 2, 3 and 4-bed condo-style villas, all recently renovated and furnished in luxury style, with fully equipped kitchens and patios or balconies. There is a blissful Villa Pool, with poolside saunas and bar, bike rentals and 2 restaurants (The Club sports bar and fine-dining Nine18 overlooking the North-South golf course), the Golf Academy for personalised lessons, plus 24hr room service. Villa guests also get full use of all the amenities of the nearby Hyatt Regency Grand Cypress (p82), a 5min ride on the free on-demand shuttle service. Literally just minutes from Disney, the villas' relaxed ambiance and lush surroundings make you feel as if you're a million miles away (407 239 4700, **www.grandcypress.com**).

Vista Cay Resort: This recent timeshare development offers some of the most extensive facilities in the I-Drive/Universal Boulevard area (behind the Convention Center North). Convenient for all the attractions but away from the main bustle, it has beautiful accommodations (2 and 3-bed executive suites and 3-bed town-homes), plus a large clubhouse with a pool set in lush, tropical landscaping; whirlpool spa, kids' pool and basketball court; games room, theatre, business centre and fitness centre. Apartments range from 1,500ft^2/140m^2 to 2,300ft^2/214m^2 and offer fully equipped kitchens, large HD TVs with DVD players and Sony PlayStations, dining rooms, master bedrooms (with separate Roman tubs and showers), private balconies and free wi-fi (407 996 4647, **www.vistacayholidays.com**).

Windsor Palms Resort: Just off west Highway 192 in Kissimmee, this popular gated community has a mix of 2-bed condos, 2 and 3-bed town-homes, and 3–6-bed private pool villas. Amenities include a large clubhouse and fitness centre, tennis courts, an Olympic-sized pool, a kiddie pool and spa, basketball, billiard room, volleyball court, video arcade, playground and a 58-seat cinema showing recent films. The (slightly newer) sister resort Windsor Hills on Old Lake Wilson Road offers the same accommodation choice and impressive amenities, like its huge lagoon-style pool with waterslide and state-of-the-art fitness centre and is even closer to the Disney parks (407 396 0642, **www.globalresorthomes.com**).

HOLIDAY HOMES

This is in many ways the biggest area of accommodation in Orlando, especially for UK visitors, as there has been a huge development of holiday homes, or villas, in the last 20 years. They provide a valuable way for large families and groups to stay together – the largest can sleep 16 – and cut costs by self-catering. The homes – individual or groups in residential communities – are sometimes gated, and most have a private pool, while some have access to communal facilities like pools and recreation areas. They are always equipped with microwaves, multiple TVs and washer-dryers. Some are classed as 'executive', and this usually means more facilities (games rooms, barbecues, Jacuzzis, etc.) rather than an increase in size. A hire car is usually essential, but the savings can be significant. Prices can be as low as $450/week off-peak, but expect to pay at least $1,600/week for a 5 or 6-bed villa in high season. A word of warning: once you've experienced pool-at-home life, you may never go back to a hotel!

If you book independently, there are several key questions to ask. Do you need to go to an office some way away to pick up the keys or is there a combination lockbox at the house? Is there a local contact if anything goes wrong (most owners do not live in Florida) and is the property maintained by a local company? Does it offer a secure bonding for your booking, and is it a member of a reputable organisation, such as the Better Business Bureau of Central Florida? In winter, is the pool heated, and what is the charge for heating? Finally, is it as close to Disney as it says (some can be in Polk County, 30mins away, but still insist they are 'just minutes from Disney')?

There are more than 25,000 villas on offer, spread across Kissimmee and out in Polk and Lake Counties to the west and south-west of Disney, most in well-established developments (such as Highlands Reserve). Be

Windsor Palms Resort

aware that homes within a particular community can still vary in quality depending on the care and attention of owners and/or property managers, hence just being in, say, stylish Cumbrian Lakes, is not a guarantee of executive quality. You can rent direct from the owners or a property management company that will look after multiple villas. For direct villa rentals, check sites like **www.vrbo. com**, **www.lastminutevillas.net** and **www. thedibb.co.uk**, plus Owner Direct, who offer villas worldwide and have a well-vetted Orlando selection of more than 500 properties and are often good for last-minute deals at **http://www. ownerdirect.com/accommodation/disney-world-central-florida**.

BRITTIP

For home-cooking comforts, the British-owned The Proper Pie Company on Ridge Center Drive (on Highway 27 in Davenport, just south of the junction with I-4) offers a fab array of home-made pies and pasties, plus British groceries, from Walkers crisps to Sharwood's chutney. See more at **www. properpiecompany.com** or call 863 438 2705. They also offer fresh fish 'n' chips every Friday!

Ironically, there are increasing numbers of terrace-style townhomes (so developers can fit in more); for a 'detached' house, ask for a 'single family home'. The bottom line is you must do your homework, shop around as you would for any big purchase, and check with organisations like the Central

Advantage Vacation Homes

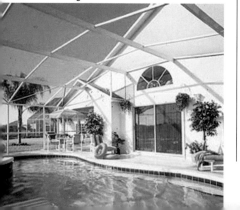

Pool heat

To heat or not to heat is a common question for those renting a villa in Florida. Typically, pools will NOT need heating from mid-May to mid-Oct, when the sun is usually enough to heat them to at least 80°F/26.6°C. But, at other times of the year, and especially Nov–Apr, you will almost certainly need pool heating. Systems can be electric or (propane) gas, with the latter usually more expensive. Expect to pay anywhere from $25–30/day for electric heating and $30–40/day for gas. It can also take up to 48hrs to heat a pool to 85°F/28°C during the colder months and, if the air temperature drops below 55°F/13°C, the heating may not function fully to more than 15°F above air temperature. Pool heat will also be in addition to the villa rental cost.

Florida Vacation Rental Managers Association. This is the only acknowledged umbrella organisation for the holiday home business and helps to provide a level of credibility.

The following companies all pass the *Brit Guide* credibility test.

Advantage Vacation Homes: In the villa rental business for more than 20 years and one of the largest companies, few of its 2–6 bed homes (the majority on west Highway 192 and Highway 27 in Clermont and Davenport) are more than 10yrs old, while many are 4–5 years at most. It also manages a range of condos (in the Bahama Bay and Venetian Bay resorts) and town-homes. It offers 24-hour management, with courteous and efficient staff at its office just off west Highway 192 (plus an attraction ticket service), open 9am–10pm daily. Its holiday homes are rated Silver, Gold or Platinum, with the difference measured in the extras rather than size (larger-screen or plasma TVs, tiled floors rather than carpeting, a Jacuzzi or games room, etc), though some of the more exclusive villas might be situated on a golf community or have tennis courts (0871 711 9531 in the UK, 407 396 2262 in the US, **www.advantage vacationhomes.com**).

Alexander Holiday Homes: Family-owned Alexander manages more than 200 properties in Kissimmee, from standard 2, 3 and 4-bed condos to luxury 7-bed executive homes sleeping 14, all with pools and immaculately furnished, within 15–20mins of Disney, including some of the closest to the parks. This company was the first of its kind in Orlando (in 1981) and still offers a personable, efficient service. It was only the third management company to earn the distinguished AAA (American Automobile Association) 3 Diamond rating, as well as being fully accredited with the official Walt Disney World Vacation Rental Home Connection (where homes are inspected quarterly) and definitely gets our approval. It shows prices in UK and US currency and even offers an airport meet-and-greet service to ensure you get to your home, as well as arrival grocery packages, barbecue rentals, scooter and wheelchair hire. Its informative website provides photo tours of all its homes, useful blogs and other features (0871 711 5371 in the UK, 1800 621 7888 in the US, **www.floridasunshine.com**).

All Star Vacation Homes: Offering an expanding collection of vacation rentals, from 2-bed condos to massive 14-bed homes, all located within 6 miles of Disney, All Star homes feature some luxurious amenities, including pools with spas, multiple master suites, game rooms and home theatres. (321 281 4966, **www.AllStarVacationHomes.com**).

Florida Leisure Vacation Homes: Another company we know well and can recommend, it is British-owned and pays great attention to detail, with an upscale, almost boutique approach, which sets them apart from the larger, more mass-market operators. With 100 homes (3–7 beds) in the Kissimmee area, most just a few years old and many in the highly regarded Cumbrian Lakes community, it prides itself on a personal touch (even down to providing personal chef, massage

Discover Vacation Homes

and concierge services) and offers some of the biggest and newest properties, as well as a full online booking system. Many are in the Executive range, with the fullest array of amenities in addition to their private, screened pools, and often in gated communities. All properties have lockboxes, so you don't need to visit the management office to check in. You can see all its homes online (in extended photo and video) plus lots of local info, while its new testimonial sections provide first-hand feedback. The sister website www.floridaleisure.com includes a regular blog, free newsletter and other useful features. Also accredited to the Walt Disney World Vacation Rental Home Connection, its office is handily placed on east Highway 192 in Kissimmee, just past Osceola Square Mall (407 870 1600; **www.floridaleisurevacationhomes.com**).

Loyalty Homes: For a luxury touch, all these homes (2–6 bedrooms) are no more than 4ml/6.5km from Disney and all offer the true 'executive' style, with the likes of digital door locks (so no key collection required), cable TV and many with games rooms. The website offers video tours, too (call 0121 468 0016 in the UK or 1877 274 2904 in the US, **www.loyaltyusa.com**).

Park Square Homes: This is actually operated by the home builder, hence it features the complete resort communities of Encantada and Bella Vida, both just off Highway 192 in Kissimmee, with a series of well-built and beautifully furnished 3 and 4-bed

Loyalty Homes

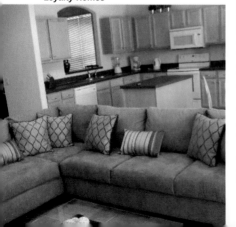

town-homes, plus larger villas at Bella Vida, all with private pools. The 2 tropically styled resorts benefit from a central clubhouse, with a large pool, cyber café, exercise room and arcade, while Encantada also has a lakefront gazebo and Romy's Bistro wine bar (1866 930 0444/1800 520 8070, **www.bvrmanagement.com** and **www.encantadaorlandoresort.com**).

Premier Vacation Homes: A good range of spacious properties with 2–7 bedrooms, sleeping up to 14, in secure residential communities within a 15–20min drive of Disney. All are privately owned and have been furnished as holiday homes, with screened pools, 2 TVs, fully equipped kitchens (including dishwasher, washer-dryer, microwave and coffee-maker), at least one king or queen bed and free local phone calls. Maid service can be added for a fee. The Luxury homes (2–4 beds) are standard accommodation, while Executive homes (3–6 beds) are bigger, with an extra TV, VCR and barbecue, and there's also a town-home and condo choice (407 396 2401, **www.premiervacationhomesorlando.com**).

BRITTIP
You'll find Marmite, Ribena, McVities and a handful of other British groceries at Publix and Winn-Dixie supermarkets, and most Wal-Marts (International aisle).

Villa Direct: Another major Orlando specialist, and one of the biggest, with an extensive range of properties in the area, from 2-bed condos to luxury 7-bed villas, and a good user-friendly website, plus an excellent range of guest services, including arrival groceries, a personalised concierge service, car hire and even mobility equipment rental. Also on the Walt Disney World Vacation Rental Home Connection, its welcome centre is easily found on west Highway 192 in Kissimmee while the head office is close by in Celebration, just off I-4 (407 409 8038, **www.villadirect.com**).

OK, that's enough accommodation advice. Now it's on to the parks…

5 The Theme Parks: Disney's Fab Four

or Spending the Day with Mickey and the Gang

Now let's prepare you for the main business of any visit to Orlando: Walt Disney World. This is the heart of all the excitement and fun in store (along with the other big theme parks of Universal Orlando, SeaWorld and Busch Gardens).

In our opinion, two weeks are barely enough to see all of Disney on its own, let alone the other theme parks and smaller scale attractions, so you start to realise the awesome scope of an Orlando holiday!

BRITTIP
Before you leave home, photocopy the back of your park passes and your passport. If your tickets are lost during your holiday you will need the information on the back of each ticket to have them replaced. A copy of your passport will suffice as photo ID in the parks, or if your passport becomes lost.

Buying your tickets in advance is highly advisable (it saves time and is often better value), but work out your requirements first – you won't get full use out of, say, a 14-day Ultimate ticket AND an Orlando Flex Ticket Plus in just a fortnight. Try to use your credit card for all purchases – there is built-in additional security (for our list of recommended ticket outlets; p10).

Discount options: You will find a welter of discount coupons for many

of the smaller attractions in tourist publications distributed in Orlando (or from your hotel Guest Services desk – it's often worth asking), while the tour operators' welcome meetings usually have special offers and tickets for the latest excursions.

BRITTIP
I-Drive has the only genuine Official Visitor Center. Offers of 'free' Disney tickets usually mean timeshare firms, which also claim to have 'official' visitor centres.

Official Visitor Center: Check this out for discounts at 8723 International Drive in the Gala Center on the corner of Austrian Row (407 363 5872, **www.visitorlando.com/uk**). The Universal Attractions booths at several shopping malls sometimes have good deals (3 days for the price of 2, 2-for-1 drinks etc.). It IS possible to bag free tickets by attending timeshare presentations but they can easily take half a day of hard-sell out of your precious holiday.

The entrance to the Magic Kingdom

Timeshare: If you DO want to check out timeshare options, look first at Disney Vacation Club for the guarantee of memorable holidays. A tour (for which you will be picked up) will take around 3 hours, and you'll receive a small parting gift (dining coupon, etc). Call 1800 500 3990 or visit **http://disneyvacationclub.disney. go.com**.

BRITTIP

Smoking is not permitted in the restaurants or in the parks, apart from in a handful of designated areas. Check park maps for their exact locations.

Ratings

Our unique rating system splits attractions into thrill rides and scenic rides, earning T or A ratings out of 5.

• **TTTTT** is as exciting as they get and, along with **AAAAA** is unmissable. These will have the longest queues, so you should plan your visit around them.

• **TTTT** or **AAAA** should be high on your 'must do' list.

• **TTT** or **AAA** should be seen if you have time.

• **TT** is worth seeing only if there is no queue, **AA** is likely to be twee and missable.

• **T** or **A** is not worth your time

Some rides have height restrictions and are not advisable for people with back, neck or heart problems or for expectant mothers. Where this is the case we say, for example, '**R**: 3ft 6in/106cm'. Height restrictions (strictly enforced) are based on

Star Wars weekend at Disney's Hollywood Studios

the average 5-year-old being 3ft 6in/106cm tall, those aged 6 being 3ft 9in/114cm and 9s being 4ft 4in/132cm. You can also refer to our Height Restriction Guide, p27.

My Magic+

In 2013, Disney introduced this high-tech system of guest interaction, designed to personalise and enhance many aspects of park visits. Free for Disney resort guests, but available for offsite guests to buy, the MagicBand wristband acts as an all-purpose ticket, optional payment card, FastPass+ and PhotoPass card, and allows various special features, like pre-booking FastPass+ and cataloguing your dining reservations. It works in conjunction with My Disney Experience (see below), where you fill in your trip details (as much or as little as you prefer) and use the mobile app for all the latest info, such as queuing wait times and dining reservations. MagicBands also come in different colours and styles and are designed to be collectible. Intended to be 'transformational' in the way we enjoy the parks, it can be difficult to navigate, somewhat glitchy, and the need to pre-book 60 days in advance for onsite guests or 30 days in advance for offsite guests makes people feel they need to plan to the nth degree (thus, actually taking some of the fun out of the whole experience), so check out the website carefully before you sign up. All Disney parks have free Wi-Fi, too. You do not have to sign up for My Magic+, but you will not be able to access all of the perks available if you choose not to participate in the programme.

Disney has an App for that

Get all the latest park updates on your mobile phone or tablet, including park hours, wait times, menus, reservations, attraction info and FastPass+ reminders, plus games and more. Available free for iPhone and Android, from **https://disneyworld. disney.go.com/plan/mobile-apps/**

Character dining

Having a meal with Mickey and Co is one of the great Disney experiences – even without children – and is often the best way to meet your favourite characters without a wait. Make reservations up to 180 days in advance by phoning 407 WDW DINE (939 3463), calling at any Guest Services desk in a hotel, or by touching *88 on any Disney pay phone or 55 from a Disney resort room phone.

Some meals are difficult to get. Breakfast at **Cinderella's Royal Table** or **Be Our Guest** at the Magic Kingdom usually sell out within minutes of the 180-day window being open. **Chef Mickey's** and the **Princess Storybook** meals also go quickly. If you cannot book in advance, try calling the day you'd like to dine or, as a last resort, show up to see if there have been any cancellations. You must check in at the podium 10mins prior to your time and you will be given the next available table. Some characters don't enter the restaurant so, if they are in the lobby, you'll want to meet them before you are seated. Dining is all-you-can-eat, served buffet, pre-plated or family-style. Inside the restaurant, characters circulate among the tables giving attention to each group (particularly when children are holding the camera!). Character interaction is top-notch, especially if you dine off-hours when the restaurant is quieter. Be sure to bring your autograph book, a fat pen or marker (easier for the characters to hold) and an extra digital card. Some characters are huge, and children may be put off by them. If you aren't sure how they'll react, see how they are with the characters in the park before booking. **Price range:** breakfast $22–58 adults, $13–35 children; lunch $32–60 and $18–38; dinner $41–73 and $21–43 (NB: beware the peak season price rises – Disney has resorted to raising its rates in high season and even at weekends, and some of those children's prices for lunch and dinner are outrageously high, in our opinion.).

My Disney Experience

This is the online platform that allows guests to make dining reservations, schedule FastPass+ times, add Photopass, and link their Disney resort reservations and theme park admission. You must have a My Disney Experience account and valid theme park admission to schedule FastPass+ selections in advance. Using the online system, guests are also able to connect Friends and Family in-park experiences. To create an account, visit **https://disneyworld. disney.go.com/plan/my-disney-experience**

Disney's FastPass+

Most of the attractions have this essential aid to queuing (free with admission), which allows you to roam while you wait for your scheduled ride time. How it works: Onsite guests can schedule three FP+ times in one park per day, up to 60 days in advance (30 days for offsite guests) using the online My Disney Experience system or Disney's free mobile app. Guests may also schedule FP+ times at in-park kiosks. Buy your park passes, create a My Disney Experience

account, and follow instructions for scheduling FP+, booking dining reservations, and adding 'reminders'. You can then link your experiences to others in your party, make changes as needed, and customise your account with additional options. However, each guest can choose their own FP+ selections if they would like to experience attractions separately.

BRITTIP
Disney's new FastPass+ system makes it essential to schedule your ride times well in advance. It is likely FP+ times for the major attractions will be gone if you leave it until the day, especially in peak seasons.

Additional FP+ times can be scheduled in the park, once you have used your 3 FP+ allotments. Park Hopping is allowed, but you must use your initial 3 FP+ in one park only, so we advise making it the park in which you begin your day. If you cancel your existing FP+ times (via Guest Services or Disney's mobile app), you cannot schedule new FP+ times until the last time scheduled for your cancelled FP+ has expired.

Character Dining: the meals

MAGIC KINGDOM: Crystal Palace for breakfast, lunch or dinner with Winnie the Pooh and Co – especially good for smaller children; and **Cinderella's Royal Table** for the (expensive) Once Upon A Breakfast, with Cinderella and her Princess Friends; Fairytale Lunch (Cinderella and Friends); and Dreams Come True Dinner (Fairy Godmother only). Breakfast (off-peak) is $53 adults, $35 children; lunch $57 and $36; dinner $67 and $41. Credit card payment in full is required to book and you WILL be charged if you cancel less than 24hrs in advance (photo package and gratuity included, additional photos for a fee).

EPCOT: Garden Grill for lunch or dinner with Farmer Mickey, Pluto, Chip and Dale; Princess Storybook Dining at **Restaurant Akershus** (Norway) for breakfast, lunch and dinner; an alternative to Cinderella's, with some of Belle, Jasmine, Snow White, Mulan, Aurora (Sleeping Beauty) and Mary Poppins. Breakfast $42 adults, $25 children; lunch $43 and $26; dinner $48 and $26. Credit card needed to book; full charge applied for cancelling less than 24hrs in advance.

DISNEY'S HOLLYWOOD STUDIOS: Hollywood & Vine for breakfast or lunch with the Play 'n Dine pals, including Doc McStuffins, Sophia the First, Handy Manny, and Jake and the Neverland Pirates.

DISNEY'S ANIMAL KINGDOM: Donald's Dining Safari Breakfast and Lunch at **Tusker House** with Donald, Goofy, Pluto and sometimes Daisy and Mickey.

DISNEY RESORTS:

Beach Club Resort: At Cape May Café, breakfast with Goofy, Minnie and Donald.

Contemporary Resort: At Chef Mickey's, breakfast or dinner with Mickey, Minnie, Goofy, Pluto, Donald Duck – peak times book up quickly.

Fort Wilderness: At Mickey's Backyard Barbecue, $59 (adults) and $33 (3–9s), games, storytelling, live entertainment, music and dancing with Mickey, Minnie and Co; chicken, hot dogs, burgers, ribs, beer, wine, iced tea and lemonade (select nights only, 6.30pm, Mar–Dec).

Four Seasons Hotel: At Ravello, Thurs and Sat (plus Tues during peak seasons) breakfast with Goofy and pals.

Grand Floridian: At 1900 Park Fare, breakfast with Alice, Mary Poppins and Mad Hatter; dinner with Cinderella, Anastasia, Drizella, Lady Tremaine and, sometimes, Prince Charming – book early. Wonderland Tea Party 2–3pm Mon–Fri, 4–12s only, $52.19, meal, activities and storytelling with Alice and friends ($10 no-show). Perfectly Princess Tea Party with Princess Aurora, 10.30am–12pm (not Tues and Sat), 3–11 with an adult, $290 for 1 adult with 1 child age 3–11. Meal (tea, cake, finger sandwiches), singalong, story time, Disney Girl doll, bracelet, necklace, rose, tiara, and scrapbook page.

Polynesian Resort: At 'Ohana, breakfast with Lilo, Stitch, Pluto and Mickey.

Walt Disney World Swan: At Garden Grove Café, Mon–Fri, Timon and Rafiki; Sat and Sun breakfast with Goofy and Pluto.

Epcot and Disney's Hollywood Studios both use a tiered system for FastPass+. Tier 1 indicates attractions from which you must choose only one; Tier 2 allows you to schedule two attractions. Watch for FP+ (choose two) and FP+1 (choose one) indications in our attraction descriptions. Guests who opt out of My Disney Experience can still use their regular ticket for park admission.

Onsite guests will each receive a MagicBand (waterproof wrist band with RFID chip) in place of an admission ticket, which can also be used to open their room door, charge purchases (if desired), allow FP+ access, and more. MagicBands will not be shipped overseas, but will be presented upon check-in. However, FP+ can still be booked in advance with a confirmation code. Offsite guests can buy MagicBands to replace their admission tickets, if they like.

 BRITTIP

Disney was experimenting with the idea of offering four initial FP+ times in 2015. Watch for this possibility in 2016.

With young ones

All Disney's parks offer pushchair ('stroller') hire, and you can save money by buying a multi-day rental at your first park. Children of ALL ages seem to get a big thrill from collecting autographs from the various Disney characters, and most shops sell autograph books. Parents wanting healthier dining options for kids in Disney parks and resorts should look on the menu for Mickey Check, a standard for more nutritious meals. You should find at least one choice at every counter service and full-service restaurant (**www.disneymickeycheck. com**). The Power Pack lunch at some counter service options also serves up healthier snacks in neatly boxed packs, containing things like juice, yoghurt, string cheese, Goldfish crackers, carrots and apple sauce.

PhotoPass

This unique and worthwhile scheme is available in all Disney's parks and (occasionally) in Disney Springs. Disney photographers take photos of guests that are linked to an online account via a card you receive with your first photo or via Memory Maker (see below). There is no charge for a card or for viewing them online, but there is if you want to download and print them. Photos can be enhanced with Disney characters and special effects, while there are 'magical' photos where photographers ask guests to pose in a fun way and Tinker Bell (or Stitch, or Simba or Mickey) balloons will appear in the frame. Guests have 30 days after the photos are taken to decide if they want to buy at **www.mydisneyphotopass.com**, or you can view at a PhotoPass studio (one at each park, plus Disney Springs Marketplace, the Grand Floridian and Polynesian resorts). Images can even be put on to mugs, mouse pads, calendars, etc. **Memory Maker** is a comprehensive digital package, linked to a My Disney Experience account (p101), that collects every PhotoPass photo, on-ride photo and character dining photo for $199 ($169 if bought 3 days in advance). This way you just swipe your card, or Magic

Band, with every photographer to add that photo. Ride photos are added automatically with a Band.

Cast Members

Disney employees are called Cast Members or CMs (never 'staff' as they all play a role in the entertainment) and they're renowned for their helpful, cheerful style, always willing to assist, offer advice or just chat. So, if you've had exceptional service or a CM has gone out of their way to help, let Disney know as it values such feedback (plus CMs get credit for it). Call in at Guest Relations or City Hall.

Child Swap

If you have children under a height restriction, you needn't queue twice. At the queue entrance, tell the operator you want to do a Child Swap. Then Mum can ride while Dad looks after junior in a quiet area and, on her return, Dad can have his go. At some attractions you may get a Child Swap ticket while you wait.

Park security

Visitors with bags must go through a security check before the turnstiles. This is a fairly cursory (but compulsory) inspection but there is a separate lane for those without bags. When you put your ticket (or MagicBand) across the electronic terminal, you must give a finger scan (which stops others from using your ticket). NB: **Selfie sticks** were banned from all Disney parks in 2015 and must be left in your car.

The Muppet Fountain at Disney's Hollywood Studios

Magic Kingdom Park

The starting point for any visit, the Magic Kingdom – the original development that sparked the Orlando tourist boom in 1971 – best embodies the genuine enchantment Disney bestows on its visitors. Similar to the Disneyland Park at Disneyland Paris and Disneyland California, outside those, it has no equal as a captivating family day out. A few rides are the same as those in Paris or LA, but there are key differences, notably on Pirates of the Caribbean, Big Thunder Mountain Railroad, Haunted Mansion and especially Space Mountain. And, even if a couple of attractions are closed for refurbishment, you won't be short of things to do! Here's our guide through a typical day, including the rides, shows and places to eat; how to park, how to avoid the worst of the crowds – and how much you should expect to pay.

The Magic Kingdom takes up just 107acres/43ha of Disney's near 31,000acres/12,555ha but attracts almost as many as the rest put together. It has six 'lands', like slices of a cake, centred on Florida's most famous landmark, Cinderella Castle. More than 40 attractions are packed into the park, plus shops and restaurants. It's easy to get overwhelmed, especially as it gets so busy (even the fast-food restaurants have long queues in high season), so plan around what most takes your fancy, but do look out for the interactive queues at some rides, including Big Thunder Mountain Railroad, Haunted Mansion, Peter Pan's Flight, Space Mountain, Little Mermaid, Winnie the Pooh and Seven Dwarfs Mine Train.

Magic Kingdom Park at a glance

Location	Off World Drive, Walt Disney World		
Size	107 acres/43ha in 6 'lands'		
Hours	9am–7pm off peak; 9am–10pm President's Day (see Brit Tip, p18), spring school holidays; 8am–11pm or midnight high season (Easter, summer holidays, Thanksgiving and Christmas)		
Admission	Under-3s free; 3–9 $99 (1–day base ticket), $295 (5–day Magic Your Way), £274 (14–day Ultimate); adult (10+) $105, $315, £299. Prices do not include tax.		
Parking	$17		
Lockers	To the right of the main entrance $12 ($5 deposit)		
Pushchairs	$15 and $31 (underneath Main Street Train Station); length-of-stay, $91/week, $130 10 days single, $189/$270 double		
Wheelchairs	$12 or $70 ($20 deposit refunded) underneath Main Street Train Station		
Top attractions	Splash Mountain, Space Mountain, Seven Dwarfs' Mine Train, Big Thunder Mountain Railroad, Pirates of the Caribbean, most rides in Fantasyland		
Don't miss	Festival of Fantasy Parade, Main Street Electrical Parade or SpectroMagic (certain nights) and Wishes fireworks (most nights)		
Hidden costs	**Meals**	Burger, chips and coke $12.69 3-course dinner (Tony's Town Square) $33.99 Kids' counter service meal $5.49–5.99	
	T-shirts	$21.95–36.95 Kids $19.95–34.95	
	Souvenirs	$1.35–32,500	
	Sundries	Chalk colour portraits $17.95, or Silhouettes $8, with oval frame $15.95	

Location

The Magic Kingdom is situated at the innermost end of Walt Disney World, with its entrance Toll Plaza three-quarters of the way along World Drive, the main entrance off Highway 192. World Drive runs north–south, while the Interstate 4 (I-4) entrance, Epcot Drive, runs east–west. Unless you are staying at a Disney resort or an Annual Pass holder, you must pay the $17 parking fee at the Toll Plaza to bring you into the massive car park.

BRITTIP
For the smoothest entry by road from Highway 192, take Seralago Boulevard (opposite the Seralago Hotel & Suites next to Old Town), turn left on to a non-toll stretch of Osceola Parkway and follow the signs to your chosen park. On West 192, turn off on Sherberth Road, go north to the first traffic lights and turn right, then pick up the Disney signs.

The majority arrive from 9.30–11.30am, so the car parks are busiest then – another good reason to get here EARLY. If you can't make it by 9am during peak periods, you might want to wait until after 1pm, or even later when the park is open as late as midnight. Remember to note exactly where you park: there are two sides to the 'parking lot', Heroes and Villains, with subsections for Woody, Simba, Rapunzel, Aladdin, Peter Pan and Mulan, then Ursula, Jafar, Zurg, Hook, Scar and Cruella. Be sure to note which side, section and number you're in – Ursula row 94, Hook 77, etc – as many hire cars look the same!

BRITTIP
Take a photo of the Section and Row number on your camera or phone so you know where you've parked.

A motorised tram takes you from the car park to the Transportation and Ticket Center. Unless you already have your ticket (which will save valuable time), you visit the ticket booths here. Then, to get to the Magic Kingdom itself, the monorail (straight ahead) is quicker if there isn't a queue, otherwise bear left and take a slower ferryboat. If you're staying at a Disney hotel, the resort buses deliver you almost to the front door (or the monorail or boat will if you are staying at one of the Magic Kingdom resorts). Finally, the Magic Kingdom is the only 'dry' park – that is, there's NO alcohol on sale (except at the Be Our Guest restaurant at dinner).

Main Street USA

Right, we've finally reached the park itself… but not quite. Hopefully, you've arrived early and are among the leading hordes aiming to swarm through the entrance. The published opening time may say 9am, but the gates can open up to 45mins earlier.

Main Street is the first of the six 'lands' and, at opening time, there is an informal Welcome Parade, with costumed singers and dancers, and the Character Train arrives at Main Street Station to bring a variety of characters for a meet-and-greet in Town Square (get those autograph books ready!). A family is then chosen at random to sprinkle some 'pixie dust' to open the park officially for the day. On your right is **Town Square Theater**, the special place to meet Magician Mickey and Tinker Bell.

BRITTIP
Meet Mickey without the long wait by scheduling your time in advance using the FastPass+ system.

The daily Flag Retreat ceremony

On your left is **City Hall**, where you can pick up a park map and daily schedule (if you haven't already got one en route) and book restaurants (highly advisable at peak periods). You can also find out where and when the characters will appear. Ahead is **Town Square**, where you can take a one-way ride on a horse-drawn bus or fire engine. The Street itself houses the park's best shopping (check out the massive **Emporium**), and the **Walt Disney World Railroad** AAA, a Western-themed steam train that circles the park and is one of the better attractions when queues are long elsewhere (though Town Square station is often the busiest).

Sorcerers of the Magic Kingdom: This interactive game takes place throughout the park (except Tomorrowland) but has its HQ at The Firehouse in Town Square (with a second station at Ye Olde Christmas Shoppe in Liberty Square), where guests sign up for a role in saving the Magic Kingdom from various Disney villains. With the help of role-playing cards, players visit special 'portals' (cleverly disguised video screens) to discover their task and use their cards to help Merlin defeat the villains. It is designed for all ages and has the ability to get quite complex for serious role-playing gamers, using multiple cards to cast 'spells' that ward off evil-doers and save the day in each land. Like an interactive scavenger hunt, it is aimed at children but adults get a kick out of it, too. AAA½

Town Square Theater

Dining: The Italian-style **Tony's Town Square Restaurant** serves lunch and dinner; **The Plaza Restaurant** offers salads and sandwiches (lunch and dinner); and **The Crystal Palace** (breakfast $26.99 adult, $14.99 ages 3–9; lunch $31.99 & $17.99; dinner $41.99 & $19.99) is buffet-style food with Winnie the Pooh and Co. Quick bites can be bought from **Casey's Corner** (hot dogs, chips and soft drinks), **Main Street Bakery** (a Starbucks coffee shop, also serving wonderful pastries), **Main Street Confectionery** (chocolate and sweets) and the **Plaza Ice Cream Parlor**. Disney characters also appear periodically throughout the Square.

Info: Check the **Guest Information Board** at the top of Main Street (on the left) as it gives waiting times for all the attractions. The **Baby Center** (for nursing mothers) is also at the top of Main Street, to the left next to Crystal Palace, along with the **First Aid** station.

BRITTIP

Can't find Mickey and Co? This is often one of the main laments of those who arrive unprepared. At City Hall they can tell you where to find the characters. In fact, City Hall is your best friend for many queries, from baby facilities to meal bookings (but there are NO baby facilities at City Hall itself). Character meet-and-greets are also shown on all park maps with a 'Mickey glove' icon.

Beating the queues: Unless you are late, skip Main Street and head for the end of the street to the real entrance to the park, where you await the official opening hour. Adopt one of three tactics, each aimed at doing some of the most popular rides before the queues build up (wait times of 2 hours for Splash Mountain are not unknown). 1: If you fancy the 5-star, log-flume ride Splash Mountain, keep left in front of the Crystal Palace with the majority, who will head for the same place. 2: If you have young children who can't wait to try the Fantasyland rides, stay in the middle and pass around the Castle. 3: If

ADVENTURELAND
1 Swiss Family Treehouse
2 Jungle Cruise
3 Magic Carpets of Aladdin
4 The Enchanted Tiki Room
5 Pirates of the Caribbean

FRONTIERLAND
6 Splash Mountain
7 Big Thunder Mountain Railroad
8 County Bear Jamboree
9 Raft to Tom Sawyer Island

LIBERTY SQUARE
10 Liberty Tree Tavern
11 Liberty Square Riverboat
12 The Haunted Mansion
13 The Hall of Presidents

FANTASYLAND
14 'It's a Small World'
15 Prince Charming Regal Carrousel
16 Mad Tea Party
17 The Many Adventures of Winnie The Pooh
18 Princess Fairytale Hall
19 Dumbo The Flying Elephant
20 Mickey's PhilharMagic
21 The Barnstormer starring The Great Goofini
22 Casey Jr Splash 'n' Soak Station

23 Peter Pan's Flight
24 Castle Forecourt Stage
25 Cinderella's Royal Table
26 Brave – Meet Merida
27 Enchanted Tales with Belle
28 Be Our Guest Restaurant
29 Under The Sea – Journey of the Little Mermaid
30 Ariel's Grotto
31 Seven Dwarfs Mine Train

TOMORROWLAND
32 Space Mountain
33 Tomorrowland Indy Speedway
34 Walt Disney's Carousel of Progress
35 Astro Orbiter
36 Tomorrowland Transit Authority
37 Stitch's Great Escape!
38 Buzz Lightyear's Space Ranger Spin
39 Monsters Inc. Laugh Floor
40 Club 626 Dance Party

TRANSPORT
41 Walt Disney World Railroad Stations
42 Boat Dock
43 Monorail Station
44 Bus Station

Parade Route

MAGIC KINGDOM PARK

the thrills of indoor roller-coaster Space Mountain appeal, move to the right by The Plaza Restaurant and go straight into Tomorrowland. Now you'll be in pole position for the initial rush (and it will be a rush; take care with children).

BRITTIP
The Move It! Shake It! Dance & Play It! Street Party begins in Town Square, but the real action takes place around the Castle Hub. Stake out a spot in advance if you want an up-front view.

Other entertainment: Watch out for the **Move It! Shake It! Dance & Play It! Street Party** up to three times daily, from Town Square, along Main Street, ending up in the Hub area as Disney characters, stilt walkers and dancers lead guests in a high-energy street party. The **Main Street Trolley Show** happens 3–4 times a day, with the horse-drawn trolley arriving on Main Street for a 6min song-and-dance interlude. The fun barbershop quartet the **Dapper Dans** and brass band **Main Street Philharmonic** (who also play in Storybook Circus) add lively musical interludes throughout the day, as does **Casey's Corner Pianist**, and don't miss the **Glass Blowing Demonstrations** at Crystal Arts Shop. There is also a daily **Flag Retreat** at 5pm each day, with a military veteran helping the Security Colour Guard to bring down the national flag.

Splash Mountain

Adventureland

If you head left (going clockwise round the park), you enter Adventureland. If you're going to Splash Mountain first, pass the Swiss Family Treehouse on your left and bear right through an archway (with toilets) into Frontierland, where you turn left and Splash Mountain is ahead. Stopping in Adventureland, these are the attractions.

Swiss Family Treehouse: This imitation banyan tree is a clever replica of the treehouse from Disney's 1960 film *Swiss Family Robinson*. It's a walk-through attraction where the queues (rarely long) move steadily if not quickly, providing a neat glimpse of the ultimate tree house. AA

BRITTIP
The special deal on autograph book and fat pen combo can be cheaper than buying them separately.

Jungle Cruise: It's not so much the scenic, geographically suspect boat ride (where the Nile suddenly becomes the Amazon) that is so amusing here as the patter of your boat's captain, who spins a non-stop yarn about your adventure. Great detail but long queues, so visit either early morning (opens 10am) or late afternoon (evening queues are shortest, but you'll miss some of the detail in the dark). AAAA FP+

Pirates of the Caribbean: One of Disney's most impressive attractions that involves Walt's pioneering work in audio-animatronics, life-size figures that move, talk and, in this instance, lay siege to a Caribbean island! Your eight minute underground boat ride visits a typical pirate adventure and the world of Captain Jack Sparrow and nemesis Captain Barbossa as they search for buried treasure. It's terrific family fun (though perhaps a bit spooky for young children, with one small drop in the dark). Queues are longest from late morning to mid-afternoon. AAAAA (**TTTT** under-10s) FP+

The Enchanted Tiki Room: A classic bird-laden, South Seas audio-animatronic show starring various parrots, macaws and other tropical feathered friends – plus the angry Tiki Gods! Queues are rare and it is air-conditioned. AA

Magic Carpets of Aladdin: In an Agrabah-themed area, this ride spins you up, down and around as you try to dodge the spitting camel! Your 'flying carpet' tilts as well as levitates, simple stuff geared for younger children (virtually identical to the Magic Carpets of Agrabah in the Paris). TT (**TTTT** under-5s), FP+.

A Pirate's Adventure: Treasure of the Seven Seas: A variation on the Sorcerers of the Magic Kingdom interactive card game (p106), with the chance to help Captain Jack Sparrow fight off his foes and locate different treasures around Adventureland, using a pirate map and magic talisman. Visit the special kiosk through the archway past the Pirates ride to get started. AAA½

Other entertainment: Outside the Pirates of the Caribbean ride (and a must for young swashbucklers), **Captain Jack Sparrow's Pirate Tutorial** runs several times daily. Captain Jack and sidekick Mack invite youngsters to join them in sword fights and treasure hunting, ending with the Pirate Oath to become honorary buccaneers. **Disney characters** also turn up at the Adventureland entrance (Peter Pan)

and next to the Magic Carpets ride (characters from Aladdin).

Shopping: The best shopping is in **Pirates Bazaar**, where **Pirates League** (9am–4pm) offers a chance for young swashbucklers to transform into fully-fledged pirates, with four packages ($29.95–49.95) that include a variety of accessories, including earrings, eye patches, swords, coin necklaces and temporary tattoos (photos sold separately).

Dining: The new **Skipper Canteen** was due to open in late 2015, offering fun 'adventure dining' themed like the Jungle Cruise and in 8 different dining rooms, with counter-service lunch and full-service dinner. It features 'World Famous Jungle Cuisine', served by Jungle Cruise skippers. **Aloha Isle** adds signature Dole Whips and **Sunshine Tree Terrace** has ice cream and drinks), and **Tortuga Tavern** (open seasonally) features tacos, empanadas and salads.

Frontierland
This Western-themed area is one of the busiest and is best avoided from late morning to late afternoon.

Splash Mountain: Based on the 1946 classic Disney cartoon *Song of the South*, this is a watery journey into the world of Brer Rabbit, Brer Fox and Brer Bear. The first part is all jolly cartoon scenery and fun with the main characters and a couple of minor swoops in your eight-

Pirates of the Caribbean

passenger log boat. The conclusion, a five-storey plummet at 45° into a mist-shrouded pool, seems like you are falling off the edge of the world! A huge adrenalin rush, but busy almost all day (try it first thing or during one of the parades to avoid the longest queues). Some riders also get VERY wet! R: 3ft 4in/101cm. TTTT FP+

Big Thunder Mountain Railroad: When Disney does a roller-coaster it will be one of the classiest, and here it is – a runaway mine train that swoops, tilts and plunges through a mock abandoned mine filled with clever scenery. You have to ride it at least twice to appreciate all the detail, but again queues are heavy, so go first thing (after Splash Mountain) or late in the day. R: 3ft 4in/101cm. TTTT FP+

Country Bear Jamboree: Now here's a novelty: a 16min musical revue presented by audio-animatronic bears! It's great family fun with plenty of novel touches (watch for the talking moose head). Crowds are rare, so it's a good one when it's busy elsewhere. AAA

Frontierland Shootin' Arcade: The park's single attraction that costs extra ($1 for 35 shots), as you take aim at a series of animated targets. T

Tom Sawyer Island: Take a raft over to an overgrown playground of mysterious caves, grottos and mazes, rope bridges and Fort Sam Clemens,

Big Thunder Mountain

where you can fire air guns at passing boats (opens 9am). A good choice in early afternoon when the queues are long elsewhere. Aunt Polly's Dockside Inn allows time off your feet, but the only drinks here are from a vending machine. TT

Other entertainment: The comic trio of The Notorious Banjo Brothers and Bob, and Hoedown Happening with the Country Bears provide musical interludes. Disney characters can be found by the Liberty Square bridge (*Princess and The Frog*) and next to Splash Mountain (*Toy Story*).

Shopping: Frontierland shops sell cowboy hats, guns and badges, as well as Native American and Mexican crafts. Look out for the nicely themed **Briar Patch** and **Prairie Outpost** for interesting gifts.

Dining: Try **Pecos Bill Tall Tale Inn & Café** (salads, sandwiches and burgers), **Golden Oak Outpost** (chicken nuggets, chicken sandwich, desserts, flatbread, fries and drinks) or **Turkey Leg Cart** (massive, smoke-grilled turkey legs).

Liberty Square

The clockwise tour brings you next to a homage to post-independence America. A lot of the historical content will go over the heads of British visitors, but it still has some great attractions.

Liberty Square Riverboat: Cruise America's 'rivers' on an authentic paddle steamer, be menaced by river pirates and thrill to the stories of How the West Was Won (10am–8pm). This is also good at busier times of the day, especially early afternoon. AAA

The Haunted Mansion: A clever delve into the world of Master Gracey's ghostly bride that is neither too scary for most kids nor too twee for adults. Not so much a thrill ride as a scenic adventure. Watch out for the fun touch at the end when the 'hitch-hiking ghosts' might drop in! Longish queues for much of the day, however, so try to visit late on. AAAA (TTTT under-6s), FP+

The Hall of Presidents: This is the attraction likely to mean least to us, a two-part show that is a film about the Constitution and an audio-animatronic parade of all 44 US presidents (opens 9am). Technically impressive, but it may bore young 'uns (though it is air-conditioned). AAA

Shopping: Look for **Ye Olde Christmas Shoppe** and the fabulous Haunted Mansion-themed **Memento Mori**.

Dining: Eating options are the full-service **Liberty Tree Tavern** (hearty soups, salads, and traditional dishes like roast turkey, carved beef and smoked ham), **Columbia Harbor House** (counter-service fried chicken or fish and some good soups, salads and sandwiches, notably for vegetarians) and **Sleepy Hollow** (a picnic area serving snacks, fruit and drinks).

Fantasyland

Leaving Liberty Square, you come into the park's spiritual heart, the area with which young children are most enchanted. The attractions, in three separate areas, are designed with kids in mind, but the shops are quite sophisticated and the Tangled 'village' (basically just a courtyard with restrooms) is wonderfully scenic.

'It's a Small World': This could almost be Disney's theme ride, a family boat trip around the world, each represented by 100s of dancing, singing audio-animatronic dolls in delightful set-piece pageants. If it sounds twee, it actually creates a surprisingly striking effect, accompanied by an annoyingly catchy theme song that young children adore. Crowds peak in early afternoon. AAAA FP+

BRITTIP

Watch for enhanced allergy-friendly menus in the parks. If you're still not sure, a chef is always happy to speak to you directly. Just ask!

Peter Pan's Flight: This may seem a rather tame ride but is another Walt classic and a big hit with kids. Its novel effect of flying with Peter Pan is good fun and there's a lot of clever detail as your ship sails to Neverland. The addition of an interactive queue in 2015 helps pass the time in air-conditioned comfort. AAA (AAAAA under-6s) FP+

Mickey's PhilharMagic: This fun-tastic 10-min 3-D film show has a host of special effects as Donald tries to conduct the Enchanted Orchestra – to comic effect. It features a 150ft/46m wide screen to immerse

The Main Street station of the Walt Disney World Railroad

guests in the 3-D world of *Beauty and the Beast, The Little Mermaid, The Lion King, Peter Pan* and *Aladdin*, with hapless Donald surviving a string of adventures before Mickey brings him back to earth. The lavish theatre, artistic animation, special effects (you can 'smell' the food!) and all-round family entertainment make for a hugely enjoyable attraction. There is no scare factor (though the sudden plunge into darkness at one point and noise of the 'orchestra' can spook young children), while you'll be enchanted when Tinker Bell seems to fly out of the screen in front of you. AAAAA FP+

Prince Charming Regal Carrousel: The Fantasyland centrepiece shouldn't need any more explanation other than it is a vintage carousel that kids love. Long queues for much of the day, though. T (TTT under-5s)

The Many Adventures of Winnie the Pooh: Building on the timeless popularity of Pooh, Piglet and Co, this family ride offers a musical jaunt through Hundred Acre Wood with some clever effects (get ready to 'bounce' with Tigger!) and an original soundtrack. Wait times are made easier by hands-on elements throughout the queue. AAA (AAAAA under-5s) FP+

Mad Tea Party: The kids will insist you take them in these spinning, oversized tea cups that have their own 'steering wheel' to add to the whirling effect. Actually, they're just a heavily disguised fairground ride. Again, go early or expect crowds. Characters from Alice in Wonderland also visit periodically. TT (TTTT under-5s) FP+

Princess Fairytale Hall: This elaborate 'royal' residence features a dramatic castle gallery area where visitors gather before they are summoned for an audience with some of the Disney princesses (choose from either Cinderella and one of Rapunzel, Aurora, Snow White, Jasmine or Tiana) or mega-popular *Frozen* duo Anna and Elsa. AAA (AAAAA under 13 girls!) FP+

BRITTIP
Anna and Elsa draw HUGE queues, while their FP+ option also books up well in advance.

Enchanted Tales with Belle: A wonderfully clever Beauty and the Beast character show, here you visit Maurice's Workshop, nestled in the shadow of the Beast's Castle, and guests are transported via a magic mirror to the Castle Library for a memorable interactive story-time with Belle and Lumière. AAAA FP+

Under the Sea – Journey of the Little Mermaid: Be a part of her world as you journey under the sea with Ariel in this lovely, gentle ride aboard stylised clamshells, past colourful

Dumbo the Flying Elephant

scenes from the movie. Ariel, Prince Eric, Flounder, Scuttle, Sebastian, King Triton and evil sea witch Ursula all make appearances, while favourite songs add to this charming adventure (with some surprising special effects!) that is sure to have a happy ending. AAAA. FP+

Ariel's Grotto: Next door is the elaborate setting for a meeting with the Little Mermaid. FP+

The Seven Dwarfs Mine Train: It's 'off to work we go' with the Seven Dwarfs in this charming dark ride through a gem-laden mine. Your trip begins as a family-friendly outdoor coaster, enters the mine for a gentle (and slightly dark) journey past the Dwarfs as they dig, dig, dig, then plunges back outside as a coaster again for the grand finale. The mine cars have the swaying motion of a real mine train (though you actually feel very little sway, as the banked turns overpower it), all the charm of the fairytale from which it originates, and the sense of being 'in the film' is completely convincing. Watch for the surprise visitor at the end! TTT (TTTTT under 10s) FP+

Storybook Circus

The former Toontown area of Fantasyland is now themed for the classic film Dumbo and features more family-friendly fun.

Dumbo the Flying Elephant: Young children cannot pass this one by and, thankfully, with all-new dual Dumbos (doubling the capacity of the old ride) and a clever interactive, air-conditioned queue, parents should be less put off by the prospect of a long wait. It's a 2min ride on the back of a swooping, circling, flying elephant, and its charm is undeniable. TT (TTTT under-5s) FP+

The Barnstormer: Get ready for a junior-sized coaster in the company of classic stunt pilot The Great Goofini as this surprisingly whizzy (but very short) ride takes some sharp twists and turns in best circus style. R: 2ft 11in/89cm. TTT (TTTTT 4–8s) FP+

Casey Jr Splash 'n' Soak Station: The Circus Train has pulled into a siding – and sprung a leak! In fact, it is just a cleverly disguised water-play area, with all manner of squirting fountains, pop-jets and dumping buckets guaranteed to get the kids good and wet – so don't forget swimsuits OR a change of clothes. AAAA (under 10s)

Pete's Silly Sideshow: More themed fun under the Big Top as Minnie, Goofy, Donald and Daisy (in circus-style character) line up for a clever meet-and-greet. AAA

Other entertainment: The superb **Dream Along With Mickey** show is staged up to six times a day on the Castle Forecourt Stage, a 20min fantasy featuring Donald, Mickey, Minnie, Goofy and various Princesses and their Princes. Peter Pan and Wendy join the battle against Maleficent and Captain Hook to help Donald remember the power of believing in your dreams (AAA). In Storybook Circus, look out for featured clown **Wowzer**, while the **Giggle Gang** are a whole posse of wacky clown fun. **The Royal Majesty Makers** are another group of strolling performers, in the Castle Courtyard, with a variety of regal routines (including the revived Sword in the Stone ceremony) and the **Fairy Godmother** meets with children periodically at Cinderella's Fountain. Other **character experiences** include Meet Merida from the 2012 film *Brave*

Big Top Treats inside Big Top Souvenirs

in the Fairytale Garden, Pooh and friends next to the Winnie the Pooh ride, Gaston outside Gaston's Tavern and Alice in Wonderland characters next to the Mad Tea Party.

Shopping: Shop at **Castle Couture**, the excellent **Sir Mickey's**, **Fantasy Faire**, **Pooh's Thotful Shop**, **Big Top Souvenirs** and **Bonjour! Village Gifts**. There is also an outlet of the **Bibbidi Bobbidi Boutique** here (the other is in Downtown Disney), where over 3-year-old 'little princesses' can choose from four makeover styles ($60–195) the Coach, Crown, Courtyard and Castle packages with three different hairstyles, Disney Diva, Pop Princess and Fairytale Princess, from 8am–8pm (reservations highly recommended on 407 939 7895).

Dining: Eating opportunities are at **Pinocchio Village Haus** (flatbreads, salads, chicken nuggets, pizza and pasta), **Storybook Treats** (ice-cream), the **Cheshire Cafe** (iced drinks and juices), **Big Top Treats** (sweets and pastries) and **Friar's Nook** (hot dogs, chicken baskets, crisps and frozen drinks). **Cinderella's Royal Table** is a fine setting for the popular character breakfast, lunch and dinner with various Disney princesses (Cinderella greets guests in the foyer only). The majestic hall, waitresses in costume and well-presented food – salads, seafood, roast beef, prime rib and chicken – provide a memorable experience. Be aware you pay in FULL by credit card when you book, there is a $10 per person fee if you cancel more than 24 hours in advance, and, if you cancel less than 24 hours in advance, there is NO refund. More fun

Pinocchio Village Haus restaurant

(and better value) is the spectacular **Be Our Guest** restaurant inside the Beast's Castle, a unique 550-seat counter service lunch option by day and a full service restaurant by night, with the addition of beer and wine (the only Magic Kingdom venue that serves alcohol). Divided into three themed sections – the Ballroom (complete with snow on the outdoor terrace!), Rose Gallery and the dark and moody West Wing – it is one of Disney's most ornate dining options. At lunch ($4.99–13.99 adults, $6.99–8.49 kids meal; 10.30am–2.30pm), choose from soups, salads, quiche, sandwiches and braised pork, while dinner ($29.69–50.69/$8.99–10.99; 4pm–10pm or park closing during low season) offers a richer range of French-influenced dishes like Ratatouille and thyme-scented Pork Rack Chop. Dinner books up FAST, though, so try to get a reservation at the 180-day mark (407 939 3463 or online at **www.disneyworld.com**; credit card deposit required, $10 charged per person if you don't turn up), lunch is also by reservation, though walk-ins may find availability before 11am. **Gaston's Tavern** is a counter-service offering featuring an eclectic menu of snacks, drinks, pastries and their signature Roasted Pork Shank, again with some great Beauty and the Beast theming.

BRITTIP

Two people can easily make a meal of the massive Pork Shank at Gaston's Tavern while the unique Le Fou's Brew (frozen apple juice with marshmallow) is a must-try drink!

Tomorrowland

This area's cartoon-like space-age styling, novel shops and varied rides provide guaranteed all-round appeal.

Space Mountain: One of the three most popular attractions, its reputation is deserved. Launching from Starport 75, this is a high-thrills, tight-turning roller-coaster, completely in the dark save for occasional flashes as you whiz through the galaxy. Don't do this on a full stomach! The only way to beat the crowds is to go either first thing, late in the day or during one of the parades (or, of course, get a FastPass+). Ride photos are available for $18.95 or $14.95 for digital delivery. R: 3ft 8in/111cm. TTTTT FP+

Tomorrowland Arcade: Children are also likely to gravitate here as you exit.

Tomorrowland Speedway: Despite the long queues, this is a rather tame ride on supposed race tracks that just putt-putts along on rails with little real steering required (children must be 4ft 4in/132cm to drive alone). T (TTTT under-6s) FP+

Astro Orbiter: A jazzed-up version of Dumbo in Fantasyland, this ride is a bit faster and higher and features rockets. Long, slow-moving queues are a reason to give this a miss unless you have young children. TT (TTTT under-10s).

Walt Disney's Carousel of Progress: This will surprise, entertain and amuse. It is a journey through 20th-century technology with audio-animatronics in a revolving theatre that reveals different periods in history. Its 22min duration is rarely threatened by crowds (open only at peak periods). AAA

Tomorrowland Transit Authority: A neat 'future transport system', this offers an elevated view of the area, including a glimpse inside Space Mountain, in electro-magnetic cars. Short queues. AAA (TTT under-8s)

Stitch's Great Escape: This 15min experience receives mixed reviews – some like it for the audio-animatronic prequel to Disney's Lilo & Stitch, with visitors being recruited into the madcap Galactic Federation prison service (where Stitch's arrival causes havoc), while others find it puzzling and rather lame. Young children can also be scared by the complete darkness at times. There are two pre-show areas before recruits are ushered into the sit-down chamber (with shoulder restraints) where Stitch is let loose to bounce, dribble and even belch over the unwary audience. R: 3ft 2in/101cm. AA

Buzz Lightyear's Space Ranger Spin: Ride into action against evil Emperor Zurg and the robot army – and shoot them with laser cannons! A sure-fire family winner, especially as you get to keep score. TTT (TTTTT under-8s) FP+

Monsters Inc Laugh Floor: With 'live' animation, special effects and high-tech voice links, guests can meet and match wits with the likes of Mike, Sulley and Roz from Monsters Inc and be entertained by their patter and amusing antics. Billy Boil opens the show, introducing various comedians (including two-headed jokester Sam-n-Ella), with the aim of capturing the audience's laughter. Guest interaction is an integral part of the show. Watch the screen – you may be featured! AAA FP+

Other entertainment: *Incredibles* fans should enjoy the **INCREDIBLES Super Dance Party** (high season) with the chance to bop along with a live DJ and various *Incredibles* characters, led by Mr & Mrs Incredible, while **Disney characters** are often on hand by the **Carousel of Progress**, notably Buzz Lightyear.

Shopping: Highlights are provided by **Mickey's Star Traders** and **Merchant of Venus**.

Dining: For food, try **Cosmic Ray's Starlight Café** (good burgers, chicken, sandwiches, soups, salads and flavoured iced coffees), **Auntie Gravity's Galactic Goodies** (ice-cream, smoothies and juices), the **Lunching Pad** (speciality hot-dogs, pretzels and frozen drinks) or **Tomorrowland Terrace** (burgers,

Gaston's Tavern

pasta, sandwiches and salads; open seasonally).

Having come full circle you're now back at Main Street USA and it's best to return here in the afternoon to avoid the crowds and enjoy the impressive shops.

Disney parades

If there is one thing Disney knows how to do well, it's a parade. Coupled with its range of special seasonal events, there is always much more to look forward to than just the rides.

BRITTIP

To watch a parade, sit on the left side of Main Street USA (facing the Castle) to stay in the shade if it's hot, or stake out a spot in the Hub or Frontierland. People start staking out the best spots an HOUR in advance.

Festival of Fantasy Parade: A dazzling and unmissable pageant of creative floats, costumes, dancers and music. The seven featured floats include The Little Mermaid, Disney Princesses (including *Frozen*'s Anna and Elsa), Maleficent (with a magnificent fire-breathing steam-punk style dragon!), Tangled and Peter Pan and friends, plus a special balloon-like vehicle for Mickey and Minnie. The energetic dancers, stilt-walkers and rather

Festival of Fantasy Parade

menacing outfits of the 'Raven' men all combine for added dramatic effect. AAAAA FP+ for special viewing area.

Main Street Electrical Parade: A mind-boggling light and sound festival full of glitter and razzamatazz, with the Disney characters at the centre of a multitude of fibre-optic effect floats. It is classic Disney, using the latest technology to enhance the heart-tugging impact of this sparkling cavalcade. Tinker Bell leads the procession, with each successive float a visual and audio treat, and the music a real highlight. A brilliant end to any Magic Kingdom day. When the park is open late (during peak periods and weekends), there are two showings per night, and the second is less crowded. AAAAA

Main Street USA closes 30mins after the rest of the park, so you can avoid the inevitable mad rush for the car parks by lingering here to shop or enjoy an ice-cream.

Celebrate The Magic!: This stunning nightly state-of-the-art projection show uses the Cinderella Castle as its backdrop, incorporating a series of animated special effects and video that make the castle seem to come alive, transforming again and again with a sequence of Disney characters and films in dynamic colour. Look for the castle's turrets to become 'rockets,' or a vine-covered fantasy or a fiery inferno as the imagery weaves visual trick after trick in a kaleidoscopic pattern that will leave your eyeballs breathless! AAAA

Wishes: Most nights also finish with this spectacular fireworks show over the Castle. With a clever soundtrack narrated by Jiminy Cricket and featuring memorable moments from various Disney classics, it is magnificently choreographed and culminates in a sequence of dazzling pyrotechnic explosions (many designed especially for this show). Starting with an appearance by Tinker Bell (from the Castle's top turret), it continues for 12mins of typical Disney emotional appeal; the perfect pixie-dust farewell to a memorable day. AAAAA FP+

MAGIC KINGDOM PARK with children

Here is a rough guide to the attractions that appeal to different age groups (height restrictions have been taken into account):

Under-5s
Buzz Lightyear's Space Ranger Spin, Prince Charming Regal Carousel, Country Bear Jamboree, Dream Along With Mickey, Dumbo the Flying Elephant, Enchanted Tales With Belle, The Enchanted Tiki Room, 'It's a Small World', Jungle Cruise, Liberty Square Riverboat, Main Street Vehicles, Many Adventures of Winnie the Pooh, Mickey's PhilharMagic, Monsters Inc Laugh Floor, Move It! Shake It! Dance & Play It! Street Party, Peter Pan's Flight, Tomorrowland Speedway (with a parent), Tomorrowland Transit Authority, Walt Disney World Railroad, Main Street Electrical Parade, Journey of the Little Mermaid, Festival of Fantasy Parade.

5–8s
Astro Orbiter, The Barnstormer, Big Thunder Mountain Railroad, Buzz Lightyear's Space Ranger Spin, Country Bear Jamboree, Dream Along With Mickey, Enchanted Tales With Belle, The Enchanted Tiki Room, Haunted Mansion, Jungle Cruise, Liberty Square Riverboat, Mad Tea Party, Magic Carpets of Aladdin, Many Adventures of Winnie the Pooh, Mickey's PhilharMagic, Monsters Inc Laugh Floor, Move It! Shake It! Dance & Play It! Street Party, Pirates of the Caribbean, Seven Dwarfs Mine Train Ride, Space Mountain (with parental discretion), Splash Mountain, Stitch's Great Escape!, Swiss Family Treehouse, Tom Sawyer Island, Tomorrowland Speedway (with a parent), Tomorrowland Transit Authority, Walt Disney World Railroad, Walt Disney's Carousel of Progress, Main Street Electrical Parade, Journey of the Little Mermaid, Festival of Fantasy Parade.

9–12s
Astro Orbiter, Big Thunder Mountain Railroad, Buzz Lightyear's Space Ranger Spin, Country Bear Jamboree, The Haunted Mansion, Mad Tea Party, Mickey's PhilharMagic, Monsters Inc. Laugh Floor, Move It! Shake It! Dance & Play It! Street Party, Pirates of the Caribbean, Seven Dwarfs Mine Train Ride, Space Mountain, Splash Mountain, Stitch's Great Escape!, Tomorrowland Indy Speedway (without a parent), Main Street Electrical Parade, Journey of the Little Mermaid, Festival of Fantasy Parade, Wishes fireworks.

Over-12s
Astro Orbiter, Big Thunder Mountain Railroad, Buzz Lightyear's Space Ranger Spin, Haunted Mansion, Mad Tea Party, Mickey's PhilharMagic, Move It! Shake It! Dance & Play It! Street Party, Pirates of the Caribbean, Festival of Fantasy parade, Seven Dwarfs Mine Train, Space Mountain, Splash Mountain, Stitch's Great Escape!, Main Street Electrical Parade, Wishes fireworks.

BRITTIP
After the fireworks crowd exits, you are allowed to take the Resort Only monorail back to the Transportation & Ticket Center, rather than queue for the main Express monorail.

Wishes Cruises: If you prefer not to fight the crowds for a fab view of Wishes, book one of three speciality cruises to view the fireworks from Seven Seas Lagoon. The Basic Cruise holds up to eight guests onboard a 21ft/6m pontoon boat and costs $292 (includes water, soft drinks and snacks); the Premium Cruise holds up to 10 on a 25ft/7.6m pontoon boat (for $346), including water, soft drinks, snacks and an audio feed to the Wishes music; or splash out for the Celebration Cruise, which adds special occasion decorations to the Basic Cruise for a total of $325 and the Premium Cruise for $375. All can be booked 90 days in advance.

Pirate and Pals Fireworks Voyage: This kid-friendly Wishes cruise includes meeting Mr Smee and Captain Hook before cruising the Seven Seas Lagoon to view the Electrical Water Pageant and Wishes.

Snacks and drinks are provided while you enjoy a retelling of the Peter Pan story, then meet Pan himself at the end of your voyage ($57/adult, $33/3–9; can be booked 180 days in advance).

BRITTIP
For a final bit of typical Disney entertainment, head outside the Magic Kingdom at 10.25pm and catch the Electrical Water Pageant passing by on Seven Seas Lagoon in front of the park.

Leaving the park

When it comes to leaving, the monorail is quicker than the ferry but it can still take up to an hour to get back to your car. Also, if the crowds get too heavy during the day, you can escape by leaving in the early afternoon (your car park ticket is valid all day) and returning to your hotel for a few hours' rest or a dip in the pool. Alternatively, catch a boat to one of the Disney resorts. Fort Wilderness is especially fun for kids and boasts the good value Trails End restaurant for lunch or dinner.

Halloween and Christmas

Two additional annual events in the Magic Kingdom provide a separate, party-style ticketed event 7pm–

Main Street USA at Halloween

midnight, with most of the rides open and extra themed fun and games.

Mickey's Not So Scary Halloween Party: Sept–Oct sees many visitors dress up for the typical American trick-or-treat fun, with plenty of treats for all. With special features, shows, Mickey's Boo To You Halloween Parade and the wonderful HalloWishes fireworks (with lighting effects), tickets ($68 adults, $63 3–9s) go on sale about 5 months in advance and sell out quickly.

Mickey's Very Merry Christmas Party: The Christmas party (Nov–Dec) sees 'snow' on Main Street and an array of magnificent festive decorations and theming. There is free hot chocolate and cookies, as well as a special parade and more fireworks. The atmosphere is enchanting, though the evening can be prone to unfriendly weather.

BRITTIP
Although the special evening parties don't start officially until 7pm, you can use the ticket to gain entry to the park from 4pm, which gives you 8 full hours to enjoy all the attractions.

Park tours: Finally, one of the park's little-known secrets is the **Keys to the Kingdom**, a 4–5-hour guided tour of many backstage areas, including the service tunnel under the park, and entertainment production buildings. It's an extra $79 (including lunch; not available for under-16s) but is a superb journey into the park's creation. **Disney's Family Magic Tour** is a 2-hour guided adventure that takes you on a search for clues throughout the park at $34/person, or you can experience the 3-hour **The Magic Behind Our Steam Trains Tour** ($52/person; no under-10s) as you join the crew that prepares the park's trains each day. **Walt Disney: Marceline to Magic Kingdom** is a 3-hour tour on how the inspiration of Walt's early years in Marceline, Missouri, culminated in the creation of the Magic Kingdom ($30/person; no under-12s).

Epcot

Epcot originally stood for 'Experimental Prototype Community of Tomorrow', but it might be more accurate to say Every Person Comes Out Tired. For this is a BIG park, with a lot to see and do, and much legwork required to cover its 300acre/122ha extent. Actually, it is not so much a vision of the future as a look at the world and technology of today, with a strong educational and environmental message. At almost three times the size of the Magic Kingdom Park, it is more likely to require a two-day visit (though under-5s might find it less entertaining) and your feet in particular will notice the difference! Remember FP+1 means you can pick only ONE of these FastPass attractions, while FP+ indicates where you can select two.

Location

Epcot opened in October 1982 and its giant car park can hold 9,000 vehicles, so a tram takes you from your car to the main entrance (though if you are staying at a Disney hotel you can catch the monorail, boat or bus service to the gates; International Gateway is a separate entrance for guests at the Epcot resort hotels). Don't forget to note where you have parked (e.g. Create, row 49). If you have your ticket or MagicBand, you pass through the gate area and wait in the immediate entrance plaza for Rope Drop, which is signalled by Mickey and Co arriving to greet guests.

Beating the queues: Epcot is divided into two distinct parts arranged in a figure of eight and there are two

Epcot at a glance

Location	Off Epcot Drive, Walt Disney World
Size	300 acres/122ha in Future World and World Showcase
Hours	9am–9pm Future World (except Universe of Energy, Imagination, Innoventions, 9am–7pm), 11am–9pm (World Showcase)
Admission	Under-3s free; 3–9 $99 (1-day base ticket), $295 (5-day Magic Your Way), £274 (14–day Ultimate); adult (10+) $105, $315, £299. Prices do not include tax.
Parking	$17
Lockers	Through the main entrance to the right hand side and at International Gateway $12 small, $14 large ($5 deposit each)
Pushchairs	$15 and $31 to the left after the main entrance and at International Gateway; length of stay $91/week, $130 10 days, $189/$270 double
Wheelchairs	$12 or $70 ($20 deposit refunded) with pushchairs
Top attractions	Mission: SPACE, Test Track, Spaceship Earth, Soarin'™, Universe of Energy, American Adventure
Don't miss	IllumiNations: Reflections of Earth, Disney Character Spot, Turtle Talk With Crush, live entertainment (including American Music Machine, JAMMitors and Voices of Liberty in America), and dinner at any of the World Showcase pavilions
Hidden costs	Meals	Burger, chips and coke $10.76 3-course dinner $39.25–49.25 (La Hacienda, Mexico) Kids' meal $8.50
	T-shirts	$24.95–39.95 Kids' T-shirts $17.95–29.95
	Souvenirs	$1.35–475
	Sundries	Epcot 'Passport' $9.95

Future World

1 Universe of Energy
2 Mission: SPACE
3 Test Track
4 Odyssey Center
5 Imagination! (including Captain Eo)
6 The Land (including Soarin'™)
7 The Seas with Nemo and Friends
8 Spaceship Earth
9 Innoventions West
10 Innoventions East

World Showcase

11 Mexico
12 Norway
13 China
14 The Outpost
15 Germany
16 Italy
17 The American Adventure
18 Japan
19 Morocco
20 France
21 International Gateway (to Epcot resort hotels)
22 United Kingdom
23 Canada
24 Friendship Boats to Italy and Morocco
25 America Gardens Theater
26 Showcase Plaza
27 Monorail Station
K Kidcot Fun Stops

EPCOT

tactics to help you avoid the worst of the crowds. The first or lower half of the park consists of Future World, with six pavilions arranged around Spaceship Earth (which dominates the skyline) and the two Innoventions centres.

The second part, or top of the park, is World Showcase, a potted journey around the world via 11 international pavilions that feature a taste of each country's culture, history, entertainment, shopping and cuisine. Once through the entrance plaza, aim to get the three big-time rides – Test Track, Mission: Space and Soarin'™ – under your belt first, then move into World Showcase for its 11am opening. Continue around World Showcase until 4–5pm, then return to Future World to catch up on the other attractions there, as the majority will have moved on (apart from at the three main rides).

As a general tactic, head first for the magnificent Soarin'™, then go across to the other side of Future World for Test Track, if you haven't got a FP in advance (and you can book only one of them with the two-tiered FP+ system). While you wait for your ride time, you can queue for Mission: SPACE and perhaps even take in Universe of Energy. Alternatively, if the rides don't appeal quite so much as a visit to such diverse cultures as Japan and Morocco, spend your first couple of hours in the Innoventions centres (busy from mid-morning), then head into World Showcase at 11am and you'll be ahead of the crowds for the first hour. Also early on, book lunch or dinner at one of the fine restaurants around World Showcase (Mexico, Italy, France and Morocco are all highly recommended). The best reservations go fast, but check in at Guest Relations (on the left after Spaceship Earth) for advice and bookings.

Planning your visit
If you plan a two-day visit, it makes sense to spend the first day in World Showcase, arriving by 11am and going straight there while the majority

stay in Future World, booking your evening meal for around 5.30pm, then lingering around the lagoon for the evening entertainment. For your second visit, try arriving in mid-afternoon and taking your time doing Future World. Queues at most of the pavilions are almost non-existent for rides like Universe of Energy, Spaceship Earth and Journey into Imagination, though Test Track, Soarin'™ and Mission: Space stay busy all day. You CAN do Epcot in a day – if you arrive early, put in some speedy legwork and give most of the detail a miss. But, of all the parks, it is a shame to hurry this one. Browse in the shops (almost 70 in all), when the rides are busiest.

Kidcot Fun Stops: At 11 activity centres around Epcot (each country in World Showcase), children can play games and collect a special Epcot Passport to get stamped as they visit each Stop.

Future World
Here's what you'll find in the first part of your Epcot adventure.

Universe of Energy: The one attraction here is a stunner. Ellen's Energy Adventure is a 35min show-and-ride with comedienne Ellen DeGeneres and Bill Nye the Science Guy exploring the creation of fuels from the age of dinosaurs to the modern day. You think you are in a conventional theatre until your seats rearrange themselves into 96-person solar-powered cars and you are off on a journey through the prehistoric era, with some realistic dinosaurs! Queues are steady but not overwhelming from mid-morning. AAAAA.

Italy Pavilion

Mission: SPACE: This is more high-tech Disney imagination, a journey into the future at the International Space Training Center. The space-age building prepares you for a major adventure as you enter through Planetary Plaza, with its giant replica planets (check out the model showing the moon landings). At the entrance you have a choice of two queues – Standby (the main queue), and FastPass+ Return, and the clever organisation keeps queues moving. As you enter the training facility, there are some superb models and graphics (like the giant revolving Gravity Wheel) to look at while you queue to reach Team Dispatch. For the ride, you form you into teams of four in the ready rooms: Navigator, Engineer, Pilot or Commander, each with different functions. You also have the choice of either the full, dynamic version of the ride (the 'orange' version) or a toned-down alternative that avoids the 'spinning' effect (the 'green' version). Once briefed (by actor Gary Sinise), you enter the Preparation Room to learn your mission – a flight to Mars. And then it's into the ride vehicle – capsules that close down tightly with outer doors, shoulder restraints and screens that move forward to just 18in/46cm from your face (this is NOT a good ride for those with claustrophobia, prone to motion sickness, or expectant mothers). The sense of realism, with the control consoles, individual speakers and countdown is magnificent.

For those on the full version, a very real blast-off simulates some of the genuine forces of a rocket launch (thanks to its huge centrifuge, which is part-ride and part-simulator). Each team member dhas to perform their duties on cue and you experience a simulated sling-shot around the moon and on to Mars, where the landing is an adventure in itself. It's a truly original, aggressive ride, but you should heed the advice to keep your head still and look straight into the screen or you WILL feel sick (unless you are on the tamer version, where the capsules just tilt and turn). We think the full-on experience is too intense for young children, and there is no backing out once you blast off (parents could try it first). R: 3ft 8in/112cm. TTTTT FP+

Elaborate post-show and activities include **Space Base** – an excellent play area for children who can't ride (and those who just like to climb, slide and crawl); **Space Race** – a great game for two teams of 60 players to propel a rocket back to Earth via a series of

Mission: Space

on-screen challenges; **Expedition Mars** – a computer game to rescue stranded astronauts; and **Postcards from Space** – where you can email a 'space video' to friends and family. There is then the inevitable (and well-stocked) gift shop. All in all, it's a terrific experience.

Test Track: This equally big-scale production – a 5½min whirl along Disney's longest, fastest track – offers a journey into the world of Chevrolet car design and technology. It starts with an interactive queue that invites riders to design their own car according to Capability, Efficiency, Responsiveness and Power, which they then carry on to their prototype vehicle. Once aboard, it is off through an elaborate digital computer world of performance tests, with the car put through its paces on hair-pin bends, rough surfaces, temperature extremes and a final high-speed section outside the building at up to 67mph/108kph. Each guest's car design is computer tested alongside the vehicle and scored according to how it fares. The final post-ride area shows more about the testing process and its four key design elements. The vivid lighting, which makes you feel as if you're inside a computer (like the film *Tron*), sharp twists and turns and other special effects add up to a unique whirl through this high-tech world (complete with Chevy gift shop), but it does draw BIG queues and the FP+ option can run out well in advance during busy seasons. If you're on your own or don't mind your family being split up, the Single Rider option is handy here. **R**: 3ft 4in/101cm. **TTTT** (**TTT** teens) **FP+1**

The Odyssey Center: Baby-care, first-aid, telephones and restrooms.

Imagination!: The two-part attraction here starts with **Journey into Imagination with Figment**, an uneven but quirky ride into experiments with imagination in the company of Eric Idle (as Dr Nigel Channing of the Imagination Institute) and the cartoon dragon Figment. The sight laboratory sees Figment having fun with a vision

chart, the sound lab is a symphony of imaginative melodies and Figment's house is a truly topsy-turvy world (watch out for the skunk in the smell lab!). It's gentle fun and rarely draws a crowd. AAA FP+ You exit into **Image Works – The 'What If' Labs**, an interactive playground of sight and sound, which usually amuses kids more than adults (though you might be tempted to buy various cartoon images and select-your-own CDs).

Captain EO: Come out and turn right for an encore presentation of this fun 3-D musical film show starring Michael Jackson, which originally debuted in Epcot in 1986 but was replaced by Honey I Shrunk The Audience in 1994. Now digitally remastered and sound enhanced, it is a 17min romp through space as Captain EO and his band of ragtag renegades set out to save the universe by bringing a special gift to the evil Supreme Leader. Jackson's signature dancing and the show's 'We Are Here To Change The World' message keep the tone upbeat, but some of the darker thematic elements may frighten young children. It's a visually thrilling trip down memory lane for Disney fans, as good conquers evil – naturally! AAAA FP+ Outside, kids are always fascinated by the Jellyfish and Serpentine Fountains that send water squirting from pond to pond. Have your cameras ready! (NB: This theatre was used to preview several Disney films in 2015, and we expect to see Captain EO pensioned off in 2016.)

The Land: A three-element entertaining and educational experience on food and nutrition

Test Track

plus the spectacular thrill-ride of Soarin'. **Living with the Land** is an informative 14min boat ride well worth the sometimes long queue. A journey through food production may sound dull, but it is informative and enjoyable, with plenty to make children sit up and take notice of its three ecological communities, especially the greenhouse finale. AAAA FP+ After the ride, you can also take the **Behind the Seeds** 1-hour guided tour through the greenhouse complex and learn more about Disney's horticultural projects ($20 adults, $16 3–9s). FP+1

The Circle of Life: This 15min animated tale features characters from *The Lion King* explaining ecological concerns that are easily digestible for kids. Queues are rare. AA

Soarin'™: One of Disney's most imaginative attractions, this 'flight simulator' offers an exhilarating ride for all ages, a breathtaking swoop over Californian icons, complete with 'aromavision' (smell those orange groves!). An elaborate queuing area leads to the departure lounge, with passengers embarking on rows of seats that are hoisted into the air over a giant screen. The feeling is like taking a hang-glider ride as the special film, sounds and scents become all-encompassing. Feet dangling, you soar over the Golden Gate Bridge, sweep through a redwood forest and glide above Napa Valley. The finale includes a close encounter with a Disney theme park in Los Angeles! The ride's realism, magnificent music and superb

View across Epcot

technology ensure a 5-star experience – but also long queues. FastPass+ may be difficult to secure on the day, so be sure to book well in advance or visit early. R: 3ft 4in/101cm. AAAAA FP+1

Dining: The **Sunshine Seasons Food Court** offers the chance to eat some of Disney's home-grown produce, while the **Garden Grill** restaurant is a slowly revolving platform that offers more traditional food, including beef, turkey, fish, and salad, all in the company of Mickey, Goofy, Pluto and Chip 'n' Dale.

> **BRITTIP**
> Anyone looking for organic or gluten-free treats and snacks should look for the selection on offer at the entrance to the Sunshine Seasons food court.

The Seas with Nemo & Friends: This pavilion does for the oceans what The Land does for terra firma, in the company of the characters from the Pixar film *Finding Nemo*. You start with the signature ride, **The Seas With Nemo and Friends**, which takes riders on an underwater journey in 'clam-mobiles' to meet Nemo and Co (brilliantly interwoven into the huge aquarium, apparently swimming with the real fish!). Nemo has gone missing (again), hence the ride becomes a quest to reunite him with teacher Mr Ray and the rest of the class in a rousing musical finale. AAAA FP+ You then exit into **Sea Base**, a two-level development offering six modules presenting stories of undersea exploration and marine life, including a research centre that provides a close encounter with the endangered manatee. Plenty of interactive elements and educational touch-screens are on offer, plus additional tanks displaying Caribbean reef fish, jellyfish and cuttlefish, while there is an excellent demonstration of a diving chamber. Crowds are steady, but queues rarely get too long – with one exception. **Turtle Talk With Crush** is a brilliantly interactive meet-and-greet with the surfer dude turtle and his friend Dory from *Finding Nemo*. Crush is the star of the show as he swims up and engages children in the audience with some fun live banter. **AAAA FP+** Next door, **Bruce's Sub House** is a kids' play area including great photo opportunities with more of the Nemo characters (**TTT** under-6s). Nemo and Friends is more hands-on fun for kids, while **Mr Ray's Lagoon** showcases some real stingrays.

Dining: The pavilion includes the highly recommended **Coral Reef Restaurant** that serves great seafood with a grandstand view of the massive aquarium. Dinner will be $28–44 (starter and main), depending on your choices, which isn't cheap, but the food is first class (kids' menu $8.99–10.99).

Spaceship Earth: Spiralling up 18 storeys, this attraction is a convincing time-travel story into various technologies narrated by Dame Judi Dench. From cave paintings to the internet (with a superb depiction of Michelangelo's Sistine Chapel), the gentle ride unfolds in imaginative historical stages, culminating in an interactive finale that invites riders to 'predict' the future. Sponsor Siemens (the electronics giant) has added a post-show interactive demonstration area (including predictive surgery and a driving challenge), which makes for an entertaining diversion after the 15min ride. Queues are heavy all morning, but almost non-existent late in the day. **AAAA FP+**

Innoventions: These two centres of hands-on exhibits are fun and educational, with interactive exercises into things like recycling, fire prevention and energy use, as well as future technologies and some of the latest video games. **Innoventions East:** Don't miss **The Sum of All Thrills** experience, where budding mathematicians and engineers can design and create their own ride using physics principles and touchscreen technology. Then, hop aboard the motion simulator for a hair-raising ride! **R:** 4ft/122cm for non-inversion ride, 4ft 6in/138cm with inversions. **TTT.** Other novelties include **Vision House** (a 15min walk through new

home technologies) and **Storm Struck** (experience a violent storm from a special viewing theatre). **Habit Heroes** is a clever series of interactive games that focus on healthy eating habits and encourage guests to have a more active lifestyle (although most kids just want to play the games!), with computers outside to record your own 'secret code'. **AA Innoventions West:** As we went to press, Innoventions West was undergoing an extensive refurbishment, with new sponsors due to arrive for 2016. Expect interesting new technologies with that special 'Disney twist' that turns learning into fun, adding the latest video games that kids tend to gravitate to, giving parents a break in air-conditioned comfort.

BRITTIP

Innoventions East and West are good places in which to spend time if you need to cool down, or if it's raining. They are usually quiet in the afternoon, too.

Other entertainment: Live fun is also provided periodically around Future World by the unique JAMMitors percussion group, while the **Epcot Character Spot** (across from Innoventions West, 9am–9pm at peak times, 10am–6pm off-peak, **FP+**) offers a fabulous themed

Epcot monorail and Spaceship Earth

meet-and-greet with many Disney characters. Daisy Duck and Goofy can often be found just inside the main entrance. The majestic Plaza Fountain choreographs to musical performances every 15min.

Shopping: Mouse Gear in Innoventions East features a massive variety of Epcot and Disney merchandise (and don't miss the wacky ceiling architecture!), while the **Art of Disney** features superb signature art and animator drawings.

Dining: Food outlets include the counter-service **Electric Umbrella Restaurant** for lunch and dinner (sandwiches, burgers and salads) and the **Fountainview Café** for signature Starbucks coffees, cold drinks, pastries and sandwiches. Look out also for **Club Cool** presented by Coca-Cola®, where you can enjoy international Coke products and souvenirs, along with various free tastes from around the world (beware the Beverly!).

World Showcase

If you found Future World amazing, prepare to be astounded by the imaginative pavilions around the World Showcase Lagoon, each featuring a glimpse of a different country in dramatic settings. Several have rides or films to showcase their main features, while the restaurants offer some outstanding fare and many character greeting spots can be found here (check the daily Times Guide for locations and timings).

Mexico pavilion

Agent P's World Showcase Adventure: 11am–8.15pm. Look out for the sign-up station for this interactive and family-friendly challenge game, based on the *Phineas & Ferb* TV series, on the bridge over to World Showcase (and with other stations at International Gateway, Norway and Italy). With the aid of the Field Operative Notification Equipment (or FONE), guest 'agents' follow the clues around each World Showcase pavilion to help the boys' pet platypus Perry (Agent P) in his bid to foil his nemesis Dr Doofenschmirtz. Complete all the tasks on your FONE and you foil the evil Dr and free Perry from his predicament.

BRITTIP
Don't waste your three precious FastPasses on attractions such as Imagination, Spaceship Earth, or IllumiNations. Queues for the two rides are generally non-existent in late afternoon, and it usually isn't difficult to find a good spot to view IllumiNations.

Mexico: Starting at the bottom left of the circular tour of the lagoon and moving clockwise, your first encounter is inside the spectacular pyramid of Mexico. Here you have the amusing boat ride **Gran Fiesta Tour Starring The Three Caballeros**, a 9min journey through the people and history of the country guided by Donald Duck, Panchito and José Carioca. Queues build up in mid-afternoon but are usually light otherwise. AAA

Other entertainment: As in all of the World Showcase pavilions, there is live entertainment, with periodic 25min music shows from **Mariachi Cobre**, while Donald Duck puts in character appearances.

Shopping: Much of the pavilion comprises market-style gift shops.

Dining: The San Angel Inn is a romantic Mexican restaurant and **La Cava del Tequila** has tempting cocktails, light bites and signature tequilas. Outside, choose from the revamped counter service **Cantina**

de San Angel (open-air lunch from 11am, serving tacos, nachos and tortillas) and full-service **La Hacienda de San Angel** (dinner from 4pm) serving a rich variety of authentic Mexican fare with a superb lagoon view and grandstand seat for the nightly IllumiNations show. This gets our thumbs-up as a stand-out choice.

Norway: A reproduction of Oslo's splendid Akershus Fortress, the interior reopens in 2016 with a new Arendelle ride as part of a retheming from the movie *Frozen*. The boat ride Frozen Ever After features a journey with all the characters, while Anna and Elsa will have an elaborate new meet-and-greet that's sure to be hugely popular. FP+ (for ride AAA) and FP+1 (for meet-n-greet AAAAA); expected.

BRITTIP

If you can't get a booking for Cinderella's Royal Table in the Magic Kingdom, the Akershus Royal Banquet (8.30am–8.30pm; $42–48 for adults, and $25–26 kids 3–9) is the next best thing and should keep most young 'princesses' happy! Call 407 939 3463 up to 180 days in advance or book online at www.disneyworld.com.

Dining: The **Akershus Royal Banquet Hall** offers the Princess Storybook dining for breakfast, lunch and dinner, complete with a host of Disney Princesses, while the counter-service café serves sandwiches, pastries and drinks.

Shopping: There is a large gift shop for all things *Frozen*.

China: The spectacular landscapes of China are well served by the main attraction of this pavilion, the stunning **Reflections of China**, a 360° film in the circular Temple of Heaven, where you are surrounded by the sights and sounds of one of the world's most enigmatic countries. Queues build up to 30mins during the main part of the day (but it is fully air-conditioned). AAAA

Other entertainment: Don't miss the periodic shows from the spectacular

Jeweled Dragon Acrobats on the plaza in front of the temple, while Disney characters from *Mulan* also appear throughout the day.

Shopping: Yong Feng Shangdian Dept Store is a warehouse of Chinese gifts and artefacts.

Dining: Two restaurants, the **Nine Dragons** and the counter-service **Lotus Blossom Café** offer tastes of the Orient,

The Outpost: Between China and Germany features hut-style shops and snacks, with crafts from Africa and the Caribbean.

Germany: There is more in the way of shopping and eating than entertainment, though you still find a magnificent re-creation of a **Bavarian Biergarten**, with lively Oktoberfest shows featuring the resident Musikanten brass band at regular intervals. It also offers hearty portions of German sausage, sauerkraut and rotisserie chicken. The Sommerfest is fast food German-style (bratwurst and strudel), while there are eight shops, more than anywhere else in Epcot, including chocolates, wines, crystal, porcelain, toys and cuckoo clocks.

BRITTIP

With seating for 400, Biergarten often takes walk-ups even when Disney's reservations system indicates the restaurant is full.

Other entertainment: An elaborate outdoor **model railway** is popular with children, and look out for character appearances from Snow White.

A view of Spaceship Earth from Japan

Italy: Similarly, Italy has pretty, authentic architecture, including a superb reproduction of Venice's St Mark's Square, three gift shops stocking wine, chocolates, Armani collectables, fine crystal, porcelain and Venetian masks, and two full-service restaurants. **Tutto Italia** is the fine-dining option, designed like the Medici Palace, complete with a gluten-free menu and a splendid cellar-style wine bar, **Tutto Gusto**, that offers small plates and light bites (reservations not required for the wine bar), while the superb **Via Napoli** is a delightfully authentic pizzeria, featuring wood-burning ovens and genuine Neapolitan style, with 300 seats, including an outdoor terrace.

Other entertainment: Watch out for the fun entertainment of **Sergio**, a madcap juggler who loves to involve his audience, and the eye-catching **Sbandieratori Di Sansepolcro** flag-waving team.

The American Adventure: At the top of the lagoon and dominating World Showcase is this huge edifice, not so much a pavilion as a celebration of the country's history and Constitution. A colonial Fife & Drum Corps and wonderful singing group add authentic sounds to the 18th-century setting, overlooked by a reproduction of Philadelphia's Liberty Hall. Inside, you have the **American Adventure** show, a magnificent half-hour film and audio-animatronic production that details the country's founding, its struggles and triumphs, presidents, statesmen and heroes. It's a glossy, patriotic display, featuring some outstanding technology and, while some of it will be unfamiliar to foreign visitors, it's difficult not to be impressed. A good choice at most times of the day – and it's all in the cool! AAAA If you have time to spare, check out the special exhibitions in the American Heritage Gallery.

Other entertainment: New in 2015 was **American Music Machine**, an outstanding *à capella* group that should not be missed. It's one of the most talented and creative groups we've seen in a long time, featuring close-harmony vocals from the 1960s to present day. Another superb à capella group, **Voices of Liberty**, appear in the pavilion's rotunda several times a day, while the **America**

Italy

Gardens Theater, next to the lagoon, presents concerts from international artists during the Flower & Garden Festival, Sounds Like Summer series and Food & Wine Festival.

Dining: Antiques and handcarts provide touches of nostalgia, along with the **Heritage Manor Gifts** store.

Shopping: Liberty Inn offers fast-food lunch and dinner and the **Block & Hans** kiosk has craft beers, wine and pretzels.

Japan: Next up on the clockwise tour, you are introduced to typical Japanese style and architecture, including a five-storey 8th-century **Pagoda**, some magnificent art exhibits, notably in the **Bijutsu-kan Gallery**, featuring art and insights into Japanese history and culture, a tranquil **Bonsai garden** (complete with carp pond) and landmark Torii gate.

Other entertainment: Live shows are key here, with periodic presentations from the superb **Matsuriza** taiko drummers.

Shopping: The huge **Mitsukoshi** store adds fascinating shopping, from traditional calligraphy, tea kettles and wind chimes to Hello Kitty souvenirs.

Dining: Great food is a real highlight, and the restaurant line-up consists of the wonderful fine dining of **Teppan Edo** (with its traditional chefs at each table) and **Tokyo Dining**, featuring typical cuisine and ingredients, showcasing sushi and innovative presentation. **Katsura Grill** is its fast-food equivalent, with great soups, teriyaki and sushi dishes while the **Kabuki Café** serves sake, beer, plum wine, tea and soft drinks.

Morocco: As you would expect, this is another shopping experience, with bazaars, alleyways and stalls selling a well-priced array of carpets, leather goods, clothing, brass ornaments, pottery and antiques. All the building materials were imported for the pavilion, which was hand-built to give Morocco a greater degree of authenticity, even by World Showcase's high standards.

The **Gallery of Arts and History** offers more historical and cultural insights, while the **Fez House** depicts a typical Moroccan home.

Other entertainment: Characters from Disney's *Aladdin* appear from time to time, while live musical show **B'net Al Houwariyate** presents Moroccan folk music, with plenty of guest interaction. Get ready to dance!

Dining: Restaurant Marrakesh provides a full dining experience, complete with traditional musicians and their own belly dancer. It's rather pricey but the lively atmosphere is entertaining. Better value can be had at **Tangierine Café**, with its healthy array of roast lamb, hummus, tabbouleh, couscous, lentil salad and Moroccan breads ($9.99–14.99; kids' meals $7.99). **Spice Road Table**, a clever indoor/outdoor café and bar, offers superb small-plate, Mediterranean-style meals and snacks plus signature cocktails and other drinks, all with a great Lagoon view (select tables are ideal for the nightly IllumiNations show).

▶ BRITTIP

The Tangierine Café in Morocco is a peaceful haven in which to enjoy a quiet, healthy lunch, especially if you are vegetarian, plus there is a tempting coffee and pastry counter.

France: Predictably overlooked by a replica Eiffel Tower, this is a clean and cheerful pre-World War I Paris, with comedy street theatre adding to the rather dreamy atmosphere and pleasant gardens, plus stylish

American Music Machine

shopping and great dining options. Don't miss **Impressions de France**, a big-film production that serves up all the grandest sights of the country to the music of Offenbach, Debussy, Saint-Saëns and Satie. Crowds get quite heavy from mid-day. AAAA

Other entertainment: Look out for the visual comedy and amazing balancing act of **Serveur Amusant** (not when it's too windy), while **Princess Aurora** (Sleeping Beauty) makes regular appearances, along with *Beauty and the Beast* characters.

Shopping: Suitably chic, there's an authentic **Wine Shop** and elegant **Guerlain** and **Givenchy** perfumeries (ask about the free perfume tour during the Flower and Garden Festival).

Dining: This is THE pavilion for a gastronomic experience provided by three restaurants, of which **Les Chefs de France** and **Monsieur Paul** are major discoveries. The former is a classic, full-service establishment featuring top-quality French cuisine for lunch and dinner, while the latter, upstairs, is named (and themed) for famous chef Paul Bocuse, with his well-trained team in charge of both. Monsieur Paul is a touch more formal and upscale, with a 4-course prix fixe menu ($89/person), and, while an expensive meal (dinner only; appetisers from $16–29 and main courses $29–44), it is a truly fabulous choice. Also here is the **Les Halles Boulangerie Patisserie**, a genuine French patisserie featuring authentic

France

freshly-made baguettes, croissants, salads, quiches and wonderful pastries, and **L'Artisan des Glaces**, an artisan ice-cream and sorbet shop, with everything made fresh in-house every day (and with liqueur treats for grown-ups!).

BRITTIP

The special dining events in the France pavilion are often the highlight of the annual Food & Wine Festival and are worth signing up for.

United Kingdom: The least inspiring of all the pavilions, and certainly with little to entertain those who have ever visited a pub or shopped for Royal Doulton or Burberry goods, it is partly offset by some good live entertainment and pleasant gardens, but that is about it.

Other entertainment: Live music is provided by **British Revolution**, offering the sounds of the 60s, 70s and 80s up to five times a day, while the **Pub Musician** performs several times daily and the **Paul McKenna Band** features traditional Scottish music. Mary Poppins, Winnie the Pooh, Tigger and Alice can also be found here.

Shopping: The best shops are the **Tea Caddy**, the **Queen's Table**, **Crown and Crest** (perfumes and heraldry), **Sportsman Shoppe** (sweaters, kilts, football shirts) and **Toy Soldier** (traditional games and toys), but prices are WAY above what you'd pay at home.

Dining: The Rose and Crown Pub is antiseptically authentic but you can get better elsewhere at these prices (New York strip steak $28.99, bangers and mash $15.99 or fish and chips $15.99, and a pint of Bass for a whopping $8.75). There's also a takeaway **Yorkshire County** fish and chippie.

Canada: Completing the World Showcase circle, the main features here are **Victoria Gardens**, based on the world-famous Butchart Gardens on Vancouver Island, some spectacular Rocky Mountain scenery,

EPCOT with children

Here is our rough guide to the attractions that appeal to different age groups:

Under-5s
Circle of Life, Gran Fiesta Tour Starring The Three Caballeros, Journey into Imagination with Figment, Kidcot stops, Living with the Land, The Seas with Nemo and Friends, Soarin'™ (if tall enough), Spaceship Earth, Turtle Talk with Crush, Universe of Energy.

5–8s
All the above, plus The American Adventure, Captain EO (with parental discretion), Image Works, Innoventions, JAMMitors, Test Track, Agent P's World Showcase Adventure.

9–12s
All the above, plus Impressions de France, Matsuriza Drummers, Mission: SPACE, O Canada!, Sergio, Le Serveur Amusant, Reflections of China, American Music Machine.

Over-12s
Living with the Land, The Seas with Nemo and Friends, Soarin'™, Spaceship Earth, Universe of Energy, The American Adventure, Captain EO, Innoventions, JAMMitors, Test Track, Impressions de France, Matsuriza Drummers, Mission: SPACE, O Canada!, Reflections of China, Bijutsu-kan Gallery, American Music Machine.

a replica French gothic mansion, the Hôtel de Canada, and another stunning 360° film, *O Canada!* As with China and France, this showcases the country's sights and scenery in a terrific, 17min advert for the Canadian Tourist Board led by comedian Martin Short. It's at its busiest in late afternoon. AAA

Other entertainment: The beefy **Canadian Lumberjacks** exhibit axe throwing, chopping, log-rolling and chainsaw skills up to six times daily.

🇬🇧 **BRITTIP**
Best way to tour World Showcase? Start in Canada and continue anticlockwise or jump on the Friendship Boats and go straight to Italy or Morocco.

Shopping: The Trading Post and **Northwest Mercantile** provide a range of Canadian clothing and souvenirs, notably wonderful glass ornaments and Deauville perfume.

Dining and shopping: Le Cellier Steakhouse is an excellent dining room, offering great steaks, prime rib, seafood, chicken and several vegetarian dishes for lunch and dinner.

IllumiNations: Reflections of Earth

The day's big finale and an absolute show-stopper, this firework and special-effects extravaganza is awesome even by Disney standards. British composer Gavin Greenaway provided the original music for a 15min performance of vivid brilliance. Some 2,800 firework shells are launched as a celestial backdrop to a series of fire-and-water effects on the World Showcase Lagoon. The central icon is a 28ft/9m video globe of Earth that opens in a spectacular climax of choreographed pyrotechnics. However, people start staking out the best lagoon-side spots up to 2 HOURS in advance.

Flower and Garden Festival

FP+1 for special viewing area. The ultimate way to view IllumiNations is by private boat on one of two speciality cruises from Disney's Boardwalk or Yacht and Beach Club Resorts, and the Grand Floridian (for non-residents, too). The price range is $325–1148 per boat (holding 4–10 guests) and can be used for special celebrations. The Basic Cruise costs $325 and the boat holds up to 10. It includes water, soft drinks and snacks (call 407 824 2682 up to 90 days in advance to book).

Behind-the-scenes tours

Epcot also has a big range of tours. Book all tours on 407 939 8687.

Dolphins in Depth: This is a 3-hour dip into the research areas of The Seas pavilion, including a chance to meet the dolphins ($199, with refreshments, photo and T-shirt; 13–17s must be accompanied by an adult; swimming costume required).

Undiscovered Future World: A 4½-hour journey into the creation of Epcot, Walt's vision for the resort and backstage areas like IllumiNations ($64).

Disney's Food and Wine Festival

Behind the Seeds: This 1-hour tour, every 45mins from 9.45am–4.30pm at The Land pavilion, looks at Disney's innovative gardening practices ($20 adults, $16 3–9s).

Dive Quest: A 3-hour experience, with a 40min dive into The Seas aquarium, plus a backstage look at the facility at 4.30 and 5.30pm daily, Must have scuba certification; park admission not required ($175/person, 10 and over, includes T-shirt and certificate).

Seas Aqua Tour: A similar tour without the scuba diving, daily at 12.30pm ($140/person, 8 and over; under-18s must be accompanied by an adult).

Backstage Magic: The most comprehensive tour goes behind the scenes of Epcot, Magic Kingdom and Disney's Hollywood Studios on a 7-hour foray into little-seen aspects, such as the backstage areas of the Studios and the tunnels below Magic Kingdom ($249, 16 and over).

Annual festivals

There are two main annual Epcot events to watch out for.

International Flower and Garden Festival: This literally puts the whole park in full bloom with an amazing series of set-pieces, topiaries, seminars and mini-exhibitions from early Mar to mid-May. All exhibits and some lectures are free, and they add a beautiful aspect to an already scenic park, along with new food kiosks around World Showcase that offer regional tastes and drinks.

Food and Wine Festival: From late Sept to around 12 Nov, this showcases national and regional cuisines, wines and beers, with the chance to attend grand Winemakers' Dinners and Tasting Events, or just sample the offerings of more than 20 food booths dotted around World Showcase. Both festivals also offer free concerts several times a day at the America Gardens Theater (weekends only for Flower & Garden).

Disney's Hollywood Studios

Welcome to a journey into the world of film and TV, an epic voyage of adventure, creation – and fun. Here you will learn plenty of tricks of the trade; movie-making secrets and behind-the-scenes glimpses that have been cleverly turned into rides, shows and other attractions with guaranteed entertainment appeal. Bigger than the Magic Kingdom at 154acres/62ha but smaller than Epcot, this is a different experience again with its rather chaotic combination of attractions, street entertainment, film sets and smart gift shops. Like the Magic Kingdom, the food may not win awards, but some of the restaurants (notably the Sci-Fi Dine-in Theater and 50s Prime Time Café) have imaginative settings. The park also has more to occupy smaller children than Epcot, but you can still easily see it in a day, especially as several attractions have closed ahead of a big change (p142).

Location

The entrance arrangements will be fairly familiar if you have already visited the other parks. Disney's Hollywood Studios is located on Buena Vista Drive (which runs between World Drive and Epcot Drive) and parking is $17. Make a note of where you park before you catch the tram to the main gates, where you wait for the official opening time. If the queues build up quickly, the gates will open early, so be ready for a running start.

Once through the gates, you are into Hollywood Boulevard, a street of gift shops, then you have to decide which

Disney's Hollywood Studios at a glance

Location	Off Buena Vista Drive or World Drive, Walt Disney World
Size	154 acres/62ha
Hours	9am–7pm off peak; 9am–10pm high season (Easter, summer holidays, Thanksgiving and Christmas)
Admission	Under-3s free; 3–9 $99 (1–day base ticket), $295 (5–day Magic Your Way), £274 (14–day Ultimate); adult (10+) $105, $315, £299. Prices do not include tax.
Parking	$17
Lockers	From the Crossroads kiosk through the main entrance; $12 small, $14 large ($5 deposit each)
Pushchairs	$15 and $31 Oscar's Super Service Station; length of stay $91/week, $130 10 days, $189/$270 double
Wheelchairs	$12 or $70 ($20 deposit refunded), from Oscar's
Top attractions	Toy Story Mania, Twilight Zone™ Tower of Terror, Rock 'n' Roller Coaster Starring Aerosmith, Star Tours, The Great Movie Ride, Voyage of the Little Mermaid, Muppet*Vision 3-D, Lights, Motors, Action!™ Extreme Stunt Show
Don't miss	Indiana Jones™ Epic Stunt Spectacular, Beauty and the Beast – Live on Stage, Fantasmic!
Hidden costs	**Meals** — Burger, chips and coke $12.98; 3-course lunch $25.50–53.97 (Mama Melrose's); Beer $6–8.50; Kids' meal $5.99
	T-shirts — $21.95–36.95 Kids' T-shirts $21.95–29.95
	Souvenirs — $1.35–5,000
	Sundries — Special effects make-up $12–$18

1 The Great Movie Ride
2 For the First Time in Forever
3 Indiana JonesTM Epic Stunt Spectacular
4 Star Tours
5 Jim Henson's Muppet*Vision 3-D
6 Honey, I Shrunk the Kids Movie Set Adventure
7 Toy Story Mania
8 Walt Disney: One Man's Dream
9 Voyage of the Little Mermaid
10 Star Wars Launch Bay (new in 2016)
11 Disney Junior – Live on Stage!
12 Rock 'n' Roller Coaster Starring Aerosmith
13 The Twilight Zone™ Tower of Terror
14 Beauty and the Beast – Live on Stage
15 Fantasmic!
16 Guest Information Board
17 Toy Story Pizza Planet
18 Lights, Motors, Action!™ Extreme Stunt Show
19 Premier Theater
20 '50s Prime Time Café
21 Hollywood and Vine
22 Hollywood Brown Derby
23 Mama Melrose's
24 Sunset Ranch Market
25 Sci-Fi Dine-in Theater Restaurant

DISNEY'S
HOLLYWOOD
STUDIOS

of the main attractions to head for first, as these are the ones where the queues will be heaviest most of the day. Try to ignore the lure of the shops as it is better to browse in the early afternoon when the attractions are at their busiest.

BRITTIP

It is crucial to schedule your Hollywood Studios FastPass+ times 60 days in advance if you are staying onsite, or 30 days in advance if you are staying offsite. Main attraction Toy Story Mania books up well in advance.

Incidentally, if you thought Disney had elevated queuing to an art form in its other parks, wait until you see how clever they are here. Just when you think you have reached the ride itself, there is another twist to the queue you hadn't seen or an extra element to the ride that holds you up. The latter are 'holding pens', which are an ingenious way of making it seem you are being entertained instead of queuing. Look out for them in particular at the Great Movie Ride, Twilight Zone™ Tower of Terror and Muppet*Vision 3-D.

The main attractions

The park is laid out in a rather more confusing fashion than its counterparts, with their neatly

packaged 'lands', so have your map handy to keep your bearings.

Beating the queues: The opening-gate crowds will all surge in one of three directions, which will give you a good idea of where you want to go. By far the biggest attraction is **Toy Story Mania**, so head here first if you don't have a FastPass+ time scheduled. The other crowd-pullers are **Twilight Zone™ Tower of Terror**, a magnificent haunted hotel ride that ends in a 13-storey drop in a lift, where queues hit 2 hours at peak periods, and **Rock 'n' Roller Coaster Starring Aerosmith**. Head straight up Hollywood Boulevard, turn right into Sunset Boulevard and you'll see it them at the end of the street. They are both **FP+** rides (p101).

Star Tours, the remodelled Star Wars™ simulator ride is another of the park's serious queue-builders (and, happily, also a FP+ attraction). If you are not up for the really big thrills, schedule a FP+ for Toy Story Mania if there are any available, then head for Star Tours (across the main square past the Indiana Jones™ show). After Star Tours and Toy Story Mania, another gentler experience (and also worth doing early on) is the hilarious Muppet*Vision 3-D show, which is another big draw later in the day. It has the benefit of being air-conditioned, too, for when you need a rest. The park's big stunt show,

Star Tours

Lights, Motors, Action!™ **Extreme Stunt Show**, plays 2–3 times a day and is a good one to catch early on or later in the day.

Hollywood Boulevard

Move around the park in a (roughly) clockwise direction, starting along this street of shops and services that are best visited in early afternoon when it's busier elsewhere. Immediately to the left through the turnstiles are the Guest Relations and First Aid offices, plus the Baby Care centre. An up-to-the-minute check on queue times at the attractions is kept on a Guest Information Board on Hollywood Boulevard, just past its junction with Sunset Boulevard, where you can also book restaurants. To the right is Oscar's Station for pushchair and wheelchair hire, while locker hire is obtained at the Crossroads kiosk in front of you.

The Great Movie Ride: This faces you as you walk in along Hollywood Boulevard and is a good place to start if the crowds are not too serious. An all-star audio-animatronics cast re-creates a number of box office smashes, including Jimmy Cagney's *Public Enemy*, Julie Andrews in *Mary Poppins*, Gene Kelly in *Singin' in*

the Rain and many more masterful set-pieces. Young children may find the menace of *The Alien* too strong, but otherwise the ride has universal appeal and features some clever live twists (there are two variations on this ride, a cowboy and a gangster version – ask a Cast Member if there's one you especially want to do). AAAA FP+

Other entertainment: A series of **Citizens of Hollywood** acts enliven Hollywood Boulevard throughout the day, staging impromptu movie shoots, casting calls or even detective investigations. Have fun with them – you just might end up the star of the show! Also by the Hat, look out for **Disney characters** during the morning.

Shopping: Hollywood Boulevard has the best of the park's shopping (nine of the 21 stores), including **Sid Caheunga's One-of-a-Kind** (rare movie and TV items, including celebrity autographs), **Keystone Clothiers** (some of the best apparel), **Mickey's of Hollywood** (souvenirs and gift items) and **The Darkroom** (for camera items).

Dining: The Brown Derby is the park's signature restaurant, offering fine dining in best vintage Hollywood style

The Great Movie Ride

(reservations usually necessary) while the **Trolley Car Café** quick-service offers breakfast-all-day, plus cakes and Starbucks coffee.

Echo Lake
Turn left out of Hollywood Boulevard and you find another area that pays homage to the movie world of the 1930s and 40s.

For The First Time In Forever: Join Anna and Elsa and the Royal Historians of Arendelle for a *Frozen* Sing-Along Celebration, with the music and film clips from the hit animated movie. AAA (AAAAA+ under 8s). FP+

Indiana Jones™ Epic Stunt Spectacular: Consult your park Times Guide for the various times this stunt cavalcade hits the stage. A special movie set creates three different backdrops for Indiana Jones'™ stunt people to put on a dazzling array of scenes and special effects from the films. Audience participation is an element and there are some amusing sub-plots. Queues for the 30min show begin up to ½hr beforehand, but the auditorium holds more than 2,000 so everyone usually gets in. TTTT FP+

Star Tours – the Adventure Continues: The popular Star Wars™ simulator ride has had a complete revamp. Climb into your StarSpeeder 1000 for a stunning high-speed journey through the worlds created by George Lucas in his award-winning films, including Coruscant, Naboo, Kashyyyk (the Wookiee planet) and Tatooine, where riders blast into the Boonta Eve Classic Podrace with dramatic results. New robot characters AC-38 ('Ace') and Aly San San prepare you for your flight, but predictably it all goes wrong, and droids R2-D2 and C-3PO must save your Speeder from disaster as they evade the Imperial Forces and a very determined bounty hunter. Master Yoda, Boba Fett, Darth Vader and a new branch of stormtroopers, called 'Skytroopers', join the pursuit, and you never know how it will all work out. With the option to change the story at four points, making for 54

ride options, the repeat factor here is huge! The realism of the Star Wars™ world, from the queue to the post-ride gift shop, is brilliant and lots of fun. R: 3ft 4in/101cm, no under-3s. TTTT AAAAA FP+

Other entertainment: Kids should make a beeline for the **Jedi Training Academy**, on the stage outside the Star Tours ride up to eight times a day. Here, young Jedi hopefuls get to try their light sabre technique under the eyes of a Jedi master, before taking on Darth Vader himself. Great fun just to watch, too (TTTT for under-12s).

BRITTIP
This area will be the focus of a big park expansion and you may see preliminary work here in 2016 (p142).

Shopping: Shop for Star Wars™ goods at **Tatooine Traders** (at the exit to Star Tours) and Indiana Jones souvenirs at the **Indy Truck and Adventure Outpost**.

Dining: There are also three good dining choices: the **'50s Prime Time Café** is a fun experience as you sit in mock stage sets from 1950s American TV sitcoms and eat meals 'just like Mom used to make' (the waiters all claim to be your aunt, uncle or cousin and warn you to take your elbows off

Indiana Jones Epic Stunt Spectacular

Lights, Motors, Action!™ Extreme Stunt Show

the table – good fun!); the **Backlot Express** features superb burgers, hot dogs and sandwiches, while a varied buffet dinner is served up at **Hollywood & Vine** in addition to the Play 'n Dine character breakfast and lunch with the Disney Junior Pals, available from 8am–2.25pm ($32 adults, $17 3–9s).

Streets of America

Three of the park's bigger attractions can all be found here, along with an often-overlooked gem of a restaurant.

Honey, I Shrunk the Kids

Muppet*Vision 3-D: The 3-D is crossed out here and 4-D substituted in its place, so be warned strange things are about to happen! A wonderful 10min holding-pen pre-show takes you into the Muppet Theater for a 20min experience with all of the Muppets, 3-D special effects and more – when Fozzie Bear points his squirty flower at you, prepare to get wet! It's a gem, and the kids love it. Queues build up through the main parts of the day, but Disney's queuing expertise makes them seem shorter. AAAAA FP+

Honey, I Shrunk the Kids Movie Set Adventure: This adventure playground gives youngsters the chance to tackle massive blades of grass that turn out to be slides, crawl through caves, investigate giant mushrooms and more. There can be long queues here, so arrive early if the kids demand it. TTTT under-10s.

Premier Theater: This fully enclosed theatre is used for the Star Wars™ Weekend meet and greets and other set-piece special events.

Lights, Motors, Action!™ Extreme Stunt Show: A direct import from the Walt Disney Studios in Paris, this is one of the most remarkable shows you will see anywhere, full of genuine high-risk stunts featuring cars, motorbikes, jet-skis and stuntmen of all kinds, that will leave you shaking your head in amazement. The magnificently crafted set is based on a Mediterranean village and seating starts 30min prior to a show. There is some amusing pre-show chat before the serious stuff starts, when you are treated to a 33min extravaganza of daredevil stunts, with a Car Ballet sequence, a Motorbike Chase and a Grand Finale that features some surprise pyrotechnics to complete an awesome presentation (keep your eyes on the windows below the video screen at the end). Each scene – featuring a secret-agent and various baddies – is explained by a movie director and the results of each shoot are played back on screen to show how the effects were created.

All the cars were specially built by Vauxhall and there are some extra tricks between the main scenes. It was designed by Frenchman Rémy Julienne, the doyen of film car stunt sequences from James Bond films *Goldeneye* and *Licensed to Kill* and other action epics like *The Rock*, *Gone in 60 Seconds* and *Enemy of the State*. The exit can be quite a scrum, though, as 5,000 people have to leave together, and it can take 15mins to clear the auditorium, hence if you can sit towards the front, you will be out quicker. Because it involves so much live co-ordination, it makes for a thrilling experience and you may want to see it more than once – another reason to see it early on. TTTTT FP+

BRITTIP
Star Wars fans visiting in late May-early June may want to attend Star Wars Weekends in costume. Dress up as your favourite character for even more interaction with the Star Wars characters that roam the Streets of America/Star Tours area of the park.

BRITTIP
If you have young children, be aware there is some (loud) mock gunfire in the Lights, Motors, Action!™ Extreme Stunt Show, which can upset sensitive ears, while the motorbike scene includes a rider catching fire, which can be frightening for them, too.

Other entertainment: Live music is provided periodically on the main street by the spectacular comedy rock band **Mulch, Sweat and Shears** (AAA; at the top of Hollywood Boulevard or Streets of America), while this is also a

Monsters Inc meet-and-greet

great place to meet **Disney characters** – look for *Cars* friends Lightning McQueen and Tow Mater at Luigi's Garage, and a Monsters University set-piece starring Sulley and Mike from the 2013 movie prequel in the building to the right of Lights, Motors, Action! Extreme Stunt Show. Disney TV stars Phineas & Ferb can be found near Luigi's Garage.

Shopping: Shop for Christmas items at **It's A Wonderful Shop**, **Stage 1 Company Store** for Muppet and Sesame Street souvenirs and **Writer's Stop** for books and speciality coffees.

Dining: Mama Melrose's Ristorante Italiano is a wonderful table-service Italian option (one of our favourites), while there are also the counter-service offerings of **Toy Story Pizza Planet** (average pizza, salads and drinks) and **Studio Catering Co.** (sandwiches, chicken wraps, salads and its own bar – with beer $8.50, wine $7.50 and cocktails $10.75).

Commissary Lane

This is just a small link between the Streets of America and the central plaza by the Sorcerer's Hat, and contains only two eating opportunities. The **Sci-Fi Dine-In Theater Restaurant** is a big hit with kids as you dine in a mock drive-in cinema, with cars as tables, car-hop waitresses and a big film screen showing old black-and-white science-fiction movie clips. The menu features gourmet burgers, ribs, chicken, pasta and sandwiches, as well as signature milkshakes and sodas ($32.50 for 3-course lunch, $8.99 kids' meal). The counter-service option **ABC Commissary** serves up standard fare that includes a Seafood Platter, Chicken Club sandwich and Asian salad.

Pixar Place

This area is styled after the real-life Pixar film studios in California, and houses one of the most popular rides.

SciFi Dine-in Theatre

Toy Story Midway Mania

Toy Story Midway Mania: A real family fun fiesta, a 3-D ride into a fantasy fairground of games with the *Toy Story* characters. To start with you are 'shrunk' to toy-size and board carnival vehicles (each equipped with individual spring-action shooters) to go through Andy's Bedroom, where the toys have set up a Midway Games Play Set with five challenges, plus a practice round. Thanks to a pair of 3D glasses, riders can 'see' everything their shooter fires at the sequence of targets (while, with the magic of Disney's special effects, they might also 'feel' objects whirring past as they burst out of the screens; and, if you hit a water balloon, watch out!). Throw virtual eggs at barnyard targets, launch darts at prehistoric balloon targets, break plates with baseballs, land rings on Buzz Lightyear's alien friends and finish up in Woody's Rootin' Tootin' Shootin' Gallery (with a bonus roundup) before totting up your scores and comparing with fellow riders. All the time, the *Toy Story* characters cheer you on (and pass on hints to boost your score, so it works for all abilities) and provide some amusing commentary. At times it is a touch raucous and chaotic, but kids are sure to love the shooting game element and the whole family can enjoy the amusing ride through the toys' world. Even the queuing area is fun, with a huge animatronic Mr Potato Head acting as a fairground barker to entertain while you wait (AAA TTTT FP+1). It draws some HUGE queues, so use the FastPass+ option here (it is crucial you book these as far in advance as possible).

Other entertainment: Look out for the *Toy Story* characters meet-and-greet here.

Shopping: For souvenirs and gifts from your favourite Pixar films visit the **Camera Dept**.

Dining: Hey Howdy Hey Take Away offers counter-service ice-cream, snacks and drinks.

Animation Courtyard
Get ready for a series of wonderful family-friendly shows in this area of the park.

Voyage of the Little Mermaid: A 17min live performance that is primarily for children who have seen the Disney cartoon. It brings together a mix of actors, animation and puppetry to re-create the film's highlights. Parents will still enjoy the special effects, but queues tend to be long, so go early or late. There is also the likelihood you will get a little wet. AAA (AAAAA under-9s; FP+)

BRITTIP
Try to sit at least halfway back in the Mermaid Theatre, especially if you are with young children, as the stage front is a bit high.

Walt Disney: One Man's Dream: This interactive show-and-tell exhibit chronicles Walt himself and his lifetime of accomplishments. From archive school records to a model of the Nautilus from *20,000 Leagues Under the Sea*, the story of the man behind the Mouse comes to vivid life. The homage ends with a preview of Disney's future developments, plus a 10min film encapsulating all Walt achieved and dreamed about. AAAA

Disney Junior – Live on Stage!: Mickey, Goofy, Donald and Daisy are throwing a surprise birthday party for Minnie, but need the help of friends like Jake and the Neverland Pirates, Doc McStuffins and Sofia the First to make this the best celebration ever. It's colourful and entertaining and pre-schoolers just love it. AA (AAAAA under-5s) FP+

Other entertainment: Youngsters can meet all their favourite Disney Junior characters in **Animation Courtyard**, several times daily and take part in the lively **Disney Junior Dance Party**, while Minnie Mouse has her own meet-and-greet in the Drawing Room in the post-show area of the Magic of Disney Animation.

Sunset Boulevard

The final part of the park contains the two high-thrill rides, and the big night-time finale, but it's also the busiest area from midday on, so try to visit here first or use FastPass+.

Rock 'n' Roller Coaster Starring Aerosmith

Disney's Hollywood Adventure

Regular park visitors will notice that several attractions have shut in recent times as part of a long-term expansion plan. American Idol Live, the Backlot Tour and The Magic of Disney Animation have all closed, but on their way are two fab new areas, a Star Wars-themed land and a Toy Story Land. These will add new rides, dining and character experiences, including scenes from the next three Star Wars films, but it will take several years. But, for 2016, there are some additions to current park experiences, with new scenes for **Star Tours** from the latest blockbuster, *Star Wars: The Force Awakens*; **Star Wars Launch Bay**, an interactive look at the latest movie with special merchandise and food (in Animation Courtyard); and a new **Jedi Training Academy**, featuring characters from the Disney XD series, Star Wars Rebels.

Rock 'n' Roller Coaster Starring Aerosmith: Disney's first big-thrill inverted coaster is a sure-fire draw for the adrenalin ride addicts, with a magnificent indoor setting and nerve-jangling ride. It features a clever holographic-style film show starring rock group Aerosmith in their recording studio. That leads to the real fun, set to specially recorded tracks from the band itself and with outrageous speaker systems, as

DISNEY'S HOLLYWOOD STUDIOS with children

Here is our guide to the attractions that appeal to the different age groups in this park:

Under-5s
Beauty and the Beast – Live on Stage, Fantasmic!, Honey I Shrunk the Kids Movie Set Adventure, Disney Junior–Live On Stage!, Voyage of the Little Mermaid, For The First Time In Forever.

5–8s
Beauty and the Beast – Live On Stage, Fantasmic!, Honey I Shrunk the Kids Movie Set Adventure, Indiana Jones™ Epic Stunt Spectacular, Lights, Motors, Action!™ Extreme Stunt Show, Muppet* Vision 3-D, Jedi Training Academy, Toy Story Mania, Voyage of the Little Mermaid, For The First Time In Forever.

9–12s
Beauty and the Beast – Live on Stage, Fantasmic!, The Great Movie Ride, Indiana Jones™ Epic Stunt Spectacular, Lights, Motors, Action!™ Extreme Stunt Show, Muppet*Vision 3-D, Rock 'n' Roller Coaster Starring Aerosmith, Jedi Training Academy, Star Tours, Twilight Zone™ Tower of Terror, Toy Story Mania.

Over-12s
Fantasmic!, The Great Movie Ride, Indiana Jones™ Epic Stunt Spectacular, Lights, Motors, Action!™ Extreme Stunt Show, Muppet*Vision 3-D, Rock 'n' Roller Coaster Starring Aerosmith, Star Tours, Toy Story Mania, Twilight Zone™ Tower of Terror, Walt Disney: One Man's Dream.

---

riders climb aboard Cadillac cars for a memorable whiz through a mock Los Angeles (watch out for a close encounter with the Hollywood sign!). The high-speed launch and inversions ensure a dynamic coaster experience. Go first thing or expect serious queues, and don't forget to check out your ride photo ($18.95, or $14.95 delivered digitally). **R**: 4ft/124cm. **TTTTT** FP+1

BRITTIP
If only one or two in your group want to ride Rock 'n' Roller Coaster, or you want to save significant time waiting, opt for the Single Rider queue. You will be split up, but the wait will be much shorter.

The Twilight Zone™ Tower of Terror:
This 199ft/60m landmark invites you to experience another dimension in the strange Hollywood Tower Hotel that time forgot. The exterior is intriguing, the interior is fascinating, the ride is scintillating and the queues are huge! Just when you think you are through to the ride, there's another queue, so spend your time inspecting the superb detail. There's a lot more to this than just the big 13-storey drop, however, as the 'Twilight Zone' theme adds a real element of invention.

Your elevator car twists and turns unexpectedly before it is time to 'drop in', and the random drop sequence provides hair-raising thrills before you exit! **R**: 3ft 4in/101cm. **TTTTT** FP+

Beauty and the Beast – Live on Stage:
An enchanting live musical song and dance performance of the highlights of this Disney classic will entertain the whole family for 30min in the Theater of the Stars. Check the daily

Twilight Zone™ Tower of Terror

schedule for show times, which are up to five times a day, usually starting at 11.45am. AAA FP+1

Fantasmic!: A not-to-be-missed special-effects spectacular. Staged nightly (twice nightly in peak periods) in a 6,900-seat amphitheatre, it features the dreams of Mickey, portrayed as the Sorcerer's Apprentice, through films such as *Pocahontas*, *The Lion King* and *Snow White*, but hijacked by the Disney villains, leading to an epic battle, with Our Hero emerging triumphant. Dancing waters, shooting comets, animated fountains, swirling stars and balls of fire combine in a breathtaking presentation, especially the giant, fire-breathing dragon! The 25min show begins seating up to two hours in advance and it's best to head there at least 30min before (watch out for the splash zones!). AAAAA FP+1

Other entertainment: Sunset Boulevard is also home to more of the park's **Citizens of Hollywood** characters.

BRITTIP
You can get a plain burger without all the trimmings at Backlot Express and Rosie's. Just ask when you reach the cashier. It's not on the menu, but it is available.

R2D2 at a Star Wars weekend

Shopping: Legends of Hollywood, **Planet Hollywood Super Store** and the **Sunset Boulevard** shops (for limited edition watches, clothing and other collectibles) are the best.

Dining: Rosie's All-American Café (chicken, burgers and salads) and **Catalina Eddie's** (pizza) are the best of Sunset Boulevard's five market-style eateries.

Skywalker and Co

Film fans will want to make a beeline for the Studios during Star Wars Weekends in late May and early June when the park becomes a playground for characters, film stars, photo-opportunities, competitions and other memorabilia based on anything to do with Luke Skywalker and Co, plus a nightly fireworks display. Much of the event is scheduled in and around the Premier Theater in the Streets of America area. There is no additional fee to rub shoulders with (and get autographs from) various Star Wars™ personalities (FP+1), and the Studios take on an extra dimension each weekend (though the park is also at its most crowded). Some Star Wars Weekend character meets and events are FP+1. Try the Star Wars Dine-In Galactic Breakfast at the **Sci-Fi Dine-In Theater** ($50 adults, $32 3–9) and Jedi Mickey Star Wars Dine at **Hollywood and Vine** for dinner ($58 adults, $35 3–9; $64/$39 adds the Fantasmic Dinner Package) featuring Jedi Mickey, Darth Vader Goofy, and more.

Frozen Summer Fun

The children's hit of each summer season (mid-June–early Sep) is this extra programme of live entertainment themed around the hit film. It brings together Princess Anna, Queen Elsa, Kristoff and Olaf with the citizens of Arendelle in a daily Royal Welcome parade, *Frozen*-themed treats and merchandise, and a spectacular Frozen fireworks display above Hollywood Boulevard nightly, in addition to the regular **For The First Time In Forever** show.

Disney's Animal Kingdom Theme Park

Disney's newest and smartest theme park opened in 1998 representing a completely different experience. With an emphasis on conservation and nature, it largely eschews non-stop thrills and attractions for more relaxing pace, although still in Disney's usual seamless entertainment style and with some excellent rides, including one of its very best. The attractions are relatively few, with just six out-and-out rides, but there are then two elaborate wildlife trails, four shows (including two that are almost worth the entry fee alone), an extravagant adventure playground, conservation station and a petting zoo.

It is also outrageously scenic, notably with the 145ft/44m Tree of Life, the Kilimanjaro Safaris and the Asian village of Serka Zong (home to the gigantic Expedition: Everest™ ride), but it won't overwhelm you with Disney's usual grand fantasy. Rather, it is a chance to explore and experience; to learn and understand; and to soak up the gentler more natural ambience. It is not a zoo in the conventional sense, but it is home to 200-plus species of birds and animals (in some wonderfully naturalistic settings). The educational tone is fairly strong, but children in particular may pick up easily on the essential conservation undertones of things like Kilimanjaro Safaris and Maharajah Jungle Trek. However, the park does get crowded, the walkways can be congested and there are fewer places to cool down. It is definitely a good idea to be here on time and use FastPass+ to minimise queuing.

Disney's Animal Kingdom Theme Park at a glance

Location	Directly off Osceola Parkway, also via World Drive and Buena Vista Drive		
Size	500 acres/203ha divided into 6 'lands'		
Hours	9am–5 or 6pm; 8 or 9am–8 or 9pm once Rivers of Light show begins in 2016		
Admission	Under-3s free; 3–9 $99 (1-day base ticket), $295 (5-day Magic Your Way), £274 (14-day Ultimate); adult (10+) $105, $315, £299. Prices do not include tax.		
Parking	$17		
Lockers	Either side of Entrance Plaza; $12 small, $14 large ($5 deposit each)		
Pushchairs	$15 and $31 at Garden Gate Gifts, through entrance on right; length of stay $91/week, $130 10 days, $189/$270 double		
Wheelchairs	$12 or $70 ($20 deposit refunded) with pushchairs		
Top attractions	DINOSAUR!, Kilimanjaro Safaris, It's Tough To Be A Bug!, Kali River Rapids, Festival Of The Lion King, Finding Nemo – The Musical, Expedition: Everest™		
Don't miss	Pangani Forest Exploration Trail, Maharajah Jungle Trek, Rafiki's Planet Watch, dining at Rainforest Café, new Rivers of Light night-time show.		
Hidden costs	Meals	Burger, chips and coke $11.68 3-course meal at Yak & Yeti $33-48 (kid's entrée and dessert $8.49) Beer $7.50–9.00 Kids' meal $6.99–$7.49	
	T-shirts	$24.95–36.95 Kids' T-shirts $19.99–29.99	
	Souvenirs	$1.35–2,000	
	Sundries	Caricatures: $20–35	

The Oasis
1 The Oasis Tropical Garden

Discovery Island
2 The Tree of Life
3 It's Tough To Be A Bug
4 Discovery Island Trails
5 Flame Tree Barbecue
6 Pizzafari
7 Adventurers' Outpost

Africa
15 Harambe
16 Kilimanjaro Safaris
17 Rafiki's Planet Watch
18 Pangani Forest Trail
19 Tusker House Restaurant
20 Festival Of The Lion King
21 Harambe Market

Asia
22 Flights Of Wonder
23 Kali River Rapids
24 Maharajah Jungle Trek
25 Expedition: Everest™
26 Yak 'n Yeti Restaurant
27 Rainforest Café
28 Rivers of Light (summer 2016)

Dinoland USA
8 DINOSAUR!
9 The Boneyard
10 Finding Nemo – The Musical
11 Chester And Hester's Dino-Rama!
12 TriceraTOP Spin
13 Primeval Whirl
14 Restaurantosaurus

DISNEY'S ANIMAL KINGDOM

Rafiki's Planet Watch

Africa

Discovery Island

Avatarland (coming 2017)

Oasis

Entrance

Rivers of Light (Summer 2016)

Asia

DinoLand U.S.A.

Location

If you are staying in the Kissimmee area, Disney's Animal Kingdom is the easiest of the parks to find. Just get on the (toll) Osceola Parkway and follow it all the way to the toll booths. Alternatively, coming down I-4, take exit 65 on to Osceola Parkway. From West Highway 192, come in on Sherberth Road and turn right at the first traffic lights. If you arrive early (which is advisable), you can walk to the Entrance Plaza. Otherwise, the usual tram system takes you in, so make a note of the row you park in (e.g. Unicorn, 67). The entrance plaza is overlooked by the Rainforest Café, with its 65ft/20m waterfall, which is open for breakfast, lunch and dinner (but is busy 12.30–3.30pm and an hour before closing). With Orlando so hot in summer, you need to be here as early as possible to see the animals before they hide in the shade.

BRITTIP
An early start is especially advised for Kilimanjaro Safaris in summer. If you don't arrive early, plan this attraction for its latest excursion of the day.

Beating the queues: For the early birds, here is your best plan of campaign. Once through the gates, animal lovers should head first for **Kilimanjaro Safaris**, through the Oasis, Discovery Island and Africa. After the Safari, go straight to **Pangani Forest Exploration Trail** and you will have experienced two of the park's best animal encounters before it gets too hot. Alternatively, thrill-seekers should walk straight through Discovery Island for Asia, where the **Expedition: Everest™** ride is the big draw. Then head to Kilimanjaro Safaris or the nearby **Kali River Rapids** raft ride, followed by the scenic **Maharajah Jungle Trek**. The best combination for the first arrivals is to get a FastPass+ for Expedition: Everest™ (if you don't already have one), then ride Kilimanjaro Safaris and, once you have done that (and depending on your FP+ time), either do your Everest ride or go straight to Kali River Rapids. Check your show schedule for **Festival of the Lion King** and try to catch one of the first two performances, as the later ones draw sizeable queues. The wait time board

Disney's Animal Kingdom

DINOSAUR!

at the entrance to Discovery Island is helpful. Those are your main tactics – here is the full rundown.

The Oasis

Tropical Garden: A gentle, walk-through introduction to the park, this is a rocky, tree-covered area featuring animal habitats, streams, waterfalls and lush plant life. Here you meet miniature deer, a giant anteater, exotic boars, macaws, waterfowl, a Patagonian cavy and wallabies in an understated environment that leads you across a stone bridge to the main park area. Visit in early afternoon when many of the rides are busy. AAA

Shopping: Stop at **Garden Gate Gifts** (on the right) for pushchair, wheelchair and locker hire, while Guest Relations is on the left.

The Tree of Life

Dining: The fun **Rainforest Café** also has an entrance inside the park here. If you haven't seen the one at Disney Springs, you should call in to view the amazing jungle interior with its audio-animatronic animals, waterfalls, thunderstorms and aquariums. A three-course meal costs $26–$60, but the setting alone is worth it and the food is above average. Try breakfast or an early dinner to avoid the crowds.

Discovery Island

This colourful village is the park hub, themed as a tropical artists' colony, with animal-inspired artwork, nature trails, four main shops and two eateries. You will also find the Baby Center and First Aid station here (look for the 'ladybird' lights).

The Tree of Life: This arboreal edifice is the park centrepiece, an awesome creation that seems to have a different perspective from wherever you view it. The trunk and roots are covered in 325 carvings representing the Circle of Life, from the dolphin to the lion. Trails lead round the tree, interspersed with habitats for flamingos, otters, ring-tailed lemurs, macaws, axis deer, cranes, storks, ducks, porcupines, kangaroos and tortoises. The tree canopy spreads

160ft/49m, the trunk is 50ft/15m wide and the diameter of the roots is 170ft/52m. It has 103,000 leaves (all attached by hand) on more than 8,000 branches! AAAA

Tree Trails: Opened after a 2015 refurbishment, these pretty trails at the foot of the Tree of Life feature habitats for the cotton-top tamarin, African crested porcupine, Galapagos tortoise, shark catfish and more.

It's Tough To Be A Bug!: Winding down among the Tree's roots brings you 'underground' to a 430-seat theatre and another example of Disney's artistry in 3-D films and special effects. This hysterical 10min show, in the company of Flick from the Pixar film *A Bug's Life*, is a homage to 80 per cent of the animal world, featuring grasshoppers, beetles, spiders, stink bugs and termites (beware the 'acid' spray!) as well as several tricks we couldn't possibly reveal. Sit towards the back in the middle (allow a good number of people in first as the rows are filled up from the far side) to get the best of the 3-D effects. Queues build up from midday, but they do move quite steadily. Don't miss the 'forthcoming attractions' posters in the foyer for some excruciating bug puns on famous films. AAAAA FP+

BRITTIP

The dark, special effects and mock creepy-crawlies in It's Tough To Be A Bug! can be extremely scary for young 'uns. Use caution.

Other entertainment: The Island is home to the lively **Viva Gaia Street Band** and various **Disney characters**, notably Daisy Duck at Character Landing (opposite Flame Tree Barbecue), Pocahontas on Discovery Island Trail, and two of the characters from *UP!* near Disney Outfitters. **Adventurers Outpost** is the setting to meet Mickey and Minnie. FP+ Children can also sign up for the novel **Wilderness Explorers** programme here (also based on *UP!*), with the chance to visit 30 locations around the park for interactive lessons and animal experiences, earning sticker badges along the way that act as a gentle educational story. **Winged Encounters – The Kingdom**

The gibbon enclosure in the Asia area

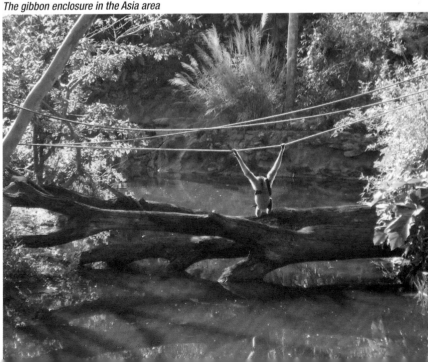

Takes Flight free-flight macaw show takes place over Discovery Island several times daily.

Shopping: You will find a huge range of merchandise, souvenirs and gifts here, notably in **Disney Outfitters** (artwork and collectables) and **Island Mercantile**.

Dining: Counter-service restaurants **Pizzafari** (pizza, salads and sandwiches) and **Flame Tree Barbecue** (barbecued ribs, beef and pork, chicken sandwiches and salads) are both good choices. If it's not too hot, the Flame Tree is a picturesque option, set among pretty gardens and fountains on the Discovery River; the air-conditioned Pizzafari is better in summer months.

Africa

The largest land in the park, it recreates the forests, grasslands and rocky homelands of East Africa's most fascinating residents in a richly landscaped setting that is part vintage port town and part savannah. The central area, Harambe Village, is a superb Imagineer's eye-view of a Kenyan port town, complete with white coral walls and thatched roofs,

and is the starting point of your adventure. The Arab-influenced Swahili culture is also depicted in the native tribal costumes and architecture.

BRITTIP

The best (i.e. the most jolting) ride with the Kilimanjaro Safaris is at the back of the truck. There is less to see from midday to late afternoon in summer when many animals take a siesta.

Festival of the Lion King: This not-to-be-missed, high-powered 25min production (up to 10 times a day in peak periods, seven at quieter times) brings the film to life in spectacular fashion, with giant moving stages, huge animated figures, singers, dancers, acrobats and stilt-walkers, plus some fun audience participation. All the well-known songs are given an airing in a fiesta of colour and sound, and it underlines the usual Disney quality Disney. However, queuing often begins an hour in advance for the new 1,000-seat (air-conditioned) theatre, so use FastPass+ or try to take in one of the early shows. AAAAA FP+ Sign language shows are performed

Harambe Village

Kilimanjaro Safaris

at 4pm each Tues and Sat; arrive at least 25 mins early and ask to sit in the Warthog section, but check with a Cast Member on arrival.

Kilimanjaro Safaris: The queuing area alone earns high marks for authenticity, preparing you for the sights and sounds of the 110acre/45ha savannah beyond. You board a 32-passenger truck, with your driver relaying information about the flora and fauna on view and a bush ranger-pilot overhead relaying facts and figures on the wildlife, including the dangers threatening them in the real world. Scores of animals are spread out in various habitats, with no fences in sight (the ditches and barriers are all well concealed) as you splash through fords and cross rickety bridges, and you should get good close-ups of lions, rhinos, elephants, giraffes, antelope, hippos and ostriches. Once again, the authentic nature of all you see (okay, some of the tyre 'ruts' and termite mounds are concrete and the baobab trees are fake) is breathtaking, with the spread of the vegetation and landscaping. The animals roam over a wide area, though, and can disappear from view. Not recommended for expectant mothers or anyone with back or neck problems. AAAAA FP+

Pangani Forest Exploration Trail: As you leave the Safari, you turn on to a serious nature trail that showcases gorillas, hippos, okapi, zebras, meerkats and rare tropical birds. You wander the trail at your own pace and visit 'research' stations to learn more about the animals, including the underwater view of the hippos (check out the size of a hippo skull and those teeth!) and the savannah overlook, where giraffes and antelope graze and the meerkats frolic. The walk-through aviary gives you the chance to meet the carmine bee-eater, pygmy goose, African green pigeon, ibis and brimstone canary, among others, but the real centre-piece is the silverback gorilla habitat (in fact, two of them). The family group is often just inches away from the plate-glass window, while the bachelor group further along can prove more elusive. Again, the natural aspect of the trail is fabulous and it provides a host of photo opportunities. Do this early or save it for late in the day when most of the crowds will have moved on. AAAAA

Rafiki's Planet Watch: This subsection of Africa involves a (rather dull) rustic train ride, with a peek into some of the backstage areas, as a preamble to the park's interactive and educational exhibits (especially for children). The three-part journey starts with Habitat Habit!, where you can see cotton-top tamarins and learn how conservation begins in your own garden. Conservation Station offers a series of exhibits, shows and information stations about the environment and threats to its ecology. Look out for Sounds of the Rain Forest (in listening booths) and the Live Animal Cams that show many of the park's inhabitants in their back-stage areas. Then observe the park's Veterinary Treatment Center (including a hatchery and neo-natal care) and Training Exhibits. You can easily spend an hour absorbing the information here, inspired by Disney's Worldwide Conservation Fund. Finally, the Affection Section petting zoo consists of a collection of goats, sheep and a miniature donkey. AAA

Expedition Everest

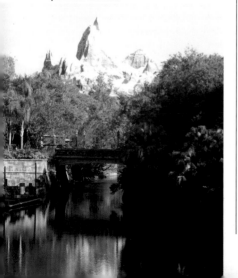

Other entertainment: There's plenty more to enjoy here, with the splendid African sounds of **The Burudika Band** and the pageantry and rhythms of **Tam Tam Drummers of Harambe**. With luck you'll also spot the wonderful **DiVine**, a 'moving' part of the foliage (also in The Oasis at times). Rafiki's Planet Watch is also home to roving musician **Gi-Tar Dan** and his fun songs, which he can personalise at the drop of a hat!

Shopping: Harambe is home to the **Mombasa Marketplace/Ziwani Traders**, where you can suit up safari-style, while Rafiki's Planet Watch has **Out of the Wild** for more gifts and souvenirs. Harambe Marketplace offers more African-inspired shopping at (name of shop and stuff they sell goes here) and (name of shop and stuff they sell goes here; both names TBC at proof stage).

Dining: Tusker House Restaurant (featuring Donald's Dining Safari for Breakfast at $30 adults, $17 children, and Lunch at $35 and $18) is one of the best diners in the park, with a mouth-watering array of salads, a hot carvery, rotisserie chicken, stews and vegetarian dishes ($42 and $20 for dinner, without characters). There are also four snack and drink bars, most notably the **Kusafiri Coffee Shop** (muffins, pastries, coffee), while **Tamu Tamu Refreshments** offers some ice cream and soft drinks, and the **Dawa Bar** is a great place to sit with a beer or cocktail and soak up the scenery. The new Harambe Marketplace has **Kitamu Grill** (chicken skewers and kebab sandwiches), **Famous Sausages** (South African-style corn dogs), **Wanjohi Refreshments** (beer, wine, speciality drinks) and **Chef Mwanga's** (ribs).

Asia

The next 'land' is elaborately themed as the gateway to the imaginary south-east Asian region of Anandapur, with temples, ruined forts, landscape and wildlife. The element of reality is startling and the architecture is full of faithful

representations of genuine locations. The elaborate ruined temple showcases for the gibbons and siamangs are worth looking out for – and you may well hear them wherever you are in the park!

Flights of Wonder: Another wildlife show, this portrays the talents and traits of the park's avian inhabitants. A trainer showcases the behaviours of various birds, including macaws and hawks, before being interrupted by a bumbling tour guide, who needs to be reminded of key conservation issues. This is the cue for some frolics with our feathered friends, including vultures, eagles, toucans and a singing parrot. The Caravan Stage is open-air, though, and can be hot in summer. AAA

Kali River Rapids: Part thrill-ride, part scenic journey, this bouncy raft ride will get you pretty wet (not great for early morning in winter). It starts out in tropical forest territory before launching into a scene of logging devastation, warning of the dangers of clear-cut burning. Your raft then plunges down a waterfall (and one unlucky soul – usually the one with their back to the drop – gets seriously damp) before you finish more sedately. Queues can be long through the main part of the day, so use FastPass+ here. **R**: 3ft 6in/106cm (a few rafts have adult-and-child seats allowing smaller children to ride). **TTT** AAAA **FP+**

Maharajah Jungle Trek: Asia's version of the wildlife trail is another picturesque walk past decaying temple ruins and animal encounters. The first few exhibits – the Malayan tapir, Komodo dragon and a bat enclosure (including the flying fox bat, the world's largest) – lead to the main viewing area, the 5acre/2ha Tiger Range, whose pool and fountains are a popular playground early in the day for these magnificent big cats. An antelope enclosure and walk-through aviary complete this breathtaking trek (which rarely draws heavy crowds). AAAAA

Expedition: Everest™: A major attraction, this clever roller-coaster takes you deep into the Himalayas for an encounter with the mythical Yeti. The queuing area alone will convince you of its authentic location (try to do the main queue at least once rather than FastPass to appreciate all the fine detail) as it delivers you to an old abandoned tea plantation railway station. Here you undertake the ride to the foothills of Mount Everest, but you must first brave the perils of the Forbidden Mountain – lair of the Yeti. Will the beast be in evidence? You bet! The ride becomes a typically fast-paced whiz (but no inversions), forwards AND backwards, as you attempt to escape the creature's domain. The final encounter with a massive audio-animatronic Yeti is jaw-dropping and underlines the

Kali River Rapids

splendidly creative nature of this ride. It has proved to be a fabulous attraction but draws equally impressive crowds all day, so make it one of the first things you do. You can also take advantage of a Single Rider queue here (at the FP entrance) if you don't mind your group being split up. You can get ride photos here, too ($18.95, or $14.99 delivered digitally). R: 3ft 8in/115cm. TTTTT FP+

BRITTIP
Although Expedition: Everest™ is a FastPass+ ride, its popularity means FP+s often run out, so schedule in advance, if possible. Don't leave it too late.

Other entertainment: Have fun with **DJ Anaan and his Bangra Dance Party** next to the Local Foods Café, along with the **Chakranadi** duo, sitar and tabla musicians, while *Jungle Book* characters can be found at Upcountry Landing.

Shopping and dining: The retail options are limited in Asia (just two minor kiosks), but it is home to the fab **Yak and Yeti** combination diner. Outside is the counter-service **Local Foods Café** (honey chicken, Teriyaki beef bowl, egg rolls, chicken salad and Korean stir-fry), while inside the two-storey structure is the full restaurant. Yak and Yeti offers some

Yak and Yeti

imaginative cuisine, from a Dim Sum basket to Chicken Tikka Masala and a Malaysian Seafood Curry, as well as more standard Asian-fusion dishes, like Kalbi Steak and Coconut Shrimp, and Spring Rolls. A good range of drinks and cocktails complement this superior eatery. Extra incentive to visit: a full range of bar drinks to go, while you can just sit at the bar for a drink or a full meal. The **Anandapur Ice Cream Truck** is also popular and the **Royal Anandapur Tea Company** features a great range of speciality teas, coffees and soft drinks.

DinoLand USA
The final area of the park is somewhat at odds with the natural theme of the rest, a full-scale palaeontology exercise, with the accent on a 'university fossil dig'. Energetically tongue-in-cheek (the students who work the area have the motto 'Been there, dug that', while you enter under a mock brachiosaurus skeleton, the 'Oldengate Bridge' – groan!), it still features some glimpses into genuine research and artefacts.

DINOSAUR!: Renamed after Disney's big animated film (it was initially called *Countdown to Extinction*), this is a herky-jerky ride experience, rather dark and intense (and often too scary for young children). It is also a wonderfully realistic journey back to the end of the Cretaceous period, when a giant meteor put paid to dinosaur life. You enter the high-tech Dino Institute for a multimedia history show that leads to a briefing room for your 'mission' 65 million years in the past. However, one of the Institute's scientists hijacks your trip to capture a dinosaur, and you career back to a prehistoric jungle in a 12-passenger Time Rover. The threat of a carnotaurus (quite frightening for children; try to sit them on the inside of the car) and the impending doom of the meteor add up to a whirl through a menacing environment. You will need to ride at least twice to appreciate all the detail, but queues build up quickly, so go either first thing or late in the day. R: 3ft 4in/101cm. TTTT AAAA FP+

DISNEY'S ANIMAL KINGDOM THEME PARK with children

Here is our guide to the attractions that appeal to the different age groups in this park:

Under-5s

Affection Section, The Boneyard, Discovery Island Trails, Festival of the Lion King, Finding Nemo – The Musical, Kilimanjaro Safaris, Maharajah Jungle Trek, Pangani Forest Exploration Trail, TriceraTOP Spin, Rivers of Light.

5–8s

All the above, plus Conservation Station, DINOSAUR! (with parental discretion), Flights Of Wonder, Habitat Habit!, It's Tough To Be A Bug (with parental discretion), Kali River Rapids, Primeval Whirl.

9–12s

All the above, plus Expedition: Everest™.

Over-12s

DINOSAUR!, Expedition: Everest™, Festival of the Lion King, Flights Of Wonder, It's Tough To Be A Bug!, Kali River Rapids, Kilimanjaro Safaris, Maharajah Jungle Trek, Pangani Forest Exploration Trail, Primeval Whirl, Rivers of Light.

The Boneyard: A hugely imaginative adventure playground, it offers kids the chance to slip, slide and climb through the 'fossilised' remains of triceratops and brontosaurs, explore caves, dig for bones and splash through a mini waterfall. The amusing signage will be wasted on most kids, but it's ideal for parents to let their young 'uns loose for up to an hour (though not just after the neighbouring Finding Nemo show has finished). TTTT (kids only).

Finding Nemo – The Musical: This lovely show is a first for Disney entertainment, taking a regular animated feature and turning it into a full musical. The show combines colourful puppets, dancers, acrobats and animated backdrops with innovative lighting, sound and special effects.

BRITTIP

Finding Nemo – The Musical is popular, but although it draws long queues, the theatre seats 1,500, so most people usually get in.

The basic idea remains faithful to the story of Nemo, his dad Marlin and friends Dory and Crush and features larger-than-life puppetry, plus rod, bunraku and shadow puppets, all designed by Michael Curry, who created the award-winning Broadway version of Disney's *The Lion King* show. It's a spectacular combination of music and grand staging, and the 30min show performs up to five times a day. AAAA FP+

Chester & Hester's Dino-Rama!: This mini-land of rides, fairground games and stalls adds a rather garish element to the park. Its main icon is a towering concretosaurus (!), and it is designed to have a quirky, tongue-in-cheek style reminiscent of 1950s' American roadside attractions. The rides are: **TriceraTOP Spin:** another version of the Dumbo/Aladdin rides in the Magic Kingdom, where a flying, twirling, spinning top bounces you up and down with a surprise at the top. AA (TTTT under-5s); and **Primeval Whirl:** coaster fans will get a laugh out of this wacky offering that sends

Primeval Whirl

its riders through a maze of curves, hills and (quite sharp) drops that make it seem faster than it actually is. It's basically a lampoon of the DINOSAUR! ride, a mock journey 'way back in time', with plenty of cartoon frippery. Extra fun is provided by the fact that the cars spin, which gives an unpredictable element to each 3min ride. The queuing area is a riot of visual gags, but the ride is not recommended for anyone with back or neck problems. **R**: 4ft/122cm. **TTTT FP+**

Other entertainment: Dino-Rama also features the **Fossil Fun Games**, six fairground-type stalls (costing $4 for a single ticket, $10/3 tickets, $3/5 or more tickets) designed to tempt you to try to win a cuddly dinosaur. **Disney characters** Goofy and Pluto meet guests across from TriceraTop Spin, with Donald Duck nearby.

Shopping: Chester and Hester's Dinosaur Treasures (the 'Fossiliferous Gift Store' – groan!) offers a wide range of dino-related souvenirs.

Dining: You can get a counter-service meal at the (you've guessed it!) **Restaurantosaurus** (burgers, hot dogs, sandwiches, chicken nuggets and salad) or ice-cream and pastries at **Dino Bite Snacks**.

Other entertainment

Rivers of Light: This new evening show is set to debut in 2016 as the park moves to extended hours and finishes with a stunning nightly special effects extravaganza in front of a brand-new seating area. Staged on the lake between Discovery Island and Expedition Everest, it will feature live music, fountains, floating lanterns, boats and an immense water-screen effect with elaborate animal imagery, all presented before an amphitheatre viewing area. **AAAAA FP+** (expected).

Tours: Finally, for a behind-the-scenes look at the park, **Backstage Tales** is a wonderful almost four-hour journey into the handling and care of all the animals (7.30am daily; $90, no under-12s, under 18s with adult). For something really different, try the **Wild Africa Trek**, a three-hour ride-and-trek into the African savannah. From a precarious rope bridge crossing high above Harambe Reserve to a VIP safari in special open-air vehicles and a visit to Harambe's private camp, this exclusive experience, in groups of no more than 12, is open to ages 8 and up (minimum 4ft/122cm tall; under 18s with adult), six times daily. Closed-toe shoes required, dresses/skirts not advised; weight limit 310lb/141kg. Seasonal pricing $189–249. Book tours on 407 939 8687.

That's the full Disney theme park story, but there is still PLENTY more in store…!

TriceraTop Spin

6 Five More of the Best

or Wizards, Wildlife and Wonders

It's time to leave the wonderful world of Disney and explore the rest of Central Florida's great attractions. And there's still a terrific amount in store, including some of the most thrilling rides and dazzling creativity. Yes, Universal Orlando and the SeaWorld parks are that good.

Universal has developed astronomically in recent years, with new hotels, entertainment, restaurants and, above all, headline attractions. In 2014, it opened the massive Cabana Bay Beach Resort, completed a major expansion of the CityWalk district and debuted the most eye-catching themed area in 15 years with the Wizarding World of Harry Potter – Diagon Alley. And there's more in store, with another new hotel for 2016 – Sapphire Falls – a new King Kong attraction, the under-construction Volcano Bay water park and more CityWalk enhancements.

With four hotels, all connected by boat, bus or path to the CityWalk hub, from where the two parks radiate, Universal is an increasingly dynamic proposition, and more centralised than Disney. It also owns the Wet 'n Wild water park and its tie-up with the SeaWorld parks via the Orlando FlexTicket offers amazing value. For UK visitors, the 2 and 3-park Bonus Tickets are also extremely well priced. It does not offer a free FastPass+ system like Disney but you can buy the Universal Express pass that covers

A raptor at Jurassic Park, Islands of Adventure

Universal Dining Plan

Visitors can choose to add a daily meal allowance to their hotel bookings, or a daily Quick Service meal plan if they are just visiting the parks. The full Dining Plan can only be booked via Universal's own reservation system – **www.universalorlandovacations.com** – and offers one Table Service meal (entrée, dessert and soft drink), one Counter Service meal (entrée and soft drink), omne Snack (popcorn, ice-cream, etc) from food carts or counter service restaurants, and 1 additional soft drink per day for $52/adult and $19/child. It can be used at most dining venues in the parks and 10 in CityWalk (but, strangely, none in the hotels). The Quick Service option costs $20/adult and $13/child per day and offers one counter service meal (entrée and soft drink), one snack and one soft drink per day. The Quick Service option can be purchased on the day or in advance online. There is also the Coca-Cola Freestyle cup at $13/person (plus $10 for additional days) with unlimited free refills all day at the special Coca-Cola Freestyle outlets (five in each park), offering more than 100 different drinks.

a one-time front-of-queue access to nearly all the rides (but not the three headline Harry Potter attractions). It is not cheap – from $35–100 depending upon time of year and $65–110 for both parks, but can save a lot of queuing at peak periods. A limited number go on sale after park opening and are snapped up, but they can also be bought online for a specific day at **www.universalorlando. com** or in the parks themselves for another day. The Park-to-Park Ticket + Unlimited Express provides park admission AND unlimited Express access for 1–4 days, from $210–390/ adult, $205–380/child (online only).

Universal hotel guests (except those at Cabana Bay Beach Resort) benefit from Express ride priority all day by showing their room key and all 4 enjoy the major perk of early access to The Wizarding Worlds of Harry Potter each day. In addition, some rides have Single Rider queues, which save time if you want to go by yourself or don't mind splitting up your group. Once again, height/health restrictions (R) are noted in ride descriptions. Universal is also home to some of the best (and most grisly!) Halloween celebrations on earth, with their Halloween Horror Nights programme (p167).

Halloween Horror Nights

© Universal Orlando Resort

Universal Studios Florida®

Universal opened its first Florida park in June 1990 and quickly became a serious rival to Disney. For the visitor, it means a consistently high standard and good value (though the choice can be bewildering), but there are few similarities to their Los Angeles park. Universal is also a different proposition to Disney, with a more in-your-face style that appeals especially to teens. Younger children are still well catered for, though. Universal parks can also need more than a full day in high season. Strategies are the same, though: arrive EARLY (up to 30mins before opening), do the big rides first, avoid main meal times and take time out for an afternoon break (try shopping, dining or visiting the cinemas at CityWalk) if it gets too crowded.

Location
Universal Studios Florida® is divided into seven main areas, set around a lagoon, but there are no great distinguishing features. The main resort entrance is just off Interstate 4 (I-4 eastbound take exit 75A; westbound take exit 74B) or via Universal Boulevard from I-Drive by Wet 'n Wild. Parking is in its massive multi-storey car park and there is quite a walk (with moving walkways) to the front gates.

Photo connect
Universal's photo sharing system allows guests to collect all their ride photos in one source and is cheaper than buying them individually. Just ask for a Photo Connect card when

Universal Studios Florida® at a glance

Location	Off exits 75A and 74B from I-4; Universal Boulevard and Kirkman Road		
Size	110 acres/45ha in 7 themed areas		
Hours	9am–6 or 7pm off peak; 9am–10pm high season (Washington's birthday, Easter, summer holidays, Thanksgiving, Christmas)		
Admission	Under-3s free; 3–9 $97 (1-day ticket), $185 (2-day Park-to-Park ticket), $316 (5-Park FlexTicket), $336 (6-Park FlexTicket); adult (10+) $102, $195, $336, $356. Prices do not include tax.		
Parking	$17 (preferred parking $22; valet parking $35)		
Lockers	Immediately to left in Front Lot $8–10		
Pushchairs	$15 and $25		
Wheelchairs	$12 and $50 (with photo ID as deposit), with pushchairs		
Top attractions	Harry Potter and The Escape From Gringotts, Hogwarts Express, Revenge of the Mummy, Men in Black, Despicable Me: Minion Mayhem, TRANSFORMERS: The Ride – 3D, The Simpsons, Hollywood Rip, Ride Rockit!		
Don't miss	Universal's Cinematic Spectacular, Universal's Superstar Parade, Curious George Playground (for kids), The Blues Brothers, Tales of Beedle the Bard		
Hidden costs	Meals	Burger, chips and coke $13 3-course dinner $25–39 (Lombard's) Kids meals $7 ($7–10 in Finnegan's)	
	T-shirts	21.95–38.95	
	Souvenirs	95c–$1,500	
	Sundries	Temporary tattoos $7–10	

Production Central

1 Main Entrance
2 Shrek-4D
3 Despicable Me
4 Hollywood Rip, Ride, Rockit!
5 Meet Shrek & Donkey
6 Monsters Café
7 Transformers: The Ride – 3D

New York

8 Twister
9 Revenge Of The Mummy
10 The Blues Brothers
11 Finnegan's Bar and Grill
12 Louie's Italian Restaurant

San Francisco

13 Fast And Furious – Supercharged (coming summer 2017)
14 Beetlejuice's Revue (closing 2016)
15 Lombard's Seafood Grill

The Wizarding World of Harry Potter – Diagon Alley

16 Hogwarts Express

17 The Leaky Cauldron
18 Diagon Alley
19 Harry Potter and the Escape from Gringotts
20 Carkitt Market

World Expo

21 Men in Black – Alien Attack
22 Fear Factor Live!
23 The Simpsons Ride
24 Kang amd Kodos' Twirl 'n Hurl
25 Duff Brewery & Shop

KidZone

26 Animal Actors on Location!
27 Fievel's Playland
28 A Day in The Park with Barney
29 ET Adventure
30 Woody Woodpecker's Nuthouse Coaster
31 Curious George Goes To Town

Hollywood

32 Universal's Horror Make-Up Show
33 Terminator 2: 3-D Battle Across Time
34 Hello Kitty
35 The Brown Derby

you buy your first ride photo and all subsequent ones will end up on the same account for that day. You can then download your pics, add fancy borders and other features, share or have them put on posters, keychains, mugs and more at the Photo Connect kiosk when you leave. Or look for the Star Card, which allows you to compile ALL your Universal photos (include ride ones) on the one card account for either one day ($39.95), three days ($59.95), an Annual Pass ($89.95) or a 14-day Digital Package ($89.99). You can pre-order it with a discount at **https://photoconnect. amazingpictures.com/** and share it on social media with their Amazing Pictures app.

◀🇬🇧▶ BRITTIP

A good way to enjoy the Universal Express perk is to book a night's stay at one of their three deluxe hotels. Check in early (they will store bags for you) and you get your hotel room key, with Express feature, for use that day AND the next day.

Beating the queues: With the opening of The Wizarding World of Harry Potter – Diagon Alley, this has become THE place to visit first, with heavy queues building up quickly and lasting all day. It is at the back of the park, so try to avoid all the other attractions if this is your top target. Turn right on Rodeo Drive, continue through Sunset Boulevard and the Springfield area of The Simpsons, and go left across the bridge straight to the Wizarding World. If you are not a Potter fan (although you should still give Diagon Alley a look at some stage) and want some of the big-time thrills, stop first at Hollywood Rip Ride Rockit (on your left in Production Central) and then take in TRANSFORMERS: The Ride – 3D and the nearby Revenge of The Mummy in New York. For interactive fun, take in Despicable Me first, then head back to the Springfield area and do The Simpsons and Men In Black. Many of the other attractions are now easy to do with the crowds flocking to Diagon Alley.

Here's a full guide to the Studios (for CityWalk, see Chapter 10). Watch out for the helpful mobile electronic Wait Times boards around both parks, too.

Production Central

Coming straight through the gates brings you into the administrative centre, with a couple of large gift stores plus Studio Sweets. Call at **Guest Services** for guides for disabled visitors, TDD and assisted listening devices, and to make restaurant bookings, which can also be made at a kiosk to the right after the turnstiles, next to the **Beverly Hills Boulangerie**. **First aid** is available here (and on Canal Street between New York and San Francisco), while there are facilities for nursing mothers at **Family Services** by the bank through the gates on the right. In addition, Universal Studios hosts **IMPACT Wrestling** (periodically), with free tickets available on a first-come, first-served basis (call 407 224 8000 for more details, or visit the Studio Audience Center – the Lost & Found office in the Guest Services courtyard through the gates to the right). Coming to the top of the Plaza of the Stars brings you to the business end of the park.

Shrek 4-D: This adds a new dimension to 3-D films as the original cast (Mike Myers, Eddie Murphy, Cameron Diaz and John Lithgow) reprise their Oscar-winning roles. The amusing 7min pre-show leads into the 500-seat main theatre, where you don your Ogre Vision 3-D glasses and prepare to enter a new world. The film is funny enough as Shrek and Donkey

Diagon Alley

save the Princess, but the special effects (watch out for the spiders!) and moving seats add a startling extra element that is hugely entertaining. State-of-the-art digital projection and audio systems, lighting effects and smoke (plus a hilarious finale featuring an out-of-control Tinker Bell) ensure a real laugh-fest. Queues stay long for much of the day. AAAAA+

Despicable Me – Minion Mayhem: This outrageously funny 3-D simulator ride is based on the animated films starring Steve Carell. You enter the home of super-villain Gru and visit his lab where you are 'shrunk' to undergo Minion training. In the company of Gru's daughters, Margo, Edith and Agnes, the zany scheme goes awry and his 'recruits' suffer some hair-raising adventures that need Gru's intervention to save the day. It ends happily, of course, with a fun Minion dance party (and gift shop). With dynamic, motion-based seats, things can get bumpy, so those with heart, neck, or back problems should ask for the stationary seats. TTT+ AAAA (TTTTT under-10s)

Hollywood Rip Ride Rockit!: This iconic ride is a high-tech colossus, with an onboard system that allows you to select your own ride music – then take home the DVD. Orlando's highest and fastest roller-coaster at a daunting 167ft/51m and almost 70mph/113kph, you can't miss this vivid red steel beast as it loops right through park. It starts with a video intro while you queue that reveals five music choices (Rap/Hip Hop,

Country, Classic Rock/Metal, Pop/Disco and Club Electronica), each with six tracks. You're then strapped into an open-sided car that goes straight up a 17-storey vertical lift-hill, then into a steep dive followed by the signature Double Take, the world's first non-inverted loop (you don't actually go upside-down but it feels like it!). You will soar over the heads of people in the queue, dive below ground level and fly around a 150° banked turn, all in the course of the 1min 40sec ride. The innovative open cars make the whole experience feel even faster and more dynamic, while the mix of pounding music (from your headrest and speakers along the track) and concert-style lighting (flashy during the day, stunning at night) ensures this is a ride that really rocks. You can buy the ride video, complete with your musical selection captured by multiple cameras (for $35; ride photos $20–70). It looks more frightening than it actually is, but it is truly exhilarating. Leave this for later in the day when queues tend to drop off. R: 4ft 3in/130cm. TTTTT+

BRITTIP
At Universal's three big coasters – Rip Ride Rockit, The Hulk and Dragon Challenge – you have to pass through metal detectors at the entrance, so ALL metal items must be placed in a (free) locker beforehand.

TRANSFORMERS: The Ride – 3D: The latest generation of Universal's dramatic 3-D technology allied with a dynamic ride vehicle, this puts guests at the heart of an explosive battle between the Autobots, led by Optimus Prime and the evil Decepticons of Megatron. It feels like walking into a movie as the long, elaborate queuing area prepares riders for joining the planet-defending forces of NEST, and then a larger-than-life whirl through a Decepticon attack in a bid to defend the AllSpark – and the earth's existence! The combination of ultra-HD film, real scenery and dramatic special effects is breathtaking (if loud). Even those who have never

Transformers: The Ride – 3D

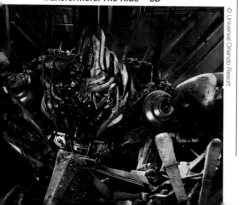

© Universal Orlando Resort

seen one of the films will not feel left out as the whole scenario is explained while you queue. Crowds build up quickly, hence you need to ride early on or late in the day. **R**: 3ft 4in/101cm. **TTTT**

Character appearances: Optimus Prime, Bumblebee and Megatron have a brilliant set-piece **Transformers photo spot** next to the ride, or meet Shrek, Fiona and Donkey at **Meet Shrek & Donkey**, well worth catching for the amusing patter. You'll find **Minion photo ops** in the Super Silly Stuff shop.

Shopping: Great shops here, including **Supply Vault** for all things Transformer, **On Location** (film, clothes, sundries and 2-way radio rentals), **Super Silly Stuff** (Despicable Me merchandise), the massive **Universal Studios Store** (with everything) and **It's A Wrap** (discounted items).

Dining: The main eating outlet is the wonderful **Monsters Café** (peak season only) offering salads, lasagne, meatloaf, burgers, hotdogs and pizza. The counter-service area is themed like Frankenstein's lab, with the dining areas showing black-and-white horror film clips.

New York

Now head to New York with its impressive architecture, street scenes and park.

Twister: Based on the hit film, this brings audiences 'up close and personal' with the awesome forces of a tornado. The 5-storey terror shatters everything in its path, with a splintering climax but the noise can be a bit much for under-10s. The pre-show area is also a work of art. **TTT**. NB: We believe this attraction will close in 2016 for something new.

Revenge Of The Mummy: This superb offering is a high-thrill, high-fun journey into the Ancient Egypt of The Mummy film series, fusing coaster technology with space-age robotics and special effects. It starts out as a slow, dark ride through curse-ridden Hamunaptra, but soon takes an

ingenious launch into something more dynamic, using the novel idea of the film studio becoming a full archaeological discovery, with a host of special effects and audio-animatronics as you brave the Mummy's realm. The high-speed whiz in the dark (backwards to start with) doesn't involve inversions but is still a thrill with its tight turns and dips, while there are several clever twists (the front row may get slightly damp!). It is a hugely immersive experience and rates 5-star with the elaborate queuing area, but may be too scary for under-8s. Preview your ride photos ($20–65) as you enter the gift shop. **R**: 4ft/122cm. **TTTT½**

BRITTIP

For the best ride experience on Revenge Of The Mummy, try to get a back row seat. You are not allowed to carry anything on the ride – loose items must be left in the (free) lockers provided.

The Blues Brothers: Fans of the film will not want to miss this live show as Jake and Elwood Blues (or pretty good doubles anyway) put on a stormin' performance on New York's Delancey Street several times a day. They cruise up in their Bluesmobile and go through a series of the film's hits before heading off into the sunset, stopping only for autographs. AAAA

Other entertainment: The energetic can try the **42nd Street Wall Climb** (rock wall) on 5th Avenue ($5). New York also boasts the inevitable **amusement arcade**. Or just grab a drink at **Finnegan's bar** and listen to the live music from their fun singer-guitarist.

Shopping: Check out **Sahara Traders** for Mummy souvenirs, as well as jewellery and toys, **Rosie's Irish Imports** for all things Irish and **Aftermath** for Twister souvenirs.

Dining: You have two main restaurants: **Finnegan's Bar and Grill** offers shepherd's pie, fish and chips, corned beef and cabbage, along with steak, burgers, fries and a good range of beers, plus Irish-tinged entertainment, while **Louie's Italian Restaurant** has counter-service pizza and pasta, ice-cream and tiramisu. There's also a **Ben and Jerry's** store for ice-cream and smoothies, and a **Starbucks** for coffee and pastries.

San Francisco

Crossing Canal Street brings you right across America to two smaller-scale attractions.

Fast And Furious – Supercharged: This fabulous new ride-and-show experience is due to open in 2017 but should be well under construction by late 2015. Based on the underground street racing world made famous in the film series starring Vin Diesel and Paul Walker, it will take visitors into an all-new adventure with the high-speed stars, using the latest ride technology and giving it an immersive twist thanks to new digital film and sound-surround effects. In addition, there will be a chance to get up close with some of the super-charged cars from the films, including *The Fast 8*, which is also due for release in 2017. AAAA/**TTTT** (expected). This also replaced the *DISASTER! A Major Motion Picture Ride…Starring YOU* attraction, which closed down in September 2015.

Beetlejuice's Graveyard Revue: Disney's Hollywood Studios has Beauty and the Beast and The Little Mermaid; Universal goes for Dracula, Frankenstein, The Wolfman and Frankenstein's Bride in this 20min live song-and-dance show compèred by Beetlejuice himself. The raucous concert shuns the

prettiness of Disney's attractions yet still comes up with a fun family show as the graveyard characters perform adapted 1980s rock and pop anthems. AAA NB: This show was due to close in late 2015 as part of the process to create space for the new Fast And Furious attraction.

Other entertainment: Although the **Jaws** ride is gone, you can still get a photo with the 'Great White' next to the Chez Alcatraz dockside bar, or try the **Amazing Pictures** kiosk and have your face added to a famous view or magazine ($30–119).

Shopping: Visit **San Francisco Candy Factory** for fab pick-n-mix.

Dining: Try the park's best dining choice, **Lombard's Seafood Grille** (high season only; reservations accepted) for great seafood, steak, pasta and sandwiches, accompanied by a wonderful view over the Central Lagoon. **San Francisco Pastry Co** offers desserts and coffee and **Richter's Burger Co** has some tempting burgers.

The Wizarding World of Harry Potter – Diagon Alley

Put simply, this is the most amazing theme park experience in the world today. The second part of Universal's hugely impressive Potter-verse not only repeats the immersive, film-like setting of Hogsmeade in Islands of Adventure (with a unique link between the two), it goes even deeper into JK Rowling's creation and leaves you in awe of the design and innovation. And that's before you get to the two rides, the live entertainment and the food offerings!

Diagon Alley: Hidden behind a realistic setting of The Embankment lies the secret wizarding street and a full array of complex theming, with the entrance next to a façade of Leicester Square tube station. The external design is modern London, right down to the ¼-scale King's Cross Station and a working version of Piccadilly's Eros Statue, where you

Beetlejuice's Graveyard Revue

© Universal Orlando Resort

will also find the iconic Knight Bus. Other elements include Grimmauld Place and the Wyndham Theatre but then visitors walk through the jumbled red-brick barrier next to the tube station and emerge in the jaw-dropping recreation of Diagon Alley, where the towering shop-fronts and mysterious businesses envelop visitors with the full visual effect of the films. Also here is the brooding Knockturn Alley, where the dark arts rule and every nook and cranny is suitably sinister as it is always night-time. Another area, Carkitt Market was created by JK Rowling purely for Universal. It is all new yet it LOOKS like it has been here for 150 years. Its mix of shops and dining are all jumbled together in a seamless way, making this as much of an attraction as the rides themselves. AAAAA+

Harry Potter and The Escape From Gringotts: Prepare to be mesmerised as you enter the vaults – and dangers – of the wizarding world's bank. A fire-breathing dragon sits high atop the building and, if that doesn't take your breath away, the stunning entry hall will as realistic goblins – the bank staff – lift the animatronic art to new heights, including an ultra-realistic head clerk who talks to visitors while you wait. The queue twists and turns through the filing office and backrooms before reaching Bill Weasley's office, where you learn you have arrived during the famous episode when Harry, Ron and Hermione break into the vaults. Then you take the elevator deep underground and climb a long flight of steel stairs into a vast cavern that only feels like it's miles below the bank. Here you board the ride to share in the perils of Harry and Co as they search for a crucial Horcrux. Half coaster and half 3-D simulator ride, it changes pace from scene to scene as riders brave the various guardians of the vaults, including the dangerous Bellatrix Lestrange, a fire-breathing dragon, an enchanted waterfall, assorted goblin guards and, finally, a close encounter with Lord Voldemort himself (which may be a touch intense for young children).

Riders do escape, of course, and the sense of realism will have you coming back for more – just be aware this draws the longest queues in the park from first thing, so head here straight away or expect a l-o-n-g wait. **R:** 3ft6in/106cm. **TTTTT+**

Hogwarts Express: This neat, realistic ride operates between the two parks, as guests journey to Hogsmeade from King's Cross Station. Again, the sense of realism is superb and, after what seems like the longest queue in theme park history, you arrive at Platform 9¾ to board an amazing replica of the famous Hogwarts train, complete with separate compartments and pulled by a Hull-class locomotive. While it runs on a special track backstage, the enclosed carriage 'windows' show highlights of the long journey north to Scotland, including a close encounter with Hagrid on his flying motorcycle, the flying Ford Anglia – and some dangerous Dementors. Oh, and look out for Harry, Hermione and Ron on the train! As this ride goes from park to park, you will need a multi-park ticket to ride, hence there is a real ticket office to check you through, or sell you a ticket to complete the journey. The queue area here is vast but waits rarely top 30mins. AAAAA+

Other entertainment: Look out for two completely original shows in Carkitt Market, where **Celestina Warbeck & The Banshees** take the stage several times a day to deliver a rollicking four-song performance. The 'Singing Sorceress' is not dissimilar to Shirley Bassey in a 1940s big-band jazz style, and the songs are

The Escape from Gringotts

© Universal Orlando Resort

all originals, including the classics 'You Stole My Cauldron But You Can't Have My Heart' and 'Beat Back Those Bludgers, Boys and Chuck That Quaffle Here'! AAAA. Also on the Market stage is the elaborate story-telling of **Tales Of Beedle The Bard**, a combination of live actor and puppetry show, with the intricate puppets created by award-winning designer Michael Curry. It's especially engaging for children, and Potter fans. AAA. Other live entertainment is provided by the essential wizard's shop of **Ollivander's**, where 'the wand chooses the wizard' and all manner of strange goings-on highlight this fun actor-staged show. AAA. Look out also for the **Knight Bus Conductor**, who will engage visitors as they enter the Wizarding World, and don't miss the bus's Talking Shrunken Head, as his wisecracks might just be aimed at YOU!

Shopping: Another key experience, with eight immersive stores to please the eye and tease the wallet. **Weasley's Wizard Wheezes** is a multi-storey joke shop with all manner of gags, then there is **Wiseacre's Wizarding Equipment** (for all your essential school gear), **Quality Quidditch Supplies**, **Madam Malkin's Robes** (school uniforms and accessories), **Borgin & Burkes** (the Dark Arts store in Knockturn Alley), **Magical Menagerie** (a soft toy emporium – listen to the animals scurrying about in the upper levels!) and **Scribbulus**, for other Hogwarts mementoes. The shops also feature interactive windows that work with the special wands on sale at **Ollivander's** and **Wands By Gregorovitch** at $45 each. Look for the markers in the pavement, say the magic command

The Leaky Cauldron

and wave your wand for a host of surprises. You can even change dollars into wizarding notes at the **Money Exchange**, complete with a Goblin host. Be ready to spend a fair bit of time here, as well as money!

Dining: The essential reality of the Wizarding World is continued into the main dining outlet of **The Leaky Cauldron**, a superb recreation of Diagon Alley's hallmark pub. The food may seem standard pub fare, but the Cottage Pie is excellent, as is the Beef, Lamb and Guinness Stew, while their Ploughman's Platter is positively indulgent with its array of three cheeses, pickle, salad, scotch egg and fresh bread (priced variously from $9–20). There is also Toad in the Hole (which Simon may just have helped with!), Fish 'n Chips, two types of sandwich (sausage and chicken) and a Fisherman's Pie. Kids can choose from a mini-pie, mac and cheese and their own fish 'n chips ($6.99). There are then three tempting desserts, of which the Sticky Toffee Pudding is to die for. All this can be washed down with signature drinks such as Fishy Green Ale (a variation on bubble tea, and non-alcoholic), Otter's Fizzy Orange Juice, Tongue-Tying Lemon Squash and Gilly Water, as well as two outstanding beers – the IPA-like Dragon Scale Ale and porter-style Wizards Brew. You order at the counter and are then given a 'magical' candle and shown to a table, where the food will find you thanks to a clever GPS device in the candle! There is a separate menu for breakfast. Still hungry? Head for Florean Fortescue's Ice Cream Parlour where Universal's culinary wizards have come up with a superb array of flavours that are all worth trying, including Earl Grey & Lavender, Apple Crumble, Chocolate Chilli and Clotted Cream. You can also grab a drink – alcoholic and otherwise – at the Hopping Pot and Fountain of Fair Fortune.

World Expo
Continuing around the park brings you to an extensive area that is home to Fear, Aliens and The Simpsons.

Halloween Horror Nights

Universal's massively popular Halloween celebration occurs through late Sept and all of Oct each year and is a wonderfully bloodthirsty – and thoroughly entertaining! – series of evening events. The Horror Nights have become a real trademark and add a suitably grisly touch to park proceedings. The park is transformed with imaginative set pieces from various horror movies, plus live shows and character interaction. The general mix is eight indoor Scare Houses, each with its own macabre theme (such as Friday The 13th and Halloween in 2015), plus open-air Scare Zones, with atmospheric dry ice and characters (zombies, chainsaw guys and various beasts!) lurking in dark corners, and two or three live presentations, including the signature Bill & Ted's Excellent Halloween Adventure (an annual comedy special that heavily satirises pop culture icons). All horror genres are well represented, and the Scare Houses feature some superb 'scare actors' and special effects. The rides are all open (and often with fairly short queues), adding more novelty to the park experience, but this over-the-top (and occasionally downright gruesome) extravaganza is definitely not for kids, especially as the atmosphere can get a bit raucous late in the evening as alcohol is widely available. It goes down a treat with adults with the right sense of humour, though, and begins every evening at 6.30pm until 1 or 2am. It is a separate event costing $102/person (but there are savings of up to $52 if you add it on to a daytime ticket of any kind). There is even a Frequent Fear Pass for multiple visits on selected evenings (not Sat, when crowds are heaviest and queues for the Scare Houses can reach 2 hours) and a HHN Universal Express pass for $70–120 (depending on dates), plus a Frequent Fear Plus Express Pass (including Friday) for $280. No costumes are allowed on any evening, though. Look up more at **www.halloweenhorrornights.com**.

Men in Black – Alien Attack: This combination thrill/dark ride takes up where the hit films, starring Will Smith, left off. Visitors are introduced to the MIB Institute in an inventive mock-futuristic setting and enrolled as trainees for a battle around the streets of New York with a horde of escaped aliens. Your 6-person car is equipped with laser zappers for an interactive shoot-out that is like a real-life arcade game, as the aliens can also shoot back to send your car spinning. The finale features a close encounter with a giant bug that is all mouth. Only your collective shooting skills can save the day, and there are numerous ride variations according to your accuracy. Fast, frantic and a bit confusing, you'll want to come back until you can top 250,000 (for Defender status). R: 3ft 6in/106cm. TTTT

BRITTIP
For a big score in Men In Black, when you meet the Big Bug – push the big red button!

Fear Factor Live: (high season only) This live-action version of the reality TV show asks audience volunteers to take part in some hair-raising (and stomach-churning!) challenges, with a head-to-head competition to find the biggest daredevil. Auditions take place 70mins before each show, and the audience then gets to see the chosen few battle it out, with clips from the TV show interspersed with live action. Some of the stunts are distinctly off-colour (anyone for a maggot milkshake?) and may not be good for young children (or anyone of a weak disposition!). TTT

The Simpsons Ride: The headline attraction in the Springfield sub-area of World Expo, this brings the TV characters to vibrant life in a colourful and amusing production, even if you're not a fan of The Simpsons. It is themed as Krustyland amusement park, brainchild of irascible Krusty the Clown, a bizarre funfair that is the setting for a hectic, breathtaking ride in the company of the Simpson clan. A wicked sound system and state-of-the-art motion simulator technology ensure a frantic race through outlandish attractions (watch out for the Tooth Chipper!). The feel of the 'ride' is amazing and the huge domed screen ensures an outrageously comical sensory experience. However, this can also be a big draw, hence you should visit early or expect a serious wait. **R**: 3ft 4in/101cm. **TTTTT**

Kang and Kodos' Twirl 'n' Hurl: A standard fairground whirligig with some clever touches as the alien duo take 'foolish humans' into 'orbit' and provide a challenge as you twirl. **TT** (**TTTTT** under 6s).

Other entertainment: In Springfield, chance your hand at a series of fairground-type games that require $5 to play, like the groan-inducing Sledge-Homer. Look out for Simpsons **character meet-and-greets** at regular intervals, and **photo ops** with Springfield icons like the Lard Lad Donuts statue, Founders statue and The Seven Little Duffs.

Shopping: Visit **MIB Gear** (at the exit to the ride) for Men In Black-themed clothing and souvenirs (plus photo opportunities with the MIB themselves). To complete the immersive Springfield effect, visit the **Kwik-E-Mart** for Simpsons souvenirs (plus more gags).

Dining: Expo Eats offers drinks and snacks, then there's the clever counter-service offerings of the food-court, where you can dine in true Homer fashion (albeit with better quality) at **Krusty Burger, Luigi's Pizza, Frying Dutchmen, Cletus' Chicken Shack** and **Moe's Tavern** (complete with the non-alcoholic Flaming Moe cocktail). For a specially-made brew, you can visit the **Duff Brewery & Shop** with a fab view of the Lagoon. **Bumblebee Man's Taco Truck** completes the picture here.

Kang and Kodos' Twirl 'n' Hurl

© Universal Orlando Resort

BRITTIP
Along the lagoon in the Springfield/KidZone area is East Green, a quiet spot where you can stop to take a break for a while.

KidZone

This is a great place to let the kids loose on their own, but it does also feature several great family attractions. This area is also likely to be next for a big refurbishment, possibly later in 2016.

Animal Actors On Location!: An amusing mix of video, animal performance and audience interaction, several children are invited to help present some unlikely feats and stunts featuring a range of wildlife, from parakeets and pigs to cats, dogs and an orang-utan. Many have been rescued from animal shelters and gone on to feature in films before finding a home at Universal. The theatre also provides an escape from the queues. AAAA

Fievel's Playland: Strictly for kids, this playground, based on the enlarged world of the cartoon mouse, offers the chance to bounce under a 1,000-gallon hat, crawl through a giant boot, climb a giant spider's web and shoot the rapids (a 200ft/61m waterslide) in Fievel's sardine can. TTTT (young 'uns only!)

A Day in the Park with Barney: Again strictly for the younger set (2–5), the purple dinosaur from kids' TV is brought to super-dee-duper life in a large arena that features a pre-show before the 15min main event, plus an interactive post-show area. AA (AAAAA under-5s)

ET Adventure: This is as glorious as scenic rides come, with a picturesque queuing area from the film and then a spectacular leap on the trademark flying bicycles to save ET's home planet. Steven Spielberg has added some special effects and characters, and you have an individual ET greeting at the end. The masses often overlook this corner of the park, hence it's a good afternoon choice. R: 4ft/122cm to ride alone, but smaller children can ride with parents. AAAAA

Woody Woodpecker's Nuthouse Coaster: Anchoring the excellent under-10s adventure land is this child-sized but still quite racy roller-coaster. The ride reaches only 28ft/8m high and 22mph, but it seems the real deal to young 'uns. However, the height restriction is still 3ft/91cm. TTTT (juniors only)

BRITTIP
If you want to let your youngsters loose in the Curious George playground, it is advisable to bring swimsuits or a change of clothing.

Curious George Goes To Town: Kids of all ages love this adventure playground with plenty of ways to get wet. It combines toddler play, water-based play stations and a huge interactive ball pool, and is a real bonus for harassed parents. The town theme includes buildings to climb, pumps and hoses to spray water, a ball factory in which to shoot, dump and blast thousands of foam balls and – the tour de force – two huge buckets of water that flood the street below at regular intervals. TTTTT (under-12s) Curious George roams the KidZone from time to time, while other characters make regular appearances.

Other entertainment: Young 'uns should head for **Barney's Backyard**, a neat indoor play area for those under 36in/91cm tall, including a **photo opportunity** with Barney himself (in addition to the one at the end of each show). It also has the parental benefit of being in the air-conditioned cool!

Shopping and dining: Shop at the fun **Spongebob Storepants** for everything to do with Spongebob and friends in an immersive environment, complete with character photo opportunity, plus the **Barney Store** and **ET's Toy Closet** and **Photo Spot**. For a quick bite, **Kidzone Pizza Company** offers pizza and chicken fingers.

Hollywood

Finally, your circular tour of Universal returns you to the main entrance via Hollywood (where else?).

Universal's Horror Make-Up Show: Not recommended for under-12s, this demonstrates some of the ways in which films have terrorised us, from classic black-and-white examples to modern horror movies. Using film clips and 2 special effects 'experts', the audience is treated to a slapstick approach to horror make-up. It's a 20min show, queues are rarely long and the special effects are largely amusing. AAA

Terminator 2: 3-D Battle Across Time: Another first-of-its-kind attraction, this is part film, part show, part experience but all action, and usually leaves its audience in awe. The 'Wow!' factor works overtime as you go through a 10min pre-show representing a trip to the Cyberdyne Systems company from the Terminator films and then into a 700-seat theatre for a 'presentation' on its latest robot creations. The show is interrupted, though, by John and Sarah Connor and mayhem ensues, with the audience subjected to an array of (loud) special effects, including real actors interacting with the screen and the audience, indoor pyrotechnics and a climactic 3-D film finale that takes the Terminator story a step further. TTTTT

Hello Kitty: Fans of the popular Sanrio character Hello Kitty (and others like Chococat and My Melody) should be thrilled to discover this extensive new retail and character

Terminator 2: 3-D

© Universal Orlando Resort

meet-and-greet opportunity, replacing the old Lucille Ball tribute exhibit.

Other entertainment: The **Hollywood Character Zone** provides numerous character appearances throughout the day along Hollywood Boulevard, from Scooby Doo and Shaggy to Dudley Do-Right, The Flintstones and Lucille Ball, along with music from the **Studio Brass Band**. The **Character Party Zone** features various members of the Superstar Parade periodically next to Mel's Drive-In.

> **BRITTIP**
> Budding magicians should make a bee-line for the small Theater Magic shop next to Mel's Drive-In, with merchandise and some terrific small-scale magic shows several times daily.

Shopping: Look for Terminator gifts and clothing in **Cyber Image**, all manner of headgear in **The Brown Derby**, Hollywood legends' jewellery in **Studio Styles** and movie memorabilia, notably for Betty Boop and Lucille Ball, in **Silver Screen Collectibles**.

Dining: There are four contrasting eateries: **Mel's Drive-In**, a re-creation from the film *American Graffiti*, serving burgers and hot dogs (though Richter's has better burgers); **Café La Bamba** for the daily Parade Character Breakfast (see right); **Schwab's Pharmacy**, with traditional ice-cream, milkshakes and sundaes; and **Beverly Hills Boulangerie** for a range of sandwiches, cheesecake, pastries, juices and coffee.

Universal's Cinematic Spectacular

© Universal Orlando Resort

Parade time!

Universal's Superstar Parade: The daily performance takes place at 3 or 5pm in a vibrant and lively style, with dozens of performers and interactive characters. The four main sets of 'superstars' are led by Gru and his Minions from *Despicable Me* and followed by Spongebob Squarepants and his Bikini Bottom pals, including skaters and stilt walkers – and with the world's biggest pineapple! EB and the bunnies from the 2011 film *Hop* take over, including some snazzy live drumming, while Nickelodeon stars Dora and Diego from *Dora The Explorer* and *Go, Diego, Go!* complete the line-up, with aerialists and other high-energy performers. The huge floats – especially for the Minions – are feature-packed, and the parade has two dance stops to allow characters to meet guests. It is just 15mins but there are up to four other meet-and-greet performances during the day when characters come into the park for their own Street Parties. AAAA

> **BRITTIP**
> The two best viewing spots for the Parade are halfway along the main New York street (opposite the Palace Arcade) or on Hollywood Boulevard, outside the Cyber Image shop.

The Parade also has a **Character Breakfast** 9–11am (Thurs–Sat), with the chance to meet the Minions, pose with Spongebob, get autographs from Dora and Diego and enjoy a full breakfast at **Café La Bamba** ($26 adults, $13 3–9s). Those booking the breakfast also receive VIP viewing for the Parade and early access to selected rides.

Universal's Cinematic Spectacular: The nightly finale is this 20min film, firework, fountain and special effect-laden performance on the Main Lagoon. With three 'stages' and numerous water effects, it celebrates 100 years of Universal movies with clips choreographed to some spectacular fountains and pyrotechnics. See how many

UNIVERSAL STUDIOS with children

Our guide to the attractions that generally appeal to the different age groups:

Under-5s
Animal Actors On Location!, Curious George Goes To Town, A Day In The Park With Barney, ET Adventure, Fievel's Playland, Kang & Kodos' Twirl 'n' Hurl, Universal's Superstar Parade.

5–8s
All the above (minus Barney), plus Disaster! and TRANSFORMERS: The Ride – 3-D (with parental discretion), Despicable Me, Hogwarts Express, Men In Black, Shrek 4-D, The Simpsons and Woody Woodpecker's Nuthouse Coaster, Universal's Cinematic Spectacular.

9–12s
All the above, plus Hollywood Rip Ride Rockit, Beetlejuice's Graveyard Revue, Fear Factor Live!, Harry Potter and The Escape From Gringotts, Revenge Of The Mummy, Terminator 2: 3-D Battle Across Time, TRANSFORMERS: The Ride – 3-D, Twister.

Over-12s
Hollywood Rip Ride Rockit, Beetlejuice's Graveyard Revue, The Blues Brothers, Disaster!, ET Adventure, Fear Factor Live, Despicable Me, Men In Black – Alien Attack, Revenge Of The Mummy, Shrek 4-D, The Simpsons, Terminator 2: 3-D, TRANSFORMERS: The Ride – 3-D, Twister, Universal's Cinematic Spectacular, Universal's Horror Make-Up Show.

movies you can spot, as well-known moments from the likes of *E.T.*, *Apollo 13*, *Jurassic Park*, *The Mummy* and *The Fast & The Furious* are projected on to the fountains, all with narration by Morgan Freeman. The show culminates in a firework frenzy, underscored by dramatic music (on 300 outdoor speakers) and superb digital projection for a truly original presentation. There is a seasonal version for Christmas, too. TTTT

For VIP viewing of the Spectacular, book the **Cinematic Dining Experience** with dinner at Lombard's Seafood Grille and reserved seats in the new VIP area on the Springfield waterfront ($45 for adults, $13 3–9s). Book on 407 224 7554 or at **www.universalorlando.com**.

BRITTIP
You need to be facing one of the three stages (they are double-sided, so can be seen from both sides of the Lagoon) of the Universal Cinematic Spectacular for a good view, notably along the waterfront of the World Expo area or in the East Green park.

Special programmes

Universal Studios features some brilliant extra seasonal entertainment for **Mardi Gras**, with a hectic, bead-throwing parade, plus music, street entertainment and authentic New Orleans food each Sat at 6pm mid-Feb–mid-Apr (and free with park admission). The day culminates in a live concert with well-known acts (including the B-52s, Kelly Clarkson and Olivia Newton-John in 2015), but it does draw HUGE crowds. Universal also throws a party for Fourth of July, when the park presents a major firework spectacular. And don't miss the Studios at Christmas (p39).

The fab Transformers meet-and-greet

© Universal Orlando Resort

172

FIVE MORE OF THE BEST

Islands of Adventure

With the arrival of Diagon Alley at Universal Studios, you'd think there might be slightly less focus on the original Harry Potter development here but not a bit of it. In fact, with the Hogwarts Express ride now connecting the two areas, it was as busy as ever in 2015 and is poised to hit the attendance jackpot again with the summer 2016 opening of the new King Kong attraction.

The Islands of Adventure opened in 1999 under the supervision of creative consultant Steven Spielberg, and it provided one of the most complete and thrilling theme parks you could imagine, containing an upbeat collection of high-adrenalin rides, shows and entertainment, plus some fine dining. Then JK Rowling's boy wizard arrived and added a whole new 'world' of excitement.

The park has a full range of attractions, from out-and-out thrills to pure family entertainment. OK, so they aren't really islands (the areas form a chain around the central lagoon), but that's the only illusion. And you get a lot for your money here, unless you have extremely timid children or under-5s. Seuss Landing will usually keep preschoolers amused for several hours, while Camp Jurassic is a clever adventure playground for 5–12s, but the rest of the park, with its nine 5-star thrill rides and other attractions, is primarily geared to kids of 10 and over, their parents and especially teenagers. There are six elements that look alarming, but don't be put off – they all deliver immense fun as well as terrific spectator value! If any one ride sums up IoA, it is Harry Potter and the Forbidden Journey, which

Islands of Adventure at a glance

Location	Off exits 75A and 74B from I-4; Universal Boulevard and Kirkman Road		
Size	110 acres/45ha in 6 'islands'		
Hours	9am–6, 7 or 8pm off peak; 8 or 9am–9 or 10pm high season (Washington's birthday, Easter, summer holidays, Thanksgiving, Christmas)		
Admission	Under-3s free; 3–9 $97 (1-day ticket), $185 (2-day Park-to-Park ticket), $316 (5-Park FlexTicket), $336 (6-Park FlexTicket Plus); adult (10+) $102, $195, $336, $356. Prices do not include tax.		
Parking	$17 (preferred parking $22; valet parking $35)		
Lockers	Immediately to left through main gates; $8–10		
Pushchairs	$15 and $25		
Wheelchairs	$12 and $50 (with photo ID as deposit)		
Top attractions	Harry Potter and the Forbidden Journey, Hogwarts Express, Amazing Adventures Of Spider-Man, Dragon Challenge, Incredible Hulk Coaster, Jurassic Park River Adventure		
Don't miss	Eighth Voyage Of Sindbad, Jurassic Park Discovery Centre, If I Ran The Zoo playground (for toddlers), Three Broomsticks restaurant and Ollivander's Wand Shop		
Hidden costs	Meals	Burger, chips and soda $13.18 3-course lunch $19–33 (Confisco Grill) Kids' meal $6.99	
	T-shirts	$21.95–37.95	
	Souvenirs	95c—$6,500	
	Sundries	Caricature drawings $15–41 (black and white and airbrush colour); Butterbeer $5 regular, $5.90 frozen	

took theme park ride technology to a whole new level.

Private nursing facilities, an open area for feeding and resting (with high chairs) and nappy-changing stations, can be found at the **Family Service Facility** at Guest Services (to the right inside the main gates), while ALL restrooms throughout the park are equipped with nappy-changing facilities. First aid is provided in Sindbad's Village in the Lost Continent, just across from Oasis Coolers, and in Port of Entry.

Port of Entry

You arrive for IoA as you do for Universal Studios, in the big multi-storey car parks off I-4 and Universal Boulevard and pass right through the CityWalk area, where you come to the main entrance plaza (head for the huge Pharos Lighthouse). As with Universal Studios, you can purchase the Universal Express pass for Islands of Adventure ($35–100, depending on time of year) at various locations throughout the park and at Guest Services. Once through the gates, the lockers, pushchair and wheelchair hire are on your left as the Port of Entry opens up before you. This elaborate 'village' consists of shops and eateries, so push straight on until you hit the main lagoon. Above all, be sure to take in the wonderful architecture throughout Port of Entry, which borrows from Middle East, Far East and African themes and uses bric-a-brac from all over the world.

Shopping: Later in the day, return to check out the extensive retail experience at places like **IoA Trading Company** and **Ocean Trader Market** for a full range of Islands of Adventure merchandise.

Dining: You can enjoy a coffee and pastry at the inevitable **Starbucks** or the **Croissant Moon Bakery** (also with croissants and sandwiches), or sample the huge cinnamon rolls and pastries of **Cinnabon**. Alternatively, try lunch or dinner at **Confisco Grille** with tastes from around the world including Italian, Mexican and Asian as well as American, and a good

range of dishes from sandwiches and burgers to salads, Fajitas, ribs, pizza and pasta. Or just grab a beverage and a snack at the **Backwater Bar** (Happy Hour 4–7pm).

Beating the queues: At the end of the street, you will need to decide which way to head first as there are nine attractions where the queues build up quickly and remain that way. If you are among the majority lured by Harry Potter, turn right (through Seuss Landing and The Lost Continent). If you're after the big thrill rides, turn left into Marvel Super-Hero Island and head straight to Spider-Man, then do Dr Doom's Fearfall and the Incredible Hulk Coaster. The new King Kong attraction (between Toon Lagoon and Jurassic Park) is sure to be a big draw when it opens in 2016, too, so you may want to head here first, and then visit Hogsmeade.

> **BRITTIP**
> There are two entrances to the Wizarding World of Harry Potter: from Jurassic Park and The Lost Continent. The latter is much more dramatic and offers the full Hogsmeade Village panorama.

Dinosaur fans should go left around the lagoon to Jurassic Park for the River Adventure before the majority arrive. Once you are nice and wet, go back to Toon Lagoon for Ripsaw Falls and the Bilge-Rat Barges. Or, if you have younger children, turn right into the multicoloured world of Seuss Landing and enjoy The Cat In The Hat and High In The Sky Seuss Trolley Train Ride prior to the main crowd build-up.

Jurassic Park River Adventure

© Universal Orlando Resort

Port of Entry
1 Ocean Trader Market
2 Confisco Grille

Marvel Super-Hero Island
3 Incredible Hulk Coaster
4 Dr Doom's Fearfall
5 Café 4
6 Captain America Diner
7 The Amazing Adventures of Spider-Man
8 Storm Force Accelatron

Toon Lagoon
9 Popeye And Bluto's Bilge-Rat Barges
10 Dudley Do-Right's Ripsaw Falls
11 Me Ship, The Olive
12 Comic Strip Café
13 Toon Lagoon Amphitheater

Jurassic Park
14 Jurassic Park River Adventure
15 Pteranodon Flyers
16 Camp Jurassic
17 Discovery Center
18 Skull Kingdom: Reign of Kong (summer 2016)
19 Raptor Encounter

The Wizarding World of Harry Potter
20 Harry Potter and the Forbidden Journey
21 Filch's Emporium
22 Flight of the Hippogriff
23 Olivander's
24 Dervish and Banges
25 Three Broomsticks
26 Zonko's
27 Dragon Challenge
28 Hogwart's Express

The Lost Continent
29 Mythos Restaurant
30 Mystic Fountain
31 The Eighth Volage of Sindbad
32 Poseidon's Fury

Seuss Landing
33 Circus McGurkus Café Stoo-pendous
34 High In The Sky Seuss Trolley Train Ride
35 Caro-Seuss-el
36 If I Ran The Zoo
37 The Cat In The Hat
38 One Fish, Two Fish, Red Fish, Blue Fish

Main Entrance

Turning right, in an anti-clockwise direction, here's what you find.

Seuss Landing

There is not a straight line to be seen in this vivid 3-D working of the books of Dr Seuss. The characters may not mean much to those unfamiliar with the children's stories, but everyone can relate to the fun here (though queues build up quickly). Take your time and try not to miss the clever detail, from squirt ponds to beach scenes, while the lagoon-front area provides a quieter corner to escape the crowds.

Caro-Seuss-el: This intricate carousel ride on some of the Seuss characters – cowfish, elephant-birds and dog-a-lopes, for example – has rider-activated features that are a big hit with children. AA (AAAA under-5s).

One Fish, Two Fish, Red Fish, Blue Fish: A fairground ride with a twist as you pilot these Seussian fish up and down according to the rhyme that plays while you ride. Get it wrong and you get squirted! More fun for the younger set. TTT (TTTTT under-5s)

The Cat in the Hat: Prepare for a ride with a difference as you board these crazy 6-passenger 'couches' to meet the world's most adventurous cat and friends Thing One and Thing Two. You literally go for a spin through this storybook world, and it may be a bit much for very young children. The slow-moving queues are a bit of a drag, so try to get here early or leave it until later in the day. AAAA/TTT

If I Ran the Zoo: Interactive playgrounds don't get much better for the pre-school brigade than with these Seuss character scenarios, some of which can be pretty wet! Hugely imaginative and great fun to watch. TTTTT (under-5s)

The High in the Sky Seuss Trolley Train Ride: This fun family adventure high above Seuss Landing has terrific appeal to youngsters as you board a trolley to journey into the world of the Sneetches, visiting the Inking and Stamping Room, the Star Wash Room and a tour inside the Circus McGurkus Café Stoo-pendous. It is slow-paced and scenic, but it does draw slow-moving queues, so head here early with under-9s. AAAA

Character appearances: Look out by The Cat In The Hat, Thing One and Thing Two and The Grinch outside the Circus McGurkus, and the character-filled celebration of the Oh! The Stories You'll Hear street show.

Shopping: If the land has captivated you, you can buy the books at **Dr Seuss' All The Books You Can Read Store**, or a full variety of character merchandise at the **Mulberry Street Store**. **Snookers and Snookers Sweet Candy Cookers** is a super sweet shop.

Dining: Snacks and drinks can be had at **Hop On Pop Ice Cream Shop**, **Moose Juice Goose Juice** and **Green Eggs and Ham Café** (sandwiches and burgers). The **Circus McGurkus Café Stoo-pendous** is a mind-boggling eatery for fried chicken, lasagne, spaghetti, burgers and pizza – with clowns and pipe organs.

The Lost Continent

This land underwent a rather drastic reduction to accommodate Harry Potter, but it still offers some eye-catching locations.

The Eighth Voyage of Sindbad: This stunt and special effects show is fun for both elaborate staging and performance. Mythical adventurer Sindbad and side-kick Kabob tackle evil witch Miseria in a bid to rescue

High in the Sky

© Universal Orlando Resort

Princess Amoura, and the action springs up in surprising places. There are several loud bangs that could scare young children but otherwise it's good family fun. The cast appear for photos and autographs post-show. TT AAAA

Poseidon's Fury: A walk-through show that puts its audience at the heart of the action as a journey in the company of a hapless young archaeologist takes a turn for the worse in the lost temple of Poseidon. You pass through an amazing water vortex before your expedition awakens an ancient demon. There is an element of suspense, but the special effects showdown between Poseidon and the demon is amazing. Queuing is tedious, but it is inside. TTT

Other entertainment: Try a bit of mystic manipulation with the **Psychic Readers**, while the Shop of Wonders houses **Theatre Magic**, with continuous live shows from 11am. But beware **The Mystic Fountain**; it can strike up a conversation – and then soak you!

Shopping: Find some original souvenirs at **The Coin Mint** (watch coins forged and struck) and **Coat Of Arms** (explore the history of your family name and coat of arms), **Treasures of Poseidon** (jewellery, clothing), and **The Pearl Factory** (pick an oyster).

Honeydukes in Hogsmeade Village

© Universal Orlando Resort

Dining: Food options include **The Fire-Eater's Grill** (chicken fingers, hotdogs, salads, fries and drinks) and **Frozen Desert** (sundaes and sodas). The ornate **Mythos Restaurant** provides the best dining in IoA; the food (seafood, salads, grills, pizza and pasta) is first class, but the setting (inside a dormant volcano with fountains and clever lighting) is a real attraction (3-course meal $22–37, kids' meals $6.99–10.99).

Wizarding World of Harry Potter – Hogsmeade

This 'Island' has significantly boosted the park's attendance since it opened in 2010 and draws BIG crowds. The magnificent edifice of Hogwarts Castle looms large over the 20acre spread of the famous Wizarding World but the whole area is completely immersive as it uses the design genius behind the films. Entering from The Lost Continent area provides the grand view, through Hogsmeade and with Hogwarts seemingly towering above (the use of architectural perspective is masterful), and you are drawn into an all-encompassing realm where chimneys smoke, icicles glitter, owls roost, visitors are warned to 'Observe the spell limits' and Butterbeer is real!

Hogsmeade Village: Walk through the grand archway into the Wizarding World and a powerful sense of realism envelops you. This is a shimmering, snow-covered version of the magical settlement Harry, Ron and Hermione inhabit. It is the shopping and dining heart of the Wizarding World, but is an attraction in itself. Here you will find a wonderful photo opportunity with the **Hogwarts Express**, while nearly all the shop windows feature 'wizardly' animatronic touches. The Owl Clock comes to life every 15mins; the wooden-raftered Owlery is a work of art; and you may just encounter Moaning Myrtle in the loos! Numerous other clever effects and design touches all help to transform this corner of Florida into J K Rowling's authentic creation (see also Shopping and dining). AAAAA+

Dragon Challenge: This towering coaster delves into the Goblet of Fire story involving the big contest between the wizarding schools of Hogwarts, Durmstrang and Beauxbatons, represented by the billowing banners at the entrance. The long, elaborate queuing area (we LOVE the Corridor of Candles!) sets the scene for your 'flight' on either a Chinese Fireball or Hungarian Horntail dragon, with perils aplenty. You choose which dragon to ride (the tracks differ slightly) and this is a suspended coaster, so your legs dangle free – the initial drop is therefore like going into free-fall! Coaster aficionados reckon the best ride is in the back of the Hungarian (blue) dragon, but both offer an awesome experience. The coaster features a 100ft/30m drop, 5 rapid-fire inversions among the intertwined tracks and hits a top speed of 60mph/96kph. **R:** 4ft 6in/137cm; all loose items must be left in the lockers by the entrance. **TTTTT+**

BRITTIP

The lockers for Dragon Challenge are in the Hogsmeade train station, but are free only for the duration of your ride. You MUST remove all metal objects from your pockets before riding.

The Flight of The Hippogriff: This junior-sized coaster is aimed primarily at youngsters and features a journey into Hagrid's realm, where his love of outlandish creatures gives rise to this swooping ride. Hagrid offers instructions and warnings as you wind through the queue, and you may even hear Fang barking from inside his hut. There are no big drops, but it delivers a surprisingly fast-paced whirl. Be sure to bow to the Hippogriff at the start of the ride. **R:** 3ft 4in/92cm. **TTT** (**TTTT** for 6–12s)

Harry Potter and the Forbidden Journey: This is the Big One: a trip inside the legendary halls of Hogwarts, and a breathtaking plunge on a state-of-the-art ride, Quidditch and all. The basic premise is that 'muggles' (non-wizarding types, i.e. you!) have been invited to tour the school for the first time and see much of the castle's interior. The queuing area is part discovery, part storytelling and part entertainment as it winds through, out, around and back in again for some 1,500ft/400m before you even get to the ride. Be ready for a LONG time on your feet as you traverse the corridors, traipse through the greenhouse, tiptoe along the Portrait Hall (where the paintings of the four founders of Hogwarts come to life in magical fashion) and tread

Harry Potter and the Forbidden Journey

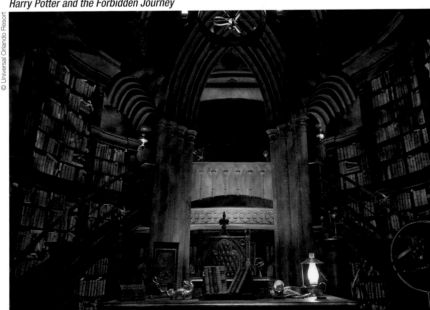

the stone floors of the Gryffindor common room. Along the way, you'll be greeted by Professor Dumbledore in his study (complete with more talking portraits), be accosted by the Fat Lady (another painting-come-to-life) and enter the Defence Against the Dark Arts classroom, where Harry, Ron and Hermione urge visitors to abandon their 'boring' tour and come to the Quidditch match (with the aid of a magic spell).

BRITTIP

Once again, this is an unpredictable, dynamic ride, with sudden twists, turns and tilts. You are strongly advised to leave all loose items in the free-to-use lockers just inside the castle.

Finally, you reach the Room of Requirement (past the Sorting Hat), where your mode of transport to the match is revealed – magical flying benches. With some pre-ride warnings, you are then strapped in to your 'bench' and are up, up and away. Only things don't go as planned and, before you can say 'Expecto Patronum' you're on a crazy dash through some of the young wizard's most dangerous adventures. Your unique ride vehicle – which moves on a giant robotic arm – sweeps

you through dramatic settings that combine clever film technology with full-scale, all-encompassing scenery, creating a totally convincing effect as you move up, down, backwards, forwards and even sideways.

BRITTIP

Look for the Single Rider queue at Harry Potter and the Forbidden Journey – it can save a LOT of time.

There is a close encounter with a fire-breathing dragon, an army of giant spiders, a Death Eater and a narrow escape from the clutches of the Whomping Willow before the big finale in a spooky underground cavern where it's up to Harry, naturally, to try to save the day. The 4min whirl will seem a LOT longer as the ride's breathtaking sequence of special effects make this an eye-popping extravaganza of sound, movement and high-tech dynamics. It is an astounding theme park experience, but it WILL scare small children (and those with arachnophobia!), and it draws HUGE queues – in excess of 2hrs at peak times – so you are strongly advised to do this early in the day. **R:** 4ft/122cm. **TTTTT+** NB: Universal's Express Pass does NOT cover this ride. You

Hogwart's Castle

exit through **Filch's Emporium of Confiscated Goods**, where you'll find plush Hedwig owls, Crookshank cats, Scabbers rats and 3-headed dogs (watch out, he growls!), plus a range of tempting Azkaban and House-related clothing and gifts. You also pick up your ride photos here ($24.95–69.95).

> ◀🇬🇧▶ **BRITTIP**
> Look out for the Marauders Map in Filch's Emporium, plus other clever Hogwarts signature gadgets and gizmos among the merchandise.

Hogwart's Express: This is the new element in Hogsmeade, the 'northern' end of the famous train ride from King's Cross Station. With its own station (and queue area), it provides the full effect of arriving at or departing from this mythical Scottish village. The station is almost completely enclosed to allow the designers to build up the illusion, and then you pass through a small section of the Forbidden Forest to reach Hogsmeade itself and enjoy your first full view of the village with Hogwarts towering behind it. The ride from Hogsmeade to King's Cross is also different, screen-wise, from the one that brings you here, with more scenes of London and some of Harry's other exploits from the films. Don't forget, you need a 2-park ticket to ride the Express, or you can pay the extra fee at the ticket office. AAAAA+

> ◀🇬🇧▶ **BRITTIP**
> Butterbeer is non-alcoholic and comes in three sweet varieties, 'regular', frozen (slushie style) and hot. Try them all as they taste quite different! It's also usually easier to get served in the Hog's Head rather than at the busy street carts.

Other entertainment: The **TriWizard Spirit Rally** celebrates the upcoming tournament, with the Beauxbatons Academy ribbon dancers and staff-fighting wizards from Durmstrang Institute. Hogwarts is represented by the **Frog Choir** (four students and two enormous frogs!), an ensemble whose vocal talents result in an entertaining show.

Shopping: As with all things here, the level of detail given to shopping and dining locations is so intricate they are attractions in their own right. Many items can be found only here in Hogsmeade, but whether you pull your wallet out or not, be sure to have a wander through each to soak up the atmosphere. When shopping, be sure to visit the famous sweetshop **Honeydukes**, the place to buy Cauldron Cakes, Bertie Bott's Every Flavour Beans, Chocolate Frogs and more. Find 136 varieties of sweets, many from the Harry Potter films or well-known British favourites (including jelly babies, humbugs and sherbet lemons). **Dervish and Banges** supplies 'students' with Quidditch gear and school related clothing, Luna Lovegood's 3-D Quibbler, and even the Nimbus 2001 broomsticks. At **Owl Post**, you can buy your wand, and don't miss sending a letter by owl! Your mail will receive one of four different Hogsmeade postmarks, a detail friends and family back home can enjoy. Also here are stationery and owl-related gifts. Every wizard needs a wand, and **Ollivander's** has 13 varieties to choose from. Here, 'the wand also chooses the wizard,' with surprising special effects similar to those Harry experienced when

Ollivander's Wand Shop

© Universal Orlando Resort

The Three Broomsticks

choosing his wand. Because the environment is interactive and the shop is small, a limited number are allowed inside for each 'show' and wait times are long all day. AAAAA

Dining: There is only one sit-down dining location here, but it's a corker. A 'Cathedral to Butterbeer', the **Three Broomsticks** menu features British favourites such as shepherd's pie, fish and chips and Cornish pasties, along with the Great Feast, a family-style meal of salad, ribs, chicken, roast potatoes and corn on the cob ($49.99 party of 4; $12.99 per extra person). Entrées $8.99–15.99, with desserts $3.49–4.99, including strawberry and

The Tri-Wizard Spirit Rally

peanut-butter ice cream, found only in the Wizarding World. They also serve a different menu for breakfast. Next door is the **Hog's Head Pub**, complete with animatronic boar's head, where you'll find Hog's Head Brew ($8 a pint).

BRITTIP

Of all the buildings, the Three Broomsticks is a must-see experience of dramatic interior design and special effects. Look up in the rafters for arriving owls, magical maids and the roaming House Elf!

All in all, it's an immense collection of dramatic and charming elements (witness the animated Prisoner of Azkaban poster in Hogsmeade) that add up to a vivid portrayal of J K Rowling's work. You don't need to be a fan to enjoy the Wizarding World and, like the Diagon Alley area in Universal Studios, the only snag is the huge crowd it draws for much of the day, as most of the shops are quite small and quickly feel congested. Arriving early is highly advisable (hence the early entry perk with Universal hotels is so valuable here), but you should also try to see it after dark, when the lighting effects make it even more dramatic.

Jurassic Park

Now travel back to the Cretaceous age and the make-believe dinosaur film world where extravagant scenery will have you looking over your shoulder for stray dinos.

Jurassic Park River Adventure: From scenic splendour, the mood changes to hidden menace as your journey into this magnificent waterborne realm brings you up close and personal with some realistic dinosaurs. Inevitably, your passage is diverted to the hazardous, and the danger increases as the 16-person raft travels through the main building – with raptors loose everywhere. You are aware of something large lurking in the shadows – will you fall prey to the T-Rex, or will your boat take the 85ft/26m plunge to safety (plus a good soaking)? Queues usually move briskly but will top an hour in mid-afternoon. **R**: 3ft 6in/106cm. The ride photo comes in various packages ($19.95–69.95). **TTTT**

BRITTIP
Keep your valuables dry on the River Adventure by leaving them in the lockers at the start of the queue.

Pteranodon Flyers: The slow-moving queues are a major turn-off, especially for a fairly average ride, which glides gently over much of Jurassic Park (though it reaches a height of almost 30ft/9m). **R**: It is designed mainly for kids, and anyone OVER the height range of 3ft–4ft 8in/91–142cm (usually 11+) must be accompanied by a child of the right height. **TT** (**TTTT** under-9s). The Universal Express pass is not valid here, either.

Camp Jurassic: More excellent kids' fare with the mountainous jungle giving way to an 'active' volcano for youngsters to explore, climb and slide down. Squirt guns and spitter dinosaurs add to the fun (for kids, but parents can explore!). **TTTT**

Discovery Center: This indoor centre offers various interactive games, like creating a dinosaur via DNA sequencing, mixing your own DNA with a dino on a touch-screen, seeing through the eyes of various large reptiles and handling 'dino eggs', plus other hands-on exhibits. It's ideal in summer as it's fully air-conditioned (10am–4pm; 5pm peak season). **AAA**

Other entertainment: The more adventurous can try the **Rock Climbing Wall** (just outside River

Skull Island, Reign of Kong

© Universal Orlando Resort

Adventure) for an extra $5, while there are also fairground games at an extra $5 a time.

Shopping: Visit **Dinostore** and **Jurassic Outfitters** for the best shopping.

Dining: Try **Burger Digs** (huge burger platters), **Pizza Predatoria**, **Thunder Falls Terrace** (counter service rotisserie chicken, ribs, burgers, turkey legs and salads, plus a great view of River Adventure) or the **Watering Hole** (hot dogs, snacks and drinks).

Skull Island

This new 'land' should open in summer 2016 featuring a chance to see the great ape himself.

Skull Island: Reign of Kong: Get ready to be at the centre of a battle between the mighty gorilla and three marauding dinosaurs in the world created by Peter Jackson's 2005 remake of *King Kong* (and the new *Skull Island* movie set for 2017). Part ride-through, part 3-D film spectacular, it will feature both indoor and outdoor sections of a large-scale truck tour that delves into the depths of a huge re-creation of Skull Island, and has a big finale with

Popeye and Bluto's Bilge-Rat Barges

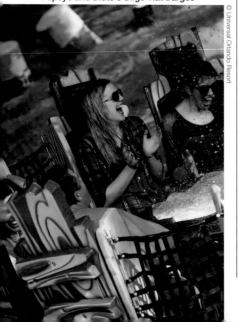

© Universal Orlando Resort

a giant animatronic version of Kong that is sure to leave riders convinced they have just escaped from a terrible fate! TTTT/AAAAA (expected). The immense nature of the queue area, with warnings of weird Skull Island creatures (think extra-large bugs!), should be worth seeing on its own.

Toon Lagoon

The thrills continue here with a watery theme and more comic-book elements from (US) newspaper cartoon characters. Children will also love the fountains, squirt pools and overflowing fire hydrants!

Popeye And Bluto's Bilge-Rat Barges: Every park seems to have a variation on the white-water raft ride, but this is one of the wettest! Fast, bouncy and unpredictable, it has water coming at you from every direction, a couple of sizeable drops and a whirl through the Octo-plus Grotto that adds to the fun. If you don't want to get wet, don't ride, because there is no escaping the deluge here. This is also one of the top five for long queues (at least when it's hot), but it's worth the wait. **R:** 4ft/ 122cm. Look for the Water Blasters (for 25c) on the bridge to give riders a wet start. TTTTT

> **BRIT**TIP
> A change of clothes is often advisable after the Barges, unless it's mega hot. Bring a waterproof bag for your valuables or leave them in a locker.

Dudley Do-Right's Ripsaw Falls: A flume ride that sends its passengers on a wild (and steep!) journey in the company of guileless Mountie Dudley Do-Right, bidding to save girlfriend Nell from the evil Snidely Whiplash. The action builds to an explosive finale at the top of a 75ft/27m abyss that drops you through the roof of a ramshackle dynamite shack to the lagoon below. Wet? You bet! **R:** 3ft 8in/111cm. TTTTT More Water Blasters on the bridge overlooking the final drop get riders even wetter.

Me Ship, The Olive: A kids' playland is designed as a three-storey boat full

ISLANDS OF ADVENTURE with children

Our guide to the attractions that generally appeal to the different age groups:

Under-5s
Caro-Seuss-el, The Cat In The Hat, High In The Sky Seuss Trolley Train Ride, If I Ran The Zoo, Jurassic Park Discovery Center, Me Ship, The Olive, One Fish, Two Fish, Red Fish, Blue Fish.

5–8s
All the above, plus Amazing Adventures Of Spider-Man, Camp Jurassic, Eighth Voyage of Sindbad, Flight of the Hippogriff, Jurassic Park River Adventure (with parental discretion), Pteranodon Flyers, Storm Force Accelatron, Harry Potter and the Forbidden Journey (if tall enough), Hogwarts Express.

9–12s
Amazing Adventures Of Spider-Man, Camp Jurassic, The Cat In The Hat, Dr Doom's Fearfall, Dudley Do-Right's Ripsaw Falls, Dragon Challenge, Eighth Voyage Of Sindbad, Flight of the Hippogriff, Harry Potter and the Forbidden Journey, Hogwarts Express, Incredible Hulk Coaster, Jurassic Park Discovery Center, Jurassic Park River Adventure, Popeye And Bluto's Bilge-Rat Barges, Pteranodon Flyers, Storm Force Accelatron, Skull Island: Reign of Kong.

Over-12s
Amazing Adventures Of Spider-Man, Dr Doom's Fearfall, Dudley Do-Right's Ripsaw Falls, Dragon Challenge, Eighth Voyage Of Sindbad, Harry Potter and the Forbidden Journey, Hogwarts Express, Incredible Hulk Coaster, Jurassic Park Discovery Center, Jurassic Park River Adventure, Popeye And Bluto's Bilge-Rat Barges, Storm Force Accelatron, Skull Island: Reign of Kong.

---

of interactive fun, including water cannons, bells and slides (ideal for squirting riders on the Bilge-Rat Barges below), in best Popeye style. **TTTT** (for youngsters)

Other entertainment: Comic Strip Lane is the place to meet the Classic Comic Book Characters like Beetle Bailey, Hagar the Horrible, Betty Boop, Popeye, and Dudley Do-Right. Plus various **fairground stall games** for $5–10.

Shopping: There is the usual array of character shops, like **Gasoline Alley**, **Boop Oop A Doop** and **Toon Extra**.

Dining: Grab a humongous sandwich at **Blondie's** (home of the Dagwood), a trademark burger at **Wimpy's**, sample the food court of **Comic Strip Café** (burgers, fish, chicken, Chinese dishes, pizza and pasta), something cool at **Cathy's Ice Cream** or a cold beverage at **Ale To The Chief**.

Marvel Super-Hero Island
Finally, you arrive at total immersion in super-hero comic-book pages, with some of the best rides in the park.

The Incredible Hulk Coaster:
Roller-coasters don't come much more dramatic than this giant green edifice that soars over the lagoon, blasting 0–40mph/64kph in 2secs, and reaching a top speed of 65mph/105kph. It looks awesome, sounds stunning and rides like a demon as you enter the gamma-ray world of Dr David Banner, aka the Incredible Hulk, and zoom into a weightless inversion 100ft/30m up.

> **BRITTIP**
> At the Hulk Coaster, keep left where the queue splits up and you will be in line for the front car for an even more extreme Hulk experience.

Just watching is mind-boggling, and the effects are brain-scrambling! Deposit ANY loose articles in the lockers at the front of the building as the ride is guaranteed to shake anything out of your pockets. Crowds build up rapidly but queues move reasonably quickly. **R:** 4ft 6in/137cm. You can also buy the DVD of your ride for $35, with extra park footage, or photo packages from $20–65. **TTTTT**

Dr Doom's Fearfall: Dr Doom's latest creation, Fearfall is a device for sucking fear out of his victims, and YOU are about to test it as 16 riders at a time are strapped into chairs at the bottom of a 200ft/60m tower. The dry ice rolls, and whoosh! Up you go at breakneck speed, only to plummet back seemingly even faster, with a split second when you feel suspended in mid-air. Summon up the courage to do this and we promise an astonishing (if brief!) experience. Substantial queues from mid-day. **R**: 4ft 4in/132cm. **TTTTT+**

The Amazing Adventures Of Spider-Man: A visit to the Daily Bugle, home of ace reporter Peter Parker (aka Spider-Man) turns into a mission in a 'Scoop' vehicle – and an audio-visual extravaganza. This roving 3-D motion simulator takes you into a battle with super-villains that includes a convincing 'drop' off a skyscraper. There are special effects aplenty and the whole ride is loaded with the 'wow' factor. Go early on or wait until late in the day – queues often top an hour by mid-morning. **R**: 3ft 4in/101cm. **TTTTT+** PS: If this seems similar to the TRANSFORMERS ride at Universal Studios, it's because they use the same ride platform.

BRITTIP
You can beat some of the queues on the Spider-Man ride at busy times by opting for the Single Rider queue.

Storm Force Accelatron: This ride, primarily for kids, puts you in the middle of a battle between X-Men heroine Storm and arch-nemesis Magneto. It's basically an updated spinning-cup ride but with some neat twists (like a 3-way rotation where the cars look set to collide). **TTT** (**TTTTT** under-12s)

BRITTIP
For some of the park's best shopping bargains, visit Port Provisions right by the exit gates (to the left as you come through) where all the merchandise is 30–50% off.

Other entertainment: The **Marvel Super-Heroes** appear here periodically for photos and autographs, while **Spider-Man** has his own meet-and-greet booth at The Marvel Alterniverse Store. A high-energy **video arcade** can be found at the exit to Dr Doom's Fearfall.

Shopping: Each ride has its own character merchandise, while the **Comic Book Shop** and **Marvel Alterniverse Shop** sell other souvenirs.

Dining: For a bite to eat, try the Italian buffeteria **Café 4** (pizza, pasta, sandwiches and salads) or a burger, chicken fingers or salad at the **Captain America Diner**.

And that, folks, is the full low-down on arguably the world's most thrilling and complete theme park. Not to be missed!

The Incredible Hulk Coaster

© Universal Orlando Resort

SeaWorld

SeaWorld is firmly established as one of the most popular parks for its more peaceful and naturalistic aspect, the change of pace it offers and lack of substantial queues. It is large enough to handle big crowds well (though it still gets busy in peak season) and is a big hit with families in particular, but it has some fabulous rides and imaginative attractions too, including Antarctica: Empire of the Penguin, and, in summer 2016, a major new roller-coaster with the huge Mako.

Part of the SeaWorld Parks & Entertainment group, along with sister parks Busch Gardens in Tampa, with its animal encounters and roller-coasters (p202); Discovery Cove, an exotic tropical 'island' with dolphin, coral reef and snorkelling adventures (p198); and water-park Aquatica (p247), this makes for excellent multi-day tickets, notably Discovery Cove's

Ultimate Ticket, which includes all four parks. SeaWorld's recent additions and brilliant Christmas overlay (p39) mean this remains a wonderfully fresh and invigorating place to visit.

Happily, this is still a park where you can proceed at a relatively leisurely pace, see what you want without too much jostling and yet feel you have been well entertained (even if the restaurants get crowded at mealtimes). SeaWorld is a good starting point if this is your first Orlando visit as it gives you the hang of negotiating the vast areas, navigating by maps and learning to plan around the show times. There are special offers for booking online at **www.seaworld.com**, where you can print your tickets to save waiting in the queue, plus a website for UK visitors – **www.seaworldparks.co.uk**.

SeaWorld at a glance

Location	7007 SeaWorld Drive, off Central Florida Parkway (Junctions 71 and 72 off I-4)
Size	More than 200 acres/81ha, incorporating 26 attractions
Hours	9am–6pm off peak; 9am–7, 8 or 9pm some weekends; 9am–9pm high season (Easter, summer holidays, Thanksgiving, Christmas)
Admission	Under-3s free; 3–9 $90 (1-day ticket), $129 (2-park ticket, with Aquatica), $139 (2-park ticket with Busch Gardens), $316 (5-Park Orlando FlexTicket), $336 (6-Park Orlando FlexTicket); adult (10+) $95, $135, $145, $336, $356.
Parking	$17, $22 preferred parking
Lockers	Inside Entrance Plaza (next to Sweet Sailin' Candy), $8 and $11 (rent from Pushchair and Wheelchair location)
Pushchairs	$15 and $25, to right of Guest Services inside park
Wheelchairs	$15 and $50; with pushchairs
Top attractions	TurtleTrek, Antarctica: Empire Of The Penguin, One Ocean, Shark Encounter, Journey To Atlantis, Kraken, Manta, Wild Arctic, Blue Horizons, Mako (summer 2016)
Don't miss	Manatee Rescue, behind-the-scenes tours, Dolphin Nursery, dining at Sharks Underwater Grill
Hidden costs	**Meals**	Burger, chips and coke $13.68 3-course lunch $43–58 (Sharks Underwater Grill) Kids' meal $6.69; $13 at Sharks Underwater Grill
	T-shirts	$22–36
	Souvenirs	$1.99–1,500
	Sundries	Ride photos $20–39

Private VIP Tour: Seven-hour tour with individual guide and reserved seats for the three main shows, just for your family or group, including preferred parking, animal interactions and lunch at Sharks Underwater Grill ($249/person).

Dolphin Encounter: Learn how SeaWorld cares for its resident dolphins with this opportunity to see the park's animal team in action at Dolphin Cove, learning about their behaviour and having a 5min interaction when you can touch a dolphin ($15/person).

Sea Lions Up-Close Tour: A 1-hour walking tour focusing on the care and training of the stars of the Clyde & Seamore show, including a photo with them and a chance to feed the Pacific Point Preserve sea lions ($44–59 and $24–39).

Penguins Up-Close Tour: This 45min family walk goes behind the scenes at Antarctica: Empire of the Penguin to learn the proper care for these cute birds and gives visitors the chance to interact with and touch a penguin ($59-79 and $39–59).

Wild Arctic Up-Close Experience: An interactive 60min tour into the care and animal interactions with the walrus, seals and beluga whales at this in-depth exhibit ($59-79/person, ages 8 and up only).

Family Fun at Christmas Tour: A 3-hour guided tour of the top children's attractions, with a penguin meet-and-greet, reserved seats at Elmo's Christmas Wish show, a meal at Santa's Fireside Feast and front-of-line access to the Polar Express Experience, finishing with an exclusive meet 'n' greet with Santa Claus ($59-79).

Marine Mammal Keeper Experience: An interactive programme, this takes two visitors daily to discover the care needed to rehabilitate injured manatees, plus bottle-feed some of them, meet the seals and walruses and prepare meals for the beluga whales (starts at 6.30am; lasts around 8hrs; $399/person including lunch, T-shirt, special book, souvenir photo and 7-day SeaWorld pass; must be 13 or older).

Behind The Scenes Tour: Join a knowledgeable tour guide for a 75min look backstage at the park's rescue and rehab facilities, including rescued manatees and sea turtles, as well as have the chance to touch a shark and interact with a penguin ($29–39 and $9–19).

Beluga Interaction Program: A unique chance to meet some of the park's biggest but most benign denizens in their own environment. Swimming isn't necessary but guests must be comfortable in the water as touching, feeding and using hand signals are part of this informative tour ($119–179/person; no expectant mothers; must be 10 or older). NB: All prices can vary seasonally.

Location
SeaWorld is located off Central Florida Parkway, between I-4 (exit 71 going east or 72 heading west) and I-Drive. It is still best to arrive before the opening time so you're in

Behind the Scenes Tour

© SeaWorld Parks

a good position to book a backstage tour, dash to one of the attractions that draws a crowd, like Manta and Antarctica, or buy QuickQueue, the park's limited number of paid-for passes that provide front-of-the-line access to each of the main rides (priced seasonally at $19–34). There is also a Signature Show Seating option at $19–29/person.

The park covers more than 200acres/81ha, with five shows, five major rides (with a sixth to come in 2016), 10 large-scale continuous viewing attractions and seven smaller ones, plus a smart range of shops and restaurants. Try to eat before midday or after 2.30pm for a crowd-free lunch, and before 5.30pm if you want a leisurely dinner (better still, book Sharks Underwater Grill).

SeaWorld is arranged in various 'seas' on the park map but they are hard to follow, hence you will need to keep the map close to hand to navigate, as there is also a fair bit of to-ing and fro-ing to catch the various shows, with the show schedule listed on the back of the map. Going in a clockwise direction, here's what you find.

Port of Entry

Coming through the turnstiles brings you to the park's main business area, including the Information & Reservations kiosk, Lost & Found, and lockers, pushchair and wheelchair hire. You will also find some good shopping and snack options here. Look for **Shamu Emporium** for the full range of SeaWorld souvenirs, while **Adventure Photos** provides all your park pictures taken by the SeaWorld photographers. You can grab a quick breakfast (tasty pastries and coffee) at **Cypress Bakery** or something colder from the **Polar Parlor Ice Cream**. This is also the place for a photo opportunity with Shamu and friends.

All Day Dining Deal: Also worth considering, a wristband gives unlimited visits to six restaurants (Spice Mill, Voyager's – excluding their baby-back ribs – Mango Joe's, Seaport Pizza, Seafire Inn and Terrace Garden Buffet), claiming an entrée, side dish or dessert and standard non-alcoholic drink each time ($34.99 and $19.99). It's good value if you eat at least twice in the park and can be booked at the Information & Reservations desk.

A rescued manatee is returned to the wild

© SeaWorld Parks

Beluga Interaction Program

Photokey: If you'd like to collect all your SeaWorld photos digitally, including ride photos and character meet-and-greets (but not backstage tours), then sign up for this new service – either online in advance or when you arrive at the park – for a one-off $74.00 (**www.seaworld.com/ photokey**).

Sea of Shallows

A whole collection of exhibits is grouped together here, as well as the eye-catching Dolphin Theater and one of the signature rides.

There is also a clever Key West theme, starting with **Stingray Lagoon**, where you can feed (for $5) and touch fully grown rays, including a nursery for newborn rays. The centrepiece, though, is the 2.1acre/0.8ha **Dolphin Cove**, a spectacular, naturalistic development that is home to a frisky community of Atlantic bottlenose dolphins, who make for great viewing, including from a special underwater window.

The whole Key West area is designed in the eclectic, tropical flavour of America's most southerly city, but it also underlines the environmental message through interactive graphics and video displays, and children will find it a fun, educational experience. AAA

Blue Horizons: This wonderful production serves up a big helping of dramatic animal behaviour in best Broadway style. It features dolphins,

exotic birds (including an Andean condor), and a lot more besides as the general (and rather abstract) theme of a girl's dream about maritime wildlife is brought to life. The elaborate set design has a 40ft/12m sea-meets-sky backdrop that also conceals the setting for a host of additional performers, from high divers to bungee jumpers and trapeze-like aerialists. There is subtle interaction between trainers and animals as the show moves from one scene to the next, both above and below the water, but there is plenty to admire as the stage is filled with graceful and daring action. A stirring score by the Seattle Symphony Orchestra underpins the complex staging and Broadway-style costumes and it makes for a magnificent 25mins that often draws a huge ovation. AAAAA

Kraken

Manta: This ride turns high-tech coaster into a unique mixture of ride and animal encounter. The elaborate queuing area winds through cool, rocky caverns, passing waterfalls and floor-to-ceiling windows showcasing some 300 rays and thousands of fish, which lead through to the 'undersea world' of the manta ray. Themed like a giant ray, riders are swung into a face-down position before being launched into an exhilarating series of four inversions along 3,359ft/1,024m of track, reaching nearly 60mph/96kph and 140ft/43m high as well as skimming the surface of the lagoon. The 'flying' nature of the coaster and smooth ride vehicles make this a true original. It has great spectator appeal and there is a separate walk-though aquarium with its own entry. Lockers located near the queue entry are available for use during your ride (50c and $1). **R:** 54in/137cm. **TTTTT.** For the most powerful effects of the Manta G-forces, opt for the back rows.

TurtleTrek: Right behind the Dolphin Theater is this thrilling experience that is part exhibit and part show. You enter down a ramp that introduces you to the undersea world of the sea turtle and marine conservation, passing by two huge man-made lagoons, the first for the endangered manatee and then some of SeaWorld's rescued turtles. A marine life host introduces the next part of the Trek and the doors open to reveal a domed cinema where you don 3-D glasses. Suddenly, you are in the world of the sea turtle, sharing the life-cycle journey from the dangers of leaving the egg to life in the open ocean and then the final return to the same beach where it was born. It all takes place in an immersive 3-D environment (you have to remember not to hold your breath!) with amazingly graphic encounters with a marauding crab, sharks and dolphins. You exit back up another ramp to two open-air pools (the top view of the lagoons you see below) where you can learn more about sea turtle life and see them and the manatees being fed. There is also a TurtleTrek video game for kids, and another open-air exhibit showcasing some Florida alligators. AAAAA NB: The menace of the crab in the early scene may be a bit scary for very young children.

Other entertainment: The **Dolphin Nursery** provides wonderful close-up views with some of the park's younger dolphins.

Shopping: There are three main gift shops here, the best being **Coconut Bay Traders** and **Trek Treasures** (apparel and soft toys), as well as **Manta Photo & Gifts**.

Manta

© SeaWorld Parks

Dining: You can grab a turkey leg, cheese nachos or chicken tenders at **Captain Pete's Island Eats** or ice cream at **Dippin' Dots**, plus drinks snacks and refills and several cart-style kiosks.

Sea of Legends

Continue past Dolphin Theater and you come to the park's serious thrill quotient.

Journey to Atlantis: This terrific water-coaster is a combination of special effects and water-ride that becomes a runaway roller-coaster. The discovery of Atlantis in your eight-passenger 'fishing boat' starts gently through the lost city. But evil spirit Allura takes over and riders plunge into a dash through Atlantis, dodging gushing fountains and water cannons, with hundreds of holographic and laser-generated illusions before the 60ft/18m drop, the entry to the roller-coaster finale back in the candle-filled catacombs. Be ready to get soaked, which is great in summer but not so clever first thing on a winter morning. R: 3ft 6in/106cm. TTTTT

Kraken: One of Florida's most breathtaking roller-coasters, based on the mythical sea monster, it is an innovative pedestal ride (you are effectively sitting in a chair without a floor) that plunges an initial 144ft/44m, hits 65mph/105kph, dives underground three times, adds seven inversions (including a vertical loop, a diving loop, a zero-gravity roll and a cobra roll) and a flat spin before riders escape the beast's lair. The ride from the front row, especially down an opening drop at an angle best described as ludicrous, is blood-curdling, and sitting in the rear is thrilling, too. R: 4ft 6in/137cm. TTTTT+

Shopping: Don't miss the **Golden Seahorse** and **Jewel of the Sea**

as you exit Journey to Atlantis, a combination gift shop and aquarium full of tropical fish (remember to look upwards), while there are coaster-orientated souvenirs in **Kraken Gifts** and **Manta Gifts**.

Dining: High Seas Market offers convenient grab-and-go snacks and drinks, and there is a **Dippin' Dots** for ice cream.

Sea of Ice

Getting back to the animal side of the park brings you to the newest development (opened May 2013), and one of the most eye-catching sections of any park. It is both an extensive, themed area in its own right – and an amazing ride. It is the biggest expansion in SeaWorld history and their most immersive environment to date, an epic journey into the snow and ice-covered realm of the South Pole and its inhabitants.

Antarctica: Empire of the Penguin: Once you walk between the towering ice-and-snow-capped 'mountains,' the (indoor) ride awaits. It begins with a dramatic presentation about penguin life and then takes visitors on a unique expedition into the heart of the continent, following the

Journey to Atlantis

© SeaWorld Parks

Antarctica: Empire of the Penguin

story and guidance of Puck, a young Gentoo penguin. Guests board special vehicles in groups of eight and choose their own level of ride experience, either 'Mild' or 'Wild', and then set off through a mix of simulation and film elements that offer a realistic taste of the polar region, above and below the penguins' icy world, moving seemingly at random and with no obvious track. The dangers – including a typical Antarctic storm – and beauty of life in this extreme realm are graphically depicted as you track Puck's own life journey through the world's most extreme landscape before you then step out through a real penguin colony (cleverly but minimally screened off) to experience more of their 'empire.' And guess what? It is cold; like, *really* cold (the temperature drops during the ride, reaching to below freezing by the end) and you may want to visit the gift shop for a scarf or some gloves before you set off! The 'Wild' version of the ride is more fast-paced, with various bumps, slides, spins and rolls, but 'Mild' is still designed for all the family, with no height restriction. AAAAA+ This is also easily the park's most popular attraction, hence if it appeals to you, go here **first**.

BRITTIP

Take a look at the main 'mountain' in Antarctica. Does the shape look familiar? Yes, that's right – the whole edifice has been shaped like a towering mother penguin on the left, with her baby to the right.

Other entertainment: After the ride, there is a spectacular two-storey **underwater viewing area** where you can see the different species of penguin – Rockhopper, King, Adelie and Gentoo – at play. Then, back out in Antarctica, you can marvel at this realistic environment, which includes a special **Penguin Wall** for photo opportunities, and flatscreen TVs that offer more info about the region's main inhabitants. It even has its own original musical score that evokes images of the windswept frozen continent.

Shopping: Lone gift shop **Glacial Collections** has a huge selection of all things penguin-orientated and cuddly.

Dining: Expedition Café provides Italian, Asian and American food choices from their show kitchen which you can then enjoy in one of two clever 'Quonset Huts' that provide a South Pole setting.

BRITTIP

Be sure to come back to Antarctica at night to see how the brilliant blue lighting makes the whole setting even more impressive.

Sea of Delight

This extensive area features two more great live shows plus some of the park's best dining and shopping.

Sea Lion and Otter Theater: The venue for another live show (new in 2015), this features the resident pinnipeds in *Clyde and Seamore's Sea Lion High*, and offers 25mins of slapstick and watery stunts, with guest appearances by Opie Otter and Sir Winston Walrus. The basic premise is that Clyde and Seamore are in danger of flunking their high school exams and need to help to get the necessary grades, which is the cue for all manner of school-type jokes and amazing antics from the animals (often at the expense of their human assistants!). The educational pre-show celebrates teachers the world over. AAAA

Pacific Point Preserve: A natural rocky habitat for the park's seals and sea lions with a hidden wave machine and lively talks from park attendants. You can also buy smelt ($5 per tray or five trays for $20) to throw feed the animals. AAA

Pets Ahoy!: Just inside the Waterfront is the air-conditioned haven of the Seaport Theater, which hosts this cute 25min giggle featuring an unlikely menagerie of dogs, cats, birds, rats, pot-bellied pigs and others, most from local animal rescue shelters. AAA. The Theater is also home to the seasonal show *Elmo Rocks!* when the Sesame Street characters get together for their own rock 'n roll concert. AAA

Sky Tower: This 400ft/122m landmark offers slowly rotating rides for a bird's-eye view of the park and surrounding areas. It used to cost extra but is now open to all-comers. NB: It will close if windy. AAA

Other entertainment: Look out for the zany antics of **The Longshoremen** periodically, as the hapless trio try their hand at various maintenance tasks.

Shopping: The **Waterfront** shops offer an extensive shopping plaza with a stylish range of souvenirs and other gift items (notably at **Allura's Treasure Trove** and **Artisans Hall**) while **Oyster's Secret** features the chance to see pearl divers in action (and buy a pearl afterwards).

Dining: The excellent eateries are: **Seafire Inn** (sandwiches, wraps, pasta, fish and chips and chicken stir-fry); **Voyagers Smokehouse** BBQ (smoked chicken, barbecue ribs, salads, turkey sandwich and a children's menu with chicken nuggets, hot dog, macaroni and cheese or junior portion of ribs); and **Spice Mill Burgers** (flame-grilled burgers, salads, sandwiches and flatbreads, plus a low-fat vegetarian

The Waterfront

chilli), plus **Seaport Pizza** for cheese and pepperoni pizza. There are also three snack bars: **Café de Mar** for pastries, coffees, smoothies and soft drinks; **Turkey Legs** for huge smoked turkey legs; and **Freezas** for frozen yoghurt and other drinks. The **SandBar** is a water's edge hideaway, serving beer, wine and snacks – THE place to watch the sun go down.

> **BRITTIP**
> Grab an evening meal at The Spice Mill, then head out on to its open-air terrace for one of the best seats in the house for the view over the central Lagoon – idyllic in summer.

Sea of Mystery

Continuing the clockwise tour brings you towards the back of the park (which usually doesn't open until 11am). Here you find more animal encounters – and a wonderful show.

Shark Encounter: Top of the bill, the world's largest collection of dangerous sea creatures can be found here, brought dramatically to life by the walk-through tubes that surround you with more than 50 prowling sharks (including sand tigers, black tips, nurse sharks and sandbars), sawfish, tropical fish and gigantic groupers. It's an eerie experience, but brilliantly presented and highly informative. Queues build up here at peak times. AAAA TTTT

The **Nautilus Theater** is home to weekend events throughout the year, notably Jack Hanna's Animal Adventure.

Mango Joe's

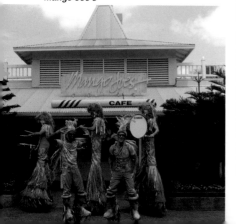

Mako: SeaWorld's dramatic new steel rollercoaster make its eye-catching appearance between the Shark Encounter and Nautilus Theater, giving the park another iconic ride for its growing collection. At 200ft high and reaching 73mph, Mako – which is the world's fastest shark – will be both the tallest and fastest in Orlando, and it should give adrenalin junkies a real blast, with multiple high dives, swoops and lots of 'air time'. TTTTT (expected).

> **BRITTIP**
> Looking for a quiet spot for a break? Seek out the terrace along the lagoon (with tables and chairs) directly behind Fins gift shop and across from Sharks Underwater Grill.

Other entertainment: The **flamingo pedal-boats** on the lagoon rent for $5 per 20min (for two). You can also feed the sharks and stingrays outside **Shark Encounter** ($5 per tray). Also nearby is the revamped **Sea Garden**, a lovely spot for some time off your feet. As well as several clever sea-creature sculptures made completely out of reclaimed rubbish washed up on America's beaches by http://WashedAshore.org, the **Animal Connections** meet-and-greets here allow for encounters several times daily with various rescued and rehabilitated animals, including two small ponies, a possum, various hawks, a Kookaburra, a great horned owl, a Crested Caracara, a groundhog and others. Bring your camera, as photos are encouraged.

Shopping: There are two small-scale shops: **Fins Gifts** and **Gulf Breeze Trader**.

Dining: At the entrance to Shark Encounter is the top dining choice, **Sharks Underwater Grill**, with an amazing backdrop for your meal in a subterranean environment (check out the mini-aquarium bar), and an upmarket menu of 'Floribbean' cuisine, blending local and spicy Caribbean fare. The emphasis is on seafood – with various wonderful creations – plus pasta, steaks and chicken, as well as fab desserts, cocktails (including non-alcoholic) and menus for under-10s. Open from 11.30am to an hour before park closing, it's busy at lunch but quieter in late afternoon, so we advise booking (at the restaurant) as soon as you arrive. The **Lakeside Panini Bistro** (high season only) offers fresh-grilled panini sandwiches, salads and drinks while the **Terrace BBQ** features delicious barbecue platters ($11.49–15.79) and the **Terrace Bar** serves craft beers.

Sea of Fun

This section is primarily for kids, with a fabulous children's play area, eight junior-sized rides, various snack kiosks and a delicious new pretzel café.

Shamu's Happy Harbor: 4acres/1.6ha of brilliantly designed adventure playground and rides await youngsters of all ages here. Activities include a 4-storey net climb, two tented ball rooms to wade through, a giant trampoline tent, a mock pirate ship and a water play area, **Water Works** (great on a hot day). The signature junior-sized coaster **Shamu Express** offers mild thrills over more than 800ft/245m of track (and a framed ride photo for $19.99). The **Jazzy Jellies** is a jellyfish-themed samba tower ride that lifts and spins, while **Swishy Fishes** features oversized seats that spin round a giant waterspout. **Flying Fiddler** (a 20ft/6.1m tower ride on a jumping giant crab), **Ocean Commotion** (a rocking tug ride), junior-sized **Seven Seas Railway** and **Sea Carousel** (a traditional carousel featuring 65 sea creatures) complete the line-up. The area gets busy from midday, but the kids seem to love it at any time. Next door is the arcade and **Games Area**, a series of fairground-type stalls for $5 as you head toward the Nautilus Theater. TTTT. At the back of the Harbor is a well equipped, comfortable **Baby Care Center** and the park's **First Aid** station.

Shopping: More cuddlies and other souvenirs at **Happy Harbor Gifts**.

Dining: Grab a tasty drink at **Seaside Coffee** and great ice cream treats at **Dippin' Dots Sundae Shop** and **Soft Serve**, while you should definitely try **Mama's Pretzel Kitchen** for a mouth-watering array of freshly-baked pretzels with a variety of dipping sauces.

BRITTIP
Busch Gardens' Twisted Tails Pretzels has proved so popular in that park that SeaWorld has copied the formula here, including the must-sample Bacon Pretzel Fury!

Sea of Power

The final main area of the park features the iconic Shamu Stadium, plus another engaging ride/animal attraction, and the high-season fireworks finale.

BRITTIP
The first 14 rows at Shamu Stadium get VERY wet (watch out for your cameras) – when a killer whale leaps into the air in front of you, it displaces a LOT of water on landing. In fact, the Splash Zones should be renamed Soak Zones!

Shamu Stadium: 'What can one person do?' That is the message One Ocean brings to SeaWorld in a spectacular show filled with brilliant splashes of colour – especially of the black and white variety! In the past, the whales' relationship with their trainers was the main focus, and while that bond remains strong, the heart of One Ocean lies with the relationship between the whales themselves. Behaviours common

One Ocean

© SeaWorld Parks

to whales in the wild combine with learned behaviours in a celebration of joyful play, reminding us we are all connected and, when we pull together, we can do amazing things. And if the biggest thrills in past Shamu shows came from seeing these magnificent animals jump, spin, and cover the Soak Zone in a wall of water, you're in for a real treat! Even better, the charming Side By Side scene features the connection between mother and baby, so have those cameras ready. Shamu Stadium is extremely popular, so try to take in an early show. And, if you think it looks good during the day, return in the evening (in high season) for an even more dramatic, music-orientated presentation under the lights, **Shamu's Celebration: Light Up The Night**. AAAAA+ NB: You may notice the big construction project to enlarge the killer whale enclosure, which will provide an extensive new state-of-the-art habitat and enlarged underwater viewing section, due to open in 2018.

BRITTIP
Be sure to arrive early for One Ocean, especially if you have a smart-phone. You may get a sneak peek behind the scenes during the pre-show!

All guests can then enjoy the **Shamu Underwater Viewing area**.

Wild Arctic: This interactive ride-and-view is an exciting simulator

Shamu's Happy Harbor

© SeaWorld Parks

jet helicopter journey into the white wilderness, where passengers see seals, beluga whales and walruses. This one is not to be missed (but avoid just after One Ocean when the hordes descend). R: 3ft 6in/106cm. TTTT AAAAA. Those who don't want to do the (quite dynamic) ride can just walk to the Base Station.

Bayside Stadium: The final element is this large outdoor arena facing the central Lagoon. It's home to various seasonal entertainments, including fireworks show **Reflections**, the Bands, Brew & BBQ concerts and an ice-skating show at Christmas. NB: Reflections did not run in summer 2015 and it was not clear if it would return at Christmas.

BRITTIP
Any purchases can be sent to Package Pick-up in Shamu's Emporium to collect on your way out, if you give at least an hour's notice.

Shopping: Wild Arctic Gifts is the best of the three stores here.

Dining: Mango Joe's Burgers offers grilled burgers, speciality salads and sandwiches, while **Dippin' Dots** features more ice cream treats and there are two snack and drinks counters at Shamu Stadium. Killer whale fans may also want to splash out (!) on the **Dine With Shamu** experience, backstage at Shamu Stadium, where a buffet lunch or dinner featuring seasonal, organic and sustainable menu items is served while some of the trainers meet with guests and show off more of the whale behaviours in spectacular, close-up fashion (times changes seasonally, with prices from $30-40 for adults and $20–30 for children; book in advance on 1888 800 5447, online at www.seaworldparks.com or at the Information Kiosk when you arrive).

BRITTIP
Learn more about SeaWorld's conservation and environmental efforts at www.seaworld.org.

SEAWORLD with children

The following gives a general idea of the appeal of the attractions to the different age groups:

Under-5s
Antarctica: Empire of the Penguin, One Ocean, Blue Horizons, Clyde And Seamore's Sea Lion High, Elmo Show, Pacific Point Preserve, Dolphin Cove, Pets Ahoy!, Shamu's Happy Harbor, Wild Arctic (without the ride).

5–8s
All the above, plus Turtle Trek, Shark Encounter, Wild Arctic (with the ride).

9–12s
All the above, plus Journey to Atlantis, Manta and Kraken.

Over-12s
Antarctica: Empire of the Penguin, One Ocean, Blue Horizons, Clyde And Seamore's Sea Lion High, Journey To Atlantis, Manta, Kraken, Shark Encounter, Wild Arctic, Turtle Trek.

Summer extras

During the official summer season (mid-June–early-Aug), SeaWorld has extended hours to 9pm and offers an array of extra live entertainment as part of its **Summer Nights** programme. The 'rock 'n' roll' party atmosphere is generated by live DJs and other entertainers and features extra shows, notably **Shamu's Celebration: Light up The Night**, which adds a more high-energy version of the main show, including new, original music and production elements, as well as new killer whale behaviours and dramatic lighting. **Summer Nights Central**, on the Bayside Stadium pathway, features live DJs (and bands at weekends) to add a family-friendly dance party from 6pm.

New for summer 2015 (replacing the previous Reflections firework show) was the **Celebrate America Concert Series,** each Sat and Sun evening in the Nautilus Theater which provides a set-piece musical show amid the rest of the animal-led fun. In 2015, artists included Trick Pony and Crystal Gayle, as well as other patriotic acts.

For SeaWorld's amazing **Christmas Celebration** (late Nov–31 Dec each year), see our Christmas section, p39.

And there's more

Other seasonal events (all FREE with park admission) include **Bands, Brew & BBQ**, weekends in Feb and Mar that provide a festival atmosphere with live music, barbecue kiosks and craft beer stalls, as well as a special guest concert (beer and barbecue extra, including a 'Sampler' package for $21/person); the Apr–May weekends of **Viva La Musica** Latin festival (with more live bands and food offerings); and the ultra child-friendly **Halloween Spooktacular**, when there are fun activities for kids of all ages, including trick-or-treating, Penelope's Party Zone, sweet treat decorating and strolling entertainers.

Turtle Trek

© SeaWorld Parks

Discovery Cove

Fancy a day in your own tropical paradise, with the chance to swim with dolphins, encounter sharks, snorkel in a coral reef and dive through a waterfall into a tropical aviary? Well, Discovery Cove is all that and more. The only drawback is the price. This mini theme park comes at a premium because it is restricted to just 1,300 guests a day, creating an exclusive experience that is reflected in the admission fee.

The weather can get distinctly cool in the winter, but the water is always heated (apart from the dolphin lagoon, which remains at 72°F/22°C) and full wetsuits are available to keep out the chill. The attention to detail is superb, guest ratings are extremely high and it is hugely popular with British visitors. However, if any element falls below expectations, it's worth bringing it to the attention of a manager as they are always keen to rectify any oversights.

The costs

In 2015, the Dolphin Swim package was $229–359/person, or you could choose the Day Resort package, without dolphin swim, for $169–219, all depending on day and season (under 3s free; 3–5s cannot do the dolphin swim but must pay the Day Resort price). So, just what do you get

for your money? Well, as you would expect, it's a supremely personal park. You check in at the beautiful entrance lobby as you would for a hotel rather than a theme park, and you have a guide to take you in and get you set. All your basic requirements – towel, mask, snorkel, wet-jacket, lockers, beach umbrellas, food and drink – are included, and the level of service is excellent. A pass for SeaWorld AND Aquatica is also included (valid for 14 consecutive days before or after your Discovery Cove visit), or you can upgrade to the Ultimate Package, which provides 14 days at SeaWorld, Aquatica AND Busch Gardens for just $22 extra (superb value). A full breakfast, snacks, beverages (including beer and cocktails) and an excellent lunch at the Laguna Grill are all included. But gift shop and photo prices reflect the entry fee – expensive. It is also an extra $199 to hire one of their swanky cabañas for the day (which include tables, chairs, loungers, towels and a fridge stocked with soft drinks) depending on position and view (must be booked in advance).

Therefore, for all its style and dolphin appeal, Discovery Cove will take a BIG bite out of your holiday budget. A family of 4, with children old enough to do the Dolphin Swim, would pay

A female dolphin born at Discovery Cove

© SeaWorld Parks

$1,436 in peak season. Even with a free SeaWorld and Aquatica pass, it's a big outlay. The charge for ages 3–5 is also pretty steep, in our opinion. Your sundries can add up, too. A 6x8in/15x20cm photo is $20; then there are photo packages at $70 and $159, while the DVD of your experience (which includes 30mins of park highlights) costs $60 and the Discovery Package (7 6x8 photos, 1 4x6 photo, 2 key chains, digital photo CD, Interaction video, photo album, 16x24 poster) is $229. Poster-size photos (16x24 and 24x36) are $30 and $40, while a marble photo-tile is $45. However, despite the fees, the feedback we get is almost unfailingly positive and most people are captivated by the experience. One handy free perk, though, is the Horticulture Tour, twice a day, which takes guests through the care and maintenance of the park's tropical plant and tree life (sign up at Guest Relations).

BRITTIP

Try to pick up your Discovery Cove photos before 4pm or you might find everyone else trying to do the same!

Trainer for a Day: This programme is an exciting opportunity to go behind the scenes into the park's training, feeding and welfare. You get to work with the experts as they interact with dolphins, birds, sharks, stingrays and tropical fish, including a behavioural training class, the chance to experience a double-foot push (ride on the front of two dolphins), a souvenir shirt, dolphin book and waterproof camera. Participants must be at least 6 and in good health, and it costs $488–558 (seasonally). For all Discovery Cove bookings, call 407 370 1280 (freephone 00800 3344 1818 in the UK) or visit **www.discoverycove.com**.

Location
Situated on Central Florida Parkway, almost opposite the SeaWorld entrance (open year-round 9am–5.30pm; parking free), the whole 30acre/12ha park is magnificently landscaped, with thatched buildings, palm trees, lush vegetation, white-sand beaches, gurgling streams – even hammocks to chill out in. The overall effect is of being transported to a relaxing tropical paradise away from the hurly-burly. The 5-star resort feel is enhanced by a high staff-to-guest ratio, there are no queues (though the restaurant may get busy at lunchtime), and the highlight Dolphin Encounter is world class. Visitors with disabilities are well catered for, with special wheelchairs that can move in sand and shallow water, and an area of the Dolphin Lagoon that allows those who can't enter the water still to touch a dolphin.

The main attractions
Freshwater Oasis: This combination of animal environment, walking trails and pools offers the chance to get a close-up of the park's otters and marmosets in realistic, natural habitats. Children especially love watching the otters, and the way the animals are incorporated into the lush tropical scenery is a real gem of clever design. AAAA

Wind-away River: This 800yd/732m circuit of gently flowing bath-warm water is a variation on the lazy river feature of many of the water parks, though with a far more naturalistic aspect and none of the inner tubes. It

Dolphin Swim at Discovery Cove

© SeaWorld Parks

is primarily designed for snorkellers and features rocky lagoons, caves, a beach section, a tropical forest segment and sunken ruins. The lack of fish makes it a bit bland after the Grand Reef, but it is as much about relaxing as having fun. It is up to 8ft/2.4m deep at points, so non-swimmers are advised to use a flotation vest. It finishes in the freeform Serenity Bay pool, which provides more idyllic relaxation. AAA

Explorer's Aviary: This three-part adventure is both an area in its own right and a 120ft/37m section of the Tropical River. You can walk in off the beach or swim in through the waterfall from Wind-away River, fun for snorkellers. Some 250 tropical birds fill the main enclosure and, if you stand still, they are likely to use you as a perch. There is a small-bird sanctuary – full of finches, honeycreepers and hummingbirds – and a large-bird enclosure, featuring toucans and the red-legged seriema. Guides will introduce you to specific birds (which you can hand-feed) and tell you about their habitats and conservation issues. AAAA

Dolphin Swim: The big headline attraction is the encounter with the park's Atlantic bottlenose dolphin community. A 20min orientation programme in one of the beach cabañas, with a film and instruction from two trainers, sets you up for this thrilling experience. Groups of 6–8 go into the lagoon with the trainers and, starting off standing in the waist-deep (slightly chilly) water as one of the dolphins comes over, you gradually become more adventurous until you are swimming with them. Timid swimmers are well catered for and there are flotation vests for those who need them. The lagoon is up to 12ft/3.6m deep so there is a real feeling of being in the dolphins' environment. You learn how trainers use hand signals and positive reinforcement to communicate, and get the chance to stroke, feed and even kiss your dolphin. The encounter concludes dramatically as you are towed ashore by one of these awesome animals (which weigh up to 600lb/272kg), though activities vary according to their attention span. You spend around 30mins in the water and it is totally unforgettable. Under-6s are not allowed in the lagoon. TTTTT+

The Grand Reef: This area features a massive 2.5acre/1ha artificial reef with 125 species of sea creatures, including fish, rays, eels, sharks, urchins, and lionfish (the dangerous ones are behind glass!). White sand beaches, meandering pathways and

The Grand Reef

scenic bridges lead to shallow wading areas, waist-deep paddling pools and deep-water snorkelling, while underwater canyons and inviting grottos combine with brightly coloured artificial coral reefs for a convincing and utterly exhilarating experience. It's like paradise, only better!

For an extra element of relaxation, stake out a hammock on the central island or consider hiring one of eight private waterside cabañas (with table, chairs, loungers and towels). There is a drinks kiosk here but no food outlets. AAAAA

BRITTIP
The Sea Venture area is not accessible to snorkellers during tours, but you can swim there when a tour is not running.

Sea Venture: One of the most innovative features of the Grand Reef is this underwater walking tour. Equipped with special dive helmets, guests make a 20min trek along the bottom of the reef, passing sharks and lionfish and interacting with schools of fish and gentle rays. This is a totally immersive experience and a sensation like no other (how often can you explore underwater while standing up straight?). There are handrails throughout the journey, which takes groups of 4–9 at a time. Total tour time is 1hr, including preparation and underwater trek (for an extra $59 per person). Ages 10 and up only. TTTT

Discovery Cove 'extras'

This isn't a cheap day out, but the extra quality is everywhere. The Laguna Grill lunch is excellent and you can visit as often as you want, while a Calypso band adds to the tropical paradise feel. Conservation Cabaña allows guests to meet a neat selection of the park's small mammals (like an anteater and tree sloth); parking is free and you also receive an 8x6in/15x20cm welcome photo. While official opening time is 9am, they will check you in as early as 8am for the free breakfast.

Special occasions

Discovery Cove has a range of options that involve dolphin interaction and private beach cabañas.

The Celebration Package ($159) includes 6x8in/15x20cm photo, photo frame or plush toy, bag, T-shirt, souvenir buoy delivered by a dolphin and 25% off Ultimate photo package. while a Premium Package ($229) adds a private cabaña.

The Elite Package ($399) includes a buoy with personalised message delivered by a dolphin; signature tote bag; choice of deluxe photo frame or plush toy; a private cabaña; Discovery Photo Package.

VIP Package ($799) offers the ultimate Discovery Cove experience as it includes a buoy with a personalised message, tote bag, photo frame, plush toy, cabana for the day, Discovery Photo Package, reserved seating at Laguna grill, a dedicated host/hostess and itinerary planner, and an additional up-close animal encounter.

Park admission and dolphin swim package are required with all special occasion packages. You are advised to book at least three months in advance as they do sell out in peak periods and, in winter, the park is closed on some midweek days. There is also a 10% advance discount periodically for online bookings. See **www.discoverycove.com**.

Freshwater Oasis

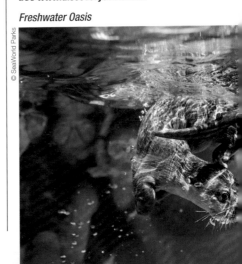

© SeaWorld Parks

Busch Gardens

While the Orlando parks may get more publicity, the 335acre/136ha Busch Gardens in Tampa offers just as much in terms of attractions and – especially – Brit appeal. In fact, the sister park to SeaWorld, which started as a mini-menagerie for the wildlife collection of the brewery-owning Busch family in 1959, is often one of the most popular of all Florida attractions with UK visitors for its nature appeal – and superb roller-coasters. It is a major, multi-faceted family park, the biggest outside Orlando and just an hour from International Drive. It is rated among the top four zoos in America, with more than 2,700 animals representing over 320 species of mammals, birds, reptiles, amphibians and spiders. But that's just the start. It boasts a safari-like section of Africa spread over 65acres/26ha of grassy veldt, with special tours to hand-feed some of the animals. Interspersed among the animals are more than 20 bona fide theme park rides, including the mind-numbing coasters Kumba, SheiKra, Montu and Cheetah Hunt, plus the dramatic new drop-tower ride, Falcon's Fury, with guaranteed fun for coaster addicts, plus plenty of scaled-down rides for children. Then there are animal shows, musicians and big-stage show productions.

The overall theme is Africa, hence the park is divided into areas like Nairobi and Morocco, and dining and shopping are just as good as the other parks. It doesn't quite have the pizzazz of Epcot or Universal, and the staff are a bit more laid back, but it has guaranteed 5-star family appeal, especially with its rides just for kids. It's a bit like the big brother of Chessington World of Adventures in Surrey, though on a grander scale

BUSCH GARDENS at a glance

Location	Busch Blvd, Tampa; 75–90mins' drive from Orlando
Size	335 acres/136ha in 11 themed areas
Hours	9 or 10am–6 or 7pm off peak; 9am–8pm Easter, Thanksgiving, Christmas; 9 or 9.30am–10.30pm summer
Admission	Under-3s free; 3–9 $90 (1-day ticket), $139 (2-park ticket with SeaWorld), $154 (3-park ticket with Aquatica and SeaWorld), $336 (Orlando FlexTicket Plus); adult (10+) $95, $145, $159, $356.
Parking	$17, $22 preferred parking, $28 valet
Lockers	$7, in Morocco, Congo, Egypt and Stanleyville
Pushchairs	$15 and $20
Wheelchairs	$15, $45 and $55, with pushchairs
Top attractions	Congo River Rapids, Kumba, Montu, Cheetah Hunt, SheiKra, Tanganyika Tidal Wave, Iceploration show, Falcon's Fury, Cobra's Curse
Don't miss	Jungala, Edge of Africa, Madagascar Live! Operation: Vacation, Animal Care Center, Myombe Reserve, Meet The Keepers talks

Hidden costs	**Meals**	Burger, chips and Pepsi $11.20 3-course meal $22-35 (Zambia Smokehouse) Kids' meal $6.99
	T-shirts	$19.95–35.95
	Souvenirs	99c–$2,100
	Sundries	Face Painting $7–13

BUSCH GARDENS

Morocco
1 Marrakesh Theater
2 Moroccan Palace Theater
3 Myombe Reserve
4 Gwazi Gliders

Cheetah Hunt
5 Cheetah Run
6 Cheetah Hunt and Skyride Station

Bird Gardens
7 Gwazi Pavilion
8 Lory Landing
9 Walkabout Way

Sesame Street Safari of Fun
10 Air Grover
11 Sunny Day Theater
12 Big Bird's 123-Smile With Me

Stanleyville
13 SheiKra
14 Stanley Falls Flume
15 Tanganika Tidal Wave
16 Stanleyville Theater
17 Skyride Station
18 Zambia Smokehouse

Jungala
19 Jungle Flyers, The Wild Surge and Treetop Trails
20 Tiger Habitat
21 Orang Outpost

Congo
22 Kumba
23 Congo River Rapids
24 Ubanga-Banga Bumper Cars

Pantopia
25 Falcon's Fury
26 Sand Serpent
27 The Phoenix
28 Grand Caravan Carousel
29 Pantopia Theater

Nairobi
30 Curiosity Caverns
31 Serengeti Plain
32 Jambo Junction
33 Edge of Africa
34 Elephant Habitat
35 Animal Care Center

Egypt
36 Montu
37 Cobra's Curse (summer 2016)

(and in a better climate). Busch Gardens is the only park to offer 1-day Tickets with a rain guarantee, which means if you get rained out on your visit, you can return FREE within seven days. Look for self-serve machines to the right of the park entrance to save time at ticket booths.

> **BRITTIP**
> Like SeaWorld, Busch Gardens offers QuickQueue, the limited number front-of-the-line pass for all the park's main rides. Price varies (seasonally), $19.99–44.99 for One-Time use, $39.99–69.99 for Unlimited use.

All Day Dining Deal: For just $29.99 ($15.99 3–9s) you can enjoy all-you-care-to-eat-and-drink privileges at five restaurants throughout the park. With your special wristband, choose one entrée, one side or dessert and a soft drink each time you pass through the dining queue (child's price valid for kids' meal only; baby back ribs excluded).

Photokey: If you'd like to collect all your park photos digitally, including ride photos and character meet-and-greets (but not backstage tours), sign up for this new service, either online in advance or when you arrive at the park, for $50 (**https://photokeyonline.com/**).

Meet The Keeper: Look out also for sessions around the park where the animal handlers explain various features of animal husbandry, notably with the gorillas, elephants and hippos. You will find them at the Alligator Habitat, Myombe Reserve, Edge of Africa, Jungala, Elephant

Pantopia

© SeaWorld Parks

and Rhinoceros Habitats and Jambo Junction (where they feature various small-animal encounters).

Location

Busch Gardens can be hard to locate on the sketchy local maps as the sign-posting is not as sharp as it could be, but from Orlando the directions are simple. Head west on I-4 for almost an hour (it is 55ml/88km from I-4's junction with Highway 192) until you hit intersecting motorway I-75. Take I-75 north for 3½ml/5.5km to the exit for Fowler Avenue (Highway 582). Go west on Fowler for another 3½ml/5.5km, then, just past the University of South Florida on your right, turn LEFT into McKinley Drive. A mile/1.6km down McKinley Drive, the car park is on your left, where it costs $17 to park (those with disabled badges should continue on then turn right).

Those without a car can use the **Busch Gardens Shuttle Express** bus, which makes several $10 round trips a day from Orlando (FREE if you have a multi-day ticket). You board at SeaWorld, Orlando Premium Outlets, Universal Studios, Ramada Maingate West, Best Western Lakeside or Old Town in Kissimmee and pick-up times range from 8.30 to 9.40am, returning at 6 or 7pm. Book at Guest Services at SeaWorld or call 1800 221 1339.

Beating the queues: Don't think you've left the high-season Orlando crowds behind. It's still advisable to be here at opening time, if only to be first in line to ride the dazzling roller-coasters, which all draw big queues (especially SheiKra and Cheetah Hunt). The Congo River Rapids, Stanley Falls Log Flume ride and Tanganyika Tidal Wave (all opportunities to get wet) are also prime draws in peak season. But queues take longer to build here, so for the first few hours you can enjoy a relatively crowd-free experience.

Adventure Tour Centre: On your left through the main gates, go here first (better still, book in advance on 1888 800 5447 or online at www.buschgardens.com) if you'd like to do the wonderful Serengeti Safari or other Adventure Tours (p213). Busch Gardens is divided into 10 main sections, with the major rides all a bit of a hike from the main entrance. Check your park map for times and locations of various small-animal encounters throughout the park – then watch for passing flamingos as they take the first of their twice-daily promenades in the main courtyard!

Coaster fans flock to SheiKra, the world's second highest and fastest dive coaster, and peak-season queues can top an hour by mid-afternoon. So, if you want to ride this first, bear left through Morocco past the Zagora Café, through the Bird Gardens and up into Stanleyville. Then continue through Stanleyville to Congo for Kumba, and retrace your steps to do Congo River Rapids and the other two water rides. To start with the superb Cheetah Hunt coaster, veer right into Morocco and go past the Moroccan Palace Theater, opposite Crown Colony. After riding the Cheetah, try the new Project 2016 Coaster in nearby Egypt, then return to take the SkyRide to Stanleyville and take on the other big rides there. Here is the full layout of the park in a clockwise direction.

Morocco

Come through the main gates to the home of all the guest services and a lot of shops. Epcot's Moroccan pavilion sets the scene better, but the architecture is still impressive and this version won't tax your wallet as much as Disney's! Turning the corner brings you to the first animal encounter, the alligator pen. Morocco is also home to 2 of the park's biggest shows.

Marrakesh Theater: In summer 2015, this venue presented **Motor City Groove**, a well-presented musical tribute to the Motown sound of the 1960s and 70s up to four times a day, with a chance to meet the performers after the show. AAA

Moroccan Palace Theater: The setting for the lavish production

Iceploration, a 25min stage show featuring ice skating, elaborate puppetry, trampoline artists and 20 live animals (including a Siberian lynx), plus in-theatre special effects. It tells the story of a technology-overdosed teen who gets to travel the world with his grandfather and learn the real-life mysteries of the African Serengeti, the Great Barrier Reef, the Arctic and the Amazon rainforest. With vivid costuming, scintillating music and eye-catching performers – plus some wonderfully cute huskies! – it offers yet another dimension to the park's live entertainment 3–4 times a day. AAAAA Stay around to meet some of the performers; you can also buy a CD of the original music.

Myombe Reserve: One of the largest and most realistic habitats for the threatened highland gorillas and chimpanzees of Central Africa, this 3acre/1.2ha walk-through has a convincing tropical setting with high temperatures, lush forest landscaping and water mist sprays. Take your time, especially as there are good, seated vantage points, and catch these magnificent creatures on their daily routine. It is also highly informative, with attendants on hand to answer any questions. AAAAA

Gwazi Gliders: This gentle circling 'hang-gliding' ride is purely for the pre-school crowd. T (TTT under-6s)

Other entertainment: Basketball fans can try the **Hoops Challenge** (for $5) next to Gwazi.

Serengeti Safari

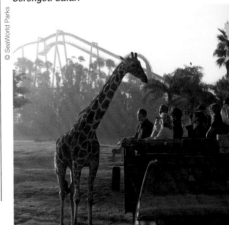

© SeaWorld Parks

Shopping: The Emporium and **Marrakesh Market** are the best of four shops.

Dining: For a quick meal, try **Zagora Café**, especially at breakfast, or the enticing **Sultan's Sweets** serves coffee and pastries.

Cheetah Hunt

This sub-area next to Morocco features the park's wonderful cheetah habitat – and signature ride.

Cheetah Hunt: This beast of a coaster re-creates the thrill of a cheetah in pursuit of its prey. Launching from the loading station out across the savannah, the hunt is on. A second launch spirals you 10 storeys up the ride's signature figure-of-eight tower (with an astonishing view) before taking an exhilarating 130ft/40m plunge into a subterranean gorge. Then you're off again, low and fast along the Serengeti. A final launch zips back across the grasslands (leaping over the heads of onlookers below and above the SkyRide!) and, just before you're completely out of breath, the hunt comes to an end. It's a sensational 2mins. The smooth ride, extensive theming and superb eye-appeal mark this out as possibly Florida's finest but it draws BIG queues, so try to do it early on.
R: 4ft/120cm; TTTTT

Skyride: Take to the air with this one-way cable car trip to Stanleyville, getting a fabulous aerial view of the park, including part of the Serengeti Plain. TT

Cheetah Hunt

© SeaWorld Parks

Cheetah Run: Here you have the chance to see these magnificent cats up close in a 250ft/7m sprint (chasing their favourite toy alongside Cheetah Hunt!), or just lounging around the splendid habitat designed especially for them. Sprints occur up to four times daily (check park map for times). Then, take time to learn more about cheetahs and the park's conservation efforts through nearby touch-screen technology.

Shopping and dining: Grab a souvenir at **Cheetah Gifts** or quick bite or drink from **Cheetah Snacks**.

Bird Gardens

The most peaceful area and the original starting point of the park in 1959, you can unwind here from the usual theme-park hurly-burly. The exhibits and shows are all family-orientated, too, with live shows, an elaborate kids' playground and more animal exhibits.

BRITTIP
The Bird Gardens area is a good place to visit in mid-afternoon when most of the rides are busy.

Lory Landing: Walk through this tropical aviary featuring lorikeets, hornbills, parrots and more, with the chance to become a human perch and feed the friendly lorikeets. A cup of nectar costs $5, but makes for a great photo opportunity. AAA

Walkabout Way: This charming Australia-themed attraction offers the chance to feed the free-roaming kangaroos and wallabies ($5, ages 5 and up only) and meet other Down Under denizens like the emu. It is a surprisingly captivating area, perfect for a relaxed stroll. AAA Other encounters include the lush, walk-through Aviary, Flamingo Island and the Backyard Wildlife Habitat.

Other entertainment: Gwazi Park is home to the seasonal live musical entertainment during summer and other special events, like the new **Food & Wine Festival** (Mar/Apr).

Shopping: A real novelty here is the eye-catching **Xcursions** eco-friendly gift shop. Its live frog and gecko displays and conservation info on interactive touch-screens make it worth visiting whether you buy or not (but all proceeds contribute to the Busch Gardens Conservation Fund). **Garden Gate** is another imaginative shop.

Dining: A pizza-and-pasta buffet with salad, dessert and non-alcoholic drinks (beer and wine extra) is on offer at the pleasant **Garden Gate Café** (excellent value at $15.99 per adult, $10.99 under 9s).

Sesame Street Safari of Fun

This impressive children's interactive play area is the cheerful 'home away from home' for much-loved Sesame Street characters, dressed in best African Safari finery. You will be hard pressed to get pre-schoolers away when they catch sight of this land's seven rides (including a junior-sized coaster, a gentle flume ride and character-themed fairground style rides), entertaining stage show and the wonderfully extensive water play and climb-and-slide areas. The huge treehouse climb, ball pools and adventure play structures alone will keep most kids busy for hours! But there's more:

Air Grover: A whizzy little dip-and-turn coaster packing plenty of junior-sized thrills, piloted by everyone's favourite blue guy, Grover. R: 2ft 9in/97cm accompanied; 3ft 5in/104cm unaccompanied.

Sunny Day Theater: Elmo, Abby, Zoe, Grover and Cookie Monster star in *A is for Africa*, a delightfully zany stage show that brings tales of adventure to life, with a gently uplifting message. Children (and adults!) can't help but sing and clap along, and it is a great photo opportunity as the characters arrive and then come out for a meet-and-greet afterwards.

BRITTIP
Arrive early and find a seat in the first five rows for an unobstructed view at the Sunny Day Theater. Seat children on the ends for the best character interaction.

Big Bird's 1-2-3 Smile with Me: Big Bird and friends have their own meet-and-greet area, near Air Grover. The big bonus here is 1-on-1 time with the character in a quiet, air conditioned room (photo packages $20–30).

Bert and Ernie's Watering Hole: Thoughtfully designed with even the smallest guests in mind, this gentle water-play area is filled with bubblers, water jets, dump buckets, geysers and splash tubs. Swimwear and sun block are available at Cookie Monster's

Dining with Elmo and friends

© SeaWorld Parks

Trading Post if you forgot yours. Convenient seating surrounds the area. TTTTT (young 'uns only!)

Shopping: Look for **Abby Cadabby's Treasure Hut** and **Cookie Monster's Trading Post** for Sesame Street gifts and souvenirs.

Dining: For a quick bite, try **Snack-n-Getti Tribal Treats**. But the big opportunity is **Dine with Elmo & Friends**, where visitors can enjoy lunch with Elmo and his chums in an outdoor covered dining area. A kid-friendly buffet along with a character song-and-dance show make this a delight for the younger set, with loads of time to meet their favourite characters ($22 for adults, $15 3–9s, including a 6x8in/15x20cm photo per family; every Saturday; Wed–Sat peak season).

Stanleyville

This brings you back into true ride territory, with the park's biggest coaster, as well as several water rides and a fabulous new show. You'll also find one of the three Train Stations here (next to SheiKra), for a gentle 35min journey round the park.

SheiKra: The park's outstanding big-thrill attraction is the giant steel structure of this monstrous coaster. At 200ft/62m tall and hitting 70mph/112kph, it puts Alton Towers' fearsome Oblivion in the shade. Higher, longer and faster, it features an initial drop at an angle as near vertical as makes no difference (with a delicious moment of stop-go balance as you teeter on the edge!), a second drop of 138ft/42m into an underground tunnel, an Immelman loop (an exhilarating rolling

SheiKra

© SeaWorld Parks

manoeuvre) and a water splashdown over 0.6ml/1km of smooth-as-silk track. As if all that isn't enough, a 2007 modification removed the coaster's floor, so there is nothing between you and the track but air! The whole ride lasts less than 3min and is almost as much fun to watch as to ride. It also draws big queues, so get here early or expect a long wait (or use the paid-for QuickQueue system). You can buy the video of your ride for $25, a 6x8in/15x20cm photo for $19.95 or packages from $20–35. R: 4ft 6in/137cm. TTTTT+

Stanley Falls: Almost identical to Log Flume rides at Chessington, LEGOLAND, Thorpe Park and Alton Towers, this guarantees a good soaking at the final 40ft/12m drop. R: 3ft 10in/116cm. TTT

Tanganyika Tidal Wave: A more scenic ride, this takes you on a journey along 'uncharted' African waters before tipping you down a two-stage drop that lands with tidal-wave force. R: 4ft/122cm. TTTT

> **BRITTIP**
> Don't stand on the bridge by Tanganyika Tidal Wave or by the SheiKra splashdown – unless you want to get seriously wet!

Stanleyville Theater: This enclosed and air-conditioned venue debuted with the 20min **Madagascar Live! Operation: Vacation** show in 2013, featuring live song-and-dance performances from the stars of the *Madagascar* film series. It follows the antics of Alex the Lion, Gloria the Hippo, King Julien, Mort and the Penguins during their holiday adventures, backed by music from a live band rocking through both classic and original songs. Superb staging, vivid lighting and the show's singers and dancers (plus the lovable penguins and outrageous King Julien) combine to provide an infectious, sing-along style that should appeal to children and anyone who enjoys the Madagascar humour. The characters are also available for meet-and-greets after the show. AAAA

Skyride: The other end of the park's cable-car ride (from Cheetah Hunt), it offers spectacular views over the Serengeti Plain (with a thrilling moment as Cheetah Hunt races above!). However, it closes when it's windy and queues can build up here in late afternoon. AA

Other entertainment: Try **Bahati Hoops** and other fairground games (next to SheiKra) for a small fee.

Shopping: The **Kariba Marketplace** has the best of the shopping.

Dining: For a hearty meal (and a great view of SheiKra), try **Zambia Smokehouse**, where its wood-smoked ribs platter is a delight among a heavily barbecue-orientated menu (also with salads, sandwiches and kids' meals).

Jungala

This 4acre/1.6ha land opened in 2008 adding a couple of small-scale rides, some superb animal habitats and a hugely elaborate children's play area, designed with older children in mind, but is one of the biggest expansions. It gets busy in the afternoon, so visit either early on or late in the day.

Jungle Flyers: This kids' ride (6–13s) is a junior-sized zipline journey over part of the Jungala area, a 1-seat there-and-back trip from the upper level of Treetop Trails. Great fun for kids, but a rather short ride, and queues build up quickly and move slowly most of the day. R: Maximum height 4ft 8in/145cm. TTT

The Wild Surge: Get ready to 'surge' four storeys into the air on this tower ride from inside a giant waterfall providing a (brief!) glimpse over Jungala before bouncing back down again. Be aware that queues here are also long and slow-moving as the ride takes just 14 at a time. R: 3ft 6in/106cm to ride solo (3ft 2in/96cm with a parent). TTT (TTTTT under-12s)

Treetop Trails: Climbing nets, elaborate bridges, crawl tubes and a multi-level maze are the basis of this fab 3-storey children's playground, with smaller-scale adventures at ground level, including squirt fountains and other watery fun (swimsuits or a change of clothes are advisable). It cleverly mixes in two different animal habitats, for the fun-loving gibbons, flying fox-bats and the rare tomistoma (an Asian crocodile). TTTT (young 'uns only)

BRITTIP
The toddler play area in Treetop Trails is very thoughtfully in the shade.

Tiger Habitat: One of the park's most creative animal environments is this multi-level tiger exhibit (including its rare white tigers). Tiger Lodge is an air-conditioned overlook including conservation info and issues, and Tiger Trail is a walkthrough section with close-up opportunities, including a unique pop-up turret (with a separate queue) in the main enclosure and a rope-pull for guests to 'test their strength' (periodically) against the big cats. Huge windows provide maximum viewing of the animals at play, especially in their plunge pool. AAAA

Orang Outpost: Another brilliant animal habitat, the orang-utans love to look in on guests, viewing them as much as vice versa. A series of close-up windows, including a glass floor over a hammock play area and a kids' tunnel, provide superb observation of the specially designed forest environment. AAAA

Tiger Habitat in Jungala

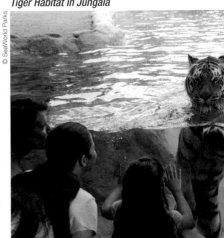

© SeaWorld Parks

Other entertainment: Look out for **Kareebu Jungala**, colourful stilt-walkers around the village area periodically (see map for times).

Shopping: Shop for gifts at **Tiger Treasures** (organic cotton T-shirts and conservation-related items) and **Cubs Closet** (kids' clothing).

Dining: Stop to eat at **Bengal Bistro** (fish, burgers, veggie wraps, salads and sandwiches) or the more snack-orientated **Orang Café** (chicken strips, hot dogs, fries, and funnel cakes).

Congo

As you continue into the Congo, this is primarily about just three rides, plus a stop on the Serengeti Railway.

Kumba: Another of the park's signature coasters, this unmistakable giant turquoise structure looms over the area. It's one of the largest and fastest in south-east USA and, at 60mph/97kph, features three high-thrill elements: a diving loop plunging a full 110ft/33m; a camel-back, with a 360º spiral; and a vertical loop. For good measure, it dives underground! It looks terrifying close up but is absolutely exhilarating, even for non-coaster fans. **R**: 4ft 6in/137cm. **TTTTT**

Congo River Rapids: These look pretty tame after Kumba, but don't be fooled. The giant rubber rafts will bounce you down some of the most convincing rapids outside of the Rockies, and you will end up with a fair soaking. **R**: 3ft 6in/106cm. **TTTT**

Falcon's Fury

© SeaWorld Parks

Ubanga-Banga Bumper Cars: Fairly typical fairground dodgems, you won't miss anything if you pass them by. **R**: 3ft 6in/106cm. **TT**

Shopping and dining: There is just the **Congo River Outfitters** gift shop here, plus three refreshment kiosks.

Pantopia

This redeveloped land opened in summer 2014 with a dramatic new look, name (formerly Timbuktu) and the park's most eye-catching ride. There is also a full back-story, as Pantopia was created by a mystical Key-Master who arrived by hot air balloon to create a place where travellers could meet. The doors of Pantopia tell a tale of the original owners and travellers who passed this way and the land includes clever kinetic sculptures and re-purposed vehicles, like an Asian tuk-tuk and various bikes and wagons. Another highlight is The Sitting Place, a modern-day watering hole where visitors can sit, relax and enjoy the views, as well as the signature food and drink offerings.

Falcon's Fury: The land's signature ride, this awe-inspiring tower lifts 32 riders at a time (slowly) up to its 300ft/91m height, tilts them forward so they are face down – then drops in best free-fall style. Yes, it's the world's highest drop-tower ride and it's for adrenalin addicts only as it really has that sky-dive feeling for several seconds before the brakes kick in and bring you more gently back to earth. It is aptly named for the vertical dive of a falcon (which can hunt its prey at up to 160mph) and provides an amazing view from the top – if you can keep your eyes open. We think it's as much a spectator opportunity as something you'll actually want to ride but it does provide an iconic look to the park. It's a relatively brief experience and queues move slowly, so you may want to try this early on – or chicken out completely! **R**: 3ft 6in/106cm. **TTTTT**

Sand Serpent: This family-orientated 'Crazy Mouse' style coaster is surprisingly energetic, rising as it does some 46ft/14m and adding tight turns and swift drops. Top speed is only 22mph/35kph, but it seems faster and thrills younger kids. **TTT** (**TTTTT** under-10s)

The Phoenix: A positively evil invention that involves sitting in a gigantic, boat-shaped swing that eventually performs a 360º rotation in dramatic, slow-motion style. Don't eat just before this one! **R**: 4ft/122cm. **TTTT**

Scorpion: A 50mph/80kph roller-coaster, this features a 62ft/19m drop and a 360º loop that is guaranteed to dial D for dizzy for a while. It lasts just 120secs, but seems longer. Queues build here from late morning. **R**: 3ft 6in/106cm. **TTTT**

Grand Caravan Carousel: Join this 'Bedouin caravan' in its layers of tapestries and tenting for a genuine kiddie carousel ride. **TT** (**TTTT** under 5s)

Pantopia Theater: This all-new indoor entertainment arena (replacing the former 3-D cinema) features a terrific animal show, *Opening Night Critters*. It follows the exploits of two wannabe stage presenters and their host of critter side-kicks, including dogs, cats, birds, pigs, a skunk and even a kangaroo, and is sure to raise a lot of laughs with all the family, while you can also meet some of the stars of the show afterwards. **AAAA**

Other entertainment: The **Games Area** offers fairground-style games that require a few extra dollars, while the all-new **Dragonfire Grill** – a Moroccan-influenced nightclub that is Pantopia's gathering place for artists from around the world – offers a show while you dine (or just sit and watch). In 2015 it was **Treasures of the Mirage**, an Arabian-inspired music and dance concoction, featuring belly dancers and a quick-change costume performer, with a chance to meet the cast after the show.

Shopping: This has been heavily redesigned for the Pantopia theme, with the **Painted Camel Bazaar** offering a wide range of creative

merchandise, some of it made from recycled materials from around the world, as well as Falcon's Fury and other souvenir items.

Dining: Headline restaurant the **Dragonfire Grill** is a new food court-style offering featuring several innovative elements and including Italian, American, Asian and Mexican cuisine, as well as a grab-and-go Starbucks coffee station and an extended selection of craft beers. Look out for rotisserie chicken, flatbread pizza, chicken teriyaki and shrimp lo mein Paninis. **Twisted Tails Pretzels** is a delightful new offering of fresh-rolled pretzels (don't miss the signature Bacon Pretzel Fury, along with the beer mustard sauce!), artisan sandwiches, pizza and pretzel dogs, as well as craft beers. **Lynx Frozen Treats** adds snowcones, smoothies and other icy delights and **Kettle Corn** is a haven for popcorn-lovers as well as serving turkey legs, potato twisters, chicken strips and drinks.

Nairobi

It's back to the animals as we enter this area, with five different habitats.

Serengeti Plain: A 49acre/20ha spread of African savannah, this is home to buffalo, antelope, zebras, giraffes, wildebeest, ostriches, hippos, rhinos and many exotic birds, and can be viewed for much of the journey on the Serengeti Express, a full-size, open-car steam train that chugs slowly from its main station in Nairobi to the Congo, Stanleyville and back. **AAA**

BRITTIP

Take the Serengeti Railway from Nairobi (or Congo or Stanleyville) in mid-afternoon to give your feet a rest when it's busy elsewhere.

Jambo Junction: The park's nursery is an interesting animal encounter, with some friendly flamingos, small critters (lemurs, sloths, possums and babies needing extra care) on view through the large windows. This is the place to meet the park's Animal

Ambassadors for education and conservation issues. AA

Animal Care Center: This is a peek into the way Busch Gardens cares for its residents, even down to performing live surgical procedures. The state-of-the-art facility is in three parts, for the Treatment Room, Nutrition Center and Pathology Lab, with live audio links to the vets and technicians working behind the big glass windows and keepers on hand to answer questions, whether it's a snake getting an ultrasound check-up or the daily preparation of mealworms for the possums! AAAA

Other entertainment: Look out for the **Elephant Interaction Wall** and periodic sessions with animal staff (notably the afternoon Elephant Wash), while you can see more park inhabitants at the **Reptile House**, **Curiosity Caverns** (nocturnal animals) and **Tortoise Habitat**. The meeting area for the Serengeti Safari is also here, next to Kenya Kanteen.

Shopping and dining: Caravan Crossing (safari apparel and hats) has the best shopping here while **Kenya Kanteen** offers drinks and snacks.

Egypt

The final area of Busch Gardens is somewhat tucked away, so it's best visited either first thing or late in the day. It sits in the park's bottom right corner and much of it is re-created pharaoh country, dominated by suspended coaster Montu, named after an ancient Egyptian warrior god. New coaster Project 2016 can also be found here.

Montu

Montu: You cannot miss the area's main attraction, another breathtaking inverted coaster, covering nearly 4,000ft/1,219m of track at up to 60mph/97kph and peaking with a G-force of 3.85! Like Kumba, it looks terrifying but really is a 5-star thrill as it leaves your legs dangling and twists and dives (underground at two points) for almost 3min of brain-scrambling fun. R: 4ft 6in/137cm. TTTTT

Cobra's Curse: Get ready for some all-new coaster thrills with this ride for summer 2016 that replaces the old Tut's Tomb exhibit and soars out into the African plain with multiple swoops and dips. It is a high-speed ride with a difference, as the cars will *spin* at various points to provide a first-of-its-kind coaster experience. The vertical lift hill will also bring riders face-to-face with a soft snake and features a 70ft drop along more than 2,100ft of track. TTTTT (expected)

Edge of Africa: This is a 15acre/6ha 'safari experience', which can also be accessed through Egypt, guarantees a close-up almost like the real thing. The walk-through puts you in an authentic setting of native wilds and villages from which you can view giraffes, lions, baboons, meerkats, crocodiles, hyenas and vultures, and even an underwater hippo habitat. Wandering naturalists offer informal talks, and the attention to detail is superb.

BRITTIP

Edge of Africa offers some fantastic photo opportunities but, in the hot months, come here early in the day as many animals seek refuge from the heat later.

Other entertainment: Youngsters can make their own excavations in the **Shifting Sands**, a neat sand play area or try some more fairground-style games.

Shopping: The high-quality **Golden Scarab** offers hand-blown glass and cartouche paintings while you can grab other souvenirs at **Montu Gifts**.

© SeaWorld Parks

Dining: Victorian-style **Crown Colony Café & Pub** overlooks Serengeti Plain and offers counter-service salads, sandwiches and pizzas, with an adjoining pub bar for an excellent selection of craft beers.

> **BRITTIP**
> We find Crown Colony Cafe a blissful lunch stop in the hotter months when its cool interior and elegant ambience offer a welcome change of pace after all the rides.

Special tours

Busch Gardens features a wide range of behind-the-scenes tours and adventure expeditions that add an extra dimension to the park. For all tours, book at the Up Close Adventure Center in Morocco or, better still, book in advance on 1888 800 5447 or at **www.seaworldparks.com**.

Serengeti Safari: A 30min excursion (five times a day, up to 20 at a time) aboard flat-bed trucks, takes you to meet some of the Serengeti Plain's residents and feed the beautiful giraffes while learning about the park's environmental efforts. It tends to fill up quickly and costs $29–39/person seasonally (children must be at least 5; 5–15s must be accompanied by an adult).

Serengeti Night Safari: (park admission not required) is a 2hr after-dark excursion into the Serengeti, with appetisers and hot and cold drinks (Nov–May, $69/person, 21 and over only).

Guided Adventure Tour: This takes just 15 at a time on a 5hr VIP trek, with your own guide, reserved seating at the Moroccan Palace Theater, front-of-line access for major rides, counter-service lunch and close encounters with many of the animals, including the Serengeti Safari ($99/person).

Elite Adventure Tour: The ultimate personal park tour, a 7hr journey with front-of-line access to all rides, the Serengeti Safari, reserved seating at shows, free bottled water throughout

and lunch at Crown Colony ($199/person, 5 and over).

Keeper for a Day: An exclusive 6½hr behind-the-scenes tour where you join the keepers as they feed, train and care for giraffes and antelope, then move on to assist the avian team on the Serengeti ($250/person, including park admission and lunch; 13 and over only, must book at least two weeks in advance).

Jungala Insider: A fascinating 45min group visit behind the scenes in Jungala to meet the keepers, see how they care for the magnificent tigers (you might even help to weigh one!) and orang-utans, and learn some zoo husbandry secrets ($29/person, ages 5+).

Animal Care Center Behind The Scenes: A 75min tour with the park's vet and zoological staff, with hands-on opportunities, as they showcase medical check-ups and other treatments ($29/person, ages 8+).

Heart of Africa Tour: A 90min behind-the-scenes walking tour to get close to hippos, cheetahs and lions with their keepers ($39/person, ages 10+).

Orang Outpost in Jungala

© SeaWorld Parks

Special programmes

Food & Wine Festival: While the park no longer stages the Viva La Musica and Buds, Brew & BBQ programmes, this new (in 2015) offering features elements of both in a completely original package (weekends Mar–Apr). Based in the Gwazi Pavilion area, it consists of a series of special food and beverage kiosks offering an array of dozens of fresh dishes and new menus created especially by the park's culinary team. The festival runs from noon–9pm and starter-size samples range from $4–7, with wine and beers from $7–8, plus live musical entertainment and an evening concert at 6pm from the likes of Daughtry, Kool And The Gang and Gavin Degraw, all as part of regular park admission. There are also food and wine sampler packages from $34–59.

Summer Nights: Busch Gardens is open until 10pm (June–Aug) for this programme featuring outdoor food and drink, live entertainment (notably at the Dragonfire Grill and Gwazi Pavilion), music and DJs, plus clever lighting effects on coasters like SheiKra. A superb nightly high-energy finale, **Kinetix**, brings together live musicians, singers, dancers and acrobats for a 30min contemporary rock show enhanced by innovative lighting and with an all-new fireworks spectacular at the end.

Baby tamandua at the Animal Care Center

© SeaWorld Parks

Howl-O-Scream: Don't miss the park's special Halloween presentation each Sept–Oct. A separately ticketed event ($55–85/person; see online for early-booking discounts) offering grisly goings-on and themed houses, it also offers the chance to ride all the big coasters at night (7.30pm–midnight or 1am). It features some imaginative shows with all the shock-horror effects, plus a dance party, but it is definitely not advised for young children. It is similar to Universal's Halloween Horror Nights programme (p167), with 8 elaborately themed haunted houses – like Blood Asylum and Zombie Mortuary – plus a series of scare zones that change annually. The Busch Gardens version is more spread out and less frenetic than Universal's, but you may well want to try both. See more at **www.howloscream.com**.

Christmas: See p39.

Adventure Island: For a really full family day out, you can combine Busch Gardens with sister water park Adventure Island (on McKinley Drive), which is blissful when it's hot. The 25acres/10ha of watery fun, in a Key West theme, offer a full range of slides and rides, such as the all-new **Colossal Curl**, a massive family raft ride, **Wahoo Run** raft ride, a 210ft/64m plunge on the body slide **Gulf Scream**, the exciting 4-lane mat slide **Riptide** and spiralling tube ride **Calypso Coaster**. Open mid-Mar to late Oct (weekends only Sept and Oct) 10am–5pm (9pm in summer). Tickets are $49 (ages 3 and up), while a Busch Gardens–Adventure Island combo is $135 (but only $95pp online).

BRITTIP

The Anheuser-Busch factory at Busch Gardens is long gone BUT you can still get a (free) brewery tour (and samples!) at the nearby Yuengling Brewery on neighbouring 30th Street (p280).

Well, that's the low-down on all the main theme parks, but there is still MUCH more to discover…

7 The Other Attractions

or One Great Leap for Tourist Kind

If you think you can 'do' Orlando just by sticking to the main theme parks, think again! There is still a LOT more to discover, starting with Kennedy Space Center, which we rate as an essential place to spend a day.

Then there's LEGOLAND Florida – ideal for the 3–12 brigade – and Gatorland, another great-value experience. There are unique venues like WonderWorks, I-Drive 360 and Ripley's Believe It Or Not and, for more individual tastes, the amazing 'skydive' experience of iFLY Orlando and WhirlyDome fun centre, plus some magnificent water parks. The choice is yours, but it's an immense selection. Let's start with One Giant Leap for Mankind.

Kennedy Space Center

Welcome to the past, present and future of NASA's space programme, and one of the most fascinating places in Florida. The KSC has undergone huge redevelopment in recent years, culminating in 2013 with the opening of their Space Shuttle Atlantis exhibit to showcase the last orbiter in the Shuttle programme that gives the whole Visitor Complex a fresh, new look. This underlines its place among the first rank of local attractions and provides even more reason to justify an all-day visit. Apart from the Space Shuttle, there are a series of exhibits and shows (including 2 splendid IMAX films),

a children's play area, an art gallery, the captivating daily Astronaut Encounter, the poignant Astronaut Memorial, and the essential Space Center bus tours, which all add up to great value. There is also the brilliant Astronaut Training Experience, an extra programme into real-life astronaut missions and simulations at the US Astronaut Hall of Fame. However, there is now a $10 parking fee, when it used to be free.

Getting there: Take the Beachline Expressway out of Orlando (Route 528, and a toll road, see map p216) for about 45mins, bear left on SR 407 (don't follow signs to Cape Canaveral or Cocoa Beach at this point) and turn right at the T-junction onto SR 405. The Visitor Center is located 9ml/14km along on the right. Tours and IMAX presentations start at 10am (**www.KennedySpaceCenter.com** – be sure to check the website for periodic online ticket discounts).

> **BRITTIP**
> Don't miss the clever water show at the Space Center's entry plaza. It runs every 15 minutes.

Once inside the Visitor Complex, the attractions are as follows. You should certainly start with the new Space Shuttle *Atlantis*, as this has proved THE big draw since it opened in June 2013. Late arrivals should do the Bus Tour first, though, then visit the Shuttle complex.

Orlando's Other Attractions
And Main Shopping Outlets

Daytona

✈ Sanford International Airport

Sanford Airport via Interstate 4 has no tolls, but can be far busier, especially during rush-hour

Sanford Airport via 417 has a few tolls, but is much quieter

Mount Dora

ALTAMONTE SPRINGS

Altamonte Mall

Sanford-Central Florida Zoo

Toll road (from 50c to $5)

Lake Apopka

Winter Park

Black Hammock Fish Camp

Leu Gardens

OCOEE

WINTER GARDEN

WEST COLONIAL DRIVE

Winter Garden Village

EAST - EAST EXPRESSWAY

Amway Center
Downtown Orlando
Lake Eola

WINDERMERE

Citrus Bowl Stadium

FLORIDA TURNPIKE

KIRKMAN RD

SEMORAN BOULEVARD

Universal Studios
Universal Citywalk
Islands of Adventure

Mall at Millenia

Orlando Premium Outlets International Drive

Cocoa Beach

Port Canaveral

Artegon Orlando
Pirates Dinner Adventure

Florida Mall

SAND LAKE RD
Sleuth's Mystery Dinner Shows

BEACHLINE

TURKEY LAKE RD

INTERNATIONAL DRIVE

Orlando Watersports Complex

Orlando International Airport

Magic Kingdom

Mickey's Backyard Barbecue,
Hoop-Dee-Doo Musical Revue

SeaWorld

ORANGE BLOSSOM TRAIL

BOGGY CREEK ROAD

WESTERN BELTWAY

Lake Buena Vista

Disney Springs

Orlando Premium Outlets Vineland Avenue

JOHN YOUNG PARKWAY

CENTRAL FLORIDA GREENEWAY

Epcot
Disney's Hollywood Studios

Buena Vista Watersports

Fantasia Gdns Mini-golf

Animal Kingdom

Winter-Summerland Mini-golf

Lake Buena Vista Factory Stores

The Loop & Loop West

FLORIDA TURNPIKE

MainGate West

OSCEOLA PARKWAY

Toll road

BOGGY CREEK ROAD

Old Town

KISSIMMEE

East Lake Fish Camp (Boggy Creek Airboats)

Celebration

Capone's Dinner Show

Osceola County Pioneer Museum
Osceola County Historical Museum

OLD LAKE WILSON RD

Medieval Times

IRLO BRONSON MEMORIAL HIGHWAY

Silver Spurs Arena

East Lake Tohopekaliga

Downtown Kissimmee

Warbird Adventures & Museum

Kissimmee Airport

Kissimmee Scenic Lake Tours

Champions Gate

Green Meadows Petting Farm

Forever Florida, Reptile World Serpentarium

Dinosaur World

Tampa, Clearwater, Gulf Coast

ST CLOUD

© Steve Munns 2015

Boggy Creek Airboat Rides

Lake Tohopekaliga

0   5 miles

Miami

N

Atlantis: This dramatic $100m, 65,000ft²/6,000m² exhibit is the core experience of the new-look KSC, offering the 30-year history of the Shuttle programme through a mix of interactive media. Both hands-on and immersive, it features one of the three surviving orbiters (*Discovery* is on show at The Smithsonian in Washington and *Endeavour* at the California Science Center in Los Angeles). The six-storey building is clad in orange and gold, to symbolise the fiery glow of atmosphere re-entry, and is dominated outside by full-size replicas of the external fuel tank and solid rocket boosters, with their 184ft/56m height illustrating the power needed to put the Space Transport System (STS) in orbit. Visitors wind up a gently sloped ramp to a film pre-show into how and why the Shuttle programme was devised, and then doors open into the main theatre, offering a vivid sense-surround presentation into the life and missions of *Atlantis* (stand about two-thirds of the way back to get the full effect of the wrap-around screens). The specially written musical score

reaches an emotional crescendo that is accompanied by a real 'wow' moment as…no, we won't reveal it! It is a breathtaking show that leads into the main exhibit hall, with the orbiter displayed with its payload bay doors open and robotic arm extended alongside an elevated viewing platform. The hall is subdivided into areas for the International Space Station, Hubble Space Telescope and Astronaut Training Simulation Gallery (complete with the chance to land a Shuttle and dock with the Space Station). In all, there are more than 60 interactive touch-screen experiences and simulators, and the climb-through Space Station, with its clear plastic tube suspended two storeys up, is quite a challenge. There are also parts of the launch platform and other support elements on show, while kids can try the Shuttle 'landing slide' and a jump-around hydrogen 'energy' game. You can easily spend a coupe of hours in here and we strongly advise heading here first as queues build up quickly on the entry ramp. AAAAA+ The gift shop offers a great variety of souvenirs.

KENNEDY SPACE CENTER at a glance

Location	Off State Road 405 in Titusville	
Size	Visitor Complex 70 acres/28.3ha	
Hours	9am–5 or 6pm) year-round (except Christmas Day)	
Admission	Under-3s free; 3–11 $40; adult (12+) $50; Atlantis annual pass $89/$71; Explorer annual pass $139/$109. Prices do not include tax but include admission to US Astronaut Hall of Fame.	
Parking	$10	
Lockers	$5 and $8, just inside turnstiles to left.	
Pushchairs	$5 and $8 at Information Central (through entrance on left)	
Wheelchairs	$10 and $25 (electric scooter) at Information Central	
Top attractions	Space Shuttle Atlantis; Shuttle Launch Experience; IMAX films; Astronaut Encounter; KSC Bus Tours	
Don't miss	Apollo-Saturn V Center on Bus Tours; Astronaut Memorial; Rocket Garden	
Hidden costs	Meals	Burger, chips and coke $12.98 Kids' meal $5.49–7.59
	T-shirts	$15.99–36.99
	Souvenirs	79c–$4,800
	Sundries	Bus tour photos – $15 and $25

Shuttle Launch Experience: After seeing *Atlantis*, visitors should also walk up the long gantry for this well-made presentation into a real-life launch – with you on board! A clever pre-show, with dry ice, moody lighting and sound and vibration effects pave the way to the 'ready room' to prepare for your own blast-off. The capsules look like crew cabins in the cargo hold of the Shuttle, and you go through the launch procedure as the vehicle moves into a near vertical position for take-off. On the command 'Go for engine start', you are at the heart of a 5min simulation providing the features of a realistic launch, with vibration generators, sound effects, cabin movements and screen visuals. You get a taste of the G-forces involved, the Rocket Booster and External Tank separations, and a moment of 'weightlessness' as you enter Earth's orbit. Finally, the cargo doors open to reveal an awe-inspiring view. There is then a 'space walk' back to Earth via a spiral walkway surrounded by the stars and more satellite views of the planet. Don't miss the plaques to mark every Shuttle flight – and the memorials to the *Challenger* and *Columbia* tragedies. **R:** 3ft 8in/112cm. **TTT AAAAA**

BRITTIP

All of the Shuttle Launch Experience is fully wheelchair-accessible, and there is a seat outside for potential riders to test their comfort level. For anyone wary of the full ride (although there is no need to be), there is a bypass room where you can experience the attraction without the motion.

Bus tours: The KSC's signature coaches depart every 15mins from 10am and are fully narrated to provide a full overview of the Space Center. They make two stops in addition to driving around much of the working area, including past the shuttle launch pad. The first is the LC39 Observation Gantry (Fri and Sat only), just 1ml/1.6km from shuttle launch pad 39A, a combination four-storey observation deck and science centre. The exhibits consist of a 10min film into how launches were prepared, plus models and videos of a countdown with touch-screen info on the shuttle programme. Next is the Apollo/Saturn V Center, one of the KSC's great exhibits, where you can easily spend 90mins. It highlights the Apollo missions and first Moon landing with 2 impressive

Shuttle Launch Experience

theatrical presentations on the risks and triumphs, a full-size 363ft/111m Saturn V rocket and a hands-on gallery of space exploration. Allow a couple of hours to do the tour justice but be aware the last bus leaves the Visitor Center at 2.20 or 2.50pm, depending on season. AAAAA

IMAX films: Back at the Visitor Complex are the IMAX cinemas, twin 55ft/17m screens that give the impression of sitting on top of the action. **Hubble 3-D** (narrated by Leonardo DiCaprio) is a fabulous 43min journey through the universe as seen by the Hubble Space Telescope. Float beside astronauts as they adjust and repair Hubble, marvel at the sensation of moving through galaxies and experience the profound dynamics of the cosmos. New in 2015 was **Journey To Space 3D**, a 42min look at the story of the space shuttle programme and what comes next – a mission to Mars. The future of space exploration is well detailed and exciting, and the film traces some amazing new developments. Both films dazzle with the spirit of human achievement and you may feel the urge to stand up and cheer at the end! AAAA Also in the IMAX building, you'll find Eye on the Universe: The Hubble Telescope Exhibit, featuring still images taken by Hubble.

Astronaut Encounter: This engaging feature is a daily talk and Q&A session, with personal observations and stories from various veterans of the space programmes, including Shuttle astronauts. It is an insightful and engrossing programme, up to 3 times a day at the Astronaut Encounter Theater. AAAA

Early Space Exploration: A clever walk-through trip into the space programme's past, including the Hall of Discovery, the Mercury Mission Control Room – the original consoles from America's first manned space flights – and the Hall of History. AAA

Exploration Space: An interactive exhibit and showcase featuring the Explorers Wanted show, an engaging NASA presentation geared toward children. Check out the computer photo stations for a neat souvenir to take home. AAA

Other exhibits: Nature and Technology (which showcases the unique balance the Center maintains with the local environment), the **Center for Space Education** (an interactive learning centre), the **Space Walk of Honor** and **NASA Art Gallery** (exhibits and artwork).

An extensive new **Education Center** is in preparation for a 2016 debut, along with the full transfer of the **Astronaut Hall of Fame** to the main Visitor Center (see below). This will involve a major new building with more interactive exhibits and hands-on opportunities. Details were limited as we went to press, so be sure to see **www.kennedyspacecenter.com** for the latest updates.

Youngsters have their own playground, the covered **Children's Play Dome**, which has a range of climbing/crawling/sliding elements. Finally, head back to the **Rocket Garden**, which has a kids' splash fountain and an Apollo capsule gantry, to give the feel of astronauts boarding the Saturn V rocket. Free tours are given up to four times a day (times vary). Don't forget to stop at the **Astronaut Memorial**, a moving tribute to the men and women who have died in the course of the space programme. AAA

Multi-axis trainer at the Astronaut Training Experience

© Kennedy Space Center

Shopping: The Visitor Complex has an excellent **Space Shop** (the world's largest store for space memorabilia and gifts – enter at your peril!), the smaller **Voyagers** just outside the main exit and **The Right Stuff Shop** at the Apollo/Saturn V Center.

Dining: Stop for lunch at **Orbit Cafe**, a revamped and modern counter-service diner where you order your food – a tempting array of salads, sandwiches, pizza, burgers and kids meals – at touchscreen kiosks (and can see some of the lettuce and herbs being grown in hydroponic towers), or the excellent **Rocket Garden Café**, for tasty sandwiches, salads, tacos and fish and chips. Quick bites and drinks, including speciality coffees, can be found at several kiosks throughout the Visitor Center. You'll also find the **Moon Rock Café** at the Apollo/Saturn V Center on the bus tour.

The Center then has five optional extra tours and three other features.

KSC Up-Close: Explore Tour: Travel nearly a ¼mile/800m within the perimeter security fence of Launch Pad 39-A and get a close view of the amazing complex, including the flame trench and emergency escape system. The highlight of the tour is the photo opportunity during a stop near the pad. Other sites on the tour include drive-by views of Launch Pad 39-B, the Vehicle Assembly Building,

A Falcon 9 rocket launch

© Kennedy Space Center

mobile launch platforms and a stop at the Apollo/Saturn V Center ($25 adults, $19 for 3–11s).

KSC Up-Close: The Launch Control Center Tour: Go inside Firing Room 4, from which all 21 shuttle launches since 2006 were controlled. See the engineers' working computerised launch control systems, main launch countdown clock and large video monitors on the walls, then enter the 'bubble room' with its wall of interior windows through which the management team viewed all of the proceedings ($25 and $19).

Cape Canaveral: Then and Now: If you want to learn more about NASA history, try this three-hour+ guided tour (daily at noon) into the early days of space exploration around the older part of the facility. Highlights include the Air Force Space & Missile Museum, Mercury launch sites and Memorial, original astronaut training facility and several active launch pads, all of which are otherwise off-limits. For this tour, international guests (including children) must present a valid passport to participate. You must check in at the Information Counter at least 30min prior to your tour ($25 and $19). Reserve online or call 1866 737 5235.

Astronaut Training Experience (ATX): Away from the main attractions, you have the choice of a thrilling ½day programme into Shuttle training, using a sequence of simulated hands-on preparations, with the input of various NASA veterans. The training provides activities from the multi-axis trainer and one-sixth gravity chair, to operating a Shuttle mock-up and taking the helm in Mission Control. You must be at least 14 (under-18s accompanied by a parent). Hardwearing clothes and athletic shoes are advised, and 'recruits' should be free of neck and back injuries. It costs $175 (including ATX gear) but guarantees a memorable day for 'space cadets'.

ATX Family: is a chance for children as young as seven, with a parent, to participate in a ½day course.

The session includes building and launching rockets, riding realistic simulators, meeting a veteran NASA Astronaut and working on a shuttle mission to the International Space Station in 'Mission Control.' It's $175/adults and $145/child (7–11) and you can book in advance on 1866 737 5235 or online (see below).

BRITTIP

The Space Center still has an extremely active rocket launch programme (2015 was the busiest since 1998) and you can see full details at **www.nasa.gov** and **www.visitspacecoast.com/launch-schedule/**.

Lunch with an astronaut: For another fully engrossing feature at the Kennedy Space Center, a small group gets to dine with the star of the daily Astronaut Encounter. The featured person gives their own special briefing, adding extra insight into their space missions, plus answers individual questions, gives autographs and poses for photos. It is $30 adults and $16 children at noon daily, and tickets may be bought online or by calling 1866 737 5235. It's a highly worthwhile opportunity and one we strongly recommend. The buffet-style lunch is pretty good, too!

US Astronaut Hall of Fame

While the Space Center tells you primarily about the machinery of putting men and women in space, this (on SR 405, just before the main entrance to KSC) gives the low-down on the people involved, with memorabilia, exhibits and explanations. The chronological sections are: Entry Experience, visions of space flight; Race to the Moon, the stories of the Mercury, Gemini and Apollo missions; Space Shuttle: The Astronaut Experience, a unique collection of testimonials, personal experiences and authentic artefacts; Astronaut Adventure room, with space-walk 'chairs', a G-force simulator, moon exploration, interactive computers and Mars Mission experience; and on to Science on a Sphere, a fascinating 3-D exhibit exploring the Earth, moon and the planets in our solar system as viewed from space. Admission: Included with Kennedy Space Center or $27 adults, $23 3–11s on its own. Open noon–5pm. If you enjoyed the KSC, try to spend a couple of hours here (it is busiest towards the end of the day). AAA. NB: The Hall of Fame will be moving in 2016 to a new site at the main KSC Visitor Complex.

US Astronaut Hall of Fame

© Kennedy Space Center

LEGOLAND Florida

Children aged 2–12, their parents and probably their grandparents will all want to make a beeline for this wonderfully bright and expansive park, which opened in 2011. In a beautiful lakeside setting on the site of the former Cypress Gardens – and including the old tropical gardens – it offers 150acres/60ha of guaranteed fun with its extensive main park and Water Park. In fact, while the typical LEGOLAND age range is 2–12, the Floridian version probably appeals to kids as old as 14 with its bigger rides and water flumes. There is plenty to do, with no fewer than 32 rides, four main shows, an extensive adventure play area, the amazing Miniland, new LEGO Friends area and, of course, great LEGO shopping, hence they offer a 2-day ticket, which is great value. Even the dining options are fresh, healthy and appealing, and there are plenty of quiet corners and gardens in which to chill out.

Getting there: take I-4 west to Exit 55, then Highway 27 south for 18 miles to State Road 540. Turn right and the park is 4 miles along, on the left.

It does require a lot of legwork to see it all, though, as it is spread round the southern shore of Lake Eloise in rather sprawling fashion and, when it's hot, there aren't so many places in the air-conditioned cool. But there is definitely something for all but older teens here and we really enjoy the clever landscaping and fun use of LEGO characters and features.

Location and tactics

LEGOLAND Florida is in the town of Winter Haven, about 45mins south-east of the Disney/Kissimmee area. Shuttle service is available from the new I-Drive 360 complex on International Drive at 9am next to the multi-storey car park, for $5/person round trip, reservations required on 1877 350 5346 or the Legoland website.

LEGOLAND FLORIDA at a glance

Location	Off State Road 540 in Winter Haven	
Size	150acres	
Hours	10am–6 or 7pm in high season (Easter, summer, Thanksgiving and Christmas), 10am–5pm off peak; closed Tues and Wed off peak; Water Park 10.30am–5 or 6pm in summer; 10.30am–5pm Apr–May (closed some weekdays); 10.30am-5pm Sept–Oct (Sat–Sun only).	
Admission	Under-3s free ($3 for water park); 3–12s $82 (1-day ticket); $97 (1-day plus water park or 2-day ticket); $112 (2-day plus water park); adults (13-plus) $89, $104, $119.	
Parking	$17 ($15 if prepaid online)	
Lockers	$5, $7 and $12	
Pushchairs	$10 and $15	
Wheelchairs	$12 and $37 ($47 with canopy)	
Top attractions	The Dragon, Coastersaurus, Technic Coaster, Driving School, Boating School, Wave Racers, Island in the Sky, The Quest for CHI, Royal Joust, Safari Trek	
Don't miss	Miniland, Heartlake City, Fun Town 4-D Theater, Pirates Cove Water Ski Show, Cypress Gardens	
Hidden costs	Meals	Burger, chips and coke $10.89 Kids' meal $5.99
	Kids' T-shirts	$14.99–27.99
	Souvenirs	$0.50–200
	Sundries	Face painting $10–15; Photopass $39.99

You arrive into the large car park where the parking fee is $17 and then walk to the entrance. Its 150acres/60ha spreads people out well but still draws queues at peak periods, hence your best bet is to head for LEGO Kingdoms, Land of Adventure, World of Chima and DUPLO Valley (girls will also want to check out the new Heartlake City), returning to Fun Town and Miniland later in the day. For day two, start with your favourite rides then cool down in the Water Park (which closes an hour before the main park). Once through the gates, here's what you'll find, moving in an anti-clockwise direction (advisable). NB: All ratings are indicated for younger children rather than adults!

The Beginning: This offers the ticket centre, Guest Relations and functional elements like the lockers, pushchair and wheelchair hire. There are no shows but the one ride, **Island in the Sky**, is a breathtaking 150ft/46m lift into the air on a gently revolving platform that affords a magnificent view over the park, lake and surrounding areas. Under 4ft/122cm must be accompanied by adult. AAAA

Shopping and dining: Immediately to the left of the entrance is **The Big Shop** (one of the largest LEGO merchandise stores in the world). Dining is found at **The Market Restaurant** (soups, salads, sandwiches; gluten free, fresh chicken and Asian stir-fry selections) with a quick-bite counter and coffee bar.

Fun Town: Here is where the squeals of delight really begin! In true LEGOLAND style, you have entered a charming village complete with a working factory, 4-D cinema and carousel. Take a **Factory Tour** and watch working machinery as it goes through the process of making LEGO bricks, from moulding to packaging, then let the kids ride **The Grand Carousel** (TT; under 4ft/122cm must be accompanied by adult). Just beyond is **Fun Town Theater**, featuring three 12min 4-D movies daily – including the LEGO

Chima 4-D Movie Xperience and all-new animated follow-up to The LEGO Movie, featuring the further adventures of Emmet and Wyldstyle – all of which provide some clever special effects as well as great film fun for kids (**TTT**).

BRITTIP

Fun Town Theater is a blissful air-conditioned haven in summer and ideal for visiting during the hottest parts of the day.

Shopping: All of your favourite themed merchandise can be found at **LEGO Studios**, including Star Wars, SpongeBob, Indiana Jones, and Batman, the **Minifigure Market** and **Pick A Brick**.

Dining: Granny's Apple Fries serves up the park's signature dessert (apples, cinnamon and a creamy sauce), and **Sunny's Ice Cream Shop** offers great cold treats. **Fun Town Pizza & Pasta Buffet** is a value-conscious choice if you have a hungry tribe to feed.

DUPLO® Valley: Next up as you turn right out of Fun Town is the perfect place for toddlers to let their imaginations run wild as they explore a village sized just for them. Completely re-themed in 2014, this area features a junior-sized train that winds through the 'countryside', passing farms, campgrounds, and fishing holes. Toddlers will love helping the 'farmer' find missing animals and plough the fields, and then cool down in the water play area. TTTT under-6s

Duplo Valley

World of Chima: This is where the large-scale fun starts for the 6-plus brigade, themed for the LEGO Legends of Chima toy range, as brought to life by the Cartoon Network. Here, visitors enter the fabulous Lion Temple on **The Quest for CHI**, a challenging water ride where they battle Cragger the Crocodile King with water cannons as he bids to steal the CHI energy orbs. The journey travels through the full mystical animal world, including imaginative habitats for **Gorilla Forest** and **Raven's Roost**. **TTTT** Also here is the **Speedorz™** Arena, where players can build LEGO Speedorz and compete to win the precious supply of CHI in group challenges. For watery fun, check out **Cragger's Swamp**, a children's play area featuring an array of interactive water spouts and fountains. Kids can then meet Laval the Lion Prince and Cragger at a special **character meet-and-greet** station.

Shopping: Having ridden the ride, of course, you can then buy the LEGO at **Razar's Bazaar**.

LEGO Kingdoms: The next large-scale land features three major rides and a cool play area. Climb aboard **The Dragon** for a backstage view of life in an enchanted castle, then take off on a thrilling flight as this scenic dark ride becomes a dynamic outdoor coaster! **R:** 4ft/122cm or 3ft 4in/102cm with adult. Child Swap and ride photo available. **TTTT** Then, saddle up on LEGO-themed horses for **The Royal Joust**, where youngsters gallop though

Meet and greet at the World of Chima

© Legoland Florida

an enchanted forest, jousting with LEGO knights along the way. **R:** 3ft/91cm; max 12 yrs and 170lb/76kg. **TT** Also here is **Merlin's Challenge**, a fairly standard but quite whizzy fairground circular ride (4ft/122cm or 3ft 4in/102cm with adult). **TTT** Kids will also want to spend time in **The Forestmen's Hideout**, a multi-level climb, scramble and crawl treehouse adventure with ropes and slides. **AAAA** There are also the **Jester's Games** for a few extra dollars.

Shopping: The Kings Market and **Princess Palace** are two suitably themed gift opportunities.

Dining: Castle Burger serves up tasty burgers and chicken sandwiches.

Land of Adventure: Next up is another BIG land, with two more major rides and three other great kiddie attractions. The excitement continues at Lost Kingdom Adventure as you hunt for treasure while fighting off baddies with laser blasters. Youngsters will want to ride several times to better their score. **R:** 4ft 6in/137cm or 2ft 10in/86cm with adult. **TTT** Child Swap, ride photos available. Next is another top thrill in the form of **Coastersaurus**, a classic wooden coaster that zips through a prehistoric jungle and past animated dinosaurs (made from LEGO, of course!). **R:** 3ft/91cm or 4ft/122cm with adult. **TTTTT** Then you can just let young 'uns loose at **Pharaoh's Revenge** multi-level climbing structure, with the added fun of being able to shoot soft foam balls at each other. **Beetle Bounce** shoots riders 15ft/4.5m high on this kid-friendly tower ride (**R:** 3ft/91cm; **TTTT**) while **Safari Trek** is the classic children's car ride, albeit through a clever LEGO-themed African savannah full of lurking animals. **R:** 2ft 10in/86cm, or 4ft/122cm with adult, max age 12; **TTT** The **Adventure Games** are more fairground side-stalls for an extra few dollars.

Dining: Adventure Snacks is a good choice for hot dogs, nachos and cheese, and beverages and **Dino Ice Cream** offers tasty desserts.

LEGO City: The first thing you see in this next area is the large-scale stage fun of **The Big Test Show**, where the madcap members of the City Volunteer Fire Department prove they are not quite a crack fire-fighting force (but also deliver some key fire safety advice) several times a day. AAAA

BRITTIP

Those sitting in the first few rows on The Big Test Show may just get a bit wet as the 'firemen' often miss their target!

The scaled-down elements of a real working town continue with **Rescue Academy**, where families race each other to 'put out the fire'. But these fire trucks only move when you pump the levers! **R**: 4ft/122cm or 2ft 10in/86cm with adult; guests in wheelchairs must transfer. TTT LEGOLAND's ultra-popular **Driving School** (ages 6–13) and **Junior Driving School** (3–5s) and **Boating School** (4ft/122cm or 2ft 10in/86cm with adult) are all here too, giving kids the chance to navigate electric cars and small boats to earn official LEGOLAND driving licences. TT–TTTT For something more dynamic, try **Flight School's** suspended steel coaster, one of the biggest thrills in the park and a major hit with coaster fans. **R**: 3ft 8in/111cm or 4ft 4in/130cm with adult. TTTTT

Shopping: Pick up some souvenirs at the **Driving School Store**.

Dining: Grab a tempting chicken lunch or dinner at the indoor **Fried Chicken Co** or a light bite and drink at **City Slush**.

BRITTIP

See LEGOLAND's website for periodic discounts. They sometimes offer $15 off ALL tickets if booked in advance for a specific day.

LEGO Technic: This area is packed with fun and thrills for older children as it offers three super rides. Project X is the stand-out offering, a tall, fast-turning steel coaster where riders race, brake and bank in life-size LEGO Technic cars. **R**: 4ft/122cm or 3ft 6in/99cm with adult; TTTTT Ride the waves and dodge soaking blasts of water on the airboat-style **Aquazone Wave Racers**, a ride so cool you'll want to queue up straight away for another go! **R**: 4ft 4in/132cm or 3ft 4in/102cm with adult; TTTT). Kids can also try the more sedate **Technicyle** (TT) and have a go at the **Extreme Games** (for a few extra dollars).

Shopping: With a great view overlooking Lake Eloise, the **Extreme Brick Bargains Shop** offers end-of-range LEGO sets, clearance deals and last-chance items.

Dining: Neighbouring **Lakeside Sandwich Co** is a fab choice for fresh sandwiches, wraps, salads and drinks. **Robot Pit Stop** features hot dogs, nachos, novelty ice creams, and drinks.

BRITTIP

Have kids who are nervous about coasters (even the junior kind)? LEGOLAND has a unique programme to help parents with 'Roller Coaster Readiness' tips, available online at **http://florida.legoland.com/PageFiles/1107/LLFBrochureWeb.pdf** and at the front gate.

Imagination Zone: Next up is the creative heart of the park, where kids put their imaginations to work at four hands-on stations. Hero Factory offers the chance to create and build your own galaxy-defending LEGO Heroes (and meet leader Preston

Granny's Apple Fries

Stormer periodically); build and race a LEGO car at **Build & Test**; try out the **Warner Bros. Games Zone**; or assemble a robot at **LEGO Mindstorms**. **Kid Power Towers** then burn off excess energy as kids (and adults!) use ropes and pulleys to ascend colourful towers – and let go for a 'free fall' back down. **R:** 4ft/122cm or 3ft 4in/100cm with adult; **TTT** Child swap available, guests in wheelchairs must transfer.

Dining: Grab a tasty toasted sandwich, salad and drink at **i-Zone Panini**.

Cypress Gardens: Just behind and to the right of the Imagination Zone are the beautiful gardens this park was originally known for, now lovingly restored and a peaceful haven for strolling, complete with beautiful gazebo and tropical displays (and yes, that banyan tree is real, unlike the Disney version!). AAAA

Pirates Cove: Come back out of the Gardens and you'll find the place where swashbuckling meets water in an exciting battle on the 'high seas' in The Battle for Brickbeard's Bounty. LEGO characters and a life-sized pirate ship add to the fun of this water stunt show, with water-skiers, ski-jumping and other stunts that young children will not want to miss. AAA

Dining: Grab a burger, chicken sandwich or snack before or after the show at **Capt Brickbeard's Snack Galley**.

Heartlake City: New in summer 2015 was this area dedicated to the LEGO Friends, with a themed character meet-and-greet area, a show and a whizzy ride. **Friends To The Rescue** is a neat interactive show featuring the five main characters, with plenty of audience involvement, while **Mia's Riding Adventure** offers junior-sized horse-themed fun on a back-and-forth disk coaster. **Stephanie's News Room** is then the perfect venue to meet all the Friends, take photos and get autographs.

Shopping: Pick up all the latest LEGO Friends collections and accessories at the **Friends Shop**.

Miniland USA: Completing the big LEGOLAND tour brings you to the park's other crown jewel, an iconic area featuring eight themed US locations in miniature – and the big bonus of a Star Wars-themed area. **Florida** shows off some of the state's gems, with separate areas devoted to a magnificent replica of the Kennedy Space Center (complete with Shuttle countdown!) and the huge Daytona International Speedway, where youngsters can race LEGO dragsters. **Las Vegas** boasts the glittering resorts and other icons of Nevada's most famous city while **Washington DC** re-creates the White

Legoland

Haven dining

After a day at LEGOLAND Florida you may like to stay in Winter Haven for dinner, in which case there are 2 great choices on Highway 17 (3rd Street SW; turn left on Cypress Gardens Boulevard out of Legoland, go 3 miles then turn right on to 3rd St SW). **Fred's Southern Kitchen** features a true southern-style buffet with the likes of skillet cornbread, chicken and biscuits, collard greens, ribs and fried catfish as well as salads, soups and fabulous home-made desserts ($15 adults, $8 kids; soft drinks only; **www.fredssouthernkitchen.com**). Then there is the Winter Haven outlet of popular local chain **Manny's Chophouse**, with its signature steaks, chops and ribs, plus lively style and eclectic decor. With a good kids' menu and full bar service, it is easily the equal of its Brit-friendly Highway 27 counterpart and, while they don't take reservations, waits rarely top 20–30 mins (p314; **www.mannyschophouse.com**).

House, US Capitol, Smithsonian museum and the Washington and Jefferson monuments. Look closely and you'll see an animated parade and the cherry trees that bloom each spring. No mini-land would be complete without **New York City**, and this representation includes Rockefeller Plaza (complete with squirt fountains!), Times Square, Lady Liberty, the Empire State building, Bronx Zoo and Grand Central Station. Finally, there is a section devoted to the ever-popular subject of **Pirates**, and another miniland that highlights the state of **California**, plus the **Star Wars** zone, complete with scenes from all six films, as well as one from animated series the Clone Wars. Miniland's detail is amazing, with a riot of visual gags and fun touches (try to spot the surprised gent in the loos at Grand Central Station!), and you can easily spend an hour or more browsing here.

BRITTIP

There is no shade in the Miniland area, so be SURE to apply lots of high-factor suncream before spending time here.

Water Park: This fabulous extra (for $15/person) is an opportunity to have fun in best LEGO style. Not as large as the likes of Blizzard Beach and Aquatica, but designed completely with young children in mind and easier to negotiate, it offers the full array of lockers, changing rooms, towel rental and gift shop (with swimming costumes for sale if you make a late decision to try it), plus its own restaurant, complete with shaded **Tiki Bar** for tired parents! There are five main areas and it will require at least half a day of your time. As ever, have plenty of high-factor, waterproof suncream.

DUPLO Splash Safari: This is Toddler Central, featuring small-scale slides and interactive DUPLO creatures, all in just 6in/15cm of water (and within view of the Tiki bar!). AAAA

Joker Soaker: Older children will be captivated by this huge water-feature adventure playground and its array of slides, fountains, climbs, squirt guns and more, including a 300-gallon bucket that fills and tips periodically! R: 3ft/91cm on 3 lower slides, 3ft 6in/99cm on upper 4; under 3ft 6in/99cm must be accompanied by an adult. AAAAA

Build A Raft River: An imaginative variation on the lazy-river idea, with riders able to build their own floating raft with special LEGO bricks and then complete the 1,000ft/330m-long 3ft/91cm deep circuit. AAA

LEGO Wave Pool: Enjoy some gentle surf fun in this wide, walk-in pool that allows young children to splash happily while their older siblings can brave the 3ft 4in/100cm-plus depths. AAA

Legoland at Christmas

© Legoland Florida

Twin Chasers: Older children will love the chance to ride these double flumes – one open, one enclosed – on individual rafts that sloosh down the 375ft/114m tubes, with a grand splash-down at the end. R: 4ft/122cm; TTTT

Splash Out: The ultimate thrill-ride for kids, a selection of 3 intertwined body-slides with a drop of 60ft/18m that afford a great view of the surrounding area – before you 'drop in'! R: 4ft/122cm; TTTTT

Take note: LEGOLAND closes on Tue & Wed at quiet times of the year and the Water Park is only open in the hotter months (and closes weekdays in the spring and autumn). Check in advance on 1877 350 5346 or **http://florida.legoland.com**.

The new **LEGOLAND Hotel** is a great way to stay right in the heart of the fun and take full advantage of those 2-day tickets. With 152 brightly coloured and fully themed rooms, there is bags of LEGO style throughout, from the giant dragon at the entrance to dozens of individual pieces in the rooms, where there is a special Treasure Hunt for kids to solve (and find a prize!). Chose from Kingdom, Adventure, Pirates and LEGO Friends for the individual room themes, which all feature bunk beds and an entertainment unit for kids, while the huge two-room Suites add a living room, pullout sofa and play

area. The VIP Suites sleep up to six. There are king-sized beds for adults, two flatscreen TVs, a mini-fridge and coffee maker in every room. Premium rooms add more LEGO décor and models for kids to play with. The hotel includes a fabulous heated outdoor pool and its own buffet-style diner, Bricks Family Restaurant. A full breakfast is included in the daily rate, along with exclusive Master Model Builder sessions (a major hit with children), early park admission, nightly LEGO building competitions and live entertainment, and there is also a lovely boardwalk on the edge of Lake Eloise. There are interactive play areas for kids throughout the hotel, and it doesn't get much better than walking straight out of the hotel – and straight INTO the park!

BRITTIP

Don't miss the 'Disco Elevators' at the LEGOLAND Hotel – you might not want to get out when it's your floor!

Gatorland

For a taste of Florida wildlife, this is as authentic as it gets and is popular with children of all ages. The 'Alligator Capital of the World' was founded in 1949 and is still family owned, so it possesses a natural, homespun charm few of its big-name rivals can match. And, when the wildlife consists of several thousand menacing alligators and crocodiles in various natural habitats and three fascinating shows – plus a fabulous Zip Line attraction that is now disabled accessible – you know you're in for a different experience (although there is a LOT more to Gatorland than just gators – including their new Bobcat Bayou). Overall, Gatorland is something you're unlikely to get anywhere else, and the sense of being in the 'real' Florida is terrific.

The nursery at Gatorland

Getting there: Gatorland is on the South Orange Blossom Trail, 2ml/3km south of the Central Florida Greeneway and 3ml/5km north of Highway 192 (see map p14). Admission: $26.99 adults, $18.99 3–12s, 10am–5pm, parking free.

Annual passes are only $45.99 and $31.99 if you plan more than one visit (407 855 5496, **www.gatorland.com**). Check website for current coupons.

BRITTIP

If you have an evening flight home from Orlando International, visit Gatorland for half a day on your final day as it is just 20mins' drive from the airport.

Gatorland Express tours: Start by taking the 15min train ride around the park to get an idea of its 110acre/45ha expanse. This has an added fee but is good for multiple rides, is amusingly narrated and is especially fun for kids. You also get a good look at the native animal habitat, which features whitetail deer, wild turkey and quail. Wander the natural beauty of the 2,000ft/610m Swamp Walk, as well as the Alligator Breeding Marsh Walkway, where a three-storey observation tower gives a neat overview. Ask yourself: are they hanging around in the hope someone might 'drop in' for lunch?

BRITTIP

If you are at Gatorland first thing in the morning, take the Swamp Walk straight away. There will be far more wildlife activity then and the peaceful ambience is quite invigorating.

Attractions: Breeding pens, baby alligator nurseries and rearing ponds are also situated throughout the park to provide an idea of the growth cycle of the gator and enhance the overall feeling that it is the visitor behind bars here, not the animals. **Jungle Crocs** features some of the deadliest animals of Egypt, Australia and Cuba, with authentic lairs and brilliant presentation (look out for Sultan and his 'harem' of lady crocs from the Nile). Many of the small-scale attractions have been designed with kids in mind and there is plenty to keep everyone amused. **Allie's Barnyard** is a petting zoo, while you can feed some friendly lorikeets at the **Very Merry Aviary**, and view the pink inhabitants of **Flamingo Island**.

White Gator Swamp: Don't miss this remarkable showcase for four rare and completely white alligators, which are totally leucistic (without pigment), with startling blue eyes, not pink like albinos. Other animals include owls, turtles, flamingos, tortoises, snakes, spiders, emus and deer; also hundreds of wading birds, providing a fascinating close-up of the nests during Mar–Aug.

Bobcat Bayou: New in 2014 was this elaborate habitat for the park's newest residents, two bobcats, while the park also showcases two rare Florida panthers in the **Panther Springs** exhibit.

BRITTIP

Lucy and Neiko, brother and sister panthers who live at Gatorland, are at their most lively first thing in the morning when they have been let out of their night quarters – just like any domestic cat!

Shows: The 800-seat **Wrestling Stadium** sets the scene for some real cracker-style feats (a 'cracker' is a Florida cowboy) as Gatorland's resident 'wranglers' catch a medium-sized gator and proceed to point out the animal's features, with the aid of some daredevil stunts that will have you questioning their sanity. The **Gator Jumparoo** is another eye-opening spectacle as some of the park's biggest creatures use their tails to 'jump' out of the water and be hand-fed tasty morsels, like whole chickens! **Up-Close Encounters** is another amusing showcase of creatures, from the expected snakes to less obvious cockroaches and scorpions. Great photo opportunities for brave children!

Gatorland Express

Gator Gully: This superb little water park features numerous ways for kids to cool down, get wet and generally have fun. The ½acre/0.2ha park features five elements, including a giant jalopy with water jets for spokes and a fountain radiator, an old shack that 'explodes' with water, and giant gators with squirt guns. The neighbouring dry play area and chairs and tables allow parents to sit and watch the kids expend some energy, perhaps with a drink from one of the kiosks.

But wait… that's not all!

Screamin' Gator Zip Line: Gatorland has fixed its eyes firmly on the brave of heart, introducing a first-of-its-kind zipline experience, with four zips soaring high above the park's most notorious residents. At 1,200ft long and up to 56ft high, the lines afford spectacular views of jumping Cuban Crocodiles and the scenic Alligator Breeding Marsh. Start at Tower One, where the 'bunny hill' builds up your courage (and your excitement!). Tower Two soars over croc pools (look down – the view is outrageous!); Tower Three is the tallest launch point at 75ft/23m, and its 600ft/182m run zips straight over the breeding marsh at up to 35mph/56kph. Take the walking bridge over to Tower Four where you're met by a double zipline for a final (and utterly thrilling) race to the finish.

BRITTIP

Book the Screamin' Gator in advance to avoid disappointment. Capacity is limited to groups of 12 4–7 times a day and demand is high. Reserve by phone or online.

Keeping cool in the mud at Gatorland

The experience includes orientation, full equipment check, the zipline and a trek across a swinging bridge. There is a separate fee, but at $69.99/person, it includes all-day admission to the park. A photographer will also chart your journey for purchase back on terra firma! **R**: Min weight 75lb/34kg, max 250lb/113kg. Must be able to climb stairs. Wear closed toe shoes and trousers or long shorts. New in 2014, Gatorland installed a brilliant wheelchair-accessible, one-segment zip line for guests with lower-body disabilities (must transfer to specially designed harness), providing a thrilling 350ft/106m glide over the gator marsh.

Shopping: In addition to three gift stores and the **Gator & Snake** photo opportunity, you should visit the **Gift Shop** complex at the entrance, which incorporates the trademark Gator Mouth entryway.

Dining: Grab a bite or drink at three snack bars: try **Gator Jake's Fudge Kitchen** or dine on smoked gator ribs and fried gator nuggets (as well as burgers and hotdogs) at **Pearl's Smokehouse**, with excellent kids' meals at $6.49.

Special events: Some unique options if you really want to get to know your gators are: **Trainer for a Day**, with the chance to work behind the scenes at the park 8am–10am, finding out what it takes to handle such dangerous animals, behavioural training and novice gator wrangling ($125 12s and over, max five people; includes park admission); **Gator Night Shine**, which takes guests into the Breeding Marsh after dark for a one-hour tour with a senior gator expert, with torches and gator food to lure the 'locals'. You can then marvel at how gator eyes shine like red beacons in the torchlight and learn more about the habits of these amazing animals – a real family treat, which kids seem to love (dusk, around 8.15pm summer, 6.30pm autumn and winter; $20 all ages; bug spray provided; reservations required); and **Adventure Hour**, a chance to go truly 'behind-the-scenes' in the Breeding Marsh to feed and pose for photos with the gators here ($10/person). Rookie Wrestling is every kid's chance to show his or her bravery and have the picture to prove it ($10 to kneel over a gator's back; extra for the photo).

INTERNATIONAL DRIVE

The 14½ml/23km tourist corridor of I-Drive (see maps p14 and 216) continues to be an ever-changing source of hotels, restaurants, shopping and fun. There are more than 42,000 hotel rooms, 150+ restaurants and almost 500 shops, as well as 15 attractions, including 6 mini-golf courses. The I-Ride Trolley links it all in transport terms and the website **www.internationaldriveorlando. com** highlights all the options.

Its Official Visitors Guide has an I-Ride map and valuable money-off coupons, which you can download to get you started, plus a hotel booking facility. The I-Ride Trolley section provides 'NextTrolley' info as well as maps and listings of what is near each trolley stop. Access to the mobile site, with live options for dining, shopping or attractions, is obtained by QR scanning, SMS texting or by simply going to **iDrive2Go.mobi** on a smart phone.

Here's a look at the area's attractions (see also Chapter 10, Orlando By Night, and Chapter 12, Shopping, to get the full picture).

BRITTIP

I-Drive 360, Ripley's, Titanic, iFly Orlando, WonderWorks and WhirlyDome are all handy retreats to keep in mind for a rainy day or if you need time out of the sun.

I-Drive 360

Now the biggest attraction on International Drive is this new (in May 2015) multi-level entertainment, restaurant and shopping complex (on the site of the old Mercado Center). It boasts five headline attractions, notably the 400ft/121m Orlando Eye, plus 12 restaurants, eight shops and two bars/nightclubs, and features free parking in its multi-storey car park.

The landscaped centre also boasts an elaborate fountain and lighting, and is worth visiting both by day and night. The most iconic element is the **Orlando Eye** observation wheel (like the London Eye), a 20min journey that lifts visitors up in air-conditioned 15-passenger capsules for a panoramic view of this part of Central Florida (all the way to the Kennedy Space Center on a clear day). The experience starts with a green-screen photo and a fabulous pre-flight 4-D multi-sensory film of Florida's highlights, then passengers are loaded on the slow-moving Wheel for their flight, which is especially impressive in early evening. There is narration of the major sights, plus information pads on each side, and the vista is fabulous from the top, including the vast spread of Walt Disney World. The Eye costs $25 for adults and $20 for 4–12s and is open 10am–10pm (midnight Fri & Sat). There is also a VIP Experience with priority boarding, fast-track access and a glass of champagne or soft drink for $32 and $27 (available 4.45–8.45pm).

On to **Madame Tussauds**, an extensive range of celebrity waxworks that allow you to rub shoulders (and take as many selfies as you want) with some of the most famous people on the planet, both past and present. The experience starts, suitably, with a Floridian entrance (and a neat photo opportunity) and a meeting with Spanish explorer Juan Ponce de Leon in 1513 as he discovers Florida.

The Orlando Eye

There is a quick history tour of the US featuring the likes of President Lincoln, Uncle Sam, President Obama (in the Oval office, no less) and Martin Luther King, and then the journey continues with famous inventors and innovators (look out for a superb chance to visit with the man who brought Mickey to Orlando in the first place!). The Madame Tussaud story is well illustrated at the half-way point – along with the chance to have your hand cast in wax – and then the centre really turns on the style with a dazzling range of modern celebrities from the world of sports (including a certain David Beckham), music (the likes of Elvis, Madonna and Beyoncé), TV (with Oprah, Jim Parsons, Neil Patrick Harris and more) and Hollywood (with classic stars like Marilyn Monroe and modern icons Jennifer Lawrence and Taylor Lautner). Your tour concludes in the A-list Party, with an amazing selection of the biggest film stars of today, from Samuel L Jackson to Brad Pitt and Angelina Jolie. Look out for some engaging interactive features along the way, notably with Edison's Challenge. You'll need at least an hour to see everything, and taking photos with the 'stars' is actively encouraged ($25 and $20; 10am–8pm, 10pm Fri & Sat).

BRITTIP

If you are worried by heights on the Eye, there is a seat in the middle of the capsule with a central pole that provides a secure vantage point to enjoy the view with an extra feeling of reassurance.

The third part of the attraction is **SeaLife Orlando**, a huge indoor aquarium that features some fabulous exhibits and hands-on displays, ideal for children of all ages. The highlight is the 360-degree immersive tunnel through the main aquarium, with fish – including giant rays and sharks – floating all around you, but there are then a variety of smaller tanks and other underwater scenes, including a Rockpool experience, Stingray Cove and Everglades tableau. In all there are more than 5,000 animals to see and investigate, along with some clever 'Talking Aquarium' interactive talks and animal feedings throughout the day, as well as the chance to see the centre's divers feeding and cleaning at regular intervals. There is a Scavenger Hunt for children to follow along the way, and the different vantage points are geared towards smaller visitors, with a strong eco-friendly message throughout. There is even a multi-level play structure for young 'uns to climb and slide over. Your ticket is valid all day, so you can come and go as you please, but you will need a couple of hours for all the exhibits ($25 & $20; 10am–8pm, 10pm Fri & Sat). There are two Behind The Scenes tours, 25mins or 60mins, for an extra $5 and $25/person.

Combo tickets for 2, 3 or 4 of these adventures (including LEGOLAND Florida, which is also owned by Merlin Entertainments) are really well priced at $39 and $34; $45 and $40; and $99 and $94 (advance booking discounts available online). There is also a Gift Shop for each of the three attractions and a central Food Court, making it a well-rounded and enjoyable half-day option, while the additional dining choice around the complex is excellent.

BRITTIP

Didn't bring a camera to Madame Tussauds? Not to worry – there are photographers at regular intervals to make sure you have great memories of the visit.

Separate to the three Merlin attractions is **Skeletons: Animals Unveiled**, a fascinating museum-with-a-difference boasting a look at some 400 animals of all types (including a great Africa section and a rare Sumatran rhino) in amazing anatomical detail, with full-size skeletons displayed in active poses and cool but educational dioramas that provide great photo opportunities. We especially like the Africa section, with the bull elephant, while the python exhibit shows off its staggering 900-plus bones, and you'll also learn the art form of turning animal carcasses into these skeletons ($19.99 adults, $12.99 3–11s; 9am–midnight; **http://skeletonmuseum.com/**). There's also **Arcade City**, high-energy games arcade with all the latest video challenges and activities, including some high-tech variations on familiar games (with prizes to match; 10am–10pm; **www.arcadecityfun.com**).

Kings Bowl: This is a neighbouring part of the complex, a bowling centre with restaurant and bar. With a plush 1950s vibe but modern styling – notably with 22 high-tech bowling lanes – it offers a grown-up atmosphere that is also family-friendly. Its elegant multi-bar and dining room set-up features 60 big-screen HDTVs, billiard tables, shuffleboard, bocce ball, serve-yourself beer booths and great cocktails. The food – from standard diner fare like burgers, pizza and fish and chips, to succulent steaks and scallops – is worth coming in for on its own, while the beer list is impressive and the desserts and sundaes nothing short of decadent. Bowling is 11–2am daily, at $5/person before 6pm and $6 after 6pm ($7 after 6pm on Fri and Sat). Shoe hire is $4 and it's 21s and over after 8pm (407 363 0200; **http://kingsbowlamerica.com/orlando/**). Parts can also be booked for private parties.

For I-Drive 360 Dining, see p317; for Shopping, see p331. Look up more at **www.i-drive360.com**.

> **BRITTIP**
> Call ahead for a Priority Lane Reservation when you dine at Kings Bowl and your group will be bumped up to the next available lane once you have finished eating.

Ripley's Believe It Or Not

You can't miss this particular attraction and its extraordinary tilted appearance as it's designed to seem as if it's falling into a Florida 'sinkhole'. However, once inside you soon get back on the level and, for an hour or so, you can wander through this quirky museum dedicated to the weird and wonderful. Robert L Ripley was an eccentric explorer and collector (a real-life Indiana Jones) who for 40 years travelled the world to assemble a collection of the greatest oddities known to man. The Orlando branch of this chain features 8,900ft^2/830m^2 of displays in 16 galleries, including authentic artefacts, interactive exhibits, illusions, video presentations and music. The elaborate re-creation of an Egyptian tomb showcases a mummy and three rare mummified animals, while the Primitive Gallery contains artefacts (some quite gruesome) from tribal societies around the world. There are then Human and Animal Oddities, Big and Little galleries, Illusions and Dinosaurs, plus extra interactive elements. The collection of miniatures includes the world's smallest violin and a single grain of rice hand-painted with a tropical sunset. Larger-scale exhibits include a balloon-powered chair that flew over the Rocky Mountains, a 2/3-scale 1907 Rolls-Royce built in matchsticks and a 26ft/8m tall 'painting' of Van Gogh made out of postcards! You can also attempt various puzzles and brain teasers, and try the shooting gallery with its odd array of targets.

Admission: $19.99 adult, $12.99 4–12s; 9am–12am (last entry 11pm; 407 345 0501, **www.ripleys.com/orlando**). AAA Included with Go Orlando Card and I-Drive 4 Pass.

> **BRITTIP**
> Receive a $3 discount/adult, $2/child (4–12s) on the regular admission price at Ripley's Believe It Or Not by visiting their website.

Ripley's Believe It or Not

Titanic –
The Artifact Exhibit

Go back in time at this fascinating attraction just north of Sand Lake Road. Guided tours of the Exhibit start on the hour and weave through full-scale re-creations of the Titanic's famous rooms, including her grand staircase, first-class parlour suite, Verandah Café, Marconi Room, third class cabin and bridge. Costumed actors portray characters such as Captain Smith and Molly Brown, sharing stories of passengers and crew during the one-hour journey of the famous ship. The 17-gallery attraction features an interactive Underwater Room, including a 15ft/4.5m 'iceberg' and a detailed replica of the vessel as she appears on the bottom of the Atlantic today. More than 400 artefacts and treasures, including memorabilia from James Cameron's blockbuster movie Titanic are also on display here, notably some ultra-rare pieces, including the 2nd-largest piece recovered from the wreck site. Both engaging and moving, it consistently gets good reviews from locals and tourists alike. PS: Make sure you keep your entry ticket – you'll need it at the end!

Admission: $21.95 adults, $12.95 3–11s ($2 off online; under-3 free); tours 10am–6pm (8 or 9pm peak seasons; **www.premierexhibitions.com**). AAAA Also with Go Orlando Card and I-Drive 4 Pass.

Titanic

Titanic Gala Dinner: For something special, try this 3hr theatre/dining occasion with the cast of the Exhibit. Starring Molly Brown, Captain Smith, Thomas Andrews and other high-society luminaries, it offers each table a front row seat for the whole Titanic story, setting the scene and delivering a dinner party with a difference, all in period style. Enjoy a sumptuous 3-course meal, featuring fillet of beef and chicken, with tea, coffee and soft drinks (extra for unlimited beer and wine) in a splendid atmosphere. The Gala Dinner recreates Titanic's first-night sailing each Fri and Sat from 6.30pm ($69 for adults, $42 for 6–11s; not recommended for under-6s; book in advance on 407 248 1166).

CSI: The Experience

This is actually a three-part attraction, headlined by a hands-on journey into the investigative world of the CSI TV series. Visitors get to pick one of three crime scenes to solve, and there are plenty of interactive activities to steer you through, including the Pathology Lab and Autopsy centre, while the stars of the TV show make various appearances via computer and TV screens as you go. After a proper briefing, guests are unleashed on the colour-coded crime scenes with clipboard and ballistics vest to discover the clues and uncover the evidence to solving the crime, before submitting your report to Supervisor Gil Grissom for praise (or admonishment!). You can choose from the standard entry or a Full Investigator package, while a printed Diploma of your work costs an extra $2.99 and there is a neat gift shop at the end (10am–6pm, Mon–Thurs, 9pm Fri & Sat, 8pm Sun; $19.99 adults, $12.99 6–11s, also included with Go Orlando Card and I-Drive Four Pass; 407 226 7220, **http://orlando. csiexhibit.com/**). After CSI, there is also the **Consumed By Art** exhibition, a fun series of 14 large-as-life 3-D paintings that put visitors literally 'in the picture' for all manner of fun photo opportunities, including sport, nature and wildlife (post your own photos on their website to win prizes – **www.consumedbyart.com**); and a travelling exhibit that changes every 14–15 months, with the latest being **Leonardo da Vinci**, an extensive showcase of his artistic and creative talents, including original drawings, recreated scale replicas of his inventions and masterpiece artwork depictions (including The Last Supper). It is $10 just for Consumed by Art or $5 with either of CSI or Leonardo da Vinci. The Da Vinci exhibit is $16.99 and $9.99 (6–12s), while all three together are $31.99.

> **BRITTIP**
>
> CSI: The Experience is not recommended for children under 12, although they will accept 6–11-year-olds. If the TV programme is too grown-up for your kids, the exhibit will be, too.

Fun Spot America

Just off I-Drive on Del Verde Way (look for the 250ft/76m SkyCoaster past the junction with Kirkman Road) is this extensive amusement park that offers a whole raft of family fun with coasters, go-karting, kiddie rides and arcade action. The go-kart thrills come from four challenging tracks, including the enlarged Quad Helix, the triple level corkscrew track of Conquest, the fiendish Thrasher and multi-level Commander. Then there are bumper cars and boats, five daring fairground-type rides (including the new Space Invader swing ride and the whizzy Scrambler), one of the largest and most up-to-date video arcades in Florida, a Big Wheel, nine Kiddie Rides – including a classic two-storey carousel – and a Cadet track for the little ones. Fun Spot also boasts the world's second-largest SkyCoaster (a massive, free-fall swing) and three coasters – the impressive long steel-wooden hybrid of White Lightning, which races along at up to 48mph/76kph with a max drop of 75ft/23m; the tight-turning suspended ride of Freedom Flyer; and the child-friendly Sea Serpent. Another fun option is the high-spinning Enterprise, while the large Food Court serves hotdogs, burgers, salads, pizza, nachos, popcorn and

ice-cream. New in May 2015 was Gator Spot, a separate area featuring almost 40 residents of Gatorland, including an albino gator, as well as a gift shop and some great photo opportunities (entry fee $6). Parking and admission are free, with a series of ride Passes geared around children's height (above and below 4ft 4in/1.32m), with younger children getting free run of all the rides (and as a passenger on the 2-seater go-karts with an adult).

Admission: Free; Go-Karts $9, other rides $3, 6 & 9; Go-Kart Armband (all day on all 4 tracks, plus all rides and unlimited Free Play arcade) $40; Rides Armband (all day on all rides plus unlimited Free Play arcade) $30; Kid Spot Armband (all day on Kid Spot rides plus unlimited Free Play arcade) $15; 4-Ride Track Sampler $27; 1-Day 2-Park ticket with Fun Spot USA (Kissimmee), $44.95 (over 54ins) and $34.95 (under 54ins). Height requirements: over 4ft 4in/1.32m for Quad Helix, Conquest, Commander; 4ft 6in/1.37m for Thrasher. Open daily 10am–midnight (2pm-midnight off-peak; 407 363 3867, **http://fun-spot. com/O_Orlando.aspx**). TTTT Also with Go Orlando card.

Magical Midway

Magical Midway back on I-Drive (just north of Sand Lake Road) offers more go-karts, games and thrill rides, including the Sling Shot (400ft straight up!), the unique StarFlyer, a 230ft/70m tower with chair swings that lift and rotate for a dizzying view at 54mph, and Space Blast, another vertical-launch monster! The two elevated kart tracks, the double uphill corkscrew of The Avalanche and sharply-banked Alpine are its signature rides (you must be at least 12 and 4ft 8in/147cm tall to drive, at least 16 to drive a passenger, and at least 5 and 3ft/91cm to be a passenger). Fast Track, a flat concrete track with a 25° bank turn (riders must be 12 and 4ft 8in/147cm to drive; single cars only) completes the line-up. There are also bumper cars, boats, a merry-go-round, trampolines, a large arcade, a pizza parlour and ice-cream counter.

Admission: Free, then 3hr Armband (unlimited go-karts and midway rides for 3hrs, not Sling Shot) $25; All-Day Unlimited Armband (not Sling Shot) $32. Or $25 Sling Shot, $7 Starflyer (ride DVD $15), $7 go-karts, $3 all other rides. Must be 4ft/121cm for Bumper Cars, 3ft 6in/106cm for Bumper Boats and Kiddie Track; 2–12pm Mon–Fri, noon–midnight Sat–Sun (407 370 5353, **www.magicalmidway.com**). TTTT See website for $2.50 off Go-Karts.

BRITTIP

I-Drive 360, WonderWorks, Fun Spot, Magical Midway and WhirlyDome are all open until at least midnight in high season, long after most theme parks are shut, so you can have a day at the park, then let the kids loose here to tire them out completely!

WonderWorks

This interactive entertainment centre is I-Drive's most unmistakable landmark, a 3-storey chamber of family fun with a host of novel elements. Unmistakable? The 82ft/25m building is upside-down! That's right, the entire edifice is constructed from the roof up, the result of a 'tornado experiment that went wrong.' You have to give full marks for imagination and, with various enhancements since it opened in 1998, there's a lot here, especially for 6–12s.

You enter through an 'inversion tunnel' that orientates you the same way round as the building (look out of the window to check!) and then progress to various chambers of entertaining and mildly educational hands-on experiences that demand several hours to explore fully. Without ever using the words 'science' or 'museum', WonderWorks steers you through six WonderZones of interactive activities, including natural disasters (earthquakes, hurricanes, famous disasters) and Google Earth virtual globe and map; physical challenges (Bubble Lab, Mind Ball bio-feedback challenge,

Bed of Nails and the chance to make an impression of your entire body in 40,000 plastic nails at Wonderwall!); Light & Sound (challenges to beat the clock, shape the music and strike a pose); the Imagination Lab (with physical and mental challenges to create and have fun); and Space Discovery, where you have Jet Fighters (virtual reality F18 fighter jet), Shuttle Landers (your chance to pilot the Discovery Space Shuttle), a Mercury capsule mock-up, an astronaut spacesuit and Wonder Coaster (a pair of enclosed 'pods' that let you design and ride your own coaster). There is also a 3-storey glow-in-the-dark ropes course with 20 obstacles, and the 4D XD Motion Theater with three simulator rides, plus the WonderWorks Gift Shop and Café. A Lazer Tag game on the top floor adds even more appeal for kids. If you have already seen DisneyQuest, WonderWorks may seem tame, while it isn't as educational as the Orlando Science Center, but it has different features from either, including the fun of The Outta Control Magic Comedy Dinner Show (p298), with a good-value combo ticket.

Admission: $26.99 adults, $20.99 seniors (55+) and 4–12s (includes 1 4-D Motion Ride and Ropes Course); $10.99 just for 4-D Motion Ride and Ropes Course; $7.99 for Lazer Tag; $25.99 and $19.99 for The Outta Control Dinner Show; $43.99 and $33.99 for WonderWorks/dinner show; $27.99 and $22.99 for WonderWorks/Lazer Tag; $48.99 and $37.99 for everything; 9am–midnight (407 351 8800, **www.wonderworksonline.com/orlando**). TTT Also with Go Orlando Card and I-Drive Four Pass.

iFLY Orlando

At the junction with I-Drive and Kirkman Road is this unmistakable blue and yellow funnel that houses one of the most fun 'rides' in town. It is billed as a 'free-fall skydiving adventure' but is much more than that – a fun, addictive, difficult but exhilarating 'flying' experience, with the bonus of a great spectator sport! It's basically a huge vertical wind tunnel, which provides the feeling of a freefall. The standard 1hr programme provides a full briefing with an instructor, then you're given helmet, pads, goggles, earplugs and flight suit, and your group of 8–12 returns to the flight deck, where you get two 1min supervised 'flights' (which seem a lot longer!). Just watching makes it seem all too easy but, as soon as you hit the tunnel, you discover how fiendishly tough it is to just 'hang' in this 125mph/200kph column of air. However, before long it becomes a fun and absorbing experience and it's almost guaranteed to make you want to try again. There is no fee for non-participating members of your group to watch from the observation deck, and you can also just turn up to see for yourself at any time (you might even see sky-dive groups practising).

Admission: Standard flight, which includes a certificate, is $59.95; add a DVD and photo CD for $19.99. Discount coupons (for return visitors) and gift certificates can be found on its website. Try a Spread Your Wings Package (double your flight time) for $99.95, Spread Your Wings for Two at $129.95, or a Family Package for up to 5 at $269.95, (all including DVD). For real addicts, a Take Flight package offers 10 1min flights or 5 double-flights for $219.95. Open 10am–10pm daily, reservations recommended (407 903 1150, **http://orlando.iflyworld.com**). TTTT.

WhirlyDome

This indoor fun centre boasts a unique game, full-service restaurant, arcade and other novel elements. Their stock in trade is the hilarious **WhirlyBall** game, a cross between bumper cars, basketball and lacrosse (!) as two teams of five battle for possession of a whiffle ball and try to hit a target at either end. There are two courts of 4,000ft²/370m² and the centre provides a ref. It is open to all-comers or groups and games are timed in periods of 10min. Guests must be at least 12 and 4ft 6in/137cm to play but it is easy to pick up and the Whirlybugs, like fancy bumper-cars,

are easy to drive. It is free just to turn up and watch (and is great spectator fun). Playing time is $8/player for 10min, or you can hire the court at $250/hr. In addition, the Dome also offers America's only genuine **F1 race simulator**, the SYM 026 from Italy ($8/3min), a huge **Laser Tag** venue ($8/10min) and a novel **Laser Frenzy** room, where players try to navigate a maze of laser beams, haze and mirrors ($3). More arcade games, two self-serve bowling lanes (bowling shoes not required; $5/person) and billiards and pool in the upstairs Bar fill out the entertainment, while the **Bloodhound Brew Pub & Eatery** is a surprisingly smart restaurant, with great local microbrews and a tempting menu (Happy Hour 4–7pm. The Dome is open 4–10pm Tues–Thurs, 4pm–midnight Fri, 11am–midnight Sat, 11am–10pm Sun, just south of Wet 'n Wild. See more, including Monthly Specials, at **www.whirlydome.com** (407 212 3030).

Helicopter rides

These are another local staple, and you can try any one of nine tours with **Air Florida Helicopters** at 8990 International Drive (just north of the big Convention Center). At least two passengers take either the local 8ml/12.87km tour over Universal and SeaWorld, Disney and Downtown Orlando or a mega 30ml/48km grand journey that adds flying over the homes of the rich and famous in

WhirlyDome

Windermere. Just $20 for the short flight to $355 for the longest, plus a $4/person fuel surcharge ($20–325 for children; see website for discounts). No need to book; just turn up and go. They fly 9.30am–7pm daily (407 354 1400, **www.airfloridahelicopter.com**).

Escape games

These have become all the rage in Orlando recently, with two major opportunities on I-Drive to test your wits in a Crystal Maze-type challenge.

America's Escape Game: Choose from Pandemic, Crisis At 1600 and Lost Tomb Of Monthu to test your ability to solve puzzles and unscramble clues in team fashion at this venue next to the Official Visitor Center on Austrian Court. In groups of 8–10, visitors undergo an explanatory briefing about their 'mission' and then have an hour to work through the Game Room, under the supervision of a game minder, who can offer three clues if you get stuck. The countdown effect is very real and some of the puzzles are fiendishly difficult, which adds to the fun. Players ideally need to be 13 or older and the rooms include props, special effects and strobe lighting – be prepared for the unexpected! Single players are welcome to make up the number with other groups. You don't have to book in advance but it is advisable (Tues– Thurs, 1–9pm, Fri & Sat 1–11pm, Sun 11am–6pm; $35/person; 407 512 5585, **http://americasescapegame.com/**).

Air Florida Helicopters

Escapology: This venue on southern I-Drive (in a shopping/office plaza just north of Sheraton Vistana Villages resort) offers a sophisticated style with a 'living room' to encourage visitors to relax before their briefing for one of four games (which change periodically), and enjoy a complimentary soft drink and debrief afterwards. Designed for families and friends in groups of 2–6, the game rooms can even be used for side-by-side games to test each group. Visitors should book online and then turn up at the allotted time, get locked into their chosen game for 60mins and have to find the clues to escape from situations like Shanghaied, Cuban Crisis and Arizona Shootout. Again it's a real test of initiative, teamwork and lateral thinking, and each room has a Game Master to monitor progress and provide a few clues if needed (Mon– Fri 12.40–9.40pm; 10am–10.50pm Sat, 10am–9.30pm Sun; $28/person; 407 278 1515, **www.escapology.com/orlando**).

> **BRITTIP**
>
> Players are advised to arrive 15mins early for escape games to allow time for paperwork and briefing. No entry once the clock has started. It's important to select a leader and work as a team. Oh, and visit the loo first!

Mini-golf

For those in need of more holiday fun, don't miss the six mini-golf outlets along International Drive (see p268).

Kissimmee

Old Town: In the heart of tourist Highway 192 in Kissimmee is this shopping and entertainment attraction. The shopping part is covered on p331, but there are also live events, rides and attractions that are worth trying in their own right. Look for the **Happy Days Extreme Bumper Cars** ($5/ride), one of the largest indoor arenas of its kind in the world, while the **Happy Days Family Fun Track** ($7/ride) is flat-track go-kart racing at its best. There is then the fun challenge of the **Happy Days Laser Blast** ($5/person) and the high-energy games **Games Arcade** and the **Rootin and Tootan's Shooting Alley**, which is great fun for kids (and dads with a competitive streak). However, the most eye-catching attraction is the two-storey **Legends: A Haunting at Old Town**, a clever, atmospheric and totally convincing walk-through haunted house with state-of-the-art horror scenes, live 'scare actors' and special effects that come straight out of Universal's Halloween Horror Nights playbook (($15/person; not recommended for under 14s). Finally, **The Great Magic Hall** offers live magic shows on the hour from 3–10pm daily ($7/person). Rides are open 2–11pm Mon–Fri, noon–midnight Sat and noon–11pm Sun (407 396 4888, **www.myoldtownusa. com**). Old Town is also known for its Saturday Classic Car Cruise, the Friday All-American Muscle Car Cruise and Little Darlin's Street Party & Cruise-In each Wednesday. Additionally, Sunday night features jeeps, trucks and SUVs.

Fun Spot USA: Next door to Old Town (but not connected) is another area of rides and fun owned by Fun Spot Attractions. There are a good selection of nine thrill rides, eight Kiddie Rides, the high adrenalin SkyCoaster and four go-kart tracks. **RockStar Coaster**, formerly in Cypress Gardens, adds another terrific ride to the line-up. But the big daddy of them all is the amazing **SkyCoaster**, a 300ft/90m tower that sends up to three riders at a time on a free-fall plunge (for the first 120ft/37m) that turns into a giant swing – at 85mph/136kph! The more down-to-earth rides consist of two; flat go-kart tracks, **Slick** and **Road Course**, and two multi-level tracks, the labyrinthine **Chaos** and **Vortex**, with its challenging banked bowl section. The other nine rides are almost as much fun – like the more fairground style of **Flying Bobs**, **Fun Slide**, **Surf's Up** and the **Paratrooper**, the giant swing of the **Hot Seat** and the tower-ride **Screamer**. More swinging fun is provided by the **Screaming Eagles** and **YoYo**, while standard **Bumper Kars** complete the line-up. There is a well-stocked

indoor **Snack Bar** when you need to cool down, as well as an **Ice Cream Kiosk**, while the kids will gravitate to the **Arcade**, with 60 games (perfect for a wet day or the heat of summer).

Admission: Free, then per-ride prices are Multi-level Tracks $9, Flat Tracks $6, Extreme Thrill Ride $6, Most Thrill and Family Rides $3; an Adult Armband is $40 (go-karts and other rides all day), Youth Armband (less than 54in/1.37m tall) $30, and a Track Sampler $27 (four goes on go-karts or rides), plus there is a Chauffeur Armband (for a parent to drive or accompany a young 'un on various suitable rides) at $10. The SkyCoaster is $40 for one rider ($35 for a second ride), $70 for 2, $90 for 3. Open 10am–midnight (407 397 2509, **www.funspotattractions.com**). There is also a special 2-park Armband for Fun Spot America and Fun Spot USA at $44.95 (over 54ins tall) and $34.95 (under 54ins).

Chocolate Kingdom: Sandwiched between Old Town and Fun Spot is this cute and ultra-child friendly opportunity to see how chocolate is made – and get some tasty samples! Sign up for their 1hr tour (on the hour) and you join a quest to help a handsome prince woo the hand of a chocolate-loving princess, while getting quite a history lesson in the process. Select the pre-tour Chocolate Bar option and you can have a custom-made bar of your own made right before your eyes at the end of the tour (11am-5pm daily, $16.95 adults, $12.95 4-12s; 407 705 3475, **www.chocolatekingdom.com**). Their new venue is on International Drive, on Hawaiian Court, and can take tours up to 20 people.

BRITTIP

Visiting the Orlando Information Center? Take exit 82B off I-4 and there are four multi-storey car parks nearby, including the Library park (take 4th right on Central Boulevard). Or just go straight across South Street (the first main road you come to), and park on the left, underneath I-4 after Church Street, where it is just $1/ hr (pay-and-display).

DOWNTOWN ORLANDO

The last few years have seen a major revitalisation of Orlando's city centre ('downtown'), with new offices, apartments, shops and restaurants. This makes it a tourist attraction in its own right and it is well served by the Information Center on Orange Avenue (10am–5pm, Mon–Fri; 407 254 4636, **www.downtownorlando.com** – click 'Visit Downtown'). Start here to get a full overview, with a 3-D city model and ultra-helpful staff (plus free wi-fi). They can provide free maps of the area, a Historic Walking Tour guide and info on riding the free LYMMO bus service around downtown. There is also a free guided tour at 9.30am on the first Fri of each month with local historian Richard Forbes (Oct-May). Much of the former Church Street Station area is also vibrant again, **www.churchstreetdistrict.com**.

Orange County History Center

Getting there: On E Central Boulevard (exit 82B off I-4, go across South St and take 3rd right; see also map p216), park at the Public Library multi-storey car park on Central Blvd. Admission: $12 adults, $10 seniors (60+), $9 5–12s; 10am–5pm Mon–Sat, noon–5pm Sun (407 836 8500, **www.thehistorycenter.org**).

This smart part of the downtown scene offers an imaginative journey into central Florida history, from the wildlife and Native Americans to today's tourist issues and space programme. The accent is on the interactive, with hands-on exhibits

Orange County History Center

and audiovisual presentations, and it is very much a journey through time, starting with the Natural Environment and First Peoples exhibits and moving on to the 1800s, with an authentic pioneer 'cracker' home, tales of Florida's ranching days, a Seminole settlement, and tourism pre-Disney to modern times. Aviation explores World War II bombers to the outer reaches of space. Orlando Remembered is a journey from the 19th century to the edge of the 21st while an exhibit on African American history and a series of travelling exhibits round things off.

Getting around: Everywhere is walkable downtown, but the free Lymmo bus service connects the central area along Magnolia Avenue, from South Street and City Hall up to the Centroplex area. Or you could try the **Orlando Juice Bike Share** service, a bike-sharing scheme that allows bike rentals from specific hubs around the city centre, for as little as $6/hr (**http://orlandobikeshare.com/**).

Theatre and more

Orlando loves its theatre, and those wishing to take in a performance should look for the lavish new **Dr Phillips Center for the Performing Arts**, which features touring Broadway shows, ballet, concerts and more (407 839 0119; **www. drphillipscenter.org**); the amazing **Amway Center**, home to the Orlando Magic basketball team, Orlando Predators Arena League outfit and Orlando Solar Bears minor-league ice-hockey team, plus major concerts (407 440 7000; **www.amwaycenter.com**); the improv of **SAK Comedy Lab** at Eola Capital Loft on S Orange Avenue (407 648 0001, **www.sakcomedylab.com**); and **CityArts Factory** featuring local and national artists and a city-wide Gallery Hop on the third Thurs each month from 6–9pm (407 648 7060, **www.orlandoslice.com**). Downtown also has a thriving public arts scheme, **See Art Orlando** (**http://seeartorlando.com/**).

Dining: The restaurant/bar choice is also pretty good here, too. Take your pick from **Frank & Steins** (with

300 craft beers, 40 on tap), **Wall Street Plaza** (a lively collection of bars and lounges that are the heart of downtown nightlife), the upscale **Kres Chophouse**, and Church Street Station, the remains of the old entertainment district, which still includes a cluster of fine restaurants and bars, notably the stylish Spanish cuisine of **Ceviche**, the fun **Harry Buffalo** and **Hamburger Mary's Bar & Grille**. See more in Orlando By Night.

Lake Eola: Once you have sampled the hustle-bustle of downtown, head out to this gem, with more restaurants and shops, plus a beautiful lakeside walk, children's play area, swan paddle-boats, new artwork and a peaceful ambience. There are regular open-air concerts at the **Disney Amphitheater** and the **Sunday Farmers Market** (around Lake Eola, 10am–4pm) is another focal point, with vendors including local artists as well as wonderful fresh produce.

Dining: Stop for a great meal, with a view, at **310 Lakeside** (407 373 0310, **www.310parksouth.net**) or **Spice Modern Steakhouse** (407 481 9533, **http://spicesteakhouse.com**). Continue on to Thornton Park Central (at the junction of Summerlin Avenue and Central Boulevard, just south-east of Lake Eola), offering a mix of unique boutiques and trendy restaurants. **Cityfish** is a casual seafood café/bar (407 849 9779, **www.cityfishorlando.com**), **Anthony's Pizzeria** is a great upmarket pizza restaurant (407 648 0009, **http://anthonyspizza.com**) and **Dexter's** is a smart café/wine bar with a fab Sunday brunch (407 648 2777, **http://thorntonpark.dexwine.com**).

BRITTIP

Don't miss the annual Spring and Fall Fiestas around Lake Eola, with hundreds of vendors, live entertainment and special fun for kids, the first weekend in April and Nov (**www.fiestainthepark.com**).

Loch Haven Park

Continue north and you travel the 'Cultural Corridor' to Loch Haven Park and the area's fine collection of theatres, museums and the Orlando Science Center.

Getting there: On Princeton Street in downtown Orlando, just off exit 85 of I-4 (go east on Princeton; the Science Center is on the left but the multi-storey car park is on the RIGHT, see map p216).

Orlando Science Center: The Orlando Science Center is more than a mere museum and far more fun than the average science centre. Here you are given a series of hands-on experiences and habitats that entertain as well as inform, and school-age children in particular will benefit greatly from it. It has seven main permanent exhibits, plus periodic travelling ones (*Dora & Diego: Let's Explore* was on offer in 2015), a night sky observatory, an inviting café, Science Store and a giant screen cinema.

NatureWorks gets you up close and personal with some of Florida's most fascinating reptiles (including gators and turtles) while you step back into the prehistoric age at **DinoDigs**. Visitors discover the dynamic forces and systems that shape Earth, and other planets, in **Our Planet, Our Universe** (don't miss the hands-on Mars Rover experience and the chance to **Ask An Astronomer** via video kiosk), and there is more to explore with electricity, magnetism, lasers, soundwaves and nature's forces in Science Park. **Engineer It** is a chance to build using all manner of structures, boats and bridges, and pre-schoolers will appreciate **All Aboard**, with child-sized trains, planes and automobiles, and no visit is complete without a trip to KidsTown, an interactive playground

Loch Haven Park

Loch Haven Park

dedicated to smaller explorers. Each Jan also sees the fun **Otronicon**, a four-day event celebrating the best in video game technology. If you like the game Rock Band, you'll LOVE Otronicon! In addition, the centre has several programmes in **Dr Phillips CineDome**, a 310-seat cinema that surrounds its audience with large-format films and digital planetarium shows. The **Digital Adventure Theater** adds educational films and Science Live! real-life experiments and interactive programmes in partnership with National Geographic.

Admission: $19 adults, $17 seniors (55+) and students with ID, $13 3–11s; parking $5, includes 1 mainscreen film (Fri, Sat and Sun). 10am–5pm daily (closed Wed, Easter Sunday, Thanksgiving, Christmas Eve and Christmas Day; **www.osc.org**) AAA

The extensive **Orlando Museum of Art** (407 896 4231, **www.omart.org**) is here, and, the diverse **Mennello Museum of American Art**, with a permanent collection by painter Earl Cunningham (407 246 4278, **www.mennellomuseum.com**), the **Orlando Philharmonic Orchestra** (407 770 0071, **www.orlandophil.org**) and **Orlando Shakespeare Theater** (407 447 1700, **www.orlandoshakes. org**). Parents should also note the superb **Orlando Rep**, a company specialising in family theatre, with youth academies and summer camps for kids. Their 2015 season included *Shrek The Musical TYA* and *Diary Of A Worm, A Spider And A Fly* (407 896 7365, **www.orlandorep.com**). Highly recommended.

Aquatica water park

THE WATER PARKS

Florida specialises in elaborate water parks, and Orlando boasts the very best. Predictably, Disney has the two most sophisticated ones, but SeaWorld's Aquatica adds real competition, while Universal-owned Wet 'n Wild is also adept at providing hours of watery fun. They adopt a variety of styles that owe much to the flair of the theme park creators, and are imaginative for both the rides and imagery around them. All require at least half a day of splashing, sliding and riding to get full value from their rather high prices. Lockers are provided for valuables and you can hire towels. Be sure to check out Universal Orlando later in 2016, too, for news of their new water park, Volcano Bay.

BRITTIP

Want a day of watery fun but don't want to purchase an extra pass for a water park? Consider **CocoKey Water Resort** on International Drive. You can purchase a day pass for $24.95–26.95; it's great for the pre-school to 10-year-old crowd, and it's partly covered, to protect kids from the harsh Florida sun (**www.cocokeywaterresort.com**).

Disney's Typhoon Lagoon Water Park

When Typhoon Lagoon opened in 1989, it was the biggest and finest of Florida's water parks. And, although it has since been superceded, in high season it is still the busiest, so be prepared for queues. Arrive half an hour early if possible as entry often begins before the official opening hour. The park's 56acres/23ha are spread out around the 2½acre/1ha lagoon fringed with palm trees and white-sand beaches. It is extravagantly landscaped and the walk up Mount Mayday provides a terrific overview as well as adding scenic touches like rope bridges and tropical flowers. Sun loungers, chairs, picnic tables and even hammocks are provided to add to the comfort and convenience of restful areas like Getaway Glen. However, you need to arrive early to bag a decent spot. Or, for $58 extra (!) you can reserve two beach loungers, two towels, an umbrella and a small table by stopping in at High 'n Dry Rentals (or calling in advance). Really want to splash out? Opt for a Beachcomber Shack (cabaña), which includes a locker, drinks mug, cooler with ice, bottled water, towels, loungers and table, and waiter service. Full day rental for up to 6 guests will set you back $345 (admission not included). Reserve in advance on 407 939 7529 (we're fans of arriving early and getting your loungers for free!).

Getting there: On Buena Vista Drive, ½ml/800m from Downtown Disney (see map, p216). Admission: $58 adults, $50 3–9s (under-3s free); included with Ultimate tickets; parking free; 9am (10am off season)– dusk daily. TTTT AAAAA

BRITTIP
Water parks provide both a great way of cooling down and an easy way of getting sunburn. So don't forget the high-factor waterproof suncream, and reapply often.

Beating the crowds: To avoid the worst of the summer crowds (when the park often reaches its 7,200 capacity), Monday morning is best (steer clear of weekends at all costs) and, on other days, arrive either before opening or in mid-afternoon, when many decide to dodge the daily rainstorm. Early evening is also pleasant when the park lights up.

BRITTIP
Want to learn to surf? Typhoon Lagoon offers Surfing School 2hrs before park opening every day. Call 407 939 7529 in advance to book at $165/person.

Slides and rides: The park is overlooked by **Mount Mayday**, on top of which is perched the luckless Miss Tilly, a shrimp boat that legend has it landed here during the typhoon that gave the park its name. Watch out for the water fountains that shoot from Miss Tilly's funnel at regular intervals, accompanied by a siren, signalling another round of BIG waves in the **Surf Pool** (and they are big; take care with toddlers). Circling the lagoon is **Castaway Creek**, a 3ft/1m deep, lazy flowing river offering the chance to float along on rubber tyres.

The slides and rides are all clustered around Mt Mayday and vary from the breathtaking body slides of **Humunga Kowabunga** that drop you 214ft/65m at up to 30mph/48kph down some steep inclines (make sure swimming costumes are securely fastened!) to **Ketchakiddee Creek**, which offers a selection of slides and pools for youngsters under 4ft/122cm. In between, you have the **Storm Slides**, body slides that twist and turn through caves, tunnels and waterfalls, **Mayday Falls**, a wild 460ft/140m single-rider inner-tube flume down a series of banked drops, **Keelhaul Falls**, a more sedate tube ride, and **Gangplank Falls**, a family ride inside rafts that take up to four people down 300ft/90m of mock rapids. **Crush 'n' Gusher** is a fabulous trio of 'water-coaster' tube rides, plus a large heated pool with zero-depth entry (great for toddlers). It also has an extensive sandy beach, ideal for sunbathing. The three different slides feature tubes for two or three riders at a time that whoosh you down and UP several inclines before dropping you into the pool with a significant splash. This is busy from midday. The imaginative (but chilly) **Shark Reef** is an upturned wreck and coral reef where you can snorkel among

Typhoon Lagoon

4,000 tropical fish and a number of (harmless) nurse sharks. Those not brave enough to get in can still get a close-up through the underwater portholes of the sunken ship. Closed during the winter. Substantial queues build up from late morning, so do this early.

BRITTIP
'Buy a disposable waterproof camera to tie around your wrist when you visit the water parks. We bought one cheap at Wal-Mart and have some lovely photos from Typhoon Lagoon,' says reader Judith Bingham.

Keeping out of the sun can also be a problem as there's not much shade. A quick plunge into Castaway Creek usually prevents overheating but do remember your sunscreen. There are height restrictions (4ft/122cm) on Humunga Kowabunga and Crush 'n' Gusher and they're not suitable for anyone with a bad back or neck, or expectant mothers.

Shopping: You can buy anything you have forgotten – even a swimsuit – at **Singapore Sal's**. You CAN'T bring your own snorkels, inner tubes or rafts, but snorkels are provided at Shark Reef.

Dining: Lowtide Lou's and **Let's Go Slurpin'** both offer snacks and drinks, while **Typhoon Tilly's** and **Leaning Palms** serve a decent mix of sandwiches, burgers, salads and ice-cream. Avoid main mealtimes if

you want to eat in relative comfort. You can bring your own picnic (unlike the main parks), although no alcohol or glass.

BRITTIP
As the busiest of the water parks, Typhoon Lagoon can hit capacity quite early in the day in summer. Call 407 824 4321 in advance to check on the crowds.

Disney's Blizzard Beach Water Park

Ever imagined a skiing resort in the middle of Florida? Well, here it is. This park opened in 1995 and is still the largest, with all 66acres/27ha arranged as if it were in the Rocky Mountains rather than the subtropics! That means snow-effect scenery, Christmas trees and waterslides cunningly converted to look like skiing pistes and toboggan runs. The same 'premium' offer at Typhoon Lagoon applies here for two beach loungers, two towels, an umbrella and a small table for $58. Or, if the price doesn't scare you off completely, you can hire a Polar Patio (cabaña), which includes a locker, drinks mug, cooler with ice, bottled water, towels, loungers and table, and waiter service. Full day rental for up to six guests is $345 (admission not included). Reserve in advance on 407 939 7529 (once again, we're fans of arriving early and getting your loungers for free).

Snow Stormers at Blizzard Beach

Getting there: Just north of Disney's All-Star Resorts off Buena Vista Drive (see map p14). Admission: $58 adults, $50 3–9s (under-3s free); included with Premium and Ultimate tickets; parking free; 9am (10am off-season) to dusk daily. TTTTT AAAAA

BRITTIP
Adjacent to Blizzard Beach are the amazing Winter Summerland Miniature Golf Courses (where Santa's elves hang out!), with 2 elaborate courses that are a great diversion for children (p268).

Slides and rides: Main features are **Mount Gushmore**, a 90ft/27m mountain down which all the main slides run. A ski chair-lift operates to the top, providing a magnificent view. Don't miss the outstanding rides, including the world's tallest free-fall speed slide, the terrifying 120ft/37m **Summit Plummet**, which rockets you down a 'ski jump' at up to 60mph/97kph. For those not quite up to the big drop, the brilliantly named **Slush Gusher** is a slightly less terrifying body slide. Then there is **Teamboat Springs**, a wild family inner-tube adventure and arguably the best of all the water rides; **Runoff Rapids**, a choice of three tube plunges; **Snow Stormers**, a daring head-first 'toboggan' run; and **Toboggan Racers**, the chance to speed down the 'slopes' against seven other head-first riders. All four provide good-sized thrills without overdoing the scare factor. The side-by-side **Downhill Double Dipper** tubes send you down 230ft/70m tubes in a timed race, with a real jolt half-way down! **Tike's Peak** is a kiddie-sized version of the park's slides and a mock snow-beach, and **Ski-Patrol Training Camp** is a series of challenges and slides for pre-teens. **Melt-Away Bay** is a 1acre/0.4ha pool fed by 'melting snow' (actually blissfully warm), and **Cross Country Creek** is a lazy-flowing 1½ml/800m river round the whole park that also floats guests through a chilly 'ice cave' (look out for the ice-water waterfalls!).

Shopping and dining: There is a 'village' area with a **Beach Haus** shop and **Lottawatta Lodge** fast-food restaurant (pizzas, burgers, salads and sandwiches), offering a grandstand view of Mount Gushmore. Snacks are also available at **Avalunch** (ouch!), the **Warming Hut**, **Polar Pub** and **Frostbite Freddie's Frozen Refreshments**.

Wet 'n Wild
The world's first water park opened in 1977 with an eye-catching array of rides and slides, and it remains a great place for high-energy thrills, especially for teens. However, Universal is closing it down in advance of its new Volcano Bay park in 2017, hence 2016 will be your very last chance to give it a try.

Wet 'n Wild is one of the best-attended water parks in the country, and its location in the heart of I-Drive makes it a major draw. Consequently, you will encounter some crowds here, though the 15 slides and rides, Lazy River attraction, elaborate Blastaway Beach kids' park, Surf Lagoon, restaurant and picnic areas absorb a lot of punters before queues develop. Waits of more than a ½hr at peak times are rare, but it is packed at weekends and throughout June and July as well. However, the park offers an **Express Pass** for limited queuing for an extra $20/person (1-time use per ride) or $50 (unlimited use).

Lazy River

Getting there: Wet 'n Wild is ½ mile/800m north of I-Drive's junction with Sand Lake Road at the intersection with Universal Boulevard (see map p14), just off exit 75A and 74B of I-4. Admission: $57 adults, $52 3–9s (half-price after 5pm; buy online in advance and save $5–10/person), under-3s free (included with Orlando FlexTicket and Universal 3-Park Ticket). Towels $5 ($3 deposit) and lockers $6–11 ($3 deposit); cabañas for up to 6, from $169–299; parking $13; open 9.30–9pm in summer, 10am–5, 6 or 7pm at other times (**www.wetnwildorlando.com**). TTTTT AAA

Slides and rides: You are almost spoilt for choice of main rides, from popular group inner-tube ride **The Surge** to the more demanding **The Flyer**, **The Blast** and single-rider **Mach 5** (head-first on a mat-slide). For body slides, try the high-energy plunge of **The Storm** and the sheer terror of **Der Stuka** and **Bomb Bay** – 276ft/23m near-vertical body slides, **Der Stuka** is the straightforward slide, while **Bomb Bay** adds the extra terror of being allowed to free-fall on to the top of the slide (both with 4ft/122cm height restrictions). Strangely, only a minority of visitors pluck up the courage to try it! New in summer 2014 was **Aqua Drag Racer**, a terrific four-lane, head-first toboggan-mat plunge down 350ft/107m of twisting track, ending in a big splash-down. Another standout is **Black Hole: The Next Generation**, a pulsating two-person ride down an enclosed flume, with a dynamic lighting package and other special effects.

Aqua Drag Racer

© Wet 'n' Wild Orlando

Our favourites? We like the thrilling toboggan-like **Flyer**, which takes four passengers in 8ft/2m in-line tubes down more than 450ft/137m of banked curves and straights, and **The Blast**, with its single or double tubes that surprise you with sudden twists and turns, explosive pipe bursts and drenching waterspouts, leading to a final waterfall plunge. And don't miss **The Storm**, a pair of identical circular slides billed as 'body coasters' – the enclosed tubes (complete with storm sound and light effects) send the rider plunging into a circular bowl, around which they spin at high speed before landing in the splash-pool below. Possibly the funniest, though, is **Disco H2O**, a superbly themed family raft ride that plunges down an enclosed tube into a swirling 'disco bowl' (featuring lights and mirror ball!) before spitting you out through a waterfall. It is all accompanied by 1970s music and commentary to add to the fun (big queues from midday to late afternoon). Equally, **Brain Wash** is a 65ft/20m funnel ride that sends riders on 2, 3 or 4-person tubes down an enclosed flume into a huge funnel that washes the tube wildly backwards and forwards before setting it up for the final splashdown.

Families should definitely head for the **Blastaway Beach** area, a full 1acre/0.4ha play structure themed like a giant sandcastle. This amazing adventure playground features a huge array of junior-sized slides and flumes, with all manner of soakers, jets, waterfalls and cannons to keep kids amused for hours. There are two pool areas, with 17 slides ranging from just small to more than two storeys high. More importantly, it has its own seating area, set amid some lush tropical beach landscaping to allow parents to relax while they supervise or just watch. There is only one exit/entry, hence it is an ideal self-contained area for younger children. It is the largest structure of its kind in Florida – at 60ft/28m high and covering a full 1acre/0.4ha – but is also extremely popular with youngsters, hence you should head here first if you have children under 12.

Take a breather in the slow-flowing **Lazy River** as you float past palms and waterfalls, or head for one of several picnic areas (though they can be crowded). The energetic can play beach volleyball. Lockers, showers and tube and towel rentals are all available; if you bring your own equipment, you must have it checked by the lifeguards.

Shopping and dining: Sportswear, swimwear, sunglasses, hats and more can all be found at the **Beach Shop**. For food, **Bubba's Fried Chicken** serves chicken, fries and drinks, the **Surf Grill** features burgers, hotdogs, salads, chicken and sandwiches, and **Manny's Pizza** has pizza and subs. **Riverside BBQ** (summer only) offers an 'Unlimited visit' BBQ option ($19 adults, $11 3–9s) while the **Wild Tiki Lounge** is a covered Polynesian-style restaurant and bar, **Carnival Treats** features various sweet treats, including candy floss and funnel cakes and six more snack bars offer ice-cream, beer and more. You can also bring your own picnic, but not alcohol or glass containers.

BRITTIP

For all the water parks, it's a good idea to bring a pair of water shoes or sandals that can be worn in water. All the local supermarkets sell them cheaply.

Aquatica by SeaWorld

This eye-catching water park has a wonderful range of children's attractions and facilities, innovative rides and an all-you-can-eat-meal option, spread over 59acres/24ha of South Seas-inspired landscaping.

Getting there: Just across the road from SeaWorld on International Drive, exit 71 or 72 off I-4. Admission: $57 adults, $52 3–9s; 2-Park Ticket (with SeaWorld) $129 and $124; (save $10 by booking online; included with Orlando FlexTicket); parking $12, locker rental $20 and $35 (plus refundable $5), towels $4; 9am–6, 7 or 8pm (late May–Aug) or 10am–5pm (winter, spring and autumn; 407 351 3600, www.aquaticabyseaworld.com) TTTT AAAAA

Slides and rides: Aquatica's signature attraction is the **Dolphin Plunge** (4ft/122cm), a twin body slide that sends riders down 300ft/91.5m of tubes and through a lagoon of playful, black-and-white Commerson's dolphins (it's a touch gimmicky as you catch only the briefest glimpse of them on the way down, but it is an exhilarating slide). You can then view the Dolphins at the end of the ride through the huge lagoon window, where the inhabitants often hang out to look at their human visitors! The other standout attraction is **Ihu's Breakaway Falls**, with three enclosed tubes featuring break-away floors (complete with heartbeat effect while you're waiting for the drop!) and one outrageous non-breakaway tube that is every bit as scary. Each offers a completely different ride. **Whanau Way** is a quadruple raft ride with two distinct variations that twist and turn before landing with a resounding splash, while **Tassie's Twisters** are double bowl rides that send riders down single or double tubes into giant bowls before splashing back into the **Loggerhead Lane** lazy river (which also has a coral reef viewing section). **Taumata Racer** (3ft 6in/107cm) is a fast-paced mat slide set up like an eight-lane racing toboggan run, partly enclosed and then with a double drop into daylight (queues can look long here but they usually move quickly). Family raft ride **Walhalla Wave** features a winding, enclosed section before a big splash finale; while **HooRoo Run** is a shorter, and straighter ride – with two distinct drops on the way (4ft/122cm must wear a life vest)!

Taumata Racer

© SeaWorld Parks

Omaka Rocka features two high-speed single-rider tube flumes, each with three sets of funnels that send you coursing up one side and down the other with a sensational 'feel it in your tummy' weightlessness before final splash-down. **Big Surf Shores** wave pool offers big dynamic waves, while sister wave-pool **Cutback Cove** features gentler rolling surf. A huge sandy beach offers a large array of sun loungers and umbrellas, and private cabañas (from $50–120 in low season to the Ultimate Cabaña, including upgraded furniture, dining table and a second cabana with couch, coffee table and additional seating for up to eight, at $275–600 seasonally). Call 1888 800 5447 to book or go online.

BRITTIP

Head for the Beach area when you first arrive to stake out a place to base yourselves and try to grab one of the bigger fixed umbrellas that offer the most shade.

As well as the gentle **Loggerhead Lane** (under 4ft/122cm must wear life vest), you should try the dynamic **Roa's Rapids** (under 51in/129cm must wear a life vest), which provides a helter-skelter whirl along this river feature, with a series of fountains, jets and other watery boosts to keep you bobbing along with no effort at all. Free life vests are on offer here and it is worth trying one for the feeling of floating along in high style!

Dolphin Plunge

© SeaWorld Parks

Kids' features: The big success of the park, though, is its extensive features for children, from the youngest to young teens. **Kata's Kookaburra Cove** is an exclusive area for those under 4ft/1.2m tall, with a whole range of scaled-down slides, rides, pools and fountains to provide a gentler experience for the young 'uns. By contrast, **Walkabout Waters** is a vast and frenzied 60ft/18m-high water play structure with every kind of climb, slide and water eruptions and outpourings, including two giant buckets that fill and dump in spectacular fashion over those below. Small animal encounters are also designed to appeal to children, so watch out for these around the park (featuring macaws, leggy spoonbills, anteaters, tortoises and a kookaburra).

Shopping and dining: The imaginative **Kiwi Traders** is the biggest of the four shops, but both **Adaptations** and **Beachies** are worth a look. For dining, try **Waterstone Grill** (chicken tenders, burgers, salads, sandwiches, wraps), **Mango Market** (chicken tenders, sandwiches, salads, fries and desserts) or **Banana Beach Cookout** buffet (pizza, pasta, chicken, pork, hotdogs, salads, desserts, non-alcoholic drinks; all-day pass $16–20 adults, $11–15 ages 3–9; add refillable souvenir bottle for $6).

BRITTIP

Youngsters can learn to swim at Aquatica, with a week-long course of 45min lessons by water safety instructors at $69/student. Book online or call 1888 800 5447.

Aquatica features elements that no other park has, like Roa's Rapids and Kookaburra Cove. And, if you buy the two-park ticket with SeaWorld, it's great value in summer, as you can spend much of the day in Aquatica and then hop over to SeaWorld for the evening.

That sums up the large-scale attractions on offer, but let's explore some alternatives to the mass-market experience…

8 Off the Beaten Track

or When You're All Theme-Parked Out

Orlando's main attractions are undoubtedly a lot of fun, but they can also be extremely tiring and you may well need a break from all the hectic theme park activity. Or you may be visiting again and looking for a different experience. If either is the case, this chapter is for you.

Hopefully, you will already have noted the relatively tranquil offerings of Gatorland in the previous chapter, but to enhance your view of the area further, the following are all guaranteed to take you off the beaten tourist track. This chapter could easily be subtitled 'A Taste of the Real Florida', as it introduces the towns of Winter Park, Celebration and Mount Dora, plus the natural delights of the area, including the state parks, day-trips, eco-tours and sports.

ORLANDO/Orange County

Winter Park: Foremost among the 'secret' hideaways is this elegant northern suburb, little more than 20mins from the hurly-burly of I-Drive yet a world away from the relentless tourism. It offers museums and art galleries, boutique shopping, numerous restaurants, walking tours, a delightful 50min boat ride around the lakes and, above all, a chance to slow down. Take exit 87 from I-4, Fairbanks Avenue; turn right on Fairbanks and go east for 2ml/3km

and turn left at the junction with Park Avenue.

Morse Museum of American Art: A must for admirers of American art pottery, American and European glass, furniture and other decorative arts of the late 19th and early 20th centuries, as it includes one of the world's foremost collections of works by Louis Comfort Tiffany. The dazzling chapel restoration from the 1893 Chicago World Expo is on display in its original form for the first time since the late 19th century and is worth the entrance fee alone. It also has special Christmas exhibitions and periodic family programmes (9.30am–4pm Tues–Sat, 1–4pm Sun, also 4pm–8pm Fri only Nov–April; adults $5, Seniors $4, students $1, under-12s free; free 4–8pm each Fri Nov–April; **www.morsemuseum.org**).

> **$ BRITBONUS**
> Bring your *Brit Guide* to the Cornell Fine Arts museum and receive a 10% discount on all purchases in the museum store.

Park Avenue: The heart of Winter Park is a classy street of restaurants, fine shops and a shaded park. At one end is Rollins College, a small but respected arts education centre housing the beautiful Cornell Fine Arts Museum, with the oldest collection of paintings, sculpture and decorative arts in Florida (10am–4pm

Tues–Fri, 12am–5pm Sat and Sun, closed Mon and holidays; admission is free; **www.rollins.edu/cfam**).

Park Avenue Walking Tour: Free maps are provided for this tour by the Welcome Center (on W Lyman Ave; 8.30am–5pm Mon–Fri, 9am–2pm Sat; 407 644 8281). The shops of Park Avenue are a cut above most and, while you may find the prices equally distinctive, just browsing is an enjoyable experience with the charm of the area highlighted by the friendliness hereabouts. For shops both unique and fun, look for **Simmons Jewellers**, **Ten Thousand Villages** (international arts and crafts), **Bebe's** (children's clothes), the eclectic **Filthy Rich** (jewellery), **Tuni** (women's clothing) and **Williams-Sonoma** (kitchenware), plus **Peterbrooke Chocolatier**. Regular craft fairs and art festivals add splashes of colour to an inviting scenario. Street parking allows three hours free, but there is a multi-storey car park on the corner of Comstock and Park Avenue, which is a better half-day option. Keep an eye out for the **Taste of Winter Park** in Apr and **Autumn Art Festival** in Oct (**www.cityofwinterpark.org**).

Scenic Boat Tour: Started in 1938, this is located on East Morse Boulevard and offers a charming, 12ml/19km narrated tour around the lakes and canals, giving a fascinating glimpse of some stunning homes, boat houses and lakeside gardens (property prices start at around $1m and several top $10m!). Tours run every hour 10am–4pm daily (closed Christmas) at $12 for adults and $6 for 2–11s, cash only; and this is one of the most relaxing hours you can spend in Orlando (407 644 4056; **www.scenicboattours.com**).

Lakeside Inn at Mount Dora

A dining delight

Winter Park boasts some of the best upmarket dining in Orlando. **Park Plaza Gardens** specialises in a modern mix of American and Continental cuisines, plus a wonderful Sunday brunch. **310 Park South** offers the epitome of elegant, European café culture. We are also big fans of the pavement bistro of **Briarpatch** (breakfast and lunch), the Italian style of **Pannullo's**, and the fabulous **Luma** on Park, a 'gastropub' featuring fresh, daily specials from simple burgers to gourmet offerings and a superb wine list (**www.lumaonpark.com**). The **Ravenous Pig** on Orange Avenue has a similar wide-ranging pub choice, from its fine micro-brewery to wonderful steaks and seafood and earns top marks from leading local restaurant critic Scott Joseph (**www.theravenouspig. com**). Two recent high-quality additions are **Scratch**, an imaginative tapas-style bistro that features fabulously fresh, locally-sourced produce that changes on a week-to-week basis (407 325 5165, **http://scratchtapas. com**), and **Cask & Larder**, a 'Southern public house' from the creators of Ravenous Pig and with a similar creative touch to typical artisan southern foods and craft beers (407 280 4200, **www.caskandlarder.com**).

Lake Tibet-Butler Preserve: This small nature reserve is in south-west Orange County (just north of Disney) on SR535 (Winter Garden–Vineland Rd) and features 4ml/6.5km of trails and elevated boardwalks where the cypress swamps, freshwater marshes, scrub and pine flatwoods are home to gopher tortoises, turtles, armadillos and especially birds (it is on the Great Florida Birding Trail). Stop by the Visitor Center to pick up a map and see its wildlife exhibits and enjoy an hour or so of peace and quiet (10am–5 or 6pm Wed–Sun).

MOUNT DORA/ Lake County

Immediately to the west and north of Orlando is this large, rural county that is home to more unspoiled Florida charms and several small-scale attractions, including a notable state park and well-known winery.

Mount Dora: This smallish town on beautiful Lake Dora is one of Florida's hidden gems; a day here is a breath of fresh air with its unique mix of pleasant shops, restaurants, bars, inns and tours. Mount Dora is also renowned as a festival city, with 19 annual galas. Visit **www.mountdora.com** to see if there is one during your visit (4 July and Christmas are especially notable, while the Sail Boat Regatta each April is one of Florida's finest).

Mount Dora Trolley: Start with a one-hour narrated trundle around the streets from the Lakeside Inn, (11am, noon, 1 and 2pm Mon–Sat, $15 adults, $13 2–13s; 352 385 1023), a fascinating tour of one of the 'Top 100 Great Towns of America', and a former key stop on the now-defunct Florida railroad. Then stroll round the compact centre, which is full of quaint shops, cafés and bars. Antique hunters are spoiled for choice but should visit **Village Antique Mall**, with more than 80 vendors, and **Pak Ratz**, plus **Uncle Al's Time Capsule**, for film and celebrity memorabilia, while other unique stores include a **Papilio** (gifts), **Gold In Art** (jewellery) and **La Petit Maison** (aromatherapy gifts). The town even boasts the **Rocking Rabbit Brewery**, with live music on Fri and Sat 8pm–11pm (**www.mountdorabrewing.com**). Other stops of interest include **Mount Dora Historic Museum** (the former town jail!), which displays more (free) local history, and the **Museum of Speed**, a homage to high-powered American sports cars of yesteryear (plus other memorabilia such as vintage juke boxes and Coca-Cola machines; 10am–5pm Mon–Fri; $12/person or $14 with tour, no under-14s, no credit/debit cards; 352 385 0049, **www.classicdreamcars.com**).

Guided Tours of Segway of Central Florida: One of the best ways to see Mount Dora is with these fully narrated tours. They use unique, state-of-the-art, 2-wheel Segways to take small groups downtown, on to the iconic **Mount Dora lighthouse** and around scenic **Palm Island Park**. They pass some of the city's many fine B&Bs (including the award-winning

Magnolia Inn on East 3rd Avenue) and the genteel 125-year-old **Lakeside Inn**, on the National Register of Historic Places, where you can stop for a drink in Tremain's Lounge or dine in the Beauclaire Dining Room (great Sunday brunch – **www.lakeside-inn.com**). The Segway is easy to master (after a brief hands-on lesson) and ideal for the quiet streets. If you enjoy the 1hr tour, there is a second guided tour of nearby Dogwood Mountain. Both cost $55/person and tours run daily 9.30am, 11.30am, and 1.30pm (reservations advised; 352 460 2039, www.segwayofcentralflorida. com; save $6 if booking online). Riders must be 14 and no more than 260lb/118kg. This is one of our favourite activities.

Premier Boat Tours: You can see more via the *Captain Doolittle* from the Lakeside Inn for a fascinating eco-tour of the lakes and Dora Canal. As well as gators, you may see raccoons, turtles, otters, birds of prey and other nesting birds along this beautiful waterway. There are narrated two-hour tours daily at 11am and 2pm ($27 adults, $15 children) and one-hour Sunset Tours 45mins before sunset daily ($17 and $12, bring your favourite beverages; reservations advised on 352 434 8040, **www.doracanaltour.com**). Pontoon rentals are also available.

CraigCat Tours: Two-hour narrated guided tours along Lake Dora and the Dora Canal aboard CraigCat, motorised two-person watercraft. Bottled water and lifejackets provided. No experience necessary, drivers must be 21 and up with valid driving licence, passengers must be 12 and up. Non-marking soft-soled shoes or sandals required ($99/person; 407 227 3388; **www.craigcattours.com**; check website for periodic discounts).

Getting there: On US Highway 441 north-east of Orlando, take the (toll) Florida Turnpike to exit 267A for the (toll) Western Beltway (429), and the Beltway north to its junction with 441, from where Mount Dora is 10ml/16km further north. For more info, contact the excellent Mount Dora Chamber of Commerce on 352 383 2165 or www.mountdora.com. The visitor centre is at 341 Alexander Street.

BRIT BONUS

$ Take a kayak tour with Central Florida Nature Adventures and, when you book for three, the fourth person paddles free! Just remember to quote the *Brit Guide* offer when you book and show your copy when you turn up.

Central Florida Nature Adventures: Head north from Mount Dora to Eustis, from where this company offer guided tours of the Dora Canal and the Lil' Amazon in Lake County, Rock Springs Run and the Wekiva River in Seminole County, Blackwater Lake in Marion County and the Silver River in Ocala; plus a winter Manatee tour and a kayak and horse-riding combo. Their two chief guides are experienced kayakers but most of these scenic trips (2–7 hours) require no experience. Tours vary from $59–125 (352 589 7899, **www.kayakcentralflorida.com**).

Lake Louisa State Park: Another gem just off Highway 27 (at the west end of Highway 192), this offers beautiful countryside, with six lakes and rolling hills. There are over 20ml/32km of hiking trails, a picnic pavilion, swimming in Lake Louisa (with lifeguards late May–Aug), plus 20 cabins, sleeping up to 6 (8am–dusk daily, entry $5/car; 352 394 3969, **www. floridastateparks.org/park/Lake-Louisa**). Further up Highway 27 is the **Citrus Tower**, built in 1956, with panoramic views from its 22-storey glass observation deck (9am–5pm Mon–Sat, $6 adults $4 3–11s; 352 394.4061, **www.citrustower.com**); and **Lakeridge Winery**, a 127acre/51ha producing some award-winning wines with free tours and tastings (10am–5pm Mon–Sat, 11am–5pm Sun; 1800 768 9463, **www.lakeridgewinery.com**).

Revolution – The Offroad Experience: Perfect for those with kids of 16+ and keen to see the real Florida, this British-run attraction is

---

Mount Dora dining

Try a leisurely lunch at the excellent **Copacabana Cuban Café** or **One Flight Up**. **Village Coffee Pot** is the place for coffee and the **Windsor Rose** is an English tea-room. For something stronger, there are notable pubs like **Tremain's Tavern** or **The Lost Parrot**. All also offer dinner, but our top two – especially if you arrive before sunset – are **Pisces Rising**, a lovely Key West-themed restaurant, with a grandstand view of sunsets over Lake Dora, plus fresh Florida seafood and steaks (352 385 2669, **www.piscesrisingdining.com**); and the charming **Goblin Market** bistro tucked away in a quiet corner of town (352 735 0059, **http://thegoblinmarketrestaurant.com/**). With a small patio dining area, a conservatory-style ground floor and clubby upper floor with bar, this renovated warehouse is ideal for a refined lunch or upmarket dinner (not Mon; 11.30am–3.30pm only Sun).

---

with a private lake. They offer ATV (Quad-Bike), Jeep and Dune Buggy off-roading, plus the amazing JetLev adventure. The purpose-built ATV trail features two 40min sessions of fab driving (must be 16+ with driving licence; 12–15 can ride with an instructor). There is a short 'test' to ensure riders are in control, then it's off over the sand-hills and grasslands on trails and dirt tracks groomed for off-road activity, but you WILL get dirty, so wear old clothes – long trousers and close-toed shoes or trainers. The **4 x 4 Experience** (in a Jeep Wrangler) can be driven by anyone with a driving licence and passengers are welcome, while the sturdy dune buggies are open to all with a valid driving licence, under 280lb/127kg and under 1.9m/6ft 3in. This is one of Florida's best off-road drives – novel, enjoyable and highly addictive! The **Mucky Duck** tour is self-drive in four-passenger amphibious vehicles. The 75min experience includes training in the 6 and 8-wheel Argo UTVs and the chance to drive around and through the main lake. Drivers must be at least 18 and hold a full licence, but passengers can be as young as 4 (with safety vests and helmets provided). Booking is essential on 352 400 1322 or **www.revolutionoffroad.com**. ATV is $75/person ($35 for ride-along); ATV & Dune Buggy or ATV & Jeep $130, or all three for $185. Mucky Duck tour $75/driver, $40/passenger. There are also 4–6-hour fishing adventures for $225 and $325 (for two) and Target Archery ($45). To get there, take Highway 192 west to Highway 27; go north on 27 for 3 traffic lights; turn left on Highway 474 it hits 33, then go right for 2ml/3km and it is on the right.

$ BRITBONUS
Get $5/person off any activity at Revolution Offroad by showing your copy of the *Brit Guide* or mentioning it when booking.

OSCEOLA COUNTY
You'll find some of Florida's most scenic and nature-orientated attractions in the Kissimmee area – you just need to know where to look!

BRITTIP
Dresses are not advisable for balloon trips and hardwearing shoes for the set-up and landing areas are essential.

Balloon trips
Florida is hugely popular for ballooning and you will often see them in Osceola County. It's a majestic experience; the utterly smooth way in which you lift off is breathtaking, but the peace and quiet, and the stunning views are awesome. It's not cheap, but it is appealing to all but young children or those with a fear of heights. It can also be a highly personal ride, with basket capacity starting at just four people.

Orlando Balloon Rides: The main operator in central Florida flies every day, weather permitting, meeting at their smart new Reception Center on Highway 27 (close to the junction with I-4) at 5.30–6.30am depending on season, as the best winds are nearly always early, then transferring in their vans to the take-off site. Here

you can help the friendly crew set up their balloons (which take up to 20 passengers in total comfort, one of which is also disabled-accessible). Then you fly off for an hour, floating serenely or sinking to skim the treetops or one of the many lakes in the south-west Disney area. After your flight, enjoy a champagne landing ceremony before returning to the Center, where there are free snacks and drinks. It lasts 3–4 hours and costs $195/adult, $99 ages 4–10 ($219 and $109 at weekends; no under-4s or expectant mothers). Select hotel pick-ups are available at $15/person for the round trip, or for $30 you can be part of the chase crew and just enjoy the champagne landing. Balloonist Certificates can be downloaded from the website. Book well in advance on 407 894 5040 or www.orlandoballoonrides.com. Orlando Balloon Rides are also part of the Orlando Adventure Collection, a group of 7 companies with an action-themed attraction. They include Revolution – The Offroad Experience (p252), Boggy Creek Airboats (p254), Forever Florida Zipline Safari (p257), Warbird Adventures (p259), Kissimmee Helicopters and Revolution Bass Fishing. Look up **www.orlandoadventurecollection.com**.

$ BRITBONUS
Mention the code BG2016 and show your copy of the *Brit Guide* with **Orlando Balloon Rides** for a 10% discount on all their flights.

Revolution Off-road Experience

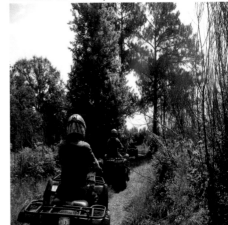

Thompson Aire: Top local pilot Jeff Thompson, a veteran with more than 35 years' flying, also flies every day (weather permitting), meeting at the Maingate Lakeside Resort on Highway 192, and returning there for a hearty buffet breakfast. Fares are $185 ($105 10–15s; 1 child 5–9 can fly free with a paying adult; discounts for four or more adults travelling together). Chase package available for non-flyers. Call 407 421 9322 or visit **www.thompsonaire.com**. Hotel pick-ups can be arranged at $15/person.

Airboat rides

The thrill of airboat rides – like flying at ground level – can be experienced on many of Florida's waterways, but especially in Osceola County. You can explore areas otherwise inaccessible to boats, skimming over the marshes to give you an alternative, close-up view. Travelling at up to 50mph/80kph means it can be loud (you will be given ear protectors) and sunglasses are also a good idea to keep stray flies out of your eyes. It is NOT the trip for you, however, if you are spooked by crickets, dragonflies and similar insects that occasionally land in the boat! In summer, a good insect repellent is essential.

BRITTIP
Look out for some great discounts and special offers on Boggy Creek's website, **www.bcairboats.com**.

Boggy Creek Airboat Rides

Boggy Creek Airboat Rides: Take your pick from two contrasting sites in different parts of Kissimmee, one more rural while the other has more facilities. The rural site is on Lake Toho at peaceful **Southport Park**, all the way down Poinciana Boulevard, off Highway 192 between markers 10 and 11, and across Pleasant Hill Road into Southport Road – about a 35min drive. Boggy Creek's half-hour ride features the most modern 18-passenger airboats in Florida, skimming over the local wetlands for a close-up of the majestic cypress trees and wildlife including eagles, ospreys, snakes and turtles, as well as the ever-present gators. Southport Park feels a million miles away from the main tourist area and it is likely you'll see a variety of wildlife, especially in spring.

You don't need to book, just turn up, as boats go every 30mins (9am–5pm daily; $26.95 adults, $20.95 3–10s). Don't forget the sunscreen as you can really burn on the water. Boggy Creek also does an hour-long Sunset Tour ($51.95 adults, $47.95 3–10s, from 6.45pm late March–late Sept) or Night Tour ($51.59 adults, $47.95 3–10s, from 7.30pm Oct–Mar, 8:30pm March-Sept) for a completely different and exhilarating experience (gator eyes glow red in the dark!), but you must book in advance. Or go all out with the 45min Swamp Excursion, exploring remote areas beyond the regular tour ($56.95/person). Round-trip hotel transport is offered (call for pricing).

BRITBONUS
Brit Guide readers qualify for 10% off any tour with Boggy Creek Airboats when showing the book at check-in or using code *BritGuide* when booking in advance.

Boggy Creek's other (rather busier) site is at East Lake Fish Camp (reservations required), a completely different experience to Lake Toho, so it is worth trying both. East Lake also offers a one-hour Scenic Nature Tour for $43.95 adult, $38.95 3–10. Stay after your ride for a live alligator demonstration – and have the chance to hold a gator and have your picture taken! To reach East Lake Fish Camp, either take exit 17 off Central Florida Greeneway – 417 – and go 3ml/5km south on Boggy Creek Road, then right into East Lake Fish Camp, or take Osceola Parkway east until it hits Boggy Creek Road. Go left and then turn right at the Boggy Creek T-junction, then right into East Lake Fish Camp after about 2ml/3km (book on 407 344 9550 or **www.bcairboats.com**).

BRITTIP

Want an airboat ride but don't have a car? Taxis are seriously expensive but *Brit Guide* partners Florida Dolphin Tours offer a special excursion package to Boggy Creek every Mon, Wed and Sat, or Gatorland plus an airboat ride (see p265).

Wild Florida: Set on tranquil Cypress Lake, this airboat ride and wildlife reserve features 30min, one-hour and night-time rides from their purpose-built dock (a great place for wildlife watching) with the chance to see gators, turtles, birdlife and even snakes from the safety of their 6- and 17-passenger airboats. It also features a self-contained 13acre/5.2ha **Wildlife Park** that is home to their own collection of gators, deer, tortoises, emus, zebras, watusi cattle and water buffalo, plus an aviary and a peaceful boardwalk cypress swamp walk. You can feed some of the animals (for a small fee) and there is an excellent gift shop (remember you can't bring alligator products back to the UK) and the **Chomp House Grill**, for a snack or lunch (we especially like their pulled pork!). Their alligator handling and photo opportunities (single photos $15–20; percentage of all photos goes to Florida Panther Conservation Society) are good, too, and you won't see any sign of human habitation out on the Lake. Again, you don't need to book for day tours as they go out regularly from 9am–6pm Mon–Sat (closed Sun). The ½hr tour is $26.50 for adults and $23 for 3–11s; 1hr is $47.50 and $37; 1hr

private tour and night-time tour $63/person (must pre-book). All tours include Wildlife Park, or $18 and $15 on its own (407 957 3135, **http://wildfloridairboats.com/**). Also watch for their new Ranch Buggy Tours ($30). To get there, take Highway 192 east to St Cloud (about 20miles/32km), turn right on Vermont Ave (12miles/19km), which becomes Canoe Creek Rd, then right on Lake Cypress Rd (a dirt road) for 2miles/3.2km. From Orlando, you can take the (toll) Florida Turnpike to 192 at Exit 244, then continue east to Vermont and follow the other directions from there.

BRITBONUS

Wild Florida offers $5 off all one-hour airboat tours, Free kids-size ice cream cone with any Wildlife Park admission, and $3 off all ranch buggy tours when you use promo code WILDBRITS to redeem online, by phone or in person. Cannot be combined with any other offers.

Paddling and Climbing

Kissimmee Paddling Center: Here's a great chance to get up close with the heart of Osceola County nature, with kayaks, canoes and paddleboards on offer at this new site ideally located on Highway 192. Shingle Creek forms the headwaters of the Everglades and is a haven of peace and quiet, perfect for a paddling adventure whether for 1hr or a half day. There are even 45min electric boat tours for those who just want to enjoy the scenery. You can just turn up and go but bookings are advisable. Open daily, 8am to 5 or 7pm, rentals are from $13–18/hr while 2hr guided tours are $55/person and 4hr round-trip to Makinson Island is $99 (located in Shingle Creek Regional Park just past Medieval Times; 407 343 7740, **http://paddlingcenter.com/**).

Orlando Tree Trek: Adventure-seekers will want to test out this challenging new aerial ropes course in a forested area of Kissimmee south of Disney. There are 2 kids courses (ages 7–11) and 4 for ages 12 and up, from beginner to advanced in skill level, plus a dual giant zipline to finish with.

There is a full instruction session then it is off into the treetops for a series of obstacles ranging from short ziplines to cargo nets, ladders, cable bridges, Tarzan swings and more. It is huge fun but the full 4-course challenge will take at least 2hrs, and bottled water, stout shoes and older clothing are essential. Priced from $29.95–49.95, it is open daily 8am–dusk (last tour 2hrs before dusk). Take Old Lake Wilson Rd south from Highway 192 to Sinclair Rd, turn right and it is on the right. Bookings advisable (407 390 9999, **www.orlandotreetrek.com**).

BRITTIP

For Celebration, don't stop at the first set of shops and services you come to off Highway 192. Keep going until you find Market Street and the centrepiece lake that is the proper downtown area.

Celebration

In 1994, the Walt Disney Company set out to build a 'new urban' neighbourhood, a model community with a friendly, welcoming spirit and strong traditional values. The result was Celebration, where picture-perfect Victorian homes mingle with smart town-houses with an array of shopping, dining and entertainment options. Today, it is a self-sufficient, bustling town with a hospital, schools, cinema and two hotels. On Disney's southern border off Highway 192, enter at the landmark water tower via Celebration Ave, then follow

Wild Florida

A cause for Celebration

Dining in Celebration is a real highlight. Try **Market Street Café**, a 50s-style diner serving down-home favourites such as turkey dinners or meatloaf and, or try award-winning **Café D'Antonio** for authentic Italian cuisine in a sleek, family-friendly atmosphere (407 566 2233, **www.antoniosonline.com**); Spanish-Cuban **Columbia** uses unique combinations of authentic ingredients (407 566 1505, **www.columbiarestaurant.com**); **Celebration Town Tavern**, a casual ambiance, specialising in New England seafood; **Ari Sushi**, is the place for sushi and hibachi dishes; and the **Imperium Food & Wine** is an excellent option for fine wines and cocktails, plus a tempting light bite menu, including soups, sandwiches, salads and flatbreads (407 566 9054, **www.imperiumfoodandwine.com**). You should also consider the **Bohemian Bar & Grill** at the Bohemian Hotel, a contemporary American steakhouse with old-world Florida charm, while **Kilwins** is great for chocolate and ice-cream treats.

signs to the Bohemian Hotel in the town centre.

Market Street shops: feature delightful boutiques like **Market Street Gallery** (Disney collectables, Swarovski crystal, Lladro and gifts), **Confetti of Celebration** (speciality and customised gifts), **Once Upon A Time** (children's clothing) and **Soft as a Grape** (casual wear for the family). Other specialists include **Enchanted Boutique** and **Woof Gang Bakery** (pet needs). There are miles of bike and walking paths, with the pretty lakefront setting, children's play area and periodic festivals. A huge event is held on American Independence Day 4 July, with picnics, entertainment and face-painting (parking is at the town entrance, with a park-and-ride bus), while the Christmas period also sees festive events and nightly snowfall on Market Street (**http://celebrationtowncenter.com**). You can also take a 20min carriage ride (Fri and Sat, 6–9.30pm and Sun 11am–3pm, weather permitting) at $45 for 1–4 people.

Segway Tours

An outstanding feature in Kissimmee/ Celebration is this super opportunity to try out the fab 2-wheeled Segway transporter and get a guided audio tour of the area as well. Ideal for young and old alike (age 14 and up), they are easy to master, fun to ride and a breeze to enjoy as you trundle along Highway 192 and around the most scenic parts of Celebration in true eco-friendly style.

ZE Tours: Choose from three separate tours in the company of a wonderfully personable guide (10am–4pm daily), heading out from their store in the Rock Church plaza on Highway 192 (by Marker 10; next to the Helicopter Tours) and rolling along for 70, 100 or 130mins to discover the heart of Celebration, its many lakes, paths and byways, plus lots of wildlife – from playful squirrels (which you can feed) to gators (which you can't!). There is a quick ride-around to get your 'Segway legs', then it is off in single-file, with the tranquil tour enabled by small walkie-talkies that clip on to your helmet. There are plenty of stops to ask questions and compare notes with your group, and your guide is a great source of knowledge about the town and the area (especially Disney). ZE Tours also offer bike rentals to tour Highway 192 at your leisure (and it's all completely flat). The Segway tours cost $55, $70 and $85/person (70, 100 and 130mins; 14–17-year-olds must be accompanied by a parent; minimum weight 100lb/45kg, max 250lb/113kg), or you can just try a ride-around on a Segway at $15 for 10min, $25 for 20mins, and $35 for 30 mins. Bike rental is from $5–25 (hourly or all day). Reservations are highly recommended for both on 863 512 0256 or online at **www.zetours.com**.

Forever Florida

For our money, this is one of the most outstanding non-theme-park attractions in Florida. Both a 4,700acre/1,900ha wilderness preserve and working ranch, it offers a close-up of the flora, fauna and conservation issues, plus a real taste of cracker-style life ('crackers' were 19th century Florida cowboys), as well as their own EcoPark, with six thrilling adventures.

Cypress Restaurant and Visitor Center: Start here with its essential 30min orientation programme into the preserve's creation. Beginning as a dream of gifted biologist and ecologist Allen Broussard, it was completed after his death (from complications of Hodgkin's disease) by his parents, Dr William and Margaret Broussard as a non-profit-making memorial to their son. The education element alone is awesome, and the two tours feature a strong conservation message. The two-hour **Coach Safari** is a tranquil trundle in a large-wheeled, open-sided buggy round much of the woods, swamp and prairie of the Crescent J Ranch and Conservancy. Your guide gives the lowdown on the history and environmental issues. A boardwalk along Bull Creek affords the chance to get up close with a typical cypress 'dome' and breathe the amazingly pure air. You are likely to see alligators, turtles, whitetail deer, armadillos and a host of bird life – including bald eagles and wild turkeys – as well as native cattle and horses, and you'll leave with a good understanding of the REAL Florida ($24.99 adults, $14.99, 6–12s; daily at 10am, 1pm, and 4pm).

Horseback Safaris: For ages 10 and over; here's the chance to enjoy Western trail rides for 90min with a native cracker guide ($69.99/person, book at least 24 hours in advance on 407 957 9794).

Forever Florida zipline

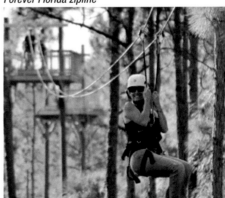

EcoPark: THE must-not-miss attraction in Central Florida for serious thrill-seekers, featuring three ziplines, tree-top cycling and two hair-raising straightaway ziplines.

Zipline Safari: This 2½-hour adventure starts with a short scenic hike to the launch point, which provides a breathtaking aerial view of the preserve at up to 55ft/16.8m high. The course includes seven different ziplines, 10 observation platforms and 3 sky-bridges over three eco-systems. The longest run is 750ft/229m and riders reach top speeds of 25mph/40kph. The final zip brings you down to its wildlife interaction area, including a Florida panther, alligators and other animals. There is also a Starlight Safari or Moonlight Safari every Sat night, but you must book in advance ($79.99/person, ages eight and up).

The Thrill Pack – The Rattlesnake, Peregrine Plunge & Panther Pounce and Swooping Crane: The Rattlesnake is 'next generation ziplining' at its best, a 1,000ft/205m long, 20mph/32kph diving and soaring 'roller-coaster' ride from the 65ft/20m high tower. Peregrine Plunge launches from a 71ft/22m tower with 1,300ft/396m of line – the longest single zipline in Florida, at up to 30mph/48kph – and not for the faint of heart. But do it once and you'll want to go again. Want to get to the ground quicker? Tethered to an overhead crane and fitted into a secure harness at Panther Pounce, step off the 68ft/21m tower and go straight into free-fall! The effect is mindboggling, with serious bragging rights when it's over.

All the adventures are covered by The Thrill Pack, at $69.99/ages 8 and up (max weight 275lb/125kg; 265lb/120kg for Panther Pounce; min weight 70lb/32kg and age 10).

The **Horseback Safaris** can also be extended to two days ($199), staying in bunk-house accommodation. Forever Florida is a good 80min drive out of Orlando, 40ml/64km east on Highway 192, through St Cloud as far as Holopaw, then 7½ml/12km south on Highway 441, but is well worth the journey to experience the charm and tranquillity (407 957 9794, reservations recommended for all experiences, **www.foreverflorida.com**).

Osceola County History Center and Pioneer Village

Highway 192 (just by Marker 15) features the **Osceola County Welcome Center** and **History Museum**, a collaboration between the County and Historical Society, providing a small-scale but engaging look at the area's history and nature. There is a 'steamboat' entryway inside, then a tour of local history from 1867 to the present, through the four main 'habitats' (swamplands, pine flatwoods, oak hammocks and lakefront) with a series of tableaux and nature exhibits that depict the true rural and agricultural nature of central Florida, plus the original Indian tribes. Outside, you can wander alongside Shingle Creek, the headwaters of The Everglades (free admission daily 9am–5pm; 407 396 8644, **www.osceolahistory.org**). After seeing the museum, cross over Highway 192 to Shingle Creek Regional Park for a chance to wander the hiking trails and experience Osceola nature at first hand.

Next, head for the all-new **Pioneer Village**, just off Highway 192 on Babb Road. This delightful discovery pays real-life homage to 19th-century Florida life, with a preserved 'cracker' homestead, blacksmith shop, Seminole Village and other buildings portraying how settlers lived in the 1880s. The charming outdoor museum traces more Osceola County history and includes an array of homes owned by historically-known Floridans, plus a citrus-packing operation from nearby Narcoossee, originally started by a family from the UK! The tours are self-guided, or volunteers who can take you round, providing a fascinating view of life here more than 130 years ago (2491 Babb Road, just off Highway 192. Take Old Vineland Rd to Babb Rd and turn left; 10am–4pm daily; $7 adults, $3 6–12s, under-6s free).

Warbird Adventures and Kissimmee Air Museum

This is the most exhilarating ride in town, bar none – guaranteed. It's the only place we know of where, 20mins after walking in with no previous experience, you can actually be flying a 1945 T-6 Harvard fighter-trainer plane… and doing all manner of aerobatics. It's enhanced by in-flight video and wingtip camera to record every moment. Roller-coasters? They're for wimps! Mind you, this is not cheap – a 15min flight costs $250, 30mins is $430, 45mins is $590 and an hour $740 (aerobatics on 30min flight $35 extra), while the DVD is $50 and photos $25. Nevertheless, the memory will last a lifetime and just the thought of it is thrilling. Max weight is 18st/115kg and minimum height is 4ft/122cm. Also on the same site at Kissimmee Gateway Airport is Kissimmee Air Museum, a combination warplane showcase and restoration centre where you can get up close with the exhibits, which include a Bell 47 helicopter, an open-cockpit Ryan PT-22, a Boeing Stearman biplane, its three T-6 Harvards and the amazing one-off Aerocar, plus small-scale offerings like a WWII rifle collection and Luftwaffe memorabilia. Other exhibits include Air Power and Pearl Harbor, with rare photos and artefacts behind the story. Other aircraft include a racing P-51 Mustang, De Havilland T11 Vampire and a Ryan STA. It can all be found just off Hoagland Boulevard, ½ml/800m south of Highway 192, on the left (Air Museum open 9am–5pm Mon–Sat; $10/person, ages 6–12 $5, under-5s free; 407 870 7366, **www.warbirdadventures.com**).

POLK COUNTY

Head south from Kissimmee/Osceola County and you head into Polk territory, another of Florida's oldest-established and most authentic areas. It is home to the large-scale attractions of LEGOLAND Florida (p222) but also has its share of off-the-beaten-track experiences.

Bok Tower Gardens

For those wishing to experience the genuine peace, tranquillity and floral ambience of Florida, there is no better recommendation than this national monument and garden centre at Lake Wales, 50ml/80km to the south-west of Orlando (go west on I-4, then south on Highway 27). With one of the most unusual attractions in the state – a majestic 205ft/62.5m pink-and-grey marble Carillon Tower: Set in 250acres/101ha of unique parkland, this is a feast for the eyes and soul. Called the Singing Tower, the 1920s-built carillon is the centrepiece and concerts are given every day at 1 and 3pm. The Tower is wonderfully photogenic and quite stunning on a cloudless day.

Gardens: Around the Tower is a wide moat, a pond and semi-formal gardens. At one of the highest points on Florida's peninsula (all of 298ft/90m above sea level), the view is inspiring and uncluttered, and retains an inherent peace and solitude that persuaded the founder,

Bok Tower Gardens

philanthropist Edward Bok, to grant the estate to the community in 1929. The gardens also provide a wildlife observatory, nature trails, an endangered plant exhibit, butterfly and woodland gardens and pine forests. There is a kids' play area, plus brass rubbing and art classes.

Education and Visitor Center: The award-winning centre illustrates the story of Edward Bok (don't miss the film about his impact on US society) and his vision for Bok Tower Gardens. The Blue Palmetto Café adds a pleasant opportunity for a light lunch and snacks, while the Tower & Garden Gift Shop offers souvenir items.

Pinewood Estate: For an additional fee ($6 adults, $5 5–12s, noon–4pm Mon–Sat, 1pm–4pm Sun), you can tour a fine example of Mediterranean-style architecture in this 20-room mansion, built as a winter retreat for a Pennsylvania steel tycoon in the early 1930s and lovingly maintained to show a slice of period opulence.

Getting there: Off US Highway 27 on Burns Avenue; take I-4 west to exit 55, go south on US 27 for 25ml/40km, then left on Mountain Lake Cutoff Road (2 traffic lights past Eagle Ridge Mall) and follow the signs. Admission: $12 adults, $3 5–12s (under-5s free), apart from occasional ticketed events (mainly carillon festivals and recitals). Open 8am–6pm daily (last entry 5pm; Visitor Center 9am–5pm only; 863 676 1408, **http://boktowergardens.org/**).

$ BRITBONUS

Receive a $3 discount off regular adult combo admission tickets at Bok Tower Gardens by producing your copy of the *Brit Guide* (includes Gardens and Pinewood Estate.)

Lake Wales

Continue on to the Lake Wales area after Bok Tower Gardens and you encounter some other local gems.

Head into the quaint 1920s town of Lake Wales and you discover **Spook Hill** (where cars mysteriously roll uphill!), **Grove House Visitor Center** (home of Florida's Natural fruit juice products – as fresh as it gets; 10am–5pm Mon–Fri; 10am–2pm Sat, seasonally. Closed Memorial Day–end of Sept) and the quaint **Museum and Cultural Center** (set in a restored 1928 Atlantic Coast Line railroad station; 9am–5pm Mon–Fri, 10am–4pm Sat).

Westgate River Ranch: Out in rural Polk County is this superb dude ranch and activity centre that boasts great accommodations (including 'glamping' for those who like to camp in style) and the chance to try horse-riding, fishing, airboating, trap shooting and archery, as well as take in the exciting Saturday night Westgate Rodeo in the 1,200-seat arena. You can visit just for the day to try any of the activities or the weekly rodeo (which is followed by live music, line dancing and a family-friendly Street Party), but the accommodations are excellent and you can sample the River Ranch Saloon without having to drive afterwards! It is guaranteed fun for all the family and a real taste of Florida's cowboy country. See more at **www.westgatedestinations.com** and click on River Ranch, FL.

SEMINOLE COUNTY

You may have flown into the airport at the historic town of Sanford and there are plenty of diversions to get you well off the beaten track. If you want to finish your holiday with a day or so in the area, there are many good hotel choices (often significantly cheaper than their big-name rivals elsewhere) and you can catch your breath after all the hectic theme-parking!

Adventures in Florida: Get into the wilds with this specialist company that features kayaking adventures along the picturesque Econlockhatchee and Wekiva rivers, with expert guides and an in-depth understanding of the flora and fauna. They offer 2–3hr trips, all-day tours and even night-time paddles, as well as expeditions and lodge-based trips further afield. Along the Wekiva River you may encounter gators, manatees, turtles and all manner of birdlife, all in total safety and with immensely personable guides. Trips must be booked in advance and cost from $40–100/person (407 924 3375; **www.adventuresinflorida.com**).

Black Hammock Fish Camp and Restaurant: One of the most fun and entertaining of the area's airboat rides is found off exit 44 of the Central Florida Greeneway (take SR 434 east, turn left on Deleon Street and left on Black Hammock Road). This quiet backwater on scenic Lake Jesup is home to Capt Joel Martin, whose 30min tour takes you into every nook and cranny of either the east or west lake (which is crammed with some of the biggest gators in Florida). The standard rides leave every 30mins (no reservation needed) and are $26.95 and $20.95 (under-11s), but there are one-hour rides ($43.95 and $38.95), a 45min private tour ($50/person, four person minimum, reservations required), and a 60min night ride at $55/person (four person minimum; reservations required; 407 365 1244, **www.theblackhammock.com**). Then grab lunch or dinner at the Black Hammock Restaurant (fine local delicacies, especially the catfish and gator tail, plus other dishes and a kids' menu; 11am–9pm Sun–Thurs, 11am–10pm Fri and Sat; 407 365 1244 ext 105) or visit the Lazy Gator Bar, with nightly drink specials.

Central Florida Zoological Park: This private, non-profit organisation puts a natural accent on the zoo theme, set in a wooded 116acres/47ha of unspoilt countryside with boardwalks and trails around all the attractions. These include more than 100 species of animal, weekend feeding demonstrations, educational programmes, a picnic area, pony rides and a butterfly garden, plus the Zoofari Outpost gift shop and, Tropical Splash Ground water play area. It's good value at $16.50 adults, $13.95 seniors (60+) and $11.95 3–12s and is open 9am–5pm daily (not Thanksgiving Day or Christmas Day). Also try **ZOOm Air Adventures**, a separate series of eco-friendly rope bridges, ziplines, guide wires and other aerial challenges through the

Zoo's treetops. The 2 courses can be taken separately or combined (4ft 6in/137cm to take part), plus there are 2 children's courses (for 3–5ft/92–152cm). It costs $30.95 for the Upland course and $19.95 for the kids' versions, while the combo Upland and Rainforest costs $50.95. ZOOm opens at 9am, last adventure 4pm (off exit 104 of I-4; 407 323 4450, **www.centralfloridazoo.org** and **www.zoomair.us/orlando**).

BRITTIP

Visit Central Florida Zoo at the weekend and you will be offered a series of educational and enjoyable animal encounters (ranging from gators and snakes to hedgehogs).

St Johns River Eco-Tours: Drive through Seminole County to the Highbanks Marina & Camp in Debary (take I-4 east to exit 104, turn right and go north on SR600 for 4ml/6.5km, then turn left on W Highbanks Rd and follow it due west for 3ml/4.5km to the Marina) and you find this wonderful opportunity to immerse yourself in Florida nature on the beautiful St Johns River, with a two-hour pontoon boat ride in the company of naturalists Jeanne and Doug. You will gain expert insight into the magnificent local flora and fauna as well as seeing an array of birdlife, gators, turtles and even manatees. There is complimentary bottled water and a restroom on the boat. Tours leave Tues–Sun at 10am and 1.30pm, and there is a sunset tour seasonally, but booking is advisable ($25 adults, $12.50 under-13s; 386 626 9004, **www.stjohnsriverecotours.com**). You can also enjoy a pre or post-cruise lunch at the fun Swamp House Riverfront Grill, with an elevated view of the river and marina and the chance to sample catfish and gator nuggets (**www.swamphousewgrill.com**).

Sanford: The heart of Seminole County, this quaint town on Lake Monroe boasts a historic centre full of brick-paved streets, antique shops and an artist colony regeneration project (Jeanine Taylor Folk Art). It is small-town America, having lost the growth battle with Orlando years ago, but it makes a peaceful diversion with the lovely Riverwalk along the lakefront. Head first for the Historic Sanford Welcome Center (230 East 1st Street (11am–2.30pm Mon, 11am–5pm Tue–Sat, noon–5pm Sun) and the **Sanford Museum** (520 East 1st Street) for an overview of city history, founded in 1877 by pioneering lawyer and diplomat Henry Sanford as a hub on the St John's River, the 'Nile of America.' The free museum (11am–4pm Tues–Fri, 1–4pm Sat) illustrates the life and times of the city's founder, its growth as the 'celery capital of the world' and recent life as a naval base. The historic port features the **Gator's Nest** airboat rides (from The Port Restaurant), where the 1hr tour gets up close with the river wildlife in great style ($45/adults, $35, 3–12s) (book in advance, 407 892 2222, **www.thegatorsnest.com**). In the evening, the restaurant makes for memorable waterfront dining, or stop for a bite on First Street, with its many restored turn-of-the-century buildings. Try **The Corner Café** (fresh sandwiches, soups and salads) or the down home family cookin' of the **Colonial Room**. For a different dining experience, **Hollerbach's Willow Tree Café** is a genuine German diner featuring wonderful traditional food, great beers and live music Thurs–Sun evenings (11am–9pm Sun–Thurs, 10pm Fri and Sat; 407 321 2204, **www.willow treecafe.com**). If you like the food, visit Magnolia Square Market, a lovely deli run by the Hollerbach family just round the corner. For a real treat, **The Imperial** at Washburn Imports (an antique

Central Florida Zoo

store by day) is a fabulous evening bar, with delightful cocktails and craft beers. For great burgers, fish and sandwiches, we also like **The Breezeway Restaurant & Bar** (11am–10pm Mon–Thurs, midnight Fri, Sat, 10pm Sun; 407 878 1284, **www.thebreezewayrestaurantandbar.com**).

The second Thurs in every month in Sanford features the **Alive After Five** street party 5–8pm on First Street, with music, street artists, restaurant samples and more. Admission is free, food and drink extra. Look up details at **www.sanfordinfo.com**.

State Parks: You could, of course, just head for one of Seminole County's splendid parks and follow the well-marked trails. **Wekiva Springs State Park** offers bike rentals, hiking, canoeing, swimming, picnic areas and shelters, and **Little Big Econ** state forest has 5,048acres/2,045ha of scenic woodlands and wetlands. **Spring Hammock Preserve** offers 1,500acres/607ha of wilderness to explore and the Lake Proctor area has 6ml/10km of equestrian, hiking and biking adventures. There are more trails along the Econlockhatchee River at the **Econ River Wilderness Area**, while Chuluota has 625acres/253ha and the **Geneva Wilderness Area** 180acres/73ha, including Ed Yarborough Nature Center.

Where to stay: At Altamonte Springs, the refurbished **Hilton** is an upmarket choice without the price-tag, with large rooms, excellent amenities, a swish bar and versatile restaurant for breakfast, dinner and lunch (407 830 1985, **www.hilton.com**). At Lake Mary, the five-year-old **Westin** still feels like new, with ultra-comfy rooms, exceptional service and the bonus of Shula's 347 Grill, a stylish, casual eatery featuring exceptional Black Angus steaks, signature salads, speciality dishes and a full bar (407 531 3555; **www.westinlakemary.com**). As a unique alternative, **Danville B&B** is an amazing creation in rural Seminole county. Built with a totally false front, the building opens to reveal the 'village' of Danville, which is a superbly-equipped guesthouse boasting its own pub and cinema! It is also a magnificent setting for the many weddings it hosts each year, so advance bookings here are essential (407 349 5742, **www.danvillebnb.com**).

More info: See **www.visitseminole.com** or go to one of the Visitor Centers at Orlando Sanford International Airport (in the Welcome Center as you exit the main building) or the office at the Heathrow junction of I-4 (exit 98, go west on Lake Mary Blvd, right on International Parkway and left at AAA Drive; 407 665 2900).

CITRUS COUNTY

If you want to travel a little further, the two state park delights of Citrus County, on the Gulf Coast north-west of Orlando, are worth seeking out.

Crystal River Preserve State Park: Just north of Homosassa Springs, the Crystal River is home to the endangered manatee and it is possible to go swimming with these wonderful creatures, either on a self-guided or an organised tour. Winter and spring are ideal times for manatee sightings, but the park offers year-round adventure, with hiking and biking trails, kayaking, canoeing and fishing – or just pack a picnic lunch and enjoy a relaxing afternoon amid the natural beauty. You can also catch a relaxing and educational ride with **Heritage Eco-Boat Tours**, with a unique 1½-hour look at local history (Mon, Wed, Fri, 10.30am and 1.30pm; call to confirm on 352 563 0450).

BRITTIP
Never touch or disturb a wild manatee. They are protected animals and there are heavy fines, strictly enforced, for harassing them.

Getting there: Take the (toll) Florida Turnpike north to I-75, then, almost immediately, take SR44 west to Crystal River. Admission: Free (8am–dusk; 352 563 0450, **www.floridastateparks.org/ crystalriverpreserve**).

Homosassa Springs Wildlife State Park: This park also showcases

the manatee (via its underwater observatory), plus whooping cranes, deer, bobcats, black bear and even a hippopotamus among an active display of rehabilitating animals. There are daily programmes on its wildlife (every hour from 10.30am–3.30pm), notably snakes and birds of prey, plus a hands-on children's education centre. The park's 210acres/85ha take in some of the state's loveliest landscape as well as the headwaters of the Homosassa River and this is extremely popular in the spring.

Getting there: As for Crystal River, but turn left on to CR490 just after Lecanta on SR44. Admission: $13 adults, $5 6–12s (9am–5.30pm, last entry 4pm; 352 628 5343, **www.homosassasprings.org**).

BREVARD COUNTY

Out on the Atlantic coast you'll find the beauty of Cocoa Beach's Thousand Islands. Tranquil canals wind past mangrove stands, wildlife flourishes in the still waters and the Indian River Lagoon Estuary is one of the most biodiverse eco-systems in the world.

Island Boat Lines: This family-owned enterprise offers eco-tours, fishing and the wonderful Indian River Queen dinner boat, recalling Mark Twain's tales of paddleboats and peaceful gentility. A relaxing two-hour In Search of Wildlife eco-tour onboard Coast Guard-certified pontoon boats departs from the Sunset Waterfront Café on Highway 520 (W Cocoa Beach Causeway), passing some of the area's most impressive homes before heading into the Thousand Islands. Here you may spot bottlenose dolphins, manatees and a variety of coastal birds. Knowledgeable guides offer a wealth of info, encouraging visitors to ask questions and move about the boat for a closer look. Tours run at 10am and 2pm Mon–Sat, 2pm Sun ($28 adults, $26 seniors and military personnel, $23 2–12s; call to book on 1800 979 3370; **www.islandboatlines.com**)

Getting there: Take the Beachline Expressway (Highway 528) to Highway 1 south, then Merritt Island Causeway (Highway 520) east, approx. 2ml/3.2km with the café on the right.

BRITBONUS

Get $8 off the regular adult price with Island Boat Lines by showing your copy of the *Brit Guide*. Book in advance, though, on 321 454 7414.

Indian River Queen: Also used for private events, this beautifully appointed triple-deck paddlewheel riverboat is open to the public at weekends, with an elegant Date Night Dinner Cruise for couples every Fri featuring a red carpet reception, live music, themed dinner buffet and full bar. Captain Georges and owners Penny and John provide memorable authentic Southern hospitality. Boarding begins at 6.30pm, sailing from 7–9pm ($120/couple, limit 40 couples). The Scenic Historical Cruise: Offers two-hour narrated tours with souvenir photo (no meal) for $35pp, select dates only (booking required on 321 454 7414 or **www.indianriverqueen.com**).

Getting there: To reach Cocoa Village Marina, take the Beachline (Highway 528) east to Highway 1, go south to Highway 520, make a slight left at Bee Line, continue to N Cocoa Blvd, turn left at King, then left at Delannoy.

Cocoa Beach Sportfishing: Board the fully equipped *Centerfold*, a 33ft/10m Tournament-rigged boat, and get ready for big game fishing! Troll for dolphin (the fish, not the mammal), sailfish, wahoo, kingfish, grouper and more with a crew who boast plenty of experience in finding 'the big one.' Captain Tim and Captain Beau share their passion for fishing with anglers of all experience levels (novice to pro), and do it with humour and professionalism. Centerfold offers nine-hour trips at $800, 5hr trips $600, 1–6 passengers; the 19ft custom in-shore fishing Flatsboat accommodates 1–3 passengers at $250 for two, $300 for three for four

hours, $50 per extra hour; and the 26ft Killer Bee takes 1–4 anglers out for four, six or eight hours at $400, $500 or $600 (fishing licence, tackle, bait included; reservations on 321 848 2662, **www.cbsportfishing.com**). For more Cocoa Beach info, p277.

Port Canaveral: This area immediately adjacent to the busy cruise port (right off Highway 528) is now well worth a visit as it boasts some great small-scale attractions as well as tempting places to eat, all with a great view of the port. Start at the new **Exploration Tower**, a seven-storey museum and exhibition centre featuring the region's history and livelihood through a range of multimedia presentations and hands-on exhibits (like the Port Navigation simulator). There is also a wonderful top-floor open-air observation deck, plus a café and gift shop (daily 10am–7pm; adults $6.50, seniors $4, children $2.50; closed public holidays; 321 394 3408, **www.explorationtower.com**). **Space Coast Segway Tours** are a great way to have fun and see the whole area on these fab two-wheel vehicles, with a tour guide who takes you round and points out the key elements of the Port and its many facilities. Tours for four run five times a day (not Tues and Thurs Sept–Feb) and can take anyone from 45–118kg/7–18st, following a short training session. Reservations required (321 652 4169, **http://spacecoastsegwaytours.com**). Another real collectors item is **Parker Brothers Concepts**, who make all kinds of amazing vehicles for TV and films (notably the *Batman* series), with tours daily (Mon–Sat 10am–5pm **www.parkerbrothersconcepts.com**). When you need lunch or dinner (and we definitely recommend dinner here), there is an excellent array of restaurants along Glen Cheek Drive. Try any of Grills Seafood Deck & Tiki Bar, Rusty's Seafood & Oyster Bar, Fishlips Waterfront Bar & Grill and, our fave, **Milliken's Reef**, a fabulous inside/outside diner and bar with a great seafood-orientated menu, superb views, live music Fri and Sat evenings, Happy Hour 4–6pm daily, and even its own beach (321 783 0100, **www.millikensreef.com**).

Excursion operators

For those without a car (or wanting to put their feet up for a bit), there are tours and day trips visiting as far afield as the Everglades, Miami, Florida Keys and even the Bahamas. You can see a lot if you don't mind a long day (up to 16 hours). However, if the main attraction of a trip to the Everglades is the airboat ride, you are better off going to Boggy Creek Airboats (p254).

> **BRITTIP**
> For more info on all tours, see our special booking section online at **www.britguideorlando.net** and look up Our *Brit Guide* partners for the full range of Florida Dolphin Tours excursions – with your exclusive 12½% discount.

Florida Dolphin Tours: Make this British-owned company first on your list to check as it offers more than 15 memorable excursions, notably its swim-with-dolphins trips to the Keys and manatee swim adventure, Gatorland and Boggy Creek Airboats, plus excursions to St Augustine and an Orlando City Tour. They also feature free wi-fi on every coach and a great Christmas Dinner option. More to the point, as a *Brit Guide* partner, it offers readers a 12½% discount on all tours (see inside back cover). Choose from: Cocoa Beach, an excellent-value all-day trip to **Cocoa beach** for an afternoon of fun in the sun, an exciting airboat ride in search of gators on the St Johns River, all with a wonderful lunch ($75 adults, $59 3–9s); the **Kennedy Space Center** trip, with transportation to both Space Center and Astronaut Hall of Fame – ask about options such as including an airboat ride, Lunch with an Astronaut, or even the Ultimate Kennedy Experience (from $104 adult, $94 3–11s); **Florida Adventure Tour**, an all-day adventure (and their No.1 attraction), featuring breakfast and a 2hr boat trip on the picturesque Crystal River

(with snorkel and mask to check out where the manatees swim). There are picnic lunches, airboat rides and trips to Homosassa State Wildlife Park, too, plus an educational briefing on manatees and a chance to see them being fed from the underwater viewing area ($119 adults, $89 3–11s); **Dolphin Adventure**, its trademark tour, a holiday within a holiday: a 2-day excursion to lovely Key Largo with a 2hr dolphin programme (and the choice of an organised or informal dolphin swim), including transport, hotel on Miami Beach, dolphin swim, Everglades airboat ride, (interactive) alligator and snake-handling show, and ½-day to see Miami with shopping at Bayside or a boat tour along the inland waterway. The dolphin programme includes a full briefing and about 30mins in the water, with dolphin contact guaranteed ($209–299, $109 non-swimmers age 3–6); there is also a Miami 1-Day & Everglades Tour, that packs a LOT in but the 2-day version is better value and less rushed.

> **BRITTIP**
> For something truly different and uplifting, book the Gospel Brunch at Downtown Disney's House of Blues, including round-trip transportation, admission, lunch buffet, and show. Sun, from $69.

Florida Dolphin Tours

© Florida Dolphin Tours

Other tours: These include limo trips to Chef Mickey's character breakfast and dinner experiences, Planet Hollywood VIP ($79–119); Clearwater Beach & Lunch, a day-trip to the Gulf Coast for a beach adventure with lunch, and options to enjoy a Pirate Cruise, see the local dolphins in their own environment, go deep sea fishing AND work on your tan! ($75 and $65, plus extra fees per option); a Shopping Extravaganza, an all-day retail adventure with brunch and stops at the Orlando Premium Outlets, Super Wal-Mart and Florida Mall ($45 and $35); and Jacksonville Jaguar games ($75–$119, Aug–Dec). For the latest details, be sure to check out **www.floridadolphintours.com**.

O-Town Tour: Experience the best of downtown Orlando with this five-hour city tour, featuring stops in Lake Eola, Leu Gardens and Winter Park. Learn about Orlando's history, take the Winter Park scenic boat tour, and indulge in boutique shopping and dining. Advanced booking required, limited availability per tour, and weather permitting. Prices start at $79 adults, $65 under 10s; private O-Town Tour starts at $119; must call for pricing and booking (407 470 6939, **http://stonevips.com/o-town-tours**).

$ BRITBONUS

Mention promo Code **otown11** when booking and receive a special *Brit Guide* reader discount of 10% on the O-Town Tour.

Further tours and day trips can be found on **www.grayline.com/Orlando/**.

Of course, you can also have a great day-trip by heading for the beaches in your hire car (see Chapter 9).

Clearwater Beach

© Florida Dolphin Tours

SPORT

In addition to virtually every form of entertainment known to man, central Florida is one of the world's biggest sporting playgrounds, with a huge range of opportunities to either watch or play your favourite sport.

Golf

Without doubt, the No.1 sport is golf, with almost 200 courses in central Florida. There are numerous packages for golfers of all abilities to enjoy the weather and some spectacular courses, many designed by legends like Greg Norman, Tom Watson, Arnold Palmer and Jack Nicklaus. With an 18-hole round, including cart hire and taxes, from as little as $25 (average around $75), it's an attractive proposition and quite different from British courses. If you go in for 36-hole days, it's possible to save up to $30 by replaying the same course, while it is cheaper to play Mon–Thurs than Fri–Sun, and there are often lower rates for afternoon tee-times in summer. Sculpted landscapes, manicured fairways, abundant water features and white-sand bunkers add up to memorable golf. Winter is the high season, hence more expensive, but many courses are busy year-round. Be aware some courses pair golfers with little thought for age, handicap etc., so, if two of you turn up, you may be paired with two strangers.

BRITTIP

Golf balls are inexpensive in Florida, so there's no need to bring your own. Good-quality clubs are usually available for hire, including top brands.

Virtually every course will offer a driving range to get you started, plus lockers, changing rooms and showers, while the use of golf carts is universal (including the GPS system, which gives the yardage for every shot). They feature comforts like iced-water stations and drink carts that circulate the course (don't forget to tip the trolley drivers). Some have swimming pools, and all offer a decent bar and restaurant.

Your best starting point is visiting one of the five **Edwin Watts** golf shops around Orlando for a free copy of the Golfer's Guide for a handy introduction to most of the courses (and perhaps some new clubs at the Watts National Clearance Center just south of Wet 'n Wild on I-Drive; 407 352 2535 **www.edwinwatts.com**). Tee-Times USA (1800 374 8633, **www.teetimesusa.com**) offers excellent advice and a reservation service. Visit Florida has its own golf section at **www.visitflorida.com/golf**.

Local golf pro (and *Brit Guide* friend) Chad Czarnecki recommends the website **www.golfnow.com** as a great source of tee times all over Central Florida, and usually at reduced rates. Then you can take your pick from the following representative selection:

Walt Disney World: Quick to attract the golf fanatic, Disney has three high-quality courses, including the 7,000yd/6,400m Palm, rated by Golf Digest in its top 25 (the 18th hole is reputedly one of the toughest in America), plus a nine-hole par-36 course, Oak Trail. Fees are $45–120 for Disney resort guests and $45–160 for visitors ($38 at Oak Trail) varying seasonally, with a third off Twilight Rate. Call 407 938 4653 for tee-times. Private and group lessons are available under PGA pro guidance, with video analysis and club rentals. Former Disney course Osprey Ridge is now part of the magnificent Four Seasons Resort.

BRITTIP
Some of the best tee-times at Walt Disney World golf courses are reserved for those staying at a Disney resort.

Champions Gate: Challenging and eye-catching, the two magnificent Greg Norman-designed courses to the south of Disney (exit 58 off I-4) are the International (a British-style links course) and the National (a more traditional style). The practice facilities, clubhouse, service and coaching (at the HQ of the renowned David Leadbetter Academy) are world class, and there are stay-and-play packages with the superb Omni Orlando Resort; $45–142 (407 787 4653, **www.championsgategolf.com**).

Dubsdread: The oldest public course in Orlando and the only municipal one, just east of the city centre, this offers a testing 18 holes ($30–54) featuring narrow fairways and 'postage stamp' greens. It offers a beautiful clubhouse, restaurant and pub, where the likes of Sam Snead and Ben Hogan rubbed shoulders in the past. They also have a free shuttle from some area hotels (407 246 2551, **www.historicaldubsdread.com**).

BRITTIP
Visit Dubsdread Golf Course and be sure to spend some time in The Tap Room, their speciality bar and restaurant, with a great setting for a memorable meal or just a beer and a burger.

Falcon's Fire: An outstanding course in Kissimmee, featuring the ProShot digital caddy system carts. Plenty of water around the course assures a testing 18 holes, but it is highly picturesque. $44–119 (407 239 5445, **www.falconsfire.com**).

Grande Lakes Orlando: This wonderful resort complex just off John Young Parkway is a Greg Norman masterpiece, offering 18 holes of Florida nature with a caddie-concierge service; $86–215 (407 393 4900, **www.grandelakes.com**).

Hawk's Landing: At the Orlando World Center Marriott, this beautiful course boasts extensive practice facilities, a superb shop, resort exclusivity and the world-class teaching of Bill Madonna's Golf Academy: $55–89 (407 238 8660, **www.marriottworldcenter.com**).

Hollywood Drive-in Golf

Hyatt Grand Cypress: A luxury experience on Winter Garden-Vineland Road ($150–175) with 3 elegant 9-hole courses and a superb 18-hole links-style offering, all designed by Jack Nicklaus; $120–150 (407 239 4700; **http://www.grandcypress. com/golf_club/**).

Kissimmee Oaks: Some majestic moss-draped oaks as well as 18 holes of memorable lakeside golf, all just 3½ml/6km south of Highway 192 in the Oaks Community off John Young Parkway $15–50 (407 930 4710, **www.kissimmeeoaksgolf.com**).

Legends Golf & Country Club: Just 25mins from Disney on Highway 27 towards Clermont, this has a pleasant layout with unusually rolling hills in a peaceful location; $20–43 (352 243 1118, **www.legendsgolforlando.com**).

Mystic Dunes: Just off Highway 192 near the Disney entrance, this course winds through native oaks and is a real test. There's a wonderful menu at the clubhouse, plus the latest equipment; $35–67 (407 787 5678; **www.mysticdunesgolf.com**).

Orange Lake Country Club: Massive vacation resort 4ml/6km from Disney offers 2 18-hole, a 9-hole and a rare par-3 floodlit 9; $30–109 (407 239 0000; **www.experienceorangelake.com/ golf**).

Shingle Creek: Arguably the cream of the crop is this world-class facility at the 5-star hotel, designed by top local architect Dave Harman and set among beautiful oaks and pines. It also boasts the superb Brad Brewer Golf Academy, which offers genuine state-of-the-art technology for novices and pros alike and is a real pleasure to spend time at; $39–149 (407 996 9933, **www.shinglecreekgolf. com** and **www.bradbrewer.com**). There are many offers. Be sure to ask if fees are negotiable, as they can be lower at quiet times of the year. There are often reductions for seniors but check the dress code, as they can vary. Typically, you need a collared shirt, Bermuda shorts and no denim.

Fans: For those just looking to see the stars in action, Orlando has a big annual event, the Arnold Palmer Invitational at the Bay Hill Club off Apopka-Vineland Road in west Orlando. Held each March, it is a major tournament on the US PGA tour, with Tiger Woods, Phil Mickelson and Justin Rose all playing in recent years (407 876 2888, **www. arnoldpalmerinvitational.com**). The Players Championship is also held at TPC Sawgrass in Ponte Vedra Beach each May, just a couple of hours from Orlando (**www.tpc.com/tpc-sawgrass**).

Mini-golf

Not exactly a sport, but Orlando's many extravagant mini-golf centres are a big hit. Several attractions and parks offer mini-golf as an extra, but for the best try the self-contained centres.

Disney's Fantasia Gardens: Next to the Swan Hotel just off Buena Vista Drive is a two-course challenge over 36 of the most varied holes of mini-golf. The style is taken from the classic film Fantasia. Fantasia Fairways is a cunning putting course, complete with rough, water hazards and bunkers. 18 holes can take more than an hour ($14 adults, $12 children, 10am–11pm daily).

Winter-Summerland Mini-Golf: At the entrance to Blizzard Beach and divided into two 18-hole courses, these mini works of art feature a 'summer' setting of surf and beach tests and a 'winter' variety of snow and ice-crafted holes. An adult round is $14 ($12 3–9s), a double round is half price (10am–11pm; Blizzard Beach admission not required).

Universal's Hollywood Drive-In Golf: This imaginative twin 18-hole set-up is at the entrance to Universal's CityWalk. The two sides are The Haunting of Ghostly Greens, a 1950s mock-horror themed selection that includes putting through a cemetery and a giant spider's lair, concluding in the basement lab of a haunted house, and Invaders From The Planet Putt, 18 holes of best sci-fi humour that feature an alien spaceship and a 30ft/9m robot. There are also special effects, surprises (you may get a little wet!), atmospheric music and a riot of visual gags. And, while it looks good during the day it positively sparkles at night under its LED lighting system. It also stays open long after the theme parks have closed, hence is ideal for saving for late in the day. Open 9am–2am daily, it costs $15 for adults, $13 (3–9s) for 18 holes, or $28 and $24 for both courses (9am–2am; 407 802 4848, **www.hollywooddriveingolf.com**).

International Drive: Mini-golf is a staple of the scene here, with no fewer than six courses in the vicinity (and be sure to see their websites for valuable discount coupons). Check out the 18-hole Congo River in front of the Four Points by Sheraton Orlando Studio City Hotel ($13 adults, $11 under-10; **www.congoriver. com**; 10am–11pm Sun–Thurs, 10am– midnight Fri and Sat); Hawaiian Rumble's 36 holes by WonderWorks on I-Drive (and in Lake Buena Vista on Apopka-Vineland Ave) 9am– 11.30pm Sun–Thurs, 9am–midnight Fri and Sat; $9.95 for 18 holes, $11.95 for 36; **www.hawaiianrumbleorlando. com**); **Pirates Cove** remains the original and most imaginative I-Drive set-up, with a whole Pirate 'village' at its entrance (including mock tavern, blacksmiths and bakery), while the eye-catching courses include caves, waterfalls and rope bridges to test your skill over twin 18-hole challenges (the Captain's Course and harder Blackbeard's Challenge; 9am– 11.30pm daily; $12.50 adults, $11.50 4–12s, or $20.50 and $18.95 for all 36; **www.piratescove.net/orlando**). There is another (unconnected) Pirates Cove set-up at Lake Buena Vista at the back of the Crossroads shopping plaza. The unique Putting Edge has indoor glow-in-the-dark mini-golf at Artegon Orlando (10am–9pm Mon 11am–9pm Tues–Thurs, 11am–11pm Fri–Sat, 11am–7pm Sun; $10.50 adults, $8.50 under-13s; unlimited play $2 extra) while Volcano Island adds two more 18-hole layouts, including a tricky par 45 (11am–11pm; $12.95 adults, $11.95 under 18s, **http:// volcanoislandgolforlando.com**). Finally, the extensive Gator Golf & Adventure Park is just past Carrier Drive, next to Murphy's Arms Pub. With a variety of gator shows daily, you can sink your teeth into some challenging mini-golf (admission to park $5; golf $9.99 adults, $7.99 3–11s; gator photos, feeding and handling for additional fees; **www.idrivegatorgolf.com**).

Kissimmee: Here you'll find the scenic 36-hole Congo River Golf & Exploration Co set-up on Highway 192 (by Marker 12; $11.99 adults, $9.99 under-10s; 10am–11pm Sun– Thurs, 10am–midnight, Fri–Sat, **www.congoriver.com**); Pirates Cove, a 36-hole course next to Old Town (behind the Red Lobster, between markers 9 and 10); Mighty Jungle Golf, with two African-themed courses on Highway 192 by Formosa Gardens Blvd (10am–10pm Sun–Thurs, 11pm Fri & Sat; $9.95 adults, $8.95 under 12s; $2 extra for 2nd 18 holes); and Pirates Island Adventure Golf, off Highway 192 between marker 14 and 15 ($11.50 adults, $9 4–12s).

Freshwater fishing
Freshwater fishing on central Florida's abundant rivers and lakes attracts enthusiasts worldwide. The primary draw is the chance to catch giant Florida bass – which grow to record sizes in the area's grassy waters – and view some of the wildlife in its natural environment.

Florida Freshwater Fishing License: To fish here you need to get this from the Florida Fish and Wildlife Commission (**http://myfwc.com/license/ recreational/freshwater-fishing/** with a credit card). You'll be issued with a temporary licence number within minutes, enabling you to fish right

Congo River mini-golf

away. A permanent licence will be mailed within 48 hours. A 3-day licence costs $17, 7-day $30. It's advisable to book at least two weeks in advance, especially at peak periods.

AJ's Freelancer Bass Guide Service: This long-running company specialises in trophy bass fishing on Lake Toho in Kissimmee. Toho is rated the best big bass lake in the USA, and AJ's holds the record for largemouth bass – 16lb 10oz/7.5kg! Saltwater trips are also offered. All guides are experienced, full-time professionals and run trips of 4–8 hours. Rates start at $250 for a 4hr guided trip, max three clients per boat ($50 for 3rd person; 12 and under free). Visit the excellent website at **www.orlandobass. com** or call 407 288 9670.

Ultimate Guide Service: Another personal guide and fishing service with 36 years' experience and with trophy bass the principal aim, this is led by Captain Jim Passmore and is great for novices and even better for those seeking a real challenge. It makes for a superb day or half day and their attitude is notably one of low environmental impact. It costs $275 for 4 hours of fishing for one or two anglers, $325 for 6 hours or $375 for 8hrs (extra person $50), excluding fishing licence and lunch (407 572 5391, **www.fishcentralfla.com**).

Go bass fishing (catch-and-release) at Walt Disney World for $235–$270 for two hours for a boat with 1–5 people. It's advisable to book 24 hours in advance on 407 939 2277. For other opportunities, see **www. experiencekissimmee.com**, click Things To Do, then Nature, then Fishing & Charters.

Kayaking in Seminole County

Water sports

Florida is mad keen on water sports so, on any area of water bigger than your average pond, don't be surprised to find the locals water-skiing, jetskiing, knee-boarding, canoeing, paddling, windsurfing, boating or indulging in many other watery pursuits.

Buena Vista Watersports: This is the place for jet-skiing ($60/30 min, $105/hr; seats two adults and one child), water-skiing, wakeboard and tube rides ($55/15 min, $95/30min, $165/hour), plus rent pontoon boats, canoes, kayaks and stand-up paddle-boards ($25–175) on Little Lake Bryan by the Holiday Inn Sunspree on Highway 535 (407 239 6939, **www.bvwatersports.com**).

Orlando Watersports Complex: Just off the Beachline Expressway (528) near Orlando International Airport, this is an elaborate facility featuring wake-boarding and water-skiing, by boat and suspended cable, for novices and experts (407 251 3100, **www.aktionparks.com**).

Walt Disney World: Disney offers all manner of boats (from catamarans to canoes and pedaloes) and activities (from water-skiing to parasailing) on Bay Lake, as well as the smaller Seven Seas Lagoon, Crescent Lake and Lake Buena Vista. Parasailing (from Disney's Contemporary Resort, p62) comes in two price categories: a Regular flight, which goes to 450ft/137m for 8–10 mins, and a Premium flight to 600ft/183m for 10–12mins. It costs $95–130 solo or $170–195 tandem, while boat rentals vary from $45/30mins (21ft/6m pontoon boat) to $135/hour (personal watercraft and wave runners), and can be found at 11 Disney resorts. To book, call 407 939 0754.

Spectator events

When it comes to spectator events, Orlando isn't as well furnished as some cities, but there's always something for those who'd like to see a local game – and a real bonus for footy fans. There are no top-flight

American football or baseball teams, but there is an indoor version of gridiron called Arena Football (the Orlando Predators at the Amway Center), plus Spring Training (pre-season) for several baseball teams (Atlanta in Disney's ESPN Wide World of Sports™ and Houston at Osceola County Stadium in Kissimmee).

Basketball: This is the main sport in town, with the Orlando Magic of the National Basketball Association (NBA). The season runs Nov–May (with exhibition games in Oct), and the only drawback is the 18,500-seat Amway Center where the team plays (on W Church Street, exit 82B off I-4) can be fully booked. Contact the Magic (407 896 2442, **www.orlandomagic.com**) to see if there are any tickets, but you'll have to call in person to buy them (from $15 in upper seats to over $1,500 courtside), or try the excellent ticket resale company StubHub (**www.stubhub.com** or 1866 788 2482). *Brit Guide* partners Florida Dolphin Tours (p265) also offer Magic packages.

◀▶ BRITTIP
We rate the local sports highly if you want to experience some real Americana. You don't need to understand the game, just turn up and enjoy the excitement and fan-friendly atmosphere. Sports are a family event here.

American football: For the real thing, the nearest teams in the National Football League (NFL) are Tampa Bay Buccaneers, 75ml/120km to the west, Miami Dolphins, 3–4 hours' drive south down the Florida Turnpike, or Jacksonville Jaguars up on the east coast past Daytona, a 3-hr drive on I-4 and I-95. Again, StubHub can usually give you ticket prices ($40–150) and availability (Sept–Dec).

For spring training each March, Osceola County Stadium for the Houston Astros is a real experience in local colour. Book online at **www.osceolastadium.com**, or TicketMaster (**www.ticketmaster.com**). However, the best opportunity is to head to St Petersburg on the Gulf Coast where

the Tampa Bay Rays play at indoor Tropicana Field (Apr–Sept). Tickets are nearly always available and the indoor stadium is superb (p281).

Orlando City Soccer Club: Orlando now has its own fully-fledged Major League Soccer team, playing Mar-Oct at the 65,000-seat Citrus Bowl in downtown Orlando (until its own purpose-built stadium is completed later in 2016). They have built up a passionate and loyal following and their games have become THE big sporting event in town, with a fabulous atmosphere, tail-gating (a huge car park party) and live music several hours before kick-off. Ticket prices vary from $25–130 and are readily available at the huge Citrus Bowl. However, once they make the move to their own arena, capacity will be limited and booking well in advance will be essential. And, if you already follow a team, you need to make 'The Lions' your No.2 club! (1855 675 2489, **www.orlandocitysc.com**).

ESPN Wide World of Sports™

Disney's big sports development is an impressive 220acre/86ha state-of-the-art complex, featuring 30 sports. It boasts a 9,500-seat baseball stadium, softball quadraplex, 10-court tennis complex, 5,000-seat indoor facility, athletics and extensive sports fields.

The Ballpark: Top of the crop for a must-see visit, this is home for spring training of baseball's Atlanta Braves, where the crowds flock for 16 pre-season games late Feb–late Mar (advance tickets highly recommended; individual tickets from Ticketmaster or the box office only). This is a big deal for American sports fans and games do sell out. The centre's extensive fields also cater for soccer, lacrosse, baseball and softball, and you can often see some keen sporting action just with college and school teams. Disney's Soccer Showcase (Sept–Jan) is a fine example of this, with some 400 skilful teams competing under the eye of various scouts. Standard admission is

$17 adults, $12 3–9s, but it is also an option with Premium and Ultimate tickets (excluding special events like baseball). ESPN Wide World of Sports™ is off Osceola Parkway, on Victory Way (**www.espnwwos.com**).

Disney Soccer Academy: This series of four-day training camps in Jun/Jul is for children 5–18, and focuses on age-appropriate coaching and technical development, small-sided games and encouragement from the stars. It costs $400/child and includes tuition by fully licensed coaches, an event T-shirt, special gift and lunch daily, plus appearances from British stars each year (1877 714 5575 or **www.midwestsoccer.net**).

Walt Disney World Marathon: A major annual event, its 17th running will be on 10 Jan 2016. Some 55,000 runners take part – including some of the world's leading athletes – drawing huge crowds and taking in all four Disney theme parks. Be aware the parks face some serious disruption but, as with the London Marathon, the Disney version is a great spectacle. The annual half-marathon takes place the same weekend.

Rodeo

An all-American pursuit straight out of the Old West, the **Silver Spurs Rodeo** is staged twice a year at the 8,300-seat Silver Spurs Arena. The biggest event of its kind in the southeast, it is held in Feb and early June (check website for dates). However, it sells out fast so book in advance on 321 697 3495 (**www.silverspursrodeo.com**). The event features classic bronco and bull riding and attracts competitors from as far as Canada. The arena is part of Osceola Heritage Park, which includes Osceola County

Stadium (for baseball) and the Kissimmee Valley Livestock Show and Fair Pavilion. The Arena is a state-of-the-art facility and there isn't a bad seat in the house. There is also a weekly Saturday Night Rodeo at **Westgate River Ranch** (p260).

Motor sport

The Richard Petty Driving Experience has closed at Walt Disney World but is still available at **Daytona International Speedway** (take I-4 east, then I-95 and Highway 92), where race fans will find some big-league thrills. The renowned Speedway hosts more than a dozen events a year, including motor-bike, stock car, sports car and go-karts. Highlights are the **Rolex 24** (a 24hr sports car event, late Jan), the famous **Daytona 500** (Feb), and **Coke Zero 400** (early July). The big events attract crowds of 200,000-plus and offer exhilarating sport. Or just try the 1hr **All Access Track Tour**, daily on the hour from 10am–3pm ($23 adults, $17 6–12s, under-6s free) and a ½hr Speedway Tour at 11.30am, 1.30pm, 3.30pm and 4pm ($16 and $10). There is even a special **VIP Tour** on specific dates (see website) at $50/person. Fascinating and fun, even for non-race fans! (800 748 7467, **www.daytonainternationalspeedway.com**). The **Richard Petty Driving Experience** is a great opportunity to sample the thrills of NASCAR racing first hand, either as passenger or driver, with a range of different on-track experiences. It costs $109/person for the high-speed, 3-lap Ride-Along (age 14 and up, under 18 must be accompanied by an adult); $69 for Junior Ride Along (6–13s); $549 for 3hr Rookie Experience (tuition plus 8 laps of the Speedway); $849 for Kings Experience (tuition plus 18 laps); $1,299 for the Experience of a Lifetime (an intense 30-lap programme) and $2,199 for Speedway Challenge (50 laps). You must be 18 or over for all but the Ride-Along (1800 237 3889, **www.drivepetty.com**).

OK, that's the local area sorted out; now let's take you further afield…

Richard Petty Driving Experience

9 The Twin Centre Option

or To Orlando – and Beyond!

While Orlando continues to get bigger and better, it is equally true there is a LOT more to see in the rest of Florida, with some magnificent twin-centre options. From St Augustine in the north-east to Key West in the extreme south (the 'Floribbean'), it's easy to find wonderful resorts, glorious beaches and more family attractions.

The beaches of the Gulf (west) coast, the Atlantic coast from Ormond Beach all the way to Miami, and the fabulous Florida Keys all feature some of the best seaside escapes in the world, while cities like West Palm Beach, Daytona, St Augustine, Fort Lauderdale, Tampa, Miami and Key West provide more Sunshine State fascination. Two-centre (or fly-drive) options are common with most tour operators, but it is also easy to arrange your own, for 1 or 2 weeks or just a night. A cruise-and-stay holiday is also a great choice, with the ports of Tampa, Port Canaveral, Fort Lauderdale and Miami within easy reach.

You can head out from Orlando in any direction in search of a great twin-centre experience. Go East to Cocoa Beach, New Smyrna Beach, Ormond Beach and Daytona Beach, all with terrific appeal and barely an hour's drive away; the sea is a degree or so cooler on the Atlantic side, and the surf and currents are more noticeable, hence this is good surfing territory, but beware possible undertows if you are travelling with children. To the north-east you have historic St Augustine about 2hrs away. To the north-west is the growing resort area of Panama City Beach. Go West for the city of Tampa and miles of pristine sands, from Clearwater Beach south to Naples and lovely Marco Island; this is better for families with younger children, while the Clearwater-St Pete Beach area is a perfect combo with Orlando (about 1½–2hrs' drive). Go South-East and you hit Vero Beach, West Palm Beach, Fort Lauderdale and Miami (about a 3½hr drive). Continue South and there are the Keys, a superb 110ml/177km chain of islands linked by roads and bridges, culminating in eclectic Key West. So, heading north-east first, here's what you find.

BRITTIP
The Florida Turnpike (toll) is the main route south-east from Orlando, but it is a dull drive. If time is not a factor, take the Beachline Expressway (528) east and then I-95 or, better still, Highway 1, south for a more rewarding journey. Or go south on Highway 27 and take in the charming town of Sebring.

St Augustine
A 2hr drive up I-4 and I-95 brings you to America's oldest city. Founded by Spanish conquistadors in 1565, St Augustine is full of authentic

buildings and signs of the original settlement around the imposing Castillo de San Marcos. Much of the original walled city still remains and 'old' is a much-revered term here, as 18th and 19th-century Mediterranean influences are everywhere. Walk the narrow, uneven streets of the Restoration Area to discover colonial architectural treasures, now home to gift shops, restaurants, pubs, ice-cream parlours, antique shops, quaint B&Bs and other attractions.

BRITTIP
Spanish adventurer Ponce de Leon was searching for the Fountain of Youth when he arrived at the site of St Augustine in 1513. The modern day **Archaeological Park** tells the story of his arrival and discovery of the continent of America – and offers the chance to drink the famous waters. Visit **www.fountainofyouthflorida.com**.

Tours: To see as much as possible, hop on a horse-drawn carriage, the **St Augustine Sightseeing Train** or the **Old Town Trolley Tours** for a narrated tour. For a spookier experience, walk the streets with **Ghost Tours of St Augustine**, with your guide in period costume. Other tours reveal the architectural heritage (also the product of British and colonial American rule).

Other attractions: Florida railway mogul Henry Flagler was another big influence, building some magnificent hotels for his 'passengers to paradise'. The ornate **Lightner Museum**, formerly Flagler's Hotel Alcazar, is home to his turn-of-the-century treasures, including Tiffany and other glass works of art. There's a modern theatre, art galleries, **Potter's Wax Museum**, **Ripley's Believe It Or Not Museum** and **Whetstone Chocolates Factory**. New in 2014 was the **St Augustine Distillery**, a chance to tour a working small-batch premium distillery and learn the history of the converted ice factory (free tours daily, 10am–6pm Mon–Sat, 11am Sun; **http://staugustinedistillery.com/**).

Restaurants: These range from **Hot Shot Bakery** and the famous, family-owned **Columbia Restaurant**, to a modern microbrewery, **A1A Ale Works**. Golf fans should visit nearby Ponte Vedra for the **World Golf Hall of Fame**.

Where to stay: The premier hotel is historic **Casa Monica** (904 827 1888, **www.casamonica.com**), while the boutique **St George Inn** (904 827 5740; **www.stgeorge-inn.com**) is also a good choice, but there are numerous B&Bs, plus chain hotels like Best Western and Hampton Inn.

BRITTIP
Festivals are an integral part of St Augustine, from monthly art walk nights to annual costumed torchlight re-enactments of British occupation and the City Birthday on 8 Sept.

More info: St Augustine Visitors & Convention Bureau (1800 653 2489 or **www.floridashistoriccoast.com**).

Volusia County

Travel south from St Augustine and you arrive in this famous beach area.

BRITTIP
Look out for Speeding Through Time, a series of memorials and plaques along Daytona's Boardwalk, highlighting the world speed records set on the beaches, including those of Britons Sir Henry Segrave and Sir Malcolm Campbell.

Daytona Beach: Only an hour from Orlando along I-4 east, this area now includes some chic hotels and restaurants, but is still family friendly. It is busiest in summer (mid-June to mid-Aug) but there is something for everyone, especially in the quieter period after Easter when there are often some good deals. The prime attraction is the good beaches (some of which you can drive on – for a $10 toll, speed limit 10mph/16kph). From these open expanses of sands, you can go boating, parasailing, biking, jet-skiing and fishing. Stay in the Oceanfront area and you are at the heart of all things beach-related, with the Pier – now including the huge Sand Blaster rollercoaster – historic Bandshell, Boardwalk and the shops and restaurants of **Ocean Walk Village**.

Ocean Walk Village: Here you have **RC Theatres' Ocean Walk Movies 10 Cineplex**, the fun of the **Mai Tai Bar**, **Johnny Rockets Diner**, **Cold Stone Creamery**, **Starbucks**, **Santora's Buffalo Pizza & Wing Est** and unique shopping at **Maui Nix Surf Shop**, **Daytona Beach Candle Gallery**, **Bath Junkie** and **Sunglass Hut**. When you're hungry, try the film-themed style of **Bubba Gump Shrimp Co** (based on the movie *Forrest Gump*). With fun decor, wonderfully casual vibe and an excellent menu, it is ideal for a quick lunch or leisurely dinner (**www.bubbagump.com** and **www.oceanwalkshoppes.com**).

BRITTIP
Spend the day on Daytona Beach, then try some water park fun at Daytona Lagoon after 3pm, when admission is only $12.99.

Daytona Lagoon: Opposite Ocean Walk Village, this is a combination water park, go-kart track, mini-golf course, arcade and laser tag centre. The water park has a wave pool and lazy river, seven different flumes and an area purely for toddlers (adults $27.99, children under 3ft 6in/108cm $20.99). The 18-hole mini-golf course ($7), single and double go-karts ($8–10), laser tag (must be above 3ft 6in/108cm, $7), Island Hopper kiddie ride ($3.49) and Rock Wall ($7) are all separate items. See more at **www.daytonalagoon.com**.

Historic Downtown Daytona Beach: The heart of the city is on Beach Street, with a museum of local history, restaurants, nightclubs, coffee bars and a performing arts theatre. **The Angell & Phelps Chocolate Factory** (established 1925, **www.angellandphelps.com**) is another notable curiosity. Head to the Riverfront in early evening when the street takes on a café society style.

There are plenty of good places to eat, but for something different try the lively **Caribbean Jack's** (right on the river at Ballough Road) or chic **Chez Paul** (on N Beach St with a view of the Halifax River). Similar upmarket choices are **Martini's Chophouse Restaurant** (on S Ridgewood Avenue) and the fine Italian dining of **The Cellar** (on Magnolia Avenue). **Vince Carter's** (on LPGA Blvd, co-owned by the basketball star) is another smart choice, with a chic Dining Room, eye-catching Highlight Zone Sports Grill and relaxing Piano Lounge (**http://vincecarters.com**).

Other highlights: Taking **The Manatee scenic river voyage** out of Ponce Inlet is a great choice. Their leisurely 2hr tours go year-round at 10am, 1 and 4pm, plus a 7pm Sunset Cruise Jun–Sept (on Inlet Harbor Rd; $25 for adults, $22 seniors, $16 children; reservations required on 386 761 2027, or **www.manateecruise.com**). Go south on Atlantic Avenue and you find even more choice of beaches and attractions, including **Sun Splash Beach**, **Frank Rendon Park** and **Lighthouse Point Park**, a 52acre/21ha stretch of nature trails, fishing, observation deck, swimming and picnicking (8am–9pm; $5/car). The tide here can retreat up to 500ft/150m and the beaches, open to the public year-round, tend to be quieter, though there can be some serious rip-tides. At the southern end of the beaches is the wonderful **Ponce de Leon Inlet Lighthouse**, with a formidable 203 spiralling steps to the top. This well-preserved monument is a magnificent re-creation of 19th-century Florida maritime life and the view from the top of America's second tallest lighthouse is superb (10am–6pm, 9pm Jun–Aug; $5 adults, $1.50 under-12s; **http://ponceinlet.org/**). It also has a lovely gift shop. Ponce Inlet has some great deep-sea fishing, too – see **www.inletharbor.com**.

BRITTIP
Try a meal at the Hidden Treasure Rum Bar & Grill at Ponce Inlet for an eclectic Floridian experience.

Marine Science Center: More family-orientated fun can be found round the corner from the lighthouse, showcasing mangrove, manatee and sea turtle exhibits, a seabird sanctuary and turtle rehab facility. It has a huge artificial reef aquarium, plus static and interactive educational displays. A boardwalk and nature trail extend through the Center, which also has a gift shop (10am–4pm Tues–Sat, noon–4pm Sun, closed Mon; $5 adults, $4 seniors, $2 under-13s; http://marinesciencecenter.com/).

Daytona Speedway: Of course, this is one of the biggest draws (p272), with two great tours of this amazing facility that is undergoing a $400m renovation.

Three Brothers Boards: This family-run business of handcrafted stand-up paddleboards offers tours and rentals on the beautiful Halifax River, with its plentiful wildlife. Choose from the two-hour Dolphin & Manatee Adventure or the Nature Tour through mangrove trails and bird sanctuaries. You may even be inspired to try paddleboard yoga! Call 386 310 4927 or visit http://threebrothersboards.com.

New Smyrna Beach: Continue south on Highway 1 to this fabulous 13ml/20km stretch of pristine white sands with great surfing, shell collecting and boating at any of the many marinas. New Smyrna Beach is also a big festival destination, notably for the **Shrimp & Seafood Festival** each August and the **Jazz Festival** over a weekend in late Sept. Other highlights include the shopping and dining of historic and pedestrian-friendly Canal Street, with a farmers'

market each Saturday (7am–1pm, www.canalstreetnsb.com), more unique shops and galleries along Flagler Avenue (www.flaglerave.com), the kid-friendly **Marine Discovery Center** and the **Atlantic Center for the Arts**. For dining, don't miss **The Garlic**, with outdoor seating under huge oaks (386 428 1600, http://nsbfla.com/).

Where to stay: You'll find some of our favourite resorts in Daytona Beach, plus a variety of Select Small Inns (www.daytonabeach.com/hotels/select-small-inns/). The **Wyndham Ocean Walk Resort** is a huge ultra-modern complex right on the beach at Ocean Walk Village, with versatile 1, 2 and 3-bed condos (all with kitchens and fab views). With three outdoor pools, waterslide and lazy river, plus a kids' water play area, two indoor pools, indoor mini-golf, kids' programmes, spa and an excellent lounge and food court, it is hugely family-friendly (386 323 4800, www.wyndhamoceanwalk.com). The nearby **Hilton Daytona Beach Oceanfront Resort** is another large, recently renovated hotel with wonderfully spacious rooms, beachfront cabañas and suites, plus a terrific dining choice (notably Hyde Park Prime Steakhouse), two pools and a modern fitness centre (386 254 8200, www.daytonahilton.com). **Shores Resort & Spa** is a boutique choice on a quieter stretch of the beaches, (386 767 7350, www.shoresresort.com), while the 10-storey oceanfront **Hyatt Place** is also a chic choice with its spacious family rooms (386 944 2010, http://daytonabeach.place.hyatt.com). Try **Flamingo Inn** for a great example of the Small Inns of Daytona Beach. With a tranquil oceanfront setting, heated free-form pool, tropical Key West styling and some rooms with kitchenettes (and all with fridges), it is a real boutique bargain here (386 252 7212, www.daytonamotel.com).

More info: 01737 643 764 in the UK, 386 255 0415 in the US or visit www.daytonabeach.com.

Ormond Beach: Immediately to the north is another happening area with more smart resorts and beaches, notably at **Bicentennial Park** (with a

Merritt Island

Breakfast with a difference!

Just north of DeLand in DeLeon Springs State Park is the unique **Old Spanish Sugar Mill** grill and griddle house, one of Florida's little restaurant treasures. Famous for hearty cook-it-yourself breakfasts (9am–4pm; 8am at weekends), each table has an inset griddle, and you choose your ingredients and get cracking. Its speciality is pancakes (pitchers of batter provided), with all manner of fillings, but it also has bacon, eggs, ham, sausage, home-made breads, French toast, sandwiches and salads. You'll struggle to pay more than $10/person and it's great fun, as well as a local institution. However, as it is inside the State Park, there is a $6/car entry fee (386 985 5644, **www.planetdeland.com/sugarmill**). You can then try the park facilities, which include canoes, kayaks, hiking trails and boat tours (**www.floridastateparks.org**).

nature walk, playground and fishing dock) and **Birthplace of Speed Park** (commemorating the first automobile race on the beach here in 1903). Don't miss **The Casements**, the restored former **Rockefeller House and Gardens**, with free tours twice a day Mon–Sat (**www.thecasements.net**). And, for a different shopping experience, **Dunn's Attic & Auction House** takes some beating (**www.dunnsattic.com**). Stop for a meal at the fun **Lulu's Oceanside Grill** with a wonderful seafood-laden menu, great cocktails and a great weekend brunch, **www.lulusoceansidegrill.com**). Or sample the chic **Fusion 43** (**www.fusion43.com**) or the eclectic **Grind Gastropub & Kona Tiki Bar** (**www.grindgastropub.com**).

The Space Coast

Further south on the Atlantic seaboard is the 'Space Coast', home to the iconic Kennedy Space Center (p215).

BRITTIP
For good info on all Kennedy Space Center rocket launches, especially good public viewing locations, see **www.visitspacecoast.com/launch-schedule/**.

Cocoa Beach: Closest to Orlando, barely 50mins east (on the Beachline Expressway 528, then south on Highway A1A), this area has two excellent public beaches plus trademark shopping at Ron Jon's Surf Shop, a massive neon emporium of all things water related. As it's the Atlantic, the sea can be chilly Nov–Apr, but its resort style ensures good facilities (**www.cocoabeach.com**). If you haven't tried an airboat ride by now, you should definitely head for **Midway Airboats** on the nearby St John River (daily from 9am; 407 568 6790, **www.airboatridesatmidway.com/**), and don't forget **Island Boat Lines** (p263).

Cocoa Village: This little town in the intracoastal waterway just inland from Cocoa beach offers a fun array of shopping and dining, with some original boutiques, the historic Cocoa Village Playhouse and two of our favourite restaurants on the coast (**http://visitcocoavillage.com/**). For casual dining, try **Murdock's Southern Bistro & Bar** (**www.murdocksincocoavillage.com/**) while **Crush Eleven** is a wonderfully chic and stylish option with a wonderfully creative cocktail list and menu (**www.crusheleven.com**).

Titusville: Head here for attractions like the US Space Walk of Fame (a river walk with displays of memorabilia, plaques and public art depicting America's history in space), **Merritt Island National Wildlife Refuge** (a 6ml/9km driving tour adjacent to the Kennedy Space Center) and the fascinating and rather moving **American Police Hall of Fame & Museum**, with all you ever wanted to know about the history of crime and law enforcement, and a tribute to police officers who have died in the line of duty (see **www.aphf.org** for $3 off coupon). For great dining, **Dixie Crossroads** is a local institution for great Florida seafood (**www.dixiecrossroads.com**).

Aviation fans will enjoy the **Valiant Air Command Warbird Museum**, with dozens of vintage warplanes and fully guided tours through the exhibits and history of military aviation, as well as their dedicated restoration programme (**www.vacwarbirds.net**). Look out especially for the 3-day **Warbird Air Show** here in Mar.

BRITTIP

For something truly unique, Valiant Air Command Warbird Museum now offers periodic flights on its beautifully restored vintage WWII C-47 paratroop transport plane for $175/person. Call 321 268 1941 or email vacwarbirds@bellsouth. net for full details and availability.

Melbourne: Family-friendly **Brevard Zoo** is well worth a visit here, with almost 500 animals in five themed areas, including the excellent Cheetah Complex in the Expedition Africa exhibit. Other highlights include Australasia, La Selva (South America), Wild Florida and Paws On Play, where children can enjoy water play, and the new Meerkat Hamlet (9.30am–5pm; $17 adults, $16 seniors, $13 2–12s; 321 254 9453, **https://brevardzoo.org/**).

BRITTIP

For top value at Brevard Zoo, consider a Young Explorer's Package (admission, train ride, giraffe and lorikeet feeding at $20.95, $19.95 and $16.95) or Wild Explorer's version (a choice of kayaking in Wild Florida or Expedition Africa, plus giraffe and lorikeet feeding at $24.95, $23.95 and $20.95).

Where to stay: Try lively, surf-themed **Four Points by Sheraton Cocoa Beach** (321 783 8717, **www.fourpointscocoabeach.com**) or **International Palms Resort** (321 783 2271, **www.internationalpalms.com**). **More info:** 321 433 4470 or **www.space-coast.com**.

Panama City Beach

For one of Florida's hidden gems (albeit not during the pre-Easter Spring Break holiday when it is Party

Central!), head north-west to the 'Panhandle' area and this charming and nature-based stretch of coastline that offers fabulous sightseeing, nature tours and downhome local style. It is a long drive, but you can also fly there for a short-break option and it is blissful from mid-Aug to late Oct. **St Andrews** and **Camp Helen State Parks** are natural wonderlands, and you can see it all via helicopter tours, sunset cruises, paddleboarding, kayaking, snorkelling and hiking. **Gulf World Marine Park** is a local institution and the sea hereabouts is often full of dolphins, turtles, rays, tarpon and even the occasional shark. Dining is full of one-off opportunities, notably the organic style of **Bridge Span 14** (**www.bridgespan14. com**), the fun beachfront vibe of **Barefoot Hide-A-Way Grill** (**http:// barefoothideawaygrill.com/**), the elegant chic of **Firefly** (**http://fireflypcb.com/**), and local seafood specialities of **Capt Anderson's** (**www.captanderson.com**).

Where to stay: The modern condo-style resorts of the **Tidewater Beach Resort**, with 1, 2 and 3-bed apartments (850 636 8000, **www. wyndhamvacationrentals.com**) and the superbly equipped **Edgewater Beach Resort** (855 874 8686, **www. edgewaterbeachresort.com**) are both worth trying. **More info:** 1800 722 3224, **www.visitpanamacitybeach.com**.

Tampa

Going west from Orlando brings you down I-4 to the bright city of Tampa, right on a major sea bay and with some excellent attractions of its own (including Busch Gardens, p202).

Dinosaur World: Right on I-4 as you head to Tampa (and a nice stopping point by exit 17) is this family-run attraction ideal for 3–8s. With more than 200 life-sized dinosaurs in a lush, natural setting, plus walking trails, picnic area, playgrounds and gift shop, it makes a good diversion for several hours. There are no rides, but there are various life-size animatronic set-pieces – including a triceratops and pterodactyl – along with a Prehistoric Museum featuring authentic fossils from dinosaur eggs to raptor claws and mammoth teeth. The different trails then feature more dino models with explanatory signs, plus a cave-themed video theatre, while the Skeleton Garden features six replica skeletons. There are also two play areas, for under 7s and older children, and an expanded fossil dig with fossils you can take home. The park is totally laid back and a nice change of pace from the main parks. There is no café (just drinks machines), but it does have picnic facilities and there are fast-food locations nearby, including a pizza delivery service (9am–5pm; $16.95 adult, $14.95 seniors, $11.95 3–12s, under-3 free; 813 717 9865, http://dinosaurworld.com/florida/).

Florida Aquarium: In the heart of Tampa is this superb journey into Florida's waterways, coast and deep-sea elements, beautifully presented and ultra child-friendly. It starts with the Wetlands, then moves on to Bays & Beaches (including Sea Turtle Corner), Coral Reef Gallery (with an amazing variety of fish) and Ocean Commotion (interactive touch-screens, videos and podcasts). The outdoor Explore A Shore water-play area adds squirt pools, fountains and pirate ship, plus an excellent tropical-themed Bar & Grill. Other highlights are the daily Penguin Promenade (meet-and-greet a penguin), and Shark Bay, where scuba-certified 15s and older can join the daily dive into the lagoon ($150/person, reservations required on 813 2713 4015). Other extras include a daily 20min non-scuba 'Swim with the fishes' reef swim ($75/person), a two-hour Shark Feeding programme every Sun, a daily 30min Behind The Scenes tour ($12) and Penguins Backstage Pass (a 30min penguin interaction opportunity at $30/person). There's also a daily (weather permitting) Wild Dolphin Cruise on their 130-passenger catamaran, leaving from the aquarium to explore the Bay where more than 500 dolphins live, along with the occasional manatee (9.30am–5pm daily, closed Thanksgiving, Christmas Day; parking $6; $23.95 adults, $20.95 seniors, $18.95 under-12s; with Dolphin Eco-Tour, $49.90, $44.90 and $40.90; 813 273 4000, www.flaquarium.org; also on Tampa CityPass, p281).

BRITTIP
Book tickets online for the Florida Aquarium and save several dollars on their regular prices.

Channelside Bay Plaza: Next door is a centre of shops and restaurants, which is well worth exploring for unique stores like **Lit Cigar Lounge**, **Surf Down Under**, **White House Gear**, **Kingdome** clothing and **Quachbal Chocolatier**, plus great entertainment and dining. Choose from the fun **Fusion Flambe**, **Hooters**, **Oishi Sushi**, **Splitsville** 10-pin bowling (who also own the Splitsville in Disney Springs), lively **Wet Willie's** bar, **Thai Tani** and **Precinct Pizza**, plus **Coldstone Creamery** (great ice-cream and shakes). Like Ybor City, this is where Tampa parties – hence the restaurants and bars, many featuring live music, are hopping at weekends. There's also an **Official Tampa Bay Visitor Center** (www.channelsidebayplaza.com).

Lowry Park Zoo: Rated one of the top zoos in America, this lush 60-scre spread showcases manatees, koalas, elephants, tigers, penguins, giraffes and orangutans among its more than 1,000 animals. Kids will also enjoy the water-play areas, educational shows and even rides, like Gator Falls flume ride and Outback Bumper Boats. There are extensive natural animal habitats and the chance (for a few extra dollars) to interact with some of them, including giraffes and lorikeets (9.30am–5pm; $27.95 adults, $25.95 seniors, $20.95 3–11s; www.lowryparkzoo.com; also on Tampa CityPass, p281). Animal lovers should also make a note of **Big Cat Rescue**, a non-profit park that sets out to rescue various lions, tigers, panthers and more that have been abandoned, ill-treated or retired from various shows. It runs 90min tours and all proceeds go into the care and rehab of the 100-plus animals. Other options include

Feeder, Keeper and Private tours (3pm Mon, Tue, Wed & Fri, 10am & 1pm Sat & Sun, $36/person, over 10s only; Under-10s tour 9am Sat & Sun for $19; other tours $65–125; 1888 316 5875, **http://bigcatrescue.org**).

Museum of Science and Industry: More family fun (especially for 4–12s) can be found at this entertaining science centre, with three floors of educational exhibits, activities and large-screen IMAX films. Highlights include the Kids In Charge science play area (under-13s), The Amazing You (a tour of the human body), Disasterville (an interactive look at natural disasters) and the High-Wire Bicycle (ride a bike on a steel cable 30ft/9m up). Permanent exhibits include Sky Trail Ropes Course (with two ziplines) and The Saunders Planetarium, while the IMAX® Dome Theatre offers a range of films daily and there are periodic travelling exhibits. Outside is the BioWorks Butterfly Garden and the Historic Tree Grove, providing more insight into natural Florida (10am–5pm Mon–Fri, 6pm Sat and Sun; $22.95 adults, $20.95 seniors, $18.95 2–12s, includes Kids in Charge, a standard IMAX film and Planetarium show; additional films $8.95, $7.95 and $6.95; SkyTrail Ropes and Zipline are $20 extra with admission; 813 987 6100, **www.mosi. org**; also on Tampa CityPass, p281).

Ybor City: Tampa's other entertainment district can be found in the rejuvenated Cuban quarter of the city, where a fine mix of shops and restaurants provide a lively vibe both by day and at night. Top dining choices include **Hamburger Mary's** (tempting burgers), **Carne Chophouse** (fine steaks and seafood) and **Samurai Blue** (sushi and sake) while the lively bar scene offers **Centro Cantina**, the **Brass Tap** (for craft beers and live music) and (our fave) the **Tampa Bay Brewing Co**, a British-run brewpub with a varied menu, great range of beers, multiple TV screens and pool table. Find more fun at **Game Time**, an upscale arcade of games and bars, the **Muvico** 20-screen cinema complex and the **Improv Comedy Theatre**, busiest

on Fri and Sat but bustling most nights (**www.centroybor.com**). Start at the **Visitor Center & Museum**, which shows a fascinating film on the history of the city, and the well-presented **Ybor City Museum** on East 9th Avenue (9am–5pm; $4/person, under-6s free; **www.ybormuseum.org**). You can also tour the area on the new **Electric Glide Segway** tours, a fabulous way to sight-see and have fun at the same time on these 2-wheeled machines (Mon–Wed at 10am, 1 and 3.30pm; $65/person; 1800 979 3370, **http://electricglidetours.com/**).

TECO Line Streetcar: Much of downtown Tampa, including Ybor City and Channelside, is linked by replicas of authentic electric trams, with one-way fares of $2.50 (cash only; $1.25 for under 17s and seniors) or $5 for an all-day card. A Family All Day Ticket ($12.50, for up to 5) is available from ticket machines.

BRITTIP

Visit the Columbia Restaurant in Ybor City. Opened in 1905, it incorporates a whole city block that was gradually absorbed into this Spanish/Cuban bar-diner. Ask at the host stand if they can give you a tour, with the story of the Gonzmart family (813 248 4961, **www.columbiarestaurant.com**).

Yuengling Brewery: For a fascinating free brewery tour, try this modern facility near Busch Gardens (on 10th street, parallel to McKinley Drive, where you enter the theme park). It brews up to nine beers (two seasonal), including a fab lager and porter. With guided tours at 10am, 11.30am and 1pm Mon–Fri (10.30am and noon Sat; closed Sun), it shows off the creative process behind the company, then offers a couple of samples! The Gift Shop is open 9am–3pm, and you are likely to see the full interior workings of the brewery, including the bottling and canning plant (813 972 8500, **www.yuengling.com/breweries/tampa/**). NB: Closed-toe shoes – no sandals or flip-flops; children welcome.

Where to stay: Try the boutique style

of historic **Don Vicente Inn** in Ybor City, a beautiful period refurbishment of a 19th-century building with just 16 individual rooms (813 241 4545, **http://donvicenteinn.com/**), or the upscale new **Le Meridien** (a gorgeous conversion of the old Federal Court building; 813 221 9555, **www.lemeridientampa.com**). More info: Visitor Center 813 223 2752 or **www.visittampabay.com**.

BRITTIP
The new Tampa Bay CityPass card can provide BIG savings on five main area attractions, including Busch Gardens, Clearwater Marine Aquarium, the Florida Aquarium and Lowry Park Zoo. It costs $99 adults and $84 3–9s. See more at www.citypass.com/tampa.

St Pete/Clearwater

Continue west and you have the gorgeous Gulf Coast, a two-hour drive down I-4 and through Tampa on I-275 south to St Pete Beach (105ml/169km) or Clearwater Beach (110ml/177km), with a string of beautiful resorts in between, all featuring white-sand beaches, water sports and fewer crowds than you would think, plus the smart Beach Walk in Clearwater. The sea is a bit warmer and calmer on this side of Florida so is more suitable for small children. The 35ml/56km stretch from St Pete–Clearwater represents the heart of the Sunshine State beach experience and is one of the most popular two-centre options. It has a wonderful array of attractions and averages 361 days of sun a year.

BRITTIP
Do the 'stingray shuffle' in the sea here from Apr–Oct. Whenever you are in the water, move your feet through the sand without lifting them up to ensure you alert the occasional stingray to your presence. They will then move away without bothering anyone. Neosporin is a good antiseptic if you are stung.

St Petersburg: This city, just across the Howard Frankland Bridge from Tampa, is a wonderful mix of the old and the new, with a fast-developing Art District (eight museums, dozens of galleries and counting) and a real café society feel. Take time for the world-renowned **Dali Museum** (10am–5.30pm, 8pm Thurs; $24 adults, $22 seniors, $17 13–18s and students, $10 6–12s; **www.thedali.org**), and the **Chihuly Collection** at the **Morean Arts Center**, a superb showcase of the American glass artist, with guided tours on the hour every 30mins. There's also a separate glass studio and hot shop nearby (10–6pm Mon–Sat, noon–6pm Sun; $15 adults, $14 seniors, $11 students and children over 5; $9 7, $5 for Hot Shop; combo ticket $20, $18, $13; 727 896 4527, **www.moreanartscenter.org**; also on Tampa CityPass, see left). Other highlights include the elegant **Museum of Fine Arts**, with its two interior gardens (**www.fine-arts.org**), the **St Petersburg Museum of History** (**www.spmoh.com**), and fascinating **Great Explorations Children's Museum** (**www.greatex.org**). Pedestrian-friendly streets provide plenty of interest, while the **Bay Walk** complex adds restaurants, shops and a **Muvico IMAX 20-screen cinema** (**www.yourbaywalk.com**). Also visit the fan-friendly **Tropicana Field**, which hosts the Tampa Bay Rays baseball team (Apr–Sept) for terrific local entertainment ($15–300; **http://tampabay.rays.mlb.com**). And try the **All About Fun Tours** from the Museum of History on 2-wheeled Segways. They are easy to master and provide a superb view of the city's miles of waterfront parks, beaches and residences with your knowledgeable guide. Ages 12 and over (max 275lb/125kg; Tues–Sat 10.30am and 2pm, Sun 12.30 and 2.30pm; 1-hour tour $35, 90min $50; call for reservations on 727 896 3640, **www.gyroglides.com**).

Weedon Island Preserve: Enjoy the rich cultural history of this 3,700acre/1,500ha seaside nature park in St Petersburg. Start at the Natural History Center (the main entrance, is at the back) and learn about the prehistoric and Native American settlements here (plus periodic exhibitions), then go up to the 3rd floor observation deck. There are several miles of boardwalks and trails around the tidal wetlands, which are home to a wildlife like ospreys, turtles, spoonbills, turtles, mangrove crabs, raccoons and gopher tortoises, and guided hikes on Sats at 9am (call to register; Center open 9am–4pm Thurs–Sat, free entry; Preserve open 7am–dusk; 727 453 6500, **www.weedonislandpreserve.org**). The more energetic may want to try a paddle round the shallow waters with **Sweetwater Kayaks**. This close encounter with nature (stingrays, jumping mullet and the occasional manatee) is offered on an hourly or four-hour basis (10am–4pm Mon–Fri, 9am and 1pm Sat and Sun; $40 for a four-hour single-kayak rental, $56 for double, or $17 and $25 hourly; booking advised on 727 570 4844 or **www.sweetwaterkayaks.com**).

BRITTIP
Insect repellent is essential for any visit to Weedon Island Preserve as it is not sprayed for mosquitoes, and the little pests will feed on tourists!

Beaches: You are spoiled for choice, from the 1,100acre/445ha **Fort De Soto Park** in the south to stunning **Caladesi Island State Park** in the north (regularly voted in America's Top 10). There is plenty to do, too, with the likes of Treasure Island, Sand Key and St Pete Beach all receiving the Blue Wave Award for cleanliness and safety. Fort De Soto Park offers free walking tours of its Spanish-American War-era fort (usually 10am; call to confirm on 727 552 1862; it costs $5 for park entry), while **John's Pass Village** is an eclectic shopping district and marina full of art galleries and restaurants, plus the fun **Pirate Cruise** – a replica sailing ship offering a 2hr party cruise ($35 adults, $30 65 and over, $25 under-20s, $10 under-3s, inclusive of beer, wine and soft drinks; 11am, 2pm and sunset; call for reservations on 727 423 7824) and 90min **Dolphin Quest** boat tour at noon, 2, 4 and 6pm daily ($19.50 adults, $17.50 seniors, $15 under 20s; call for reservations on 727 392 7090).

Seminole Central

Head west out of Fort Lauderdale to Big Cypress and you find the rewarding **Ah-Tah-Thi-Ki Museum**, home to the Seminole tribe of Florida. Here you can learn about Native American culture, from its customs to the bitter 19th century Seminole Wars and its modern face as 'Guardians of the Everglades.' See the **Living Village** and walk the 1ml/1.6km Boardwalk over the Cypress Swamp. Then try the Billie Swamp Safari, a 2,200-acre/1.6ha **Cypress Reservation** featuring close-ups of the wildlife (including snakes and gators) via its giant-wheeled buggy, airboat rides and swamp critter shows. And you can even stay overnight in its Chickee huts (1800 683 7800, **www.floridaseminoletourism.com**).

Parasailing, jet-skiing, fishing, boat rentals and tours are also popular (**www.johnspass.com**).

Dolphin Landings: A 'Don't miss' in St Pete Beach, with a pair of 51ft/15.5m yachts that sail on 2hr trips along the calm inland waterway (9.30am, noon & 2.15pm, Mon–Sat, noon & 2.15pm Sun; $35 adults, $25 children) for close-up dolphin-watch cruises and sunset sailings, plus a Sunset Sail, 4hr trip around beautiful Egmont Key and a 3½-hour trip to Shell Key, with up to two hours on the beach ($40-45; 727 367 4488, **www.dolphinlandings.com**).

BRITTIP
Most public beaches will have toilets, changing facilities and picnic tables, but there is usually a parking fee.

Suncoast Seabird Sanctuary: Further north at Indian Shores is America's largest wild bird hospital, caring for injured birds including birds of prey, pelicans, spoonbills and egrets. No charge but donations to visit this non-profit-making rehabilitation centre (9am–sunset, 727 391 6211, **www.seabirdsanctuary.com**).

Clearwater Beach: Continue north to acres of clean, white sands and the **Clearwater Marine Aquarium**, a wonderful non-profit organisation

Miami nice

If you see nothing else in Miami, do spend some time in **South Beach** (or SoBe as it is known) and über-cool Ocean Drive, full of open-air cafés, art galleries and pulsating nightclubs. Tranquil during the day, non-stop at night, this is where the beautiful people hang out, or just cruise in their Ferraris and Hummers. The restored Art Deco gems twinkle at night and will use up lots of capacity on your camera's memory card.

BRITTIP

Don't leave without visiting the area's top attraction, a dolphin called Winter, the star of films *Dolphin Tale* and *Dolphin Tale 2* with Morgan Freeman. Rescued from a crab trap, her tail had to be amputated and she was not expected to survive. Happily, she not only lived but has learned to swim with a prosthetic tail!

that rescues and rehabilitates injured dolphins, turtles, river otters and more (especially good for under-12s). There are 17 main exhibits, including Turtle Cove, Otter Oasis, Shark Pass and Shipwreck Alley but much of the focus is on the area's Hollywood 'star', Winter the tail-less dolphin (see Brit Tip) in the Winter Zone. There are dolphin presentations (into behaviour and care – not 'shows') three times a day and other interactive animal encounters, plus a Trainer For A Day option at $325/person. You can also do their behind-the-scenes tour, with access to all the rehab areas and a close-up of the dolphins, or two-hour Sea Life Safari (great for kids) that goes out on the coastal waterway. There are also another seven animal encounter options, including dolphins, pelicans and sharks, and an Assistant Trainer with Winter opportunity ($5–449/person). The Dolphin Tale Adventure – with re-built scenes, film images, interactive kids area and mini-theater all based on the original movie – in downtown Clearwater is also included in the price if you buy tickets at the Aquarium, from where there is also a free trolley ride to the Adventure (Aquarium hours 9am–6pm daily, 10am–6pm for Dolphin Tale Adventure; $22 adults, $20 seniors, $17 3–12s; behind-the-scenes tour $17, $15 and $12; Sea Life Safari $26, $23, $17; Aquarium plus backstage tour $35, $32, $27; Aquarium plus Safari $41, $38, $30; or all 3 $54, $50, $40; 727 441 1790, **www.seewinter.com**; also on Tampa CityPass, p281).

The Beach Walk: The heart of the area is a winding beachside promenade of lush landscaping and artistic touches that links a ½-mile stretch of resorts, shops and restaurants (like the fun **Frenchy's** and **Crabby Bill's**) to Pier 60 where the daily sunset celebration (with craft stalls and music) is held. Also here is the marina where you can catch the two-hour **Captain Memo's Pirate Cruise** (10am and 2pm daily; $36 adults, $33 seniors, $31 teens, $28 under-13s, $11 under 3s) or the **Sunset Champagne Cruise** (at 4.30, 5, 6 or 7pm, $39, $33, $31, $28, $11; online discounts available at **www.captainmemo.com**).

Caladesi Island: Further north is another of the world's most picturesque beach spots. Don't miss the annual 10-day Pier 60 Sugar Sand Festival each April, with even more family-friendly fun (**www.sugarsandfestival.com**).

Suncoast Beach Trolley: For those not wanting to drive, this is the perfect option (6.10am–11.25pm daily) both along the beaches and into St Petersburg for $2 a ride, $4.50 for an all-day pass and $20 for a week pass (info line 727 540 1900, **www.psta.net**).

Restaurants: The area also boasts 2,000 restaurants, of which the Key West bistro style of the five **Frenchy's Cafes** (Original Café, Rockaway Grill, South Beach and Salt Water Café all in Clearwater Beach, plus **Frenchy's Outpost** in Dunedin), the **Daiquiri Shak** (Madeira Beach), **Crabby Bill's Seafood** (in Clearwater Beach) and the **Moon Under Water** (St Petersburg) are all worth visiting. The chic **Parkshore Grill** in downtown St Pete is ideal for a relaxing lunch or elegant dinner (727 896 3463, **www.parkshoregrill.com**), as is **400 Beach Seafood & Tap House**, which also features a fabulous Sunday brunch (727 896 2400, **www.400beachseafood.com**).

Where to stay: A range of **Superior Small Lodgings** combine beachfront locations with small-scale service. Weekly rates can be from $800 for a 3-room apartment (727 367 2791, **http://floridassl.com/**). Upscale hotels include family-friendly **Tradewinds Island Resorts** on St Pete Beach, a 743-room complex with great facilities and dining in a blissful location (1800 360 4016, **www.tradewindsresort.com**); the superb **Sandpearl Resort**, a 4-star choice on Clearwater Beach, with a mix of stylish standard rooms and spacious suites. The pool, bar and grill are a beachfront sanctuary, and the modern Spa has a fab array of treatments. Caretta on the Gulf offers memorable dining with an inventive fusion cuisine (727 441 2425, **www. sandpearl.com**); and the **Hyatt Regency Clearwater Beach Resort & Spa**, an all-suite hotel at the heart of Beach Walk with fantastic pool facilities and picturesque Gulf views, plus the eco-friendly Sandova Spa, state-of-the-art gym and 2 wonderful restaurants (727 373 1234, **www. clearwaterbeach.hyatt.com**). By contrast, the **Vinoy Resort** (in St Petersburg) is the area's oldest formal hotel, a 1920s treasure that is well worth a look just for its Spanish Revival style (727 894 1000, **www.marriott. com**). Another personal favourite is the **Grand Plaza Hotel** right on St Pete Beach, where the ultra- friendly

service and fresh style are ideal for a beach getaway, especially with the revolving restaurant and bar of Spinners on the 12th floor providing grandstand Gulf views (727 360 1811, **www.grandplazaflorida.com**). **Sunset Vistas Beachfront Suites** on Treasure Island, with 1 and 2-bed suites and fully- equipped kitchens, is a top self-catering choice (727 360 1600, **www. providentresorts.com**). **More info:** 0208 651 4742 in the UK, 727 464 7200 in the US, or **www.visitstpeteclearwater.com**.

BRITTIP
Don't miss the chance to dine at the Hyatt Regency's SHOR Seafood Grill, with its dramatic show kitchen and superb local seafood dishes.

The south-west

Bradenton/Sarasota: Around two hours' drive from Orlando is this artsy area (take I-4 then I-75), which features the superb beachfronts of Anna Maria Island (charming and secluded beaches), Longboat Key and Venice ('the shark tooth capital of the world' and great for fossil hunters). Sarasota is year-round home to the Ringling Circus, and there are many circus-influenced offerings here, including the unmissable **Ringling Estate and Museum of Art**, which includes the unique Circus Museum and Tibbals Learning Center (the world's largest scale model of a classic circus). The Museum of Art features a multi-million-dollar collection of Old Masters in a palatial setting while the former family home, the dazzling Ca d'Zan Mansion, grounds and gardens are also part of the entry fee (daily 10am–5pm, 8pm Thurs; closed Thanksgiving, Christmas, New Year's Day; $25 adults, $20 seniors, $5 6–17s and students; **www.ringling.org**). There is superb shopping at **St Armand's Circle** in Lido Key, and the **Mote Aquarium** is also worthy of note. In Bradenton, look out for the **Village of Arts**, and the sophisticated **South Florida Museum**, which includes the **Parker Manatee Aquarium** and **Bishop Planetarium**. The Aquarium is home to Bradenton's mascot, Snooty, the world's oldest living

Cocoa Beach

© Florida Dolphin Tours

manatee (10am–5pm Mon–Sat, noon–5pm Sun; closed Mon in May, Jun and Aug–Dec; $19 adults, $17 seniors, $14 4–11s; 941 746 4131, **www.southfloridamuseum.org**). Good food is always on the menu, and you should try another outlet of the excellent Spanish-Cuban **Columbia Restaurant** in St Armand's Circle (941 388 3987, **www.columbiarestaurant.com**), the al fresco dining of **Mattison's City Grille** in downtown Sarasota (941 330 0440, **www.mattisons.com**) and **Siesta Key Oyster Bar** in Siesta Key Village (941 346 5443, **www.skob.com**).

Where to stay: Anna Maria Island is full of small-scale B&Bs and cute beachfront inns. The **Hyatt Regency Sarasota** is one of the top resorts in the area (941 953 1234, **www.sarasota. hyatt.com**), while the **Ritz-Carlton** is a Gulf Coast landmark (941 309 2000, **www.ritzcarlton.com**). For a great self-catering option, try the **Beach Club at Siesta Key** (941 552 9810, **www.beachclubatsiestakey.com**). **More info:** Sarasota, call 941 957 1877 or **www.visitsarasota.org**; **Bradenton and Anna Maria Island**, 941 729 9177 or **www.bradentongulfislands.com**.

Charlotte Harbor: Go further south (170ml/272km from Orlando) and you have the lower-key destinations of Punta Gorda, Port Charlotte, Englewood and Boca Grande. Port Charlotte is the place to be for some of the best shelling in Florida, while kayakers should try the 'tunnel of love' mangrove tunnels and other nature adventures with **Phoenix Rising Kayak Tours** (941 586 2836; **www.prkayak.com**). To immerse completely in nature, try an overnight stay on **Little Gasparilla Island**, where there are no roads, cars or shops, just miles of beaches and exceptional bird-watching and tarpon fishing. Eco-adventures can be found at **Babcock Wilderness Adventures**, with swamp buggy tours through the Telegraph Swamp (1800 500 5583; **www.babcockwilderness.com**). Downtown Punta Gorda has free bike rentals and a lovely walk along the Peace River where you'll feel miles off the usual tourist trail. If you are looking for 'small town America', this

is it. **More info:** 941 743 1900 or **www.charlotteharbortravel.com**.

Fort Myers/Sanibel: It's only a short drive to the mini tropical paradise of the Lee Island Coast, featuring history and nature-rich Fort Myers and funky Pine Island. Among the many highlights are bustling family-orientated Fort Myers Beach; Sanibel Island, centred around its shell-strewn beaches; the bird-watching Mecca at the **Darling National Wildlife Refuge**; the jumble of shops and restaurants in Captiva Island; and Bonita Beach. Sanibel is home to the unique **Bailey-Matthews Shell Museum**, plus a quaint **Historical Museum & Village**, several wildlife attractions, canoeing, kayaking and nature tours.

Where to stay: There is a good mix of vacation homes and cottages in Fort Myers Beach and Sanibel, while the top hotels are **Lovers Key Resort** (239 765 1040, **www.loverskey.com**) and **Sanibel Harbor Marriott Resort & Spa** (239 466 4000, **www.marriott. com**). **More info:** 239 338 3500 or **www.fortmyers-sanibel.com**.

Paradise Coast: Continue south to the magnificent 'Paradise Coast' of Naples and Marco Island. Naples is a fresh, modern city with plenty of attractions (notably the **Museum of Art**, **Naples Nature Center** and **Corkscrew Swamp Sanctuary**, plus ultra-chic shopping) and a top beach destination. Its art-tinged ambience is well-evidenced in its two main areas of Fifth Avenue South, with boutique shops, sidewalk cafés and art festivals, and Third Street South, with more distinctive stores, galleries and café society atmosphere (try the **Old Naples Pub** for fine food in a relaxed ambience with an outdoor patio and live music Thurs–Sat). The beaches are mere steps away; at the municipal beach, Naples Pier juts into placid Gulf waters, while Lowdermilk Beach is family-friendly, with volleyball and other facilities. Marco Island is the largest of the Ten Thousand Islands, consisting of two main communities: Marco, known for its wide-coved beach and fine resorts, plus a multitude of fishing charters; and Goodland, with its eclectic fish house restaurants, plus fishing charters into the Everglades.

Where to stay: Pick from high-quality resorts like **Marco Island Marriott Beach Resort** (239 394 2511, **www.marcoislandmarriott.com**), **Marco Beach Ocean Resort** (239 393 1400, **www.marcoresort.com**) and **Naples Grande Beach Resort** (239 227 2182, **www.naplesgrande.com**). We also like the small-scale Caribbean-tinged **Lemon Tree Inn** in Naples (239 262 1414, **http://lemontreeinn.com/**). **More info:** 001 239 225 1013 or **www.paradisecoast.com**.

BRITTIP
The Naples/Marco Island area is the perfect base from which to explore the amazing Florida Everglades, though you can also reach them from Fort Lauderdale on the east coast.

Treasure Coast

Returning to the Atlantic Coast, heading south on Highway 1 brings you to an often-overlooked Florida jewel, Vero Beach. Nicknamed the Treasure Coast (for its history of shipwrecks), it boasts the intriguing **McLarty Treasure Museum** and the **Pelican Island National Wildlife Refuge**. Vero Beach itself is located on the barrier island of North Hutchinson but spreads to the mainland, with art galleries, smart shops, restaurants, small resorts and beach parks, including a boardwalk atop the dunes. Go south for another hour and you reach the **Palm Beaches** and the mainland city of West Palm Beach, foremost among Florida's chic cities. A playground of the rich and famous, the fabulous **Flagler Museum** (formerly the rail tycoon's 1902-built Whitehall mansion) is a highlight, while the many restaurants are places to go celebrity-watching and **Worth Avenue** is one of America's most iconic shopping streets. Don't miss dining at Italian style **Bice** (561 835 1600, **http://palmbeach.bicegroup.com/**), the ultra-chic **Meat Market** (561 354 9800, **www.meatmarket.net/palm_**

beach/), small-plate specialist **Buccan** (561 833 3450, **www.buccanpalmbeach.com**) and indulgent **HMF** at The Breakers, plus the celebrity bistro of **Ta-boo** (561 835 3500, **www.taboorestaurant.com**). This is also a great place to take a fishing charter or yacht hire, like **Palm Breeze Charters** (561 368 3566, **www.airandsea.com**), while, for something different, check out the **International Polo Club** (games from Jan–Apr; 561 282 5290, **www.internationalpoloclub.com**) and **National Croquet Center** (lessons every Sat, plus a great bar-restaurant; 561 478 2300, **www.croquetnationalcom**). Also here is **Lion Country Safari**, with lions, elephants and giraffes (**www.lioncountrysafari.com**).

Where to stay: Disney's Vero Beach Resort doesn't always have availability (it is a Disney Vacation Club hotel), but is the ideal family resort on this coast (772 234 2000, **http://disneyvacationclub.disney.go.com**). The Palm Beaches boasts an array 5-star hotels, notably the blissful **Eau Palm Beach** (561 533 6000; **www.eaupalmbeach.com**), the period style of **The Brazilian Court** (561 655 7740, **www.thebraziliancourt.com**), the gorgeous **Four Seasons** (561 582 2800, **www.fourseasons.com**) and the ultimate opulence and style of **The Breakers**, one of America's legendary resort destinations, with breathtaking décor and design (561 655 6611, **www.thebreakers.com**). **More info:** 1800 554 7256 or **www.palmbeachfl.com**.

Miami and Fort Lauderdale

From Palm Beach, you reach increasingly built-up resort territory – Delray Beach, chic Boca Raton, Deerfield Beach, Pompano Beach and Fort Lauderdale. This latter has become one of Florida's most upmarket destinations in recent years, with a great mix of resorts, shopping, attractions and beaches. It also has a canal and waterway network that makes it the 'Venice of America', with water taxis being more plentiful than the wheeled variety. Top things to see are the **Museum** of **Discovery & Science** (one of the state's finest), **Bonnet House Museum & Gardens**, **Old Fort Lauderdale Village & Museum** and **Las Olas Boulevard**, full of boutiques and restaurants. Shop at **Sawgrass Mills**, Florida's largest mall, which has more than 300 outlet-style stores from big-name designers. Fort Lauderdale is also a perfect stay for a few days before or after a cruise, as both Port Everglades and Miami are only a short distance away.

Where to stay: Look for their **Superior Small Lodgings** or the many high-class resorts now dotting the beachfront, like **Fort Lauderdale Marriott Harbor Beach Resort & Spa** (954 525 5000, **www.marriott.com**) and the dramatic 5-star **Ritz-Carlton** (954 465 2300, **www.ritzcarlton.com**). **More info:** 954 765 4466 or **www.sunny.org**.

Miami: If you have taken the 3½-hour drive south from Orlando, you will finally arrive in the state's biggest and most glamorous city, Miami. With superb high-rise resorts, miles of open, accessible beaches, the ultra-chic **South Beach** area (with its Art Deco District), fantastic shopping, sports, restaurants and nightlife, and an array of outstanding attractions, you could easily spend a week here. The city is actually 5ml/8km from the beach area, which runs north for almost 15ml/24km along the sprawling corridor of Collins Avenue, where you have most of the resorts and nightlife. High style is almost everywhere – a narrated boat tour (from the Bayside Marketplace) will show off the mansions of the rich and famous, while you should also tour Coral Gables and the older, neater Coconut Grove, with its **CocoWalk** shopping district and ornate **Vizcaya Museum**.

Other attractions include **Miami Seaquarium** on the island of Key Biscayne (**www.miamiseaquarium.com**), the amazing Venetian Pool at **Coral Gables** and the surprising and entertaining family attraction **Jungle Island**, a combination of zoo, animal shows and gardens with great up-close encounters (**www.jungleisland.**

com). You are spoiled for choice for shopping, from fashion-conscious **Bal Harbor Shops**, to the massive **Aventura Mall** and funky **Lincoln Road** in South Beach. Or try the **Village of Merrick Park** in Coral Gables, a Mediterranean-style outdoor mall with more designer style, including the iconic **Nordstrom** department store and superb dining, notably at fab Italian restaurant **Villagio** and gastropub **Yard House** (305 529 0200, **www.villageofmerrickpark.com**).

Miami Food Tours: Try this fascinating insight into the Art Deco district's architecture and eclectic dining. Sample 'neighbourhood specialities' at six South Beach restaurants and cafés along this fun walking tour, while learning about the area's culture, history and unique building style. (212 209 3370; **www.miamifoodtours.com**)

Dining: This is a strong feature of Miami these days. Consider the sumptuous Latin American cuisine of **Ola Miami** (305 695 9125; **www.olamiami.com**); fresh and authentic Northern Italian trattoria offerings at **Salumiera** 104 (305 424 9588; **www.salumeria104.com**); ultra-swanky **Casa Tua** (the place to see and be seen; 303 673 1010, **www.casatualifestyle.com/miami**); and the casual comforts at eclectic **Soyka**, a train station turned car collector's warehouse turned restaurant, with live jazz each Fri (305 759 3117; **www.soykarestaurant.com**).

Where to stay: There are boutique hotels and dazzling resorts aplenty, but two we like a lot are **The Beacon** in the heart of bustling South Beach on Ocean Drive, and an iconic

Ola Miami

breakfast location (305 674 8200; **www. beaconsouthbeach.com**) and the new **Miami Beach Edition**, a wonderfully chic conversion of the 1950s Seville Hotel (786 257 4500, **www.editionhotels. com/miami-beach/**). **More info:** 305 539 3000 or **www.miamiandbeaches.com**.

Florida Keys

Leaving Miami behind on Highway 1 brings you to the unique realm of the Keys, a loose archipelago of 1,700 islands that arc down into the Caribbean. If you thought mainland Florida was easy-going, just try the laid-back 'Conch Republic', where shorts and flip-flops are official wear and the mix of influences merges into a 'Floribbean' culture. Scuba divers enjoy some of the world's best coral reefs, with renowned **John Pennekamp Coral Reef State Park** the highlight of miles of National Marine Sanctuary. Or try Vandenberg Artificial Reef off Key West, an old US Navy ship intentionally sunk in 2009 to create a man-made reef. The first city you encounter is **Key Largo**, followed by **Islamorada**, where you should stop to see Theater To The Sea, with its dolphin and sea-lion programmes. For fishing, some of the best charters are at Islamorada, Marathon and Big Pine Key.

Marathon is the starting point of the amazing **Seven Mile Bridge**, the unofficial eighth wonder of the world, which connects the biggest gap between the islands, while **Big Pine Key** is home to **Bahia Honda State Park**, one of Florida's finest beaches. Finally, the 375ml/600km drive from Orlando brings you to America's southernmost city. **Key West** is possibly the most eclectic city in the US, a mix of the laid-back and outrageous, with street performers, sidewalk artists, cafés and bars,

Disney cruise ship Fantasy

plus the former home of Ernest Hemingway, whose residence and museum are essential viewing. You should also see **Key West Aquarium** and **Shipwreck Historeum**, and the wonderfully diverse array of shops. You must be on the harbour front, though, for the daily Sunset Celebration, when Key West's party spirit is in full force. The other great feature of Key West is its myriad ways to get around – you can try the **Conch Tour Train**, **Old Town Trolley Tours**, pedicabs and bicycles. Just don't expect your stay to be sedate!

Where to stay: Guest houses, inns and B&Bs are plentiful. Try **Old Customs House Inn** (305 294 8507, **www.oldcustomshouse.com**) in Key West's Old Town or charming **Banyan Resort** (305 296 7786, **www.thebanyanresort.com**). **More info:** 1800 352 5397 or **www.fla-keys.com**.

Cruise-and-stay

Taking a cruise is increasingly popular with an Orlando stay and there are well-priced 3, 4, 5 and 7-day sailings out of Port Canaveral, Tampa, Fort Lauderdale and Miami. From here, you can visit the Bahamas, much of the Caribbean, Mexico and even Central America.

Select from **Disney Cruise Line** (from their own dedicated cruise terminal at Port Canaveral and Miami), with four fabulous ships and voyages from 3–7 days (0800 028 3179, **http:// disneycruise.disney.go.com**); party-style **Carnival** (from Port Canaveral, Miami and Tampa), 3–7 days (0843 374 2272 in the UK, **www.carnival. co.uk**); **Royal Caribbean**, with some of the biggest ships (from all four ports) for 3–14 days (0844 493 4005, **www.royalcaribbean.co.uk**), **Norwegian Cruise Line** (from Port Canaveral, Miami and Tampa) from 3–7 days (0845 201 8900, **www.ncl.co.uk**) and **Princess Cruises**, 7–14 days (from Fort Lauderdale; 1800 774 6237, **www.princess.com**).

Well, that represents pretty much the full range of holiday choices. Now we need to tell you about how to enjoy all the night-time entertainment…

10 Orlando by Night

or Burning the Candle at Both Ends

If Orlando and the parks are hot during the day, they positively sizzle at night, with yet more diverse and thrilling entertainment, much of it extremely family friendly. Disney and Universal lead the way, but there is much to enjoy in the after-dark scene generally.

The full range runs from purpose-built entertainment complexes and an amazing range of dinner shows to a unique array of bars and nightclubs. The choice is widespread and almost always high quality. Downtown Orlando has some unique offerings, while there is more being added to International Drive all the time. Disney Springs – which raised the bar for the big evening entertainment concept with the opening of Pleasure Island in 1987 – is experiencing a massive makeover, which will double the current array of choice. Disney's Boardwalk Resort is also a good evening option.

BRITTIP
Photo ID is essential for most bars and clubs, even if you happen to be the 'wrong' side of 30. No ID equals no alcohol, and there are no exceptions.

DISNEY SPRINGS
Disney's big shopping, dining and entertainment district is transforming into a 4-part adventure that is due to be complete in 2016. The original Marketplace and West Side were joined in 2015 by The Landing (the old Pleasure Island area), with the Town Center the final part, featuring an iconic new restaurant, bar and live entertainment venue, **The Edison**. This latter is a massive 1920s-themed 'Industrial Gothic' destination that will offer classic American food, cocktails and a range of cabaret-style shows, as well as contortionists, palm readers, DJs and more. Other details of the Town Center had still to be announced as we went to press but we expect more one-off shops and signature dining opportunities. (see also Dining, p304; Shopping, p328).

The Landing
Raglan Road: This pub features traditional live Irish music each night in its Grand Room 4pm–1.30am Mon–Fri, 12pm–1.30am Sat–Sun,

Hogwarts at night

© Universal Orlando Resort

plus hourly Irish dancing Mon–Sun, 5–10pm. Enjoy its full bar, ample collection of genuine Irish whiskey, 9 European beers, 4 beer flights, plus local brews, great bartenders and an even better menu (p305) (407 938 0300, **www.raglanroad.com**).

Paradiso 37: This expansive, split-level bar-restaurant offers a fine array of food from the Americas (all 37 countries) plus an amazing Tequila Bar featuring 37 varieties. Live music adds to its picturesque waterfront location (p304).

The Boathouse: This new bar-restaurant venue offers live music most evenings, but the real feature here is the Amphicar rides. Each land-to-water car accommodates up to 3 guests and a Car Captain (driver), with these 20min rides costing a whopping $125, but it's a rare opportunity to try these fascinating vehicles. Tickets can be purchased at The Boathouse. For the best spectator value, watch the Amphicars on the lake from the comfort of the Boathouse bar, situated waterside. Tours run 10am-10pm, weather permitting.

BRITTIP
Want to 'splash out' on a special occasion? Try The Boathouse's special water-taxi *The Venezia* for a guided tour of Disney Springs, complete with chocolate-covered strawberries, champagne and music ($75 per person, $50 under 13s).

Jock Lindsey's Hangar Bar: Indiana Jones fans will definitely want to 'hang' out here as this bar is themed for the pilot of the Indy films, Jock Lindsey. There will be a boat-themed patio and plenty of aircraft memorabilia, as well as a range of craft beers, cocktails and a small-plate dining menu.

West Side
AMC® Dine-In Theaters Complex: With 24 screens and 6,000 seats plus a huge choice of snacks, drinks and even its own bar, this superb cinema multiplex shows first-run films

in state-of-the-art surroundings, including the Enhanced Theatre Experience (a bigger screen, with 3D technology, 12-channel audio and digital projection) and the new feature Dine-In option, with 6 of the auditoriums converted to serve meals and drinks while you watch. The menu includes starters like wings, potato skins and onion rings, then salads, fish and chips, chicken pasta, sandwiches and burgers and yummy desserts, plus wine, beer and cocktails (tickets $8–18, prices vary by show; food and drink extra; call 1 888 262 4386 for show times; under 18s must be accompanied by an adult in Dine-In theatres; **www.amctheatres.com**). Disabled accessible; assisted listening devices available at Guest Services.

BRITTIP
Some films have added features, such as enhanced sound, larger screen, or 3-D that will increase your ticket price. However, you can save $2 on adult tickets at the AMC® cineplex by visiting before 3.55pm.

Bongos Cuban Café: The 'big pineapple' restaurant with Latin flair has salsa music and a live band nightly after 6pm. Sit on the outdoor balcony on a balmy evening and soak up the atmosphere (407 828 0999; **www.bongoscubancafe.com**).

DisneyQuest: This indoor house of games is home to 11 major adventures, such as CyberSpace Mountain (design and ride your own roller-coaster), Mighty Ducks Pinball Slam (a fun life-size pinball game), Ride the Comix! (a virtual-reality battle, this time with super-villains), Virtual Jungle Cruise (shooting the rapids, prehistoric style) and Aladdin's Magic Carpet (more virtual-reality fun in best cartoon fashion), a host of old-fashioned video games in Replay Zone, the latest sports games, a test of imagination in Animation Academy, the Wonderland Café, with computers and internet tables, and Food Quest, straight out of a space-age comic book.

Two more interactive experiences are

Pirates of the Caribbean: Battle for Buccaneer Gold, a 3-D immersion in a swashbuckling quest for pirate treasure). **Buzz Lightyear's Astro Blasters** (inter-galactic bumper cars with cannonball action! R: 4ft 3in/129cm). You enter via the Cybrolator to Ventureport and then you explore: **Score Zone** (for most of the game-playing); **Explore Zone** (role-playing and virtual-reality games); **Create Zone** (hands-on activities to be your own 'Imagineer'); and **Replay Zone** (a 'moonscape' of classic games and rides). Admission: 11.30am–10pm Sun–Thurs, 11.30pm Fri and Sat. Go during the day to avoid the queues (the building admits only 1,500). A 1-day ticket costs $45 ($39 3–9s. NB: There were strong rumours DisneyQuest would close in 2016, removing it as an option with the 7, 14 and 21-Day Ultimate tickets).

House of Blues: Free live music every night at the Front Porch bar, with full concerts at the separately accessed music venue next to the restaurant. The main venue offers a mix of big-name headliners (the likes of Duran Duran, My Chemical Romance, The Cult and Fall Out Boy have all appeared in recent years), up-and-coming bands and local acts. All concerts are standing room only. Tickets required, no discounts for children ($20–60 and up; 407 934 2583, **www.houseofblues.com**).

Cirque Du Soleil: The greatest show we've seen anywhere is Cirque du Soleil's *La Nouba*™. Twice a day, five times a week, the company's purpose-built, 1,671-seat theatre stages the most stupendous combination of dance, circus, acrobatics, comedy and live music in a 90min show by more than 60 performers. Unique styling, outrageous costumes and captivating sounds make this a stunning multi-dimensional assault on the senses.

The show title comes from the French *faire la nouba*, to live it up, and this it does in grand style. It features trampolines, acrobatics, trapezes, juggling and even mountain bikes, woven with comedy, innovative

dance, spellbinding music and magnificent staging. Some of the stunts are jaw-dropping, notably the Chinese diabolo acrobats, BMX cycling stunts and the high-energy final act, Power Track/Trampoline, which features a 3D building and performers flipping and twisting in and out of the structure in quick succession. A kaleidoscopic explosion of talent that never fails to amaze, it is just as exciting as when it opened in 1998. It is not cheap, but we believe it is worth every cent and a highlight of any visit to Orlando. Booking is vital and can be done up to 6 months in advance on 407 939 7328 (or **www.cirquedusoleil.com**). Shows are at 6pm and 9pm Tues–Sat, but try to be early for some excellent pre-show fun. Admission: Golden Circle at $139 for adults, $115 3–9s; Front & Center, $124, $102; Cat 1, $99, $80; Cat 2, $80, $64; Cat 3, $75, $60; and Cat 4, $59, $48 (but there is hardly a bad seat in the house).

Splitsville: An imaginative venue in which to 'dine, dance, drink – and bowl'. Yes, it's a 10-pin bowling centre, but not like anything you've seen before. Built in best 1950s period style, this twin-level entertainment palace offers 30 lanes of bowling, multiple bars, billiard tables and a full-service restaurant, along with elegant indoor and outdoor seating, including a 1st-floor patio for a great

La Nouba

view over Disney Springs. The upper floor also has more of a grown-up style in the evening, with DJs adding a nightclub vibe. Walk-in rates are $15/person Mon–Fri 10am–4pm and $20 after 4pm; $20/person all day Sat and Sun, with Early Bird specials until 12:30pm. Book a lane in advance by calling or online (10.30–1am Mon–Fri; 10–2am Sat and Sun; 407 938 7467, www.splitsvillelanes.com).

Other entertainment: The evening sees a variety of live music performers throughout Disney Springs, from flamenco guitarists to classical quartets and more. Look for them in all four sections.

Disney Resorts

Disney's Boardwalk: Disney's other big evening entertainment offering is part of its impressive BoardWalk Resort, where the waterfront entertainment district contains several notable venues (not counting the excellent micro-brewery and restaurant of the Big River Grille and Brewing Works, the thrilling ESPN Club for sports fans and 5-star Flying Fish Café). **Jellyroll**s is a variation on the duelling piano bar, with the lively pianists conjuring up a humorous and often raucous evening of audience participation (7pm–2am, music from 8pm; $12 cover charge; 21 and over only).

The **Atlantic Dance** club features mainly modern dance music with house and guest DJs, plus occasional live music, a huge dance floor and a great bar service and ambience. Video DJs feature on Tue, Wed and Sat, with 'duelling DJs' on Thurs and Fri, and it's especially popular on Fri and Sat nights (9pm–2am; closed Sun and Mon). It's strictly 21 and over, so bring your ID (no ID, no entry, no exceptions). The Boardwalk also features some amusing stalls and live entertainers, which add to the carnival atmosphere, while the ESPN Club features regular celebrity (American) sports guests.

Coronado Springs Resort: A hidden gem here is the **Rix Lounge**. A bar-nightclub with a smooth ultra-lounge vibe, it features its own cocktail list, from martinis to shooters and tequila and margarita flights, plus a light-bite menu of appetisers and flatbreads. With a live DJ Thurs–Sat, it is a cool place just to go for an early-evening drink or a great full-on nightclub later on (6pm–midnight; www.rix-lounge.com).

Electrical Water Pageant: This is another nightly (and free!) alternative, an eye-catching 'parade' that circles Bay Lake and the Seven Seas Lagoon, passing by each of the Magic Kingdom resorts in turn. It lasts just 10mins, but it's almost a waterborne version of the Main Street Electrical

Universal's CityWalk

Parade, with thousands of twinkling lights on a cavalcade of pontoons, all set to its own music. The usual schedule is 9pm at the Polynesian Resort, 9.15 at Grand Floridian Resort & Spa (get a grandstand view in Narcoosee's restaurant), 9.35 at Wilderness Lodge, 9.45 on the shores of Fort Wilderness Resort and 10.05 at Contemporary Resort. It can also be seen outside the Magic Kingdom at 10.20pm during extended hours.

UNIVERSAL'S CITYWALK

As part of the big Universal Orlando development, this 30acre/12ha spread offers a bustling expanse of restaurants, snack bars, shops, open-air events and nightclubs. It offers a huge variety of cuisines, from fast food to fine dining, an unusual blend of speciality shops and an eclectic nightclub mix, from reggae and rock 'n' roll to salsa, jazz and high-energy disco, plus the superb **Blue Man Group** show and a karaoke theatre/bar. There's a $7 entry fee at the six clubs but you can buy a **CityWalk Party Pass** ($12) or **Party Pass with Movie** (one free film at the 20-screen Universal Cineplex; $15) for entry to all of them, while most multi-day tickets include a Party Pass. The area splits into the Main Plaza (shopping and dining), Lagoon Front (dining, live music and theatre) and the Promenade (dining and nightclubs). For dining, see p307.

Blue Man Group: The most entertaining element here at the Sharp AQUOS Theatre offers a unique brand of comedy, music and multi-media theatrics, adding something completely novel to the Universal line-up. In the hands (or mouths!) of the Blue Men, mundane items like pipes, paintballs, cereal, GI-Pads, and even audience members become the instruments of wild creativity with sometimes stunning, occasionally slightly gross but always hilariously gratifying outcomes. There is a strong live music element and it can feel a bit like a rock concert. Their ability to drum up a tune on various bits and pieces is truly amazing. The wild finale, involving the whole

theatre, is a real corker, and don't worry if you're seated in the 'poncho section'; the Blue Men will make sure you have adequate protection. An unforgettable evening of family entertainment, from $70 adults, $30 3–9s. Tickets are available at **www.universalorlando.com** or from the theatre box office (book online for a $10 discount).

◀◆ BRITTIP
Park in Universal's multi-storey car park for all CityWalk venues – only $5 after 6pm (except during special evening events), free on weekdays after 10pm. For more info, call 407 363 8000.

Bob Marley – A Tribute to Freedom: A clever re-creation of Marley's Jamaica home is turned into a courtyard music venue and restaurant. The bands are excellent, the atmosphere authentic and the place comes alive at night (bar open until 2am, 21 and over only after 9pm; cover charge after 9pm).

The Groove: For club-minded visitors this is a high-tech dance venue designed like a Victorian theatre but with the latest in club music, lighting and special effects (9pm–2am; 21 and over only; attire casual chic, no hats, no tank-tops).

Hard Rock Live: A massive mock-Coliseum styled 2,500-seat theatre with high-tech staging and sound, big-name artists are on stage several times a week (Boston, Alanis Morrisette and the fantastic Classic Albums Live all appeared in 2015) in this slightly retro rock 'n' roll venue (407 351 5483, **www.hardrock.com**).

Jimmy Buffet's Margaritaville: Live music and 3 bars (11.30am–2am). Band (and cover charge) starts at 10pm.

Red Coconut Club: This retro dance club has a trendy, tropical vibe. With live music, signature cocktails, tapas-style menu and eclectic South Seas décor, it is a popular venue (7pm–2am Mon–Sat; 8pm–2am Sun; free admission for ladies on Thurs; 21 and over only). DJ daily, live music Thurs–Sat.

Rising Star Karaoke: It's karaoke taken to the next level, with a live band, back-up singers and a host who makes every volunteer singer feel like a star. There is a full bar with speciality cocktails, appetisers and a large selection of songs (8pm–2am nightly; 21 and over; 18 and over on Thurs only). Tues–Sat live band, back-up singers and host; back-up singers and host only on Sun and Mon.

Not breathless yet? Well, there's still the 20-screen Universal Cineplex with a capacity of 5,000 and the latest in movie comfort. There's also a Meal & Movie Deal for a film and dinner at one of the 8 restaurants for $21.95. And, of course, there's the new Hollywood Drive-In Golf (p268).

POINTE ORLANDO

This eye-catching development on I-Drive, almost opposite the Convention Center, is a mix of shops, cinema, restaurants, live entertainment and the WonderWorks fun centre (with its magic-themed dinner show). The Pointe is open all day but has notable evening appeal.

Adobe Gila's: Especially popular with locals and often packed at weekends, it stays open late and features live outdoor music and DJs several days a week. On Fri and Sat the place should be kicking from 6.30pm: on weekdays, it's likely to be 8.30pm (407 903 1477; **www.adobegilas.com**).

BB King's Blues Club: Live jazz and blues make this a fine choice for a

meal or drinks and a show in this imaginative venue, featuring a main 2-storey concert hall and a variety of bars. If what you want is a real party, BB King's takes some beating, with live music nightly from 7.30pm with one of its 2 excellent house bands, plus guests (407 370 4550, **www.bbkingclubs.com**).

Cuba Libre Restaurant and Rum Bar: Offers live Latin music on Sat nights (**www.cubalibrerestaurant.com**).

Minus 5° Ice Bar: Don a Minus 5° parka or Faux Fur and a pair of gloves and party until your nose turns blue! The entire bar is made of ice—and so are the glasses—in this deep-freeze setting with LED light show, music and themed ice rooms. (**www.minus5experience.com**).

Orlando Improv Comedy Club and Fat Fish Blue: The Improv pulls in top name comedians from across the country, with shows ranging from mildly risqué to downright raucous. The theatre is intimate, making it easy for entertainers to interact with guests (often with hilarious results) and it is a terrific change of pace for a grown-up night out. Seating is first-come, first-seated, full food and drinks menu available, all shows 21 and over, with two performances on Fri and Sat (no shows Mon and Tue). Connected to the Improv is the bistro-style Fat Fish Blue, featuring American fare with a New Orleans accent. Full bar, a good range of speciality beers, and live music five nights per week. All ages welcome (407 480 5233, **www.theimprovorlando.com**).

Taverna Opa: A lively Greek option, with belly-dancing, other live entertainment and a great ouzo bar! (407 351 8660, **www.opaorlando.com**).

Regal Cinema: Also here is a 21-screen movieplex (one an IMAX) that features state-of-the-art stadium seating and sound systems, where you can often see a new film before it arrives in the UK. Look for the ticket office on the ground level. For more on Pointe Orlando, 407 248 2838 or **www.pointeorlando.com**. For more on the restaurant choices, see p319.

Blue Man Group

DOWNTOWN ORLANDO

The heart of the city of Orlando is once more a thriving area of bars, restaurants and nightlife, with a tempting array of possibilities for a memorable evening out. Church Street is the epi-centre, a core street with a wide variety of dining choice (from the distinctive supper-club of **Kres Chophouse** and its elegant bar, the award-winning **Rusty Spoon**, featuring an award-winning gastropub style, and the all-American burger bar frenzy of **Graffiti Junktion** to the full-on German vibe of **Schumann's Jager Haus**, with live entertainment Wed, Fri & Sat), high-energy bars (notably **Don Jefe's Tequila Parlor**, **Dubliner**, **Native Social Bar**, rooftop **Latitudes** and the **Church Street Tavern**), plus cabaret, theatre and live music, making it Party Central at weekends and fairly lively Wed and Thurs, too. Don't miss the eclectic **Mad Cow Theatre**, which presents major plays and theatrical events, including an annual Cabaret Festival (Apr–May; 407 297 8788, **www.madcowtheatre.com**) and the atmospheric **Ceviche** lounge, offering live flamenco dance shows, outstanding cocktails with a Mediterranean twist and an extensive wine list (to go with the restaurant's high-end cuisine; **http://ceviche.com/**). For the ultimate in party style, the outrageous **Hamburger Mary's** takes some beating, with its drag acts and live comedy (distinctly R-rated but lots of fun), in addition to its diner style of great burgers, sandwiches, decadent desserts and signature cocktails. They feature Twisted Sisters Bingo on Tue, Trivia with Doug on Weds, the Facebook Friday Show ('an interactive drag show'), Leigh Shannon's Cabaret on Sat and a signature Broadway Brunch on Sun (shows variously 6.30–8pm, booking highly advised; 321 319 0600, **http://hamburgermarys.com/orlando/**). Nearby, **Wall Street Plaza**, between Orange Ave and N Court Ave, is equally lively Thurs-Sat as the locals bar-hop along the series of seven different bar venues – including live music at Sideshow – all night long! (**http://wallstplaza.net/**). More downtown entertainment can be had at **The Social**, an indie club staging eclectic bands most nights, plus a busy bar, the **Bosendorfer Lounge** (for great live jazz; inside The Grand Bohemian Hotel), and **The Beacham**, a new nightclub and concert venue next to The Social. The Speakeasy phenomenon can also be found here, with the 1920s 'hidden bar' style well evidenced by **Hanson's Shoe Repair** (call in advance on 407 476 9446 and they will contact you with the nightly password!) and **The Treehouse** (407 205 2062, **http://thetreehouseorlando.com/**).

DINNER SHOWS

Another source of evening entertainment comes in the various dinner shows that are a major Orlando phenomenon. From murder mysteries to full-scale medieval battles, it's all wonderful, imaginative fun, even if the food is usually quite ordinary. It is live entertainment coupled with dinner and free soft drinks in a fantasy environment, where even the waiters and waitresses are in costume. They have strong family appeal and you are usually seated at large tables where you get to know other people, but at $40–74, they are not cheap (especially with taxes and tips). Be aware, too, of the attempts to extract more from you with photos, souvenirs and upgrades.

BRITTIP

American cinema popcorn is invariably SALTED. Sweet popcorn in the US is usually called Kettle Corn.

Disney shows

Visitors often overlook Walt Disney World's offerings unless they are staying at one of the hotel resorts, but they are certainly worth considering.

Disney's Spirit of Aloha: For an excellent night of South Seas entertainment, go to Luau Cove at Disney's Polynesian Resort. It's a bit expensive – $73 for adults (Category 1 main floor centre seating) and $36–40 for under-10s; or Cat 2 upper floor and sides $68 and $37; Cat 3 extreme sides or extreme upper level $61 and $34 – but good value as the 2hr show features some splendid entertainment, such as Hawaiian singers and dancers, and an amazing Samoan fire juggler, and tax and gratuity are included. The food is plentiful, with salad, BBQ ribs, roast chicken, pulled pork, vegetables, pineapple and rice, plus a pineapple bread pudding (limited kid-friendly menu). Beer, wine and soft drinks are included, and shows are at 5.15 and 8pm Tues–Sat. Make reservations up to 180 days in advance, with full payment when booking.

Hoop-Dee-Doo Musical Revue:

At Disney's Fort Wilderness Resort & Campground, this is a popular nightly dinner show that maintains the resort's Western theme, and has great food (all-you-can-eat ribs, fried chicken, seasonal vegetable, baked beans, corn bread and strawberry shortcake, plus unlimited beer, wine, sangria and soft drinks). Especially loved by children, it features the amusing song and dance of the Pioneer Hall Players in a merry American hoedown. We're slightly biased but we love this show as it's been running since 1974 and remains a Disney tradition, full of genuine wit and humour, plus a hugely energetic cast that keep things fresh every night. The Revue plays at 5, 7.15 and 9.30pm at the authentic Pioneer Hall, Category 1 seating (main floor centre) is $68 for adults, $37 for under-10s; Cat 2 (back and balcony) $65 and $34; Cat 3 (side balconies) $59 and $33 (under-3s free; prices include tax and gratuity) and the show lasts almost two hours. Reservations are ALWAYS

Men in Black Alien Attack

© Universal Orlando Resort

necessary and can be made up to 180 days in advance (full payment at booking).

Mickey's Backyard Barbecue: If you can't get enough of the Disney characters, try this dinner show (select dates, Mar–Dec at 6.30pm, at Disney's Fort Wilderness Resort). It features Mickey and the gang in a country buffet-style dinner at picnic tables under an open-air pavilion with live music, line dancing, rope tricks and other entertainment, and plenty of character interaction (great for younger children). The all-you-can-eat buffet offers barbecued pork ribs, baked chicken, hot dogs, hamburgers, macaroni and cheese, ice-cream and more. Like all Disney dining, this is a no-smoking environment. The show may be cancelled if bad weather threatens ($59 adults, $33 3–9s). To book a Disney show, call 407 939 3463.

BRITTIP

Most dinner shows can be quite chilly, especially those with animals like Medieval Times, so bring a jacket or sweater to beat the air-conditioning.

Medieval Times

Spain in the 11th century is the entertaining setting for this two-hour extravaganza of medieval pageantry, falconry and robust horseback jousts that culminate in furious hand-to-hand combat among six knights. It's worth arriving early to appreciate the clever mock castle design and the staff's costumes as you are ushered into the pre-show hall before being taken into the arena. The show features jousting, sword-fighting and other well-scripted hand-to-hand combats, along with some superb horsemanship, with the basic idea of cheering on one of the 'Knights of the Realm' in the six colour-coded sections. The show also includes a dramatic musical score by award-winning film composer Daniel May, the weapons are all real and used with great skill, and there are some neat special effects. You need to be in full audience participation mode as you cheer on your knight in the traditional Good-v-Evil scenario, but kids (and many adults) get a huge kick out of it and they'll also love eating without cutlery (the soup bowls do have handles, though!). Soft drinks are included, but alcohol is Cash Bar Only. The elaborate staging is backed up by a succulent chicken, corn and baked potato dinner (vegetarian meal available) and the serfs and wenches who serve you make it a fun experience. Prices, which include the Medieval Life exhibit, are $62.95 for adults and $36.95 for 3–12s. A basic Royalty Package upgrade for $10/person includes preferred seating, knight's cheering banner, commemorative programme and behind-the-scenes souvenir DVD. The King's Royalty Package adds VIP first-row seating all sections or second row in the centre seating area, plus a framed group photo ($20), and the birthday Celebration Package adds a group photo per person, VIP seating, programme, banner, DVD, personalised announcement during the show and a slice of cake ($16 more). Doors open 90mins prior to show time. Times vary seasonally, so call 1866 543 9637 or visit **www. medievaltimes.com** for reservations and details. The Castle is on Highway 192, 5ml/8km east of the junction with I-4.

If you have 45mins to spare before the show, the Medieval Life exhibit is an interesting diversion. This mock village portrays the life and times of 900 years ago (with some gruesome dungeon and torture chamber scenes not for young 'uns!). Stay on after the show (the 2nd show only on busy nights) for The Knight Club, full bar service, music, dancing and the chance to meet royalty and knights for autographs and photos.

Pirates' Dinner Adventure

This show, sub-titled Rise of the Sea Dragon, features one of the most spectacular settings, with a life-size pirate ship 'anchored' in a huge indoor lagoon – and a giant animatronic dragon! It delivers good value with its pre-show elements, plentiful food, soft drinks and beer (with the main show, plus a cash bar during the pre-show). A kids' meal choice (chicken fingers or mac and cheese) is available if the hearty main meal of beef kebabs or chicken with rice and seasonal vegetables doesn't appeal. The story starts in period style at the Seaport Village where the Governor's Annual Gala is taking place, with entertainment provided by the magic and stories of Raddu the

Medieval Times

Gypsy King before guests are spirited off to the pirates' realm. Here, Captain Sebastian the Black is preparing to raid Treasure Bay for the booty that awaits him if he can get past the fearsome sea serpent that guards the way. The evil captain thinks he can win the day with a royal sacrifice, but the kind-hearted Benjamin Blue is ready to save the imperilled princess, even if it means fighting off the whole band of scurvy pirates. That's the cue for all manner of fights, duels, acrobatics, fights, trapeze acts and more fights, with plenty of audience participation and cheering. Highly family friendly and a big hit with kids ($65.95 adults, $39.45 3–11s, includes one round of beer or two of soft drinks during the show; see website for savings).

There is a Treasure Experience upgrade that adds second row seating, guaranteed pirate interaction, unlimited soda and beer during the show, and gift shop discount ($25 extra); a Governor's VIP Upgrade ($30) adds exclusive pre-show lounge, restroom and cash bar, front-row seating, special appetiser buffet, and champagne toast; or a Captain's Upgrade, with third row seating ($15) and discounts at the gift shop. It is located on Carrier Drive between I-Drive and Universal Boulevard, and runs at 7.30pm or 8.30pm, with appetisers served for 45mins prior to seating (407 206 5102, **www.piratesdinneradventure.com**). There is a fee for parking but also a special Pirates Christmas Dinner Adventure show, which adds suitably festive themes.

Pirates' Dinner Adventure

© Pirates' Dinner Adventure

Sleuth's Mystery Dinner Shows

This is a live version of Cluedo acted out before your eyes in hilarious fashion while you enjoy a substantial meal (with a main course choice of honey-glazed poussin (Cornish hen), lasagne with or without meatballs, or, for $6 extra, prime rib) and unlimited beer, wine and soft drinks. You can choose between three theatres and 12 different plot situations (several of which have amusing British settings), including Squires Inns, Roast 'Em & Toast 'Em and Lord Mansfield's Fox Hunt Banquet (mayhem at an English banquet), that add up to some elaborate murder mysteries. The action takes place all around you and members of the audience can take some cameo roles. The quick-witted cast keep things moving and keep you guessing during the theatrical part of the 2½-hour show, then during the main part of dinner you think up questions for interrogation (but the real murderer is allowed to lie!). Solve the crime and you win a prize, but that is pretty secondary to the overall enjoyment and this is a show we enjoy a lot, plus it's a terrific choice with teens ($59.95 adults, $28.95 3–11s; times vary; 407 363 1985, **www.sleuths.com**). Also check out their periodic Stand Up Comedy Spotlight (see website for dates, times, and comedians). Sleuth's is in the plaza just past Ripley's Believe It Or Not on I-Drive, with 3 different theatres, a smart pre-dinner bar area and gift shop.

WonderWorks: Outta Control Magic Comedy

On a smaller scale but no less fun, this dinner show is at WonderWorks on I-Drive (on one corner of Pointe Orlando). A novel mixture of improvised comedy and magic, the show is accompanied by all-you-can-eat pizza, salad, popcorn and dessert, plus beer, wine and coke. Set in the intimate Shazam Theater, it features live music, special lighting effects and some slick magic tricks from illusionist (and funny guy) Tony Brent. The tricks are relatively small-scale but are served up with terrific style and plenty of audience participation. Beware of sitting too close to the stage – you WILL end up as part of the act! Twice nightly at 6pm and 8pm, it costs a good-value $25.99 for adults, $19.99 4–12s and seniors. A Magic Combo ticket for the show and access to WonderWorks (open until midnight, p236) is $49/$38 (407 351 8800, **www.wonderworksonline.com**).

Capone's Dinner & Show

This 1930s gangland version of Chicago is home to Al himself and a 'family gathering' that goes hopelessly wrong. Try to keep track of local gangster Fingers Salvatorio and his ditzy wife, Bunny-June, as they look to provide for Fingers Jnr, aka Little Pinky, and fail miserably, causing all manner of mayhem for the hapless parents, Bunny-June's sisters Babs and Bubbles, and a vengeful – if slightly dim – beat cop, ex-detective Marvel. The audience can often be at the centre of the action and there is a hilarious 'shoot-out' finale it would be wrong to reveal (but you won't mind if you are 'hit'!). A huge Italian-American buffet offers four types of pasta, meatballs, pizza, salad bar, a carvery and side dishes. Unlimited Bud Light, a selection of wines and cocktails, plus soft drinks, juice, Kiddie Cocktails and Mama Capone's 'dessert surprise' round out the all-you-can-eat-and-drink menu ($64 adults, $40 4–12s, 3 and under free; 407 397 2378, **www.alcapones.com**).

Live music

Orlando's live music scene is lively and always changing but several venues can be relied on for quality entertainment. As already noted, the House of Blues and Hard Rock Live provide regular big-name concerts, while international acts appear at the state-of-the-art **Amway Center** in downtown (as well as the Orlando Magic, Orlando Predators and Orlando Solar Bears sports teams), including New Kids on the Block and Ricky Martin in 2015 (**www.amwaycenter.com**). The new **Dr Phillips Performing Arts Center** also features big-name concert performers as well as touring Broadway performances and the Orlando Ballet company (1844 513 2014, **www.drphillipscenter.org**).

Sports bars

The Sports Bar is a particularly American invention and is well served hereabouts if you'd like to sample the way the locals follow their sport (American football is usually the biggest at weekends Sept–Jan, but basketball is also popular, along with baseball and ice-hockey).

Orlando Ale House Group: Among the multitude of sports bars, one of our favourites has fine examples on Kirkman Road, opposite Universal Studios (407 248 0000) at Lake Buena Vista on Highway 535 near Downtown Disney (407 239 1800), on I-Drive (407 370 6688) and the newest location, Miller's Ale House in Winter Park Village (321 214 1505). The Ale Houses feature more than 30 TVs (each!), classic American bar food, including their signature spicy 'chicken zingers' and an above-average range of beers (**www.millersalehouse.com**).

ESPN Club

Buffalo Wild Wings: Another chain worth noting has five Orlando locations (notably on I-Drive just south of Wet 'n Wild, 407 351 6200; Lake Buena Vista near Downtown Disney, 407 827 0444; and their newest at I-Drive 360), where masses of chicken-orientated dishes (watch out for the Blazin' sauce – it's seriously hot!) are served up in a casual, lively atmosphere, highlighted by its Buzztime Trivia System at each table and multiple big-screen TVs (**www.buffalowildwings.com**).

Other options: Also look out for the revamped **Uno Chicago** chain (**www.unos.com**) or any TGI Fridays, Beef O'Brady's or BJ's Brewhouse outlet. Then there is **Frank & Steins Eatery & Pub** in downtown Orlando (**www.frankandsteins.com**) and The Pub and Marlow's Tavern, both at Pointe Orlando (p319).

Disney boasts the excellent **ESPN Club** at Disney's BoardWalk Resort, a full-service restaurant with sports broadcast facilities, video games, more than 70 TV monitors, giant scoreboards and even a Little League menu for kids. Universal CityWalk boasts **NBA City** (for basketball fans) and the forthcoming new **NBC Sports Grill & Brew**, with more big-screen TV style. The various British-style pubs also offer sports bar style. Try the **Orlando George & Dragon** on International Drive next to Wet 'n

The George & Dragon

© The George & Dragon

Wild (**www.orlandogeorgeanddragon. com**) and **Frankie Farrell's Irish Pub** at Lake Buena Vista Resort & Spa (next to the Factory Stores).

Something different

Icebar: Spend 45mins surrounded by 50 tons of carved ice while sipping a chilled vodka beverage, then warm up in the Nordic-inspired Fire Lounge, at the unique venue on I-Drive just north of WonderWorks. Coats and gloves are provided or you can upgrade to a glam mock fur coat for $10, and entry fee is $19.95 (drinks not included; save $5–8 by booking online). Open 7pm–12am Sun–Wed, 7pm–1am Thurs, 7pm–2am Fri–Sat, with the first ICEBAR entry time at 7.15pm; ages 8 and up allowed 7pm-9pm only. No cover charge for Fire Lounge (which also features DJs), but no children. Happy Hour 7–9pm Sun–Thurs, and Expedition Package at $29.95, including one premium drink in ICEBAR and one in Fire Lounge (407 426 0361 or **www.icebarorlando.com**).

$ BRITBONUS

Pay for entry to the Icebar and receive a FREE pint in the Fire Lounge afterwards. Just show your copy of the *Brit Guide* for the free drink.

Howl at the Moon: If you're looking for a serious party, try Howl at the Moon on I-Drive, where the live music doesn't stop until the wee hours! An energetic piano-playing duo pound out a rockin' good time, highlighted by 'Showtime', when the whole bar joins in a choreographed dance-fest. Signature cocktails are available by the glass or the bucket(!), with drink specials nightly (21 and over only; 7pm–2am Sun–Thurs, 6pm–2am Fri–Sat; cover charge $5 Mon–Wed, $7 Thurs, $10 Fri and Sat, $7 Sun; 407 354 5999, **www.howlatthemoon.com**).

Now you'll want to know a lot more about where, when and how to tackle that other holiday dilemma – where to eat. Read on…

11

Dining Out

or Eat, Drink and Eat Again!

The options for dining out are omnipresent and large scale, which is excellent news as it means it's impossible to go hungry and easy to feed the family – without breaking the bank.

Variety

The variety, quantity and quality of restaurants, cafés, fast-food chains and snack bars is in keeping with the local tradition of convenience and value.

As a rule, food is plentiful, relatively cheap, available 24 hours a day, and nearly always appetising and filling. You will encounter an increasing number of fine-dining possibilities, but the basic emphasis is on value. Portions are large, service is efficient and friendly, and it's hard to come by a bad meal. The one real exception is if you dine mainly at fast food places and the likes of Dennys and Co, you won't find much fresh veg. But if you look up the vegetarian options, visit outlets like Sweet Tomatoes and ask for the vegetable option instead of fries or potatoes at other restaurants, you will find a more balanced choice. Plus, salads are almost always on the menu.

Exceptional deals

Most restaurants tend towards the informal (T-shirts and shorts are nearly always acceptable) and cater readily for families; you will always find a kids' menu, and many have activity packs. Many hotels and restaurants offer Kids-eat-free deals (from under-10 to under-14), provided parents are also dining. The age limits vary. The all-you-can-eat buffet is another common feature, where you can probably eat enough at breakfast to keep you going to dinner! Some places offer early-bird specials – a discount to dine before 6pm. Be aware that 5.30–7.30pm is peak time for many restaurants, though, and you may have to wait for a table if you arrive between 6 and 8pm.

BRITTIP

Portions are often so large, you can save money by sharing a main course. Your waiter or waitress should be happy to oblige (but keep their tip up to the full rate).

Don't be afraid to ask for the leftovers 'to go' and don't hesitate to say if something isn't right; the locals will readily complain (politely) if they are not happy, so restaurants are keen to ensure everything is to their diners' satisfaction. And, please, don't forget to tip; the basic wage for waiters and waitresses is low, so they rely heavily on tips as part of their income and are taxed on an assumed level of tips. Unless service really is shoddy (in which case mention it), the usual tip rate is 10% of your bill at buffet-style restaurants and 15–20% at full-service restaurants. Check whether service is already added to your bill, though this is not common.

You will encounter a huge array of food types. Florida is renowned for its seafood, which comes much cheaper than in the Mediterranean: crab, lobster, shrimp (what we call king prawns), clams and oysters, as well as several dozen varieties of fish, many unusual (like mahi mahi and grouper). Latin-style cuisines, notably Cuban and Mexican, are common, and the South American influences mean the delicious citrus-marinated seafood called ceviche is often featured. There is also plenty of Asian fare, from Chinese and Indian to Japanese, Thai and Vietnamese. The big shopping malls all offer good value food courts. 'Cracker' cooking is original Floridian fare, and the speciality is alligator, either stewed, barbecued, smoked, sautéed or braised. Fried gator tail 'nuggets' are a local favourite, as are catfish and frogs' legs. And do try key lime pie!

> **BRITTIP**
>
> An excellent section of the All Ears website run by Deb Wills lists places that cater for special diets, including veggie, at www.allearsnet.com/din/special.htm. Many restaurants now offer gluten-free options, too.

How to order

Ordering food can be an adventure in itself. The choice for each item is often the cue for an inquisition! You can never order just 'toast' – it has to be white, brown, whole wheat, rye, muffin or bagel; eggs come in a baffling variety (order them 'sunny side up' for a traditional British fried egg; 'over easy' is fried both sides but still soft); an order of tea or coffee often brings the query, 'Hot, iced, lemon, green or herbal? Regular or decaf?'; and salads have more dressings than the NHS. Feel free to ask if what you fancy isn't shown on the menu.

Vegetarian options

In a country where beef is king, vegetarians often find themselves hard done by. However, there are some bright spots. Largely vegetarian

restaurants include the Indian cuisine of **Woodlands** on S Orange Blossom Trail (407 854 3330, www.woodlandsusa.com; closed Mon), the popular Chinese of the **Garden Café** on Highway 50 close to downtown Orlando (407 999 9799), and the trendy duo of **Ethos Vegan Kitchen** on N Orange Ave, just north of downtown (407 228 3898, www.ethosvegankitchen.com) and **Cafe 118** in Winter Park (407 389 2233, www.cafe118.com) with its all-organic menu. The tapas-style **Café Tu Tu Tango** on I-Drive also serves a good variety of veggie dishes. However, most upmarket restaurants can offer a vegetarian option and will be happy for you to ask in advance. In Walt Disney World, the **California Grill** (in Disney's Contemporary Resort), **Citricos** (Grand Floridian Resort & Spa), **Le Cellier** (Canada pavilion in Epcot) and **Jiko** (Animal Kingdom Lodge) feature good vegetarian choices, while the seafood-orientated **Flying Fish** (Disney's Boardwalk) and 'Ohana (Disney's Polynesian Resort) also serve up decent veggie fare if asked. Two good Mediterranean-style choices with vegetarians in mind are **Anatolia** (p315) and **Cedar's** (p316). Most full-service restaurants (notably **Bongos Cuban Café™** and **Wolfgang Puck® Café** in Disney Springs; p307) and even some counter-service outlets can cater for non-menu requests. It's always worth asking.

> **BRITTIP**
>
> Sweet Tomatoes is a restaurant chain we recommend highly, and you can benefit from its enhanced dinner menu by arriving a little before 4pm but still paying only the lunch buffet price.

However, **Sweet Tomatoes** (with five outlets, notably on I-Drive by Kirkman Road, in the Crossroads Plaza at Lake Buena Vista and just off West Highway 192 in Kissimmee on Rolling Oaks Blvd) is a great vegetarian-friendly outlet. A buffet restaurant with some great meal deals, it has an all-you-can-eat lunch for $9.99 ($11.79 at dinner, after 4pm)

Belly up to the bar!

If you'd like just a snack or sample of a restaurant's fare, many places offer a bar or appetiser menu, including Bar Louie, Big Fin Seafood, Bongos Cuban Café, Bravo, Bonefish Grill, Capital Grille, Carrabba's, Eddie V's, Emeril's Tchoup Chop, Fishbones, Fleming's, Fulton's Crab House, Hillstone, House of Blues, Kres Chophouse, Luma on Park, Moonfish, Morton's, The Oceanaire, Old Hickory, Portobello, Rainforest Café, Ravenous Pig, Roy's, Seasons 52, Tommy Bahama Café and T-Rex Café, plus Brio Tuscan Grille (weekdays only, in the bar), Landry's Seafood House (3pm–6pm Mon–Thurs) and The Palm (5–7pm Sun–Fri).

that includes a vast salad counter, freshly made soups, pizza, pasta, bread and pastries, plus fruit and frozen yoghurt. The menu is healthy and the quality is consistently first class, while its website lists nutrition info. Drinks are $2.79 (refills free) and kids' meals are $3.99 3–9s and $5.99 9–12s (11am–9pm Sun–Thurs, 11am–10pm Fri–Sat), **www.soupplantation.com**).

Chamberlin's Market & Café: With six Orlando outlets, notably in the Dr Phillips Plaza just off Sand Lake Rd, this is another choice, with home-made soups, salads, sandwiches and fruit smoothies (**www.chamberlins.com**). The **Panera Bread** chain also offers some decent veggie options (plus free wi-fi).

BRITTIP

American bacon is always streaky and crisp fried, and sausages are chipolata-like and slightly spicy. Very different from the British versions.

Eating 24/7

It's not unusual to find restaurants open around the clock (or 24/7, as they say). So here is where you can go for a snack or even a full-scale meal at four in the morning. **Chain restaurants:** Denny's, Waffle House, Steak & Shake, some McDonald's. **Individuals:** B-Line Diner (Hyatt Regency Orlando, I-Drive), Planet Java (Gaylord Palms Resort), Sundial 24–7 (Wyndham Lake Buena Vista) and Mainstreet Market (Hilton at Walt Disney World Resort).

Drinking

American big-label brewery beer is generally lager, bottled or on draught, which goes down great when it's hot, but is weaker and fizzier than our own. Of course, there are exceptions (try Killian's Red, Michelob's Amber Bock, Leinenkugel's or Sam Adams beers for a fuller flavour). The good news is, there is a huge market in excellent craft beers, which are readily available at nearly every bar and restaurant (look for Sam Adams, Kona, Magic Hat, Goose Island, Sierra Nevada, Bells, Shock Top, Leinenkugel, Orlando Brewing Co and many more). You should also look out for The Big River Grille at Disney's BoardWalk Resort and Orlando Brewing (on Atlanta Ave, just south of downtown Orlando), an organic micro-brewery with a range of distinctive brews, plus free brewery tours Mon–Sat at 6pm (407 872 1117, **www.orlandobrewing.com**). Yuengling – America's oldest brewery – has a plant in Tampa near Busch Gardens that also offers free tours – as well as samples! (p280). Spirits (called 'liquor') come in a large selection, but beware of ordering just 'whisky' as you'll get bourbon. Specify if you want Scotch or Irish whiskey and demand it 'straight up' if you don't want it with a mountain of ice. When you order a soft drink from a counter-service outlet, ask for 'no ice' or 'light ice' unless you want a drink with lots of ice.

There is a massive choice of cocktails and most bars and restaurants have lengthy happy hours with good prices. Good-quality Californian wines are better value than European. If you stick to soft drinks ('sodas') or coffee, most bars and restaurants give free refills. You can also run a tab in the majority of bars and pay when you leave. But be aware US licensing laws are stricter than ours and you MUST be 21 to drink alcohol in a bar or lounge. You'll often be asked for proof of age before you are served (or allowed into a club), so take your passport or photo driving licence. Don't bother to argue – no photo ID, no beer!

Magical Dining Month

Orlando has become a foodie's paradise in recent years and, to celebrate, each Sept is dedicated as Magical Dining Month, with an array of special events and a selection of top restaurants offering a three-course prix fixe menu at $33/head, a great saving on regular prices. In recent years these have included A Land Remembered (Rosen Shingle Creek), Seasons 52, and Emeril's Tchoup Chop. Check out more at **www.visitorlando.com/magicaldining**.

⚜ BRITTIP
If there are several of you drinking beer, ordering a pitcher will work out cheaper than buying it by the glass.

Where to eat

That gives you the inside track on HOW to eat and drink like the locals. Now you need to know WHERE. There are 4,000-plus restaurants in the area, so the following selection covers the main ones, grouped by style. You'll find the Fast Food and Family Favourite type in all the main areas. We also indicate a budget:

$	= most main courses under $10
$$	= most main courses $10–15
$$$	= most main courses $15–20
$$$$	= most main courses $20–30
$$$$$	= most main course $30-plus

Emeril's Orlando

© Universal Orlando Resort

We also have a special section on each of the three main areas of I-Drive, Highway 192/Kissimmee and Lake Buena Vista. But, as ever, we start with Walt Disney World.

DISNEY SPRINGS DINING

The heart of Disney dining can be found at Disney Springs.

The Landing

Fulton's Crab House: Good seafood is not hard to come by, but great seafood is the preserve of a handful – like Fulton's. This mock riverboat has 6 dining rooms (each with the same menu), plus the Stone Crab Lounge, which features a busy raw bar. The recently refurbished interior is filled with nautical props, photos and lithographs, giving it an eclectic atmosphere, but the real attraction is some of the freshest and most tempting fish, crab and lobster dishes in Florida, including fresh daily specials and a kid's menu. Try their excellent calamari steak or pan-roasted mussels pasta. The Stone Crab Lounge serves lunch and dinner 11.30am–11pm, while the restaurant is open for dinner only ($$$–$$$$$; 4–11pm; 407 394 2628; **www.fultonscrabhouse.com**).

⚜ BRITTIP
Fulton's Crab House began life as the paddleboat *Empress Lilly* (named for Walt's wife, Lillian). In the original Pleasure Island story, it was the boat Merryweather Pleasure arrived on (hence the name Pleasure Island). It originally had a paddlewheel and funnel, which were removed after it became Fulton's.

Paradiso 37: This 'Taste of the Americas' offers a wide variety of foods, much with a Latin-tinged flavour, and live music nightly. A tempting menu includes Argentinean skirt steak, Chilean salmon, Mexican fare, plus signature cocktails and tequila. The lively style, split-level restaurant, chic bar area (inside and out) and lakeside setting mark this out for a relaxing lunch or upbeat dinner, or just somewhere to kick back with a drink or speciality coffee ($$–$$$$; 11am–11pm Sun–Thurs, 12am Fri and Sat; 407 934 3700).

Portobello: Don't overlook this Tuscan trattoria on the edge of the Marketplace and The Landing. From the fresh bread with oven-baked garlic to the family-style menu and full wine list, there's everything from pizza to zucchini ribbons in a tomato seafood broth. We are big fans of their insistence on locally sourced fresh produce, and it really shines through in the great taste of things like the Rigatoni and Black Linguini with Florida Rock Shrimp. Old World flavours mix with New World style, while a great wine list and speciality beers complete an impressive picture, with reservations not always necessary. ($$–$$$$; 11.30am–11pm; 407 934 8888; **www.portobellorestaurant.com**).

BRITTIP
For a great light lunch at Portobello, try the antipasti platter ($16), which serves two. Their Cafe Shakerato (Italian iced coffee) is also a real treat.

Raglan Road: This Irish-themed pub, with lively music, food to match and a genuine Emerald Isle style, is where you really can enjoy the craic. Much of the restaurant's interior was shipped over from Ireland (including 4 reclaimed 130-year-old bars, plus 9 European beers on draft), establishing an authentic backdrop to an original menu created by celebrity master chef Kevin Dundon. Fresh, simple ingredients with an imaginative twist: shepherd's pie, mussels, beef stew, Irish sausages, plus excellent curries, a range of original sandwiches at lunchtime and a Portobello mushroom vegetarian entrée. They also feature a great Weekend Brunch (Sat–Sun 10am–3pm) and special dining events (see the website). Stop in at the gift shop and check out Kevin Dundon's Full On Irish cookbook ($$–$$$; 11am–2am, 407 938 0300, **www.raglanroad.com**).

The Boathouse: This new (in 2015) addition to the Disney Springs scene is nautically themed, with the obvious focus on great seafood, but other menu items include chicken, chops, salads, raw bar and some of the best steaks in Florida. A well-presented kids menu is also available, and the whole presentation is wonderfully stylish, with a period ambience but fully modern sensibilities. The service is suitably upscale and the seafood is simply some of the freshest you'll find. There are three themed bars, as well as outdoor dining, live music, gift shop, boat rides, and a water view from each dining room, which all adds up to truly memorable dining. And don't forget about dessert – their S'Mores Baked Alaska is big enough for a family of four! ($$$$$; 11am–2am daily, 407 939 2628).

BRITTIP
The signature dish at The Boathouse is a 32oz/900g Tomahawk Chop bone-in ribeye steak at $115 – but it IS for two people. It actually makes for a great special-occasion meal.

Morimoto Asia: Another newcomer in 2015 was the Pan-Asian style of Chef Masaharu Morimoto (of TV's Iron Chef fame), which puts the emphasis on Japanese cuisine, seafood and elaborate sushi offerings in a sleek two-storey setting. Exhibition kitchens, a contemporary cocktail lounge and waterside dining add to the ambiance, while the menu features classics such as Peking Duck and Dim Sum, plus plenty of contemporary twists ($$$$$; 4–11pm; 407 939 2628).

STK Orlando: The third new arrival at Disney Springs, this is a modern steakhouse given a novel twist by the STK group, who are renowned for taking their vibrant, edgy style to a very traditional area, combining restaurant and lounge (with great cocktails). Instead of dark, brooding and formal, STK goes for bright, playful and innovative (including a live DJ), with a creative touch to the décor – and a truly decadent depth to their flavours. Rooftop dining – perfect for warm Floridian evenings – is another feature, along with trendy menu items that include grilled octopus, spiced duck breast and seared foie gras, along with large, medium, and small steaks, plus some intriguing signature cocktails ($$$$$; 4–11pm; 407 939 2628).

T-Rex Cafe: Enter the audio-animatronic world of the people who created the Rainforest Café chain: a vast series of themed areas like the Ice Cave and Jurassic Forest, which are home to all manner of roaring dinos, with meteor strikes and thunderstorms for good measure! The food is straightforward (albeit with fancy names like Woolly Mammoth Chicken and Boneyard Buffet) but portions are suitably large and it is also somewhere you can pop into just for a drink – including great cocktails – and snacks at the hugely imaginative bar area ($$–$$$; 11am–11pm, midnight Fri and Sat, 407 828 8739, **www.trexcafe.com**).

Other choices: To one side of Raglan Road is **Cookes of Dublin**, a chippie serving up real chips, beer-battered fish, gourmet battered sausages and 'Do bars' (deep-fried Snickers bars!).

BRITTIP
For reservations at any Disney restaurant, call 407 939 3463 (407 WDW DINE), or book online at **www.disneyworld.co.uk**.

The Marketplace
While The Marketplace is largely the shopping heart of Disney Springs (p328), it also offers tempting dining.

Rainforest Café: With its safari-style 'adventures' under a spectacular volcano-topped exterior (that belches fire and smoke!), this is the place to entertain the family while they fill up on huge platefuls of chicken, pasta, steak, seafood and burgers, surrounded by audio-animatronic animals and periodic 'rainstorms', with an excellent menu for 10s and under. Stop by the Lava Lounge for a selection of small-plate appetisers from the main menu and great cocktails and other drink specials in

this lakeside setting ($$–$$$; 11am–10.30pm Sun–Thurs, 11.30pm Fri–Sat; 407 827 8500, **www.rainforestcafe.com**).

Other choices: Ghirardelli Ice Cream & Chocolate Shop is a great option for dessert or a milkshake. **The Earl of Sandwich** serves great sandwiches and lighter meals, and **Wolfgang Puck Express** has quick-service Californian cuisine, while several food trucks now offer quick-bite meals, which add a fun flavour to proceedings.

BRITTIP
We think the best value at Disney Springs is the excellent Earl of Sandwich, where one of their hot sandwiches is often enough for two.

West Side
Back in the more hip night-time district of Disney Springs are another five options.

Bongos Cuban Café: Co-owned by Gloria and Emilio Estefan, the sounds and tastes of Old Havana enliven this imaginative setting, with red-hot Latin music and excellent Cuban fare. You'll struggle to get a tastier – or more eye-catching – platter than their speciality seafood skillet while the Skirt Steak and Roasted Chicken are equally flavour-packed ($$–$$$$, 11am–11pm, Sun–Thurs, midnight Fri and Sat; 407 828 0999, **www.bongoscubancafe.com**).

BRITTIP
Disney is rolling out new-style menus, geared toward assisting guests with **food allergies** in making appropriate selections. Look for them at all full-service restaurants, with counter service offerings in 2016 and buffets to follow.

House of Blues®: This cavernous combination live music venue and restaurant in backwoods Mississippi style is a must for anyone even vaguely interested in blues, rock 'n' roll, R&B, gospel and jazz – while its trademark Gospel Brunch on Sun serves up some fab food with a full gospel show (10.30am and 1pm; $40.50 adults, $20.50 3–9s). The big restaurant (11am–11pm) offers some fine fare, including seafood jambalaya, fresh fish and a host of Cajun delicacies, with live music Thurs–Sat ($$–$$$$; 11.30am–11pm Sun–Thurs, 1am Fri–Sat; 407 934 2583, **www.houseofblues.com**).

Planet Hollywood: The largest and busiest of this worldwide chain offers lashings of its film-related fun style, with a fairly standard burger-and-steak orientated menu and wonderful cocktails. Our faves – the Chicken Crunch starter and outrageously calorific LA Lasagna! ($$–$$$; 11am–12am; 407 827 7827, **www.planethollywood.com**). Planet Hollywood is also due for a major makeover in 2016 as part of the big changeover to Disney Springs.

Splitsville: OK, so it's a bowling alley, but the food and drink are good, so you might want to consider this as a dining option on its own. Fresh sushi is their speciality, but the menu also features gourmet burgers, sandwiches, pizza, entrée salads and main-course dishes like pulled pork, fish 'n' chips, chicken parmesan and succulent steaks. They feature signature sundaes for dessert and the cocktail menu is extremely tempting. Head upstairs of an evening and enjoy the nightclub vibe where the bowling is purely incidental and the open-air patio is a great place to chill out and watch the world go by ($$–$$$; 10.30–1am Mon–Fri, 10–2am Sat–Sun; 407 938 7467, **www.splitsvillelanes.com**).

Wolfgang Puck® Café: A rich experience from the top Californian chef: the Café, gourmet food in a casual setting; Wolfgang Puck Express, the fast-food version; the Sushi Bar for seafood and pizzas; and the Dining Room, an upscale restaurant featuring top international cuisine. It caters for just about every taste (the sushi is excellent) and is highly family friendly ($$–$$$$; 11.30am–11pm, 6–10pm in Dining Room; 407 938 9653, **www.wolfgangpuckcafeorlando.com**).

Other choices: Grab a snack at **Wetzel's Pretzels**, with the choice of pretzels, hot dogs and lemonade; try **Haagen-Dazs** ice-cream, or coffee at the inevitable **Starbucks**; or sample more fun offerings at the **Food Truck Park**.

Universal CityWalk

Universal completely revamped its dining choice in CityWalk in 2014, making for even more great possibilities. There are 12 main restaurants, plus fast-food options.

Antojitos Authentic Mexican Food: New in 2014, Antojitos runs the culinary gambit from street food (tacos, enchiladas, fajitas) to refined twists on traditional dishes such as Paella Mexicana and Churrasco Steak, along with 203 authentic tequilas. Downstairs is the more 'street party' atmosphere while upstairs is more formal and family-style. The cocktails are superb and you can enjoy their modern Mariachi band Tue–Sat (11am–11pm Sun-Thurs, 12am Fri-Sat; 407 224 3663).

Bob Marley: Jamaican cuisine in a funky setting, featuring entrées such as curry, oxtail stew and Jamaican Jerk Chicken (4–10pm Sun–Thurs, 11pm Fri–Sat and Sun; 21 and up after 9pm; 407 224 3663).

Bubba Gump's Shrimp Co: This has the full Forrest Gump theme, and is heavy on seafood but also includes chicken, sandwiches, ribs, salads and more, with catchy names like Bubba's After the Storm 'Bucket of Boat Trash' (11am–midnight; 407 903 0044, **www.bubbagump.com**).

> **BRITTIP**
> Mention you are celebrating a birthday at Bubba Gump's and you'll find you quickly become the centre of attention!

Cowfish Sushi Burger Bar: Fresh and innovative, this claims to be the world's first restaurant to feature the best sushi AND the best burgers (and the trademark 'Burgushi'), with a wide variety of both in an eclectic, lively setting – including fun touchscreens at the sushi bar (11am–midnight; 407 224 2691, **www.thecowfish.com**).

Emeril's: This is a sophisticated and vibrant 5-star journey into the cuisine of New Orleans with master chef Emeril Lagasse. Fine wines and a cigar bar enhance Emeril's Creole-based gourmet creations, and if you don't try the Louisiana oyster stew you'll have missed a real treat (lunch 11.30am–3pm; dinner 5–10pm Sun–Thurs, 5–10.30pm Fri and Sat; 407 224 2424, **www.emerils.com**).

BRITTIP

Can't get a booking at Emeril's for dinner? Consider lunch there instead, which rarely books up. Or try its daily Happy Hour (4–8pm) with reduced prices and special small-plate dishes at the bar.

Hard Rock Café: The largest example of this worldwide chain, with its collection of rock 'n' roll memorabilia (including a pink 1959 Cadillac) and full concert venue is hugely popular, so try to get in early for lunch or dinner, with their signature burgers, steaks, fajitas, ribs and sandwiches all well worth trying. You'll also find prices in the gift shop friendlier than in the UK (11am–midnight; 407 351 7625, **www.hardrock.com/cafes/orlando/**).

BRITTIP

After dining at the Hard Rock Café, ask for one of their Backstage Tours with a special 'rock guide'. You'll get a great insight into much of their unique memorabilia, the history of the Café (which began in London), a look inside the John Lennon-themed VIP room and a tour of the music venue's back-stage areas. An amazing – and free – treat, available 1–9pm most days.

Hot Dog Hall of Fame: All manner of hot dog styles, frankfurters and stuffed dumplings from around the USA, allied to 100s of condiment variations make this a fun and unique offering (11am–10pm Sun–Thurs, 11am–1am Fri–Sat; 407 224 4233, **www.hotdoghalloffame.com**).

Jimmy Buffet's Margaritaville: An island homage to Florida's laid-back musical hero, with 'Floribbean' cuisine (a mix of Key West and Caribbean), with the Volcano Bar, which 'erupts' margarita mix (!) when the blender needs filling (9am–1am Sun–Thurs, 2am Fri-Sat, bar and live music until midnight; 407 224 2155, **www.margaritavilleorlando.com**)

NBC Sports Grill & Brew: This will open in 2016, adding a totally modern sports bar vibe as well as memorable food and the chance to enjoy all the big games in a lively but sophisticated setting. There will be 90 TV screens (including large, stadium-style screens on the outside of the building), plus more than 100 beers and an outdoor beer garden (11am–late daily). NB: The former NBC City restaurant and bar closed in 2015 with Universal set to bring in another new venture.

Pat O'Brien's: This is a reproduction of the famous New Orleans bar and restaurant with its Flaming Fountain courtyard, main bar and duelling piano bar. Excellent Cajun food and world-famous Hurricane cocktails! (4pm–2am; 5pm–2am for the piano bar, with a $7 cover charge after 9pm; 21 and over only; 407 224 3663, **www.patobriens.com/patobriens/orlando/**).

Red Oven Pizza Bakery: Authentic artisan pizza – five varieties of white and red Neapolitan style – are on offer at this chic new restaurant, with some imaginative flavours all baked in their signature 900° Red Oven (11am–2am).

Vivo Italian Kitchen: Fine Tuscan dining gets a workout here, with wonderful fresh ingredients all served from an open kitchen that offers a fully customisable menu for its pasta and other featured dishes (11am–11pm; 407 224 3663).

Other choices: Try **Menchie's** for fab frozen yoghurt, **Breadbox** for great sandwiches, **Cinnabon** for cinnamon rolls and other pastries, **Cold Stone Creamery** for indulgent ice-cream creations and the inevitable **Starbucks** coffee house. **The Top of the Walk** food court also features the **Burger King Whopper Bar**, **Panda Express**, **Moe's Southwest Grill** and **Fusion Bistro Sushi &**

Rockin' Robin

We are delighted the **Red Robin** chain is now in Orlando, with their first restaurant in Winter Garden Village and a big new venue at the I-Shops on International Drive. We think they feature the best burgers (and overall value) of any chain restaurant, and their variety, quality and sheer fun style is hard to beat, especially at their prices. A big menu is highlighted by almost 20 burger choices, all accompanied by endless steak fries, and they also offer fab milkshakes, sundaes and desserts, plus cocktails and drink specials. They also offer Boozy Milkshakes that are truly heavenly – but not for kids! (**www.redrobin.com**).

Sake Bar. Look up more details at **www.universalorlando.com/Restaurants/CityWalk-Restaurants.aspx**.

 BRITTIP

Can't get in any of the CityWalk restaurants? Jump on one of the boats to the Hard Rock Hotel or Portofino Bay Hotel and you can usually dine without a wait at The Kitchen (Hard Rock), Trattoria del Porto or Mama Della's (Portofino Bay).

FAST FOOD

While it's hard to fault Disney and Universal's quality, many of their prices can be tough on the wallet. Happily, you can eat a lot cheaper in the other tourist areas and we'll now take a look at the rest of your options, starting with some familiar names. This first section is primarily fast-food outlets, all in the $ category.

The big names: You'll find plenty of **McDonalds**, plus other standards like **Burger King**, **Wendy's**, **KFC**, **Pizza Hut**, **Subway** and **Domino's**. Local variations include **Checkers** or **Hardees** for burgers, **Popeye's Famous Fried Chicken & Biscuits**, **Bojangles** or **Chick-fil-A** as a KFC alternative, **Taco Bell** if you'd like the cheap and cheerful Mexican option, or **Arby's** for a range of roast beef sandwiches that make a change from burgers. **Dairy Queen** offers burgers, hot dogs, pork sandwiches and ice-cream dishes, while **Little Caesar's**

and **Hungry Howie's** are pizza alternatives. A more health-conscious choice is **Tijuana Flats**, with fresh Tex-Mex style in a lively atmosphere. Check out its burritos, quesadillas, enchiladas, tacos and salads – and you'll struggle to spend more than $10/person (**www.tijuanaflats.com**). Another happening local chain is **Five Guys Burgers & Fries**, who use only fresh-ground beef (never frozen), peanut oil and no trans fats. They serve up just four basic burgers (plus Little Burgers), hotdogs and sandwiches, and you can add your own extras from a 16-item toppings bar (**www.fiveguys.com**).

Yes, you can find proper chips in the States. They are called 'steak fries', and you will find them in most grocery stores and on some restaurant menus, (notably at **Outback Steak House**). **Raglan Road** and **Red Robin** serve up arguably some of the best, though.

FAMILY FAVOURITES

After all the fast food, there is a huge selection specialising in more regular fare, still with all-American style but more variety and family-friendliness. They vary from buffet to full service, and you'll see them in many locations.

The breakfast specialists

Need to start the day by stoking up with a big breakfast? Look no further.

Bob Evans: Notable for its friendly, country-style, hearty menus (plus low-carb options) and delicious desserts, it also offers takeaway and country store choice ($; 6 or 7am–10pm; **www.bobevans.com**).

Cracker Barrel: Delightful old country store style, with mountainous breakfasts, well-balanced lunch and dinner menus, Kid's Stuff choices and an old-fashioned charm that belies the usual tourist frenzy ($; 6am–10pm Sun–Thurs, 6am–11pm Fri and Sat; **www.crackerbarrel.com**).

Denny's: A classic 24-hour restaurant, its wide selection makes a traditional bacon-and-egg breakfast seem ordinary and it does an excellent range of toasted sandwiches and dinner meals, like grilled catfish, as well as a Senior Selections menu, with smaller portions for over-55s ($; **www.dennys.com**).

International House of Pancakes (or IHOP) and **Waffle House:** You will struggle to spend more than $10 on a full meal, whether on their huge breakfast platters or a sandwich with fries. Both are open 24/7 ($; **www.wafflehouse.com**) and ($; **www.ihop.com**).

Panera Bread: As well as wonderful pastries, fresh-baked breads and sandwiches, it serves a terrific (and healthy) array of soups and salads, including vegetarian options (7am–10pm; **www.panerabread.com**).

Perkins: Also a great breakfast choice; for a hearty meal try Perkins Eggs Benedict (two eggs and bacon on a toasted muffin with hash browns and fresh fruit), while its bread-bowl salads are equally satisfying (some branches open around the clock; **www.perkinsrestaurants.com**).

Village Inn: Massively popular with the tourist crowd is this unassuming outlet on Westwood Boulevard, just off I-Drive near SeaWorld. Unpretentious but fab value for breakfast, lunch and dinner, it serves up heaps of basic fare with friendly service, plus decadent desserts (we dare you to try their Boston Cream, French Silk or Key Lime pies!). Huge breakfast plates, all at around $7, great kids' menus and salads, sandwiches and burgers ($–$$; 6am–11pm, midnight Fri-Sat; **www.villageinn.com**).

Character dining at The Kitchen

Buffet style
The value of the all-you-can-eat restaurants is much in evidence here.

CiCi's Pizza: With more than a dozen locations all offering a 20-item pizza spread – all made fresh every hour – plus salad and pasta options, and a couple of delicious desserts, this is an absolute bargain at $5.99 adults and $4.99 kids (11am–10pm, **www.cicispizza.com**).

BRITTIP
A buffet breakfast should keep you going until tea-time and is a good way to start a theme-park day.

Golden Corral: The buffet theme continues with this popular choice, where the accent is again on masses of food in a pleasant setting. Golden Corral tends to be slightly fresher, with a Carver's Choice of roast meats, plus good vegetable selections and dessert bar (around 20 choices). There's a weekend supplement at some outlets as they add steak to the menu ($–$$; 7.30am–10.30pm; **www.goldencorral.com**).

Ponderosa Steakhouse and **Sizzler:** These popular, identikit, consistent but unspectacular big-chain offerings feature huge breakfast, lunch and dinner buffets. You order and pay as you enter and are then seated, before being unleashed on the help-yourself serveries. You'd be hard pushed to tell whose food was whose, but there IS a difference in price depending on location, with I-Drive tending to be a dollar or so dearer. Standard dinner fare includes chicken wings, meatballs, chilli, ribs, steaks (for a small supplement) and seafood, plus immense salad bars ($–$$; 7am–late evening, **www.sizzler.com** and **http://ponderosasteakhouses.com**).

The big chains
Moving up in terms of price, quality and options is this extensive array.

Applebee's: Self-styled 'neighborhood bar and grill', this offers a rather more health-conscious menu with

Pop into our 'local'

The nearest thing to a typical pub in these parts is the **Orlando/Miller Ale House** chain. Hugely popular with the locals, it features pool tables, multiple TV screens for all the sports action and a friendly, efficient style with a varied menu. It can be rowdy on weekend big-game days but is a great place to hang out with friends, bring the family or just pop in for a drink. The Ale House in Lake Buena Vista on Winter Garden-Vineland Road is also our 'local', and the new-style Miller's Ale House on I-Drive is positively vast ($–$$$; 11am–2am; **www.millersalehouse.com**).

good salads and weight-watchers' choices as well as an array of steaks and chicken dishes, and great-value lunches ($–$$; 11am–2am; **www.applebees.com**).

BRITTIP
Take advantage of Applebee's 2-for-$20 specials, which include one starter to split, and two mains.

Bahama Breeze: Lively Caribbean food and surroundings, there is a pleasing individual touch and you will get good value for money here. The decor is refreshing and entertaining, and it's worth popping in just for a drink. Try the Key West Fish Tacos, calypso shrimp linguine or jerk chicken pasta ($$–$$$$; 11am–midnight Sun–Thurs, 11am–1am Fri–Sat; **www.bahamabreeze.com**).

BRITTIP
The Bahama Breeze restaurants don't take reservations and are extremely popular in the evening. Try to arrive before 5.30pm to avoid a wait or try the Lake Buena Vista location, which can be quieter.

BJ's Brewhouse: An impressive chain that features a great menu, craft beers, lively atmosphere and ultra-friendly service. The extensive menu ranges from pizza, pasta, salads and sandwiches to impressive steaks, ribs and fish dishes, hence they cater for a lot of tastes. And did we mention

the great beer choice?! Look for them on I-Drive, at Lake Buena Vista and at The Loop shopping centre in Kissimmee ($$–$$$$; 11am–midnight Sun–Thurs, 1am Fri & Sat; **www.bjsbrewhouse.com**).

Boston Market: Typical home cooking, café style, they specialise in fresh-carved meats, rotisserie chicken, decent vegetables and excellent value ($–$$; 11am–10pm; **www.bostonmarket.com**).

Buffalo Wild Wings: A huge sports bar and grill, featuring chicken wings, tenders, wraps, salads, burgers and ribs. Simple but tasty, and popular with its many large-screen TVs ($–$$; 11am–1am Mon–Thurs, 2am Fri & Sat, midnight Sun; **www.buffalowildwings.com**).

Café Tu Tu Tango: Another original local restaurant high on style and quality, the accent is artist-colony Spanish, with an original tapas-style menu, live music and artwork on the walls that changes daily. Vegetarians are well catered for, and you can try some succulent pizzas, seafood, salads and soups plus imaginative Mexican dishes and a well-thought-out kids' menu (11.30am–11am, Mon, Wed, Thus, Sun; midnight Tues, Fri and Sat; **www.cafetututango.com**).

Cheesecake Factory: While its prime feature is desserts (with more than 30 cheesecakes!), the rest of a substantial menu is striking in an eclectic, high-tech setting. Mexican dishes jostle with pizza, pasta, seafood, burgers, steaks and salads, plus it offers a great Sun brunch. Beware – portions are HUGE! ($$–$$$; 11am–11pm Mon-Thurs, 11am–12.30am Fri–Sat, 10am–11pm Sun; **www.thecheesecakefactory.com**).

Chevy's: A healthy slice of Mexicana while still providing American selections, its salsa is fresh-made every hour and the tortilla chips, fajitas and tortillas are delicious ($–$$; 11am–11pm Sun–Thurs, 11am–1am Fri, Sat; **www.chevys.com**).

Chili's: Also in Tex-Mex territory, it places the emphasis more on meat dishes like steak and ribs and less on tortillas and spices. Service is usually highly efficient ($–$$; 11am–11pm Sun–Thurs, midnight Fri-Sat; **www.chilis.com**).

Chuys: More Tex-Mex style, but done just that bit more authentically and fresher, with lively style and décor to back up an extensive menu that features enchiladas, tacos and fajitas as well as signature dishes like their Steak Burrito, Chuychanga and Green Chile Fried Chicken. Plus the margaritas to go with them! ($$–$$$; 11am–10pm Sun–Thurs, 11pm Fri & Sat; **www.chuys.com**).

Don Pablo's: A fairly elaborate Mexican offering with clever theming, a fun, lively atmosphere (especially round the Cantina bar) and classic, well-explained menus ($$; 11am– 10pm Sun–Thurs, 11pm Fri and Sat; **www.donpablos.com**).

Fuddruckers: Excellent burgers, with a huge choice (including veggie, buffalo, elk and wild boar!) and a kid-friendly style. Make your selection, find a table and wait for your burger to be cooked fresh, or choose from salad and sandwich options, plus tempting shakes, cookies and desserts ($–$$; 11am–10pm Sun–Thurs, 11pm Fri, Sat; **www.fuddruckers.com**).

Hooters: A lively place that makes no bones about its style – 'delightfully tacky yet unrefined' – this is popular with the beach-party crowd, and for the famous Hooter Girl waitresses. The entertaining menu features seafood, salads and burgers, plus Hooters Nearly World Famous Chicken Wings in 8 strengths – beware of the Samurai! ($–$$; 11am–11pm Sun–Thurs, midnight Fri and Sat, **www.hooters.com**).

Houlihan's: Classic bar-restaurant with plenty of style, cheerful service, an extensive and appetising menu (try the great entrée salads) – and huge portions (but also a mini-dessert option; $–$$; 11am–10pm; **www.houlihans.com**).

Logan's Roadhouse: A fun, rustic atmosphere includes masses of peanuts in their shells (which are meant to end up all over the wooden

The cream of America

Orlando boasts outstanding ice-cream parlours: check out Carvel, Baskin Robbins, Dairy Queen, Marble Slab Creamery and Cold Stone Creamery, all of which make Mr Whippy seem extremely ordinary. But the perennial favourite remains **Ben & Jerry's** who have 4 shops in the main tourist areas – in Universal Studios; at Pointe Orlando; inside the food court at Orlando Premium Outlets at Vineland Ave; and at The Loop shopping centre in Kissimmee.

floor!), plus a menu featuring burgers, chicken, steaks and ribs, kids' meals and express lunch selection ($$; 11am–10pm Sun–Thurs, 11pm Fri and Sat; **www.logansroadhouse.com**).

Lone Star Steakhouse: Head to Texas for its mesquite-grilled steaks, ribs, chicken and fish, with a friendly welcome and roadhouse ambience (plus more huge portions! $$–$$$; 11am–10pm Sun–Thurs, 11pm Fri and Sat; **www.lonestarsteakhouse.com**).

Longhorn Steakhouse: The newer, fancier version of the Texas steakhouse and 'Flavour of the West', this features fresh-grilled steaks, chops and ribs, plus chicken and seafood that is hard to beat at the price, with a good menu for under-10s ($$–$$$$; 11am–10pm, 11pm Fri and Sat; **www.longhornsteakhouse.com**).

Olive Garden: A rather identikit approach to Italian fare, but the light, airy dining rooms create a relaxing environment and it does a modest menu well and in generous portions. Pasta is the speciality but there is also chicken, veal, steak and seafood, plus great salads and garlic breadsticks (with unlimited refills) ($$–$$$; 11am–10.30pm Sun–Thurs, 11pm Fri and Sat; **www.olivegarden.com**).

Outback Steakhouse: An Australian slant on American steakhouse style, with some of the best fare – and biggest portions. Its thick, juicy, well-seasoned steaks, ribs and seafood are great, while its trademark is a large fried onion with a dipping sauce, and all at moderate prices. Good kids' menu and a real Brit visitor favourite

A Florida steak-out

America serves great steaks and it is hard to get a BAD sirloin, T-bone or filet. For those who really want to indulge, the following (totally unofficial) ranking should help (NB: the US Dept of Agriculture grades its meat quality Standard, Select, Choice and, for the top 2%, Prime).

Standard: Beef O'Brady's, Golden Corral, Great Western, O'Charley's, Ponderosa, Sizzler, Western Sizzlin'. **Select:** Applebee's, Black Angus, Chevy's, Chili's, Copper Canyon Grill, Colorado House of Beef, Logan's Roadhouse, Lone Star, Miller's Ale House, The Pub, Rainforest Café, Red Lobster, Ruby Tuesday, Santa Fe Cattle Co, , Smoky Bones, TGI Fridays, Tony Roma's, Uno Chicago Grill. **Choice:** Amura's, BJ's Brewhouse, Brio Tuscan Grill, Cantina Laredo, Carrabba's, Jack's Place, Johnnie's Hideaway, Kobe, Le Cellier (Epcot), Longhorn Steakhouse, Marlow's Tavern, Nona Blue, Outback, Shogun, Vito's Chophouse. **Prime:** Capital Grille, Charley's, Christini's, Everglades, Fogo de Chao, A Land Remembered, Morton's, The Oceanaire, Old Hickory, Fleming's, The Palm Restaurant, Ruth's Chris, Shula's, Spencer's, Texas de Brazil, The Venetian Room, The Yachtsman (Disney's Yacht Club Resort).

($$–$$$; 11am–11pm Sun–Thurs, 11.30pm Fri, Sat; **www.outback.com**).

Santa Fe Cattle Co: a recent arrival in Lake Buena Vista and on Highway 27, this Western-style offering has some surprisingly neat touches in the décor and menu (and more peanuts!). Great burgers, steaks, ribs and fajitas are their stock in trade, but the chicken-fried steak, quesadillas and El Toro burrito are worth considering and the Margaritas are killer! ($$–$$$; 11am–10pm Sun–Thurs, 11pm Fri and Sat; bar to 1am; **www.santafecattleco.com**).

Smokey Bones: With a rustic, log-cabin touch and succulent, deep-smoked BBQ, it serves up fire-grilled steaks, salmon, chicken, burgers and salads. Try the BBQ platters and rib combos especially. Sports fans can also enjoy a huge array of TVs ($$–$$$; **www.smokeybones.com**).

Sonny's Real Pit Bar-B-Q: A national chain with no great pretensions, just masses of food of the slow-cooked barbecue persuasion served up in friendly, let's-get-messy style. The good kids' menu makes it ideal for families, and you should definitely try the ribs and coleslaw ($$–$$; 11am–10pm; **www.sonnysbbq.com**).

TGI Fridays: Lively, eclectic style, Orlando boasts multiple offerings of this popular chain. The drinks menu is huge and the main menu is heavy on wings, ribs, burgers and steaks ($–$$; 11am–2am; **www.tgifridays.com**).

Tony Roma's: 'Famous for ribs', the airy decor and ambience, clever kids' menu, junior meals and melt-in-the-mouth ribs are a winning combo. You can still get chicken, burgers and steaks, but why ignore a dish that's done this well? ($$–$$$; 11am–11pm Sun–Thurs, midnight Fri and Sat; **www.tonyromas.com**).

Uno Chicago Grill: The place to go if you're bored with Pizza Hut, it specialises in deep-dish pizzas plus pastas, chicken dishes, steaks and salads. A recent style makeover gave Uno's a fresh, inviting new look, with extra menu choices and great lunch specials making them especially good value ($–$$; 11am–2am daily; **www.unos.com**).

Wildside BBQ: Another local success threatening to become a major chain, this can be found in Thornton Park and on West Highway 192 in Kissimmee, featuring delicious pulled pork, excellent ribs and their own 'secret' barbecue sauce, as well as

Fuddruckers

signature salads, fresh fish and pasta. Lively bar style also offers live entertainment and sports specials ($–$$$$; 4pm–11pm; **www.wildsidebbq. com**).

INTERNATIONAL FLAVOURS

Your food choice extends beyond the obvious to an international array, featuring Chinese and Indian, but also Thai, Japanese and Italian. Some are still chains, others are one-offs.

Indian, Chinese and more

There is a wide range of Asian restaurants in Orlando, from ordinary Chinese to 5-star Japanese. Take your pick from this selection.

Aashirwad: A decent Indian choice, with an excellent lunch buffet and some seriously spicy Mughlai dishes ($–$$$; 11.30am–2.30 pm and 5.30–10.30pm ; 407 370 9830; **www.aashirwadrestaurant.com**).

Dragon Court Buffet: This locals' Chinese favourite in Lake Buena Vista serves a huge spread of fresh, appetising dishes at a terrific lunch price. With 100 items, including sushi, this is well worth trying ($$–$$$; 11am–11pm; 407 238 9996).

India Palace: An unassuming location tucked in a small shopping plaza in Lake Buena Vista, this serves good food in large amounts and with family-friendly service ($–$$$; 11.30am–11pm Tues–Sun, 5–11pm Mon; 407 238 2322).

Kobe: This brings a touch of Americana to its Japanese- themed dining, but still achieves individuality with the chef preparing the food at your table ($$$; 4.30pm–10.30pm, hours vary by location; **www.kobesteakhouse.com**).

◀▶ BRITTIP

Orlando features a handful of good Indian restaurants, but you'll find more – and better – curry offerings at home.

Ming Court: The Rolls-Royce of Chinese is this beautiful place on

Handy Manny

A perennial Brit favourite is eclectic American diner **Manny's Original Chophouse**, on Highway 27 near Haines City (8ml/13km south of the junction with I-4 and in Winter Haven). Great value and great fun, it features a steak-orientated menu with bags of local style and original décor, as well as an amazing 2-for-1 Happy Hour daily from 4–7pm. It is often packed by 6pm as locals and tourists alike flock here for the lively style and well-priced food (all steaks under $20, and many just $14–18), which also include fab burgers, ribs, fajitas, seafood and chicken, as well as their signature dishes. It may be a bit of a drive but, trust us, it's worth it. Save time with Call-Ahead seating (not a reservation). ($–$$$; 4–10pm Mon–Thurs, 10.30pm Sat, noon–9.30pm Sun; 863 422 3910, **www.mannyschophouse.com**).

I-Drive, opposite Pointe Orlando, with its magnificent setting and live music most evenings. The menu is extensive and beautifully presented by friendly servers. Many dishes can be had as a side order rather than a full main course and there are extensive dim sum and even sushi and sashimi choices, plus an imaginative kids' menu. The Salt & Pepper Chicken is one of our all-time favourites and, after 27 years in business, this is I-Drive's longest-serving restaurant ($$–$$$; 11am–3pm, 4.30pm–11pm; **www.ming-court.com**).

New Punjab: Another decent Indian on I-Drive, with fine tandoori dishes and good vegetable selection ($–$$$; 5–11pm Mon, 11.30am–11pm Tues–Sun; 407 352 7887; **www.punjabindianrestaurant.com**).

PF Chang's China Bistro: This mixes classic Chinese fare with American bistro style that makes fans of virtually all who sample it. You should try the spicy ground chicken and eggplant (aubergine), Cantonese roasted duck or Oolong marinated sea bass. There is also a good veggie selection ($$–$$$$; 11am–11pm, midnight Fri-Sat, 10pm Sun; **www.pfchangs.com**).

International Drive

The majority of restaurants in this busy tourist area are of the Fast Food or Family Favourite type, but there are several individuals.

The **North** section (from Orlando Premium Outlets International Dr to Sand Lake Road) features *Fast Food:* Baskin Robbins, Burger King, Cold Stone Creamery, Dairy Queen, Dunkin' Donuts, Five Guys Burgers & Fries, KFC, McDonald's, Quiznos, Pizza Hut, Popeye's Chicken, Sonic, Starbucks, Subway and Taco Bell. *Family Favourites:* Buffalo Wild Wings, Chili's, CiCi's Pizza, Denny's, Fuddruckers, IHOP, Sizzler, Sweet Tomatoes, TGI Fridays. *International Flavours:* Aashirwad, New Punjab Indian Restaurant, Thai Silk, Shogun Steakhouse. *Home From Home:* Orlando George & Dragon. *Seafood Specials:* Red Lobster. *Deluxe Dining:* Texas de Brazil.

The **South** section (from Sand Lake Rd to Orlando Premium Outlets Vineland Ave) has *Fast Food:* McDonald's, Pizza Hut, Subway, Flippers Pizza, Taco Bell, Dunkin Donuts. *Family Favourites:* Bahama Breeze, BJ's Brewhouse, Buffalo Wild Wings, Café Tu Tu Tango, Chuy's, Cici's Pizza, Denny's, Don Pablo's, Golden Corral, Houlihan's, IHOP, Longhorn Steakhouse, Miller's Ale House, Olive Garden, Outback Steakhouse, Ponderosa, Red Robin, TGI Fridays, Tony Roma's, Uno Chicago, Village Inn. *International Flavours:* Benihana, Kobe Steakhouse, Ming Court. *Seafood Specials:* Boston Lobster Feast, Red Lobster. *Tastes of the Med:* Carrabba's. *Deluxe Dining:* Charley's Steakhouse, Everglades, Fogo de Chao, Vito's Chophouse and Spencer's.

Saffron: Smart and stylish Indian choice in the Plaza Venezia along Sand Lake Road, with some fab-value lunch deals and classic dinner menu that takes it into fine-dining territory. All dishes can be prepared to individual levels of spiciness and the Chicken Xacutti and Rajasthani Hara Maas are worth coming in for on their own ($–$$$; 11.30am–2.30pm, 5.30–10.30pm; **www.saffronorlando.com**).

Seito Sushi: Another Japanese offering from this great chain, with a formal sushi bar and a more inviting, small-scale approach ($$–$$$$; 5–10pm Sun–Thurs, 11pm Fri & Sat; 407 248 8888; **www.seitosushi.com**).

Shogun Steakhouse: This is ideal for those a little unsure of Japanese food as it is totally family-friendly with its Teppanyaki-style service, at long, bench-like tables with the chef cooking in front of you. But you can still order a no-nonsense steak or chicken ($$$–$$$$; 6–10pm Sun–Thurs,10.30pm Fri and Sat; 407 352 1607, **www.shogunorlando.com**).

Tamarind: Up in Winter Park is this authentic Indian choice that features an extensive range of starters and some fabulous main courses, including excellent vegetarian dishes. Look out in particular for the imaginative Tandoori options and rice crepes or Doasa ($$$; 11.30am–3pm and 5–10pm, 10.30pm Fri–Sat (321 207 0760, **www.tamarindfl.com**).

Thai Silk: Authentic Thai flavours and contemporary décor, with soups and curries to die for. House speciality Smokey Pot is a superb stew of marinated prawns, vegetables and glass noodles in chilli ($$–$$$$; 11am–2.30pm and 5–10pm Mon–Fri, noon–10pm Sat and Sun; 407 226 8997; **www.thaisilkorlando.com**).

Tastes of the Med

Italy, Turkey and Greece are all represented in this selection.

Anatolia: For something exotic, head for some Turkish flavours in the Dr Phillips Plaza off Sand Lake Road. With a delicious range of authentic breads, hot and cold appetisers, salads, soups, pides (Turkish pizzas), kebabs and specialities like moussaka and baklava, you can dine royally without breaking the bank. Try the babaghanoush (char-grilled aubergine with fresh herbs and spices), tabouli, kofte kebab or chicken adana ($–$$; 11am–10pm Sun–Thurs, 11pm Fri and Sat; 407 352 6766, **www.anatoliaorlando.com**).

Bravo Cucina Italiana: This fresh, inviting twist on classic Italian fare features home-made pasta, pizza, flatbreads, steaks, chops and seafood in an inviting 'Roman-ruin' decor. Casual and chic, and fun for the grown-up crowd ($$–$$$$; 11am–10pm, to 11pm Fri and Sat; 407 351 5880; **www.bravoitalian.com**).

Carrabba's: Direct from Sicily, here's casual-but-elegant dining in a festive atmosphere. House specialities include crispy calamari, chicken marsala, pasta and hand-made pizzas. The kids' menu is one of the best and the style is ultra child friendly ($$–$$$; 4–10.30pm; hours vary by location; **www.carrabbas.com**).

Cedar's: Lebanese cuisine is the name of the game here, and it's some of the best chicken and lamb in town. In 'Restaurant Row' on Sand Lake Rd, this family-run Middle Eastern delight offers the full range of kebabs, falafel and hummus as well as specialities like fish tagine, grilled quail and baked kibbeh. A really different alternative and aromatic treat, with the bonus of live music and belly dancing Fri and Sat ($$–$$$$; 407 351 6000; **www.orlandocedars.com**).

Greek Flame Taverna: Another stylish offering in the Dr Phillips plaza off Sand Lake Rd, featuring Saganaki (flamed cheese), dolmades (stuffed vine leaves) and spanakopita (spinach pie), plus other classic dishes, including salads, gyros and souvlaki, ensuring a smooth taste of the Med ($$–$$$; 407 370 4627; **www.greekflametaverna.com**).

Macaroni Grill: Like Carrabba's, this chain restaurant also features a taste of Italy, with stylish, spacious dining rooms and excellent à la carte and family-style menus (serving 8–10). The pasta and wood-oven pizzas are first class and the wine list is impressive ($$–$$$$; 11am–10pm Sun–Thurs, 11am–11pm Fri and Sat; **www.macaronigrill.com**).

Pacino's: A Highway 192 feature in Kissimmee for more than 20 years, this 'taste of Sicily' features a signature open-flame oven that

delivers great pizza, seafood and steaks, as well as offering an authentic array of pasta dishes. Couples can also take advantage of their Wine Cellar setting for a romantic evening out ($$–$$$$; 12pm–11pm; 407 396 8022, **www.pacinos.com**).

HOME FROM HOME

Having extolled the virtues of the all-American choices, there is an array of British-style pubs that should appeal to UK visitors. All offer predictable pub grub and beers and you can happily take the kids.

Frankie Farrell's: Inside the Lake Buena Vista Resort Village & Spa is this smart pub-style restaurant and bar with an imaginative menu, excellent range of beers and live entertainment ($$–$$$; 9am–2am daily; 407 597 0214).

Hagan O'Reilley's: Rather off the beaten track in Winter Garden (about 20mins north of Disney) is this genuine Irish pub, boasting good beers, classic fare and traditional entertainment most nights. With 15 beers on tap and Happy Hour from 11am–7pm, you could easily be in the Emerald isle, although the beer garden is pure Florida! ($–$$$; 11am–2am; 407 905 4782; **www.haganoreillys.com**).

Orlando George & Dragon: This I-Drive staple serves a hearty breakfast as well as pub fare. It stocks Guinness, Stella, Boddingtons,

Dining 360 Style

I-Drive 360 brought a great variety of dining choice to I-Drive in 2015, ideal for a meal before or after enjoying the complex's attractions.

Tin Roof: Country music fans will love the live entertainment here, with a smattering of rock, soul, Americana and Pop. The menu features Tex-Mex favourites, and specialties include O-Eye Mac and Cheese, Shrimp and Grits, and succulent Baby Back Ribs. Full bar, funky style, and a somewhat raucous atmosphere after 10pm ($$; 11am-2am; 407 270 7926; **www.tinroofbars.com/home/orlando**).

Cowgirls Rock Bar: Another country-style offering with an emphasis on Hooter's style "cowgirl" servers, this one may not be appropriate for some families. The limited menu features burgers, hot dogs, soups, salads, and sandwiches, but you're there for the 'sassy banter' more than the food. ($; 407 930 6739; **www.cowgirlsorlando.com**).

Naru Restaurant and Sushi Bar: Japanese cuisine with an innovative touch. The highlights are their sushi offerings, which can be custom ordered for those with allergies or 'particular' tastes. ($$$; 4–11pm; **www.narusushibar.com**)

Paramount Fine Foods: Authentic Middle Eastern cuisine, this is a terrific choice for vegetarians, though meat-lovers are well catered for, too. Delicious Shawarma, crisp, fresh salads, and all the expected Middle Eastern favourites. Family Platters are available and watch for Weekend Specials. ($$; 407 930 8645; **www.paramountfinefoods.com**).

Shake Shack: Based on a 'modern day roadside burger stand' this full-service restaurant features burgers, hot dogs, crinkle fries, and frozen custards, with craft beers and wine available. ($; 11am–11pm; **www.shakeshack.com**).

Sugar Factory: An 'American brasserie' catering to guests' sweet tooth with crepes, burgers, all things ice cream, plus candy-inspired cocktails. Want to try a 'tourist v food' challenge? Go for their 16 scoop King Kong Sundae ($$; 407 930 6739; **www.sugarfactory.com**).

Tapa Toro: Classic and contemporary Spanish specialties with a focus on tapas and paella, plus live music and tableside flamenco dancers ($$; 4–11pm; 407 226 2929; **http://tapatoro.restaurant**)

Yard House: With a huge selection of beers on tap and a wonderfully inventive menu, this isn't your typical bar. Its air of comfortable refinement is also family-friendly, and the menu is several steps above the norm, featuring twists on bar favourites, such as Pear and Gorgonzola Flatbread, Black Truffle Burger, and Vodka Shrimp Pasta, plus other gourmet offerings. There is a good selection of healthy/vegetarian dishes, along with steaks, ribs, seafood and pasta. ($$; 11am–12.30am Sun–Thurs, 1.20am Fri-Sat; 407 351 8220; **www.yardhouse.com**).

The I-Drive 360 plaza also features **Outback** steakhouse, **Buffalo Wild Wings**, **Carabba's**, **Ben and Jerry's** ice cream, **Pretzlemaker**, **Bar du Jour**, **Cafe De Paris**, and a food court in the Orlando Eye terminal. Next to the main car park is **McFadden's**, a huge Irish-tinged pub-style bar and lounge, with patio dining, live music, TVs showing all the sports action and DJs to make it party central from 8pm most nights (4pm–2am; 407 930 2550; **www.mcfaddensorlando.com**).

Fosters, Newcastle Brown, Bass, Magners and Carlsberg, and features darts, pool, karaoke, Sky Sports and live entertainment on its outdoor patio. A good option for viewing English Premier League games and for St George's Day, celebrated in style, plus Happy Hour daily $–$$$; 9am–2am; 407 351 3578; **www.orlandogeorgeanddragon.com**).

The Pub: This huge pub-style offering in Pointe Orlando comes from an American company with impeccable British tastes! With a magnificent bar and wide variety of cosy seating nooks, it features a fantastic mix of UK and US beers (including the fab Orlando Brewing Co), a sharp menu and multiple TV screens for all the sports action. The unique 'Pour Your

Own Beer Walls' are a fun feature, as is Happy Hour Mon–Thurs 3–7pm, and Wine Down Wednesdays (half-price select bottles of wine). They are also a Pub Partner of Orlando City Soccer club ($$–$$$; 11am–2am; **www.experiencethepub.com/orlando**).

SEAFOOD SPECIALS

The choice of seafood eateries is equally wide and features some fun chains and excellent individuals.

Big Fin Seafood: One of Orlando's most imaginative and award-winning seafood options, in the Dellagio complex just off Sand Lake Rd. Refined but relaxed, this is a big-scale experience that offers special-occasion atmosphere, from the entrance seafood kitchen to the elegant outdoor bar (the Bar-A-Cuda – groan!). The main dining room features a grand salon style but two smaller rooms are more intimate, while the Trophy Bar is ideal for a pre-dinner drink.

BRITBONUS

$ Show your copy of the *Brit Guide* upon arrival at Big Fin Seafood Kitchen to receive a Chef's Tasting for each guest at the table. Not valid with any other offers/specials.

The menu is an impressive collection of sushi, sashimi, oysters and ceviche; classic salads and chowders; meat, chops and chicken; their exclusive crab and lobster dishes; fresh fish; and tempting pastas. You can push the boat out with the $79 Shells and Tails dinner or opt for their Famous

Big Fin Seafood

© Big Fin Seafood

Fish & Chips at $24. Notable are the succulent signature Swordfish Filet Mignon, lobster mac-n-cheese, crab cakes and the Shrimp or Scallop Orleans. A good kids' menu, delectable desserts (don't miss the bread pudding) and superb service all add up to a high-quality experience – but without the price tag. There is Happy Hour 5–7pm Mon–Sat, 9pm Sun, at the Bar with $6 drink selections and a reduced price Happy Hour menu ($$$–$$$$$; 5–10pm Sun–Thurs, 11pm Fri & Sat; **www.bigfinseafood.com**).

Bonefish Grill: This chic choice can be found throughout Florida and offers both casual dining and an upmarket dinner experience, with some of the freshest fish and a terrific range of martinis and other cocktails. Non-fish fans can choose from chicken, chops, steak and main-course salads ($$–$$$$; 11am–10.30pm, hours vary by location; **www.bonefishgrill.com**).

Boston Lobster Feast: The place for a real blow-out on an unlimited lobster and seafood buffet. There are usually early-bird specials (4–6pm Mon–Fri, 2–4.30pm Sat and Sun), and, while it is not gourmet fare, its 40-item Lobster Feast is guaranteed to stretch the stomach ($$–$$$$; 4–10pm Mon–Fri, 2–10pm Sat and Sun; **www.bostonlobsterfeast.com**).

Eddie V's: This supper-club style venue features succulent seafood with live jazz-inspired music most evenings. It is a more stylish option than many counterparts but also has a more informal V Lounge that is first come, first served. The menu is a mouthwatering collection of the freshest fish and shellfish from all over the world, as well as fine steaks, backed up by a superb wine list and signature cocktails, all delivered with smooth service as befits 5-star dining (4–11pm Sun–Thurs, midnight Fri & Sat; 407 355 3011, **www.eddiev.com**).

Flying Fish: At Disney's BoardWalk Resort, the menu of this superb seafood experience is select but brilliantly presented. Its Chardonnay-steamed mussels starter is a taste

Try it all at Pointe Orlando

Dining choice doesn't come more varied than at Pointe Orlando on I-Drive. The headline restaurants are as follows:

The Capital Grille: A truly elegant dining option (also now at Mall at Millenia), with an extensive wine menu. Food includes magnificent chops, dry-aged steaks and seafood – perfect for a special night out or an upscale lunch. Complimentary valet parking (11.30am–10pm Mon–Thurs, 11pm Fri, 5pm–11pm Sat, 5pm–10pm Sun; 407 370 4392, www.thecapitalgrille.com).

Copper Canyon Grill: This appeals to hearty appetites with its wood-fired rotisserie chicken, hearty chicken pot pie, steaks and barbecued ribs ($$–$$$$; 11am–10.05pm Sun–Thurs, 11.05pm Fri and Sat; 407 363 3933; www.ccgrill.com).

Cuba Libre: This bar/restaurant adds a touch of 1940s Havana, featuring Latin-inspired cuisine with an exciting twist, from tasty tapas and ceviche to honey-mango glazed salmon – and wicked cocktails! (5pm–10pm daily, bar until 2am weekends; 407 226 1600, www.cubalibrerestaurant.com).

Maggiano's Little Italy: Serving exceptional family-style Italian dining with a vintage 1940s Chicago ambience – and large portions. The Flatbread appetisers are easily main-course sized, while the Family Style meals feature all-you-can-eat refills ($$–$$$$; 11.30am–10pm Mon–Thurs, 11pm Fri and Sat, noon–10pm Sun; 407 241 8650; www.maggianos.com).

Marlow's Tavern: A classic American bar-restaurant style, with (rather loud) live music. The menu is above-average (great burgers and sandwiches, but also more gourmet fare such as honey-glazed salmon, pan-seared trout and steak frites), with an imaginative cocktails and wine list ($$–$$$$; 11.30am–midnight Sun–Thurs, 1am Fri and Sat; 407 351 3627, www.marlowstavern.com).

The Oceanaire Seafood Room: See Top 10, p325.

The Pub: see p317.

RA Sushi Bar Restaurant: Japanese fusion cuisine and sushi bar with a varied menu, including Bento Boxes, Crispy Asian Tacos, Tempura and some creative twists on traditional favourites. Lunch and dinner, plus Happy Hour specials ($$; 11.30am–midnight Sun–Thurs, 1am Fri & Sat; 407 454 5600, www.rasushi.com).

Taverna Opa: Lively Greek option, with an appetising menu, from hot and cold meze to moussaka, souvlaki and signature lamb chops, but much more besides, like fine steaks, fresh seafood and a great ouzo bar. Watch for table dancing and napkin throwing! ($$–$$$$; noon–11pm Sun–Thurs, 2am Fri & Sat; 407 351 8660, www.opaorlando.com).

Tommy Bahama's Tropical Café: Inspired dining in a laid-back, tropical setting. The menu is refreshing for lunch or dinner, with highlights being its coconut shrimp and tuna appetisers and seafood entrées, plus sandwiches, chicken, steaks and fab salads ($$–$$$; 11am–11pm Sun–Thurs, to midnight Fri and Sat; 321 281 5886, www.tommybahama.com).

Other choices: Adobe Gila's: this lively bar and Mexican cantina style features more than 50 tequilas (!), plus south-of-the-border dining delicacies like the signature Gila Wraps. ($$–$$; 407 903 1477; www.adobegilas.com). **BB King's Blues Club:** Live jazz and blues (see p294) with a Southern comfort-food menu, such as Fried Shrimp Po Boy and Southern Fried Catfish, and a full bar ($$–$$$$; 4pm–midnight Sun–Fri, 11am–1am Sat; 407 370 4550, www.bbkingclubs.com). **Blue Martini:** Upmarket bar with 42 signature martinis, plus beer, wine, and cocktails. Light Fare, flatbreads and signature dishes such as Lollipop Lambchops and Main Lobster Salad (4pm–2am Mon–Fri, 1pm–2am Sat and Sun; www.bluemartinilounge.com). **Funky Monkey:** Eclectic restaurant/wine bar that features an imaginative Asian–American fusion menu of tapas-like appetiser plates, steaks, seafood and hand-rolled sushi ($$–$$$, 407 418 9463, 11.30am–11pm Mon–Thurs, midnight Fri and Sat, 5–11pm Sun, www.funkymonkeywine.com). **Johnny Rockets:** a fun, 1950s-style diner for burgers and shakes ($; 11am–9pm Sun–Thurs, 11am–11pm Fri and Sat; 407 903 0762, www.johnnyrockets.com); **Itta Betta** Southern cuisine and piano bar, and **Lafayette's** Southern cuisine and live music.

sensation while the signature Potato-wrapped Red Snapper is an absolute delight, along with great scallops, steak and a vegetarian option. The Chef's Tasting Wine Dinner (Sun–Thurs, 5.45 and 8.15pm, reservations required; no under 10s) is another stand-out feature with five courses plus paired wines at the chef's counter in front of the show kitchen at $157/person for groups of up to six (5pm–10pm; 407 939 3463).

Joe's Crab Shack: Another chain restaurant but with individual style, it is highly family friendly with its kids' play area and there's a lot more than shellfish on the menu ($–$$$; 11am–12pm; **www.joescrabshack.com**).

Landry's Seafood: This big-name company boasts a genuinely elegant touch, featuring a Fresh Fish of the Day, magnificent seafood platters and excellent salad bowl with each dish, while the service and wine list are top notch. For a special occasion, the Stuffed Flounder and Surf & Turf are ideal. Happy Hour 3pm–6pm Mon-Fri, noon–4pm Sat–Sun, with drinks specials and appetisers. Oh, and don't miss their Bananas Foster dessert and speciality Mango Mojito cocktail! ($$$–$$$$; 3–10pm Mon–Thurs, 11pm Fri, 11.30am–11pm Sat 11.30am–10pm Sun; **www.landrysseafood.com**).

Moonfish: Another great place for seafood, you could make a feast of its appetisers alone, while its sushi, sashimi and raw bar are inspired. It's a touch avant-garde but it works well ($$–$$$$; 5pm–10.30pm, 11pm Fri and Sat; 407 363 7262; **www.talkofthetownrestaurants.com**).

BRITTIP
For something different, check out Moonfish's Sushi Chef Seasonal Creations. It also has a Happy Hour Mon–Sat (4.30–6.30pm) with bar specials and half-price sushi.

Red Lobster: Part of the Olive Garden chain and for the family market, with a varied menu, lively atmosphere and one of the best kids' menu/activity

books. While lobster is the speciality, the wood-fired steaks, chicken, salads and other seafood are equally appetising, and it does a variety of combination platters ($$–$$$$; 11am–10pm Sun–Thurs, 11am–11pm Fri and Sat; **www.redlobster.com**).

BRITTIP
If the Marlow's Tavern style appeals to you, they have a second location in Winter Park on S Orlando Ave, just north of Park Ave.

DELUXE DINING
This is where you can really go to town with your dining choice.

Bohème Restaurant: A magnificent menu at this tucked-away gem at the Grand Bohemian hotel in downtown Orlando. Fine seafood mixes with superb lamb, duck and seafood, with some eclectic twists and a great Sunday Brunch ($$$–$$$$; 6.30am–10pm, 11pm Fri and Sat 407 313 9000; **www.grandbohemianhotel.com**).

Brio Tuscan Grille: With two Orlando locations (Mall at Millenia and Winter Park Village), this stylish Italian offering makes for a superb casual lunch or romantic dinner, with delicious flatbreads, luscious salads, superb steaks and surf & turf, creative pastas and regional specialities like chicken limone and grilled pork chops, plus daily fish specials. The Tuscan country-style ambience and fresh kids' menu all add up to memorable dining. Great weekend brunch, too ($$–$$$$; 11am–10pm Mon–Thurs, 11pm Fri and Sat, 10am–10pm Sun; 407 351 8909/622 5611; **www.brioitalian.com**).

BRITTIP
At Brio Tuscan Grille, don't miss the melt-in-the-mouth beef carpaccio starter, the bistecca insalata and Shrimp Mediterranean as a fab dinner combo.

Cala Bella: At the stylish Rosen Shingle Creek Resort is this superb Italian-influenced restaurant, heavy on pasta and seafood, but with signature dishes like its sensational

Kissimmee/Highway 192

The long stretch of this tourist corridor offers the greatest density of restaurants in Central Florida.

East section from the junction with I-4 to John Young Parkway: *Deluxe Dining:* Charley's Steakhouse. *Family Favourites:* Applebee's, Bob Evans, Chevys, Chili's, CiCi's Pizza, Cracker Barrel, Denny's, Golden Corral, IHOP, Logan's Roadhouse, Longhorn Steakhouse, Olive Garden, Perkins, Ponderosa, Ruby Tuesday, Shoney's, Smokey Bones, TGI Fridays, Uno Chicago, Waffle House. *Fast Food:* Arby's, Burger King, Chick-Fil-A, Domino's, Dunkin' Donuts, KFC, McDonald's, Pizza Hut, Quiznos, Subway, Taco Bell, Wendy's. *International Flavours:* Kobe Steakhouse, Punjab Indian Restaurant. *Seafood Specials:* Boston Lobster Feast, Joe's Crab Shack, Red Lobster. Tastes of the Med: Pacino's.

West section from I-4 all the way to Highway 27: *Family Favourites:* Applebees, Black Angus, Bob Evans, Bahama Breeze, Buffalo Wild Wings, Carrabba's, CiCi's Pizza, Colorado House of Beef, Cracker Barrel, Denny's, Golden Corral, IHOP, Longhorn Steakhouse, Miller's Ale House, Olive Garden, Outback Steakhouse, Perkins, Ponderosa, Shoney's, Sizzler, Sweet Tomatoes, TGI Fridays, Waffle House, Wildside BBQ. *Fast Food:* Burger King, Chick-Fil-A, Domino's, Dunkin' Donuts, Flippers Pizza, McDonald's, Pizza Hut, Quiznos, Subway, Taco Bell, Wendy's. *Home From Home:* Stage Door. *International Flavours:* Passage to India. *Seafood Specials:* Bonefish Grill, Joe's Crab Shack, Red Lobster.

Cala Bella Lamb, veal piccata and Mediterranean pork. Save room for dessert – the pastry chefs are among the best in America ($$$–$$$$; 5.30–10pm; 407 996 3663; **www.calabellarestaurant.com**).

Capa: The signature 17th floor rooftop restaurant at the new Four Seasons hotel in Walt Disney World, this is superb for style, elegance – and the nightly views of the Magic Kingdom fireworks. A contemporary Spanish streakhouse, dishes range from delightful small plates, freshly shucked oysters and fine Florida seafood to succulent steaks from the wood-burning grill in the show kitchen ($$$$–$$$$$; 6–10pm; **www.fourseasons.com/orlando/dining/restaurants/capa/**).

Charley's Steak Houses: Cooking over a specially built wood-fire pit earns high marks from US meat-lovers. All the meat is specially aged, hand-cut and seasoned, making for a superb array of steaks and chops and, while it also offers fine seafood, you'd be foolish to overlook its stock-in-trade ($$$–$$$$$; 5–11pm; **www.talkofthetownrestaurants.com**).

Everglades: Tucked away inside the Rosen Centre Hotel is this beautiful Florida speciality restaurant, specialising in great steaks and fine seafood. Don't miss the Broiled Florida Grouper and melt-in-the-mouth Filet Key Largo ($$$–$$$$$; 5.30–10.30pm; 407 996 2385; **www.evergladesrestaurant.com**).

Fleming's: Check in here for finest aged prime beef and an inventive array of fresh seafood, chops, generous sides and salads, plus tempting desserts. Its award-winning wine list features 100 wines by the glass and a magnificent Reserve List for the real connoisseur ($$$–$$$$; 5–10pm Sun–Thurs, 11pm Fri and Sat; 407 352 5706; **www.flemingssteakhouse.com**).

Hillstone: A real special-occasion venue in Winter Park, the lakeside location provides a relaxed but upscale choice for a casual lunch, evening drink or full-scale dinner. Where the locals go for a 'power lunch,' it is also an evening oasis of calm and gracious service, with the chance to enjoy a drink on their pier or grab a window or patio table with a wonderful view of Lake Killarney. The menu varies from simple burgers and salads to epic fresh fish dishes, rotisserie chicken, succulent steaks and more. An equally good wine list, daily soup specials and signature desserts round out a superb offering, and this really is THE place to be when the sun goes down! ($$–$$$$$; 11.30am–10pm Sun–Thurs,

11pm Fri and Sat; 407 740 4005, **www.hillstone.com**).

Johnnie's Hideaway: Stylish lakefront supper club in the Crossroads plaza at Lake Buena Vista, serving a rich mix of salads, premium seafood, stone crabs, veal and succulent, dry-aged steaks. The menu is colossal, and there is also a raw bar and some of the biggest desserts we've seen, along with a charming bar area, outdoor terrace and Happy Hour 4.30–6.30pm Mon–Sat ($$$–$$$$$; 5pm–10.30pm, 11pm Fri and Sat; 407 827 1111; **www.talkofthetownrestaurants.com**)

Luma on Park: Head to Winter Park for this trendy 'gastropub', where the cuisine can be as simple as a well-cooked burger or pizza or a fabulous filet mignon. The mix of outdoor patio, lounge bar and restaurant makes it a chic and lively venue, with fresh contemporary cuisine. Fine lamb, duck and fish are among the highlights, along with a great wine cellar. It also features a 3-course prix fixe menu Sun–Tue, and a special Chef's Table that should be booked in advance ($$–$$$$$; lounge bar 4–11.30pm Mon–Thurs, 11.30am Fri and Sat; dining room, lunch 11.30am–3pm Fri–Sun, dinner 5.30–10.30pm; 407 599 4111; **www.lumaonpark.com**).

Morton's of Chicago: A more upmarket style following a recent refurbishment, with a lively ambience that adds to the enjoyment of its trademark steaks, cooked on an open range. Memorable, although not cheap, especially as vegetables are extra ($$$$; 5.30pm–11pm Mon–Sat, 5pm–10pm Sun; **www.mortons.com**).

BRITTIP

American restaurant terminology calls a starter an 'appetizer' and a main course an 'entrée'. 'Broiled' means 'grilled'.

Old Hickory Steakhouse: In the Gaylord Palms Resort with elaborate Everglades theming, their steak needs few gimmicks as the house speciality of certified prime-aged beef is cooked to perfection. Side dishes are extra, but the attentive service

and alternatives such as oven-roasted swordfish and Maine lobster provide a memorable experience ($$$–$$$$$; 5pm–10pm; 407 586 1600).

The Palm Restaurant: Inside Universal's Hard Rock Hotel is this upmarket New York original, famous for prime-aged steaks and jumbo lobsters, served in elegant surroundings. The house speciality, jumbo Nova Scotia lobster, is spectacular. All this is reflected in the prices, and vegetables are extra, but non-hotel guests qualify for free valet parking ($$$$–$$$$$; 5–9pm Sun–Mon, 10pm Tues–Sat, 407 503 7256; **www.thepalm.com**).

Rocco's Tacos: This wildly eclectic but quality-conscious Mexican offering on Restaurant Row is great for a fun lunch or a lively evening out. Definitely start with their prepared-at-the-table guacamole and then consider one of their signature Molcajete dishes – a sizzling fajita choice served in a lava rock bowl with fresh flour tortillas. Their taco choice is equally tempting, while there is a dazzling array of margaritas and speciality drinks from their Tequila Bar, where it is party night every night! ($$–$$$; 11.30am–2am Mon–Fri, 11am–2am Sat–Sun; 407 225 0550, **www.roccostacos.com**).

Roy's: Go upmarket Hawaii style at this grand choice, where the Asia–Pacific fusion cuisine is as spectacular as the decor and service. Creator and celebrity chef Roy Yamaguchi displays his sense of style in every dish and the specialities include Macadamia-Nut Crusted Mahi-Mahi, Blackened Island Ahi and Braised Short Ribs as well as their own cocktails and an 'Aloha Hour' menu (4.30pm–6.30pm at the bar), with $7 appetisers, wines and cocktails. ($$$$–$$$$$; 5–10pm, 11pm Fri and Sat, 9pm Sun; **www.roysrestaurant.com**).

Ruth's Chris Steak House: Another major chain, this also offers prime beef in a mouth-watering variety. It isn't cheap, but you'll be hard pushed to get a better steak. Simply seared, seasoned and served, they are the reason it has more than 80 locations

Lake Buena Vista

The third main tourist area, this features the broadest range of choice.

East of I-4: *Family Favourites:* Bahama Breeze, BJ's Brewhouse, Carraba's, CiCi's Pizza, Golden Corral, Lone Star Steakhouse, Santa Fe Cattle Co. *Home From Home:* Frankie Farrell's. *Seafood Specials:* Landry's Seafood. *Fast Food:* Dunkin' Donuts, Subway, Wendy's.

West of I-4 (in the Crossroads area, SR 535 and Palm Parkway): *Deluxe Dining:* Johnnie's Hideaway. *Family Favourites:* Black Angus, Buffalo Wild Wings, Chevys, Chili's, CiCi's Pizza, Denny's, Fuddruckers, Hooters, IHOP, Macaroni Grill, Olive Garden, Orlando Ale House, Perkins, Shoney's, Sizzler, Sweet Tomatoes, TGI Fridays, Uno Chicago, Waffle House. *Fast Food:* Dunkin' Donuts, McDonald's, Pizza Hut, Quiznos, Steak 'n Shake, Subway, Taco Bell. *International Flavours:* Dragon Court Buffet, India Palace, Kobe Steakhouse, The Knife (South American churrascaria). *Seafood Specials:* Joe's Crab Shack, Red Lobster. *Plus:* Giordano's, a fabulous Chicago-style pizzeria serving some of the best deep-dish pizza pies, plus salads, sandwiches and pasta ($–$$$, 11am–11pm; 407 239 8900, **www.giordanos.com**).

worldwide, including in Sand Lake Rd's 'restaurant row' ($$$$–$$$$$; 5–10pm Mon–Sat, 9pm Sun; **www.ruthschris.com**).

Sanaa: This wonderfully themed dining experience is in the Kidani Village section of Disney's Animal Kingdom Lodge and features a novel take on Indian cuisine, with some imaginative variations, many served as sampler platters and, for once, not the usual huge portions. It also offers great animal savannah views ($$$$; 11.30am–3pm, 5–9.30pm; 407 939 3463).

Shula's Steak House: Expansive and expensive, the porterhouse and prime rib steaks are outstanding, and this chain (owned by ex-American football coach Don Shula) is popular with locals at the Walt Disney World Dolphin Hotel ($$$$$; 5–11pm; 407 934 1362; **www.donshula.com**).

Spencer's: The Hilton by the Convention Center on I-Drive is home to this beautiful restaurant that features magnificent steak, chops and seafood. Side dishes (all organic, local produce) are extra, but the natural steaks are all pasture-raised without hormones or antibiotics, aged for 21 days and cooked in a custom-made grill. The prime porterhouse for two is outstanding, and the bittersweet chocolate soufflé is a taste sensation ($$$$–$$$$$, 5.30–10.30pm Tues–Sat; 407 313 4300; **www.thehiltonorlando.com**).

Texas de Brazil: A top-quality Brazilian-style churrascaria, with a wonderfully upmarket touch. Its variety of meats – each carved at the table off sword-like skewers – is superb, all beautifully cooked over its open-flame grill ($$$–$$$$$; 5–10pm Mon–Thurs, 5–10.30pm Fri, 4–10.30pm Sat, 4–9.30pm Sun, plus brunch noon–3pm Sat and Sun; 407 355 0355; **www.texasdebrazil.com**).

Zen: Asian-themed Zen at the Omni Orlando Resort at Champions Gate features a sake and sushi bar to go with its full restaurant style. An oasis of oriental charm, highlights include the Szechwan-style Beef Tenderloin and Sautéed Shrimp in Black Pepper Sauce and Spinach. Or try the superb Zen Experience – a multi-course feast ($$$–$$$$$, 6–10pm; 407 390 6664; **www.omnihotels.com**).

Our Top 10

Finally, if you fancy really splashing out, why not book in advance at one of our all-time faves for that really memorable dining experience?

A Land Remembered: This is simply the best steakhouse we've visited. Inside the golf clubhouse of the Rosen Shingle Creek Resort (but open to non-residents), it is a superbly refined venue boasting exquisite service and an outstanding wine list. The menu oozes class and even features local specialities like frogs' legs, gator stew, a fresh fish selection and key lime pie. But, while the lamb, chicken and short ribs are outstanding, the steak choice is out of this world (featuring all-natural prime black Angus beef from the Harris Ranch in California). Filet mignon, New York strip, ribeye, porterhouse, prime rib, chateaubriand and a surf & turf (with lobster) are among the most succulent meat dishes you will find and, while it is pricey, we really believe it is worth every cent ($$$$–$$$$$; 5.30–10pm; 407 996 1956; **www.landrememberedrestaurant.com**).

Bice: Anyone looking for the most authentic Italian dining experience outside Italy should head to the Portofino Bay Hotel at Universal Orlando where this is as smart and smooth as they come. Genuine Tuscan style oozes out of every facet, from the formal welcome, the classic dining room, live balcony music and the authentic menu. They use only the freshest ingredients, with everything made from scratch, and it shows in dishes like the Burrata mozzarella and vine-ripened tomato starter, papardelle pasta and braised veal shank. Signature risottos are superb and roast rack of lamb a masterpiece, while the soft chocolate soufflé cake is heavenly. The wine list is impressive and Italian-orientated and the whole experience is to be savoured slowly thanks to exceptional wait staff. A three-course meal will top $130 for two, but it's worth it for a special occasion ($$$$–$$$$$; 5.30–10pm; 407 503 1415; **http://orlando.bicegroup.com**).

Bice

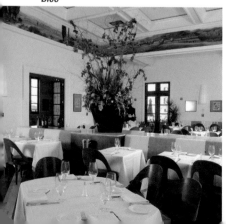

bluezoo: One of the hippest places in town (at the Walt Disney World Dolphin Hotel), bluezoo not only looks the part, but also serves some of the finest food in the Disney realm thanks to celebrity chef Todd English. With an undersea theme that benefits from superb lighting (dine later for the full effect), it has a soothing feeling, whether you are just at the bar or in one of the three dining rooms. Both the service and staff's knowledge are impeccable, so feel free to let them steer you around a mouth-watering menu, which includes ceviche and a raw bar. Fish is the signature dish (though chicken, beef, pork and pasta are also on offer) and seafood lovers will struggle to narrow down the choice: miso-glazed Hawaiian sea bass, swordfish, Cantonese lobster and more, or just try your choice of freshly caught fish, whole-roasted on its Teppenyaki grill with a choice of sauces ($$$$–$$$$$; 5.30–11pm; 407 934 1111; **www.thebluezoo.com**).

BRITTIP

For a great lunch or dinner alternative, visit Fogo de Chao and just sample their 30-item Salad Buffet at $24.50 per person. It is WAY more than just salad, with the likes of aged Parmesan, Italian salami and smoked salmon, and is wonderfully fresh and appetising.

Fogo De Chao: This Brazilian churrascaria is superbly authentic and flavourful, with an enchanting mix of elaborate serving style and succulent cuts of meat, all cooked on the traditional 'churrasco' skewer grill. It is a set-fee lunch or dinner, including a huge Salad Buffet (see Brit Tip), and you have a two-sided card (red or green) to indicate to the 'gaucho' servers if you are ready for more meat. When you flip the card to green, you will be offered freshly cooked skewers of 14 different meats, from filet mignon to linguica (Brazilian sausages), along with a selection of side dishes like crispy polenta, caramelised plantains, rice, beans and heavenly garlic mashed potato. Many of the meat cuts are seasoned with garlic, sea salt, mint, Parmesan or their own special spices and they can be cooked to order, as rare or well-done as you prefer. The bacon-wrapped filet is worth coming in for on its own while the lamb chops are outrageously delicious and the marinated chicken another taste sensation. The weekday set lunch is a bargain $31.50 for the full churrascaria experience while dinner is $48.50 ($$$–$$$$$; noon–2.30 and 5–10pm Mon–Thurs, 5.30–10.30pm Fri, 5–10.30pm Sat, 9.30–10pm Sun; 407 370 0711, **www.fogodechao.com**).

Jiko: This favourite of ours is at Disney's Animal Kingdom Lodge and is possibly Disney's most imaginative culinary offering. Jiko ('the cooking place') features twin wood-burning ovens, a masterful menu and an exclusive selection of South African wines. The menu has Indian, Asian and African influences, with dishes like Braised Beef Short-Rib and Piri Piri Swordfish, plus a couple of excellent vegetarian choices and a cheese plate that can be ordered as an appetiser or dessert. Its flatbreads are also a speciality and the dessert selection is totally decadent. The personal service and ethnic ambience underline the adventure of eating here, and it's the perfect venue for a romantic meal (5.30–10pm; 407 939 3463).

Monsieur Paul: Epcot's fine-dining array hits the heights with this 5-star dinner choice in the France pavilion. Under executive chef Francesco Santini and Maitre D' Phillipe Girard, this stylish but casual dining room is a true oasis of calm refinement in the theme park frenzy, with a French gourmet flair that isn't off-putting for non-foodies. Under the oversight of legendary chef Paul Bocuse, it ranges from classic dishes to innovative cuisine at the hands of Santini, with the opportunity for off-menu adventures for special occasions. Start with the Ravioli Escargot, then consider the Red Snapper in Potato Scales with braised fennel in a rosemary sauce, or the amazing Seared Scallops with ginger lobster consommé and cream of cauliflower.

Or just opt for a simple steak, superbly presented, as the grilled Beef Tenderloin is tastebud-teasingly flavourful. But then every dish is a well-balanced taste sensation and the desserts should not be missed at any cost! There is also an excellent 4-course prix fixe menu at $89/person ($$$$$; 5.30–8.30pm, 407 939 3463).

The Oceanaire: Step back in time at this relaxed and stylish seafood room at Pointe Orlando. The decor, reminiscent of a classic 1930s ocean liner, and mood music lead you into a fish and shellfish wonderland, complete with a superb oyster bar. Shrimp, crab, scallops, clams, lobster and as many as 15 types of fish all jostle for attention on a sumptuous menu that also offers great salads, steaks and chicken (though you'd be crazy to ignore the seafood here). The selection varies daily according to the freshest produce available, but typical examples include 'Black & Bleu' Grouper, Fin & Shell Fish Stew, Pan-seared Queen Snapper and stuffed Atlantic lobster, as well as a surf & turf option and a dozen types of oyster. Its grand shellfish platter (at $45 per person) is an extravaganza of shrimp, crab, lobster and oysters and it has an impressive wine list. Service is top-notch ($$$$–$$$$$; 5–10pm Sun–Thurs, 11pm Fri and Sat; 407 363 4801; **www.theoceanaire.com**).

Seasons 52: A trendy national chain (in the Plaza Venezia on Sand Lake Road and next to the Altamonte Mall), this offers some of the best dining in the state with a creative, seasonal, health-conscious menu. All appetisers, salads and soups range from 100–250 calories, the majority being either grilled or oven-roasted, and all mains are less than 475 calories. Its fish and seafood are a highlight but lamb, chicken and steaks are equally tempting and there are good vegetarian choices. The 'mini indulgence' desserts are ideal to finish a meal in style. The bar area and outdoor terrace are equally stylish, ideal for a romantic occasion ($$– $$$$; 4pm–10pm Sun–Thurs, 11pm Fri–Sat, lunch 11.30am–4pm Sat–Sun; 407 354 5212; **www.seasons52.com**).

Highball and Harvest: This exquisite new venue in the Ritz-Carlton resort features Southern cuisine with an upscale twist, and is one of the most exciting finds we've come across in a long time. Lightened-up favourites such as Shrimp and Grits, Chicken and Dumplings, and Peel-and-Eat Bayou Shrimp vie with Braised Lamb Shank and an utterly gorgeous Grilled Cauliflower Steak for a menu that offers inspired dining amid relaxed elegance. Belly up to the bar for a funky handcrafted cocktail (11am-11pm), drop by for lunch, and don't miss the Boiled Peanuts appetiser. They're addictive! (6.30am–10pm, 407 393 4422; **www.ritzcarlton.com/ en/Properties/Orlando/Dining/Highball_ Harvest/Default.#**)

BRITTIP

Need expert local advice on dining? Check out our good friend, restaurant critic and keen foodie Scott Joseph for up-to-date news, views and insight at **www.scottjosephorlando.com**. Not only is his 'Flog' (a Food Blog) essential reading, he also offers periodic special deals for ½-price coupons at a great range of restaurants. His Orlando Restaurant Guide is great reading and has a free app for iPhone, iPod and iPad at the iTunes store. Just look up Scott Joseph Orlando.

Tchoup-Chop

© Universal Orlando Resort

And our No 1… Tchoup-Chop

While it's practically impossible to single out one restaurant from this wealth of culinary delight, if pushed we'd nominate Tchoup-Chop (pronounced chop-chop) at Universal's Royal Pacific Resort. From the gourmet stable of New Orleans master chef Emeril Lagasse, it offers Asian-Pacific fusion cuisine in the most eye-catching setting. Service is a team effort at each table and the superb menu is well presented and explained. Blending aromatic and flavoursome elements of Thai, Chinese, Japanese, South Seas and other Pacific Rim cuisines, Lagasse has conjured up a delectable array of dishes. We're big fans of the Iron Skillet Seared Edamame and Pork Belly Tocino, followed by Kona Coffee Spice Pork Tenderloin or a selection of Maki and Sashimi. (The desserts are equally fragrant and the whole experience is a 5-star treat ($$$–$$$$$; 11.30am–2.30pm and 5pm–10pm; 407 503 2467; **www.emerils.com**).

Or… take a tip from Scott Joseph, who rates the **Ravenous Pig** in Winter Park his number one (and he's hard to argue with!). Taking the British gastropub idea, local restaurateurs James and Julie Petrakis have crafted a cosy hideaway that oozes charm and style, and with a menu that is superbly simple or simply superb, depending on if you just want great pub food or the full gourmet experience. Creative salads jostle with fresh pastas and a house-made charcuterie and cheese platter, as well as standards like a Pub Burger, Tacos and Steak Frites. Bookings here are highly advisable though, as its popularity is spreading ($$–$$$$; 11.30–2pm Wed-Sat, and 5.30–9.30pm Tues–Thurs, 5.30pm-10.30pm Fri-Sat; 407 628 2333; **www.theravenouspig.com**).

But now on to another of our favourite topics – shopping…

12 Shopping

or How to Send Your Credit Card into Meltdown

As well as being a theme park wonderland, this vast area of Florida is a shopper's paradise, with a dazzling array of specialist outlets, malls, flea markets and discount retailers. New centres spring up all the time, from smart malls to cheap gift shops – and you can't go a few paces in the tourist areas without a shop insisting it has the 'best bargains' of one sort or another.

With so much good shopping to be had for UK visitors, there's a danger of exceeding your baggage allowance for the flight home – or your duty-free allowance. American stores are genuinely fun just to browse, let alone splash out in, and you can expect to pay roughly the same in dollars as you do in pounds for items like clothes, books and jewellery, and real bargains are to be had in jeans, trainers, sports equipment and cosmetics. Almost everywhere offers free, convenient parking, while shop assistants are polite and helpful.

Sales tax: Be aware of the hidden extra costs of shopping. Unlike our VAT, Florida sales tax is NOT part of the displayed purchase price, so you must add on 6% or 7% (it varies by county) for the final price. Also, some shops will ask for photo ID with credit card purchases, so have a photo driving licence or photo ID with you.

Allowances: Your limit in the catch-all duty category of 'gifts and souvenirs' is only £390 per person. If you exceed that, you need to keep your receipts and go through the 'goods to declare' channel (though paying the duty and VAT can still be cheaper than buying the same items at home). Some items, such as clothing and footwear for children, do not incur a VAT rate. However, restrictions apply to all reduced-rate VAT items, so be sure to check details with HM Revenue & Customs. Your ordinary duty-free allowances from America include 200 cigarettes and 1 litre of spirits or 2 litres of fortified wine or sparkling wine and 4 litres of still wine.

> **BRITTIP**
> Don't buy electrical goods in the US – they won't work in the UK without a converter. Most games systems (notably X Box, Wii and PS4) are also NOT compatible with UK players. Hand-held games are fine.

Universal Studios Store

© Universal Orlando Resort

Customs duty: You pay duty (which varies depending on the item) on the total purchase price (i.e. inclusive of Florida sales tax) once you have exceeded £390, plus VAT at 20%. You CANNOT pool your allowances to cover one item that exceeds a single allowance. Hence, if you buy a digital camera that costs £400, you have to pay the duty (at 4.9%) on the full £400, taking the total to £419.60 and then VAT on that figure. However, if you have several items that add up to £390, and then another that exceeds that, you pay the duty and VAT only on the excess item (and customs officers usually give you the benefit of the lowest rate on what you pay for). Duty rates are updated regularly and vary from 2.2% (e.g. video games) to 14% (e.g. a computer monitor) keeping in mind VAT rates change. For more info, contact the Customs and Excise National Advice Service on 0845 010 9000, **www.hmrc.gov.uk**.

BRITTIP
Pick up the *Orlando Sentinel* newspaper on Sunday and you will get the full local lowdown on all the great sales for the coming week.

Alligator products constitute those of an endangered species (to UK authorities) so require an import licence. Consult the Global Wildlife Licensing and Registration Service for more info.

Disney Springs

In many ways, the heart of Walt Disney World is its Disney Springs district (10–12am), split into four linked sections: Disney Marketplace, The Landing, Town Center, and West Side. This is typical Disney, a beautiful location, imaginative architecture and a host of one-off elements that make shopping a pleasure, with 150 shops and dining opportunities. A handy water-taxi also links the ends of Disney Springs, as well as to Disney's Old Key West and Port Orleans Resorts.

Disney Springs can be found off exits 67 and 68 of I-4 and is well signposted

Up, up and away!

In Disney Springs West Side, across the bridge from The Landing, is **Characters In Flight**, a wonderful tethered balloon ride that gently soars up to 400ft/122m high carrying up to 30 at a time in a 19ft/5.7m gondola on 6min rides. It provides a fab panorama of much of the huge extent of Walt Disney World and is a great photo opportunity by day or night (8.30am–12am). It costs $18/adult and $12/3–9s. In certain weather conditions the number of passengers is limited, while it is grounded in high winds or heavy rain.

(exit 68 can be congested at peak periods).

Disney Marketplace: Don't miss the **World of Disney** store, the largest of its kind, which includes Bibbidi Bobbidi Boutique (where young girls can have hair, make-up and nails done in true Princess style), the **LEGO Imagination Center** (an interactive playground and shop), the amazing **Art of Disney** and the new **Marketplace Co-Op** (a number of small shops under one roof). **Once Upon A Toy** is a gigantic toy emporium complete with a host of classic games, many with a Disney theme, for kids to try. Other worthwhile one-offs are the blissful **Basin** (for toiletries) and **Disney's Wonderful World of Memories** (for all scrapbook fans).

BRITTIP
Parents beware! The Bibbidi Bobbidi Boutique hair and make-up shop is hideously expensive. Packages range from $55–$245, so you may want to steer your Princess gently away!

Princess Parade: Young girls in the princess mood may want to take part in the daily parade from the World of Disney store. 1–2pm each day (weather permitting), it marches in full pomp from the Princess Hollow end of the store through the Marketplace, finishing at the Carousel, where all children get a free ride. Girls can dress up (or not) as they wish, and there is NO fee to take part.

Arribas Brothers: A big, attractive gift store, those keen on pin-trading should check out **Pin Traders**. Then there's **Disney Design-A-Tee**, **Tren-D**, a cutting edge Disney fashion store for women, **Little Miss Matched** for fun and funky socks, bedding and more (popular with young girls), and **Disney's Days of Christmas**. For bargain-hunters, a section by **Goofy's Candy Company** offers **Marketplace Fun Finds** – everything at reduced prices. Dancing fountains and squirt pools (where kids tend to get seriously wet) and the lakeside setting all add to the appeal.

The Landing: Take your pick from a variety of imaginative shops, including **Art of Shaving** (upscale shaving products), **Sanuk** (footwear), **Sound Lion** (headphones, music players), **Apex by Sunglass Hut**, **Chapel Hats** (funky/vintage hats), **Havaianas** (flip-flops), and **Erin McKenna's bakery NYC** (vegan/gluten free baked goods). They all opened in 2015, along with several new restaurants (see dining chapter, p301). Raglan Road and Paradiso 37 restaurants also have their own gift shops here.

West Side: Continuing into West Side gives you the superb **AMC 24** cinema complex (p290), plus another 27 retail and dining outlets, notably the big **Harley-Davidson** store. **D Street** features Vinylmation figurines and collectables while **Pop Gallery** is also highly original for collectable artwork. **Goofy's Candy Cauldron** is a big hit with kids, but other shops, including **Something Silver** (contemporary jewellery), **Curl by Sammy Duvall** (water sports), S**osa Family Cigars**, **Sunglass Icon** and **Fit2Run** are all places you could find in the average mall and are rather dull. There are gift shops for **House of Blues**, **Bongos Cuban Café**, **Cirque du Soleil**, **Splitsville** and **DisneyQuest**, though. This is also where the new **Food Truck Park** opened in late 2014.

Town Center: The final addition to Disney Springs – with parking in two immense new multi-storey car parks, which indicate where individual spaces are open with a clever lighting system – was due to open in spring 2016, adding even more shopping and dining. Look for full details at https://disneyworld.disney.go.com/destinations/downtown-disney/.

International Drive

This core tourist area is awash with shopping of all kinds, from the cheapest and tackiest plazas, full of tourist gift shops, to four purpose-built centres. Some of the shops just north of the Sand Lake Road junction are best avoided, while the northern end of I-Drive has undergone a major redevelopment. This area is also renowned for discount outlet shopping – a local speciality – offering name brands at heavily reduced prices.

Universal CityWalk: Among the most original of the 12 shops are **Quiet Flight**, for radical surf and beachwear; the retro-American decor of **Fossil** for leather goods, watches and sunglasses; **Fresh Produce** for swimwear, casual clothing and accessories; the large **Island Clothing Company** for Tommy Bahama clothing and merchandise; **Hart & Huntington Orlando Tattoo Shop** with an array of permanent tattoos, as well as clothing and accessories; and the skate-boarding chic of **Element**. Again, none of these are anything special but the huge new **Universal Studios Store** offers a wide range of park souvenirs and merchandise.

Promenade at Premium Outlets

Artegon Orlando: Formerly Festival Bay, this large development at the top of International Drive is undergoing a 2-stage makeover to change it into an artisan market, shopping, dining and entertainment complex. Anchor stores are **Bass Pro Shops**, **Ron Jon Surf Shop**, **Shepler's Western Wear** and the **Cinemark** cinema, plus iconic new **Gods and Monsters** comic, collectibles and pop culture mega-shop. Then there are the **Artegon Sky Trail** ropes course and **Sky Zone** trampoline park, as well as **Putting Edge** indoor 'glow-in-the-dark' mini-golf and a variety of dining opportunties, notably the fab burgers at **Fuddruckers**. In 2016 we should see the Oak Ridge Market (farmers market stalls selling local produce) added to the Marketplace, which features a collection of 165 arts and crafts stalls, including a wonderful glass-blowing studio and a unique array of gifts and artwork (407 351 7718, **www.artegonmarketplace.com**).

Orlando Premium Outlets International Dr (formerly Prime Outlets): At the top of I-Drive, this attractive 175-shop 'lifestyle centre' has gone all out for the big, semi-open-air style that encourages people to wander the long interior promenades full of shop fronts and big-name brands. Boasting a landscaped canal running through the centre, outdoor seating, cafés, a Market Place food court and a Guest Services centre, it provides a luxury touch. Major brands include the **Neiman Marcus Last Call Clearance Center**, which will attract the fashion-conscious, as will the **Hugo Boss Factory Store**, **Kate Spade New York**, **Lacoste** and **Jones New York Outlet**. Other familiar names include **Nike Factory Store**, **Tommy Hilfiger**, **Crabtree & Evelyn**, **Banana Republic**, **Bath & Body Works**, **Aeropostale**, **Coach** and **Brooks Brothers**, plus, inevitably, a Starbucks. New in 2015 were **Basler Outlet** (designer fashions), **Diesel** (clothing), **American Eagle**, **Vera Bradley** and **DC Shoes**. With its attractive food court, including the popular Five Guys Burgers, Panera, plus Jack's Steakery restaurant and the smart Italian-styled Vinito, you have one of the area's brightest shopping centres that is also at the top of the I-Ride Trolley route (10am–11pm Mon–Sat, 10am–9pm Sun; **www.premiumoutlets. com/orlando**).

Pointe Orlando: Easily accessible from I-Drive, this is a good choice for an evening out with a bit of retail therapy. With 16 smart stores, you can indulge your passion for fashion at **Victoria's Secret**, **Armani Exchange**, **Chico's** and **Hollister** or stock up on gifts and souvenirs at **Bath & Body Works**, **Tommy Bahama**, **SGH Sunglass Hut**, **Design By You**, **Brighton Collectibles** and the excellent **Tharoo & Co** jewellery.

Pointe Dining: For the full rundown on where to eat at Pointe Orlando – **Capital Grille**, **The Oceanaire**, **Johnny Rockets**, **Maggiano's**, **Cuba Libre**, **Copper Canyon Grill**, **Funky Monkey**, **Fat Fish Blue**, **Tommy Bahama Café**, **Taverna Opa**, **The Pub** and **Marlow's Tavern**, plus recent additions **Itta Bena speakeasy** and **Lafayette's** (see p319).

Parking is at The Pointe's multi-storey car park, but several stores and restaurants will redeem your parking ticket if you shop here. It's open noon–10pm Mon–Sat, noon–8pm Sun Oct–May; noon–9pm Fri–Sat, noon–8pm Sun–Thur June–Sept; later at the bars and restaurants (407 248 2838, **www.pointeorlando.com**).

Pointe Orlando

© Pointe Orlando

A Kissimmee tradition

Old Town is home to some weekly events that appeal to locals and tourists alike and are well worth catching. The **Saturday Nite Cruise** at 8.30pm is a trademark drive-past of 300-plus vintage and collector cars (the biggest in America; viewing starts at 1pm). A **Friday Nite All American Muscle Car Cruise** features cars built between 1964 and today (viewing starts at 4pm, cruise starts at 8.30pm), **Sunday Show N' Shine** (4pm) features trucks, Jeeps, and SUVs, while Wed night's 5pm **Little Darlin' Street Party and Cruise In** brings out the pre-1988 cars. There is live music, fairground-type stalls and prizes, and it can get fairly raucous later on, with plenty of alcoholic libations (witness the Sun on the Beach bar!).

I-Drive 360: Orlando's newest entertainment and dining complex (see p213) has a selection of shops, including the big chemist and general store **Walgreens**, **Tervis** (durable drinkware), **Expo Electronics**, **360 Gifts** (I-Drive 360 souvenirs), and **Flip Flop Shop** (sandals and flip-flops). Nearby are the I-Shops, which include another **Walgreens**, **O'Neill** swimwear, **US Gift Factory** (souvenirs), a jewellery store and **World of Electronics** (discount electronics).

Kissimmee

Down along the tourist territory of Highway 192, you will again find a complete mix of outlets, with a profusion of the cheap and cheerful, but also several highly enticing possibilities.

BRITBONUS

Brit Guide readers receive a FREE Florida Mall discount booklet with the cut-out ad on the back flap of this book. Take advantage of this exclusive opportunity for added savings on your holiday shopping.

Old Town: This is Kissimmee's version of the purpose-built tourist shopping centre, an antique-style offering with an eclectic mix of shops, restaurants, bars and fairground attractions, set out along brick-lined streets. The shops range from standard souvenirs and novel T-shirt outlets to sportswear, and collectibles (check out the **Old Town General Store** for a step back in time, or the **Old Town Portrait Gallery** for period-style photos). The individual style of **Out Of This World Embroidery** offers a 'you name it, we'll stitch it' service, while, **Filthy Rich** jewellery, **Wild Billie's Gifts** and **Lucky Mouse** are all great for gift ideas. There are also 18 restaurants or snack bars. For lunch or dinner try **Tex Mex Mexican** cuisine or **Blue Max Tavern**, another fun alternative. **Flippers Pizzeria** and **Bamboo Court** are also worth trying, while there are other snack outlets, with offerings from popcorn to candy and the wonderful **Sweet Dreams Ice Cream Café**. **Sun on the Beach** is a good nightclub in evenings (until 2am, like Blue Max). Parking is free (10am–11pm daily; ride hours vary monthly (407 396 4888; **www.myoldtownusa.com**).

Downtown Kissimmee: This offers the more local, authentic face of shopping in Florida, with the charming Main Street area featuring a range of antique shops, one-off boutiques, cafés and restaurants. Much attention has been paid to the historic district in recent years, and it is now a relaxing place for a wander and a meal. **The Welcome Station** on Main Street (formerly an old-fashioned petrol station) is a great place to start, and even has local crafts, keepsakes, and books focusing on Floridian history (9am–5pm Mon–Fri). Then look into the likes of local landmarks **Lanier's**, **Makinson Hardware** (the oldest hardware store in Florida), and **Gallery One Artists**. The authentic Mexican family style of **Azteca's** is worth trying, along with the casual sports-bar style of **Broadway Pizza**, while we're fans of the smart **3 Sisters Speakeasy** wine bar and café, which has an **Antique Car Show** on the first Fri every month and live music Fri and Sat from 9pm–12am; 407 201 3270, **www.3sistersspeakeasy.com**). Every Tue you can also sample Kissimmee Valley

Farmers' Market in the Kissimmee Civic Center (10am-2pm; hours may change without notice, so be sure to check **www.experiencekissimmee.com**).

BRITTIP

For something really different, don't miss Abracadabra Ice Cream Factory, just outside Kissimmee town centre (on North Main Street). Here, they mix fantastic creamy creations using a wonderful variety of ingredients – and flash freeze it all with liquid nitrogen for a true taste sensation! It's open 11am–10pm daily.

The Kissimmee area is largely short of quality shopping otherwise, but head up to the Osceola Parkway (at the junction with John Young Parkway), which runs parallel to Highway 192, and you find the extensive developments of **The Loop** and **Loop West**, which help redress the balance. This double open-air plaza offers a unique mix of shops and restaurants, plus a 16-screen Regal Cinema, in a pedestrian-friendly setting, with the shops grouped around two large car parks. Many of the shops may not be familiar but are worth visiting. Of note at The Loop are **Ross** (a huge discount warehouse of clothes, shoes, linens, cosmetics and more), **Kohl's** (a well-priced department store), **Bed, Bath & Beyond** (household wares), **Pacific Sunwear** (beach and casual wear), **Old Navy** (clothing), **Michaels** (arts and crafts), **Sports Authority** and **Famous Footwear** (discounted shoes). There is also a hairdresser, nail salon and chemist (CVS). At The Loop West, look for the big department stores of **JC Penney** (clothing and

Abracadabra Ice Cream Factory

housewares) and **Kirkland** (home goods), plus **Ulta** (cosmetics), **TJMaxx** (clothing) and **DSW** (shoes), plus 16 additional shops.

In all, The Loop and Loop West boast 75 shopping and dining outlets and this has quickly become a major proposition, especially for the extensive dining choice. Take your pick from classic 1950s diner **Johnny Rockets**, **Ben & Jerry's** ice cream, the counter-service of **Pei Wei Asian Diner**, Mexican choice **Abuelo's**, **Tropical Smoothie Café** and the big-name chains of **Macaroni Grill** (p316), **Chili's** (p311), **Panera Bread** (p310), **Bonefish Grill** (p318) and the distinctive **BJ's Brewhouse** (p311 great burgers, sandwiches, salads and steaks, plus an impressive beer choice; 407 932 5245, **www.bjsbrewhouse.com**). The shops are open 10am–9.30pm Mon–Sat, 11am–6pm Sun, later at the restaurants and cinemas (407 343 9223; **www.experiencetheloop.com**).

Lake Buena Vista

The Lake Buena Vista area offers two of the best discount outlet centres, with great range and great prices.

Orlando Premium Outlets Vineland Ave: High on your 'must visit' list, this is a huge hit with UK visitors. With a fresh look and style, and a legion of big-name designers, it can be found on Vineland Avenue between I-Drive and I-4 (just south of SeaWorld; or exit 68 off I-4).

BRITTIP

Don't try to battle with the crowds in the main open-air car park at Orlando Premium Outlets Vineland Ave. Instead, head towards the back of the centre where you will find the 1,600-car multi-storey car park.

In all, it offers more than 170 stores of well-known brand names (like **Timberland**, **Diesel**, **Burberry**, **Armani Exchange**, **Kenneth Cole**, **Banana Republic**, **Prada** and **Calvin Klein**) in a semi-covered pedestrian plaza, with free parking and the

Disney connection

Disney collectors and lovers of theme park memorabilia will want to make note of this specialist store. **Theme Park Connection** is an amazing repository of past merchandise, collectors' items, cast-offs, old park signs, artwork, books and MUCH more. It is a touch pricey as most of its stock is rare or discontinued, and it can take *hours* to search through its warehouse-sized quarters, but you are bound to turn up a real treasure or two and revel in the astounding collection of Disney material. It is tucked away on a small industrial estate at 2160 Premier Row in Orlando, hence you should check its exact location on its website (**www.themeparkconnection.com**) or call 407 284 1934. Open 10am–5pm Mon–Fri, 10am–3pm Sat; closed Sun.

convenience of being at the south end of the I-Ride Trolley (main line). Other signature shops are **Samsonite Company Store**, **Ecko Unltd** (jeans and sportswear), **Fendi** (stylish women's clothing and handbags), **OshKosh B'Gosh** (baby/toddler clothes), **Famous Footwear** (a mini-warehouse of footwear fashion) and **Perfumania**. Watch out also for big Disney bargains at the **Character Warehouse**. In all, there are 82

clothing and fashion stores, 35 for shoes, 25 jewellers and accessories, 12 for children's clothing and eight for luggage. The adjoining expansion of The Promenade adds 12 additional stores, including a two-storey **Sak's Fifth Avenue Off 5th**, **Tommy Bahama** and **Forever 21**, plus the eclectic (and distinctly lively) bar/restaurant style of **Dick's Last Resort** (**www.dickslastresort.com**).

BRITTIP
Brit Guide Touring Plan clients will receive Orlando Premium Outlets' special Premier Platinum VIP Passport voucher, for significant extra savings at many shops (p41).

The food court is quite tempting, too, with 15 outlets, from **Villa Fresh Italian Kitchen** and **Maki of Japan** to **Starbucks**, **Taco Bell** and **Subway**. There is even a beer and wine café. Call 407 858 3008 for reservations, which are required at least 2hrs in advance. The Lynx bus service also stops here (407 841 2279), while **Star Transport** has on-site taxi stands (407 857 9999). Premium Outlets is open daily 10am–11pm (9pm Sun; 407 238 7787; **www.premiumoutlets.com/orlando**).

Orlando Premium Outlets Vineland Avenue

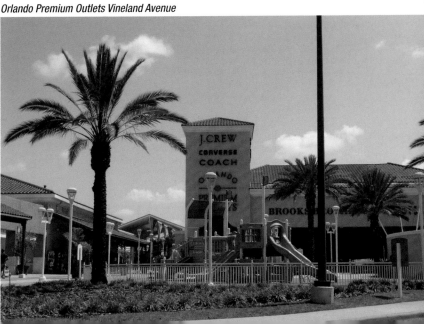

Lake Buena Vista Factory Stores: Get
ready for more big-name products
at discount prices here, from **Fossil,
Converse, Reebok, Jones New York,
OshKosh B'Gosh** superstore and (the
better-priced) **Carter's For Kids**. It
is another open-air plaza, with 46
stores spread over 6acres/2.5ha and
with plentiful parking. It's slightly off
the beaten track and therefore not
quite as busy as some of the others.
A recent addition is **Theme Park
Outlet**, which replaced the Disney
Character Outlet. There is also a
decent food court with a pleasant
outdoor deck, and a kids' playground.
Some of the stores and brand names
may not be well known to us, but
the likes of **Old Navy** (excellent-
value casual clothing), **Easy Spirit**
(super-comfortable shoes), **SAS
Shoes** (think Hush Puppies, only

cheaper!), **Travelpro** (luggage and
travel accessories) and **Rack Room
Shoes** (big names at serious savings)
are worth discovering. **Eclectic World
of Coffee** is both an internet café
and one of the best places you could
find to sip a latte and enjoy a cake or
pastry, with its outdoor terrace and
bird cages (plus some British snacks
and chocs!). Worth noting at the
neighbouring Lake Buena Vista Resort
Village and Spa are the luxurious
Reflections Spa for a bit of pampering
after your day of shopping, and
Frankie Farrells Irish Pub (p316).

The Factory Stores are on SR 535
(2ml/3km south off exit 68 on I-4) and
are open daily 10am–9pm (to 7pm
Sun). Their shuttle service picks up
at 60 participating hotels and condos
in a 10ml/16km radius (407 238 9301,
www.lbvfs.com).

Crayola Experience at the Florida Mall

Our shopping tips

As we live locally, shopping is close to our hearts and we recommend the following.

Bookshop: Barnes & Noble

Chemist: Walgreens

Clothing: Marshall's and Ross stores

Disney store: Theme Park Connection

Electronics: Best Buy

Home goods: Home Goods

Mall: Mall at Millenia

Open-air centre: Winter Garden Village

Outlet shopping: Orlando Premium Outlets

Specialist store: Shepler's Western Wear

Supermarket: Whole Foods Market

Malls

Head out slightly beyond the main tourist territory and you will discover the further choice and style of the area's many malls. They contain a huge range of shops and, if you take advantage of their periodic sales, you will be firmly back on the bargain trail. The top two locally are the Florida Mall and the Mall at Millenia, and both offer a contrasting experience.

BRITTIP

Need a good book? Make a beeline for Barnes & Noble, on West Sand Lake Road in the Venezia Plaza, on the South Orange Blossom Trail opposite the Florida Mall, or at the new Winter Garden Village shops. Each has a great coffee shop, too.

Florida Mall: The largest in central Florida, this features more than 260 shops, with five large department stores and a 16-counter food court, plus a children's play area, the lively bar-restaurant **Ruby Tuesday**, the popular fresh offerings of **Nature's Table**, **California Pizza Kitchen** and hearty **Buca di Beppo**. Located on the South Orange Blossom Trail, on the corner of Sand Lake Road, this

spacious and smart mall is open 10am–10pm Mon–Sat, noon–8pm Sun. Highlights are the department stores, led by the upmarket **Macy's**, plus **JC Penney**, **Sears** and **Dillard's**. Other shops worth looking out for are **Bath & Body Works**, **Gap**, **PacSun** (beachwear and more) and, for kids, the **Build-a-Bear Workshop**, **Game Stop** and the fun **M&M's World** store. New in 2015 were the expanded **Zara** (apparel), **American Girl** (books and educational products), **XXI Forever** (girl's clothing) and the massive **Crayola Experience** (interactive fun and design for kids). Guest services offers a discount booklet with a handy international size chart to help with American sizing, while there is also free wi-fi throughout the mall, free wheelchair use, pushchair rental and foreign currency exchange. There are even spa and beauty treatments in the Lancôme Institut de Beauté in **Dillard's**, and the **JC Penney** styling salon (407 851 7234; **www.simon. com**). The Mall also benefits from the integral **Florida Hotel**, with **Cricket's Grille & Bar**.

BRITTIP

With 25 hands-on attractions – from melting, moulding, spinning, and painting to drawing, doodling, and digital design – Crayola Experience is a good distraction when it's too hot or wet for the parks. There is even a Crayola Café for lunch or a snack. Admission is $19pp, under-3s free.

Florida Mall

© Florida Mall

Mall at Millenia: If the Florida Mall is the biggest shopping venue, this is the smartest. Just off I-4 to the north of Universal Orlando (exit 78), it is the most upmarket, dramatic and technologically advanced shopping complex in Florida, with New York's most famous department stores – **Bloomingdale's**, **Neiman Marcus** and **Macy's** – among a select number of other top-name boutiques such as **Louis Vuitton**. The entrance features a 60ft/18m glass rotunda with a flowing water garden theme and a concierge desk (valet parking is available). Then you can head in one of four directions over the marble and terrazzo floors or go upstairs to the high-quality 12-outlet food court. Try any of **Bistro Sensations** (salads, soups, wraps), **Firehouse Subs**, **Haagen-Dazs** (decadent ice cream), the authentic Mandarin-style of **Chinatown**, the fresh **Chipotle Mexican Grill** (salads, tacos and burritos) and **Southwest Grill** (succulent chicken, barbecue beef and salads), plus **Tony's & Bruno's** for Italian specialities (pasta, pizza, salads and cheesecake).

BRITTIP

Visit The Mall at Millenia Concierge, located inside the main entrance on level 1, and show this book to receive a complimentary savings book.

The grand architecture is also focused on five separate courts along a flattened, serpentine S-shape, topped by an arched glass roof like a gigantic conservatory. On two airy levels (three in Bloomingdale's and Macy's) and with eight Juliet balconies connecting the two sides, the mall consists of a colossal amount of glass, plus a stunning Grand Court, featuring a dozen 20ft/6m columns capped by curved plasma video screens. And, while around 20 per cent of the 150 stores are upmarket (**Cartier**, **Chanel**, **Jimmy Choo**, **Burberry** and **Gucci**), there are many unexpected options, such as **Urban Outfitters**, **Apple**, **MAC Cosmetics** and **Anthropologie**. You will also find plenty of mainstream names like **Abercrombie & Fitch**, **Hollister**, **Gap**, **Banana Republic** and **Victoria's Secret**. The five main restaurants are also first class: the heavenly **Cheesecake Factory**, **PF Chang's China Bistro**, the stylish Italian of **Brio Tuscan Grille** (p320), chic **Blue Martini**, and the swanky **Capital Grille** (for that special evening out). On top of that there is the excellent fresh sandwich style of **Panera Bread**, the **California Pizza Kitchen** and a **Johnny Rockets** diner. This is also the only mall with a US post office inside (NB: Standard postcards to the UK cost $1.15). A currency exchange is available, as are international phone cards.

The Mall at Millenia

All in all, this takes the Florida shopping experience to a new level, and there is even a new Personal Shopper service to provide individual guidance to the stores and their latest collections, and help when trying on the latest styles (10am–9pm Mon–Sat, 11am–7pm Sun; 407 363 3555; **www.mallatmillenia.com**).

Other malls: There are three alternatives to these popular (and busy – especially at weekends) malls. The **Altamonte Mall** is on Altamonte Avenue in the suburb of Altamonte Springs (take exit 92 off I-4 and head east for ½ml/800m on Route 436, then turn left); **Seminole Towne Center**, just off I-4 to the north of Orlando on the outskirts of Sanford (exit 101C off I-4); and **Oviedo Marketplace**, to the east of Orlando (right off exit 41 of Central Florida Greeneway, 417). The Altamonte Mall is the best of the bunch and well off the beaten tourist track, featuring 160 speciality shops, four major department stores – **Macy's**, **Dillard's**, **JC Penney** and **Sears** – and 23 eateries, including the fun **Bahama Breeze** (p311), upmarket **Seasons 52** (p325) and pub-style **Orlando Ale House** (p311). An 18-screen cinema and children's soft-play area round out the offerings. Open 10am–9pm Mon–Sat, 12pm–6pm Sun, the Customer Service Centre offers a VIP savings book to visitors (**www. altamontemall.com**). Shop during the week and you'll feel as if you have the place to yourself!

Winter Garden Village: A final recommendation, 10ml/16km north of Walt Disney World on Highway 535 at the junction with toll road 429, which is primarily a locals' centre but still has visitor appeal. The expansive open-plan design, set around key stores like **Super Target**, **Best Buy**, **Ross**, **Marshall's**, **Home Goods** and **Beall's**, features a mix of the big names and smaller boutiques, as well as a tempting array of 21 cafes and restaurants sprinkled throughout. Look for the upmarket seafood choice of **Bonefish Grill**, the elegant **Longhorn Steakhouse**, family-style **Chili's**, **Cracker Barrel**, **UNO Chicago**

Grill and **Mimi's Café**, or the counter-service options like **Five Guys Burgers**, **Panda Express**, **Coldstone Creamery** and **Chick-Fil-A**, and the first Orlando outlet of our favourite burger restaurant, **Red Robin** (**www.wintergardenvillage.com**).

Specialist shops

Wal-Mart: High on many people's lists, this warehouse-like store sells just about everything. There are 21 Wal-Marts in central Florida, 16 of which are 24hr Supercenters. The main tourist area stores are on Highway 27 (just north of 192); Highway 192 by Medieval Times (between markers 14 and 15); Osceola Parkway (at Buenaventura Lakes); John Young Parkway (at Sand Lake Road); on Kirkman Road (north of Universal Boulevard); by Highway 535 and Osceola Parkway; and on Turkey Lake Road.

Other supermarkets: There are plenty of other supermarkets and you will find rather better quality at the likes of **Publix** (throughout the main tourist areas, notably on Highway 192 and 27) and **Winn-Dixie** (a major south-east US chain). But the real Rolls-Royce of food stores, **Whole Foods Market** has an Orlando branch on Turkey Lake Road, with its signature superb fresh produce emporium and plenty of chances to sample, plus a magnificent hot-food counter to grab a meal (**www.wholefoodsmarket.com**).

Winter Garden Village

© TCA Project

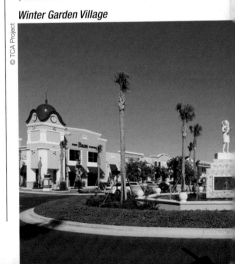

BRITTIP
Whole Foods Market has a small, funky beer and wine bar, which also serves food and offers fresh daily specials. A great choice for a sophisticated bite when you're stocking up on groceries.

Track Shack: This eye-catching new store on N. Mills Avenue in downtown Orlando is central Florida's premier running and walking HQ, with the region's largest selection of apparel, nutrition, accessories and technology for runners and walkers. They even offer bio mechanical evaluations and expert shoe fitting to ensure those trainers or walking shoes are suited to your exercise programme, along with every kind of keep-fit accessory (10am-87pm Mon-Fri, 9am-5pm Sat; 407 896 1160; **www.trackshack.com**). Their website also lists the local race calendar and running routes.

BRITBONUS
Brit Guide readers can use this code – RunTS77 – to receive $12 off any purchase at Track Shack.

For clothes, DIY, home furnishings, electrical goods, household items, gifts, toys and groceries, visit **Target** (its superstores on Highway 192 just west of Highway 535, near Mall at Millenia and Winter Garden Village are fine examples). The big chemists ('drug stores') of **Walgreens** and **CVS** also carry a surprisingly wide range of goods and almost resemble mini-supermarkets in their own right.

BRITTIP
Wal-Mart offers 1hr photo printing at great savings on UK prices, as do branches of Walgreens.

Individual outlets: Keen shoppers will want to check out other unfamiliar options. **Ross** (10 in Orlando, see **www.rossstores.com**) carries a huge range of discounted brand-name clothes, shoes, linens, towels, etc (hours vary by store, roughly 9.30am–9.30pm), while **Marshalls** (five in Orlando, **www.marshallsonline.com**) and **TJ Maxx** (also five, **www.tjmaxx.com**) are similar. For American sports gear visit **Sports Authority** stores (**www.sportsauthority.com**), while golfers should visit the **Edwin Watts Golf** stores (including the I-Drive clearance centre; **www.edwinwatts.com**), or any of the **Special Tee Golf & Tennis** shops. You can pick up some great deals on golf clubs in particular. By the same token, anglers can stock up on the latest gear at bargain prices at **Bass Pro Shops** (at the Artegon Orlando centre; **www.basspro.com**).

But now the shopping is done, it's time to think about the journey home…

World of Disney store

13 Going Home

And so, dog-tired, lighter in the wallet but (hopefully) blissfully happy and with a wealth of lovely memories, it's time to deal with that bane of all holidays – the journey home.

Now you have come through the last two weeks relatively unscathed, here's how to avoid any last-minute pitfalls.

The car

Returning the hire car can take time if you used an off-airport car depot, so allow an extra half hour; the process is much slicker with firms that operate directly from the airports, as nearly all now do. Most airlines require you to arrive 3hrs before an international flight, so don't be tempted to leave your check-in until the last minute. The off-airport check-in facility for Virgin Holidays (at Disney Springs by Cirque du Soleil®) is a major bonus in making this process smoother. Now you'll have time to kill, so here is a guide to the two main Orlando airports.

Orlando International Airport

Orlando International is 46ml/74km from Cocoa Beach and 54ml/87km from Daytona Beach on the east coast, 84ml/135km from Tampa and 110ml/177km from Clearwater and St Petersburg to the west, 25ml/40km from Walt Disney World and 10ml/16km from Universal Orlando; so always allow plenty of time for the return journey, check-in and security procedure. The Beachline Expressway (528) can get congested in late afternoon, for example, and the Central Florida Greeneway (417) is often better.

This modern airport is one of America's biggest and rated top for passenger satisfaction. It handles more than 35 million passengers a year, busier than Gatwick and San Francisco. It can get busy at peak times, but its 1,000acre/405ha terminal complex usually handles crowds with ease, and this is one of the most comfortable airports you could find. It boasts great facilities and its wide, airy concourses make it feel more like an elegant hotel (one end is actually the airport-owned Hyatt Hotel).

Ramps, restrooms, wide lifts and large open areas ensure easy wheelchair access, and there are features like

Orlando International Airport

TDD and amplified telephones, wheelchair-height drinking fountains, Braille lift controls and companion-care restrooms to assist any travellers with disabilities.

The airport always aims to stay a step ahead, with environmentally friendly enhancements, smart restrooms and a wide selection of food and drink outlets. It boasts a major food court, multiple restaurant options and superb shops. A convenient 'quick turnaround' area for hire cars allows 96 per cent of hire car companies to have onsite locations, a huge boon to visitors' ease in pick-up and drop-off.

Should you have more than 3hrs to spare, it's worth taking the 15min taxi ride to the Florida Mall.

BRITTIP

You are advised to leave all luggage unlocked (no combination locks or padlocks) when you check in for your flight, as the TSA security staff open a LOT of bags during screening and have the right to access any case, locked or not. TSA-approved locks are suggested, if you prefer to lock your cases.

Landside

As with all international airports, there is a division between LANDSIDE (for visitors) and AIRSIDE (where you must have a ticket). There are three levels to Orlando's Landside.

- Level 1 is for ground transportation, tour operator desks, parking, buses and car rental agencies, plus the Virgin Atlantic baggage claim.

- Level 2 is for main Baggage Claim and private vehicles meeting passengers.

- Level 3 is where you enter on your return journey, as it holds the check-in desks, shops and restaurants.

The main area of Level 3 is then further divided into interconnected sections:

Landside A: This houses the check-in for Gates 1–29 and 100–129. Here you'll find Aer Lingus, Southwest,

JetBlue, Norwegian, Virgin America and Virgin Atlantic (though Virgin Atlantic departs from Gates 70-99).

Landside B: Check-in here for Gates 30–99 and American Airlines, Air Canada, BA, Delta, Lufthansa, United, Spirit, and Thomas Cook.

Once you've checked in, you can explore the East and West Halls of the Level 3 concourse. These house a good mix of shops and restaurants, plus currency exchange, information desks and ATMs, while the Hyatt Hotel is in the East Hall. The East and West Halls are linked by the restaurants, shops and services of the North and South Walks. In total, there are 109 places to shop and eat, including the food court, and it's almost like being in a smart shopping mall. Many shops feature outstanding design and even photo opportunities: see the two **Disney** stores, **Harley-Davidson**, **Universal**, SeaWorld/**Busch Gardens** and **Kennedy Space Center**. Other notable shops are **Lush** bath products, **Sanrio** (for all your Hello Kitty needs), **Sunglass International**, **Brookstone**, **Ron Jon Surf Shop**, **Lids** (sports hats and apparel) and **Hudson Booksellers**.

Dining: Another pleasure here, the eight-counter food court features **Carvel** ice-cream, **Sbarro** pizza, **Quiznos** subs, **McDonalds** and **Panda Express**, plus the slightly healthier option of **Chick-Fil-A**. **Macaroni Grill** is a tasty full-service Italian restaurant option, while **Fox Sports Sky Box** adds a multi-screen TV set-up plus counter and table service. Upstairs at the West Hall is **Chili's Too**.

The East Hall is quieter and more picturesque as it is dominated by the eight-storey Hyatt Hotel atrium. Up the escalator is the main entrance, and, to see out your visit in style, **McCoy's Bar & Grill** (up and turn right) is a smart bar-restaurant with a superb airport view, refurbished and with a menu that includes a **Sushi Bar** and fresh salads, sandwiches, flatbreads and small plates ideal for sharing or lighter appetites (11am–12:30am, Sushi Bar 4–11pm; 407 825 1234, **www.orlandoairport.hyatt.com**).

To go really upmarket, take the lift to the 9th-floor **Hemisphere** steakhouse (breakfast and dinner only). You'll have an even more impressive view, and its five-star cuisine offers some of the best fare in the city, but it's pricey.

BRITTIP

If the queues at security for Gates 70–99 look long, you can use the other side, for Gates 100–129, as you end up in the same place after screening. Just remember to get the tram to Gates 70–99.

Airside

Once it's time to move to your departure gate, be aware of the four satellite 'arms' that make up the airport's Airside. This is where you will probably need to queue as the security screening takes time, and you should allow AT LEAST 30mins. The arms are divided into Gates 1–29 and 30–59 at the West end, and 70–99 (UK international departures) and 100–129 (all American domestic flights) at the East. All the departure gates are here, plus duty-free shops and more cafés.

The four satellites are each connected to the main building by an automated tram, so you need to be alert when it comes to finding your departure gate. There are no Tannoy announcements for flights, so you should check your departure gate and time when you check in. However, there are large monitors in the terminal with all the departure info. The usual gates are:

- **1–29:** American, Aer Lingus, Norwegian and JetBlue.

- **30–59:** Spirit, Bahamasair and United.

- **70–99:** Air Canada, British Airways, Delta, Thomas Cook and Virgin.

- **100–129:** AirTran, Southwest and Virgin America.

Airside is clean and efficient. There's less choice than the main terminal but there are two duty-free shops (your purchases are delivered to the departure gate for you to collect as you board). Both stores include designer sunglasses, jewellery, handbags, fashion watches, new perfumes and a selection of travel retail exclusives.

BRITTIP

Orlando International Airport offers free wi-fi throughout its main concourse and satellite arms.

Gates 1–29: The first duty-free shop, **Keys Gift Shop** (newsagent), two **Cibo Express** gourmet markets, **Za-Za's Cuban Café** and a mini food court featuring **Starbucks, Burger King, Cold Stone Creamery, Brioche Doree, On the Border Mexican Grill Cantina** and **Famous Famiglia**.

Gates 30–59: These have **Cibo Express, Qdoba Mexican Grill, Nature's Table, Wendy's, Freshens Treats, Za-Za's Cuban Coffee**, full-service **Ruby Tuesday** and **Hudson News**.

Gates 70–99: The main satellite for UK flights offers a good duty-free shop, currency exchange, **Stellar News & Gifts**, the speciality **Zoom System** shop, and a mini play area. A food court contains **Burger King, Nathan's Hot Dogs, Carvel, Starbucks** and **Fresh Attractions** deli, plus the excellent table-service **Outback Steakhouse** and bar.

Gates 100–129: Offer two **Johnny Rivers Grill and Market** outlets, a food court with **Freshens Treats**, and **McDonald's**, plus **Starbucks** coffee shop, **Au Bon Pain** café, **Kafe Kalik** bar/lounge and 10 shops. For more details, see **www.orlandoairports.net**, which includes live flight departure and arrival info.

Airside at Orlando International Airport

ORLANDO INTERNATIONAL AIRPORT

ORLANDO SANFORD INTERNATIONAL AIRPORT

Your chance to give something back

After a wonderful trip, you might be interested in two charities that help children with serious illnesses to have an equally memorable holiday.

Give Kids the World Village is an amazing organisation in Kissimmee, providing a week's holiday for children with life-threatening illnesses. GKTW works with wish-granting foundations worldwide to provide an unforgettable visit for children and their families. It is set up as a resort and includes meals, accommodation, transport, themed venues, donated park tickets and many other thoughtful touches in a magical setting. It's a charity we support ourselves and we hope you will, too. You can donate via its website, **www.gktw.org**.

DREAMFLIGHT takes seriously ill and disabled children from the UK on a 'Holiday of a Lifetime' to the theme parks of Orlando. They aim to bring fun and joy into the lives of children whose illnesses and treatments have brought pain, distress and disruption to their lives.

Each October Dreamflight takes 192 children in the 8–14 age group from all over the UK. For many, it will be their first time away from home and, of course, most will require medical treatment or supervision. One adult escort accompanies every two children, a high proportion from the medical professions. Helpers in Orlando accompany each child in the parks on a one-to-one basis.

Since 1987, more than 5,000 children have enjoyed what in many cases is a life-changing experience. Priority is given to children who would not otherwise be able to have such an opportunity due to their medical conditions and/or social circumstances. They meet others with similar experiences, and return with increased confidence and self-esteem. Many long-term friendships are formed between children in the groups.

For further information or to make a donation please see **www.dreamflight.org**

Thanks in advance for any contributions to these worthwhile organisations.

Orlando Sanford International Airport

Returning to the gateway for some British charter flights should be relatively simple, providing you retrace your route on the Central Florida Greeneway (following signs for Orlando Sanford Airport, NOT Orlando International) and come off at exit 49. Turn first right at the lights, then first right again on to Lake Mary Boulevard and follow it to the airport. The efficiency of Alamo and Dollar's car return adds to the simplicity.

BRITTIP

The airport turn-off sign is right after the toll plaza before exit 49 and is easy to miss; once you go through that toll plaza, take the very next turn-off.

Orlando Sanford was created as a full international airport in 1996, as an initiative between the airport

authorities and British tour operators. Thomson and the scheduled services of Icelandair both use this simpler option, as well as Belgian and Dutch charter flights. You are further north, so your journey time is 35mins longer with an extra $4–5 in tolls compared with the journey to and from Orlando International, but providing you follow the simple directions, you should have no problem retracing your steps here.

Orlando Sanford Airport

And, while this charter gateway is smaller than Orlando International, it boasts a spacious check-in area and works hard to make the departure as painless as the arrival, especially with its **Royal Palm Lounge** facility. Icelandair usually uses Terminal B for check-in; Thomson (and Cosmos customers) check in at Terminal A. But all passengers use the same international departure lounge in Terminal A. It continues to grow, and has an increasingly busy domestic side from Terminal B.

There are no food or beverage outlets at the check-in level at Terminal A, but you can walk across to Terminal B where there is a **Café Ritazza** and a food court. Once checked in, you need to pass through security (allow at least 30mins) to reach the International Departure Lounge. Here you have the **Budweiser Tap Room**, which serves a good selection of international beers, and the handy food court. The four-part outlet offers **American Grill**, **C**, **Sweet Endings** and the aptly named **Grab-N-Go** (soft drinks, bottled water and snacks). There is then an extensive duty-free store (also with an increased range of merchandise), **Hudson News** for sundries, **KidWorks** for educational games, books, and toys, plus **Indulgences**. There is also an information and currency exchange kiosk. No smoking inside the lounge, but there is an extensive outdoor deck for smokers.

Royal Palm Lounge: The big extra here, this premium space is available

We await your return!

to all passengers for a modest fee. It's in a separate annexe from the main lounge and is an oasis of comfort and quiet, perfect for relaxing for the last few hours of your holiday (the only things it doesn't have are beds and shower facilities!). Split into two halves, it boasts a pleasant café bar, where you can enjoy unlimited tea, coffee, soft drinks and snacks (plus two glasses of beer or wine per over-21 plus two home theatre lounges, with widescreen TV and surround-sound, for recently released films; two quiet reading rooms; 11 computer terminals for email and internet access; a youth entertainment centre with 14 Sony PlayStation 2 consoles; a separate toddlers' playroom with soft toys and games; a smoking lounge; and a left-luggage area. The Royal Palm is billed as an airport lounge with the comforts of home and is well worth the extra cost ($30/adult, $20 4–20s, under-4s free) if you're likely to be here for 1hr or more. Most tour operators offer it in advance at a discount, or you can book on arrival or through your resort reps. With its extra capacity and facilities, this is a very satisfying way to conclude a holiday. See the Royal Palm Lounge and more about the airport at **www.orlandosanfordairport.com** or email royal.palm@tbiusinc.aero.

Whether you are using Orlando International or Orlando Sanford, you can also expect the return flight to be about 1hr shorter than the journey out, thanks to the Atlantic jetstreams. Nevertheless, you'll land back home rather more jetlagged than on the trip out because the time difference is more noticeable on eastward flights, and it may take a day or so to get your body clock back on local time. It is important not to indulge in alcohol on the flight if you will be driving when you land. By far the best way to beat Florida jetlag is to enjoy the memories from this trip – then start planning your next Orlando holiday!

Believe us, the lure of this theme park wonderland is hard to resist – you WILL be back!

Example: 2 weeks with Disney's 14-Day Ultimate Ticket and Orlando FlexTicket Plus

(Disney's Ultimate Tickets give 7, 14 or 21 days of unlimited admission at their 4 main theme parks, plus visits to Blizzard Beach, Typhoon Lagoon, DisneyQuest and/or Disney's ESPN World Of Sports™, valid for 7/14/21 days from first use. The Orlando FlexTicket Plus is valid for Universal Orlando's 2 parks, CityWalk and Wet 'n Wild, plus SeaWorld, Aquatica and Busch Gardens for 14 days from first use)

Day	Our Example	Your Planner
1 (Mon)	Arrive 2.40pm local time, Orlando Sanford airport; transfer to resort – check out local shops and restaurants	
2 (Tues)	Attend tour operator Welcome Meeting; rest of day at MAGIC KINGDOM	
3 (Wed)	All day at UNIVERSAL STUDIOS for the Wizarding World of Harry Potter	
4 (Thurs)	Chill out day at Disney's Blizzard Beach water park	
5 (Fri)	All day at BUSCH GARDENS	
6 (Sat)	DISNEY'S ANIMAL KINGDOM Park. Eve: Medieval Times Dinner Show (8pm)	
7 (Sun)	Have a lie-in, then go shopping at Orlando Premium Outlets and Lake Buena Vista Factory Stores	
8 (Mon)	ISLANDS OF ADVENTURE Eve: City Walk and dinner at Hard Rock	
9 (Tues)	All day at DISNEY'S HOLLYWOOD STUDIOS (Fantasmic! show at 8.30pm)	
10 (Wed)	Kennedy Space Center Eve: International Drive	
11 (Thurs)	All day at SEAWORLD (One Ocean at 3pm)	
12 (Fri)	Enjoy a UNIVERSAL ORLANDO highlights day; or chill out at Aquatica water park	
13 (Sat)	All day at EPCOT Park (IllumiNations at 9pm)	
14 (Sun)	Have a lie-in, then head for MAGIC KINGDOM Park (Wishes fireworks at 9pm)	
15 (Mon)	Gatorland/Back to airport; return flight at 5.30pm	

Busy Day Guide

NB: This is a *general* guide only as the parks do change their hours frequently and often without notice. However, this guide will still be accurate for the busiest times of the year.

Day	Busiest	Average	Lightest
Mon	Magic Kingdom, Animal Kingdom, Universal Studios	Disney's Hollywood Studios	Epcot, Islands of Adventure, SeaWorld, Busch Gardens; Kennedy Space Center, water parks
Tues	Epcot, Universal Studios	Disney's Hollywood Studios, Kennedy Space Center	Magic Kingdom, Animal Kingdom, Islands of Adventure, SeaWorld, Busch Gardens, water parks
Wed	Animal Kingdom	Magic Kingdom, Disney's Hollywood Studios, Islands of Adventure, SeaWorld	Epcot, Universal Studios, Busch Gardens, Kennedy Space Center, water parks
Thurs	Magic Kingdom	Epcot, Islands of Adventure, Kennedy Space Center, SeaWorld	Disney's Hollywood Studios, Animal Kingdom, Universal Studios, Busch Gardens, water parks
Fri	Islands of Adventure	Disney's Hollywood Studios, Animal Kingdom, Universal Studios, Kennedy Space Center, Busch Gardens, water parks	Magic Kingdom, Epcot, SeaWorld
Sat	Disney's Hollywood Studios, Universal Studios, Islands of Adventure, SeaWorld, Busch Gardens, Kennedy Space Center, water parks	Magic Kingdom, Epcot	Animal Kingdom
Sun	Epcot, Universal Studios, Islands of Adventure, SeaWorld, water parks	Magic Kingdom, Animal Kingdom, Busch Gardens	Disney's Hollywood Studios

Only here for a week? Here's our suggestion for an action-packed 7 nights in Orlando:

Day 1: Arrive; visit Epcot in evening for IllumiNations

Day 2: Up early for Magic Kingdom

Day 3: All day at Universal and Islands of Adventure

Day 4: Epcot for the day; Disney's Hollywood Studios for evening

Day 5: Disney's Animal Kingdom for the day; Magic Kingdom evening

Day 6: SeaWorld with mid-day break at Aquatica

Day 7: Hollywood Studios for the day, Epcot evening

Day 8: Shopping and return flight

Index

Acknowledgements

The authors wish to acknowledge the help of the following in the production of this book: Visit Orlando, Experience Kissimmee, Walt Disney Attractions Inc., Universal Orlando, SeaWorld Parks & Entertainment, Visit Florida, St Petersburg/Clearwater Area Convention and Visitors Bureau, Seminole County Convention & Visitors Bureau, Visit Tampa Bay, Space Coast Office of Tourism, Mount Dora Chamber of Commerce, Greater Orlando Aviation Authority, Orlando Sanford International Airport and Alamo Rent A Car. In person: Danielle Courtenay, Amy Rodenbrock (Visit Orlando), Larry White, Sylvia Oliande, Rochelle Siegel (Experience Kissimmee), Pam Forrester (Visit Florida) Danny Trosset, Stephanie Hunicke, (Seminole County), Patrick Harrison (Visit Tampa Bay), Duncan Wardle, Todd Heiden, Dave Coombs (Walt Disney), Kalina Subido-Person, Damian O'Grady (Space Coast), Lindsey Towers (Alamo Rent A Car), Fiona Duncan, Kevin Gibson, Meredith Bandy (Universal), Andrea Farmer, Angelica Deluccia Morrisey (Kennedy Space Center), Brittany Williams (LEGOLAND Florida), Carolyn Fennell, Larry Ell (Orlando Aviation Authority), Sandy Sweatt (Forever Florida), Lorraine Ellis (Get Married In Florida), Andy James, James Brown (Florida Dolphin Tours), Emily Kruse, Travis Claytor, Lucy Dalton, Natalie Eales (SeaWorld Parks & Entertainment), Rose Vignetti-Garlick (Downtown Orlando), Debra Ray (Church Street Business District), Sam Haught (Wild Florida), Dana Gonzalez, Matt Tuchman (Medieval Times), Dana Berry (Four Seasons Orlando), John Stine, Dipika Joshi (I-Drive 360), Sandy Wade StaySky Resort Management), Laura Richeson (Richeson Communications), Scott Joseph (ScottJosephOrlando.com), Michael Caires (Orlando Sanford International Airport), Allan Oakley (Alexander Homes & Associates), Nigel Worrall (Florida Leisure), Wrenda Goodwyn (International Drive), Michelle Harris (Gatorland), Donna Ernbro (Sleuths), Gene Columbus (The Orlando Rep), Mary Deatrick (Deatrick PR for Rosen Hotels), Michelle Peters (Boggy Creek Airboats), Lorraine Gorham (Raglan Road), Lorena Garcia (Orlando Premium Outlets), Terry Lynn Morris, Jennifer Bisbee (Lake Buena Vista Factory Stores), Steve Sless (Paragon Outlets), Judy Perry (Dreamflight), plus all our ATD friends! Reader feedback via email: Michael Eppy, Rob Bryars, Roger Low, Phyllis Drozd, Johnnie Strachan, Sheila Scoines, Debbie Morgan, Andrew Morgan, Martin Coombs and Sally Spawforth. Other publications: Check out *Orlando Attractions Magazine* for information and features on this great destination, **www.attractionsmagazine.com**, and don't forget to join us on the discussion forums at **www.attraction-tickets-direct.co.uk**. Got a red-hot Brit Tip to pass on? We want to hear from YOU to keep improving the guide each year. Drop us a line at: Brit's Guide (Orlando), W. Foulsham & Co. Ltd, The Old Barrel Store, Drayman's Lane, Marlow, Bucks SL7 2FF. Or e-mail britsguide@yahoo.com.

Photograph acknowledgements

With thanks to everyone for their help in supplying photographs for this edition.